Catholic High School Entrance Exams
Seventh Edition

RELATED TITLES FOR HIGH SCHOOL-BOUND STUDENTS

SSAT & ISEE: For Private and Independent School Admissions

SHSAT: New York City Specialized High School Admissions Test

Catholic High School Entrance Exams

COOP • HSPT • TACHS

Seventh Edition

KAPLAN PUBLISHING

New York

© 2016 by Kaplan, Inc.

Published by Kaplan Publishing, a division of Kaplan, Inc.
750 Third Avenue
New York, NY 10017

Printed in the United States of America

10 9 8 7 6 5 4

ISBN 13: 978-1-5062-0339-3

Table of Contents

Available Online

FOR ANY TEST CHANGES OR LATE-BREAKING DEVELOPMENTS

kaptest.com/publishing

The material in this book is up to date at the time of publication. However, the test makers may have instituted changes in the test after this book was published. Be sure to carefully read the materials you receive when you register for the test. If there are any important late-breaking developments—or any changes or corrections to the Kaplan test preparation materials in this book—we will post that information online at kaptest.com/publishing.

How to Use This Book

The COOP, TACHS, and HSPT are the most common admissions exams used by Catholic schools. You should check with the specific schools you are interested in attending to see when they administer the exam and which test they use. You'll have to register to take the test, using an application form the school can provide. After you register, you will receive a handbook of instructions and an admission ticket for the test. Be sure to bring the ticket with you on the day of the test.

You should know that the COOP, HSPT, and TACHS cover a lot of material. To learn more specific information, read chapter 1, chapter 2, or chapter 3, depending on which test you will be taking.

Next, read chapter 4, "Test-Taking Strategies." Whether you are taking the COOP, the HSPT, or the TACHS, this chapter will provide you with tips on how to answer every question, no matter what its level of difficulty or the subject area that it covers.

To find out which of your skills need the most improvement, take the diagnostic quiz for the test you will be taking. Once you have reviewed the answer explanations and determined what your strengths and weaknesses are, read the skill review chapters. Use them to strengthen and hone your skills. Then, test your understanding with the practice set at the end of each skill review chapter.

Though you should complete the skill review in your problem areas first, be sure to work through all of them, since each one will give valuable strategies and practice on the various content areas of the tests.

Finally, be sure to take the Practice Tests at the end of the book. We've provided answer explanations for each question to help you build a systematic and effective approach that will help you do your best on whichever test you take.

Good luck!

Section 1
About the Exams

chapter one

Facts about the COOP

The COOP, or Cooperative Admissions Examination, is given each year in October or November to eighth-graders seeking admission to specific Catholic high schools. The high schools use the exam results to make decisions about admitting applicants and to group prospective ninth-grade students into classes.

The COOP contains seven subtests and lasts about two and a half hours. The subtests are: Sequences, Analogies, Quantitative Reasoning, Verbal Reasoning—Words, Verbal Reasoning—Context, Reading and Language Arts, and Mathematics. The COOP measures academic achievement as well as academic aptitude.

COOP EXAM FORMAT

The COOP contains approximately 180 multiple-choice questions. Most questions have four answer choices, A, B, C, D (odd-numbered questions) or F, G, H, J (even-numbered questions). However, some questions in the mathematics subtest have five answer choices, A, B, C, D, E (odd-numbered questions) or F, G, H, J, K (even-numbered questions). A separate answer sheet is provided to fill in your answer choices. The answer sheet is divided up into sections; each section is for a different subtest. Be careful when you fill in the answer bubbles—be sure that you're filling in the bubbles for the correct subtest!

 KAPLAN TIP

The structure and contents of the COOP change slightly from year to year, but expect to see approximately seven subtests on the exam. Be sure that the bubbles you're filling in on your answer sheet match up with the subtest you're working on in your question booklet.

You are allowed to write in the question booklet; use this to your advantage when working through problems. Cross off answer choices as you eliminate them, circle problems you decide to skip and come back to, write out a mathematics problem as you solve it, or underline important information that helps you answer a question.

The COOP changes from year to year so that no students are more familiar than others with the test format and contents. You may see new question styles or a different number of questions within a section. However, the content areas that the test covers remain basically the same. These are broken down into seven subtests:

Subtest	Number of Questions (approximate)	Time Allotted (approximate)
Sequences	20	15 minutes
Analogies	20	7 minutes
Quantitative Reasoning	20	15 minutes
Verbal Reasoning—Words	20	15 minutes
Verbal Reasoning—Context	20	15 minutes
Reading and Language Arts	40	40 minutes
Mathematics	40	35 minutes

QUESTION TYPES

Here are explanations and examples of question types you will most likely see on the COOP exam. Directions are given for each section. Be sure to read the directions carefully before starting a subtest or section, especially since the specific question format you see may vary slightly from that presented in this book.

Test 1: Sequences

Sequence questions measure your ability to understand a rule or principle shown in a pattern or sequences of figures, letters, or numbers.

Your job is to analyze the pattern and then select the answer choice that would continue or complete the pattern.

Directions: Choose the answer that best continues the sequence.

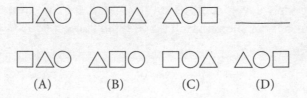

(A)   (B)   (C)   (D)

Answer: **(A)**. Each piece of the sequence contains a square, a triangle, and a circle. Each subsequent piece of the sequence moves the last figure to the beginning of the group. In the final missing piece, the square should be moved in front of the triangle and the circle.

Test 2: Analogies

COOP analogy questions measure your ability to detect various types of relationships among picture pairs, then extend that relationship to an incomplete picture pair. Pictures may be made up of scenes, people, animals, objects, or symbols.

Directions: Look at the two pictures on top. Then, choose the picture that belongs in the space so that the bottom two pictures are related in the same way that the top two are related.

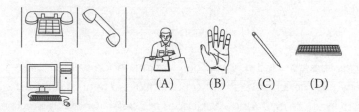

Answer: **(D)**. The receiver is a part of the entire telephone. A keyboard is part of an entire computer system.

Test 3: Quantitative Reasoning

Quantitative reasoning questions measure your aptitude for thinking with numbers. These are intentionally unlike other mathematics questions you will see on the exam since they are intended to test your reasoning ability, rather than any skills you have learned.

There are three types of quantitative reasoning questions: number relationships, visual problems, and symbol relationships. We'll cover all of them in the quantitative reasoning chapter of the book, but here is an example of one type, the visual problem.

Directions: Find the fraction of the grid that is shaded.

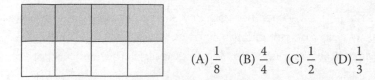

(A) $\frac{1}{8}$ (B) $\frac{4}{4}$ (C) $\frac{1}{2}$ (D) $\frac{1}{3}$

Answer: **(C)** is the correct answer choice. In this diagram, the grid is sectioned into 8 smaller squares, 4 of which are shaded. This 4 out of 8 can be expressed in fraction form as $\frac{4}{8}$ or reduced, $\frac{1}{2}$. Counting the shaded sections carefully will help you avoid errors. Create a fraction by placing the number of shaded portions as a numerator over the number of pieces in the whole in the denominator. If possible, reduce.

Test 4: Verbal Reasoning—Words

Verbal reasoning questions measure your ability to solve verbal problems by deductive reasoning, and by discerning relationships and patterns. This subtest contains several question types. Some require you to identify essential elements of objects or concepts, and others require you to classify words according to common characteristics. Another question type requires you to infer relationships between separate but related sets of words. We'll cover all of these in the Verbal Skills chapter of the book, but here is one example.

Directions: Find the word that names a necessary part of the underlined word.

liberty

(A) travel
(B) choice
(C) vote
(D) wilderness

Answer: **(B)**. *Liberty* means freedom, and a necessary part of freedom is the ability to choose. While a person who enjoys liberty may travel, *travel* is not an essential element of liberty. Likewise, we think of voting as an expression of freedom and liberty, but it does not define what the word means. *Wilderness*, which is related to the wild and nature, is related to freedom but does not define *liberty*.

Test 5: Verbal Reasoning—Context

This subtest measures your ability to solve verbal problems by reasoning deductively. This question type is also known as logic questions. You are required to identify essential elements of ideas presented in short passages and draw logical conclusions.

Directions: Find the statement that is true according to the given information.

Marisol sings in the choir. Her sister Lena takes ballet lessons. Their brother Alex plays the drums.

(A) There are exactly three children in Marisol's family.
(B) All of Marisol's family is musical.
(C) Marisol is the oldest child in her family.
(D) Lena is probably interested in dance.

Answer: **(D)**. The short statements do not tell us whether there are any other children in Marisol's family, nor whether all of them are musical. We are also not told the ages of Marisol and her brothers and sisters. The only thing we can say for certain, according to the statements, is that Lena is probably interested in dance.

Test 6: Reading and Language Arts

This subtest measures your ability to understand the central meaning of a passage as well as its details. It also tests your ability to understand the structure of sentences and paragraphs and how they work together to convey ideas. It tests language conventions such as punctuation and capitalization, and may cover aspects of the writing process such as topic selection, editing, and proofreading.

Directions: Read the following passage and answer the questions that follow.

"If only Moppits weren't so short!" Gadsolo exclaimed. He was standing on his tippy-toes, if you could call the little claws at the bottom of his furry legs "toes," but still he couldn't reach the rope dangling before him.

"Hurry!" Padlotto cried from the top of the cliff. "Grab on and I'll pull you up. There isn't much time."

The Moppit hopped up and down, trying to get his hands around the rope. "Ump! Harumph!" he cried as he hopped. And the hopping made him laugh.

"What in the twelve pink seas are you laughing about?" Padlotto shouted angrily.

"I can't help it," Gadsolo replied. "We Moppits are not only short, but also very silly."

"Well, you'd better wipe that smile off your face and find a way to climb up this rope," Padlotto said. "The Mucklurkers are coming."

"No!" Gadsolo gasped. He spun around and sure enough, there they were. Two slinky, slimy Mucklurkers were slithering on their green, oozy bellies toward him.

"Eek!" Gadsolo cried. With that, he jumped and grabbed on to the bottom of Padlotto's rope.

Where would you expect to find this passage?

(A) in a textbook about Moppits
(B) in an autobiographical book
(C) in a newspaper
(D) in a science fiction novel

Answer: **(D)** is the best choice. Moppits are not real creatures, so you would not expect to find them in a textbook, an autobiographical book, or a newspaper. Also, textbooks and newspapers generally don't include a lot of dialogue.

Directions: Choose the sentence that best combines the following three sentences:

Moppits are short. Moppits are silly. And Moppits are also quite heavy!

(F) Moppits are short; they are silly and they are, also, quite heavy!
(G) Moppits are: short, silly, and quite heavy!
(H) Moppits are short, silly, and quite heavy!
(J) Moppits they are short, they are silly, and they are quite heavy!

Answer: **(H)** is the best choice. Since the sentences all have the same subject, *Moppits*, and each contains an adjective describing the subject, the clearest and most concise way to combine the sentences is by listing the adjectives.

Test 7: Mathematics

Mathematics questions measure your understanding of math concepts. These questions include number relations, computation, estimation, operations, measurement, geometry, spatial sense, data analysis, probability, patterns, functions, and reasoning.

Directions: Read each problem and find the answer.

Mr. Wolfe drives 45 minutes to work each day. His average speed is 50 miles per hour. How far does he drive round trip?

(A)   37.5 miles

(B)   75 miles

(C)   225 miles

(D)   250 miles

Answer: **(B)**. Use the formula Rate × Time = Distance.

50 miles per hour × 45 minutes = Distance

Convert minutes to hour: 45 minutes = $\frac{3}{4}$ hour

$$50 \times \frac{3}{4} = \text{Distance} = 37.5$$

The question asks how far he *drives round trip*; 37.5 × 2 = 75 miles.

Memory

Another question type that has appeared on the COOP in the past is the memory section. At the beginning of the test, students were given 20 vocabulary words to memorize in 12 minutes, like this:

1. Spikenard is a fragrant ointment.
2. A scupper is a drainage opening.
3. Holt means a small woods.
4. To burke means to suppress.
5. Pia is a membrane of the brain.

6. A nacelle is an enclosure on an airplane.
7. A rabato is a high, lace-edged collar.
8. Calix means cup.
9. Hessite is a type of mineral.
10. Tussah is a silk fabric.

In a later section, they were asked about these definitions, in this form:

1. Which word means an enclosure on an airplane?

    (A) calix
    (B) burke
    (C) nacelle
    (D) scupper
    (E) rabato

2. Which word means cup?

    (F) calix
    (G) nacelle
    (H) pia
    (J) tussah
    (K) hessite

3. Which word means a fragrant ointment?

    (A) holt
    (B) burke
    (C) pia
    (D) spikenard
    (E) tussah

4. Which word means to suppress?

    (F) holt
    (G) spikenard
    (H) burke
    (J) rabato
    (K) scupper

5. Which word means a membrane of the brain?

    (A) nacelle
    (B) rabato
    (C) spikenard
    (D) tussah
    (E) pia

6. Which word means silk fabric?

    (F) holt
    (G) tussah
    (H) hessite
    (J) pia
    (K) rabato

7. Which word means a type of mineral?

    (A) scupper
    (B) nacelle
    (C) holt
    (D) pia
    (E) hessite

8. Which word means a small woods?

    (F) holt
    (G) rabato
    (H) scupper
    (J) hessite
    (K) calix

9. Which word means a high, lace-edged collar?

    (A) nacelle
    (B) rabato
    (C) tussah
    (D) calix
    (E) burke

10. Which word means a drainage opening?

    (F) tussah
    (G) nacelle
    (H) holt
    (J) scupper
    (K) rabato

As you see, students weren't expected to know these words; this was a test of short-term memory. (The correct answers are: 1. C, 2. F, 3. D, 4. H, 5. E, 6. G, 7. E, 8. F, 9. B, 10. J). This section has not appeared on recent tests, but the important thing is not to be thrown if such a section appears on your test. The COOP may introduce new question types, but they will test the same general skills that you are developing with other questions. Just do your best and move on.

HOW THE COOP IS SCORED

You will receive one point for every question that you answer correctly on the COOP. There is no penalty for incorrect answers, and each question, regardless of how difficult it is, is worth only one point. This is important since it means that it is in your best interest to guess on questions for which you are not sure of the answer. Also, since you win no additional points for answering more difficult questions, you should always answer the questions that are easier for you first in order to rack up the most points.

KAPLAN TIP

Be sure to fill in an answer for every question. If you don't know the answer, guess.
If you can't make an educated guess, make a random guess—you may just get it right!

The points you earn, known as your **raw score**, are tallied and then converted to a **scaled score** according to a formula determined by the test developers. Converting raw scores to scaled scores allows schools to compare a student's performance on one part of the exam with his or her performance on other parts that may have included a greater or lesser number of questions. Finally, scaled scores are reported as **percentile rank**. Percentile rank shows where students stand in relationship to one another on various sections and on the test as a whole.

chapter two

Facts about the HSPT

The HSPT, or Scholastic Testing Service High School Placement Test, is given to eighth-graders seeking admission to specific Catholic high schools. Like the COOP, it is used by schools to make decisions about applicants, to place them, and to determine scholarship awards. Generally, the HSPT is administered at the school to which you want to apply. Be sure to contact the school to find out where and when the test is offered.

The standard HSPT contains five parts and lasts about two and a half hours. The sections of the test are Verbal, Quantitative, Reading, Mathematics, and Language Skills. The Scholastic Testing Service also provides a choice of one optional test in Mechanical Aptitude, Science, or Catholic Religion. Because many schools do not choose to administer these tests, and because the results are not included as part of your percentile ranking, this book does not cover the optional exams. If the school you are interested in does use one of these tests, be sure to ask the school for more details about its contents.

HSPT EXAM FORMAT

The HSPT contains 298 multiple-choice questions, numbered from 1 through 298. All questions have four answer choices, A, B, C, D. Some questions in the Verbal Skills section on the HSPT have only three answer choices, A, B, and C.

KAPLAN TIP

Since the questions on the HSPT are numbered consecutively, it is easier to avoid filling in an answer choice on the wrong part of the bubble sheet. For example, there is only one question 5, regardless of which section of the exam you're in.

You are allowed to write in the question booklet. You can use this to your advantage when working through problems. Cross off answer choices as you eliminate them, circle problems you decide to skip and come back to, write out a mathematics problem as you solve it, or underline important information that helps you answer a question.

QUESTION TYPES

Unlike the COOP, the format of the HSPT remains relatively stable from year to year. The breakdown of sections, question types, and time allotted is as follows:

Test Section	Number of Questions	Time Allotted
Verbal Skills	60	16 minutes
Quantitative Skills	52	30 minutes
Reading	62	25 minutes
Mathematics	64	45 minutes
Language Skills	60	25 minutes

VERBAL SKILLS

This section includes synonyms, antonyms, analogies, logic, and verbal classifications. All five question-types will appear, mixed in together, on the Verbal Skills section. Knowing the directions for each question type is important, since it will enable you to move through the section without pausing to ponder what the question requires. We will review each question type and the directions for each in detail in chapter 5 of this book.

Analogy

Mechanic is to automobile as plumber is to

(A) electricity
(B) house
(C) pipe
(D) water

Answer: **(C)**. This is a functional relationship: A *mechanic* repairs an *automobile*, and a *plumber* repairs a *pipe*.

Synonym

Conclusion most nearly means

(A) finale
(B) ideal
(C) stickiness
(D) continuation

Answer: **(A)**. *Conclusion* means *ending*, which is closest to *finale*.

Logic

Kangaroo A jumps farther than kangaroo B. Kangaroo C jumps farther than kangaroo A. Kangaroo C jumps farther than kangaroo B. If the first two statements are true, the third is

(A) true
(B) false
(C) uncertain

Answer: **(A)**. If the first two statements are true and kangaroo C jumps farther than kangaroo A and A jumps farther than B, then C must also jump farther than B.

Verbal Classification

Which word does *not* belong with the others?

(A) poet
(B) engineer
(C) musician
(D) actor

Answer: **(B)**. An engineer is a technical profession, while the other choices are artistic professions.

Antonym

Pretense means the *opposite* of

(A) honesty
(B) love
(C) beauty
(D) contentment

Answer: **(A)**. *Pretense* means *trickery* or *falsehood*. The opposite is *honesty*.

QUANTITATIVE SKILLS

This section includes series, geometric comparisons, non-geometric comparisons, and number manipulations.

Number Series

Look at this series: 15, 17, 19, 21, … What number comes next in the series?

(A) 22
(B) 23
(C) 24
(D) 25

Answer: **(B)**. The pattern in this series is +2; 21 + 2 = 23.

Geometric Comparisons

Examine figures A, B, and C and find the best answer.

(A)   (B)   (C)

(A)   A > B + C
(B)   C < 2B
(C)   A + B < C
(D)   A − B = C

Answer: **(D)**. (A) contains 4 squares, (B) contains 1 square, and (C) contains 3; 4 − 3 = 1.

Non-Geometric Comparisons

Examine (a), (b), and (c) and find the best answer.

(a) $2(4 − 1)$ = 6
(b) $2 × 4 − 1$ = 7
(c) $2(−1 × 4)$ = −8

(A)   (b) < (a) + (c)
(B)   (b) = (a)
(C)   (a) + (b) > (c)
(D)   (b) + (c) > (a)

Answer: **(C)**. Determine the value of (a), (b), and (c) using order of operations.

(a) $2(4 − 1) = 2(3) = 6$
(b) $2 × 4 − 1 = 8 − 1 = 7$
(c) $2 (−1 × 4) = 2(−4) = −8$

Then, test each answer choice to see which is true.

(A)   (b) < (a) + (c)   Is $7 < 7 + (−6) = 7 < 1$? **false**
(B)   (b) = (a)   Does $7 = 6$? **false**
(C)   (a) + (b) > (c)   Is $6 + 7 > −8$? **true**
(D)   (b) + (c) > (a)   Is $7 + (−8) > 6 = −1 > 6$? **false**

Number Manipulation

What number is 10 more than $\frac{1}{3}$ of 21?

(A) 18
(B) 15
(C) 17
(D) 24

Answer: **(C)**. First find $\frac{1}{3}$ of 21; $\frac{1}{3} \times 21 = 7$. Then add 10: $7 + 10 = 17$.

READING

This section asks you to answer questions on short passages of varying styles on a range of topics.

By the late 1800s, many native peoples were being pushed off their traditional lands to make way for American expansionism. There were numerous battles of resistance, and many brave tribal leaders led the fight to keep their ancestral lands. Chief Joseph of the Nez Perce, a peaceful nation that spread from Idaho to Northern Washington, was one such leader.

Chief Joseph, known by his people as In-mut-too-yah-lat-lat (Thunder coming up over the land from the water), assumed the role of chief from his father, Old Joseph. Old Joseph was on friendly terms with the American government, and he signed a treaty that allowed his people to <u>maintain</u> most of their traditional lands. In 1863, however, following the discovery of gold in Nez Perce territory, the federal government took back almost six million acres of territory. Chief Joseph argued that his people never agreed to this second treaty and he refused to move them.

The Nez Perce were terribly outnumbered though. After months of fighting and forced marches, many of the Nez Perce were sent to a reservation in what is now Oklahoma. Many died from malaria and starvation. Chief Joseph tried every possible appeal to the federal authorities to return the Nez Perce to their land.

According to this passage, native peoples were forced off their land by

(A) gold diggers
(B) tribal leaders
(C) the growing American nation
(D) lack of food

Answer: **(C)**. The first paragraph of the passage explains that *native peoples were being pushed off their traditional lands to make way for American expansionism.* Choice (C) is a paraphrase, or rewording, of that information.

<u>Maintain</u> as it is used in the passage, most probably means

(A) keep
(B) settle
(C) care for
(D) give back

Answer: **(A)**. The passage discusses how the Nez Perce and Chief Joseph fought for their lands. *Old Joseph . . . signed a treaty that allowed his people to <u>maintain</u> much of their traditional lands.* From the context, we can understand that *maintain* most nearly means *keep*.

MATHEMATICS

Mathematics includes mathematical concepts and problem solving drawn from arithmetic, elementary algebra, and basic geometry.

Concepts

How many degrees does a right angle contain?

(A) 180
(B) 360
(C) 90
(D) 50

Answer: **(C)**. A right angle contains 90 degrees. A straight line contains 180 degrees, and a circle contains 360 degrees.

Problem Solving

Two years ago, Michael was four years older than half his father's age. If his father is 54 now, how old is Michael now?

(A) 30
(B) 32
(C) 26
(D) 27

Answer: **(B)**. Find the math within the story. Start with the fact Michael's father is now 54. Two years ago (54 − 2 = 52), Michael was four years older than half his father's age: $\frac{52}{2} + 4 = 30$. Don't forget the final step. The question asks how old Michael is now: 30 + 2 = 32.

LANGUAGE SKILLS

Language skills questions test capitalization, punctuation, usage, spelling, and composition.

Punctuation and Capitalization

Choose the sentence that contains an error in punctuation, capitalization, or usage. If there is no error, select choice (D).

(A)   Christine ordered a salad for lunch on Tuesday.

(B)   What time is it? Keshia asked.

(C)   We toured the Metropolitan Museum of Art on a field trip.

(D)   No mistake.

Answer: **(B)** has an error in punctuation. There should be quotation marks around the question: "What time is it?" Keshia asked.

Usage

Choose the sentence that contains an error in punctuation, capitalization, or usage. If there is no error, select choice (D).

(A)   Thomas is taller then his uncle.

(B)   Can penguins fly?

(C)   Lay the baby in the crib carefully.

(D)   No mistake.

Answer: **(A)** has an error in usage. *Than* should be used for comparisons, not *then*. *Then* means *next* or *afterwards*.

Spelling

Choose the sentence that contains an error in spelling. If there is no error, select choice (D).

(A)   Our neighborhood has many parks.

(B)   Please call me tomorrow to give me your answer.

(C)   Let's schedule our meeting for Sunday.

(D)   No mistake.

Answer: **(D)**. There are no spelling mistakes in any of the answer choices. Don't be tempted into selecting answers (A) through (C) even if you find no error. There is not always an error among the answer choices.

Composition

Choose the best word or words to complete the sentence.

Dolphins seem to communicate through the use of high-pitched sounds, _____ no one knows what these sounds mean.

(A) though

(B) and

(C) in addition

(D) because

Answer: **(A)**. The second half of the sentence contradicts the first, so a word of contrast such as *but* or *though* must be used.

HOW THE HSPT EXAM IS SCORED

Each question that you answer correctly on the HSPT earns you one point. There is no penalty for incorrect answers, so it is worthwhile to guess if you are not sure of the answer. Also, since each question is worth one point regardless of how easy or difficult it is, you should always answer the questions that are easier for you first. Rack up as many points as you can, then spend any remaining minutes on questions that require more time.

KAPLAN TIP

Since there is no penalty for wrong answers, you should answer every question on the HSPT. Do your best to eliminate wrong answer choices and make an educated guess.

Your **raw score**, or the total number of points you earn, is tallied and then converted to a **scaled score** ranging from 200 to 800. The Scholastic Testing Service will also determine your **percentile rank** according to your scaled score. Percentile rank shows where you stand in relationship to other students and allows the schools to more easily compare candidates. There is no passing or failing score on the HSPT, although each school determines what is a desirable score for its candidates.

chapter three

Facts about the TACHS

The TACHS, or Test for Admission into Catholic High Schools, is given in New York City and a number of other New York counties each year in November to eighth-graders seeking admission to specific Catholic high schools. The high schools use the exam results to make decisions about admitting applicants and to group prospective ninth-grade students into classes. The test measures academic achievement in reading, language arts, and mathematics, and assesses general reasoning skills.

The TACHS includes four subtests and lasts about two and a half hours. The subtests are: Reading (testing vocabulary and reading comprehension), Language (testing spelling, capitalization, punctuation, and usage/expression), Math (testing concepts, estimation, problem solving, and data interpretation), and Ability (testing abstract reasoning).

TACHS EXAM FORMAT

The TACHS contains about 200 multiple-choice questions. Most questions have four answer choices, marked A, B, C, D (odd-numbered questions) or J, K, L, M (even-numbered questions). Ability questions and some Language and Math questions have five answer choices, A, B, C, D, E (odd-numbered questions) or J, K, L, M, N (even-numbered questions). A separate answer sheet is provided to fill in your answer choices. Be careful when you fill in the answer bubbles—be sure that you're filling in the bubbles for the correct subtest!

KAPLAN TIP

Be sure that the bubbles you're filling in on your answer sheet match up with the subtest you're working on in your question booklet.

You will have space for scratch work (except for Math estimation questions); use this to your advantage when working through problems. Cross off answer choices as you eliminate them, circle problems you decide to skip and come back to, write out a mathematics problem as you solve it, or underline important information that helps you answer a question.

Like the HSPT, the TACHS intends to remain relatively stable from year to year, with four subtests—Reading, Language, Math, and Ability—each having several sections. Depending on the precise number of questions of each type, you can expect the timing to be something like this:

Subtest	Number of Questions (approximate)	Time Allotted (approximate)
Reading: Vocabulary	20	10 minutes
Reading: Comprehension	30	25 minutes
Language: Spelling, Capitalization, Punctuation, and Usage/Expression	40	23 minutes
Language: Paragraphs	10	7 minutes
Math: Concepts, Data Interpretation, and Problem Solving	32	33 minutes
Math: Estimation	18	7 minutes
Ability: Similarities and Changes	40	25 minutes
Ability: Abstract Reasoning	10	7 minutes

QUESTION TYPES

Here are explanations and examples of question types you will see on the TACHS exam. Directions are given for each section; read them carefully before starting a subtest or section, especially since the specific question format you see may vary slightly from that presented in this book.

Reading Part 1: Vocabulary

Each vocabulary question in the first part of the Reading test presents a word in a short phrase or sentence, and asks which answer choice is the closest in meaning.

Directions: For each question decide which of the four answers has most nearly the same meaning as the underlined word(s).

A violet sky

(A) long
(B) purple
(C) forceful
(D) dramatic

Answer: **(B)** is correct. The word *violet* means a light purple. Choices (C) and (D) are included to trap those who hastily read the word as *violent* instead of *violet*.

Reading Part 2: Reading Comprehension

This subtest measures your ability to understand the central meaning of a passage and to recall or locate its details. About three-fourths of the questions will require that you draw inferences or generalize about what you read.

Directions: Read the following passage and answer the questions that follow.

> If you received mail prior to 1840, you would have had to pay for its delivery. Postage stamps alleviated this burden, but how did the fee shift to the sender?
>
> In 1837, Rowland Hill, an English schoolmaster, noted that postal revenues were falling even though mail rates had increased. The simple reason was that if someone sent mail, free of charge, and the receiver would not or could not pay for delivery, the postal service then had to return the item. And all this for not a single penny.
>
> Hill proposed that a pre paid, flat-rate stamp be issued, regardless of the distance the mail was to travel. In tribute to their monarch, the British printed stamps carrying the likeness of Queen Victoria.

Why did England first make the postage stamp?

(J) To commemorate Queen Victoria

(K) To ensure payment for the mail service

(L) To make the recipient pay for delivery

(M) To standardize the appearance of the mail

Answer: **(K)** is correct. The second paragraph suggests that the existing payment was not working, and the third paragraph follows with a direct solution: the postage stamp.

Language Part 1: Spelling, Capitalization, Punctuation, and Usage/Expression

The Language section tests your ability to understand the structure of sentences and paragraphs and how they work together to convey ideas. The first three groups test language conventions such as capitalization and punctuation, each in its own group of questions. The first group presents four words, one of which may be misspelled.

Directions: Look for mistakes in <u>spelling</u>.

(A) vizhun

(B) perish

(C) dearth

(D) preserve

(E) (*No mistakes*)

Answer: **(A)** is wrong, therefore the correct choice; the word intended is *vision*. (B), (C), and (D) are correctly spelled.

The second and third groups require you to recognize over- or under-capitalization or errors in punctuation in short written contexts.

Directions: Look for mistakes in <u>capitalization</u>.

(J)   Even if you didn't remember
(K)   the pythagorean theorem, you would
(L)   be able to solve the problem
(M)   (*No mistakes*)

Answer: **(K)** is correct. The adjective *Pythagorean* should be capitalized, since it is based on a proper name.

Directions: Look for mistakes in <u>punctuation</u>.

(A)   We all know that
(B)   wood is porous. Did you also
(C)   know that some woods float.
(D)   (*No mistakes*)

Answer: **(C)** contains the error. The first sentence correctly ends with a period, but the second sentence is a question, so there should be a question mark.

The next group, testing usage and expression, presents one or more sentences in three lines in which you must identify usage errors—or select *No mistakes* if you believe there is no error in the use of verbs, pronouns, modifiers, or word choice.

Directions: Look for mistakes in <u>usage and expression</u>.

(J)   We were all ready for dinner.
(K)   Bill and Megan were working in the kitchen.
(L)   The others waited patiently in the den.
(M)   (*No mistakes*)

The right choice is **(M)**. *No mistakes* answers will be correct about as often as any other choice.

A second type of Language question offers a short paragraph followed by one or more questions about conciseness, clarity, appropriateness of expression, or organization of ideas.

Directions: For question 5–8, choose the best answer based on the following paragraph:

[1]In 1837, Rowland Hill, an English schoolmaster, noted that postal revenues were falling <u>in spite of the fact that</u> mail rates had increased. [2]The simple reason was that if someone sent mail, free of charge, and the receiver would not or could not pay for delivery, the postal service then had to return the item. [3]And all this for not a single penny.

What is the best way to write the underlined part of sentence 1?

(A) and

(B) but

(C) although

(D) (*No change*)

Answer: **(C)** is correct. "In spite of the fact that" is a needlessly wordy way of saying "although." The other choices show the wrong relationship between the ideas in the sentence.

Math

The two parts of the Math test measure your understanding of math concepts, problem solving and data interpretation, and estimation.

The first part includes questions about number relations, or asks you to solve problems based on stories, tables, or graphs.

Directions: Choose the best answer from among the four given for each problem.

Tobor wants to buy a new CD player that costs $185. He has $150. His father's friend will pay him $7 a week to rake the leaves. **What is the fewest number of weeks Tobor will need to rake the leaves to earn enough money to buy the CD player?**

(A) 4

(B) 5

(C) 6

(D) Not given

Answer: **(B)** is right. Tobor needs $35 ($185 minus the $150 he has already). At $7 per week, that will take him 5 weeks.

The second part asks you to estimate computations you aren't given enough time to complete:

Directions: For this question, estimate the answer in your head. No scratch work is permitted. Do not try to compute an exact answer.

The closest estimate of 9,173 – 6,920 is _____.

(J) 1,000

(K) 2,000

(L) 3,000

(M) 4,000

Answer: **(K)** is correct. Since the answer choices are in thousands, you only have to round to the nearest thousands; 9,173 is just over 9,000, while 6,920 is nearly 7,000, and 9,000 minus 7,000 is 2,000.

Ability

Intended to assess abstract reasoning ability, some Ability questions ask you to recognize a rule or principle shown in a sequences of figures. Your job is to analyze the pattern and then select the answer choice that would continue or complete the pattern.

Directions: The first three figures in each question are alike in certain ways. Choose the answer that goes with them.

(A)

(B)

(C)

(D)

(E)

Answer: **(A)** is the correct answer choice. The figures in the question stem all consist only of straight lines.

Other Ability questions offer two figures, the second a changed version of the first. A third figure is presented, and the answer choice will be a version of that figure that is changed in the same way as figure 2 was changed from figure 1.

Directions: The second figure shows a particular change from the first figure. The third figure, if changed in the same way, will become which of the answer choices?

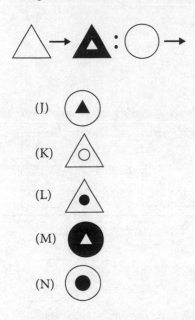

Answer: **(M)** is the correct choice. If you didn't see that, the question is explained in the Reasoning Skills chapter of this book.

A third type of Ability question shows a piece of paper and gives directions for folding it and punching holes. The correct answer shows how the paper will look when unfolded.

Directions: For each question, you can see in the top row how a square piece of paper is folded and where holes are punched in it. From the bottom row, select the choice that shows how the paper will look when unfolded again.

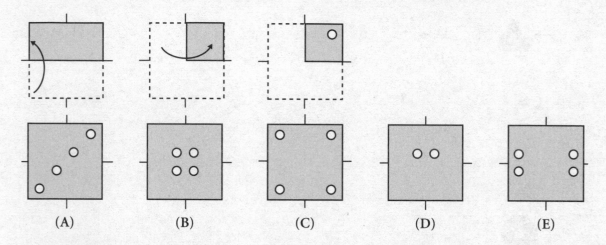

(A)   (B)   (C)   (D)   (E)

Answer: **(C)** is right. These questions are discussed in the Reasoning Skills chapter.

 KAPLAN TIP

Since you win no additional points for answering more difficult questions, you should always answer the questions that are easier for you first in order to rack up the most points.

HOW THE TACHS IS SCORED

You will receive one point for every question that you answer correctly on the TACHS. This is your **raw score**, which is tallied and then converted to a **scaled score** according to a formula determined by the test developers. Converting raw scores to scaled scores allows schools to compare a student's performance on one part of the exam with his or her performance on other parts that may have included a greater or lesser number of questions. Finally, scaled scores are reported as **percentile rank**. Percentile rank shows where students stand in relationship to one another on various sections and on the test as a whole.

chapter four

Test-Taking Strategies

Whichever test you take, the COOP, TACHS, or HSPT, there are some important things you need to know that have nothing to do with vocabulary words or isosceles triangles. Namely, you need to know how to be a good test taker. A good test taker:

- Understands the structure and content of the test
- Approaches questions systematically
- Stays calm in order to score the most points possible

Understanding the nature of the test is important in two ways. Obviously, you need to know the content in order to do well. Additionally, understanding the structure of the test, and the traps it commonly sets for you, will allow you to gain points that you might otherwise miss. This book will help you become familiar with the exams, while at the same time working on the skills tested. Subject area content is taught using test like examples. In addition to practical techniques and strategies to use on all question types, we give you targeted review.

USE THE TEST STRUCTURE TO YOUR ADVANTAGE

Answer Easier Questions First

Whether you are taking the COOP, TACHS, or HSPT exam, you will notice pretty quickly that these are lengthy tests with a lot of questions. You may find some of the questions quite difficult. Others, you'll find easier. But each one is worth the same number of points. Therefore, it is always to your advantage to answer the easier questions first. Get them out of the way, rack up as many points as you can, and spend the rest of your time on the questions that you find harder.

Don't get discouraged if you find a lot of questions that you can't answer or if you are unable to finish a section. Keep a positive attitude and do your best with each new question.

Know the Basic Question Types, but Always Read the Directions

It sounds obvious, but reading the directions and knowing what each question requires is essential.

The HSPT remains relatively stable from year to year, but the COOP may undergo changes. Knowing the basic structure of your test and the skills tested will help you answer question types without wasting too much time trying to figure out how the question type works.

Nonetheless, it is still important to read all the directions carefully on each section and on each question so as not to miss necessary key words, such as EXCEPT, NONE, ALL, etc.

Skip Around

Since time is of the essence, move through each section at a reasonable pace—no more than 30 seconds per question. If you find you can't answer a question immediately, mark it and come back to it later. Don't dwell on any question, especially a hard one, until you have tried each question at least once. And remember, expect to see several questions that you won't be able to answer. The test is intentionally set up that way, so don't let difficult questions discourage you.

If You Don't Know, Guess

When should you guess? Whenever you can't solve a problem.

There is **no wrong answer penalty**. That means you should **answer every single question on the test**, even if you have no idea of the correct answer. Of course, you should do your best to solve a problem and select the correct answer. Throughout this book, we'll give you strategies to narrow down the answer choices and improve your chances of selecting the correct answer. Since every question on each exam is multiple-choice, your odds of selecting the correct answer are 1 in 4. (Some questions on the TACHS or COOP Mathematics test give you five answer choices. In that case, your odds are 1 in 5.) If you eliminate just one wrong answer choice, your odds of selecting the correct answer improve.

If you're running out of time, you might as well quickly fill in an answer bubble. You never know what you might get right by luck!

Gridding—The Answer Grid Has No Heart

Be careful when you mark your answers on the answer grid! When time is short, it's easy to get confused going back and forth between your test book and your answer grid. If you know the answer, but mark it incorrectly on the answer grid, you won't get any points, so be careful. Here are some tips to help you avoid making mistakes on the answer grid.

Always Circle the Questions You Skip

Put a big circle in your test book around any question numbers you skip. When you go back, these questions will be easy to locate.

Always Circle the Answers You Choose

Circling your answers in the test book makes it easier to check your grid against your book.

Grid Five or More Answers at Once

Don't transfer your answers to the grid after every question. Transfer your answers after every five questions, or wherever might be a good breaking point. That way, you won't keep breaking your concentration to mark the grid. You'll save time and you'll gain accuracy. But be careful at the end of a section, when time may be running out. You don't want to have your answers in the test booklet and not be able to transfer them to your answer grid.

APPROACHING COOP, TACHS, AND HSPT QUESTIONS

Apart from knowing the setup of the COOP, TACHS, or HSPT, you need to have a system for attacking the questions. Approach your high school admissions test with a plan. What follows is the best method.

Think About the Question before You Look at the Answers

The people who write the tests love to put distracters among the answer choices. Distracters are answer choices that look like the right answer, but aren't. If you jump right into the answer choices without thinking first about what you're looking for, you are more likely to fall for one of these traps.

Work Backwards if Necessary

There are usually a number of ways to get to the right answer on a question. All of the questions are multiple-choice, so the answer is right in front of you—you just have to find it. But, if you can't figure out the answer in a straightforward way, try other techniques. We'll talk about specific Kaplan methods in later chapters.

Pace Yourself

The COOP, TACHS, and HSPT give you a lot of questions in a short period of time. In order to get through an entire section, you can't spend too much time on any one question. Keep moving through the test at a good speed; if you run into a hard question, circle it, skip it, and go back later if there's time.

Don't rush through the easy problems just to save time for the harder ones. The easier problems are points in your pocket, and you don't want to work through them in such haste that you end up making careless mistakes.

Locate Quick Points if You're Running Out of Time

Some questions can be done quickly; for instance, some reading questions will ask you to identify the meaning of a particular word in a passage. These can be done at the last minute, even if you haven't read the passage. When you start to run out of time, locate and answer any of the quick points that remain.

When you take the COOP, TACHS, or HSPT, you have one clear objective in mind: to score as many points as you can. It's that simple. The rest of this book will help you do that.

STAY CALM

The countdown has begun. Your test date is approaching. Perhaps your anxiety is on the rise. Maybe you think you won't be ready. Maybe you already know your stuff, but you're going into panic mode anyway. Don't get carried away! It's possible to tame that anxiety and stress—before and during the test.

Remember, a little stress is good. Anxiety is a motivation to study. The adrenaline that gets pumped into your bloodstream when you're stressed helps you to stay alert and think more clearly. But if you feel that tension is preventing you from using your study time effectively, here are some things you can do to get it under control.

Take Control

Lack of control is a prime cause of stress. Research shows that if you don't have a sense of control over what is happening in your life, you can easily end up feeling helpless and hopeless. Try to identify the sources of the stress you feel. Which ones of these can you do something about? Can you find ways to reduce the stress you are feeling about any of these sources?

Focus on Your Strengths

Make a list of your qualities that will help you do well on the test. Don't be modest and underrate your abilities. You will be able to draw on your strengths as you need them, helping you to solve difficult questions, maintain confidence, and keep test stress at a minimum. Every time you recognize a new area of strength, solve a challenging problem, or score well on a Practice Test, you will increase your strengths.

Imagine Yourself Succeeding

Close your eyes and imagine yourself in a relaxing situation. Breath easily and naturally. Now, think of a real-life situation in which you scored well on a test, or did well on an assignment. Focus on this success. Now, turn your thought to the exam, and keep your thoughts and feelings in line with that successful experience. Don't make comparisons between them; just imagine yourself taking the test with the same feelings of confidence and relaxed control.

Set Realistic Goals

Facing your problem areas gives you some distinct advantages. What do you want to accomplish in the study time you have remaining? Make a list of realistic goals. Perhaps it's adding 10 words a day to your vocabulary or mastering square roots. Taking active steps to improve in a particular area will boost your confidence.

Exercise Your Frustrations Away

Whether it's jogging, biking, pushups, or a pickup basketball game, physical exercise will stimulate your mind and body, and improve your ability to think and concentrate. A surprising number of students fall out of the habit of regular exercise, ironically because they are preparing for exams. A little physical exertion will help you keep your mind and body in sync and sleep better at night.

Eat Well

Good nutrition will help you focus and think clearly. Eat plenty of fruits and vegetables, low-fat protein such as fish, skinless poultry, beans, and whole grains such as brown rice, whole wheat bread, and pastas. Don't eat a lot of sugar and high-fat snacks or salty foods. Avoid stimulants, such as coffee or cola. Although sometimes they can help keep you alert as you study, too much of these can also lead to agitation, restlessness, and insomnia. Better to have a large glass of water.

Keep Breathing

Conscious attention to breathing is an excellent way to manage stress while you are taking the test. Most of the people who get into trouble during tests take shallow breaths: they breathe using only their upper chest and shoulder muscles, and may even hold their breath for long periods of time. Breathe deeply in a slow, relaxed manner.

Stretch

If you find yourself getting spaced out or burned out as you study or take the test, stop for a brief moment and stretch. Flex your feet and arms. Even though you will be pausing on the test for a moment, it's a moment well spent. Stretching will help to refresh you and refocus your thoughts.

Now, apply these strategies as you work through the review chapters and Practice Tests in this book.

"Managing Stress" adapted from *The Kaplan Advantage Stress Management System* by Dr. Ed Newman and Bob Verini, ©1996 by Kaplan, Inc.

Section 2
Diagnostic Quizzes

COOP Diagnostic Quiz
Answer Sheet

Remove or photocopy this answer sheet and use it to complete the Practice Test.

Sequences

1. Ⓐ Ⓑ Ⓒ Ⓓ   3. Ⓐ Ⓑ Ⓒ Ⓓ   5. Ⓐ Ⓑ Ⓒ Ⓓ

2. Ⓐ Ⓑ Ⓒ Ⓓ   4. Ⓐ Ⓑ Ⓒ Ⓓ

Analogies

1. Ⓐ Ⓑ Ⓒ Ⓓ   3. Ⓐ Ⓑ Ⓒ Ⓓ   5. Ⓐ Ⓑ Ⓒ Ⓓ

2. Ⓐ Ⓑ Ⓒ Ⓓ   4. Ⓐ Ⓑ Ⓒ Ⓓ

Quantitative Reasoning

1. Ⓐ Ⓑ Ⓒ Ⓓ   3. Ⓐ Ⓑ Ⓒ Ⓓ   5. Ⓐ Ⓑ Ⓒ Ⓓ

2. Ⓐ Ⓑ Ⓒ Ⓓ   4. Ⓐ Ⓑ Ⓒ Ⓓ

Verbal Reasoning—Words

1. Ⓐ Ⓑ Ⓒ Ⓓ   3. Ⓐ Ⓑ Ⓒ Ⓓ   5. Ⓐ Ⓑ Ⓒ Ⓓ

2. Ⓐ Ⓑ Ⓒ Ⓓ   4. Ⓐ Ⓑ Ⓒ Ⓓ

Verbal Reasoning—Context

1. Ⓐ Ⓑ Ⓒ Ⓓ   3. Ⓐ Ⓑ Ⓒ Ⓓ   5. Ⓐ Ⓑ Ⓒ Ⓓ

2. Ⓐ Ⓑ Ⓒ Ⓓ   4. Ⓐ Ⓑ Ⓒ Ⓓ

Reading and Language Arts

1. Ⓐ Ⓑ Ⓒ Ⓓ   4. Ⓐ Ⓑ Ⓒ Ⓓ   7. Ⓐ Ⓑ Ⓒ Ⓓ   10. Ⓐ Ⓑ Ⓒ Ⓓ

2. Ⓐ Ⓑ Ⓒ Ⓓ   5. Ⓐ Ⓑ Ⓒ Ⓓ   8. Ⓐ Ⓑ Ⓒ Ⓓ

3. Ⓐ Ⓑ Ⓒ Ⓓ   6. Ⓐ Ⓑ Ⓒ Ⓓ   9. Ⓐ Ⓑ Ⓒ Ⓓ

Mathematics

1. Ⓐ Ⓑ Ⓒ Ⓓ Ⓔ   4. Ⓐ Ⓑ Ⓒ Ⓓ   7. Ⓐ Ⓑ Ⓒ Ⓓ   10. Ⓐ Ⓑ Ⓒ Ⓓ

2. Ⓐ Ⓑ Ⓒ Ⓓ Ⓔ   5. Ⓐ Ⓑ Ⓒ Ⓓ   8. Ⓐ Ⓑ Ⓒ Ⓓ

3. Ⓐ Ⓑ Ⓒ Ⓓ Ⓔ   6. Ⓐ Ⓑ Ⓒ Ⓓ   9. Ⓐ Ⓑ Ⓒ Ⓓ

SEQUENCES

Directions: For questions 1–5, choose the answer that best continues the sequence.

1.  ⊡ ⊞   ⊞ ⊠   ⊠ __

   ⊞   ⊡   ⊠   ⊠
   (A)   (B)   (C)   (D)

2. △○○○   △○△○   △○△△   _____

   △○○○   ▲○▲○   △△○●   △○△□
   (A)   (B)   (C)   (D)

3. 18   16   ___   12   10   8

   (A) 15
   (B) 13
   (C) 14
   (D) 11

4. 1   3   9   ___   81   243

   (A) 54
   (B) 27
   (C) 21
   (D) 45

5. Z1   Y2   X3   W4   ___

   (A) V5
   (B) V4
   (C) S4
   (D) X5

ANALOGIES

Directions: For questions 1–5, look at the two pictures on top. Then, choose the picture that belongs in the space so that the bottom two pictures are related the same way that the top two are related.

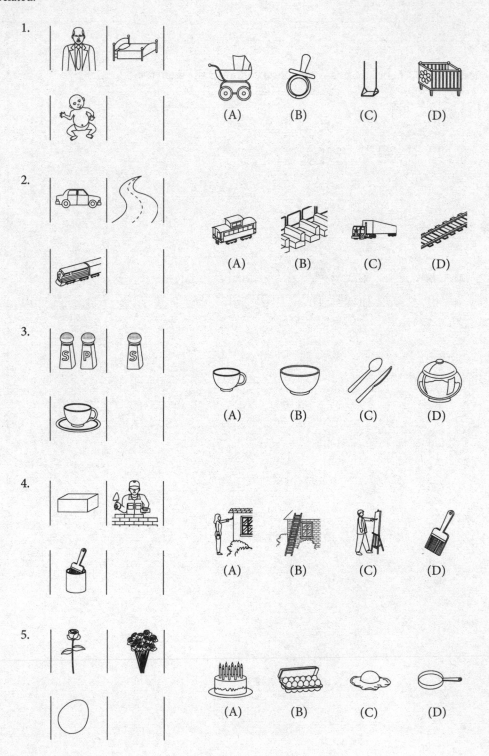

QUANTITATIVE REASONING

Directions: For questions 1–2, find the relationship of the numbers in the left column to the numbers in the right column. Choose the number that should replace the blank.

1. 3 → ☐ → 8

    10 → ☐ → 15

    11 → ☐ → __

12	15	17	16
(A)	(B)	(C)	(D)

2. 7 → ☐ → 14

    4 → ☐ → 8

    9 → ☐ → __

18	3	20	19
(A)	(B)	(C)	(D)

Directions: For question 3, find the fraction of the grid that is shaded.

3.

    (A) $\dfrac{4}{16}$

    (B) $\dfrac{5}{5}$

    (C) $\dfrac{5}{8}$

    (D) $\dfrac{1}{2}$

Directions: For questions 4–5, the scale shows sets of shapes of equal weight. Find a set that would also balance the scale.

4.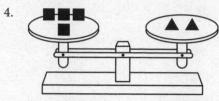

    (A) ■▲▲   ■■▲

    (B) ■■   ▲

    (C) ■▲   ▲■■

    (D) ▲▲▲   ■▲▲

5.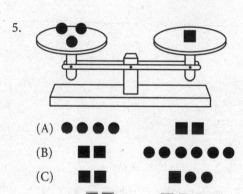

    (A) ●●●●   ■■

    (B) ■■   ●●●●●●

    (C) ■■   ■●●

    (D) ●■■   ■●●●

VERBAL REASONING—WORDS

Directions: For questions 1–3, find the word that names a necessary part of the underlined word.

1. restriction

   (A) forbid
   (B) strict
   (C) contract
   (D) sign

2. celebration

   (A) balloon
   (B) cake
   (C) party
   (D) birthday

3. wisdom

   (A) age
   (B) knowledge
   (C) books
   (D) teacher

Directions: For questions 4–5, the words in the top row are related in some way. The words in the bottom row are related in the same way. Find the word that competes the bottom row of words.

4.
bread	slice	crumb
water	puddle	

   (A) pebble
   (B) lake
   (C) river
   (D) drop

5.
pen	pencil	paint
drawing	photograph	

   (A) paper
   (B) painting
   (C) camera
   (D) clay

VERBAL REASONING—CONTEXT

Directions: For questions 1–5, find the statement that is true according to the given information.

1. Jane attends high school at Lincoln High. She bicycles to school every day.

   (A) Jane knows how to ride a bicycle.
   (B) Jane is a fast bicyclist.
   (C) There is no bus service from Jane's house to school.
   (D) Jane locks up her bicycle outside school.

2. The weather forecast says it will probably rain on Saturday. The Browns are planning a picnic on Saturday.

   (A) The Browns will change their picnic to Sunday.
   (B) The Browns will not go on their picnic.
   (C) The Browns should bring umbrellas if they go on their picnic on Saturday.
   (D) The Browns will get wet on their picnic.

3. The Blue Ridge Mountains are in Tennessee. Coby has hiked in the Blue Ridge Mountains.

   (A) Coby is from Tennessee.
   (B) Coby is a good athlete.
   (C) The Blue Ridge Mountains are high.
   (D) Coby has been to Tennessee.

4. Miss Battle is a kindergarten teacher. In order to attend kindergarten, a child must be at least five years old.

   (A) Miss Battle is five years old.
   (B) None of the children in Miss Battle's class are six years old.
   (C) The children in Miss Battle's class are at least five years old.
   (D) Miss Battle loves children.

5. Daffodils bloom only in spring. Daffodils are blooming.

   (A) Crocuses are also blooming.
   (B) Daffodils wilt easily.
   (C) Daffodils are yellow.
   (D) It is spring.

READING AND LANGUAGE ARTS

Directions: Follow the directions for questions 1–10.

Read the following passage and answer questions 1–7.

If you have never heard of the tulip craze, you won't believe it's true. The story begins in the 1550s when Dutch botanist Carolus Clusius brought the first tulip bulbs from Turkey to Holland. Clusius planted the flower bulbs in his own small garden and refused to give any to the locals. The rarity of the flower, of course, only made it more desirable to Clusius's neighbors. It wasn't long before some of them broke into Clusius's garden and stole his tulip bulbs. This is how the Dutch tulip trade started.

People fell in love with these colorful flowers. Because they were beautiful and hard to get, tulips soon became a status symbol for the well-to-do. For the next 70 years, the price of tulips increased dramatically. Everyone wanted them.

Though the early tulip buyers were people who loved flowers, later buyers were interested in trading tulip bulbs for money. By 1636, tulips were established as a trading commodity on the Amsterdam Stock Exchange. People were willing to spend vast amounts of money to obtain one rare tulip bulb in the hopes that they could trade it for profit. Though tulips had no practical use, no perfume, and no medicinal benefit, some people sold everything they owned just to buy one tulip bulb. At the height of tulip mania, the price of a single bulb could range from $17,000 to $76,000 in today's value. Tulip clerks were appointed to record tulip transactions, and laws were passed to control the tulip craze.

It wasn't long before the bubble burst. When some people began to sell their tulip holdings, tulip prices slowly began to weaken. The public's confidence in the value of tulips suddenly declined. People panicked and everyone tried to sell their tulips at once. In a period of just six weeks, tulip prices crashed dramatically. Although the Dutch government tried to pass regulations to help the market, tulip prices continued to fall. Tulip prices plummeted so that a bulb that had been worth the equivalent of $76,000 was suddenly worth less than $1. Trade in Holland took years to recover from this great shock.

1. In the last paragraph, the *word plummeted* means

    (A) rose slowly
    (B) fell rapidly
    (C) stayed steady
    (D) grew quickly

2. The selection suggests that after the early buyers, people bought tulips

    (A) as an indication of their wealth
    (B) because they loved the flowers
    (C) to annoy Clusius
    (D) to prevent people from stealing them

3. The title that best expresses the main idea of this selection is

    (A) The First Stock Market
    (B) Why People Do Crazy Things
    (C) The History of the Tulip
    (D) The Tulip Craze

4. The writer of this selection most likely feels that

    (A) people are always reasonable and predictable
    (B) flowers are a good investment
    (C) the tulip craze can teach us about human behavior
    (D) the tulip craze was a strange event that would never happen today

5. Here are two sentences related to the passage:

    People used to keep tulip bulbs in their homes.
    Tulips were considered too valuable to plant in gardens.

    Select the answer choice that best combines these sentences into one.

    (A) People used to keep tulip bulbs in their homes; tulips were considered too valuable to plant in gardens.
    (B) People used to keep tulip bulbs in their homes and that is why the tulips were considered too valuable to plant in gardens.
    (C) People used to keep tulip bulbs in their homes however tulips were considered too valuable to plant in gardens.
    (D) People used to keep tulip bulbs in their homes because tulips were considered too valuable to plant in gardens.

6. Choose the sentence that is written correctly.

    (A) During tulip mania, outsiders found it difficult to understand the great popularity of the flower.
    (B) During tulip mania; outsiders found it difficult to understand the great popularity of the flower.
    (C) During tulip mania. Outsiders found it difficult to understand the great popularity of the flower.
    (D) During tulip mania—outsiders found it difficult to understand the great popularity of the flower.

7. Choose the sentence that best completes this paragraph.

    Tulips are still popular today in Holland. They are also an important export product for the Dutch.

    (A) Tulip mania will never be forgotten.
    (B) There are many varieties of tulips.
    (C) Today, Holland exports 1.2 billion tulip bulbs a year.
    (D) Almost every Dutch garden boasts at least one type of tulip.

Here is a story a student wrote about visiting Holland. Read the story then answer questions 8–10.

(1) Last summer my family visited Holland. (2) We flew to Amsterdam. (3) Amsterdam is the capital city. (4) We spent a week there, touring many interesting sites. (5) Amsterdam is very different from New York City. (6) There are bicycles everywhere they ride bikes.

8. Which is the best way to write sentence 4?

   (A) We spent a week there, and toured many interesting sites.
   (B) We spent a week there, where we have toured many interesting sites.
   (C) We spent a week there, touring many interesting sites.
   (D) Best as is.

9. Which is the best way to write sentence 6?

   (A) People ride bicycles everywhere.
   (B) Everywhere people are there riding bicycles.
   (C) There are bicycles everywhere riding.
   (D) Best as is.

10. What is the best way to combine sentences 2 and 3?

   (A) We flew to Amsterdam, capital city.
   (B) We flew to Amsterdam, the capital city.
   (C) We flew to the city which is the capital and that city is Amsterdam.
   (D) Best as is.

MATHEMATICS

Directions: Read each problem and find the correct answer.

1. $\dfrac{2}{3} + \dfrac{1}{8} =$

   (A) $\dfrac{19}{24}$
   (B) $\dfrac{1}{8}$
   (C) $\dfrac{3}{4}$
   (D) 11
   (E) none of these

2. $12.2 - 3.5 =$

   (A) 7.5
   (B) 10.7
   (C) 9.7
   (D) 8.7
   (E) none of these

3. $8 \times -2 =$

   (A) 12
   (B) 16
   (C) −16
   (D) 6
   (E) none of these

Read the chart, then answer questions 4–6.

The ninth grade at Youngstown High put on a play. The table shows the total amounts in ticket sales for each of the three performances.

	Student Ticket Sales	Adult Ticket Sales
Friday night	$220	$280
Saturday night	$260	$375
Sunday night	$140	$225

4. Which number below best shows the part of the total ticket sales brought in on Friday night?

(A) $\dfrac{3}{10}$

(B) $\dfrac{1}{3}$

(C) 30%

(D) .03

5. If each student ticket costs $2.50, how many students attended the play in all?

(A) 1,040

(B) 520

(C) 248

(D) 210

6. If half of the 196 adults who attended also bought a bag of popcorn for 50 cents, how would you find the amount of money raised in popcorn sales?

(A) Divide 196 by 2 and add 0.5.

(B) Divide 196 by 2 and multiply by 0.5.

(C) Multiply 196 by 2 and multiply by 0.5.

(D) Divide 196 by 0.5 and multiply by 0.5.

7. What is the area of the rectangle?

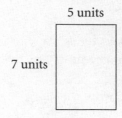

5 units

7 units

(A) 27 square units

(B) 24 square units

(C) 30 square units

(D) 35 square units

8. Farrah jogs 2 miles every morning. It takes her 40 minutes to finish her morning jog. About how fast is she jogging?

(A) 8 miles per hour

(B) 6 miles per hour

(C) 3 miles per hour

(D) 80 miles per hour

9. If $-1 < x < 3$, and x is an integer, which of the following represents the set of possible values of x?

(A) {1, 2}

(B) {1, 2, 3}

(C) {0, 1, 2}

(D) {–1, 0, 1, 2}

10. Rene has 3 dollars less than twice as much as her sister. If x represents the amount of money her sister has, which expression could represent the amount of money Rene has?

(A) $\dfrac{1}{3(2x)}$

(B) $2x - 3$

(C) $\dfrac{(x - 3)}{2}$

(D) $2x + 3$

ANSWERS AND EXPLANATIONS

Answer Key

Sequences

1. D
2. A
3. C
4. B
5. A

Analogies

1. D
2. D
3. A
4. A
5. B

Quantitative Reasoning

1. D
2. A
3. D
4. B
5. B

Verbal Reasoning—Words

1. A
2. C
3. B
4. D
5. B

Verbal Reasoning—Context

1. A
2. C
3. D
4. C
5. D

Reading and Language Arts

1. B
2. A
3. D
4. C
5. D
6. A
7. C
8. C
9. A
10. B

Mathematics

1. A
2. D
3. C
4. B
5. C
6. B
7. D
8. C
9. C
10. B

Sequences

1. D

Each square has one more line than the previous one. The next in the sequence should have another diagonal line, choice (D).

2. A

The pattern consists of triangles and circles. Only (A) contains triangles and circles. There is no reason to believe the next in the pattern should be shaded or contain squares.

3. C

The pattern is –2; 16 – 2 = 14.

4. B

The pattern is ×3; 9 × 3 = 27.

5. A

Letters are decreasing toward A and the numbers are increasing. The next letter should be V and the next number, 5.

Analogies

1. D

An adult sleeps in a bed, a baby sleeps in a crib.

2. D

A car rides on a road, a train rides on a track.

3. A

A salt shaker is one item of the pair pictured to the left. A cup is one item of the pair pictured to the left.

4. A

The brick is used by the man to lay bricks; the paint can and brush are used by the woman to paint. It is not the same kind of paint and brush that an artist would use.

5. B

Roses are usually sold by the dozen, and eggs are also usually sold by the dozen.

Quantitative Reasoning

1. D

Each number in the right column is 5 more than the number in the left column. The relationship is +5. The missing number is 11 + 5 = 16.

2. A

The number in the right column is two times the number in the left column. The relationship is ×2. The missing number is 9 × 2 = 18.

3. D

Count the total pieces of the rectangle and count the number of pieces shaded. There are 8 large pieces and 3 of them are shaded. Also, two halves of 2 more pieces are shaded. So, 4 pieces of 8 are shaded, or $\frac{4}{8}$, which reduces to $\frac{1}{2}$.

4. B

The diagram shows that 4 squares equal 2 triangles. Therefore, 2 squares = 1 triangle, or answer choice (B).

5. B

Three circles equal 1 square, so 2 squares equal 6 circles.

Verbal Reasoning—Words

1. A

A restriction forbids some action. That is the necessary part of the word since it defines what the word does. While a sign may post a restriction, such as "no swimming" this is not a necessary part of the word. Likewise, a contract is not necessary to have a restriction. Choice (B), strict, is a distracter choice. Restrictions may be strict, but again, this is not what defines the word.

2. C

A celebration marks a festive event. A party is a celebration. All the other elements, balloon, cake, birthday, are not necessary parts of a celebration.

3. B

Wisdom is the state of being wise or knowledgeable. Therefore, knowledge is a necessary part of wisdom. One doesn't have to be old to be wise, and wisdom can be found without books. Likewise, a teacher is not necessary to acquire wisdom.

4. D

The words above the line are related because they are decreasing parts of a whole; a slice is a smaller piece of bread; a crumb is the smallest bit. The words below the line are related in the same way; a puddle is made up of water and a drop is the smallest component of a puddle.

5. B

Above the line are all types of things to create art. Below the line are all pieces of art. Only choice (B) is another type of art.

Verbal Reasoning—Context

1. A

Since Jane bicycles to school, she must know how to ride a bicycle. This is the only conclusion we can draw with certainty from the information given.

2. C

It is said that it will *probably* rain. There is no certainty. The information does not state whether or not this forecast will cause the Browns to cancel or postpone their picnic. However, they should bring umbrellas in case they decide to go.

3. D

If Coby has hiked in the Blue Ridge Mountains, and the Blue Ride Mountains are in Tennessee, Coby has been to Tennessee.

4. C

The information states that *in order to attend kindergarten, a child must be at least five years old.* Some of the students may be older than that. Choice (C) is the correct answer.

5. D

Daffodils bloom only in spring and they are blooming. Therefore, it must be spring.

Reading and Language Arts

1. B

The paragraph explains that in just six weeks, tulip prices *plummeted* to less than one dollar. They fell rapidly.

2. A

The passage explains that at first, people bought tulips because they loved them. As prices grew, they later bought the flowers as a way to show off and prove that they were wealthy.

3. D

This selection is mainly about the tulip craze in Holland. The title should reflect the selection's main idea.

4. C

This is the best answer choice because the theme of the passage is that the tulip craze was an interesting example of how people behaved.

5. D

These two sentences have an effect-cause relationship. The word *because* best connects them.

6. A

The phrase *during tulip mania* should be set of with a comma.

7. C

The second sentence brings up the idea of tulips as an export product. The last sentence should expand on this idea.

8. C

The word *spended* is incorrect. The correct past tense verb is *spent*.

9. A

This sentence is the clearest because it has a simple subject and verb.

10. B

This is the most clear and correct way to combine the two sentences.

Mathematics

1. A

Change the fractions to a common denominator. The lowest common denominator is 24.

$$\frac{2}{3} + \frac{1}{8} = \frac{16}{24} + \frac{3}{24} = \frac{19}{24}$$

2. D

Line up the decimal points and subtract. You will have to borrow.

$$\begin{array}{r} 12.2 \\ -\ 3.5 \\ \hline 8.7 \end{array}$$

3. C

A positive number multiplied by a negative one will give a negative product. $8 \times -2 = -16$.

4. B

Total ticket sales = all student tickets + all adult tickets, so $620 + 880 = 1{,}500$. Friday night sales = $280 + 220 = 500$; $\frac{500}{1{,}500} = \frac{1}{3}$.

5. C

Add all student tickets, \$220, \$260, \$140, and divide by 2.50.

$$\frac{620}{2.5} = 248$$

6. B

Translate the word problem into math. "Half of the 196 adults" $= \frac{196}{2}$ "bought a bag of popcorn for 50 cents" $\frac{196}{2} \times 0.5$.

Divide 196 by 2 and multiply by 0.5

7. D

Area of rectangle = length × width = $5 \times 7 = 35$ square units.

8. C

Distance = Rate × Time

$$40 \text{ minutes} = \frac{40}{60} = \frac{2}{3} \text{ hour}$$

$$2 \text{ miles} = \text{rate} \times \frac{2}{3} \text{ hour}$$

$$\text{rate} = 2 \div \frac{2}{3}$$

$$\text{rate} = \frac{2}{1} \times \frac{3}{2} = \frac{6}{2} = 3 \text{ miles per hour}$$

9. C

The statement says that x is greater than -1 and less than 3, therefore x could be 0, 1, or 2.

10. B

Translate the word problem into math. Three dollars less than twice as much as x is equivalent to: $2x - 3$.

HSPT Diagnostic Quiz
Answer Sheet

Remove or photocopy this answer sheet and use it to complete the Practice Test.

Verbal Skills

1. Ⓐ Ⓑ Ⓒ Ⓓ   4. Ⓐ Ⓑ Ⓒ Ⓓ   7. Ⓐ Ⓑ Ⓒ Ⓓ   10. Ⓐ Ⓑ Ⓒ Ⓓ

2. Ⓐ Ⓑ Ⓒ Ⓓ   5. Ⓐ Ⓑ Ⓒ Ⓓ   8. Ⓐ Ⓑ Ⓒ Ⓓ   11. Ⓐ Ⓑ Ⓒ Ⓓ

3. Ⓐ Ⓑ Ⓒ Ⓓ   6. Ⓐ Ⓑ Ⓒ Ⓓ   9. Ⓐ Ⓑ Ⓒ Ⓓ   12. Ⓐ Ⓑ Ⓒ Ⓓ

Quantitative Skills

13. Ⓐ Ⓑ Ⓒ Ⓓ   16. Ⓐ Ⓑ Ⓒ Ⓓ   19. Ⓐ Ⓑ Ⓒ Ⓓ   22. Ⓐ Ⓑ Ⓒ Ⓓ

14. Ⓐ Ⓑ Ⓒ Ⓓ   17. Ⓐ Ⓑ Ⓒ Ⓓ   20. Ⓐ Ⓑ Ⓒ Ⓓ

15. Ⓐ Ⓑ Ⓒ Ⓓ   18. Ⓐ Ⓑ Ⓒ Ⓓ   21. Ⓐ Ⓑ Ⓒ Ⓓ

Reading

23. Ⓐ Ⓑ Ⓒ Ⓓ   26. Ⓐ Ⓑ Ⓒ Ⓓ   29. Ⓐ Ⓑ Ⓒ Ⓓ   32. Ⓐ Ⓑ Ⓒ Ⓓ

24. Ⓐ Ⓑ Ⓒ Ⓓ   27. Ⓐ Ⓑ Ⓒ Ⓓ   30. Ⓐ Ⓑ Ⓒ Ⓓ   33. Ⓐ Ⓑ Ⓒ Ⓓ

25. Ⓐ Ⓑ Ⓒ Ⓓ   28. Ⓐ Ⓑ Ⓒ Ⓓ   31. Ⓐ Ⓑ Ⓒ Ⓓ   34. Ⓐ Ⓑ Ⓒ Ⓓ

Mathematics

35. Ⓐ Ⓑ Ⓒ Ⓓ   38. Ⓐ Ⓑ Ⓒ Ⓓ   41. Ⓐ Ⓑ Ⓒ Ⓓ   44. Ⓐ Ⓑ Ⓒ Ⓓ   47. Ⓐ Ⓑ Ⓒ Ⓓ

36. Ⓐ Ⓑ Ⓒ Ⓓ   39. Ⓐ Ⓑ Ⓒ Ⓓ   42. Ⓐ Ⓑ Ⓒ Ⓓ   45. Ⓐ Ⓑ Ⓒ Ⓓ   48. Ⓐ Ⓑ Ⓒ Ⓓ

37. Ⓐ Ⓑ Ⓒ Ⓓ   40. Ⓐ Ⓑ Ⓒ Ⓓ   43. Ⓐ Ⓑ Ⓒ Ⓓ   46. Ⓐ Ⓑ Ⓒ Ⓓ

Language Skills

49. Ⓐ Ⓑ Ⓒ Ⓓ   52. Ⓐ Ⓑ Ⓒ Ⓓ   55. Ⓐ Ⓑ Ⓒ Ⓓ   58. Ⓐ Ⓑ Ⓒ Ⓓ

50. Ⓐ Ⓑ Ⓒ Ⓓ   53. Ⓐ Ⓑ Ⓒ Ⓓ   56. Ⓐ Ⓑ Ⓒ Ⓓ   59. Ⓐ Ⓑ Ⓒ Ⓓ

51. Ⓐ Ⓑ Ⓒ Ⓓ   54. Ⓐ Ⓑ Ⓒ Ⓓ   57. Ⓐ Ⓑ Ⓒ Ⓓ   60. Ⓐ Ⓑ Ⓒ Ⓓ

VERBAL SKILLS

Directions: Choose the answer that most nearly means the given word.

1. Humble most nearly means

    (A) weak
    (B) modest
    (C) poor
    (D) proud

2. Emulate most nearly means

    (A) copy
    (B) brag
    (C) tease
    (D) omit

Directions: Choose the answer that does *not* belong with the others.

3. Which word does *not* belong with the others?

    (A) ample
    (B) considerable
    (C) miniscule
    (D) substantial

4. Which word does *not* belong with the others?

    (A) transmit
    (B) inhibit
    (C) broadcast
    (D) communicate

Directions: Choose the answer that matches the relationship given.

5. Calendar is to date as map is to

    (A) location
    (B) time
    (C) appointment
    (D) identity

6. Counselor is to advice as teacher is to

   (A) instruction
   (B) blackboard
   (C) student
   (D) law

Directions: Choose the answer that means the same as the underlined word.

7. A <u>nomadic</u> tribe

   (A) agricultural
   (B) savage
   (C) settled
   (D) wandering

8. An <u>intricate</u> pattern

   (A) colorful
   (B) complex
   (C) vivid
   (D) traditional

Directions: Choose the answer that most nearly means the opposite of the given word.

9. Aggravate means the *opposite* of

   (A) improve
   (B) annoy
   (C) decline
   (D) anger

10. Reveal means the *opposite* of

    (A) uncover
    (B) conceal
    (C) display
    (D) convey

Directions: Choose the best answer to each question.

11. Mrs. Rangal cooks dinner for the Rangal family on weeknights. Mr. Rangal cooks dinner for the Rangal family on the weekend. Mr. Rangal cooks dinner more often than Mrs. Rangal. If the first two statements are true, the third is

    (A) true
    (B) false
    (C) uncertain

12. Carl runs faster than Joseph. Monty runs faster than Carl. Monty runs faster than Joseph. If the first two statements are true, the third is

    (A) true
    (B) false
    (C) uncertain

QUANTITATIVE SKILLS

Directions: Choose the best answer to each question.

13. What number is 3 more than 30% of 90?

    (A) 33
    (B) 30
    (C) 3
    (D) 16

14. Look at this series: 1, 8, 15, ____, 29… What number belongs in the blank in the series?

    (A) 20
    (B) 22
    (C) 21
    (D) 23

15. What number is $\frac{1}{3}$ the average of 10, 14, 11, and 13?

    (A) 5
    (B) 6
    (C) 4
    (D) 12

16. Examine (a), (b), and (c) and find the best answer.

    (a) 100% of 20
    (b) 20% of 100
    (c) 20% of 100%

    (A) (b) is greater than (a).
    (B) (a) is greater than (b) and (c).
    (C) (c) is greater than (a) but less than (b).
    (D) (a) and (b) are equal.

17. A small flower store earns $450 dollars per day. If the store is open six days a week, how many dollars does the store earn in four weeks?

    (A) $10,800
    (B) $8,800
    (C) $10,000
    (D) $10,050

18. On a field trip to the zoo, 60 eighth-graders visit the reptile exhibit. This is $\frac{3}{4}$ of the students in the entire eighth grade. How many students are in the eighth grade?

    (A) 90
    (B) 45
    (C) 20
    (D) 80

19. Which of the following sets of integers may replace the * to make the sentence below true?

    $6 < * < 10$

    (A) {5, 6}
    (B) {7, 8, 9}
    (C) {8, 9, 10}
    (D) {6, 7, 8, 9, 10}

20. If a box of chocolates costs y dollars, then 3 boxes of chocolates, in dollars, cost

    (A) $3 - y$
    (B) $3y$
    (C) $\frac{y}{3}$
    (D) $y + 3$

21. In which case are the numbers arranged in order of value with the smallest one first?

    (A) 0.53, $\frac{1}{3}$, 50%
    (B) 0.90, $\frac{1}{9}$, 33%
    (C) 0.25, $\frac{2}{3}$, 85%
    (D) 47%, $\frac{2}{5}$, 0.70

22. What is the next number in the series 72, 36, 18, 9, ...

    (A) 8
    (B) 4
    (C) 3
    (D) 4.5

READING

Directions: Read the passage and answer the questions that follow.

The name Fort Knox brings to mind images of solid gold bricks, stretching as far as the eye can see. However, very few people have ever laid eyes on the gold bullion reserves stored in Fort Knox, Kentucky. The bullion depository is a classified facility. No visitors are permitted inside and no gold is removed.

The gold bricks in Fort Knox are an <u>asset</u> of the United States government. Gold was originally put there to insure the U.S. dollar for other nations. During the Gold Acts of 1933 and 1934, the federal banks began collecting gold coins. By late 1934, the Treasury Department realized it needed a safe place to house this gold. Fort Knox was chosen because it is far from the country's borders. It is a safe distance from any possible invaders, and it has rough <u>terrain</u> that makes it easy to protect. Also, the First Cavalry, one of the fastest moving military units, is located in Fort Knox.

The first gold shipment arrived at Fort Knox in 1937. Forty trains, each with 200 cars, brought the gold to Fort Knox. The largest amount of gold held at Fort Knox was 649.6 million ounces. This record amount was reached in December of 1941. Worried that the war raging in Europe might spill over the into United Sates, officials decided to temporarily move the gold, as well as the Declaration of Independence, from Washington, D.C., to Fort Knox. In 1944, when danger of enemy attack had passed, the Declaration was returned to Washington, D.C.

Presently, there are 147.3 million ounces of gold housed in Fort Knox. Each ounce is valued at $42.22. One standard gold bar weighs 27.5 pounds, or about 400 ounces. A standard bar is 7 inches by $3\frac{5}{8}$ inches and 1 and $\frac{3}{4}$ inches. Each bar is worth over $16,000.

This gold is well protected. Fort Knox is built from granite that has been lined with concrete and reinforced with steel. The gold bars are kept within a concrete vault. The vault door weighs more than 20 tons. That's over 40,000 pounds! No one person knows the combination to the vault. Several members of the depository staff must dial separate combinations known only to them. The depository contains its own emergency power plant, water system, and other facilities in case of attack.

23. As used in the passage, the word <u>terrain</u> most nearly means

   (A) landscape
   (B) features
   (C) rocks
   (D) inhabitants

24. A good title for this passage might be

   (A) A Safe Place
   (B) The Combination to the Vault
   (C) The Gold Standard
   (D) All the Gold in Fort Knox

25. How much does one gold bar weigh?

    (A) 400 ounces
    (B) 25 pounds
    (C) 7 pounds
    (D) 42 pounds

26. Which of the following is correct?

    (A) The Declaration of Independence was moved to Fort Knox in 1937.
    (B) The Declaration of Independence was moved to Fort Knox during World War II.
    (C) The Declaration of Independence is still in the vault at Fort Knox.
    (D) George Washington put the Declaration of Independence in the vault at Fort Knox.

27. You would expect to find the kind of information in this passage in

    (A) a science book
    (B) a thesaurus
    (C) an encyclopedia
    (D) none of these

28. As used in the passage, the word underline{asset} most nearly means

    (A) insurance
    (B) protection
    (C) possession
    (D) tax

29. According to the passage, if you were comparing the gold kept in Fort Knox 1941 to the gold kept in Fort Knox today, you would find

    (A) each gold brick is heavier today
    (B) there is more gold now
    (C) the gold today is less valuable
    (D) there is less gold now

30. Why did the author write this passage?

    (A) to tell a funny story
    (B) to teach about Fort Knox
    (C) to persuade readers to buy gold
    (D) to explain why gold is valuable

Directions: Choose the answer that means the same as the underlined word.

31. A celebrity underline{endorsement}

    (A) advertisement
    (B) declaration
    (C) scandal
    (D) portrait

32. A casual underline{acquaintance}

    (A) friend
    (B) statement
    (C) contact
    (D) outfit

33. A underline{mutinous} crew

    (A) strong
    (B) rebellious
    (C) magnificent
    (D) competitive

34. A underline{grave} mistake

    (A) serious
    (B) unimportant
    (C) careless
    (D) accidental

MATHEMATICS

Directions: Choose the best answer to each question.

35. Which of the following represents the total number of degrees in the measure of a circle?

    (A) $36\pi°$
    (B) $90°$
    (C) $180°$
    (D) $360°$

36. The measure of angle A in the figure below is

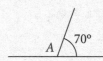

    (A) $110°$
    (B) $90°$
    (C) $80°$
    (D) $100°$

37. When multiplying a number by 10^3, the decimal point will move

    (A) one place to the right
    (B) three places to the right
    (C) three places to the left
    (D) four places to the left

38. Which of the following pairs contain a number and its reciprocal?

    (A) $\frac{1}{3}, \frac{2}{3}$
    (B) $\frac{2}{3}, \frac{3}{2}$
    (C) $(23, 32)$
    (D) $(-2, 2)$

39. Which fraction shows the greatest value?

    (A) $\frac{6}{7}$
    (B) $\frac{7}{8}$
    (C) $\frac{4}{5}$
    (D) $\frac{5}{6}$

40. The least common multiple of 3 and 8 is

    (A) 12
    (B) 4
    (C) 24
    (D) 16

41. A theater sold 120 tickets for the afternoon show at $20 per ticket and 155 tickets for the evening show at $24 per ticket. How much did the theater earn in ticket sales that one day?

    (A) $3,960
    (B) $5,120
    (C) $6,120
    (D) $2,720

42. Solve: $11 - 2\frac{1}{2} =$

    (A) $7\frac{11}{12}$
    (B) $8\frac{11}{12}$
    (C) $9\frac{11}{12}$
    (D) $10\frac{1}{12}$

43. Solve: $8 + (-4) + 6 + (-7) =$

    (A) 3
    (B) 11
    (C) 25
    (D) -2

44. Mrs. Jones paid $326.52 for her cable bill last year. Approximately how much, on average, did she pay per month?

    (A) $30.10
    (B) $28.00
    (C) $27.00
    (D) $30.50

45. If $5(2x - 3) = 42$, then $x =$

    (A) 57
    (B) 42
    (C) 4.7
    (D) 5.7

46. Three years ago, Marisa's mother was three times as old as Marisa. How old is Marisa's mother now if Marisa is 15?

    (A) 39
    (B) 36
    (C) 24
    (D) 30

47. If the 8% sales tax on a sweater is $4.16, what is the price of the sweater, not including the tax?

    (A) $56.16
    (B) $62
    (C) $60.02
    (D) $52

48. The ratio of $\frac{2}{7}$ to $\frac{5}{4}$ is

    (A) 36:8
    (B) 8:35
    (C) 5:14
    (D) 10:28

LANGUAGE SKILLS

Directions: For questions 49–52, choose the sentence that contains an error in punctuation, capitalization, or usage. If there is no error, select choice (D).

49. (A) Neither the blue nor the red pen is on the table.
    (B) I always prefer to arrive on time.
    (C) She is certainly more talkative than her sister.
    (D) No mistake.

50. (A) A letter is in the mailbox now.
    (B) Their's nothing I can do at the moment.
    (C) How many cans are in the cupboard?
    (D) No mistake.

51. (A) Aunt elisa is visiting us tomorrow.
    (B) We won't be late if we leave now.
    (C) Does he play on the team?
    (D) No mistake.

52. (A) We requested a room with a view.
    (B) I never agreed to that.
    (C) Which sweater do you like better?
    (D) No mistake.

Directions: For questions 53–56, choose the sentence that contains a spelling error. If there is no error, select choice (D).

53. (A) I received the bill yesterday.
    (B) Jack always reads the sports colum.
    (C) Compared to Louise, I am punctual.
    (D) No mistake.

54. (A) The job will take approximately two hours.
    (B) Please include specific examples.
    (C) All of the merchundise is on sale.
    (D) No mistake.

55. (A) We highly recommend the movie.
    (B) I made a note on my calender.
    (C) Maxine canceled the appointment.
    (D) No mistake.

56. (A) Please stop tapping your toes; you are irratating me.
    (B) The delivery is scheduled for noon.
    (C) Have you noticed how hazy it is today?
    (D) No mistake.

Directions: For questions 57–60, choose the best answer to each question.

57. Choose the words that best complete the following sentence.

    The club needs to decide _____.

    (A) where to go on its spring trip this year
    (B) this year where to go on its spring trip
    (C) about its spring trip this year and where to go
    (D) to go where on its spring trip

58. Choose the word that is a clear connective to complete the sentence below.

    Jonathan believed that he had done his best; ____ _____, he was content when he received his score.

    (A) however
    (B) therefore
    (C) moreover
    (D) none of these

59. Which sentence does not belong in the paragraph below?

    (1) Located north of Afghanistan, in central Asia, Uzbekistan is a dry, landlocked country. (2) Only 10% of the country consists of irrigated river valleys. (3) The capital, Tashkent, lies in the valley of the River Chirchik. (4) During the period of Soviet occupation, it was one of the poorest areas of the region. (5) It is now the third largest cotton exporter in the world, as well as a major producer of gold and natural gas.

    (A) sentence 1
    (B) sentence 2
    (C) sentence 3
    (D) sentence 5

60. Where should the following sentence be placed in the paragraph below?

    However, if Shakespeare did not invent the stories, he did pen the marvelous words that make his writings poetic and unique.

    (1) Though William Shakespeare is renowned as a brilliant playwright, many of his readers are not aware that the Bard did not completely invent his works. (2) Many of his plots and themes were borrowed from Renaissance literature. (3) In fact, most can be directly attributed to popular dramas of the day.

    (A) before sentence 1
    (B) before sentence 2
    (C) after sentence 1
    (D) after sentence 3

ANSWERS AND EXPLANATIONS

Answer Key

Verbal Skills

1. B
2. A
3. C
4. B
5. A
6. A
7. D
8. B
9. A
10. B
11. B
12. A

Quantitative Skills

13. B
14. B
15. C
16. D
17. A
18. D
19. B
20. B
21. C
22. D

Reading

23. A
24. D
25. A
26. B
27. C
28. C
29. D
30. B
31. B
32. C
33. B
34. A

Mathematics

35. D
36. A
37. B
38. B
39. B
40. C
41. C
42. B
43. A
44. C
45. D
46. A
47. D
48. B

Language

49. D
50. B
51. A
52. D
53. B
54. C
55. B
56. A
57. A
58. B
59. C
60. D

Verbal Skills

1. B

Humble means polite, reserved, or modest.

2. A

To emulate is to imitate or copy.

3. C

Miniscule means small, while all the other choices mean large amounts.

4. B

These words have to do with sharing information. However, *inhibit* most nearly means to prohibit.

5. A

A calendar shows dates, a map shows locations.

6. A

A counselor's job is to give advice; a teacher's job is to give instruction.

7. D

A nomadic tribe wanders from place to place.

8. B

An intricate pattern is complex.

9. A

To aggravate means to make worse. Choice (A), *improve*, is the opposite.

10. B

To reveal is to show something hidden. The opposite is (B), *conceal*.

11. B

Because the first two statements are true and Mrs. Rangal cooks five nights a week as compared with Mr. Rangal's two nights a week, she must cook dinner more often than Mr. Rangal.

12. A

Because the first two statements are true and Carl runs faster than Joseph, Monty must run faster than Joseph too.

Quantitative Skills

13. B

30% of 90 = 0.30 × 90 = 27; 27 + 3 = 30.

14. B

Each number is 7 more than the preceding one. The number in the blank should be 15 + 7 = 22.

15. C

First, calculate the average of the four numbers:

$$10 + 14 + 11 + 13 = \frac{48}{4} = 12.$$

Then, multiply by $\frac{1}{3}$:

$$12 \times \frac{1}{3} = 4.$$

16. D

Calculate the value of (a), (b), and (c).

(a) 100% x 20 = 20

(b) 20% of 100 = 0.2 x 100 = 20

(c) 20% of 100% = 0.2 x 1 = .2

Evaluate each answer choice; (a) and (b) are equal. Therefore, choice (D) is correct.

17. A

6 days a week × 4 weeks = 24 days.

24 × 450 = 10,800

18. D

$\frac{3}{4}$ of the students in the eighth grade = 60 students.

$\frac{1}{4}$ of the students in the eighth grade $= 60 \div 3 = 20. \frac{4}{4}$, or

all the students on the trip = 20 x 4 = 80 students.

19. B

The sentence states that the numbers that may be placed in * are greater than 6 and less than 10. The numbers 7, 8, and 9 are greater than 6 and less than 10. Therefore, the members 7, 8, and 9 may replace *.

20. B

In order to obtain the cost of three boxes you must multiply the number of boxes bought by the cost per box, 3y.

21. C

By writing all the numbers as decimals, you can compare them easily.

(A) 0.53, 0.33, 0.50—the smallest one is not first.

(B) 0.90, 0.11, 0.33—the smallest one is not first.

(C) 0.25, 0.66, 0.85—the smallest one is first here.

(D) 0.47, 0.40, 0.70—the smallest one is not first.

22. D

The pattern is that each number is divided by 2. The next number is 9 divided by 2, or 4.5.

Reading

23. A

As it is used in the passage, the word *terrain* means a piece of land, or a landscape.

24. D

A good title should contain the main idea of the passage. This passage is about the gold in Fort Knox. Therefore, choice (D) is the best answer.

25. A

This is a detail question. The answer, 400 ounces, is found in paragraph 4.

26. B

This is a detail question. Information about the Declaration of Independence is found in paragraph 3. The Declaration was moved to Fort Knox for safekeeping in 1941 during World War II and was returned to Washington, D.C., after the war.

27. C

This passage is factual. It could be found in an encyclopedia article.

28. C

Reread the sentence containing the word *asset* and a few sentences after it to figure out the meaning of the word. The gold is kept in Fort Knox by the government. It belongs to, or is a possession of, the government.

29. D

Paragraph 3 states: *The largest amount of gold held at Fort Knox was 649.6 million ounces. This record amount was reached in December of 1941.* Paragraph 4 states: *Presently, there are 147.3 million ounces of gold housed in Fort Knox.* Thus, there is less gold in Fort Knox now.

30. B

The information in the passage is not funny, nor does it persuade the reader to do something. Although it tells about the value of the gold, it does not explain why the Declaration of Independence is valuable. This passage was written to inform readers about Fort Knox.

31. B

A celebrity endorsement is a declaration given by a celebrity.

32. C

A casual acquaintance is a contact.

33. B

A mutinous crew is rebellious.

34. A

A grave mistake is serious.

Mathematics

35. D

A circle measures 360 degrees.

36. A

A straight line measures 180 degrees. Since the measure of the given angle is 70 degrees, 180 − 70 = 110.

37. B

$10^3 = 1,000$. To multiply by 1,000, move the decimal point three places to the right. The number is getting larger.

38. B

Reciprocals are fractions turned upside down so that one fraction is the inverse of the other.

39. B

To compare more readily, convert all answer choices to decimals.

Thus, $\frac{6}{7} \approx 0.85$

$\frac{7}{8} \approx 0.87$

$\frac{4}{5} \approx 0.80$

$\frac{5}{6} \approx 0.83$

$\frac{7}{8}$ is the largest.

40. C

The least common multiple of 3 and 8 is 24; in other words, 24 is the smallest number in which both 3 and 8 divide evenly without a remainder.

41. C

$(20 \times 120) + (155 \times 24) = 2,400 + 3,720 = 6,120$

42. B

Convert 11 into $10\frac{12}{12}$, then subtract $2\frac{1}{12} = 8\frac{11}{12}$.

43. A

When adding two numbers with different signs, subtract the absolute values and keep the sign of the number with the larger absolute value. $8 + (−4) = 4$; $4 + 6 = 10$; $10 + (−7) = 3$.

44. C

Round 326.52 to 327 and divide by 12 because there are 12 months in a year.

$\frac{327}{12} = 27.25$, which is approximately equal to 27.

45. D

Isolate x to solve. First, multiply using the distributive property; $10x − 15 = 42$. Add 15 to each side of the equal sign; $10x = 42 + 15$; $10x = 57$. Divide each side by 10; $x = \frac{57}{10} = 5.7$.

46. A

Let x equal Marisa's mother's age.

Marisa is now 15. Three years ago her mother was three times as old as Marisa. Thus, three years ago:

$$3(15 − 3) = x$$

$$3(12) = x$$

$$36 = x$$

Marisa's mother's age now = 36 + 3 = 39.

47. D

$$0.08x = 4.16$$

$$x = \frac{4.16}{0.08} = 52$$

48. B

Ratios can be expressed as fractions:

$$\frac{\frac{2}{7}}{\frac{5}{4}}$$

To divide a fraction by a fraction, multiply by the reciprocal of the number being divided by. The problem becomes $\frac{2}{7} \times \frac{4}{5} = \frac{8}{35}$, which can also be expressed as 8:35.

Language

49. D

There are no mistakes.

50. B

Their's is incorrect. The correct word is *there's*, the contraction for *there is*.

51. A

Elisa, a proper name, should be capitalized.

52. D

There are no mistakes.

53. B

The correct spelling is *column*.

54. C

The correct spelling is *merchandise*.

55. B

The correct spelling is *calendar*.

56. A

The correct spelling is *irritating*.

57. A

The meaning of the sentence is clearest when the adverbial phrase follows the verb.

58. B

The first phrase is the reason for the second. *Therefore* is the correct connective.

59. C

Information about the capital is not related to the general flow of the paragraph that introduces the topic of Uzbekistan and then discusses its economic status.

60. D

The word *however* indicates a change in direction of the ideas of the paragraph. It should come at the end of the paragraph, after sentence 3.

TACHS Diagnostic Quiz
Answer Sheet

Remove or photocopy this answer sheet and use it to complete the Practice Test.

Reading

1. Ⓐ Ⓑ Ⓒ Ⓓ	7. Ⓐ Ⓑ Ⓒ Ⓓ	13. Ⓐ Ⓑ Ⓒ Ⓓ	19. Ⓐ Ⓑ Ⓒ Ⓓ	25. Ⓐ Ⓑ Ⓒ Ⓓ
2. Ⓐ Ⓑ Ⓒ Ⓓ	8. Ⓐ Ⓑ Ⓒ Ⓓ	14. Ⓐ Ⓑ Ⓒ Ⓓ	20. Ⓐ Ⓑ Ⓒ Ⓓ	26. Ⓐ Ⓑ Ⓒ Ⓓ
3. Ⓐ Ⓑ Ⓒ Ⓓ	9. Ⓐ Ⓑ Ⓒ Ⓓ	15. Ⓐ Ⓑ Ⓒ Ⓓ	21. Ⓐ Ⓑ Ⓒ Ⓓ	27. Ⓐ Ⓑ Ⓒ Ⓓ
4. Ⓐ Ⓑ Ⓒ Ⓓ	10. Ⓐ Ⓑ Ⓒ Ⓓ	16. Ⓐ Ⓑ Ⓒ Ⓓ	22. Ⓐ Ⓑ Ⓒ Ⓓ	28. Ⓐ Ⓑ Ⓒ Ⓓ
5. Ⓐ Ⓑ Ⓒ Ⓓ	11. Ⓐ Ⓑ Ⓒ Ⓓ	17. Ⓐ Ⓑ Ⓒ Ⓓ	23. Ⓐ Ⓑ Ⓒ Ⓓ	29. Ⓐ Ⓑ Ⓒ Ⓓ
6. Ⓐ Ⓑ Ⓒ Ⓓ	12. Ⓐ Ⓑ Ⓒ Ⓓ	18. Ⓐ Ⓑ Ⓒ Ⓓ	24. Ⓐ Ⓑ Ⓒ Ⓓ	30. Ⓐ Ⓑ Ⓒ Ⓓ

Language

1. Ⓐ Ⓑ Ⓒ Ⓓ	6. Ⓐ Ⓑ Ⓒ Ⓓ	11. Ⓐ Ⓑ Ⓒ Ⓓ	16. Ⓐ Ⓑ Ⓒ Ⓓ	21. Ⓐ Ⓑ Ⓒ Ⓓ
2. Ⓐ Ⓑ Ⓒ Ⓓ	7. Ⓐ Ⓑ Ⓒ Ⓓ	12. Ⓐ Ⓑ Ⓒ Ⓓ	17. Ⓐ Ⓑ Ⓒ Ⓓ	22. Ⓐ Ⓑ Ⓒ Ⓓ
3. Ⓐ Ⓑ Ⓒ Ⓓ	8. Ⓐ Ⓑ Ⓒ Ⓓ	13. Ⓐ Ⓑ Ⓒ Ⓓ	18. Ⓐ Ⓑ Ⓒ Ⓓ	23. Ⓐ Ⓑ Ⓒ Ⓓ
4. Ⓐ Ⓑ Ⓒ Ⓓ	9. Ⓐ Ⓑ Ⓒ Ⓓ	14. Ⓐ Ⓑ Ⓒ Ⓓ	19. Ⓐ Ⓑ Ⓒ Ⓓ	24. Ⓐ Ⓑ Ⓒ Ⓓ
5. Ⓐ Ⓑ Ⓒ Ⓓ	10. Ⓐ Ⓑ Ⓒ Ⓓ	15. Ⓐ Ⓑ Ⓒ Ⓓ	20. Ⓐ Ⓑ Ⓒ Ⓓ	25. Ⓐ Ⓑ Ⓒ Ⓓ

Math

1. Ⓐ Ⓑ Ⓒ Ⓓ	4. Ⓐ Ⓑ Ⓒ Ⓓ	7. Ⓐ Ⓑ Ⓒ Ⓓ	10. Ⓐ Ⓑ Ⓒ Ⓓ
2. Ⓐ Ⓑ Ⓒ Ⓓ	5. Ⓐ Ⓑ Ⓒ Ⓓ	8. Ⓐ Ⓑ Ⓒ Ⓓ	11. Ⓐ Ⓑ Ⓒ Ⓓ
3. Ⓐ Ⓑ Ⓒ Ⓓ	6. Ⓐ Ⓑ Ⓒ Ⓓ	9. Ⓐ Ⓑ Ⓒ Ⓓ	12. Ⓐ Ⓑ Ⓒ Ⓓ

Ability

1. Ⓐ Ⓑ Ⓒ Ⓓ Ⓔ	4. Ⓐ Ⓑ Ⓒ Ⓓ Ⓔ	7. Ⓐ Ⓑ Ⓒ Ⓓ Ⓔ	10. Ⓐ Ⓑ Ⓒ Ⓓ Ⓔ
2. Ⓐ Ⓑ Ⓒ Ⓓ Ⓔ	5. Ⓐ Ⓑ Ⓒ Ⓓ Ⓔ	8. Ⓐ Ⓑ Ⓒ Ⓓ Ⓔ	11. Ⓐ Ⓑ Ⓒ Ⓓ Ⓔ
3. Ⓐ Ⓑ Ⓒ Ⓓ Ⓔ	6. Ⓐ Ⓑ Ⓒ Ⓓ Ⓔ	9. Ⓐ Ⓑ Ⓒ Ⓓ Ⓔ	12. Ⓐ Ⓑ Ⓒ Ⓓ Ⓔ

READING PART 1

Directions: This section is about the meaning of words. For each question, decide which choice has most nearly the same meaning as the underlined word or words given. Fill in the corresponding letter on your answer sheet.

1. To <u>insinuate</u> doubt

   (A) introduce
   (B) dispel
   (C) attribute
   (D) assume

2. An <u>avuncular</u> gentleman

   (A) senile and forgetful
   (B) decrepit and ill
   (C) solitary and lonesome
   (D) kindly and genial

3. A form with tremendous <u>volume</u>

   (A) containing great mass
   (B) brightly or loudly colored
   (C) evocative of deep emotion
   (D) intricately or finely constructed

4. To <u>accost</u> a stranger

   (A) whisper to
   (B) approach aggressively
   (C) acknowledge in friendship
   (D) introduce to others

5. A <u>despicable</u> person

   (A) inept
   (B) contemptible
   (C) admirable
   (D) cunning

6. An <u>incised</u> outline

   (A) sketched
   (B) written
   (C) carved
   (D) painted

7. A <u>libelous</u> accusation

   (A) laudatory
   (B) defamatory
   (C) commendatory
   (D) adulatory

8. A <u>matte</u> surface

   (A) lustrous
   (B) rough
   (C) flat
   (D) smooth

9. <u>Tarnished</u> silver

   (A) gleaming
   (B) luxurious
   (C) plated
   (D) dull

10. To <u>coerce</u> a confession

    (A) pressure
    (B) accept
    (C) dismiss
    (D) concoct

READING PART 2

Directions: Read the passages below and the questions relating to them. Choose the best answer from among the four given for each question and mark the corresponding space on your answer sheet.

Read the following passage and answer questions 11–15.

The Brooklyn Bridge, a steel wire suspension bridge which links the boroughs of Brooklyn and Manhattan in New York City, was at the time of its completion in 1883 the largest structure of its kind in the world. For many years, the two impressive neo-Gothic supports of limestone and granite, which anchor the span on either side of the East River, were the tallest towers in the world. The bridge was engineered by John Augustus Roebling, and construction was finished by his son, Washington, when the father succumbed to complications caused by tetanus after an accident on the building site. The Roeblings had designed an open truss system to support the deck of the bridge, and overbuilt their structure to four times the needed capacity to ensure its functional integrity. This foresight has enabled the bridge to remain standing, even as many similar successive bridges have been demolished and replaced due to the relative weakness of their original construction. Today, the Brooklyn Bridge features a six-lane roadway for vehicular use, with an elevated walkway above for pedestrians and bicyclists. The bridge is always floodlit at night, and its stunning architectural features are a spectacular part of the glittering New York City skyline.

11. Why was Washington Roebling entrusted with the building of the Brooklyn bridge?

   (A) He had an excellent understanding of engineering principles.
   (B) He understood the need for the bridge to have both vehicular and pedestrian access.
   (C) His father was unable to complete the project.
   (D) His feeling for materials such as stone and steel added beauty to the structure.

12. What is the primary reason that the Brooklyn Bridge is still in use today?

   (A) There is need for a bridge that enables people to travel between the boroughs of Brooklyn and Manhattan.
   (B) The original overbuilt structural character of the bridge has ensured its continued stability.
   (C) The neo-Gothic features of its towers have achieved landmark status.
   (D) The bridge is unique in that it allows access to both vehicles and pedestrians.

13. An open truss system served what purpose in the construction of the bridge?

   (A) It was a means of support.
   (B) It anchored the span of the bridge.
   (C) It allowed for the construction of the two tall towers.
   (D) It was a suspension system of steel wire.

14. Which engineered feature of the Brooklyn Bridge ensured that it has remained standing?

   (A) The stone towers that support the span
   (B) The overbuilt character of the bridge
   (C) The novel use of steel suspension wires
   (D) The open truss system that supports the roadway

15. Lighting the Brooklyn Bridge at night serves what purpose?

   (A) It enables pedestrians to cross its span during dark hours.
   (B) It is safer for bicyclists to use its roadway.
   (C) It highlights the architectural features of the bridge.
   (D) It enables vehicular traffic to move more smoothly.

Read the following passage and answer questions 16–20.

The Whiskey Rebellion of 1794 arose in the United States following the American Revolution, and it tested the constitutional powers of the Federal government. The Rebellion was a popular uprising led by farmers on the far western frontier of the young nation. Appalachian settlers resisted new excise taxes placed on distilled spirits, which were more easily traded than grain, and provided farms with a source of ready cash. The Secretary of the Treasury, Alexander Hamilton, proposed the tax on liquor as a way for the newly consolidated government to reduce the war debt. The rural populace found whiskey taxes to be a predatory discrimination against their livelihood. Vocal protests soon turned to outright violence.

Tax collectors were tarred and feathered, the mail was robbed, and civil proceedings were routinely disrupted, sometimes by armed force. President George Washington crushed the revolt by calling in the army, and several protesters were ordered to appear in Federal district courts. Rebels were arrested and imprisoned. Some fled farther west, to territories that would eventually become Kentucky and Tennessee. The suppression of the Whiskey Rebellion demonstrated to the citizens of the United States that efforts to challenge the laws of the land would henceforth be done peacefully and legally, though constitutional means enacted and enforced by the Federal government.

16. When did the Whiskey Rebellion arise?

   (A) When settlers moved to the western frontier of the United States
   (B) Immediately preceeding the American Revolution
   (C) When Alexander Hamilton proposed a new excise tax
   (D) Before the Federal government had any constitutional powers

17. What was a ready source of cash for most Appalachian farmers?

   (A) Harvested grain
   (B) Parcels of land
   (C) Produce and livestock
   (D) Distilled spirits

18. Why did the Appalachian farmers resist the excise tax proposed by Alexander Hamilton?

   (A) They claimed it reduced their income.
   (B) The revenue was used to pay the war debt.
   (C) They did not support Secretary Hamilton and President Washington.
   (D) The Federal government had no authority to impose new taxes.

19. How were rebellious farmers punished?

   (A) Their farms were seized by the Federal government.
   (B) They were conscripted into the army.
   (C) They were forced to move farther west of the frontier.
   (D) They were arrested and imprisoned.

20. What was the primary outcome of the Whiskey Rebellion?

   (A) The widespread dissent among Appalachian farmers was controlled.
   (B) The western frontier of the United States was subjected to the power of the Federal government.
   (C) The Federal government demonstrated its ability to enact and enforce laws according to its Constitution.
   (D) The Constitution of the United States was challenged by the citizens of the land.

Read the following passage and answer questions 21–25.

Jackie Robinson was the first African-American to break the race barrier in Major League Baseball. In 1946, the Brooklyn Dodgers general manager Branch Rickey selected Robinson, and initially assigned him to the Dodgers' minor league Montreal Royals. Robinson's play was impressive enough that he was called up to the major league the following year. Throughout the 1947 season, he suffered harassment from both his own teammates and opposing players, as well as torrents of racist abuse from fans. The Brooklyn clubhouse eventually rallied around Robinson when management suggested that players find other employment if dissatisfied with the situation. The young infielder had an outstanding first season, leading the National League in stolen bases, and winning the Rookie of the Year award. Two years later, Robinson was named the NL Most Valuable Player, and in 1955 he led the Dodgers to a World Series victory over the hated New York Yankees. He left the game in 1957, rather than accept a trade that would have sent him from Brooklyn to the rival New York Giants. His career statistics placed him as a peer among the best who have ever played the game of baseball. In 1997, at the 50th anniversary of Robinson's debut, his jersey number 42 was retired by all MLB teams. Jackie Robinson, who once stated he cared not whether he was liked or disliked, received the simple respect he'd demanded as a brave and wonderful human being.

21. For which team did Jackie Robinson play when he was first selected to play Major League Baseball?

    (A) The Brooklyn Dodgers
    (B) The New York Giants
    (C) The Montreal Royals
    (D) The New York Yankees

22. How many years did Robinson spend in the minor leagues before moving up to the major league?

    (A) One year
    (B) Two years
    (C) Three years
    (D) None, as he went straight to the major league

23. Why were Robinson's teammates initially dissatisfied with his presence in the clubhouse?

    (A) Because he was a rookie
    (B) Because he was slow on the base paths
    (C) Because he was favored by management
    (D) Because he was African-American

24. What was Jackie Robinson's jersey number?

    (A) 46
    (B) 42
    (C) 47
    (D) 44

25. Jackie Robinson ended his stellar professional career with which team?

    (A) The New York Giants
    (B) The Brooklyn Dodgers
    (C) The Los Angeles Dodgers
    (D) The New York Yankees

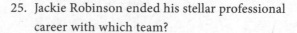

Read the following passage and answer questions 26–30.

Walt Whitman's *Leaves of Grass* appeared in a first edition published by the poet in 1855. The frontispiece featured an engraving of the rough and tumble Brooklyn native, clad in a coarse shirt and rakish hat, standing with a jauntily cocked elbow, hand on hip. This image mirrored the sensible yet confrontational poems contained within the volume's covers. With these poems, Whitman chose to eschew the classical English traditions of allegory and symbolism. In their place, he offered an exaltation of the human body and the frankly material aspects of the everyday condition. Such candid displays of sensation were considered immoral, if not obscene, and Whitman quickly found himself mired in scandal. Attempts were made to censor the book, which an indignant Whitman greatly resisted, the public be damned. He considered his poems spiritual paeans to the unbridled emotional self, and fought all attempts to suppress them. Whitman received a laudatory response from the eminent Transcendentalist Ralph Waldo Emerson, and within time the book even found its way to Abraham Lincoln, who greatly admired it. Whitman continued to scrupulously maintain, revise, and add to subsequent editions of his book. By his death, it had grown from a slim twelve poems to a lush four hundred, and *Leaves of Grass* was on its way to becoming, as Emerson had presciently called it, 'the most extraordinary piece of wit and wisdom America has yet contributed.'

26. The image of Walt Whitman, which appears in his book, presented him how?

   (A) As a stylish dandy
   (B) As a common fellow
   (C) As an eminent poet
   (D) As a mysterious sage

27. What was the primary subject of *Leaves of Grass*?

   (A) Studies of nature
   (B) Classical symbolism and literary allegories
   (C) Mystical, transcendental visions
   (D) Everyday human sensation

28. Why was Whitman's book so scandalous when it appeared?

   (A) It was self-published, which was highly unusual.
   (B) The image of Whitman in the book was deemed coarse and insulting.
   (C) The bodily and material aspects of the poems were thought obscene.
   (D) The small book only contained twelve poems.

29. What was the initial public reaction to Whitman's book?

   (A) It became a classic of American literature.
   (B) It was so popular that even President Lincoln read it.
   (C) It had only a small following among other writers, such as Emerson.
   (D) It was a target of censorship and suppression.

30. How did Whitman follow the public release of *Leaves of Grass*?

    (A) He withdrew the poems from circulation.
    (B) He largely rewrote most of the poems.
    (C) He continued to add new poems to the volume.
    (D) He sought to reconcile the public to his poetic vision.

LANGUAGE PART 1

Directions: This is a test of how well you can find errors in a piece of writing. The directions below tell what type of mistake may be present. If no mistake is made, choose the last answer.

Directions: Look for spelling mistakes.

1. (A) tropical
   (B) activate
   (C) monkies
   (D) (*No mistakes*)

2. (A) beleive
   (B) perpetual
   (C) diversity
   (D) (*No mistakes*)

3. (A) conventional
   (B) acrobatic
   (C) scratchs
   (D) (*No mistakes*)

4. (A) relinquish
   (B) inflammatory
   (C) grocerys
   (D) (*No mistakes*)

5. (A) stupendous
   (B) customary
   (C) pricing
   (D) (*No mistakes*)

Directions: Look for capitalization mistakes.

6. (A) The coffee shop employee did not
   (B) know whether or not they were open
   (C) on the President's birthday.
   (D) (*No mistakes*)

7. (A) The committee was making plans for
   (B) the easter parade, but they couldn't
   (C) find a good marching band.
   (D) (*No mistakes*)

8. (A) When my mom was a cheerleader,
   (B) her High School football team
   (C) won the State Championships.
   (D) (*No mistakes*)

9. (A) When mercury was in retrograde, I
   (B) had to give two of my friends rides to
   (C) school because their Jeeps broke down.
   (D) (*No mistakes*)

10. (A) The James family goes to Vancouver
    (B) to celebrate the Fourth of July every year.
    (C) They always bring home Canadian coins.
    (D) (*No mistakes*)

Directions: Look for punctuation mistakes.

11. (A) If we never would have gone
    (B) to Hawaii then I wouldn't
    (C) know how to surf.
    (D) (*No mistakes*)

12. (A) My mom told me to go to the store
    (B) before dinner. She needed green peppers,
    (C) bread, and onions, for her dish.
    (D) (*No mistakes*)

13. (A) My dad says that eating candy will
    (B) spoil your appetite. Furthermore,
    (C) its bad for your teeth.
    (D) (*No mistakes*)

14. (A) The ballet class meets every Tuesday,
    (B) Thursday, and Saturday. Other than
    (C) those days, practice is optional.
    (D) (*No mistakes*)

15. (A) "I have to leave for school now,"
    (B) Carrie yelled up the stairs, "The
    (C) bus is coming in twenty minutes."
    (D) (*No mistakes*)

17. (A) We hardly never run into bears
    (B) when we go camping, but we
    (C) saw two this last trip.
    (D) (*No mistakes*)

18. (A) If they win the next three games,
    (B) the soccer team are on their way
    (C) to the championship playoffs.
    (D) (*No mistakes*)

19. (A) Between the three girls in the family,
    (B) Jennifer is the singer, Malika is the
    (C) writer, and Sarah is the musician.
    (D) (*No mistakes*)

20. (A) What makes winter so unbearable
    (B) is neither the snow or the wind.
    (C) It's the lack of sunlight.
    (D) (*No mistakes*)

Directions: Look for <u>usage</u> mistakes.

16. (A) While their parents are in the office,
    (B) the box of toys provided by the doctors
    (C) keep the kids entertained.
    (D) (*No mistakes*)

LANGUAGE PART 2

Directions: For questions 21–25, choose the <u>best</u> answer based on the following paragraph.

[1]Five thousand years ago, a giant turtle came out of the Yellow River and exposed the secrets of writing and the ways of the oracle. [2]Both were systems using symbols and are written on the back of its huge shell. [3]The emperor was the first to recognize the importance of the black markings on the turtle's shell. [4]He saw correctly that the symbols stood for writing and offered prophecies. [5]The two activities has been closely linked ever since. [6]And the mythic turtle that crawled out of the river becomes the foundation of the ancient belief that a cosmic tortoise holds up the whole world.

21. Where should the *correctly* be placed in sentence 4?

    (A) after he
    (B) before symbols
    (C) before he
    (D) (*No change*)

22. Which word doesn't belong in sentence 2?

    (A) were
    (B) and
    (C) are
    (D) using

23. Sentence 5 has

    (A) an incomplete thought
    (B) a verb not in agreement with its subject
    (C) an adjective modifying the wrong noun
    (D) a verb in the wrong tense

24. In sentence 6, which word should be replaced?

    (A) becomes
    (B) crawled
    (C) belief
    (D) (*No change*)

25. What is the adverb in sentence 5?

    (A) linked
    (B) been
    (C) ever
    (D) closely

MATH PART 1

Directions: Choose the best answer from the four given for each problem

1. Seventy percent of the eligible voters in the town voted in the general election. If 4,410 people voted, how many eligible voters are in the town?

    (A) 1,323
    (B) 3,087
    (C) 6,300
    (D) 14,700

2. Josh has $360 to spend on fitness. He uses $120 of this for a gym membership. In addition to the membership fee, the training classes are $20 every month. How many months can Josh take training classes with the money he has set aside?

    (A) 6
    (B) 12
    (C) 18
    (D) 24

3. What value of x will make the equation $2x + 5 = 11$ a true statement?

    (A) 3
    (B) 6
    (C) 8
    (D) 12

4. Order these fractions from least to greatest:

    $$\frac{5}{6}, \frac{2}{3}, \frac{1}{2}, \frac{7}{12}$$

    (A) $\frac{1}{2}, \frac{7}{12}, \frac{2}{3}, \frac{5}{6}$

    (B) $\frac{1}{2}, \frac{2}{3}, \frac{5}{6}, \frac{7}{12}$

    (C) $\frac{2}{3}, \frac{5}{6}, \frac{1}{2}, \frac{7}{12}$

    (D) $\frac{5}{6}, \frac{2}{3}, \frac{7}{12}, \frac{1}{2}$

5. The circle graph below shows the method of transportation that city workers use to get to their place of employment. If a worker is chosen at random, what is the probability that he takes the bus to work?

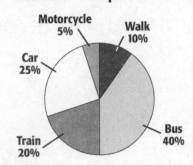

Method of Transport to Work

(A) $\dfrac{1}{10}$

(B) $\dfrac{1}{5}$

(C) $\dfrac{1}{4}$

(D) $\dfrac{2}{5}$

6. The bar graph below shows the frequency of modes of communication per week. Which age groups had about the same usage of email per week?

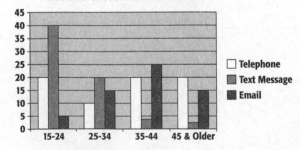

Modes of Communication

(A) 15–24 and 35–44

(B) 25–34 and 35–44

(C) 25–34 and 45 & Older

(D) 35–44 and 45 & Older

7. The line graph below shows the average high temperature in two cities for selected months. In which month does Vancouver have a higher temperature than Sydney?

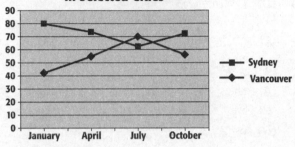

Average High Temperature in Selected Cities

(A) January

(B) April

(C) July

(D) October

MATH PART 2

Directions: For questions 8–12, estimate the answer; no scratch work is allowed. Do <u>not</u> try to calculate exact answers.

8. The number 2,637.185 rounded to the nearest hundredth place is

    (A) 2,600
    (B) 2,637.2
    (C) 2,637.18
    (D) 2,637.19

9. The closest estimate of 327 + 279 + 312 + 261 is

    (A) 1,000
    (B) 1,200
    (C) 1,300
    (D) 1,500

10. The closest estimate of $29.98 – $6.89 is

    (A) $22.00
    (B) $23.00
    (C) $24.00
    (D) $25.00

11. The closest estimate of 49.7 × 10.27 is

    (A) 360
    (B) 400
    (C) 500
    (D) 5,000

12. The closest estimate of 8,116 ÷ 89 is

    (A) 90
    (B) 100
    (C) 900
    (D) 1,000

ABILITY PART 1

Directions: For questions 1–3 below, the three figures in the question are alike in some way. Select the answer choice that shares the similarity.

	(A)	(B)	(C)	(D)	(E)

1.

2.

3.

Directions: For questions 4–7 below, the second figure shows a particular change from the first figure. The third figure, if changed in the same way, will become which of the answer choices?

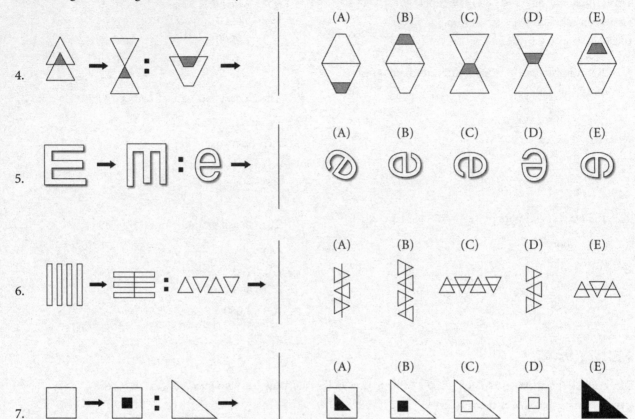

ABILITY PART 2

Directions: The top row shows how a piece of paper is folded, and then where hole(s) are punched after folding. Choose the figure from the bottom row that shows how the paper will look when it is completely unfolded.

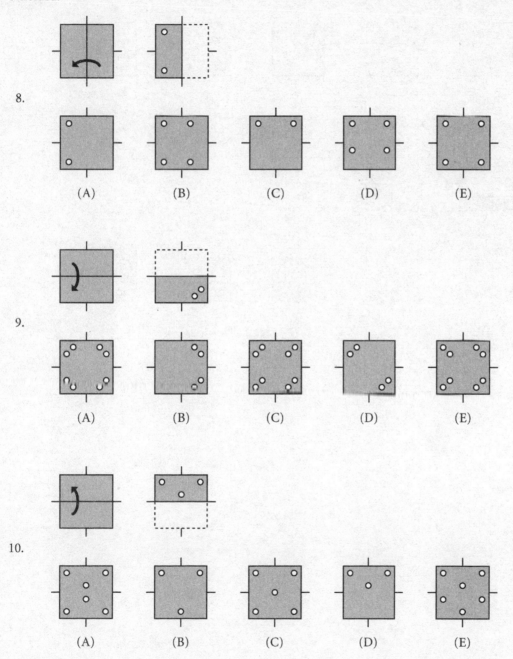

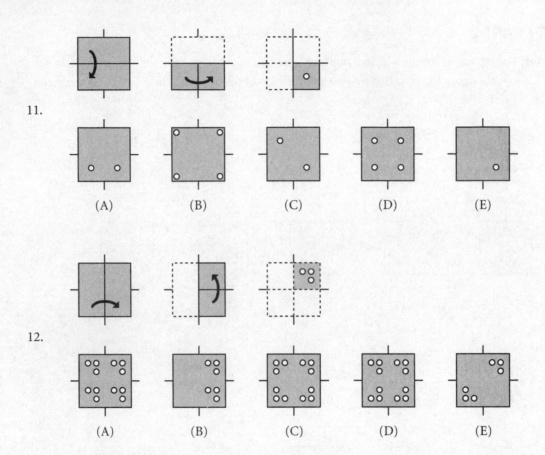

ANSWERS AND EXPLANATIONS

Answer Key

READING, Part 1
1. **A**
2. **D**
3. **A**
4. **B**
5. **B**
6. **C**
7. **B**
8. **C**
9. **D**
10. **A**

READING, Part 2
11. **C**
12. **B**
13. **A**
14. **B**
15. **C**
16. **C**
17. **D**
18. **A**
19. **D**
20. **C**
21. **C**
22. **A**
23. **D**
24. **B**
25. **B**
26. **B**
27. **D**
28. **C**
29. **D**
30. **C**

LANGUAGE, Part 1
Spelling
1. **C**
2. **A**
3. **C**
4. **C**
5. **D**

Capitalization
6. **C**
7. **B**
8. **B**
9. **A**
10. **D**

Punctuation
11. **B**
12. **C**
13. **C**
14. **D**
15. **B**

Usage
16. **C**
17. **A**
18. **B**
19. **A**
20. **B**

LANGUAGE, Part 2
21. **A**
22. **C**
23. **B**
24. **A**
25. **D**

MATH, Part 1
1. **C**
2. **B**
3. **A**
4. **A**
5. **D**
6. **C**
7. **C**

MATH, Part 2
8. **D**
9. **B**
10. **B**
11. **C**
12. **A**

ABILITY, Part 1
1. **B**
2. **D**
3. **C**
4. **B**
5. **C**
6. **D**
7. **B**

ABILITY, Part 2
8. **E**
9. **B**
10. **A**
11. **D**
12. **C**

Reading, Part 1

1. A

To *insinuate* doubt is to introduce it where it may not exist. Choices B, C, and D are incorrect. To *dispel* doubt is to banish it. To *attribute* meaning is to assign it based on specific characteristics or qualities. To *assume* culpability is to accept responsibility for deeds or actions.

2. D

An *avuncular* gentleman is kindly and genial, much like a beloved uncle, from which the word is derived. Choices A, B, and C are incorrect. An *absent-minded* gentleman may be senile and forgetful. A sickly man would likely be decrepit and ill. A *monkish* man would be solitary and lonesome.

3. A

A sculpture of great weight may contain tremendous *volume*. Choices B, C, and D are incorrect. A brightly colored painting may be said to be *garish*. A *moving* story evokes deep emotion. An intricately constructed instrument is executed with great *precision*.

4. B

A drunken person may *accost* other drinkers in a tavern. Choices A, C, and D are incorrect. One *whispers* quietly in order to avoid being overheard. One may *hail* friends upon meeting them unexpectedly. One *introduces* an acquaintance to another so he/she may be known.

5. B

A *despicable* person is held in contempt by others. Choices A, C, and D are incorrect. An *inept* person is one who lacks the competence or skill for a particular task. An *admirable* person is held in great esteem by others. A *cunning* person acts in secret with great care.

6. C

An *incised* outline is a shallow mark carved into a surface. Choices A, B, and D are incorrect. A *sketched* outline may be loosely drawn on a surface. A *written* outline employs the alphabetic characters of a language. A *painted* outline may be brushed on a surface in color.

7. B

A *libelous* accusation contains defamatory content. Choices A, C, and D are incorrect. A *laudatory* exclamation contains great praise. A *commendatory* word acknowledges well-earned merit. An *adulatory* remark recognizes a high degree of achievement.

8. C

A *matte* surface is one that is dull and flat. Choices A, B, and D are incorrect. A *lustrous* surface has a deep gloss. A *rough* surface is irregular and bumpy. A *smooth* surface is continuous and uninterrupted by incident.

9. D

A metal that is *tarnished* has a dull appearance. Choices A, B, and C are incorrect. A *gleaming* metal is one that is bright and reflects light. A *luxurious* metal has a sumptuous and expensive quality. A metal that is *plated* consists of a thin coat of precious material over an inexpensive base.

10. A

To *coerce* a confession is to pressure one to admit something. Choices B, C, and D are incorrect. To *accept* guilt is to admit to wrongdoing. To *dismiss* evidence is to render it irrelevant to the discussion at hand. To *concoct* an alibi is to fabricate a tale that is usually not true.

Reading, Part 2

11. C

Although the Brooklyn Bridge was, at the time of its construction, one of the largest man-made structures in the world, this was not the primary reason for building the bridge. Its purpose was to link the boroughs of Brooklyn and Manhattan. The Roeblings had a solid engineering background which was tempered by a fine aesthetic sense. The bridge was a structural marvel, but John Augustus Roebling did not live to see it completed, and his son, Washington, was entrusted with finishing it. Choices A, B, and D are each relevant to the discussion, but are nonetheless incorrect.

12. B

The Brooklyn Bridge is a unique structure, in that it is both functional and beautiful. It continues to serve New York City even as it has now been recognized as a historical landmark. Choices A, C, and D are relevant to the discussion, but the primary reason the bridge is still operational is due to its solid structural character. Indeed, many similar bridges of inferior construction have long been demolished and replaced.

13. A

Choices B, C, and D each attest to the engineering features of the bridge and to how it is used, but choice A specifically describes a unique structural characteristic of the bridge, in that the truss system was designed as a means of support.

14. B

Choices A, C, and D each attest to specific engineering features of the bridge, but choice B mentions the overbuilt structure which has enabled the bridge to remain standing, even as many similar successive bridges have been demolished and replaced due to the relative weakness of their original construction.

15. C

It could be inferred that the bridge is lit at night for the reasons given in choices A, B, and D, but these are not stated as such in the passage. The Brooklyn Bridge is lit at night to call attention to its dramatic qualities and to integrate it with the nighttime New York skyline. This is explicitly stated in the passage, making choice C the correct one.

16. C

Peaceful settlers on the far western frontier of the new American Republic rebelled when Alexander Hamilton proposed a tax on distilled spirits. Collection of the taxes tested the constitutional powers of the new government in the years immediately after the Revolution. Choices A, B, and D are incorrect.

17. D

Farmers often distilled excess grain into spirits, which were easily transported and represented a ready source of cash. Choices A, B, and C are incorrect, as no mention is made in the passage of other sources of income.

18. A

Farmers claimed that excise taxes on spirits were a predatory drain on their income and resisted efforts to collect the taxes. The passage makes no note of the farmers' refusal to recognize the Federal government, even if they disagreed with its policies. Choices B, C, and D are incorrect, as the passage makes no note of other sources of discontent.

19. D

Rebellious farmers were arrested, imprisoned, and forced to stand trial in Federal court. Choices A, B, and C are incorrect, as other penalties levied against the rebels are not mentioned in the passage.

20. C

The Whiskey Rebellion presented the first serious challenge to the Federal authority of the new American government. Although dissent challenged the power of the government and forced a review of its laws, the primary outcome of the Rebellion was a demonstration of Federal power in enacting and enforcing the law according to its Constitution. Choices A, B, and D are incorrect, as they are secondary outcomes of the Rebellion.

21. C

Although Jackie Robinson was selected for the major league by the Brooklyn Dodgers, he spent his first season with the Montreal Royals. Choices A, B, and D are incorrect.

22. A

Robinson spent one year with the Montreal Royals before joining the Brooklyn Dodgers. Choices B, C, and D are incorrect.

23. D

Robinson's performance as a rookie player was outstanding, and management forced his teammates to accept his presence on the Dodgers regardless of his race. Choices A, B, and C are incorrect.

24. B

The passage clearly states that Robinson's jersey number 42 was retired from use in 1997. Choices A, C, and D are incorrect.

25. B

Jackie Robinson played with the Brooklyn Dodgers throughout his career, defeating the New York Yankees in the World Series and refusing a trade to the rival New York Giants. Choices A, C, and D are incorrect.

26. B

An engraving which appears as the frontispiece to Whitman's book shows him in the coarse shirt and rakish hat of a common fellow. Choices A, C, and D, other images of poets prevalent at the time, are incorrect.

27. D

Whitman's book treated everyday human sensation as the subject of its poetry. In doing so, it broke with classical tradition and the typical subjects of poetry of its day. Choices A, B, and C are incorrect.

28. C

The subject matter of Whitman's book, with its focus on bodily sensation and the material aspects of being, were thought to be obscene when it first appeared. The furor raised and the calls for its censorship outshone the book's other qualities. Choices A, B, and D are incorrect.

29. D

Although Whitman's book eventually came to be appreciated as a great masterwork, the initial public response was one of outrage, and attempts were made to suppress the book. Choices A, B, and C are incorrect.

30. C

Whitman was shocked at the public reaction to his book, yet he refused to withdraw or censor its contents. In fact, he continued to revise the existing poems and add new ones up until his death. Choices A, B, and D are incorrect.

Language, Part 1

Spelling

1. C

Monkies should be spelled *monkeys*. Words ending in *y* following a vowel retain the *y* and add an *s*.

2. A

Beleive should be spelled *believe*. *I* precedes the *e* in most words except when following the letter *c*.

3. C

Scratchs should be spelled *scratches*. Words ending in *ch* add an *es* when in the plural form.

4. C

Grocerys should be spelled *groceries*. Words ending in *y* following a consonant are formed by dropping the *y* and adding an *ies*.

5. D

There are no spelling mistakes.

Capitalization

6. C

President is only capitalized when used as a title preceding a person's name, such as President Kennedy. Otherwise, the *p* is lowercase.

7. B

All holidays are capitalized. *Easter* should be capitalized.

8. B

There is no reason for *High School* to be capitalized. It is not a proper noun, and it is not following the name of the high school. *State Championships* is the name of the event; thus, it is capitalized.

9. A

Mercury should be capitalized because all planets are capitalized.

10. D

There are no mistakes in capitalization in this sentence.

Punctuation

11. B

There should be a comma after *Hawaii* because it is the last word in the introductory phrase beginning with *if*. In *if/then* constructions, a comma separates the two phrases.

12. C

There should not be a comma after *onions* in this sentence. The serial comma separates the items of the list but is not used further after the list is complete.

13. C

Its is a contraction for *it is* and thus requires an apostrophe.

14. D

There are no punctuation mistakes in these sentences.

15. B

There should be a period after *stairs* instead of a comma. The first quote is a complete sentence, and the second quote is a complete sentence. Therefore, the first sentence requires a period before the second sentence can begin.

Usage

16. C

This is an error in subject/verb agreement. The verb *keep* is modifying *box* which is singular. Thus, the verb should be *keeps*.

17. A

The error in this sentence is a use of the *double-negative*. *Hardly* carries a negative charge, meaning *barely* or *not any*. Thus, *never* should be changed to *ever* to avoid this error.

18. B

There is a problem with the subject/verb agreement in this sentence. The verb *are* should be *is* because it is modifying the singular noun *team*.

19. A

Between is only used with two things or people. This sentence is describing three girls, so the appropriate word to use would be *among*.

20. B

The word *or* should be changed to *nor* in this sentence. This rule is the *neither/nor* construction. Likewise, *or* is part of the *either/or* construction.

Language, Part 2

21. A

Correctly is an adverb that is modifying the verb *saw*. Modifiers should be placed directly before the word they modify. Thus, *correctly* should be before *saw*, or after *he*.

22. C

Verbs in a sentence must be in the same tense. The first verb is *were*, which is in the past tense; therefore, all remaining verbs must be in the past tense. *Are* is in the present tense and does not belong.

23. B

The subject in the sentence is *activities*, which is plural. The verb *has* is singular and is not in agreement with its subject. It should read "activities have."

24. A

If it is an "ancient belief," then this subject is placed in the past. *Becomes* is in the present tense. The correct verb is *became*.

25. D

An adverb describes a verb and tells why and how the action is performed. *Closely* (adverb) is explaining how the activities are *linked* (verb).

Math, Part 1

1. C

Let *n* represent the number of eligible voters in the town. It is given that 70% of those voters amounted to 4,410 people.

Set up an equation: $\quad 0.70n = 4{,}410$

Divide both sides by 0.70: $\quad \dfrac{0.70n}{0.70} = \dfrac{4{,}410}{0.70}$

Simplify: $\quad n = 6{,}300$

Answer choice A is 30% of 4,410. If you chose B, you multiplied 4,410 by 0.70, instead of dividing. Answer choice D would be the number of voters if 4,410 was 30% of the voters having voted.

2. B

Josh has $360 available for a gym membership and monthly training classes. Write an expression to represent the fitness costs. The costs are given as a one-time membership fee of $120, plus $20 every month. Let *m* represent the number of months, so the costs are $120 + 20m$. Now, set this equal to the money available.

The equation is: $\quad 20m + 120 = 360$

Subtract 120 from both sides:
$$20m + 120 - 120 = 360 - 120$$

Simplify: $\quad 20m = 240$

Divide both sides by 20: $\quad \dfrac{20m}{20} = \dfrac{240}{20}$

$$m = 12$$

Answer choice A is the number of months of training classes if $120 is available. Choice C is the number of months if there were no membership fee subtracted. If you chose D, you most likely added $120 to $360 instead of subtracting.

3. A

This is a two-step equation. Solve by performing opposite operations to isolate the variable x:

The equation is:	$2x + 5 = 11$
Subtract 5 from both sides:	$2x + 5 - 5 = 11 - 5$
Simplify:	$2x = 6$
Divide both sides by 2:	$\dfrac{2x}{2} = \dfrac{6}{2}$
	$x = 3$

Another method to solve this problem is to substitute in the given value choices to see which produces a true statement. By substituting in choice A, you get $2 \times 3 + 5 = 11$. Multiply to get 6, and then add $6 + 5 = 11$, which makes $11 = 11$, a true statement. If you chose choice B, you may have forgotten to divide by 2. Choice C would result from adding 5 to both sides of the equation instead of subtracting 5.

4. A

The best way to order fractions is to convert each fraction to have a common denominator. The least common denominator of these fractions is 12. $\frac{5}{6} \times \frac{2}{2} = \frac{10}{12}$, $\frac{2}{3} \times \frac{4}{4} = \frac{8}{12}$, $\frac{1}{2} \times \frac{6}{6} = \frac{6}{12}$. Now that all fractions have the common denominator of 12, order them by the numerators from least to greatest: $\frac{6}{12}$, $\frac{7}{12}$, $\frac{8}{12}$, $\frac{10}{12}$. This is choice A, as written in the original fraction form: $\frac{1}{2}$, $\frac{7}{12}$, $\frac{2}{3}$, $\frac{5}{6}$. Choice D is the fractions ordered from greatest to least.

5. D

Probability is expressed as a fraction that compares the number of ways an event can occur to the total number of possible outcomes. Look at the circle graph; the percent of workers who take the bus is 40%. This means that 40 out of every 100 workers ride the bus to work. Express this percent as a fraction and simplify, which is choice D. Choice A is the probability that the worker is a walker, choice B is the probability that the worker takes the train,

and choice C is the probability that the worker takes a car.

6. C

The problem asks you to find which age groups had about the same usage of email per week. Look at the key on the bar graph to determine that email is represented as the darkest bar. Then, look at the bars to find two dark bars that are the same length. The number of emails for both age groups 25–34 and 45 & Older is 15. If your choice was D, you may have read the bars that represent telephone, not email.

7. C

Look at the key to this line graph to determine that the line with the diamond points represents Vancouver, and the line with the square points represents Sydney. Now, look at the line graph to find the month in which this diamond-point line has a higher value than the line that represents Sydney. This is the month of July, choice C.

Math, Part 2

8. D

The hundredth place is two spaces to the right of the decimal point. In this number, you must round to the underlined place value: 2,637.1<u>8</u>5. Look at the digit to the right of this place. Because it is a digit that is 5 or greater, you round the 8 up to a 9, to get 2,637.19, choice D. Choice A is the number rounded to the hundreds place, not the hundredth place. Choice B is rounded to the tenth place. Choice C is not rounded correctly.

9. B

You are asked to estimate. Look at the answer choices, which are all numbers rounded to the hundreds place. Therefore, round the numbers in the problem to the hundreds place. Each of these numbers will round to 300. 327 rounds down to 300 because the digit to the right of the 3 is a 2 which is less than 5. 279 rounds up to 300 because the digit to the right of the 2 is a 7, which is greater than or equal to 5. 312 rounds down to 300 because the digit to the right of the 3 is a 1, which is less than 5. 261 rounds up to 300 because the digit to the right of the 2 is a 6, which is greater than or equal to 5. Because each number rounds to 300, the sum is $300 \times 4 = 1,200$.

10. B

Round each monetary value to the nearest dollar to estimate, which is the underlined place value: $29.98. The digit to the right of the underlined place value is a 9, which is greater than or equal to 5. This directs you to add 1 to the underlined value. $29.98 rounds to $30.00. In the same way, $6.89 rounds to $7.00. Now the subtraction is easy: 30 – 7 = 23, or $23.00.

11. C

Round each value to the nearest whole number, by rounding 49.7 up to 50, because the digit to the right of the 9 is a 7, which is greater than or equal to 5. Round 10.27 down to 10 because the digit 2 is less than 5. Now, the multiplication is easy: $50 \times 10 = 500$, choice C.

12. A

First, round the divisor up to 90 to make the division easier. Then look at the dividend. This can be rounded down to 8,100, which is easily divided by 90, because $9 \times 9 = 81$. $8,100 \div 90 = 90$.

Ability, Part 1

1. B

All figures are regular polygons. They all have congruent side lengths and congruent angles. Figure B is a regular pentagon. Size is not relevant. You may have been tempted to choose choice A, which has congruent angles, but this rectangle is not a regular polygon; the sides are not all congruent.

2. D

All figures have only diagonals drawn in the interior. Diagonals are line segments that connect non-adjacent vertices.

3. C

All figures have six sides. Choice C is the only figure with six sides. Don't be confused that figures B and E have a similar looking shape. The number of sides is the common characteristic.

4. B

The congruent shapes are "pulled apart," and then the top polygon is flipped vertically. The bottom figure stays the same. Choice A is the correct shape, but the shaded shape should be on top. Choices C and D have the bottom polygon flipped vertically.

5. C

The figure is rotated 90° clockwise, to the right. Don't be confused by choice A; the capital "E" only looks slanted after the transformation because it is slanted in the original. Choice B is rotated 90° counterclockwise. Choice E is rotated and then flipped horizontally.

6. D

The figure is made up of four congruent shapes. It is transformed to three of these shapes, that are then rotated 90°. It is further altered by the addition of a segment that runs down the middle, ending at the edges of the figure. In choice A, the segment extends out of the figure. Choice B has four shapes. Choices C and E are not rotated.

7. B

The only change is that a black square is placed inside the polygon. The missing figure must be a triangle, so choices A and D can be eliminated. Choice B is the only choice left with a black square inside.

Ability, Part 2

8. E

The square is folded once to the left, to make two layers. Two holes are punched through two layers, to make a total of four holes when unfolded. Therefore, eliminate choices A and C. The holes are punched in the corners, which is choice E.

9. B

The square is folded down once, to make two layers. Two holes are punched through two layers, to make a total of four holes when unfolded. Eliminate choices A, C, and E because they do not have four holes. Because it was folded down, the correct choice is B. Choice D would have resulted from a diagonal fold.

10. A

The square is folded up once, to make two layers. Three holes are punched through two layers, to make a total of six holes when unfolded. This leaves choices A and E as the only possibilities. The correct answer is A, because two of the holes are punched in corners; the resultant square will have every corner punched.

11. D

The square is folded down and then to the right to make four layers. One hole is punched through four layers, to make a total of four holes when unfolded. Eliminate choices A, C, and E because they do not have four holes. Eliminate choice B because the hole is not punched in the corner.

12. C

The square is folded right and then up to make four layers. Three holes are punched through four layers, to make a total of 12 holes when unfolded. This leaves choices A, C, or D as the only possibilities. The correct choice is C because all of the holes are close to a corner or an edge.

Section 3
Skill Review

Verbal Skills

Verbal Skills—that is, vocabulary—questions account for a sizeable portion of your raw score on the HSPT, TACHS, and COOP. There are 60 Verbal Skills questions on the HSPT, approximately 20 on the TACHS, and approximately 30 on the COOP. These questions can appear in several formats: synonyms, antonyms, words-in-context, analogies, and verbal classification. (On the HSPT, short logic questions will also appear on the Verbal Skills section; we'll cover these in the Reasoning Skills chapter of this book.)

In this chapter, we'll review each of the vocabulary-based question types. TACHS only has vocabulary-in-context questions, but many are essentially the same as synonym questions. On both the COOP and HSPT, several formats of Verbal Skills questions will appear mixed in together, so it is really important that you feel comfortable with each type of question and are able to switch gears quickly between question types in order to answer as accurately as possible.

No matter what the question type, a strong vocabulary is a large part of doing well on these sections, and we'll discuss how to build your vocabulary at the end of the chapter. Obviously, the more words you know, the better. But our goal is to rack up points on the test, not to memorize every word in the dictionary. The strategies covered here will help you get closer to the correct answer choice, even if you don't always know the exact meaning.

QUESTION TYPE 1—SYNONYMS

A synonym is a word that is similar in meaning to another word. *Fast* is a synonym for *quick*. *Garrulous* (whether you know it or not) is a synonym for *talkative*. Many of the TACHS vocabulary questions involve selecting a synonym. On the COOP or HSPT, a synonym question will read: "Fast most nearly means…" It will be followed by four answer choices.

Genuine most nearly means

(A) authentic

(B) valuable

(C) ancient

(D) damaged

KAPLAN TIP

Questions with the phrase "most nearly means" are synonym questions. Look for a word in the answer choices that means the same as the word in the question.

Sometimes you will know the word in the question. Sometimes you won't. Sometimes you'll know all the words in the answer choices, and sometimes you won't. We'll give you Kaplan's 3-Step Method for Synonyms. Then, we'll give you some great tactics to use when you don't know all the words in the question.

Kaplan's 3-Step Method for Synonyms

Step 1. Define the stem word.

Step 2. Find the answer choice that best fits your definition.

Step 3. If no choice fits, think of other definitions for the stem word and go through the choices again.

Let's take another look at the example above, using Kaplan's 3-Step Method.

Step 1—Define the Stem Word

What does *genuine* mean? Something genuine is something real, such as a real Picasso painting, rather than a forgery. Your definition might be something like this: *Something genuine can be proven to be what it claims to be.*

Step 2—Find the Answer Choice That Best Fits Your Definition

Go through the answer choices one by one to see which one fits best. Your options are: *authentic, valuable, ancient,* and *damaged.* Something genuine could be worth a lot or not much at all, old or new, in good shape or bad, or even recent or historical. The only word that really means the same thing as *genuine* is (A) *authentic.*

Step 3—If No Choice Fits, Think of Other Definitions for the Stem Word and Go Through the Choices Again

In this instance, one choice fits. Now, take a look at the following example:

Grave most nearly means

(A) regrettable

(B) unpleasant

(C) serious ⬅

(D) careful

Maybe you defined *grave* as a burial location. You looked at the choices and didn't see any words like *tomb* or *coffin*. What to do? Move to Step 3, and go back to the stem word, thinking about other definitions. Have you ever heard of a "grave situation"? *Grave* can also mean *serious* or *solemn*, so you can see that (C), *serious*, now fits perfectly. If none of the answer choices seems to work with your definition, there may be a secondary definition you haven't considered yet.

Avoiding Pitfalls

Kaplan's 3-Step Method for Synonyms should always be the basis for tackling every question, but there are a few other things you need to know to perform your best on synonym questions. Fortunately, there are only two pitfalls to watch out for.

Pitfall 1—Running Out of Time

Pace yourself. You have a limited amount of time, so make sure you use it wisely. Never waste time on a question you don't know; just circle it and come back to it later. Be careful, since question types may be mixed together. Be sure to read the question again before answering it. You don't want to make the mistake of answering a synonym question as an antonym, or vice versa!

Pitfall 2—Choosing Tempting Wrong Answers

The test makers choose their wrong answer choices very carefully. Sometimes that means throwing in answer traps that will tempt you, but that aren't right. Be a savvy test taker; don't fall for these distracters!

What kinds of wrong answers are we talking about here? In synonym questions, there are two types of answer traps to watch out for: answers that are almost right and answers that sound like the stem word. Let's illustrate both types to make it concrete.

deceptive contempt
insipid
vigorous
pompous
anguish

Delegate most nearly means

(A) delight

(B) assign

(C) decide ⬅

(D) manage

Favor most nearly means

(A) award

(B) prefer

(C) respect

(D) improve

In the first example, (A) and (C) might be tempting, because they all start with the prefix *de-*, just like the stem word, *delegate*. It's important that you examine all the answer choices, because otherwise you might choose (A) and never get to the correct answer, (B).

In the second example, you might look at the word *favor* and think, oh, that's something positive. It's something you do for someone else. It sounds a lot like choice (A), *award*. Maybe you pick (A) and move on. If you do that, you would be falling for a trap! The correct answer is (B), *prefer*, since *favor* is being used as a verb, and *to favor* someone or something is to like it better than something else—in other words, to prefer it. If you don't read through all of the choices, you might be tricked into choosing a wrong answer.

At this point, you have a great set of tools for answering most synonym questions. You know how to approach them and you know some traps to avoid. But what happens if you don't know the word in the question? Should you just give up and move on? No way! Here are some techniques to help you figure out the meaning of a tough vocabulary word and answer a hard synonym question.

What to Do if You Don't Know the Word

Technique 1: Look for familiar roots and prefixes.

Technique 2: Use your knowledge of foreign languages.

Technique 3: Remember the word in context.

Technique 4: Use word charge.

Let's examine each technique more closely.

Technique 1—Look for Familiar Roots and Prefixes

Having a good grasp of how words are put together will help you tremendously on synonym questions, particularly when you don't know a vocabulary word. If you can break a word into pieces that you do understand, you'll be able to answer questions that you might have thought too difficult to tackle.

Look at the words below. Circle any prefixes or roots that you know.

benevolence   conspire

insomnia   verify

inscribe

Bene means good; *somn* has to do with sleep; *scrib* has to do with writing; *con* means doing something together; and *ver* has to do with truth. So, if you were looking for a synonym for *benevolence*, you'd definitely want to choose a positive, or "good" word.

Technique 2—Use Your Knowledge of Foreign Languages

Do you know or study a foreign language? If so, it can help you decode lots of vocabulary words on the COOP, TACHS, or HSPT, particularly if it's one of the Romance languages (French, Spanish, Italian, Portuguese). Look at the example words below. Do you recognize any foreign language words in them?

> facilitate
> dormant
> explicate

Facile means easy in Italian; *dormir* means to sleep in Spanish; and *expliquer* means to explain in French. A synonym for each of these words would have something to do with these general meanings.

Technique 3—Remember the Word in Context

Sometimes a word might look strange sitting on the page by itself, but if you think about it, you realize you've heard it before in other phrases. If you can put the word into context, even if that context is cliché, you're on your way to deciphering its meaning.

Illegible most nearly means

(A) illegal
(B) twisted
(C) unreadable
(D) eligible

Have you heard this word in context? Maybe someone you know has had his or her handwriting described as illegible. What is illegible handwriting?

Remember to try to think of a definition first, before you look at the answer choices.

Some of the answer choices here are tricks. Which ones are tempting wrong answers, meant to remind you of the question word? The correct answer is (C). 2020

Here's another example:

Laurels most nearly means

(A)   vine

(B)   honor

(C)   lavender

(D)   cushion

Have you heard the phrase "don't rest on your laurels"? What do you think it might mean?

The phrase "don't rest on your laurels" originated in ancient Greece, where heroes were given wreaths of laurel branches to signify their accomplishments. Telling someone to not rest on his laurels is the same thing as telling him to not get too smug, living off the success of one accomplishment, rather than striving for improvement. The correct answer is (B).

Technique 4—Use Word Charge

Even if you know nothing about the word, have never seen it before, don't recognize any prefixes or roots, and can't think of any word in any language that it sounds like, you can still take an educated guess by using word charge.

Word charge refers to the sense that a word gives you as to whether it's a positive word or a negative word. Often words that sound harsh have a negative meaning, while smooth-sounding words tend to have positive meanings. If *cantankerous* sounds negative to you, you would be right: it means difficult to handle.

You can also use prefixes and roots to help determine a word's charge. *Anti, mal, de, dis, un, in, im, a,* and *mis* often indicate a negative, while *pro, ben,* and *magn* are often positives.

Not all words sound positive or negative; some sound neutral. But, if you can define the charge, you can probably eliminate some answer choices on that basis alone. Word charge is a great technique to use when answering antonym questions too.

QUESTION TYPE 2—WORDS-IN-CONTEXT

We already discussed how trying to recall the context, or situation, in which you've heard a word can help you answer synonym or antonym questions. On the HSPT and TACHS, there are questions that already put the vocabulary word in context for you. These words-in-context questions appear on the Reading section, and they look like this:

grant a <u>reprieve</u>   <u>annual</u> earnings

strict <u>regulations</u>   <u>valid</u> argument

Of course, each question is followed by four answer choices. It is essential to realize that you are looking for a word or definition that means the same (or most nearly the same) as the underlined word. In essence, these are fancy synonym questions, in which the context is already provided for you.

Approach words-in-context questions as you would any other synonym question, but use the context to your advantage. It may help jog your memory of an otherwise unknown word, or help you clarify your definition.

Kaplan's 3-Step Method for Words-in-Context

Step 1. Define the word.
Step 2. Find the answer choice that best fits your definition.
Step 3. Refocus the definition. Use the context provided to help you clarify the word.

Use all the techniques at your disposal if you don't know the question word.

Hey, wait a minute! What if you don't know the word *disposal* used in the sentence above? Let's treat that as a words-in-context question and use Kaplan's 3-Step Method for Words-in-Context to find the answer.

Step 1—Define the Word

Techniques at your <u>disposal</u>

Use the context, the surrounding words, to help you determine your definition. (Notice the context is not "garbage disposal"—if it were, *disposal* would have a different meaning.) The context given is *techniques at your disposal*. These must be techniques you can use. So our definition of *disposal* is *something that you can use, useable,* or *at hand.*

Step 2—Find the Answer Choice That Best Fits Your Definition

Techniques at your <u>disposal</u>
(A) worthless
(B) dislikeable
(C) available
(D) memorable

Which of the answer choices is most like our definition *at hand* or *useable*? (C) fits best.

What if our definition doesn't fit?

Step 3—Refocus the Definition. Use the Context Provided to Help You Clarify the Word.

Here's another example:

Field of study

(A) garden
(B) area
(C) space
(D) object

A field is an open space. However, using the context *of study* can help us avoid going down a wrong path to begin with. Since *field* is used in the phrase *field of study*, we are not talking about a real open space with grass, but rather a general area or region. Given that definition, move on to Step 2. Which answer choice fits best? Choice (B).

Backsolving

What if you just can't think of a definition for the underlined word? Try backsolving.

What is backsolving? It may sound like an obscure form of chiropractic medicine, but it's actually just a nifty way of approaching questions when you can't answer them directly. Basically, you skip past the question and head straight for the answer choices.

Working backward means plugging in your answer choices and asking yourself if they could possibly mean the same as the underlined word. This technique is especially useful for words-in-context questions. Let's examine how this works.

Dry wit

(A) sarcastic
(B) moldy
(C) unusual
(D) pathetic

Given the context, we know that *dry* here can't mean the opposite of *wet*. The context already clues us in to the fact that *dry* has something to do with wit, or being clever.

Let's say you just don't know what *dry wit* could be. Go to the answer choices and ask yourself if each one could apply to the context, and therefore mean the same as the word *dry*.

Choice (A): Could you have *sarcastic wit*? Yes, someone could be sarcastically witty.

Choice (B): Could you have *moldy wit*? Moldy wit? That doesn't make sense. Eliminate this answer choice.

Choice (C): Could you have *unusual wit*? Perhaps, but it doesn't sound as good as choice (A).

Choice (D): Could you have *pathetic wit*? No, that doesn't make sense. *Pathetic* means *pitiable*. *Pitiable cleverness* doesn't make sense. Eliminate this answer choice.

Choice (A) is the best answer. You've got it!

QUESTION TYPE 3—ANTONYMS

Antonyms are words that have the opposite meaning of one another. *Slow* is the antonym of *fast*; *taciturn* is the antonym of *garrulous*. (Remember *garrulous* from our synonym section? Just throwing in a little review here…)

Antonym questions are clearly identifiable on the HSPT since they include the word *opposite*. An antonym question will read: "Generous means the *opposite* of…"

Use the Kaplan 3-Step Method for Synonyms when dealing with antonym questions. But just remember, now you're looking for a word that means the OPPOSITE of the one given. It's a good idea to circle the word *opposite* in the question, to make sure you don't accidentally look for a synonym.

Kaplan's 3-Step Method for Antonyms

Step 1. Define the word. Then, think of a word that means the opposite.
Step 2. Find the answer choice that best fits your definition.
Step 3. If no choice fits, think of other definitions for the stem word and go through the choices again.

Use roots, context, or word charge to help you if you don't know the definition of the question word.

Let's practice with an example:

Dear means the opposite of

(A) beloved
(B) close
(C) cheap
(D) family

Step 1—Define the Word. Then, Think of a Word That Means the Opposite.

Dear is a pretty familiar word. You know it from the beginning of a letter as in "Dear Aunt Sue." So, you might define *dear* as *a term for someone you love*. The opposite might be *a term for someone you hate or dislike*.

Step 2—Find the Answer Choice That Best Fits Your Definition

When we look at the answer choices—*beloved, close, cheap, family*—none of them fits our definition of the opposite of *dear* as *someone disliked or hated.* Since *dear* is an "easy" word, we have to figure that perhaps our definition is a little off. We have to refocus it.

Step 3—If No Choice Fits, Think of Other Definitions for the Stem Word and Go through the Choices Again

When we use the term "Dear Aunt Sue," or "Dear Sir," what are we saying about that person? We say that we care about them and think that they are valuable. Okay, so let's use *valuable* as our new definition of *dear.* Our antonym would then be the opposite of *valuable—worthless,* perhaps. Choice (C), *cheap,* is closest to worthless. That's the correct answer.

When you don't find an obvious answer choice for a word you know, there is probably an alternate meaning for that word. Use your knowledge of the word's primary meaning and see if you can expand on it to arrive at the correct answer.

You can also use your knowledge of word roots, familiarity with the word in context, and word charge to help you select the answer to antonym questions.

When using word charge on antonym questions, don't forget you're looking for words with the **opposite** charge. If the question word has a positive charge, your answer choice should have a negative one, and vice versa.

QUESTION TYPE 4—VERBAL CLASSIFICATION

Verbal classification questions on the HSPT ask you to find the word that is different from the rest of the choices, and doesn't belong with them. Synonym, antonym, and words-in-context questions all require you to define one word. Verbal classification questions require you not only to define a word, but also to figure out whether it belongs in a category with a group of other words. Verbal classification on the HSPT looks like this:

Which word does *not* belong with the others?

(A) approve
(B) scorn
(C) criticize
(D) deride

Three of the answer choices fit into the same category, and one of them does not. Your job is to find the one that does not belong.

The best approach to use? Kaplan's 3-Step Method for Verbal Classification!

Kaplan's 3-Step Method for Verbal Classification

Step 1. Define the words in the answer choices.

Step 2. Think of the category, and find the answer choice that does not belong to that category.

Step 3. If necessary, refocus and go through the choices again.

Although Kaplan's 3-Step Method is slightly different for verbal classification questions, the foundation remains the same. Define first, and find and answer second. By doing this, you will avoid becoming confused by wrong or trick answers.

Let's revisit some of our examples and see how the method works on verbal classification questions.

Step 1—Define the Words in the Answer Choices

Yes, you need to define each answer choice. It doesn't have to be an extensive or complicated definition, just a brief "label" to help you focus on what the word means.

Your labels might look something like this:

Which word does *not* belong with the others?

(A)   approve—*says okay*
(B)   scorn—*says bad things about*
(C)   criticize—*says bad things about*
(D)   deride—?

Step 2—Think of the Category, and Find the Answer Choice That Does Not Belong to That Category

Assuming that you don't know the word *deride*, you at least know that (B) and (C), have to do with disapproval. So let's define your category as *disapproval*.

Which word doesn't belong? Choice (A), *approve*. Notice how you were able to arrive at the right answer choice even though you didn't know all the words in the answer choices.

Let's try another one.

Which word does *not* belong with the others?

(A)   gloomy
(B)   depressed
(C)   hazy
(D)   fair

Step 1—Define the Words in the Answer Choices

Read all four answer choices, and jot down a brief definition next to each one.

- (A) gloomy—*sad, dark*
- (B) depressed—*sad*
- (C) hazy—*foggy*
- (D) fair—*bright? pretty?*

Step 2—Think of the Category, and Find the Answer Choice That Does Not Belong to That Category

On a quick first reading, *gloomy* and *depressed* both have to do with dark moods. You might define the category as *dark moods*.

But remember, we're looking for the choice that doesn't belong. If you initially defined the category as *dark moods*, you would find that two answer choices—*hazy* and *fair*—don't belong. Since there can be only one correct answer choice (only one word that does not belong), we know that our initial definition of the category as *dark moods* is not on target. Therefore, we need to move on to Step 3.

Step 3—If Necessary, Refocus and Go through the Choices Again

Look at the answer choices. (C) and (D) have to do with weather. So does (A). Three out of four answer choices fall into the same category. Let's refocus our definition then and call the category *types of weather*.

Therefore, (B) doesn't belong. This is the correct answer choice.

The example above illustrates an important point. Although it might seem helpful to move quickly, cutting out steps or selecting an answer without reading all the answer choices carefully can actually cost you more time in the end.

On the other hand, recognizing types of categories, such as members of a group or parts of a whole, will help you arrive more quickly at a correct answer choice on verbal classification questions.

KAPLAN TIP

Trying to select an answer in a verbal classification question without carefully reading all the answer choices can lead you down the wrong path and cost you more time in the end.

QUESTION TYPE 5—ANALOGIES

Analogy questions, which appear on the COOP and HSPT, ask you to compare two words and then extend the relationship to another set of words.

Simply put, an analogy is a comparison. When you say, "She's as slow as molasses," or "He eats like a horse," you're making an analogy.

Analogy questions on the HSPT are mixed in with the rest of the Verbal Skills questions we covered. HSPT analogies look like this:

Bird is to nest as bear is to

- (A) cub
- (B) paw
- (C) tree
- (D) cave

One set of words—*bird* and *nest*—is given. The second set—*bear* and ?—is incomplete. Your job is to find an answer choice that will create the same relationship between the second set of words as exists in the first set.

Analogies may seem pretty weird at first glance. However, once you become familiar with the format, you'll find that they are pretty straightforward and very predictable. With practice, you can learn to get analogy questions right even when you don't know all of the vocabulary words involved.

KAPLAN TIP

On the COOP, analogy questions actually use pictures instead of words. Don't panic! Kaplan's 3-Step Method for Analogies works just as well for pictures as it does for words. Go to the Reasoning Skills chapter in this book to learn more about COOP analogies.

Kaplan's 3-Step Method for Analogies

Step 1: Build a bridge.
Step 2: Predict your answer choice, and select an answer.
Step 3: Adjust your bridge if necessary.

A bridge is a sentence you create to express the relationship between the words in the stem pair. Building a bridge helps you zone in on the correct answer and helps you avoid falling for wrong answer traps. Let's take a closer look to see how it works.

Step 1—Build a Bridge

In every analogy question, there's a strong, definite connection—a bridge—between the two stem words. Your first task is to figure out this relationship.

A bridge is a short sentence that relates the two words in the question, and every pair of words will have a strong bridge that links them. In our original example, a good bridge would be "A bird lives in a nest."

Step 2—Predict Your Answer Choice, and Select an Answer

Now, you need to determine which answer choice relates to *bear* in the same way. Use your bridge to do that.

Our bridge was: A bird lives in a nest. Apply the same bridge to the incomplete pair: A bear lives in a _____. So when you predict the answer choice, you come up with a place where a bear lives: a cave.

Bird is to nest as bear is to

(A) cub
(B) paw
(C) tree
(D) cave

Cave, your predicted answer, is indeed among the answer choices, (D). Take a moment to look at the incorrect answer choices: *cub*, *paw*, and *tree*. They are all related in some way to the words in the question, but not in the way our bridge defined. Building a strong bridge is essential to predicting an answer, selecting a correct answer choice, and avoiding traps.

What if your bridge doesn't work? Sometimes you may find that even though you came up with a bridge, none of the answer choices fits. In this case, your bridge is either too broad or too narrow. You'll need to refocus it. That's where Step 3 comes in.

Step 3—Adjust Your Bridge if Necessary

Let's see how you can adjust a weak bridge using the example below.

Fish is to gill as mammal is to

(A) arm
(B) wing
(C) foot
(D) lung

Let's say you create this bridge: "A fish has a gill." Then you went to the answer choices and plugged in the bridge:

(A)   A mammal has an arm.

(B)   A mammal has a wing.

(C)   A mammal has a foot.

(D)   A mammal has a lung.

Every choice fits! (Though few mammals have wings, bats do.) In this case, the bridge was too general, so you'll need to adjust your bridge.

What would a good adjustment be? Try to create a more specific relationship between the words, because the more specific your bridge is, the fewer choices will match it. A good bridge for this pair might be: "A fish uses a gill to breathe." Now try plugging that bridge into the answer choices.

(A)   A mammal uses an arm to breathe? No.

(B)   A mammal uses a wing to breathe? No.

(C)   A mammal uses a foot to breathe? No.

(D)   A mammal uses a lung to breathe? Yes!

It should now be easier to see the correct answer: fish is to gill as mammal is to lung, (D).

KAPLAN TIP

When making a bridge, a good rule is to relate the words in such a way that you'd be able to insert the phrase "by definition" and the relationship would hold true. For example: "A poodle, by definition, is a type of dog." If you can't use "by definition" in the sentence that relates the words, your bridge isn't strong, and it needs to be reworked.

Building Classic Bridges

Because relationships between items in analogy questions need to be strong and definite, there are some bridges that appear again and again. We call these **classic bridges**. Get to know them; you'll save yourself a lot of time getting to the correct answer choice on analogy questions. As you read through each one, use the space provided to come up with an example of your own.

Bridge 1: Character

One word characterizes the other.

Quarrelsome is to argue… Someone quarrelsome is characterized by a tendency to argue.

Vivacious is to energy… Someone vivacious is characterized by a lot of energy.

Your example: _____

Bridge 2: Lack

One word describes what someone or something lacks (or does not have).

Coward is to bravery... A coward lacks bravery.

Braggart is to modesty... A braggart lacks modesty.

Your example: _____

Bridge 3: Function

One word names an object; the other word defines its function or what it is used for.

Scissors is to cut... Scissors are used to cut.

Pen is to write... A pen is used to write.

Your example: _____

Bridge 4: Degree

One word is a greater or lesser degree of the other word.

Deafening is to loud... Something deafening is extremely loud.

Hovel is to mansion... A hovel is a mansion of a poor degree. (Including the specific "poor degree" might help you hone in on the right answer choice.)

Your example: _____

Bridge 5: Example

One word is an example of, or type of, the other word.

Measles is to disease... Measles is a type of disease.

Apartment is to home... An apartment is a type of home.

Your example: _____

Bridge 6: Group

One word is made up of several of the other word.

Forest is to trees... A forest is made up of many trees.

Bouquet is to flowers... A bouquet is made up of many flowers.

Your example: _____

What to Do if You're Stuck

1. Backsolve.
2. Use classic bridges.
3. Remember the context.
4. Use word charge.

Even with your arsenal of tools, you may run into analogy questions where you don't know what to do. Perhaps you won't know what a word in the question means, or how the words relate to one another. What should you do?

There are a few strategies that will really up your chances of getting the question right, even if you're stuck.

Backsolve

You may be wondering, "How can you figure out the answer without knowing what the question is?" Well, you can't necessarily figure out the answer, but you can eliminate clearly wrong answer choices, leaving fewer options to choose from, so the odds are better that you'll pick the right choice.

Awl is to tool as rose is to

(A) vase
(B) flower
(C) bird
(D) daisy

Even if you didn't know that an awl is a type of tool, what could you rule out? Well, in (A), there's no definite connection between *rose* and *vase*. A rose could be put in a vase, but it also could be in the wild. Additionally, any other flower could also be put in a vase. Rule out (A) as a weak bridge. There is also no relationship by definition between *rose* and *bird*, choice (C). Choice (D) is also not a strong relationship by definition: although *rose* and *daisy* are both flowers, one is not defined in terms of the other. ("Both are" is NOT a good bridge—it's an answer trap!)

So in this example, only (B) has a strong, definite relationship to *rose*. The words *rose* and *flower* are joined by a classic "type of" bridge: a rose is a type of flower.

KAPLAN TIP

Watch out for the "both are" trap on analogy questions. For instance, bread and bananas are both types of food, but what exactly is their relationship? Bananas aren't a type of bread, a lack of bread, or a function of bread.

Use Classic Bridges

What if you reach the point where you can't figure out the bridge, and you can't rule out wrong answer choices?

You know the six classic bridges. So, even if you don't know the exact definition of one (or both!) words, you could make an educated guess about the bridge. For example, say you saw this question:

Word is to philologist as bug is to

What might the bridge be? Well, a *philologist* sounds like a type of person (since it ends in *-ologist*), and a *word* is a thing, so maybe a philologist does something with words. *Philologist* is a tricky word, but you could make a great guess by saying that a philologist studies words, which is exactly right!

Remember the Context

Sometimes a word sounds familiar, but you can't remember why. If that happens, use the context to help you determine its meaning. For example:

Crescendo is to music as climax is to

What does *crescendo* mean? Maybe you don't know. But the fact that it is already linked to music in the question clues you in to the fact that *crescendo* has something to do with music. *Climax* therefore has something to do with... Predict your answer choice, then look at the answers to see which one fits best.

Use Word Charge

As you saw in Question Type 1—Synonyms, some words give you the feeling that they're either positive or negative. Use this sense to help you figure out the bridge between words in the question when you don't know what one or both of them mean!

Once you determine the charge of the words in the question, you can look for a word in the answer choices that completes the second phrase with the same charge relationship. If the words in the question have the same charge (+, +) or (−, −) the two next words should have the same charge. That charge can be either both positive, or both negative, but it must be the same. If the words in the question have opposite charges (+, −) or (−, +), the two following words should have opposite charges.

VOCABULARY-BUILDING STRATEGIES

You have a lot of strategies and skills at your disposal for the Verbal Skills questions on the COOP, TACHS, or HSPT. You should be ready to handle any Verbal Skills question that comes your way if you put your knowledge into practice.

One of the best ways to prepare for the COOP, TACHS, HSPT, and many other standardized tests is to expand your vocabulary. Don't sit down and memorize the dictionary. Just spend about 30 minutes a day using any of the techniques below. We recommend dividing your vocabulary study into two daily sessions. Spend some time learning new words during the first session, and review them again later before the end of the day. Scientific research shows that this is the best way to optimize retention. (Don't know the meaning of *retention*? Look it up!)

KAPLAN TIP

Expanding your vocabulary is a great way to prepare for the COOP, TACHS, or HSPT. Divide your daily vocabulary study time into two sessions: spend around 15 minutes learning new words during the first session, and review them again later in the day.

Look It Up

Challenge yourself to find at least five words a day that are unfamiliar to you. You could find these words listening to a news broadcast or reading a magazine or novel. In fact, books that you choose to read for enjoyment normally contain three to five words per page that are unfamiliar to you. Write down these words, look them up in the dictionary, and record their definitions in a notebook.

But don't only write the word's definition. Below your definition, use the word in a sentence. This will help you to remember the word, and to anticipate possible context questions. Ask a teacher, parent, or someone else with a strong vocabulary to check your sentences to make sure you've used the word correctly.

Use Flash Cards

Periodically transfer the words from your notebook to flash cards. On one side of the card write the word, on the other side record its definition. You might find it helpful to put your context phrase on either side of the card as well. Keep your flash cards in your bag or backpack and practice with them during the day.

Make Lists of Synonyms and Antonyms

Another great way to expand your vocabulary is to list groups of words with the same meaning. Use a thesaurus to find synonyms (and antonyms) of common words.

For example, you might look up the word *talkative*. Then fold a piece of paper in half lengthwise; in one column make a list of all the synonyms you find for *talkative*, and in the other column record all the antonyms. (Make some mark on the paper to remind you that the two columns are opposites!)

Study Word Roots, Prefixes, and Suffixes

Knowing word roots, prefixes, and suffixes will expand your vocabulary and will help you guess the meaning of a word if you are not sure. You can pick up a book with word roots from the library, or ask your librarian to help you find a list on the computer and print it out. As you memorize roots, record words that use them in a notebook, write them in sentences, and put them on your flash cards.

Use Your New Words in Conversation

As much as possible, use your new words in everyday conversation. This is a great sign that you've mastered the new words and will ensure that you don't forget them.

While it's impossible to know exactly which of the many words you'll study may appear on the COOP, TACHS, or HSPT, expanding your vocabulary isn't important only on test day. A rich vocabulary will stand you in good stead for future study, work, and simply expressing yourself—not to mention that a million-dollar vocabulary is just plain impressive!

VERBAL SKILLS PRACTICE SET

1. Usurp most nearly means

    (A) seize
    (B) grease
    (C) admit
    (D) attack

2. Unscrupulous most nearly means

    (A) moral
    (B) clever
    (C) tidy
    (D) dishonest

3. Fatigued means the *opposite* of

    (A) argumentative
    (B) fragile
    (C) energetic
    (D) exhausted

4. Which word does *not* belong?

    (A) river
    (B) lake
    (C) waterfall
    (D) brook

5. Furtive is to secret as blatant is to

    (A) controlled
    (B) hurried
    (C) obvious
    (D) complex

6. Destitute means the *opposite* of

    (A) wealthy
    (B) hungry
    (C) hopeless
    (D) plentiful

7. Business acumen

    (A) sharpness
    (B) zeal
    (C) cruelty
    (D) competition

8. Ample supplies

    (A) stored
    (B) plentiful
    (C) moldy
    (D) delayed

9. Iota is to amount as miniature is to

    (A) dollhouse
    (B) size
    (C) drop
    (D) number

10. Which word does *not* belong?

    (A) kick
    (B) grasp
    (C) grab
    (D) pitch

ANSWERS AND EXPLANATIONS

1. A

This is a synonym question. Come up with your own definition first, if you know the word. Your definition might be something like this: *usurp* means *to grab*. If you can define the word, move on to the answer choices. If you haven't, try to use other means to come up with a definition. Maybe you've heard the word used in this context: "usurp a throne." This context could help you define *usurp* as *take without permission*. Even if you are unable to come up with a definition, you could eliminate (B) which sounds suspiciously like a trick, the *-surp* somehow making you think of grease. The answer choice closest in meaning to *usurp* is (A), *seize*.

2. D

This is a synonym question. *Unscrupulous* means *without scruples or morals*. The answer choice that best fits this definition is *dishonest*. Perhaps you've heard the word used in the context, "He has no scruples." Having no scruples is negatively charged. If you don't know the meaning of the word *unscrupulous*, look for an answer choice that is also negatively charged. Only choice (D) fits. It is the correct answer.

3. C

This is an antonym question. Define the word, and think of an opposite. *Fatigued* means tired or worn out; the opposite is *energetic*, choice (C).

4. B

This is a verbal classification question. Read all the answer choices and think about what three out of four of them have in common. *River, waterfall*, and *brook* are bodies of water that flow. A lake is contained. *Lake* does not belong.

5. C

This is an analogy question. Build a bridge between the first two words, and use it to determine what the missing word should be. Your bridge here might be: *Furtive* is in a *secret* manner. *Blatant* is in a *clear* manner. Which answer choice means the closest to *clear*? Choice (C), *obvious*.

6. A

This is an antonym question. *Destitute* means *poor*, the opposite is *wealthy*. If you did not know the meaning of the question word, use word charge to help you hone in on the right answer. *Destitute* has a negative charge. The opposite, or antonym, should have a positive charge. Choices (A) and (D) have a positive charge. Take your best guess from these remaining answer choices.

7. A

This is a words-in-context question. Think of a definition first. *Acumen* is *intelligence* or *cunning*. Choice (A) best fits the definition. If you are unable to think of a definition, work backward plugging in the answer choices. *Business sharpness*? Makes sense. *Business zeal*? Possibly, but it doesn't sound as good. *Business cruelty*? Doesn't really make sense. *Business competition*? That sounds good. Now that you've ruled out choice (C), take your best guess.

8. B

This is a words-in-context question. If you are able to, think of a definition first. *Ample* means *enough*. Choice (B), *plentiful* best fits this definition. If you are unable to think of a definition, try using word charge to eliminate poor answer choices. *Ample* is positively charged. The strongest positively charged answer choice is (B). Choices (C) and (D) are both negatively charged, while (A) does not really carry any charge.

9. B

This is an analogy question. Build a bridge first, then think of a word that fits into the relationship you defined. An *iota* is *a small amount*, a *miniature* is *a small size*. *Size*, our definition, is actually one of the answer choices, choice (B).

10. A

This is a verbal classification question. *Grasp*, *grab*, and *pitch* are all done with the arms, but *kick* is an action performed with the legs. Be sure to read through each item and think about what they have in common before rushing to select a choice. If you worked too quickly, you might have chosen *pitch*, since it sounds more sporty than the other choices.

Reading Comprehension

chapter six

Reading Comprehension skills are important to have when you take the COOP, TACHS, or HSPT tests. You'll be presented with five to eight passages ranging in length from one to six paragraphs. Each passage has approximately five questions that test your ability to understand what you've read.

In previous years, the COOP Reading Comprehension subtest included only passages. Currently, some language mechanics and organization skills are tested in this section as well. We'll address those topics in chapter 7. For now, we'll focus on the passages and the questions that accompany them.

Because time is of the essence on the COOP, TACHS, and HSPT exams, it's important to approach the passages in a systematic way. Reading habits that serve you well in school can prove too time-consuming for this type of exam. Avoid these common reading traps:

- Reading too slowly
- Rereading things you do not understand
- Spending more time on the passages than on the questions

All of these traps involve pacing. Normally, it's a good idea to read slowly and deliberately and to stick with something you are reading until it makes sense. However, what normally works will not help you on test day.

READING ON TESTS IS DIFFERENT FROM EVERYDAY READING

You don't usually read to gather points, do you? Remember as you approach the COOP, TACHS, or HSPT reading passages that the points come from the questions, not the passages. If you spend your time focusing on all the subtle nuances or details of a given passage, you may not have time to answer the questions (and earn points) when you are finished.

Yes, you may know all the details of 12th century manuscript illumination, but this won't help you get into the school of your choice.

Therefore, as you work through this chapter, there are two things you need to do:

- Be aware of your reading habits. Notice how you approach each passage and whether you are getting bogged down in the details.
- Make the questions your priority.

How do you do that? Use our systematic approach to focus on the questions and the points.

Kaplan's 4-Step Method for Reading Comprehension Questions

Step 1. Read the passage.

Step 2. Decode the questions.

Step 3. Research the details.

Step 4. Predict the answer, and check the answer choices.

Read passage very carefully

Like Kaplan's Method for the other question types, Kaplan's 4-Step Method for Reading Comprehension Questions requires you to do most of your work *before* you actually look at the answer choices. It's very tempting to read the questions and immediately dive into the answer choices. Don't do this. The work you do up front will save you more time in the long run and increase your ability to avoid tempting wrong answer choices.

Step 1—Read the Passage

The first thing you're going to do is read through the passage, but don't memorize it or take it apart. Instead, look for the main idea and paragraph topics (note the general idea and where it seems to be going).

For example, if you saw the following passage on the COOP, TACHS, or HSPT, these are some things you might want to note.

Franklin was remembered for many things; he was also a diplomat.

Benjamin Franklin is well-known as a founding father, an inventor, and a philosopher. He is remembered for the clever yet humorous writings of *Poor Richard's Almanac*, which offered advice such as "Early to bed, early to rise makes a man healthy, wealthy and wise." The scientist Franklin discovered electricity through his experiments with lightning. He was also the first American diplomat. From 1776 to 1778, Benjamin Franklin led a three-man envoy to France in an effort to win French support for American independence.

In Paris, Franklin charmed French aristocrats and intellectuals. They welcomed him as the embodiment of the New World Enlightenment thinking. His likeness was etched on medallions, rings, watches, and snuffboxes. Fashionable upper-class ladies wore their hair in a style imitating Franklin's fur cap. Franklin used his popularity and diplomatic talent to convince France to recognize American independence and sign the Treaty of Alliance with the thirteen states. The treaty was brilliantly negotiated, and Franklin managed to include an article stating that no payment would need to be made to secure the alliance.

Franklin was popular and successful in France.

After the American Revolution, Franklin became the first American Minister to be received by a foreign government. He was aged 73 at the time. In 1785, Thomas Jefferson followed Franklin as ambassador to France. When the French Foreign Minister asked Jefferson, "It is you who replace Dr. Franklin?" Jefferson replied, "No one can replace him, Sir; I am only his successor."

Jefferson followed Franklin, but respected the man who came before him.

Notice that we've kept our comments very broad on this initial reading of the passage. The goal is to recognize the major themes and perhaps a few details. There's no reason to focus too closely on any particular thing because we don't know yet whether the questions will ask about it or not.

Step 2—Decode the Questions

A few questions will follow each passage. The first thing you'll need to do with each question is figure out exactly what it is asking before you can answer it.

Here's an example of a question that might follow the Benjamin Franklin passage:

According to the passage, what was the goal of Franklin's first mission to France?

(A) to charm the French people
(B) to win support for the American Revolution
(C) to get help drafting the Constitution
(D) to be received by a foreign government

In other words, why did Franklin go to France?

This is a detail question. However, we did not originally note details when we first read the passage. We were waiting to see which ones were asked about in the questions. Now that we know, we can move on to Step 3.

Step 3—Research the Details

Now that you know the detail that is being questioned—why Franklin went to France—you can go back and find it. You should have noted when you read the passage that the first paragraph is about Franklin's role as a diplomat. Scan this paragraph for details about where he went and why.

Even if you have some memory of the detail, avoid answering based solely on your recollection. Check the passage to make sure your memory is right. This technique will also keep you from trying to memorize details. Memorizing details is a waste of time on the test.

Step 4—Predict the Answer, and Check the Answer Choices

When you find the detail in the passage, think about the purpose that it serves. Why does the author mention Franklin's *effort to win French support for American independence*? What does that mean? It could mean he wanted financial support or to form an alliance against the British. Now that you have an idea of the correct answer, look for an answer choice that matches your idea.

    (A)   to charm the French people
    (B)   to win support for the American Revolution
    (C)   to get help drafting the Constitution
    (D)   to be received by a foreign government

Answer choice (B) is the only one that fits the idea you've already come up with.

THE QUESTIONS

Knowing what type of questions to expect will help you constructively read the passage. There are four question types that you could be asked.

① What title expresses selection/main idea best?

Main Idea Questions

A main idea question asks you to summarize the topic of the entire passage. You may see a main idea question in a variety of forms. Some examples of these forms are as follows:

* questions about the intention of writer *

- What is this passage mostly about?
- Which of the following is a good title for this passage?
- The information in this passage could help you answer which of these questions?

② general questions abt paragraph

Decode the questions and you realize that they are asking the same thing.

③ questions abt main character & purpose

> **KAPLAN TIP**
>
> **A key strategy for main idea questions is to look for an answer choice that summarizes the entire passage, not just a detail or a paragraph.**

④ other general (non vocab) terms (definitions)

Detail Questions

A detail question asks you to research information that is directly stated in the passage. For example:

- Which of the following is a result of photosynthesis?
- What is the first stage of child development?
- Which Roman emperor conquered the Celts?

All you have to do is locate the information in the passage. A key strategy is to research the details by relating the facts from the question to a specific paragraph and then rereading that paragraph to find the detail you're looking for.

Inference Questions

The answers to inference questions will not be stated in the passage, but will be hinted at strongly. It is your job to figure out what those hints mean when put together. Here are some examples of inference questions:

- This passage is most likely found in a
- The author of this passage is probably
- The next thing that will most likely happen is

Inference questions usually ask you to predict what might happen next or what would be a logical next paragraph. Likewise, questions that ask you about the author's purpose or the author's attitude toward the topic are inference questions.

For instance, if a passage goes on about the wonders of exploring archeological excavations, the author is, most likely, an archeologist. If, on the other hand, the passage discusses the negative impact of archeological digs, the author is probably not an archeologist.

We will discuss what skills are involved in answering inference questions more in this chapter.

Vocabulary-in-Context Questions

Vocabulary-in-context questions ask you the meaning of a word used in the passage. Although it may be a word that you recognize, treat vocabulary-in-context questions as a type of research question. Often, the obvious meaning is not the correct answer.

- What does the author mean by choosing the word *misguided* to describe the plan?
- In this passage, the word *futile* most nearly means
- Based on the passage, a good definition for *exorbitant* is

Even if you think you know the meaning of the word, always go back and locate the word within the passage. Read a sentence or two before the word, the sentence in which it is used, and a sentence or two after it. The context of the word will provide enough clues to its meaning.

CRITICAL READING SKILLS

As you learned earlier, reading for the COOP, TACHS, or HSPT is not exactly like the reading you do in school or at home. In general, you usually read to learn or for pleasure. It's a pretty safe bet that you're not reading the passages on the test for the fun of it. You are reading them to answer questions and earn points. Anything that doesn't help you get a point is a waste of time. The questions will ask you about the main idea, a few details, and a few inferences. Keep in mind that you need to get enough out of the passage to help you deal with the questions. Here are some strategies to do just that.

there will be tricky questions..... take your time & rlly think abt it

COOP, TACHS, and HSPT Reading Strategies

Mark It Up

You can write in the test booklet, so use this to your advantage. You do not need to take a lot of notes, but do not leave the passage and surrounding space blank. Use it to keep track of the main idea of the whole passage and of the various paragraphs. Your notes will help you to find the information you need to answer the questions later.

Focus on the First Third of the Passage

Although you cannot count on being entertained, you can count on being presented with a well-organized passage. This means that the author is overwhelmingly likely to present the important information at the beginning of the passage. Odds are that you'll be able to answer the inevitable main idea question based on the first third of the passage.

Look for the Main Idea

All you really need to understand is the main idea and the paragraph topics. Remember that you can research the details as you need them, as long as you have an idea of where to look.

Use the Paragraph Topics

The first two sentences of each paragraph should tell you what it's about. The rest of the paragraph is likely to be detail. Just as you should pay more attention to the beginning of the passage, you should also pay more attention to the beginning of each paragraph.

Don't Worry About the Details

Don't waste time rereading parts that you don't understand. As long as you have a general idea of where the details are, you don't have to know what they are. Remember, you can look them up later. As long as you've made a note of the paragraph topic, you should be able to go back and find the detail within it.

Break It Down

Sometimes you'll come across difficult language or technical jargon in the passages, especially in the science passages. Don't get bogged down by language that you find confusing. The underlying topic is usually pretty straightforward. It can be very helpful to put confusing language into your own words. Remember, you don't have to understand every word to summarize or paraphrase. All you need is a general understanding.

Keep Moving

Aim to spend no more than two to three minutes reading a passage. Remember, reading the passage doesn't earn you points.

Summarizing

For the purposes of the COOP, TACHS, or HSPT, summarizing means capturing in a single phrase what the entire passage is about. We've already shown you the types of main idea questions you could see; these questions ask about the passage as a whole. Wrong answers will include choices that deal only with one paragraph or some other smaller component of the passage. You will need to look for the answer that deals with the entire passage. If you've thought about the main idea ahead of time, you're more likely to go directly to the correct answer choice.

The Homestead Act was one of the most important bills passed in the history of the United States. Signed into law in 1862 by Abraham Lincoln, this act made vast amounts of public land available to private citizens. Under the Homestead Act, 270 million acres, or 10% of the area of the United States, was claimed and settled. For a small filing fee of $18, five years of residency, and a lot of back-breaking labor, anyone dedicated to land ownership could win an impressive 160-acre parcel of land.

explains affect the act hand on land ownership

The qualifying requirements were seemingly scant. A homesteader simply had to be the head of a household and at least 21 years old. Each homesteader had to build a home, make improvements to the land, and farm it for five years. After this time, the settler would be eligible to "prove up," or prove all the conditions had been met. If successful, he or she would be able to keep the land. Hopeful people from all walks of life came to the West lured by the promise of "free" land.

main idea question

This passage is mainly about

(A) how to apply to be a homesteader
(B) proving requirements for homesteaders
details abt the paragraph
(C) the Homestead Act's effect on land ownership
(D) all the acts that Abraham Lincoln signed ✗

The question basically asks which choice best summarizes what the entire passage is about. Only one answer choice sums up the contents of both paragraphs. (A) and (B) are both details. (D) is too broad; all the acts that Lincoln signed are not discussed in the passage. (C) summarizes the whole passage, which discusses the importance of the Homestead Act making public land available for people to own. Although there are a few details explaining how the land was given out, the main idea of the passage is that this act made it possible for people to own land.

Researching

Whereas summarizing is important in helping you answer main idea questions, researching is important in helping you answer detail questions. Generally, if you jot down paragraph topics in the blank space around the text, you should have a good map to help you locate the details. Once you know where to look, just scan the paragraph for key phrases found in the question.

extratropical storms, layers of cold and warm air

From fall through winter, extratropical storms dominate the weather across much of the United States and other parts of the globe. These extratropical storms originate outside the tropics and generally move west to east across the oceans and continents. In areas of the storm that are ahead of a warm front, warm air flows over colder air that is closer to the ground. Thus, one layer of air that is above 32 degrees Fahrenheit is caught between a layer of colder air near the ground and a layer of colder air higher up.

rain, sleet, or snow determined by temperature of layers

Whether we experience snow, sleet, or freezing rain is determined by the temperatures of the layers of air when precipitation begins. Precipitation that begins as snow in the higher level of colder air will become rain if it meets a layer of air that's above 32 degrees Fahrenheit. However, if the layer of cold air near the ground is relatively thick, the falling rain will freeze into ice pellets, which are generally called sleet. On the other hand, if the layer of cold air near the ground is relatively thin, the falling rain will not become ice unless it hits something. This is freezing rain. In places where there is no layer of warm air, precipitation falls all the way to the ground as snow. Often, rain, freezing rain, and snow will fall together as a storm moves by, leaving an icy coating on exposed surfaces.

Take a look at the passage and paragraph topics above. The topics are very general. If you saw the following questions, would you know where to locate the answers?

Which of the following is true of extratropical storms?

(A) They dominate winter weather.
(B) They originate in the tropics.
(C) They move from east to west.
(D) They cause tornados.

According to the passage, what causes precipitation to fall as snow?

(A) It meets a layer of ice as it hits the ground.
(B) It begins high in the atmosphere.
(C) It does not meet any layer of warm air as it hits the ground.
(D) It moves from west to east as it travels the globe.

The first paragraph deals with extratropical storms. The second paragraph deals with why precipitation becomes either rain, freezing rain, sleet, or snow.

Making an Inference

Making an inference means coming to a conclusion that is not directly stated, based on the information given. In other words, making an inference means reading between the lines. What did the author almost say, but not state outright?

Inferences will not stray too far from the language of the text. Wrong answer choices on inference questions often fall beyond the subject matter of the passage.

> As the saying goes, Rome wasn't built in a day. Writing a top-notch essay takes time, planning, and careful revision. But in order to revise, you must first have something down on paper. Many students feel that this is the most difficult part of the composition process.
>
> Brainstorming is often a helpful way to overcome writer's block. Sit quietly somewhere with a piece of blank paper and your chosen topic. Note all the things that occur to you on that topic. For example, if you were writing an essay about horses, you might jot down *fast, beautiful, Arabian Stallion, work horses,* or anything else that jars your imagination. Once you have some ideas down on paper, you can begin to organize them.

According to the passage, the first step in the writing process is

(A) carefully revising
(B) purchasing necessary supplies
(C) daydreaming about the topic
(D) jotting down ideas

This short passage discusses the writing process. The question asks what the first step in the process is. Yet, there is no sentence in the passage that states directly: *The first step of the writing passage is...* However, in the first paragraph, the author mentions that *in order to revise, you must first have something down on paper.* Getting something down must be the first step.

(D) is the only choice that is close to your predicted answer. *Revising* (A) can't occur until writing has been done. *Purchasing supplies* (B) is not getting something down on paper; neither is *daydreaming* (C).

A Word About Types of Passages

There are several passage types you may see on the COOP, TACHS, or HSPT. The topics of interest can be from any field. Here are a few areas that the passages may be about.

Science

These passages are about a scientific topic such as life science, physical science, or earth science. They may be packed with details. Remember not to worry about the details or try to memorize them. Use paragraph topic sentences to help you relocate the details you need later.

Social Science

These passages are about such areas as history, linguistics, or culture. The author may have a point of view. There may be a comparison between old and new ideas about the topic. Try to notice the author's tone, but treat these passages as you would any other. Keep your first reading broad and avoid focusing on detail.

Fiction

These may be short stories or first- or third-person narratives. A selection may discuss the actions or internal thoughts of a character. The exact identity of the characters or the precise location of the story may only be hinted at. Don't let this bother you. As always, keep your initial reading general. Notice the tone or the type of story. *Mystery story about a girl*, for example, could be a helpful main idea notation for this type of passage.

Different passages may lend themselves better to different question types, i.e., science passages are full of details for detail questions, and short stories are great for inference questions about a character or what might happen next. But it is important to read every passage in the same strategic way. Note the main idea, jot down the topic of each paragraph, and circle or underline details you believe may be asked about later.

A Reminder About Timing

Plan to spend approximately two to three minutes reading the passage and no more than 30 seconds on each question. When you start practicing, you'll probably find yourself spending more time on the passages. That's okay. However, you need to pay attention to your timing, and cut the time down as you improve. Get through the passage and get on to the questions, where the points lie.

Now it's time to practice some Reading Comprehension passages and questions. Make sure you mark up the passage, noting the main idea and paragraph topics. Research the details and predict your answers. Most importantly, remember that it's all about the questions.

READING COMPREHENSION PRACTICE SET

Directions: Read the passages and answer the questions that follow.

A nuclear reaction is a change in the structure of the nucleus, or center, of an atom. The energy created during a nuclear reaction results in nuclear energy, or atomic energy. Some nuclear energy is produced naturally. The Sun and stars, for example, continually generate heat and light by nuclear reactions. The nuclear reactions that occur on the Sun, as on all other stars, are nuclear fusion reactions. In these reactions, the nuclei of atoms are joined together or fused. This occurs only at extremely high temperatures.

The nuclear energy that is produced by humans in nuclear reactor power plants is based on a different type of nuclear reaction. These plants depend on the energy released during nuclear fission to generate power. In nuclear fission, energy is released by the splitting of atomic nuclei.

Because of its many favorable properties, the element uranium is the primary fuel used in nuclear power plants. Uranium nuclei can be easily split. One split uranium nucleus can release many fragments, which then split other nuclei. This is known as a chain reaction. In addition, uranium is also a cost-efficient energy producer. One ton of uranium can be used to produce more energy than is produced by several million tons of coal or barrels of oil.

1. A good title for this passage would be

   (A) The Power of the Sun
   (B) What Is Nuclear Energy?
   (C) Favorable Properties
   (D) Explaining Nuclear Fission

2. According to the passage, nuclear reactions on the Sun differ from those of nuclear power plants because

   (A) they release more energy
   (B) they use more uranium than power plants
   (C) they join rather than separate atomic nuclei
   (D) they occur at higher temperatures

3. This text could probably be found in

   (A) a magazine article on the history of nuclear power plants
   (B) a brochure put out by a group opposed to nuclear energy
   (C) a scientific textbook explaining various types of energy
   (D) a debate about the pros and cons of nuclear energy

Although history has referred to Genghis Khan and the Mongolian army as Mongolian hordes, Mongolian superiority was most likely not a result of their overwhelming numbers. The quality, not the quantity, of the Mongolian warrior was the key to Mongolian military victories. Each Mongolian warrior was extremely well trained, disciplined, and prepared.

The Mongolian army was tightly organized according to a decimal system. The largest unit of fighters was a *tjumen*, which consisted of 10,000 soldiers. A large army would be made up of three *tjumens*: one of infantry troops who would perform close combat and two others whose job was to encircle the opponent. Each *tjumen* consisted of ten regiments. Each of these 1,000-strong regiments, or *mingghans*, was further broken down into squadrons of 100 men. The 100-men *jaghun* was then broken down further into groups of ten. Each group of ten, known as an *arban*, elected its commander by a majority vote. The Khan was personally appointed by the leaders of the *tjumen*, based on ability, rather than age or social status.

On the battlefield, each unit was expected to participate in a major co-ordinated effort and at the same time be able to act independently. Therefore, warriors carried an extensive collection of equipment, including a battle-axe, a curved sword, a lance, and two Mongolian bows. One bow was designed for rapid use on horseback. The other was heavier and more useful from a long-range ground position. Each rider also carried a sharpening stone for his metal arms, a knife, an awl, and a needle and thread in case he needed to repair his equipment in the field.

The warrior's dress was extremely important military equipment, too. Because the winter temperatures in Siberia and Mongolia fell well below zero, warm clothing was essential. Mongols wore felt socks and heavy leather boots. They would typically don a coat of fur or sheepskin, under which they wore several layers of wool. Even a Mongolian warrior's underclothes were designed for military use. They preferred Chinese silk for this purpose. Not only was it warm, but heavy silk could also prevent an arrow from piercing human skin. If an arrow did penetrate into a warrior's arm or chest, it could be drawn out by pulling the silk thread around it. If the arrow were poisoned, this technique might also keep the poison from entering the bloodstream.

4. The author's attitude toward the Mongolian army is one of

   (A) fear
   (B) respect
   (C) disbelief
   (D) awe

5. The smallest unit of the Mongolian army was

   (A) a *jaghun*
   (B) a *tjumen*
   (C) a *mingghan*
   (D) an *arban*

6. This passage is mostly about

   (A) Mongolian battle equipment
   (B) Genghis Khan's victories in China
   (C) the organization of the Mongolian army
   (D) reasons for Mongolian military success

7. According to the passage, Mongolian warriors were expected to be

   (A) excellent farmers and horsemen
   (B) well-dressed and fashionable
   (C) independent yet cooperative
   (D) competitive and mistrustful

8. As used in the passage, the word hordes most nearly means

   (A) leaders
   (B) barbarians
   (C) masses
   (D) warriors

Originally, the plaid, coarse wool of the Scottish tartan was only intended to be a decorative fabric. However, because they were made of coarse local wool and relied on a limited range of color dyes, the tartan soon became associated with particular districts and communities. In areas such as the Scottish Highlands, where there was a strong clan presence, the clan of a visitor from another area could be deduced by the color of his tartans. Thus, the tartan came to symbolize clan membership.

After the rebellion of Charles Edward Stuart, wearing the tartan of the Scottish Highlands was prohibited by law. The Highland Regiments, independent companies of soldiers who policed the area, were the only ones allowed to wear it. They used a dark tartan, which came to be called the Black Watch. The Black Watch was the basis of many patterns involving white, red, and yellow. It is still the official government tartan, and is considered a universal one that everyone may wear.

9. This passage could help you answer which of the following questions?

   (A) Why are tartans associated with clan membership?
   (B) Who is Charles Edward Stuart?
   (C) How many tartan patterns are there?
   (D) How many people wear tartans today?

10. What is the Black Watch?

   (A) a Highland Regiment
   (B) the tartan pattern of Charles Edward Stuart
   (C) a pattern of tartan
   (D) a group of pirates

ANSWERS AND EXPLANATIONS

1. B

This is a main idea question. The notes you made while reading this passage should help you hone in on the correct answer. Notice that the wrong answer choices are details from the passage. Whereas the passage does discuss the power of the Sun, uranium's favorable properties, and nuclear fission, these are not the main idea of the entire passage.

2. C

This is a detail question. Use your paragraph topics to locate information about nuclear reactions on the Sun. Then, do the same to locate information about reactions in power plants. In reactions on the Sun, the nuclei of atoms are joined together, whereas reactions in power plants use nuclear fission in which energy is released by the splitting of atomic nuclei. Notice how the wrong answer choices take details out of context from the passage. The passage mentions releasing energy, uranium, and high temperatures of the Sun, but this information does not serve as a comparison between the reactions on the Sun and those that occur in power plants.

3. C

This is an inference question. Use your knowledge of the main idea of the passage together with clues based on the style of the text. This is about nuclear energy; the information is presented in a factual way. Choice (A) is not information included in the passage, and choices (B) and (D) both would contain strong opinions not expressed in the passage.

4. B

This is an inference question. Although the author does not state his or her attitude about the Mongolian army directly, there are many clues in the passage that allow us to reach a logical conclusion. The first paragraph alone uses the adjectives *superior*, *well trained*, *disciplined*, and *prepared*. The author obviously respects the Mongolian army.

5. D

This is a detail question. You should not have memorized the definitions of each of these foreign words or spent too much time on them as you read. Instead, you should have circled or underlined them so that you could find them more easily. Remember to research detail questions by locating the information you need using your topic sentences, and then rereading them before you answer the question.

6. D

This is a main idea question. Choices (A), (B), and (C) take details from the passage (although victories in China are not discussed). Only choice (D) is the main idea of the entire passage.

7. C

This is a detail question. Use your topic sentences to help you locate the answer to this question in paragraph 3. The correct answer is a rephrasing of sentence 1 from paragraph 3, which states: *On the battlefield, each unit was expected to participate in a major coordinated effort and at the same time be able to act independently.* Notice that the wrong answer choices are either not mentioned at all in the passage (*farmers* or *mistrustful*), or are taken out of context (*well-dressed*). Only (C) works for this question.

8. C

This is a detail question. Locate the information in the passage. Sentence 1 of paragraph 1 states: *Although history has referred to Genghis Khan and the Mongolian army as Mongolian hordes, Mongolian superiority was most likely not a result of their overwhelming numbers.* If superiority is not a result of overwhelming numbers, a horde must be an overwhelming number or a mass. The wrong answer choices are taken out of context and are not directly supported by research within the passage.

9. A

This is a main idea question. Noting the main idea and the paragraph topics could help you answer this question quickly. The first paragraph of the passage explains why tartans are associated with membership in different clans. The passage does not explain who Charles Edward Stuart is. It also does not discuss how many tartan patterns there are today or how many people currently wear tartans.

10. C

This is a detail question. Remember to research the detail using your paragraph topics. Sentences 2 and 3 of paragraph 2 provide the information necessary to answer this question.

chapter seven

Language Arts

Language Arts includes spelling, punctuation, grammar, usage, and composition.

On the HSPT there are 60 Language Arts questions and on the TACHS approximately 50, all of which ask you to identify an error from among the answer choices. If all of the choices are correct, select (D).

    (A) Fridays and Saturdays we play field hockey.
    (B) Franklin Elementary School is located on birch street.
    (C) Miss Hampton discussed the situation with Peter's coach.
    (D) No mistake.

The composition questions require you to choose the answer choice that best expresses a particular idea.

    Choose the group of words that best completes the sentence.

    The children had been playing in the park; _____ .

    (A) they were covered in mud
    (B) and because of that they were covered in mud
    (C) covering them in mud
    (D) covered in mud

On the TACHS, these questions follow a short paragraph with numbered sentences that may be corrected or improved in the questions.

On the COOP, Language Arts questions follow reading passages. They test the same skills of punctuation, spelling, grammar, usage, and composition, but they tend to follow the theme of the passage rather than introduce new ideas.

For example, if the reading passage is about camels, you might see a question like this:

Read the paragraph below.

> There are two kinds of camels, the Arabian and the Bactrian camel.
> The Arabian camel has only one hump, whereas the Bactrian camel has
> two humps. The humps store fat, which the camel can absorb as nutrition
> when food becomes scarce.

Which of the answer choices would be the best introductory sentence to the paragraph?

(A) The camel is native to the desert regions of Asia and northern Africa.

(B) A camel can survive without water for several days.

(C) The Arabian camel usually stands taller than the Bactrian camel.

(D) Both types of camels have been domesticated for hundreds of years.

HOW TO APPROACH LANGUAGE ARTS ERROR QUESTIONS

On the HSPT and TACHS, this question type can be challenging because you are given three lines of answer choices and are required to decide whether there is an error in any. Because, by nature, we suspect that there *is* an error, many test takers spend too much time searching for an elusive error. How do you approach these questions without driving yourself crazy or wasting too much time? (Remember, there are 60 questions to get through.) Use Kaplan's 3-Step Method.

Kaplan's 3-Step Method for Language Arts Error Questions

Step 1. Read each sentence one time carefully, looking for identifiable mistakes. (We'll point out some common mistakes as we go through the punctuation, grammar, and usage review that follows.)

Step 2. Circle the mistake within the incorrect answer choice if there is one. If there is no error, circle choice (D). Blacken the appropriate box on your answer sheet and move on.

Step 3. If the question is really confusing you, put a check mark next to it and come back to it later, only if you have more time after finishing the entire section.

To do your best on Language Arts questions, you'll have to work at a good pace, zero in on the error, and have confidence in your chosen answer so you avoid wasting time rereading all the choices. You've got to have a firm grasp of correct punctuation, grammar, spelling, capitalization, and usage. You also need to be able to recognize common errors.

This chapter will give you the skill review you need to succeed in these areas. We'll review punctuation, grammar, and usage, and then discuss proper composition. Even if you think you've seen the material in English class, don't give in to the temptation to rush through it.

PUNCTUATION REVIEW

Commas

Use commas to separate the last two items in a long series.

If more than two items are listed in a series, they should be separated by commas. The final comma—the one that precedes the word *and*—may be omitted. An omitted final comma would not be considered an error on the COOP, TACHS, or HSPT.

> EXAMPLE: My recipe for cornbread includes cornmeal, butter, eggs, and milk.
> ALSO CORRECT: My recipe for cornbread includes cornmeal, butter, eggs and milk.

Look out for commas placed before the first element of a series, or after the last element.

> INCORRECT: Jason watches television, morning, noon, and night.
> INCORRECT: Action programs, cartoons, and soap operas, are his favorite shows.

Use commas to separate two or more adjectives before a noun, but not after the last adjective in a series.

> EXAMPLE: It was a long, dull novel.
> INCORRECT: The novel was a long, dull, travesty.

If a phrase or clause is not necessary to the main idea expressed by a sentence, it is parenthetical and should be separated by commas.

> EXAMPLE: Heather, who always attends practice, is the best athlete on the team.

The phrase *who always attends practice* is not necessary information. The main idea here is that Heather is the best player on the team. The clause in the middle merely serves to further describe her; it is therefore set off by commas.

Use commas after introductory phrases.

> EXAMPLE: Having driven 200 miles in one day, we were exhausted.

When combining independent clauses with *and, but, for, nor, or, so,* and *yet,* use a comma before the conjunction.

> EXAMPLE: Lena tried to make a pot roast, but she burned it.
> EXAMPLE: The question of who built the pyramids of Egypt has been an ongoing debate, yet one historian believes she has the answer.

Semicolons

Like commas, semicolons can separate independent clauses where no conjunction is used.

> EXAMPLE: The question of who built the pyramids of Egypt has been an ongoing debate; scholars and Egyptologists continue to argue about the number and identity of the workers.

Colons

In standard written English, the colon is used only as a means of signaling that what follows is a list, definition, explanation, or restatement of what has gone before. A word or phrase such as *like the following, as follows, namely,* or *this* is often used along with the colon to make it clear that a list, summary, or explanation is coming up.

 EXAMPLE: The rules are as follows: no running, horseplay, or splashing is permitted in the pool area.

The Apostrophe

The apostrophe has two distinct functions. It is informally used with contractions to indicate that one or more letters have been eliminated, e.g., *he's* (*he is*), *they're* (*they are*), *there's* (*there is*), *let's* (*let us*), etc.

EXAMPLE: The girl's a member of the varsity basketball team. (The girl is a member of the varsity basketball team.)

The apostrophe is also used to indicate the possessive form of a noun.

EXAMPLE: The boy's uniform was covered in mud.

With plural nouns that end in *s*, the apostrophe is placed on the end of the word to indicate possession.

EXAMPLE: The girls' team sang victory songs all the way home.

look out!!! **Careful:** *It's* is the contraction for *it is*. The possessive *its* does not have an apostrophe.

EXAMPLE: It's getting late. (It is getting late.)
EXAMPLE: The dog drank all the water in its bowl.

Punctuation with Quotation Marks

Direct quotes should be placed within quotation marks. If there is an introductory clause, a comma precedes the first quotation mark and the first word of the quotation is capitalized. The ending punctuation goes within the quotation mark. If the quotation is followed by a clause, end it with a comma.

 EXAMPLE: John asked, "How do you do?"
EXAMPLE: "I'm fine," Sue replied.
↑ doesn't have to be a comma, can be any punctuation

If the quotation is broken, punctuate as follows:

EXAMPLE: "How often," Carlos asked, "do you walk your dog?"

On the HSPT, grammar is tested along with punctuation and usage in the same question type. Of the statements given in a multiple-choice question, you might find that the punctuation in all statements is correct, but there could still be a mistake in grammar in one of the sentences.

GRAMMAR REVIEW

Subject-Verb Agreement

The form of a verb must agree with its subject in person and number.

Agreement of Person

When we talk about *person*, we're talking about whether the subject and verb of a sentence show that the author is making a statement about him or herself (first person), the person he or she is speaking to (second person), or some other person, place, or thing (third person).

The first person subjects are *I* and *we*.

> EXAMPLE: We are bicycling from New York to Vermont. I am training every other day.

The second person subject is *you*.

> EXAMPLE: Are you sure you wouldn't like to join us?

The third person subjects are *he, she, they, it,* and names of people, places, and things.

> EXAMPLE: The dog yaps day and night.

Agreement of Number

When we talk about *number*, we're talking about whether the subject and verb show that one thing (singular) or more than one thing (plural) is being discussed.

> INCORRECT: The children catches the bus to school every morning.
> CORRECT: The children catch the bus to school every morning.

Be especially careful when the subject and verb are separated by a long string of words.

> INCORRECT: Truth, the ultimate goal of all researchers, are elusive.
> CORRECT: Truth, the ultimate goal of all researchers, is elusive.

 KAPLAN TIP

Underline the subject and verb in each answer choice, and make sure they agree.

Pronouns

A pronoun is a word used in place of a noun. The antecedent of a pronoun is the word to which the pronoun refers. A pronoun must clearly refer to and agree with its antecedent.

> EXAMPLE: Research shows that green tea prevents cavities because it reduces bacteria.

Occasionally, the antecedent will appear in a sentence *after* the pronoun.

> EXAMPLE: Because it helps prevent cavities, tea is a healthy beverage.

KAPLAN TIP

Make sure you're clear on what antecedent a pronoun refers to. Ask yourself what is *it* or who is *she* or *he* or *they* referring to.

Number Agreement

	Singular	**Plural**
First Person Pronouns	I, me, my, mine	we, us, our, ours
Second Person Pronouns	you, your, yours	you, your, yours
Third Person Pronouns	he, him, she, her, it, one, his, her, hers, its, one's	their, theirs

Pronouns must agree in number with their antecedents. A singular pronoun should stand for a singular antecedent. A plural pronoun should stand for a plural antecedent. Here's a typical pronoun error.

> INCORRECT: The school refused to let Ann Marie attend the class field trip because their rules required her to have a permission letter.

What does the plural possessive *their* rules refer to? The singular noun *school*. The singular possessive *its* is what we need here.

Helpful Hints

Each, every, either, anybody, everybody, or *much* (or similar forms) requires a singular verb.

> EXAMPLE: **Everyone admires** her extensive vocabulary.

Both, few, several, many, or *others* require a plural verb.

> EXAMPLE: **Many comment** on her writing ability as well.

All, any, more, most, some, or *a part of* requires a singular or plural verb depending on the number being referenced.

> EXAMPLE: **All** of the guests **had** checked out of the hotel by noon. (singular verb)
> EXAMPLE: **Most** citizens **vote** on election day. (singular verb)
> EXAMPLE: When times are difficult, **most rise** to the challenge. (plural verb)

Person Agreement

A first-person pronoun should stand for a first-person antecedent, and so on.

> EXAMPLE: Caroline and Joe completed their laboratory report yesterday.

Relative Pronouns

Never use the relative pronoun *which* to refer to a person. Use *who, whom,* or *that.*

> INCORRECT: The woman which is waving is my sister.
> CORRECT: The woman who is waving is my sister.

Pronouns and Case

A more subtle pronoun error is that the pronoun is in the wrong case.

	Subjective Case	Objective Case
First-Person Pronouns	I, me, my, mine	me, us
Second-Person Pronouns	you	you
Third-Person Pronouns	he, she, it, they, one	him, her, it, them, one
Relative Pronouns	who, that, which	whom, that which

When to Use Subjective-Case Pronouns

As the name implies, use the subjective case for the **subject** of a sentence or clause.

> EXAMPLE: She is a daring mountain climber.
> INCORRECT: Danny, Cary, and me are going to the town fair.
> EXAMPLE: Sylvester, who is afraid of the dark, sleeps with a nightlight on.

KAPLAN TIP

Incorrect case is a typical error on the COOP, TACHS, and HSPT. Watch out for incorrect case pronouns when there is a long list of names. People often use incorrect case when they are *speaking*, so such errors might *sound* right to you; don't just trust your ear.

Use the subjective case after a linking verb, such as *to be.*

> EXAMPLE: It is I.

Use the subjective case when making comparisons to the subject of a verb that is not stated but understood.

> EXAMPLE: Wilson is faster than they (are).

When to Use Objective-Case Pronouns

Use the objective case when the pronoun is the **object** of a verb, of a preposition, or of an infinitive or gerund.

> EXAMPLE: I told him.
> EXAMPLE: I smiled at her.

EXAMPLE: I sat between Mark and her.

EXAMPLE: Sylvester, whom I gave a nightlight, thanked me.

EXAMPLE: To give him a nice gift, we all contributed five dollars.

EXAMPLE: Writing her was a good idea.

Myself/Me and Yourself/You

Use the reflexive pronoun if the subject is acting on *his/her/itself* or the action was performed *by oneself* (alone).

INCORRECT: He met with Barbara and myself. (Should be *Barbara and me*.)

CORRECT: I discovered the answer myself.

Sentence Structure

A **sentence** is a group of words that expresses a complete thought. To express a complete thought, a sentence must contain a subject and a verb.

EXAMPLE: Lions roar.

EXAMPLE: Searching through the cupboards, John found an old can of soup.

Every sentence contains at least one **clause**—a group of words that contains a subject and verb. *Lions roar*, and *John found* are both clauses.

A **phrase** is a group of words that does not have both a subject and a verb. *Searching through the cupboards* is a phrase.

Sentence Fragments

On the COOP, TACHS, or HSPT, some of those innocent-looking groups of words beginning with capital letters and ending with periods are only masquerading as sentences. In reality, they are sentence fragments: *grammatically incomplete* because they lack a subject or verb or are not complete thoughts.

INCORRECT: Arches and vaulted ceilings typical of Romanesque architecture.

This is not a complete sentence because there is no verb.

INCORRECT: Because we arrived late.

Even though this fragment contains a subject (*we*) and a verb (*arrived*), it's not a complete sentence because it doesn't express a complete thought. We don't know what happened *because we arrived late*.

Careful: Don't let strings of long, difficult words distract you. Read carefully to be sure whether or not a sentence contains a verb.

Run-On Sentences

A run-on sentence is actually two (or more) complete sentences stuck together with just a comma or with no punctuation at all.

INCORRECT: The team practiced diligently, it received a gold ribbon.
INCORRECT: The team practiced diligently it received a gold ribbon.

There are a number of ways to fix this kind of problem.

Join the clauses with a semicolon.
CORRECT: The team practiced diligently; it received a gold ribbon.

Join the clauses with a coordinating conjunction (*and, but, for, nor, or, so,* or *yet*) and a comma.
CORRECT: The team practiced diligently, and it received a gold ribbon.

Join the clauses with a subordinating conjunction (*after, although, if, since,* or *while*).
CORRECT: Since the team practiced diligently, it received a gold ribbon.

Finally, the two halves of a run-on sentence can be written as two separate complete sentences.
CORRECT: The team practiced diligently. It received a gold ribbon.

Verbs

On the COOP, TACHS, and HSPT, you'll find items that are wrong because a verb is in the wrong tense. To spot this kind of error, you need to be familiar with the way each tense is used. English has six basic tenses, and each of these has a simple form and a progressive form.

	Simple Form	Progressive Form
Present	I walk	I am walking
Past	I walked	I was walking
Future	I will walk	I will be walking
Present Perfect	I have walked	I have been walking
Past Perfect	I had walked	I had been walking
Future Perfect	I will have walked	I will have been walking

Using the Present Tense

Use the present tense to describe a state or action occurring in the present time.

EXAMPLE: I am happy.
EXAMPLE: They are studying the Holy Roman Empire.

Using the Past Tense

Use the simple past tense to describe an event or state that took place at a specific time in the past and is now finished.

> EXAMPLE: The class dissected a frog in biology class yesterday.

Using the Future Tense

Use the future tense to describe actions expected to take place in the future.

> EXAMPLE: It will rain tomorrow.
> EXAMPLE: I will call you tonight.

Future actions may also be expressed this way:

> EXAMPLE: I am going to call you tonight.

Using the Present Perfect Tense

Use the present perfect tense for actions and states of being that start in the past and continue into the present time.

> EXAMPLE: I have been attending Jefferson Junior High for the last two years.

Use the present perfect for actions and states of being that happened a number of times in the past and may happen again in the future.

> EXAMPLE: We have visited the planetarium several times.

Use the present perfect to describe an event that happened at an unspecified time in the past.

> EXAMPLE: Anna has given me her opinion already.

Using the Past Perfect Tense

The past perfect tense is used for past actions or states that were completed before other past actions or states.

> EXAMPLE: When the alarm clock rang this morning, I noticed that I had set it for eight o'clock.

Using the Future Perfect Tense

Use the future perfect tense for a future state or event that will take place before another future time or event.

> EXAMPLE: By Saturday, I will have finished the entire novel.

Using the Proper Past Participle Form

Perfect tenses use a participle form of a base verb.

> EXAMPLE: I have planted tomatoes in the garden.

The past participle is formed by adding -ed to the base form, unless it is an irregular verb. Irregular verbs have two different forms for simple past and past participle tenses. If you use the present, past, or future perfect tense, make sure that you use the past participle and not the simple past tense.

INCORRECT: I have swam in that lake before.

CORRECT: I have swum in that lake before.

The following are some of the most common irregular verbs.

IRREGULAR VERBS

Infinitive	Simple Past	Past Participle	Infinitive	Simple Past	Past Participle
arise	arose	arisen	give	gave	given
become	became	become	grow	grew	grown
begin	began	begun	hang	hung	hung
blow	blew	blown	know	knew	known
break	broke	broken	ride	rode	ridden
come	came	come	rise	rose	rise
do	did	done	run	ran	run
draw	drew	drawn	see	saw	seen
drink	drank	drunk	shake	shook	shaken
drive	drove	driven	shrink	shrank	shrunk
eat	ate	eaten	sing	sang	sung
fall	fell	fallen	speak	spoke	spoken
fly	flew	flown	take	took	taken
freeze	froze	frozen	throw	threw	thrown

Could Have, Should Have, Would Have, Might Have

The words could, should, would, and might which express possibility, impossibility, or necessity must be followed by have.

Careful: People often incorrectly say could of. This is incorrect.

INCORRECT: I could of gone if I had enough money.

CORRECT: I could have gone if I had enough money.

Adjectives and Adverbs

On the COOP, TACHS, and HSPT, you may find an occasional item that's wrong because it uses an adjective where an adverb is called for, or vice versa.

An **adjective** modifies or describes a noun or pronoun.

EXAMPLE: A man with a gray beard sat on an old tree stump.

An **adverb** modifies a verb, an adjective, or another adverb. Most, but not all, adverbs end in *-ly*. (Don't forget that some adjectives—*friendly, lovely*—also end in *ly*.)

>   EXAMPLE: The builders finished surprisingly quickly. (*Surprisingly* describes the adverb *quickly*.)

Adverbs such as *almost, nearly, hardly,* and *about* may also modify determiners, numerals, and pronouns.

>   EXAMPLE: Hardly anyone has purchased a ticket yet.

Careful: The word *hardly* means *barely*. The adverbial form of the adjective *hard* is *hard*.

>   EXAMPLE: We worked hard planting the hedges.

Parallel Structure

Make sure that when a sentence contains a list or makes a comparison, the items being listed or compared exhibit parallel structure.

Items in a List

>   INCORRECT: I love skipping, jumping, and to play tiddlywinks.
>   CORRECT: I love to skip, jump, and play tiddlywinks
>   ALSO CORRECT: I love to skip, to jump, and to play tiddlywinks.
>   ALSO CORRECT: I love skipping, jumping, and playing tiddlywinks.

Logical Comparison

Comparisons must do more than just exhibit parallel structure; they must make sense. You can't compare apples and oranges.

>   INCORRECT: The rules of chess are more complex than checkers.
>   CORRECT: The rules of chess are more complex than those of checkers.
>   ALSO CORRECT: Chess is more complex than checkers.

Comparatives and Superlatives

Use the **comparative form** when comparing two items.

>   EXAMPLE: They finished more quickly than we. (*Than we did* is understood.)

Careful: Remember to use the correct form of the pronoun.

Careful: Avoid repetitiveness in comparisons.

>   INCORRECT: The oil painting is more prettier than the watercolor is.
>   CORRECT: The oil painting is prettier than the watercolor is.

The **superlative** form of the adjective is used comparing more than two items.

> EXAMPLE: August is the hottest month.

Careful: *Good, better, best* is the correct progression of this adjective. *Bad, worse, worst* is the correct progression of this adjective.

STYLE REVIEW

Good writing is not only grammatically correct, but also stylistically clear. We'll review some problems with style in the following pages and show you how to correct them.

Pronoun Ambiguity

A problem exists when a pronoun doesn't refer to any antecedent at all or doesn't refer clearly to one, and only one, antecedent.

> UNCLEAR: Francesco likes the music they play on this radio station.

Who are *they*? We can't tell because the pronoun has no antecedent.

> CORRECT: Francesco likes the music played on this radio station.

Careful: Sometimes a pronoun seems to have an antecedent until you read more closely and realize that the word it seems to refer to is not a noun, but an adjective, a possessive form, or a verb. Remember, the antecedent of a pronoun should be a noun.

> INCORRECT: When you are cooking, be careful to watch it.
> CORRECT: When you are cooking dinner, be careful to watch it.
> INCORRECT: Veronica has always been interested in medicine and has decided to become one.
> CORRECT: Veronica has always been interested in medicine and has decided to become a doctor.
> INCORRECT: Joe started jogging, and as a result lost a lot of weight. It was very good for his heart. (What does the pronoun *it* refer to? Losing weight or jogging?)
> CORRECT: Joe started jogging because it was very good for his heart, and as a result he lost a lot of weight. (The antecedent of *it* is clearly *jogging*.)

Misreference

Remote antecedents can also cause confusion in the following way:

> POOR: The president sent a memo to Charlie, and he will address the problem right away.
> (In this sentence it is unclear what *he* refers to, Charlie or the president.)
> BETTER: The president sent a memo to Charlie, who will address the problem right away.

Dangling Modifiers

In order to avoid confusion, clauses and phrases should be close to the elements they modify.

INCORRECT: To write a clear sentence, subject and verb should agree.
                    phrase   clause

Who is writing the sentence? Certainly not the subject and verb; they can't write.

CORRECT: To write a clear sentence, you should make sure the subject and verb agree.

Here's another example:

INCORRECT: When driving across the bridge, the sun blinded him.
CORRECT: When driving across the bridge, he was blinded by the sun.

Redundancy

Redundancy means repetitiveness. Words or phrases are redundant when they have basically the same meaning as something already stated. Don't use two words or phrases when one is sufficient.

INCORRECT: Blackmore University was established and founded in 1906.
CORRECT: Blackmore University was established in 1906.

Double Negatives

In standard written English, double negatives are redundant and wrong.

INCORRECT: "I didn't say nothing!" he protested.
CORRECT: "I didn't say anything!" he protested.

Relevance

A good sentence contains only related or relevant ideas. Unrelated information, even when set off in parentheses, should be avoided. If an idea is unrelated to the main point of the sentence, it should be cut.

IRRELEVANT: Constructing the new baseball field will cost the community over 40 thousand dollars (though the entire town loves to watch the Tigers play).
RELEVANT: Constructing the new baseball field will cost the community over 40 thousand dollars. Decision makers feel this investment is worthwhile, however, since the entire town loves to watch the Tigers play.

Wordiness

Wordiness also creates a style and clarity problem.

WORDY: We were in agreement with each other that Max was charitable to a fault.
CONCISE: We agreed that Max was charitable to a fault.

Commonly Misused Words

Accept/Except

To *accept* means to receive or agree to something, whereas *except* is usually a preposition meaning excluding, although it can also mean to leave out.

> INCORRECT: Can you except my apology? (Should be *accept*.)
> CORRECT: Everyone except Sam will attend the meeting.

Affect/Effect

These are easy to confuse. To *affect* means to have an *effect* on something. When the word is being used as a verb, the proper word to use is almost always *affect;* when it's being used as a noun, the proper word to use is almost always *effect*.

> INCORRECT: The news effected me deeply. (Should be *affected me.*)
> CORRECT: What are the effects of the new medicine on rats?

Already/All Ready

Already means earlier or previously. *All ready* means all of us are ready.

> INCORRECT: Are you ready all ready?
> CORRECT: I've already finished the assignment.

Altogether/All Together

Altogether means completely. *All together* means as one group.

> CORRECT: Carlene was altogether happy with the experiment's results.
> CORRECT: Let's go all together.

Among/Between

In most cases, use *between* for two items and *among* for more than two.

> EXAMPLE: The rivalry between the Tigers and the Bears has gone on for years.
> EXAMPLE: Among the various choices, I prefer the first.

Amount/Number

Amount is used to refer to an uncountable quantity, *number* to refer to a countable quantity.

> EXAMPLE: The amount of food he threw away would feed a substantial number of people.

Anyway

Anyway means in any way possible, or regardless. *Anyways* is incorrect. Don't use it.

> INCORRECT: Anyways, I hope we can still go.
> CORRECT: Anyway, I hope we can still go.

As/Like

Like is a preposition; it takes a noun object. *As*, when functioning as a conjunction, introduces a subordinate clause. Remember, a clause is part of a sentence containing a subject and a verb.

> EXAMPLE: He sings like an angel.
> EXAMPLE: He sings as an angel sings.

As...as...

The idiom is *as...as....*

> INCORRECT: That dress is as nice than this one.
> CORRECT: That dress is as expensive as this one.

Beside/Besides

Beside means by the side of or next to. *Besides* means moreover.

> INCORRECT: Set the book besides the photo album.
> CORRECT: Set the book beside the photo album.
> CORRECT: Besides being an excellent athlete, I am also a brilliant mathematician.

Fewer/Less

Use *fewer* before a plural noun; use *less* before a singular one.

> EXAMPLE: There are fewer people in the audience tonight than there were last night.
> EXAMPLE: We paid less money for our ticket than you did.

Neither...nor...

The correlative conjunction is *neither...nor...*

> EXAMPLE: We are neither tired nor hungry.

Avoid the redundancy caused by using *nor* after a negative.

> INCORRECT: Alice's departure was not noticed by Sue nor Debby.
> CORRECT: Alice's departure was not noticed by Sue or Debby.

Its/It's

Many people confuse *its* and *it's*. *Its* is possessive; *it's* is a contraction of *it is*.

> EXAMPLE: The cat licked its paws.
> EXAMPLE: It's raining cats and dogs.

Lay/Lie/Laid

Lay means to put or to place. The past tense of *lay* is *laid*, the past participle *has laid*, and the continuous form *is/was laying*. *Lie* means to recline, to stay, or to rest. The past is *lay*, the past participle *has lain*, the continuous form, *is/was lying*.

Careful: *Lay* is both the present tense of *lay* (as in *put* or *place*) and the past tense of *lie* (as in *lie down*).

EXAMPLE: Please lay the tablecloth over the picnic table.

EXAMPLE: We laid the tarp over the sofa so it wouldn't get dirty when we painted the room.

EXAMPLE: The cat is lying on the table, and he doesn't want to be bothered.

EXAMPLE: Duncan lay down because he was feeling tired.

Than/Then

Use *than* in making comparisons. Use *then* for time.

INCORRECT: Dolores is more graceful then I. (Should be *than*.)

CORRECT: First wash the one, then the other.

Their/They're/There

Many people confuse *their, there,* and *they're*. *Their* is possessive; *they're* is a contraction of *they are*.

EXAMPLE: The girls rode their bikes home.

EXAMPLE: They're training for the marathon.

There has two uses: it can indicate place, and it can be used as an expletive—a word that doesn't do anything in a sentence except delay the subject.

EXAMPLE: Put the book over there.

EXAMPLE: There will be 15 runners competing for the prize.

Passive Voice

The passive voice uses the verb *to be* with a past participle. The subject is affected rather than acting. Although passive voice is grammatically correct, excessive or unfounded use of the passive voice is considered poor style. It is often clearer to state the information with an active subject and verb.

PASSIVE: My finger was bitten by the gerbil.

ACTIVE: The gerbil bit my finger.

SPELLING

Approximately ten questions on the Language Arts section of the TACHS and HSPT will ask you to identify mistakes in spelling. Unfortunately, it is impossible to predict which of the thousands of words in the English dictionary will appear on these questions.

Spend some time studying lists of commonly misspelled words. Ask your English teacher or local librarian to help you find these lists. The words on them are the ones you're most likely to see on the HSPT or TACHS.

Improving your spelling requires a time commitment, and there are few spelling rules in English. Sounding things out may help. However, remember:

i before *e*, **except after** *c*, **except when it sounds like** *a* **as in** *neighbor* **and** *weigh.*

> EXAMPLE: society, transient, receive, beige

A word that ends in a single vowel and a single consonant, and that has the accent on the final syllable, doubles that consonant before a suffix beginning with a vowel. If the final syllable has no accent, do not double the consonant.

> EXAMPLE: occur—occurring
> EXAMPLE: prefer—preferred
> EXAMPLE: benefit + *ing* = benefiting

If a word ends with a silent *e*, **drop the** *e* **before adding a suffix that begins with a vowel.**

> EXAMPLE: hope—hoping, like—liking

If a word ends in *e*, **drop the final** *e* **before a suffix beginning with a vowel.**

> EXAMPLE: small + *er* = smaller
> EXAMPLE: move + *able* = movable

Do not drop the *e* **when the suffix begins with a consonant.**

> EXAMPLE: manage—management, like—likeness, use—useless

When *y* **is the last letter in a word and the** *y* **is preceded by a consonant, change the** *y* **to** *i* **before adding any suffix except those beginning with** *i.*

> EXAMPLE: pretty—prettier, hurry—hurried, deny—denied

Knowing your own strengths and weaknesses is important. If you tend to have trouble spelling, you may decide to go against your instinct when selecting an answer choice. In other words, if a word looks right to you, but you know you are a terrible speller, you may guess that the word is actually spelled incorrectly.

Finally, if you are not certain whether or not a word is spelled correctly, take your best guess and move on. Remember, you have a one-in-four chance of picking the correct answer choice.

Capitalization

Capitalize proper names.

> George lives on Front Street. ("Street" is capitalized because it is part of the proper name.)
> The Tigers won five of their last 10 games.

Capitalize holidays.

> Independence Day is July 4th.
> Vincent cooked an enormous turkey for Thanksgiving.

Capitalize the first letter of a person's title when it precedes their proper name.

> Principal Young
> Dr. McCullough
> Aunt Rose

However, when the title is used without the proper name, it remains lowercase. See the following example:

> Tim's aunt is the coach of the baseball team.

Because the coach is not mentioned by name, *coach* is not capitalized.

Capitalize days of the week and months of the year.

> We walk to school Mondays, Tuesdays, and Wednesdays. In July, we often go to the shore.

Capitalize the first word of a direct quotation.

> Henry told us, "Sit on the bench outside the office."
> "Sit on the bench," Henry told us, "outside the office."

COMPOSITION

Some questions on the COOP, TACHS, or HSPT will ask you how to best organize a paragraph, sentence, or theme. Keep these four principles in mind.

Four Tests of Clear Composition

1. Each paragraph should be limited to a single topic or major idea.
2. The topic sentence should reflect the content.
3. The writing should be concise.
4. Transitions should be used when shifting ideas.

Each Paragraph Should Be Limited to a Single Topic or Main Idea

It is preferable that each paragraph address one major idea rather than jump around among various thoughts or points. Extraneous ideas should be removed.

POOR: The Browns are looking forward to their holiday in Australia next week. Mrs. Brown is excited about snorkeling in the coral reefs, and Mr. Brown is happy to have a week away from work to relax. **Mr. Brown used to sing opera when he was younger.** They hope to visit the opera house in Sydney. (Notice how the third sentence is unrelated to the theme of the Brown's holiday in Australia.)

BETTER: The Browns are looking forward to their holiday in Australia next week. Mrs. Brown is excited about snorkeling in the coral reefs, and Mr. Brown is happy to have a week away from work to relax. **They'd also like to see that famous Australian animal, the kangaroo.** They also hope to visit the opera house in Sydney. (This sentence better fits the general theme of the paragraph.)

A Topic Sentence Should Reflect the Content

A topic sentence should appropriately reflect the content of the paragraph.

EXAMPLE: **Many Americans know about the pyramids of Egypt, although they may not realize that there are pyramids much closer to home in Central America.** Deep within the jungles of Mexico and Guatemala lie the mysterious pyramids of the Maya. The Mayan were noted for their skill with astronomy and farming, as well for their elaborate and highly decorated ceremonial architecture. The Maya built temple-pyramids, palaces, and observatories all without metal tools. (This paragraph is organized well: all sentences relate to the topic sentence, which introduces the idea of pyramids in Central America.)

Writing Should Be Concise

Most sentences should be no more than two lines in length. A paragraph should be between three to five sentences long.

EXAMPLE: Senator Robbins is running for re-election on a platform of economic reform. She intends to reduce city spending and increase taxes so that more citizens can benefit from additional services. She plans to improve transportation, street cleaning, and safety. (Notice how the last sentence keeps parallel construction. All the items in the list are nouns.)

Transitions Should Be Used

Transitional words and phrases show how sentences or paragraphs are logically linked. A poorly chosen or incorrect transitional word can completely alter the meaning of a sentence or paragraph.

POOR: John is tired, so he will not rest until he finishes the job at hand. (This is not a logical transition.)
BETTER: Although John is tired, he will not rest until he finishes the job at hand. (The transitional word *although* makes the idea clear.)

Transitional Words

Words that show an idea is moving in the **same direction**: *and, also, besides, moreover, in addition*

Words that show **contrast**: *but, meanwhile, on the other hand, yet, however, on the contrary*

Words that show **emphasis**: *in fact, most of all, in any, even*

Words that **illustrate** a point: *for example, for instance*

Words of **conclusion**: *accordingly, so, therefore, consequently*

Words of **concession**: *of course, naturally, in fact*

Words of **time**: *formerly, meanwhile, after, later, at the same time, in the first place, first, second, finally*

Words that express a **condition**: *nevertheless, even though, although*

Words to point out **cause/effect**: *it follows that, accordingly, for this reason*

Words of **comparison**: *similarly, in comparison, still*

On the COOP, TACHS, or HSPT, some questions will ask you to find a logical transitional word to complete an idea or sentence. Look for clues within a sentence or paragraph that tell you how the first clause or phrase of a sentence is related to the second.

EXAMPLE: It is raining, _____ we will still go to the beach.

A word of contrast is required here. Look for an answer choice that contains a word of contrast such as *but, however,* or *yet.*

Practice, Practice, Practice

Way to go! You've worked through the basic rules. The more you practice, the more these principles will become second nature to you. Be sure to complete the practice set. Try to work at a good pace, spending no more than a minute on each question. Read each sentence carefully, circling mistakes as you spot them. Put a check mark next to the questions that cause you difficulty, but don't leave any question unanswered. Finally, check your answers, read the answer explanations, and see whether your instincts were correct on the questions that caused you difficulty.

[Shortest + expressed most clearly]

LANGUAGE ARTS PRACTICE SET

Directions: In questions 1–3, look for errors in punctuation, capitalization, or usage. If there is no error, select choice D.

1. (A) "Is there room for me in the car?" Janet asked.
    (B) The shore is three miles from the center of town.
    (C) The Hawks beat the bluejays two to one.
    (D) No mistake.

2. (A) There's no business like show business.
    (B) Sue's mother warned her to be careful.
    (C) What are the chances of winning?
    (D) No mistake.

3. (A) Who has my briefcase?
    (B) If there ready, let's go.
    (C) Uncle Tito plays the bongo drums.
    (D) No mistake.

Directions: For questions 4–6, look for mistakes in spelling only.

4. (A) I'd like to address your concerns immediately.
    (B) Please register your complaint with customer service.
    (C) Ocassionaly, we update our records.
    (D) No mistake.

5. (A) We separated the blue papers from the red ones.
    (B) Heather communicated the message to Dawn.
    (C) Knowledge is the key to power.
    (D) No mistake.

6. (A) I am including a photo of our trip.
    (B) The coach encouraged us to do our best.
    (C) It is unecessary to call before you come.
    (D) No mistake.

Directions: For questions 7–10, follow the directions for each question.

7. Choose the words that best complete the following sentence.

    The school's tennis team is _____

    (A) known for its competitive players.
    (B) known for the competitiveness of its players when they compete.
    (C) known because its players are said to be competitive.
    (D) known to be competitive and have competitive players.

8. Choose the best word to complete the sentence.

    We left our house on time, _____ we still arrived late.

    (A) consequently
    (B) therefore
    (C) so
    (D) none of these

9. Choose the sentence that is correctly written.

    (A) The pizza, as we know it, was developed in the late 18th century.
    (B) Pizza as we know it now, was developed before in the late 18th century.
    (C) Pizza, as we now know it, was developed by its developers in the late 18th century.
    (D) As we know it, the current pizza, was developed in the late 18th century.

10. Read the two sentences.

    In about 1889, Queen Margherita toured her kingdom and saw many people eating this large, flat bread.

    The people were mostly peasants.

    Which of the following sentences best combines the two sentences above?

    (A) In about 1889, Queen Margherita toured her kingdom and saw many people eating this large, flat bread; the people were mostly peasants.

    (B) In about 1889, Queen Margherita toured her kingdom and saw many people, the people were mostly peasants, eating this large, flat bread.

    (C) In about 1889, Queen Margherita toured her kingdom and saw many peasants eating this large, flat bread.

    (D) In about 1889, Queen Margherita toured her kingdom and saw many people eating this large, flat bread and the people were mostly peasants.

ANSWERS AND EXPLANATIONS

1. C
The word *Bluejays* should be capitalized since it is the name of a team.

2. D
There are no mistakes.

3. B
Look at the use of *there* in choice (B). It should be *they are,* or *they're.* Although you've spotted the error, read the final answer choice just to be sure.

4. C
The correct spelling is *occasionally.*

5. D
There are no mistakes.

6. C
The correct spelling is *unnecessary.*

7. A
The most concise and clearest answer choice is (A). Choices (B), (C), and (D) are unnecessarily wordy.

8. D
The first clause states that *we left on time,* the second clause contradicts this since *we arrived late.* The linking word must show a contrast. There are no contrasting transition words, so (D) is the best answer.

9. A
Good writing must be grammatically correct and clear and to the point. Choice (B) is redundant. Choice (C) is also redundant. Choice (D) implies that we already know pizza was developed in the late 18th century.

10. C
When combining these sentences, avoid creating a run-on sentence. Choice (C) best combines the two ideas by making the direct object *peasants.* Choice (A) is a run-on sentence. It is better to keep these two sentences separate than combine them with a semicolon. Choice (B) is too wordy. Choice (D) is a run-on sentence.

spelling+vocab

chapter eight

Math Skills

Math counts for a large portion of your score on the test. On the HSPT there are approximately 110 mathematics questions, which is about $\frac{1}{3}$ of the test. On the TACHS, Math questions will make up about $\frac{1}{4}$ of the test, or about 50 questions. On the COOP, there are approximately 40 Mathematics questions, which is about $\frac{1}{4}$ of the test.

The good news is:

- A limited amount of concepts are tested.
- This is most likely math you've already been exposed to in school.

HOW TO APPROACH MATH QUESTIONS

Before we dive in to the actual math, let's take a step back and build some strategies for how to approach math problems in general. You've most likely seen most of the math concepts you'll encounter on the COOP, TACHS, or HSPT. However, you need to approach math a little differently on the test than you would in another situation.

Remember, you'll have a limited amount of time, so use it wisely. Also, remember that each question is worth the same amount of points. You need to decide whether spending more than 30 seconds on any one question is the best use of your time. Since there is no penalty for guessing, you should answer all the questions; however, you may choose to set a problem aside and come back to it later.

Read Through the Question and Make Your Decision

You need to read the question carefully and deliberately before you start solving the problem. If you don't, it's easy to make careless mistakes.

Consider the following problem:

Jane is a salesperson for PDQ Carpet Company. In the last three years she earned $36,000, $38,000, and $40,000 dollars annually. What is her approximate average monthly income?

(A) 36,000

(B) 3,000

(C) 30,000

(D) 12,000

It's crucial that you pay close attention to precisely what the question asks. This question contains a classic trap that's very easy to fall into if you don't read carefully. You are asked to solve for Jane's *monthly* income, rather than her yearly income. Solving for her yearly income would be careless.

A second reason to read the entire question carefully before you start solving is that you may save yourself some work. If you start answering too quickly, you may assume a problem is more or less difficult than it actually is.

Decide Whether to Do the Problem or Skip It for Now

Another reason to read carefully before answering is that you probably shouldn't solve every problem on your first pass. Each time you approach a new math problem you have the option of doing it or putting it aside.

1. If you can solve the problem quickly and efficiently, do it! This is the best option.
2. If you think you can solve it, but it will take you a long time, circle the number in your test booklet and go back to it later. When you go back to problems you have skipped, fill in an answer, even if it's a random guess. Don't underestimate your ability to eliminate wrong answer choices even when you don't know how to solve a problem.
3. If you have no idea what to do, circle the problem and move on. Save your time for the problems you can solve.

Here's an example:

Which value of x would make the following equation true?

$$\frac{1}{2} = \frac{x^3}{12}$$

(A) $\sqrt[3]{6}$

(B) $\sqrt{2}$

(C) 9

(D) 28

Some students may quickly see the process they need to use in order to solve this. Others may see the exponent (the little 3 above the x) and run screaming from the room. We don't recommend this approach. However, if you know that you habitually have difficulty with exponents, save this problem for later.

Here's the solution to the question. Don't worry if any of this is unfamiliar to you, we'll review working with fractions and other math concepts later in this chapter.

First, multiply each numerator by the denominator on the other side of the equation.

$$12 = 2x^3$$

Next, isolate the unknown x by dividing each side of the equation by 2.

$$\frac{12}{2} = \frac{2x^3}{2}$$

This leaves you with $6 = x^3$. To find the value of x divide each side by its cube root.

$$x = \sqrt[3]{6}$$

If you choose to tackle any given problem, look for the method that is fastest for you.

> Patricia is a years old and her brother Mark is 5 years older than she. In terms of a, how old will Mark be in 3 years?
>
> (A) $3(a + 5)$
> (B) $a + 5 - 3$
> (C) $a + 3$
> (D) $a + 5 + 3$

You could solve the problem using algebra. If Patricia is a years old, then Mark is $a + 5$ years old. In three years, he will be $a + 5 + 3$ years old. Thus, (D) is the correct choice.

You could also solve the problem by picking numbers. Let's say Patricia is 12 years old, that makes Mark, who is 5 years older, 17. In 3 years, he'll be 20. Now, substitute Patricia's age, 12, for the unknown a in all the answer choices and see which equation gives us the result we're looking for—20. Once you try all the answer choices, only (D) works.

As you see, there is often more than one way to do a particular problem. The best method is the one that will help you arrive at the correct answer accurately and quickly.

Some people *get* algebra. Others have a harder time with it. The same is true for geometry, word problems, ratios, etc. Know your strengths and make decisions about how to approach math problems accordingly.

Make an Educated Guess

Don't leave any answers blank on the COOP, TACHS, or HSPT. Since there's no penalty for wrong answers, there is no harm in guessing when you don't know the answer.

Random guessing doesn't hurt, but you should guess strategically whenever possible. Remember, each answer choice you eliminate increases your odds of choosing the correct answer.

What is the greatest prime factor of 26 and 273?

(A) 13
(B) 4
(C) 2
(D) 5

If you read this problem and either could not remember how to find a factor, let alone a prime factor, or if you were running out of time and wanted to save your time for other questions, you should be able to eliminate at least one answer choice pretty easily. Do you see which one?

Since all multiples of 5 end in either 5 or 0, the number 5 cannot be a factor of 26. So, choice (D) must be wrong. You could also easily eliminate choices (B) and (C) since multiples of 4 and 2 must be even numbers.

ARITHMETIC REVIEW

On the COOP, TACHS, or HSPT, math skills include basic computation, using whole numbers, fractions, decimals, and percentages. You need to have a firm grasp of arithmetic concepts such as number properties, factors, divisibility, units of measure, ratio and proportion, percentages, and averages. These skills may be tested in basic operations or in word problems. Even if you feel that you know them, spend time on this section. The more you practice, the more comfortable you will feel working with numbers on these tests.

First, take a look at a few definitions.

Number Type:	Definition:	Examples:
Integers	*Whole numbers, including zero and negative whole numbers.*	$-500, -2, 0, 1, 53$
Fractions	*A **fraction** is a number that is written in the form $\frac{A}{B}$ where A is the numerator and B is the denominator. An **improper fraction** is a number that is greater than 1 (or less than –1) that is written in the form of a fraction. Improper fractions can be converted to a **mixed number** (a whole number and a fraction).*	$\dfrac{-5}{6}, \dfrac{3}{17}, \dfrac{1}{2}, \dfrac{899}{901}$ $\dfrac{-65}{64}, \dfrac{9}{8}, \dfrac{57}{10}$ $-1\dfrac{1}{64}, 1\dfrac{1}{8}, 5\dfrac{7}{10}$
Positive/ Negative	*Numbers greater than zero are positive numbers; numbers less than zero are negative; zero is neither positive nor negative.*	Positive: $1, 5, 900$ Negative: $-64, -40, -11, \dfrac{-6}{13}$
Even/Odd	*An even number is an integer that is a multiple of 2. NOTE: Zero is an even number. An odd number is an integer that is not a multiple of 2.*	Even numbers: $-6, -2, 0, 4, 12, 190$ Odd numbers: $-15, -1, 3, 9, 453$
Prime Numbers	*An integer greater than 1 that has no factors other than 1 and itself; 2 is the only even prime number.*	$2, 3, 5, 7, 11, 13, 59, 83$
Factors	*A positive integer that divides evenly into a given number with no remainder.*	The complete list of factors of 12: $1, 2, 3, 4, 6, 12$
Multiples	*A number that a given number will divide into with no remainder.*	Some multiples of 12: $0, 12, 24, 60$

Odds and Evens

Even ± Even = Even $2 + 2 = 4$ Even × Even = Even $2 \times 2 = 4$

Even ± Odd = Odd $2 + 3 = 5$ Even × Odd = Even $2 \times 3 = 6$

Odd ± Odd = Even $3 + 3 = 6$ Odd × Odd = Odd $3 \times 3 = 9$

Positives and Negatives

There are a few things to remember about positives and negatives.

Adding a negative number is basically subtraction.

$\qquad$ $6 + (-4)$ is really $6 - 4$ or 2. $\qquad\qquad$ $4 + (-6)$ is really $4 - 6$ or -2.

Subtracting a negative number is basically addition.

$\qquad$ $6 - (-4)$ is really $6 + 4$ or 10. $\qquad\qquad$ $-6 - (-4)$ is really $-6 + 4$ or -2.

Multiplying and dividing positives and negatives is like all other multiplication and division, with one catch. To figure out whether your product is positive or negative, simply count the number of negatives you had to start. If you had an odd number of negatives, the product is negative. If you had an even number of negatives, the product is positive.

$$6 \times (-4) = -24 \ (1 \text{ negative} \rightarrow \text{negative product})$$

$$(-6) \times (-4) = 24 \ (2 \text{ negatives} \rightarrow \text{positive product})$$

$$(-1) \times (-6) \times (-4) = -24 \ (3 \text{ negatives} \rightarrow \text{negative product})$$

Similarly:

$$-24 \div 3 = -8 \ (1 \text{ negative} \rightarrow \text{negative quotient})$$

$$-24 \div (-3) = 8 \ (2 \text{ negatives} \rightarrow \text{positive quotient})$$

Absolute Value

Absolute value describes how far a number on the number line is from zero. It doesn't matter in which direction the number lies—to the right on the positive side or to the left on the negative side.

For example, the absolute value of both 3 and –3 is 3.

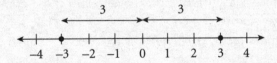

To find the absolute value of a number, simply strip the number within the vertical lines of its sign.

$$|4| = 4 \qquad\qquad |-4| = 4$$

When absolute value expressions contain different arithmetic operations, perform the operation first, and then strip the sign from the result.

$$|-6 + 4| = |-2| = 2 \qquad |(-6) \times 4| = |-24| = 24$$

Factors and Multiples

To find the prime factorization of a number, keep breaking it down until you are left with only prime numbers.

To find the prime factorization of 168:

$$168 = 4 \times 42 = 4 \times 6 \times 7 = 2 \times 2 \times 2 \times 3 \times 7$$

To find the greatest common factor (GCF) of two integers, break down both integers into their prime factorizations and multiply all prime factors they have in common. The greatest common factor is the largest factor that goes into each integer.

For example, if you're looking for the greatest common factor of 40 and 140, first identify the prime factors of each integer.

$$40 = 4 \times 10 = 2 \times 2 \times 2 \times 5$$
$$140 = 10 \times 14 = 2 \times 5 \times 2 \times 7 = 2 \times 2 \times 5 \times 7$$

Next, see what prime factors the two numbers have in common and then multiply these common factors.

Both integers share two 2s and one 5, so the GCF is $2 \times 2 \times 5$ or 20.

If you need to find a common multiple of two integers, you can always multiply them. However, you can use prime factors to find the least common multiple (LCM). To do this, multiply all of the prime factors of each integer as many times as they appear. Don't worry if this sounds confusing; it becomes pretty clear once it's demonstrated. Take a look at the example to see how it works.

To find a common multiple of 20 and 16:

$$20 \times 16 = 320$$

320 is a common multiple of 20 and 16, but it is not the *least* common multiple.

To find the least common multiple of 20 and 16 first find the prime factors of each integer:

$$20 = 2 \times 2 \times 5 \qquad 16 = 2 \times 2 \times 2 \times 2$$

Now, multiply each prime integer as many times as it appears in the integer it appears in the greatest number of times: $2 \times 2 \times 2 \times 2 \times 5 = 80$.

The Order of Operations (PEMDAS)

You need to remember the order in which arithmetic operations must be performed. PEMDAS (or Please Excuse My Dear Aunt Sally) may help you remember the order.

Please = Parentheses

Excuse = Exponents

My Dear = Multiplication and Division (from left to right)

Aunt Sally = Addition and Subtraction (from left to right)

$$3^3 - 8(3 - 1) + 12 \div 4$$
$$= 3^3 - 8(2) + 12 \div 4$$
$$= 27 - 8(2) + 12 \div 4$$
$$= 27 - 16 + 3$$
$$= 14$$

Divisibility Rules

Even if you learned the rules, take a moment to refresh your memory. There are no easy divisibility rules for 7 and 8.

Divisible by	The Rule	Example: 558
2	The last digit is even.	a multiple of 2 because 8 is even
3	The sum of the digits is a multiple of 3.	a multiple of 3 because 5 + 5 + 8 = 18, which is a multiple of 3
4	The last 2 digits comprise a 2-digit multiple of 4.	NOT a multiple of 4 because 58 is not a multiple of 4
5	The last digit is 5 or 0.	NOT a multiple of 5 because it doesn't end in 5 or 0
6	The last digit is even AND the sum of the digits is a multiple of 3	a multiple of 6 because it's a multiple of both 2 and 3
9	The sum of the digits is a multiple of 9.	a multiple of 9 because 5 + 5 + 8 = 18, which is a multiple of 9
10	The last digit is 0.	not a multiple of 10 because it doesn't end in 0

Properties of Numbers

Here are some essential laws or properties of numbers.

Commutative Property for Addition

When adding two or more terms, the sum is the same regardless of which number is added to which.

$$3 + 2 = 2 + 3 \qquad a + b = b + a$$

Associative Property for Addition

When adding two or more terms, the sum is the same, regardless of the order in which the terms are added.

$$2 + (5 + 3) = (2 + 5) + 3 \qquad a + (b + c) = (a + b) + c$$

Commutative Property for Multiplication

When multiplying two or more terms, the result is the same regardless of which number is multiplied by which.

$$2 \times 4 = 4 \times 2 \qquad ab = ba$$

Associative Property for Multiplication

When multiplying, the product is the same regardless of the order in which the terms are multiplied.

$$2 \times (4 \times 3) = (2 \times 4) \times 3 \qquad a \times (b \times c) = (a \times b) \times c$$

Distributive Property of Multiplication over Addition

When multiplying, the product of a first number and the sum of two other numbers is equal to the sum of the product of the first and second number plus the product of the first and third numbers.

$$a(b + c) = ab + ac \qquad 2 \times (1 + 1 + 1) = 2 + 2 + 2 = 2 \times 3$$

Fractions and Decimals

Generally, it's a good idea to reduce fractions when solving math questions. To do this, simply cancel all factors that the numerator and denominator have in common.

$$\frac{28}{36} = \frac{4 \times 7}{4 \times 9} = \frac{7}{9}$$

To add fractions, get a common denominator and then add the numerators.

$$\frac{1}{4} + \frac{1}{3} = \frac{3}{12} + \frac{4}{12} = \frac{3+4}{12} = \frac{7}{12}$$

To subtract fractions, get a common denominator and then subtract the numerators.

$$\frac{1}{4} - \frac{1}{3} = \frac{3}{12} - \frac{4}{12} = \frac{3-4}{12} = \frac{-1}{12}$$

To multiply fractions, multiply the numerators and multiply the denominators.

$$\frac{1}{4} \times \frac{1}{3} = \frac{1 \times 1}{4 \times 3} = \frac{1}{12}$$

To divide fractions, invert the second fraction and multiply. In other words, multiply the first fraction by the reciprocal of the second fraction.

$$\frac{1}{4} \div \frac{1}{3} = \frac{1}{4} \times \frac{3}{1} = \frac{1 \times 3}{4 \times 1} = \frac{3}{4}$$

To convert a fraction to a decimal, divide the numerator by the denominator.

To convert $\frac{8}{25}$ to a decimal, divide 8 by 25.

$$\frac{8}{25} = 0.32$$

To convert a decimal to a fraction, first set the decimal over 1. Then, move the decimal point over as many places as it takes until it is immediately to the right of the digit farthest to the right. Count the number of places that you moved the decimal. Then, add that many 0's to the 1 in the denominator.

$$0.3 = \frac{0.3}{1} = \frac{3.0}{10} \text{ or } \frac{3}{10}$$
$$0.32 = \frac{0.32}{1} = \frac{32.0}{100} \text{ or } \frac{8}{25}$$

Comparing Fractions

To compare fractions, multiply the numerator of the first fraction by the denominator of the second fraction to get a product. Then, multiply the numerator of the second fraction by the denominator of the first fraction to get a second product. If the first product is greater, the first fraction is greater. If the second product is greater, the second fraction is greater.

Here's an example:

Compare $\frac{2}{5}$ and $\frac{5}{8}$.

1. Multiply the numerator of the first fraction by the denominator of the second.

$2 \times 8 = 16$

2. Multiply the numerator of the second fraction by the denominator of the first.

$5 \times 5 = 25$

3. The second product is greater; therefore, the second fraction, $\frac{5}{8}$, is greater than $\frac{2}{5}$.

Common Percent Equivalencies

Being familiar with the relationships among percents, decimals, and fractions can save you time on test day. Don't worry about memorizing the following chart. Simply use it to review relationships you already know (e.g., $50\% = 0.50 = \frac{1}{2}$) and to familiarize yourself with some that you might not already know. To convert a fraction or decimal to a percent, multiply by 100%. To convert a percent to a fraction or decimal, divide by 100%.

Fraction	Decimal	Percent
$\frac{1}{20}$	0.05	5%
$\frac{1}{10}$	0.10	10%
$\frac{1}{8}$	0.125	$12\frac{1}{2}\%$
$\frac{1}{6}$	$0.16\overline{6}$	$16\frac{2}{3}\%$
$\frac{1}{5}$	0.20	20%
$\frac{1}{4}$	0.25	25%
$\frac{1}{3}$	$0.33\overline{3}$	$33\frac{1}{3}\%$
$\frac{3}{8}$	0.375	37.5%

Fraction	Decimal	Percent
$\frac{2}{5}$	0.40	40%
$\frac{1}{2}$	0.50	50%
$\frac{3}{5}$	0.60	60%
$\frac{2}{3}$	$0.66\overline{6}$	$66\frac{2}{3}\%$
$\frac{3}{4}$	0.75	75%
$\frac{4}{5}$	0.80	80%
$\frac{5}{6}$	$0.83\overline{3}$	$83\frac{1}{3}\%$
$\frac{7}{8}$	0.875	87.5%

Rounding

TACHS will have a number of questions requiring estimation; you might be asked to estimate or round a number on the COOP or HSPT. Rounding might also help you determine an answer choice.

There are a few simple rules to rounding. Look at the digit to the right of the digit in question. If it is a 4 or less, leave the digit in question as it is and replace all the digits to the right with zeros. If the digit to the right of the digit in question is 5 or greater, increase the digit by 1 and replace all the digits to the right of it with zeros.

For example, round off 765,432 to the nearest 100. The 4 is the hundreds digit, but you have to look at the digit to the right of the hundreds digit, which is the tens digit, or 3. Since the tens digit is 3, the hundreds digit remains the same, and the tens and ones digits both become zero. Therefore, 765,432 rounded to the nearest 100 is 765,400.

Place Units

Rounding requires that you know the place unit value of the digits in a number.

$$\text{hundred millions} \longleftarrow 192,453,726 \longrightarrow \text{ones}$$

ten millions — tens

millions — hundreds

hundred thousands — thousands

ten thousands

Symbols of Inequality

An inequality is a mathematical sentence in which two expressions are joined by symbols such as ≠ (not equal to), > (greater than), < (less than), ≥ (greater than or equal to), ≤ (less than or equal to). Examples of inequalities are:

$5 + 3 \neq 7$	5 plus 3 is not equal to 70.
$6 > 2$	6 is greater than 2.
$8 < 8.5$	8 is less than 8 and a half.
$x \leq 9 + 6$	x is less than or equal to 9 plus 6.
$c \geq 10$	c is greater than or equal to 10. (c is an algebraic variable. That means it varies and could be any number greater than or equal to 10.)

Exponents and Roots

Exponents are the small raised numbers written to the right of a number or variable. A variable is the letter term used in algebra. We'll get to that in the next chapter. For now, remember that an exponent indicates the number of times that a number (or variable) is to be used as a factor. On the COOP, TACHS, or HSPT, you'll usually deal with numbers or variables that are squares (multiplied by itself) and cubes (multiplied by itself two times).

You should remember the squares of 1 through 10.

square = a number to the second power

2^2	$2 \times 2 = 4$	7^2	$7 \times 7 = 49$
3^2	$3 \times 3 = 9$	8^2	$8 \times 8 = 64$
4^2	$4 \times 4 = 16$	9^2	$9 \times 9 = 81$
5^2	$5 \times 5 = 25$	10^2	$10 \times 10 = 100$
6^2	$6 \times 6 = 36$		

cube = a number to the third power

2^3	$2 \times 2 \times 2 = 8$	4^3	$4 \times 4 \times 4 = 64$
3^3	$3 \times 3 \times 3 = 27$	5^3	$5 \times 5 \times 5 = 125$

To add or subtract terms consisting of a coefficient (the number in front of the variable) multiplied by a power (a power is a base raised to an exponent), both the base and the exponent must be the same. As long as the bases and the exponents are the same, you can add the coefficients.

$x^2 + x^2 = 2x^2$ —the base (x) and the exponent (2) are the same, so you can add these.

$3x^4 - 2x^4 = x^4$ —again, the base (x) and the exponent (4) are the same, so you can subtract these.

$x^2 + x^3$ cannot be combined. The exponents are different: (2) and (3).

$x^2 + y^2$ cannot be combined. The bases are different: (x) and (y).

To multiply terms consisting of coefficients multiplied by powers having the same base, multiply the coefficients and add the exponents.

$$2x^5 \times (8x^7) = (2 \times 8)(x^{5+7}) = 16x^{12}$$

To divide terms consisting of coefficients multiplied by powers having the same base, divide the coefficients and subtract the exponents.

$$6x^7 \div 2x^5 = (6 \div 2)(x^{7-5}) = 3x^2$$

To raise a power to an exponent, multiply the exponents.

$$(x^2)^4 = x^{2 \times 4} = x^8$$

A square root of a non-negative number is a number that, when multiplied by itself, produces the given quantity. The radical sign $\sqrt{}$ is used to represent the positive square root of a number, so $\sqrt{25} = 5$, since $5 \times 5 = 25$.

To add or subtract radicals, make sure the numbers under the radical sign are the same. If they are, you can add or subtract the coefficients outside the radical signs.

$$2\sqrt{2} + 3\sqrt{2} = 5\sqrt{2} \quad (\sqrt{2} + \sqrt{3} \text{ cannot be combined.})$$

To simplify radicals, factor out the perfect squares under the radical, unsquare them, and put the result in front of the radical sign.

$$\sqrt{32} = \sqrt{16 \times 2} = 4\sqrt{2}$$

To multiply or divide radicals, multiply (or divide) the coefficients outside the radical. Multiply (or divide) the numbers inside the radicals.

$$\sqrt{x} \times \sqrt{y} = \sqrt{xy} \qquad \frac{\sqrt{x}}{\sqrt{y}} = \sqrt{\frac{x}{y}}$$

$$3\sqrt{2} \times 4\sqrt{5} = 12\sqrt{10} \qquad 12\sqrt{10} \div 3\sqrt{2} = 4\sqrt{5}$$

To take the square root of a fraction, break the fraction into two separate roots and take the square root of the numerator and the denominator.

$$\sqrt{\frac{16}{25}} = \frac{\sqrt{16}}{\sqrt{25}} = \frac{4}{5}$$

The Power of 10

When you raise 10 to a power, the exponent tells you how many zeros to add after the 1. For example, $10^4 = 10,000$ (4 zeros).

When multiplying a number by a positive integer power of 10, move the decimal point to the right the same number of places as the number of zeros.

$$0.0123 \times 10^4 = 123$$

When dividing by a positive integer power of 10, move the decimal point to the left.

$$43.21 \div 10^3 = 0.04321$$

Multiplying by a power with a negative exponent is the same as dividing by a power with a positive exponent. Therefore, when you multiply by a number with a positive exponent, move the decimal to the right. When you multiply by a number with a negative exponent, move the decimal to the left.

For example:

$$10^3 = 1,\underset{\underbrace{}}{000} = 1,000$$

Percents

Remember these formulas: Part = Percent × Whole, or Percent = $\dfrac{\text{Part}}{\text{Whole}}$

From Fraction to Percent

To find part, percent, or whole, plug the values you have into the equation and solve.

$$44\% \text{ of } 25 = 0.44 \times 25 = 11$$

42 is what percent of 70?

$$42 \div 70 = 0.6 = 60\%$$

To increase or decrease a number by a given percent, take that percent of the original number and add it to or subtract it from the original number.

To increase 25 by 60%, first find 60% of 25. Then add the result to the original number.

$$25 \times 0.6 = 15$$
$$25 + 15 = 40$$

To decrease 25 by the same percent, subtract the 15.

$$25 - 15 = 10$$

Average, Median, and Mode

$$\text{Average} = \frac{\text{Sum of the mode}}{\text{Number of the terms}}$$

The average of 15, 18, 15, 32, and 20 is $\frac{15+18+15+32+20}{5} = \frac{100}{5} = 20$.

When there are an odd number of terms, the **median** of a group of terms is the value of the middle term, with the terms arranged in increasing order.

Suppose that you want to find the median of the terms 15, 18, 15, 32, and 20. First, put the terms in order from small to large: 15, 15, 18, 20, 32. Then, identify the middle term. The middle term is 18.

When there is an even number of terms, the median is the average of the two middle terms with the terms arranged in increasing order.

Suppose that you want to find the mode of the terms 15, 18, 15, 32, and 20. The **mode** is the value of the term that occurs most; 15 occurs twice, so it is the mode.

Ratios, Proportions, and Rates

Ratios can be expressed in different forms.

One form is $\frac{a}{b}$.

If you have 15 dogs and 5 cats, the ratio of dogs to cats is $\frac{15}{5}$ (the ratio of cats to dogs is $\frac{5}{15}$). Like any other fraction, this ratio can be reduced; $\frac{15}{5}$ can be reduced to $\frac{3}{1}$. In other words, for every three dogs, there's one cat.

Another form is *a:b.*

The ratio of dogs to cats is 15:5 or 3:1. The ratio of cats to dogs is 5:15 or 1:3.

Pay attention to what ratio is specified in the problem. Remember that the ratio of dogs to cats is different from the ratio of cats to dogs.

To solve a proportion, cross multiply and solve for the variable.

$$\frac{x}{6} = \frac{2}{3}$$
$$3x = 12$$
$$x = 4$$

A rate is a ratio that compares quantities measured in different units. The most common example is miles per hour. Use the following formula for such problems. (although not all rates are speeds, this formula can be adapted to any rate):

$$\text{Distance} = \text{Rate} \times \text{Time or } D = R \times T$$

Units of Measurement

You will most likely see at least a few questions that include units of measurement on the test. You are expected to remember these basic units of measurement. Spend some time reviewing the list below.

Distance

1 foot = 12 inches

1 yard = 3 feet = 36 inches

1 kilometer = 1,000 meters

metric: 1 meter = 10 decimeters =
100 centimeters = 1,000 millimeters

(Remember the root *deci* is 10; the root
centi is 100, the root *milli* is 1,000.)

Volume

8 ounces = 1 cup

2 cups = 1 pint

1 quart = 2 pints

4 cups = 1 quart

1 gallon = 4 quarts

metric: A liter is a unit of volume. A kiloliter is
1,000 liters.

Weight

1 pound = 16 ounces

metric: A gram is a unit of mass. A kilogram is 1,000 grams.

Don't worry, you won't be expected to remember the formulas for converting metric and U.S. equivalents, or vice versa. On questions such as these, the formula is provided.

But be careful when approaching a problem that includes units of measurement. Be sure that the units are given in the same format. You may have to convert pounds to ounces or feet to yards (or vice versa) to arrive at the correct answer choice.

A Word About Word Problems

You can expect to see a lot of word problems on the test. Some of these will be algebra problems, asking you to solve for an unknown. We'll get into these in the next chapter. Some of them, however, will just be asking you to perform arithmetic. Your job is to find the math within the story.

Here's an example:

> A grocery store charges $0.99 for a liter of milk, $1.49 for a half pound of tomatoes, $0.49 for a jar of tomato sauce, and $1.25 for a box of pasta. If Reggie buys two liters of milk, one pound of tomatoes, a jar of tomato sauce, and two boxes of pasta, what is his bill?

> (A) $7.90
> (B) $7.95
> (C) $6.36
> (D) $8.36

If you sort through the story, you realize that the question is asking you to add the amounts of each item that Reggie bought. Read the question carefully to make sure you have the correct number of each item he bought, then add the amounts.

$0.99 \times 2 = 1.98$ (the price of two liters of milk)

$1.49 \times 2 = 2.98$ (the price given was per half pound; Reggie bought 1 full pound)

0.49 (the price of one jar of sauce)

$1.25 \times 2 = 2.50$ (the price of two boxes of pasta)

Now, add these numbers together to get the total.

1.98

2.98

0.49

<u>2.50</u>

$7.95, choice (B)

Often, word problems can seem tricky because it may be hard to figure out precisely what you are being asked to do. It can be difficult to translate English into math. The following table lists some common words and phrases that turn up in word problems, along with their mathematical translation.

When you see:	Think:
sum, plus, more than, added to, combined total	+
minus, less than, difference between, decreased by	−
is, was, equals, is equivalent to, is the same as, adds up to	=
times, product, multiplied by, of, twice, double, triple	×
divided by, over, quotient, per, out of, into	÷

MATH SKILLS PRACTICE SET

1. Which of the following demonstrates the commutative property of addition?

    (A) $1 + 3 = 4$

    (B) $1 + 3 = 3 + 1$

    (C) $1 + 3 = \frac{1}{3} \times \frac{3}{1}$

    (D) $1 + 3 = 1 - (-3)$

2. What is the least common multiple of 12 and 8?

    (A) 12

    (B) 24

    (C) 18

    (D) 96

3. Which of the following is an even multiple of both 2 and 6?

    (A) 435

    (B) 247

    (C) 322

    (D) 426

4. All of the following can be a product of a negative integer and a positive integer EXCEPT

    (A) −6

    (B) 1

    (C) −1

    (D) −2

5. What is the sum of five consecutive integers if the middle one is 9?

    (A) 50

    (B) 55

    (C) 45

    (D) 30

6. $2^3(3 - 1)^2 + (-4)^2 =$

    (A) 48

    (B) 32

    (C) 136

    (D) −48

7. If x is an even integer and $8 < x < 17$, what is the mean of all possible values of x?

    (A) 10

    (B) 11

    (C) 13

    (D) 12

8. Which of the following is closest to the product of 52.3×10.4?

    (A) 5,000

    (B) 500

    (C) 6,000

    (D) 60

9. Which of the following is 53,298 rounded off to the nearest 100?

    (A) 53,290

    (B) 52,000

    (C) 53,300

    (D) 53,000

10. If 40% of x is 8, what is x% of 40?

    (A) 80

    (B) 30

    (C) 10

    (D) 8

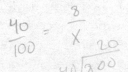
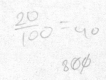

ANSWERS AND EXPLANATIONS

1. B

The commutative property of addition states that when adding two or more terms, the sum is the same, no matter the order in which the terms are added.

2. B

The least common multiple of two integers is the product of their prime factors, each raised to the highest power with which it appears. The prime factorization of 12 is $2 \times 2 \times 3$, the prime factorization of 8 is $2 \times 2 \times 2$. So their LCM is $2 \times 2 \times 2 \times 3 = 24$. You could also find their LCM by checking out the multiples of the larger integer (12) until you find one that's also a multiple of the smaller.

3. D

If a number is a multiple of both 2 and 6, it must satisfy the divisibility rules of both: its last digit must be even, its digits must add up to a multiple of 3. Only choice (D) fits both requirements: $4 + 2 + 6 = 12$. You could have quickly eliminated choices (A) and (B) which are not even numbers.

4. B

Remember to count the number of negatives to determine whether the product of negative and positive integers is either negative or positive. An odd number of negatives will yield a negative number, while an even number of negatives will yield a positive number. Since choice (B) is a positive integer, it is not the product of a negative and a positive integer.

5. C

This is a simple addition problem. If the middle integer is 9, place them in order. You would have: $7 + 8 + 9 + 10 + 11 = 45$.

6. A

Remember PEMDAS. Perform the operation in parentheses first.

$2^3(3 - 1)^2 + (-4)^2 = 2^3(2)^2 + (-4)^2$. Exponents next, $8(4) + 16$. Multiplication next, and addition or subtraction last: $32 + 16 = 48$.

7. C

x is an even integer greater than 8 but less than 17. Thus, x could be 10, 12, 14, or 16. The mean of all its possible values $= \dfrac{(10+12+14+16)}{4} = \dfrac{52}{4} = 13$. Be sure to read each question carefully. This question required two steps. If you read too quickly, you might have missed the second step that was finding the mean of all the possible values of x.

8. B

This is a rounding off question. You can round off 52.3 to 50 and 10.4 to 10; $50 \times 10 = 500$.

9. C

To round off to the nearest 100 look at the tens digit. If it is 5 or greater, round the hundreds digit up. If the tens digit is 4 or smaller, keep the same hundreds digit. Here, the tens digit is 9, so you must round the hundreds digit up to 3 and replace the digits to the right with zeros.

10. D

This problem is not difficult if you remember that $a\%$ of $b = b\%$ of a. In this case, $x\%$ of b (the number 40) = b (the number 40)% of $x = 8$. If you didn't remember this, you could have solved for x with the formula Percent $\times$ Whole = Part. Thus, $\dfrac{40}{100} = \dfrac{8}{x}$. When you cross multiply and solve for x, you get $40x = 800$, $x = \dfrac{800}{40}$, so $x = 20$. You now need to determine $x\%$ of 40. $x = 20$; 20% of $40 = 20 \times 40 = 8$.

Algebra Basics

This chapter will give you a chance to review the basic algebra concepts that you'll see on the test. (Word problems are covered in the next chapter and will build on the concepts from this chapter.)

Algebra has been called *math with letters*. Just like arithmetic, the basic operations of algebra are addition, subtraction, multiplication, division, roots. Instead of numbers though, algebra uses letters to represent unknown or variable numbers. Why would you work with a variable? Let's look at an example.

> You buy two bananas from the supermarket for 50 cents total.
> How much does one banana cost?

That's a simple equation, but how would you write it down on paper if you were trying to explain it to a friend?

Perhaps you would write: $2 \times \underline{?} = 50$ cents. Algebra gives you a systematic way to record the question mark.

> $2 \times b = 50$ cents or $2b = 50$ cents, where b is the cost of one banana, in cents.

Algebra is a type of mathematical shorthand. The most commonly used letters in algebra are a, b, c and x, y, z. The number 2 in the term $2b$ is called a **coefficient**. It is a constant that does not change.

To find out how much you paid for each banana, you could use your equation to solve for the unknown cost.

$$2b = 50 \text{ cents}$$
$$\frac{2b}{2} = \frac{50}{2}$$
$$b = 25 \text{ cents}$$

ALGEBRAIC EXPRESSIONS

A **term** is the product of a constant and one or more variables, like $2x$ or $74ab$. An **expression** is a collection of terms linked by operations signs such as + and –.

Let's go back to our fruit example. Let's say you have two bananas and you give one to your friend. You could express this as:

$2b - b$

This is a **binomial** expression because it has only two terms. A binomial expression is one type of polynomial expression: those having two or more terms (like $2 + ba - 4y$). A **monomial** expression has a single term (like $2x^2$).

On the COOP, TACHS, or HSPT, an algebraic expression is likely to look something like this:

$(11 + 3x) - (5 - 2x) =$

In addition to algebra, this problem tests your knowledge of positives and negatives, and the order of operations (PEMDAS).

The main thing you need to remember about expressions is that you can only combine like terms.

Let's talk about fruit once more. Let's say in addition to the two bananas, you also bought three apples and one pear. You spent four dollars total. You can express your purchases as $2b + 3a + 1p = 4$. Now, b = the cost of one banana, a = the cost of one apple, and p = the cost of one pear.

However, let's say that once again you forgot how much each banana cost. You could NOT add the six items, divide $4 by 6 to get the cost of each one. They're different items.

 KAPLAN TIP

Remember you can only combine like terms. Combine a's with a's , x's with x's, or coefficients that have the exact same variable.

While you cannot find the values of expressions with unlike terms, you can simplify them. For example, to combine monomials or polynomials, add or subtract the coefficients of terms that have the exact same variable. When completing the addition or subtraction, do not change the variables.

$6a + 5a = 11a$
$8b - 2b = 6b$
$3a + 2b - 8a = 3a - 8a + 2b = -5a + 2b$ or $2b - 5a$

> **Coefficient** = The number that comes before the variable. In $6x$, 6 is the coefficient.
>
> **Variable** = The variable is the letter that stands for an unknown. In $6x$, x is the variable.
>
> **Monomial** = One term: $6x$ is a monomial.
>
> **Polynomial** = More than one term: $7xy + 5y^2$ is a polynomial.

To review, you cannot combine:

$6a + 5a^2$ —Why not? The variables are not raised to the same exponent. (One is a, the other is a^2.)

or

$3a + 2b$ —Why not? The variables are different. (One is a, the other is b.)

Multiplying and dividing monomials is a little different. Unlike addition and subtraction, you can multiply and divide terms that are different. When you multiply monomials, multiply the coefficients of each term. Add the exponents of like variables. Multiply different variables together.

$$(6a)(4b) = (6 \times 4)(a \times b) = 24ab$$
$$(6a)(4ab) = (6 \times 4)(a \times a \times b) = (24)(a^{1+1} \times b) = 24a^2b$$

Use the FOIL method to multiply and divide binomials. FOIL stands for **F**irst **O**uter **I**nner **L**ast.

$$(y + 1)(y + 2) = (y \times y) + (y \times 2) + (1 \times y) + (1 \times 2)$$
$$= y^2 + 2y + y + 2$$
$$= y^2 + 3y + 2$$

EQUATIONS

The key to solving equations is to do the same thing to both sides of the equation until you have your variable isolated on one side of the equation and all of the numbers on the other side.

$$8a + 4 = 24 - 2a$$

First, subtract 4 from each side so that the left side of the equation has only variables.

$$8a + 4 - 4 = 24 - 2a - 4$$
$$8a = 20 - 2a$$

Then, add $2a$ to each side so that the right side of the equation has only numbers.

$$8a + 2a = 20 - 2a + 2a$$
$$10a = 20$$

Finally, divide both sides by 10 to isolate the variable.

$$\frac{10a}{10} = \frac{20}{10}$$
$$a = 2$$

Treat Both Sides Equally

Always perform the same operation to both sides to solve for a variable in an equation.

Sometimes you're given an equation with two variables and asked to solve for one variable in terms of the other. This means that you must isolate the variable for which you are solving on one side of the equation and put everything else on the other side. In other words, when you're done, you'll have x (or whatever the variable you're looking for is) on one side of the equation and an expression on the other side.

Solve $7x + 2y = 3x + 10y - 16$ for x in terms of y.

Since you want to isolate x on one side of the equation, begin by subtracting $2y$ from both sides.

$$7x + 2y - 2y = 3x + 10y - 16 - 2y$$
$$7x = 3x + 8y - 16$$

Then, subtract $3x$ from both sides to get all the xs on one side of the equation.

$$7x - 3x = 3x + 8y - 16 - 3x$$
$$4x = 8y - 16$$

Finally, divide both sides by 4 to isolate x.

$$\frac{4x}{4} = \frac{8y - 16}{4}$$
$$x = 2y - 4$$

SUBSTITUTION

If a problem gives you the value for a variable, just plug the value into the equation and solve. Make sure that you follow the rules of PEMDAS and are careful with your calculations.

If $x = 15$ and $y = 10$, what is the value of $4x(x - y)$?

Plug 15 in for x and 10 in for y.

$$4(15)(15 - 10) =$$

Then, find the value.

$$(60)(5) = 300$$

INEQUALITIES

Solve **inequalities** like you would any other equation. Isolate the variable for which you are solving on one side of the equation and everything else on the other side of the equation.

$$4a + 6 > 2a + 10$$
$$4a - 2a > 10 - 6$$
$$2a > 4$$
$$a > 2$$

The only difference here is that instead of finding a specific value for a, you get a range of values for a. That is, a can be any number greater than 2. The rest of the math is the same.

There is, however, one crucial difference between solving equations and inequalities. **When you multiply or divide an inequality by a negative number, you must change the direction of the sign.**

$$-5a > 10$$
$$\frac{-5a}{-5} > \frac{10}{5}$$
$$a < -2$$

If this seems confusing, think about the logic. You're told that –5 times something is greater than 10. This is where your knowledge of positives and negatives comes into play. You know that negative × positive = negative, and negative × negative = positive. Since –5 is negative and 10 is positive, –5 has to be multiplied by something negative to get a positive product. Therefore, a has to be *less* than –2, not *greater* than it. If $a > -2$, then any value for a that is greater than –2 should make –5a greater than 10. Say a is 20; –5a would be –100, which is certainly NOT greater than 10.

PICKING NUMBERS AND BACKSOLVING

Picking numbers is a very useful strategy for avoiding lots of tedious calculations.

Kaplan's 3-Step Method for Picking Numbers

Step 1: Pick simple, easy-to-use numbers for each variable.

Step 2: Solve the problem using the numbers you pick.

Step 3: Plug your numbers into each answer choice. The choice that gives you the same numerical solution you arrived at in Step 2 is correct.

A few things to remember:

- You can pick numbers only when the answer choices contain variables.
- Pick easy numbers rather than realistic ones. Keep the numbers small and manageable, but avoid 0 and 1.
- Remember that you have to try all the answer choices. If more than one works, pick another set of numbers.
- Don't pick the same number for more than one variable.
- Always pick 100 for percent questions.

Some typical questions that can be solved by picking numbers are:

- Age stated in terms of variables
- Remainder problems
- Percentages or fractions of variables
- Positive and negative variable calculations
- Questions with algebraic expressions as answers

Backsolving

- You can backsolve when the answer choices contain only numbers.
- Always start with an answer choice with a middle value. For example, if your choices are 1, 7, 35, and 12, you should start with 12.
- If the middle value is not correct, you can usually eliminate two or more choices simply by determining whether the value must be higher or lower.

ALGEBRA BASICS PRACTICE SET

1. What is the value of $a(b-2) + \dfrac{bc}{a}$ if $a = 2$, $b = 6$, and $c = 4$?

    (A) 20
    (B) 12
    (C) 24
    (D) 32

2. If $\dfrac{c}{d} = 5$ and $d = 2$, then $2c + d =$

    (A) 32
    (B) 20
    (C) 22
    (D) 35

3. What is the value of x in the equation $6x - 7 = y$, if $y = 11$?

    (A) 12
    (B) 8
    (C) 4
    (D) 3

4. If $x = \sqrt{3}$, $y = 2$, and $z = \dfrac{1}{2}$, then $x^2 - 5yz + y^2 =$

    (A) 1
    (B) 2
    (C) 4
    (D) 7

5. $(3d - 7) - (5 - 2d) =$

    (A) $d - 12$
    (B) $5d - 2$
    (C) $5d + 12$
    (D) $5d - 12$

6. If x is an odd integer and y is an even integer, which of the following expressions MUST be odd?

    (A) $2x + y$
    (B) $2(x + y)$
    (C) $x^2 + y^2$
    (D) $xy + y$

7. If $90 \div x = 9n$, then what is the value of nx?

    (A) 10
    (B) $9x$
    (C) 900
    (D) $90xn$

8. For what value of y is $4(y - 5) = 2(y + 3)$?

    (A) -13
    (B) 13
    (C) 7
    (D) -8

9. What is the value of x in the following equation?
   $\dfrac{1}{2} + x = 6.5$

    (A) 3.5
    (B) 3.25
    (C) 5.5
    (D) 6

10. If $2(a + m) = 5m - 3 + a$, what is the value of a, in terms of m?

    (A) $\dfrac{3m}{2}$
    (B) 3
    (C) $4m + 33$
    (D) $3m - 3$

ANSWERS AND EXPLANATIONS

1. A

Plug in $a = 2$, $b = 6$, and $c = 4$.

$$2(6-2)+\frac{6(4)}{2}$$
$$2(4)+\frac{24}{2}$$
$$8+12=20$$

2. C

Since we're told the value of d, we can plug it into the equation $\frac{c}{d} = 5$ to find the value of c. We are told that $d = 2$, so $\frac{c}{d} = 5$ can be rewritten as $\frac{c}{2} = 5$. Since $\frac{c}{2} = 5$, multiply both sides of the equation by 2 to isolate c and determine its value. $\frac{c}{2} \times 2 = 5 \times 2$. $c = 10$. Now, we can plug the values of c and d into the expression: $2(10) + 2 = 20 + 2 = 22$.

3. D

We are told that $y = 11$, so first we'll replace the y in the equation with 11, and then we can solve for x.

$$6x - 7 = y$$
$$6x - 7 = 11$$

Now, we can add 7 to both sides:

$$6x - 7 + 7 = 11 + 7$$
$$6x = 18$$

Next, we divide both sides by 6:

$$\frac{6x}{6} = \frac{18}{6}$$
$$x = 3$$

4. B

Remember, $5yz$ means $5 \cdot y \cdot z$. First, we will replace x, y, and z with the values given. Then, we will carry out the indicated operations using the PEMDAS order of operations—Parentheses, Exponents, Multiplication and Division, Addition and Subtraction.

$$x^2 - 5yz + y^2 = (\sqrt{3})^2 - 5 \cdot 2 \cdot \frac{1}{2} + 2^2$$
$$= 3 - 5 \cdot 2 \cdot \frac{1}{2} + 4$$
$$= 3 - 5 + 4$$
$$= -2 + 4$$
$$= 2$$

5. D

Subtract:

$$3d - 7 - 5 - (-2d)$$

Combine like terms:

$$3d - (-2d) - 7 - 5$$
$$5d - 12$$

Note that $3d$ minus $-2d$ equals $+5d$, because subtracting a negative is the same as adding a positive.

6. C

We know that x is odd and y is even. Let's say that $x = 3$ and $y = 4$.

(A) $2x + y$; $2(3) + 4 = 6 + 4 = 10$; 10 is even, so this isn't correct.
(B) $2(x + y)$; $2(3 + 4) = 2(7) = 14$; 14 is even.
(C) $x^2 + y^2$; $3^2 + 4^2 = 9 + 16 = 25$; 25 is odd, so (C) is correct.

7. A

This problem looks harder than it really is. If $90 \div x = 9n$, then $9n \cdot x = 90$, or $9nx = 90$, and $nx = 10$.

8. B

Multiply through and solve for y by isolating it on one side of the equation:

$$4(y-5)=2(y+3)$$
$$4y-20=2y+6$$
$$4y-20-6=2y$$
$$4y-26-4y=2y-4y$$
$$\frac{-26}{-2}=\frac{-2y}{-2}$$
$$13=y$$

9. D

Isolate x on one side of the equation:

$$\frac{1}{2}+x=6.5$$
$$\frac{1}{2}-\frac{1}{2}+x=6.5-\frac{1}{2}$$
$$x=6$$

This problem is easy when you remember the decimal equivalent of $\frac{1}{2}$ is 0.5.

10. D

Multiply through and then find a in terms of m by isolating a on one side of the equation:

$$2(a+m)=5m-3+a$$
$$2a+2m=5m-3+a$$
$$2a+2m-a-2m=5m-3+a-2m-a$$
$$a=3m-3$$

chapter ten

Algebra Word Problems

Understanding Algebra Word Problems is probably one of the most useful math skills you can have. The great thing about word problems is that, unlike some other areas tested, they're not only important on test day, they're useful in everyday life. Whether you're figuring out how much a piece of clothing will cost you with sales tax, or calculating your earnings, algebraic word problems help you figure out unknown amounts.

Kaplan has a systematic approach to help you do your best.

TRANSLATING ENGLISH INTO ALGEBRA

Kaplan's 3-Step Method for Word Problems

Step 1: Decode the question.
Step 2: Set up an equation.
Step 3: Solve for the unknown.

Step 1—Decode the Question

As with non-algebraic word problems, in order to solve a question, any question, you must know what it is asking you to do. You need to translate the English into math.

When you see:	Think:
sum, plus, more than, added to, combined total	+
minus, less than, difference between, decreased by	−
is, was, equals, is equivalent to, is the same as, adds up to	=
times, product, multiplied by, of, twice, double, triple	×
divided by, over, quotient, per, out of, into	÷
what, how much, how many, a number	x, n, a, b, etc.

In the table you see how algebraic variables come into play solving word problems. The letter, or variable, stands for the unknown amount we need to find.

Let's translate one:

> In a class of 30 students, 12 have birthdays in the summer, 8 have birthdays in the fall, and 6 have birthdays in the winter. How many students have their birthday in the spring?

The *how many* in the phrase clues us in to the fact that we can use an algebraic equation to help us solve this problem.

Here's another example:

> Amy is 18 months older than her brother Sean and 3 years older than her sister Katie. If the sum of their ages is 20 years, how old is Amy?

What is the question looking for? Amy's age.

Step 2—Set Up an Equation

Now that we know what's being asked of us, we have to set up an equation to find Amy's age.

Let x = Amy's age. That means that Sean's age is $x - 18$ (If x = Sean's age, then Amy's age would be $x + 18$) and Katie's age is $x - 3(12)$.

The sum of all their ages is 20, so:

$$x + x - 18 + x - (3 \times 12) = 20 \times 12$$

Hopefully you noticed that this is a trick question. Ages are given in months and in years. We have to convert everything to the same measurement in order to solve correctly. That's why we multiplied the 3 and the 20 by 12, because there are 12 months in a year.

Step 3—Solve for the Unknown

We know what's being asked of us, we set up an equation, and the only thing left to do is the math. Make sure you do your calculations in the right order and properly.

$$x + x - 18 + x - (3 \times 12) = 20 \times 12$$
$$3x - 54 = 240$$
$$3x - 54 + 54 = 240 + 54$$
$$3x = 294$$
$$x = 98$$

Amy is 98 years old? How could that be?

Remember, we were working with months. Don't forget to translate the number of months back into years when you are finished.

$$\frac{98}{12} \approx 8 \text{ years old}$$

WORD PROBLEMS WITH FORMULAS

Some of the more challenging word problems may involve translations with mathematical formulas. For example, you might see questions dealing with averages, rates, or areas of geometric figures. (More about geometry later.) Since the COOP, TACHS, and HSPT do not provide formulas for you, you have to know them. For example:

If a truck driver travels at an average of speed of 50 miles per hour for 6.5 hours, how far will the driver travel?

To answer this question, you need to know the distance formula.

Distance = Rate × Time or $D = R \times T$

Once you know the formula, you can plug in the numbers:

$D = 50 \times 6.5 = 325$ miles

Here's another example:

Thomas took an exam with 60 questions on it. If he finished all the questions in two hours, how many minutes on average did he spend answering each question?

The time it took for Thomas to finish the exam is given in *hours*, but the question is asking how many *minutes* each question took. Be sure to read each question carefully so you don't fall for tricks like this.

$$\text{Average} = \frac{\text{Sum of terms}}{\text{Number of terms}}$$

There are 60 minutes in an hour. In 2 hours (120 minutes) he answered 60 questions. The number of minutes on average is 120/60 = 2.

WORD PROBLEM STRATEGIES

Picking numbers and backsolving may be the quickest way to the answer in word problems; if you need to, review those strategies at the end of chapter 9.

KAPLAN TIP

Don't be afraid to pick numbers out of thin air if the answer choices contain variables. Also, remember to pick easy, workable numbers. Avoid 1 and 0, as these values may cause you problems.

ALGEBRA WORD PROBLEMS PRACTICE SET

1. Andrew bought a camera on sale at a 20% discount. It was marked down from its regular price of $120. If there is an 8% sales tax on the sale price, how much did Andrew pay for the camera?

    (A) $24.00
    (B) $103.68
    (C) $127.68
    (D) $105.68

2. Edward has $400 more than Robert. After Edward spends $60 on groceries, he has three times more money than Robert. How much money does Robert have?

    (A) 140
    (B) 120
    (C) 90
    (D) 170

3. A dry cleaning store charges $3.50 to clean men's shirts, $4.00 to clean men's pants, and $5.00 to clean men's jackets. If Jose brings ten items for cleaning and pays a total of $48.00, what is the average price he has paid per item?

    (A) $3.50
    (B) $2.22
    (C) $5.00
    (D) $4.80

4. Rene's dress shop is suffering from slow business. Rene decides to mark down all her merchandise. The next day, she sells 33 winter coats. Now, only 70% of the winter coats she had in stock remains. How many winter coats were in stock before the sale?

    (A) 990
    (B) 99
    (C) 110
    (D) 1,110

5. The price of a stock decreased by 20%. By what percent must the price increase to return to its original value?

    (A) 25%
    (B) 50%
    (C) 20%
    (D) 120%

6. Mrs. Bailer divides the amount of money she has between her four children. Mr. Bailer then adds $2.00 to the amount each one receives so that each child now has a total of $5.25. Which of the following equations shows this relationship?

    (A) $4x + 2 = 5.25$
    (B) $\frac{x}{4} + 2 = 5.25$
    (C) $4x = 5.25 + 2$
    (D) $4(x + 2) = 5.25$

7. A worker earns $16 per hour for the first 40 hours she works each week, and one and a half times this much for every hour over 40 hours. If she earned $700 for one week's work, how many extra hours did she work?

    (A) 3.3
    (B) 3
    (C) 2.5
    (D) 4

8. Liza has 40 less than three times the number of books that Janice has. If B is equal to the number of books that Janice has, which of the following expressions shows the total number of books that Liza and Janice have together?

    (A) $4B - 40$
    (B) $3B - 40$
    (C) $4B$
    (D) $4B + 40$

9. The Tigers had five times as many losses as they had ties in a season. If the Tigers did not win any of their games, which could be the total number of games they played in the season?

    (A) 16
    (B) 5
    (C) 10
    (D) 12

10. Ruth has finished three chapters of an eight-chapter novel in just one evening of reading. If she reads an additional $\frac{1}{10}$ of the novel tomorrow night, what part of the novel will she have finished?

    (A) $\frac{4}{10}$

    (B) $\frac{1}{2}$

    (C) $\frac{19}{40}$

    (D) $\frac{36}{80}$

ANSWERS AND EXPLANATIONS

1. B

This problem has several steps. First, find out what the sale price of the camera was.

It was discounted 20% from $120.00.

$x = 0.20 \times \$120.00 = \$24.00$

Next, subtract the discount from the total amount to find out the sale price.

$\$120.00 - \$24.00 = \$96.00$

(You could also arrive at the sale price by using the formula Part = Percent × Whole.)

Since the camera was discounted 20%, Andrew really paid 80% of the whole.

$x = 0.80 \times \$120.00 = \$96.00$

Now, multiply the sale price by the tax of 0.08 to find out how much tax Andrew paid.

$\$96.00 \times 0.08 = \$7.68$

Finally, add the tax to the sale price to find the total Andrew paid for his purchase.

$\$96.00 + \$7.68 = \$103.68$

2. D

Translate the words into math and solve for the unknown. Let x = the unknown amount of money Robert has.

"Edward has 400 more than Robert": $x + 400$
After he spends $60 on groceries": $x + 400 - 60$
"he has three times more than Robert": $x + 400 - 60 = 3x$

Now that you've set up an equation, solve for x.

$$x + 400 - 60 = 3x$$
$$x + 340 = 3x$$
$$340 = 2x$$
$$170 = x$$

3. D

$$\text{Average} = \frac{\text{Total sum}}{\text{Number of items}}$$

Let x equal the unknown average.

$$x = \frac{48}{10} = \$4.80$$

Notice that the information about how much is charged per item is extraneous. You don't need it to solve the problem.

4. C

Let x = the unknown number of coats in stock before the sale. Use the formula Part = Percent × Whole. Since the coats sold left 70% of the stock, the coat sold were 30%.

$$33 \text{ winter coats} = 0.30x$$
$$\frac{33}{0.3} = 110$$

5. A

The key here is that while the value of the stock increases and decreases by the same amount, it doesn't increase and decrease by the same percent since the "whole" is different once the stock has lost value.

If it seems confusing, this is a good question to pick numbers for. Let's pick $100 for the price of the stock. If the price decreases by 20%, the price is now $80. For the price to return to its original value of $100, it must be increased by $20. What percent of 80 equals $20?

$$x\%(80) = 20$$
$$x\% = \frac{20}{80}$$
$$x\% = \frac{1}{4}$$

$\frac{1}{4}$ is equal to 25%.

6. B

Translate this question using the verbal clues provided. Let the amount of money Mrs. Bailer has = x.

Mrs. Bailer divides the amount of money she has between her four children: $\frac{x}{4}$.

Mr. Bailer then adds $2 to the amount each one receives:

$\frac{x}{4} + 2$ so that each child now has a total of 5.25:

$$\frac{x}{4} + 2 = 5.25$$

7. C

This question has several steps. First, determine the amount of overtime dollars the worker earned. Do this by figuring how much she earned over a 40-hour work week. If she makes $16 per hour for 40 hours, she would earn $16 × 40 = $640. However, she earned $60 more than that ($700 − $640 = $60). How many extra hours did she work to earn that $60 if she earns time and a half for each hour over 40? If she earned $16 per hour, then she made $16 × 1.5 = $24 per hour in overtime. Therefore, $\frac{\$60}{\$24} = 2.5$ hours worked overtime.

8. A

This is a simple translation problem. You're told that Janice has B books. Lisa has 40 less than 3 times the number of books Janice has, which you can translate as $L = 3B - 40$. The total number they have together equals $B + 3B - 40$ or $4B - 40$ which is choice (A).

9. D

Let x = the number of ties the Tigers had. It lost 5 times as many games as it tied, $5x$. It had no wins so the total number of games played by the Tigers $= 5x + x = 6x$. So, the number of games the Tigers played must be a multiple of 6; the only choice that is a multiple of 6 is choice (D).

10. C

Let x = the part of the novel Ruth has finished.

$$x = \frac{3}{8} + \frac{1}{10}$$

Change these two fractions to a common denominator of 80 and add them.

$$\frac{30}{80} + \frac{8}{80} = \frac{38}{80}$$

Reduce the fraction to $\frac{19}{40}$.

chapter eleven

Geometry

You will definitely see some basic geometry on the COOP or HSPT. You can count on seeing questions that test your knowledge of lines and angles, triangles, and circles. You'll also see a little coordinate geometry. You might also see geometry in word problems that don't include diagrams.

If you're concerned about your geometry skills, take some time to review this chapter, spending more time with the subjects that are less familiar to you. Make sure you do all of the problems in the practice set, and that you read and understand the answer explanations even for questions you answer correctly.

It's important to know that unless it's specified, diagrams that accompany Geometry questions are NOT drawn to scale. Keep this in mind so that you don't just eyeball the diagram and come to a conclusion. In other words, don't judge the answer just by looking at the size of the diagram.

LINES AND ANGLES

There are 180 degrees in a straight line.

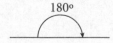

Line Segments

Some of the most basic Geometry problems deal with line segments. A **line segment** is a piece of a line, and it has an exact measurable length. A question might give you a segment divided into several pieces, provide the measurements of some of these pieces, and ask you for the measurement of the remaining piece.

$$P \qquad Q \qquad R$$

If $PR = 12$ and $QR = 4$, $PQ =$

$PQ = PR - QR$

$PQ = 12 - 4$

$PQ = 8$

KAPLAN TIP

Don't assume figures or diagrams are drawn to scale.

The point exactly in the middle of a line segment, halfway between the endpoints, is called the midpoint of the line segment. To bisect means to cut in half, so the **midpoint** of a line segment bisects that line segment.

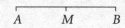

$$A \qquad\qquad B \qquad A \qquad M \qquad B$$

M is the midpoint of AB, so $AM = MB$.

Angles

A **right angle** measures 90 degrees and is usually indicated in a diagram by a little box. The figure above is a right angle. Lines that intersect to form right angles are said to be **perpendicular**.

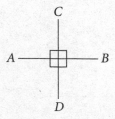

In the figure above, line AB and line CD are perpendicular.

Angles that form a straight line add up to 180 degrees. In the figure above, $a + b = 180$.

Angle b is less than 90 degrees; it is an **acute angle**. Angle a is greater than 90 degrees. Angles greater than 90 degrees are called **obtuse**.

> right angle = 90 degrees
> acute angle < 90 degrees
> obtuse angle > 90 degrees

When two lines intersect, adjacent angles are **supplementary**, meaning they add up to 180 degrees. In the figure above $a + b = 180$.

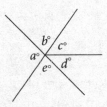

Angles around a point add up to 360 degrees. In the figure above $a + b + c + d + e = 360$.

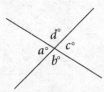

When lines intersect, angles across the vertex (the middle point) from each other are called vertical angles and are equal to each other. Above, $a = c$ and $b = d$.

Parallel Lines

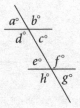

When parallel lines are crossed by a transversal:

- Corresponding angles are equal (for example $a = e$, $d = h$).
- Alternate interior angles are equal ($d = f$).
- Same side interior angles are supplementary ($c + f = 180$).
- All four acute angles are equal, as are all four obtuse angles (a, c, e, g are equal, b, d, f, h are equal).

TRIANGLES

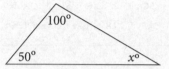

The three interior angles of any triangle add up to 180 degrees. In the figure above $x + 50 + 100 = 180$, so $x = 30$

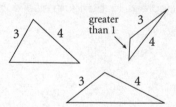

An exterior angle of a triangle is equal to the sum of the remote interior angles. In this figure, the exterior angle labeled y is equal to the sum of the remote interior angles: $y = 40 + 95 = 135$.

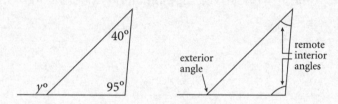

The length of one side of a triangle must be **greater than the positive difference** and **less than the sum** of the lengths of the other two sides. For example, if it is given that the length of one side is 3 and the length of another side is 4, then the length of the third side must be greater than $4 - 3 = 1$ and less than $4 + 3 = 7$.

Triangles—Area and Perimeter

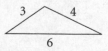

The **perimeter** of a triangle is the sum of the lengths of its sides. The perimeter of the triangle in the figure above is $3 + 4 + 6 = 13$.

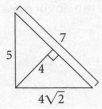

Area of triangle = $\frac{1}{2}$(base)(height) or $A = \frac{1}{2}bh$.

The height is the perpendicular distance between the side that is chosen as the base and the opposite vertex. In this triangle, 4 is the height when 7 is chosen as the base.

Area = $\frac{1}{2}bh = \frac{1}{2}(7)4 = 14$

Similar Triangles

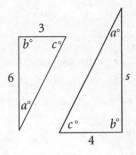

Similar triangles have the same shape: **corresponding angles are equal**, and **corresponding sides are proportional**. The triangles above are similar because they have the same angles. The 3 corresponds (or relates to) the 4, and the 6 corresponds to the unknown s. Because the triangles are similar, you can set up a ratio to solve for s.

$\frac{3}{4} = \frac{6}{s}$

$3s = 24$

$s = 8$

Special Triangles

Isosceles Triangles

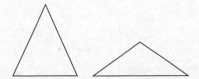

An isosceles triangle is a triangle that has **two equal sides**. Not only are two sides equal, but the angles opposite the equal sides, called base angles, are also equal to one another.

So, if you were asked to determine angle a in the isosceles triangle above, you could set up an equation. Since the sum of the degree measures of the interior angles in a triangle is 180, and you are given one angle of 40 degrees: $2a = 180 - 40$, $2a = 140$, $\dfrac{2a}{2} = \dfrac{140}{2}$, $a = 70°$.

Equilateral Triangles

Equilateral triangles are triangles in which **all three sides are equal**. Since the sides are equal, all the angles are also equal. If all three angles are equal, and the sum of the degree measures of the angles in a triangle = 180, what is the measure of each angle in an equilateral triangle?

$$\frac{180}{3} = 60$$

60 degrees!

Right Triangles

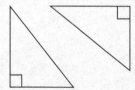

A right triangle is a triangle with a right angle. (Remember, a right angle equals 90 degrees.) Every right triangle has exactly two acute angles. The sides opposite the acute angles are called the legs. The side opposite the right angle is called the hypotenuse. Since it is opposite the largest angle, the hypotenuse is the longest side of a right triangle.

The Pythagorean Theorem

The Pythagorean theorem states the following:

$$(\text{leg}_1)^2 + (\text{leg}_2)^2 = (\text{hypotenuse})^2$$

It is also sometimes written as:

$$a^2 + b^2 = c^2$$

If one leg is 2 and the other leg is 3, then:

$$2^2 + 3^2 = c^2$$

This is where your knowledge of squares and square roots will really come in handy.

QUADRILATERALS

A quadrilateral has four sides. The perimeter of a quadrilateral (or any polygon) is the sum of the lengths of its sides.

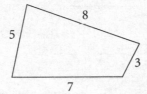

The perimeter of the quadrilateral in the figure above is: $5 + 8 + 3 + 7 = 23$.

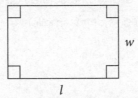

A **rectangle** is a parallelogram containing four right angles. Opposite sides are equal. The formula for the area of a rectangle is: Area = (length)(width), which is sometimes abbreviated as $A = lw$. In the diagram above, l = length and w = width, so area = lw, and perimeter = $2(l + w)$.

A **square** is a rectangle with four equal sides. The formula for the area of a square is: Area = (side)^2. Notice this can also be written as $A = lw$. However, since $l = w$ in a square, you can use the notation s^2.

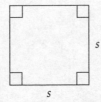

In the diagram above, s = length of a side, so area = s^2, and perimeter = $4s$.

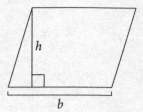

A parallelogram is a quadrilateral with two sets of parallel sides. Opposite sides are equal, as are opposite angles. The formula for the area of a parallelogram is:

$$\text{Area} = (\text{base})(\text{height}) \text{ or } A = bh$$

In the diagram above, h = height and b = base, so you can use the formula $A = bh$.

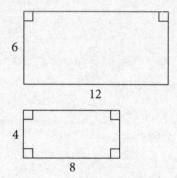

If two rectangles (or squares, since squares are special rectangles) are similar, then the corresponding angles are equal (90 degrees) and corresponding sides are in proportion. In the figures above, the two rectangles are similar because all the angles are right angles, and each side of the larger rectangle is $1\frac{1}{2}$ times the corresponding side of the smaller.

CIRCLES

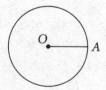

A **circle** is a figure in which each point is an equal distance from its center. In the diagram, O is the center of the circle.

The **radius** (r) of a circle is the direct distance from its center to any point on the circle. All radii of one circle have equal lengths. In the figure above, OA is the radius of circle O.

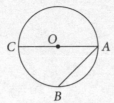

A **chord** is a line segment that connects any two points on a circle. Segments AB and AC are both chords. The largest chord that may be drawn in a circle is the diameter of that circle.

The **diameter** (d) of a circle is a chord that passes through the circle's center. All diameters are the same length and are equal to twice the radius. In the figure above, AC is a diameter of circle O.

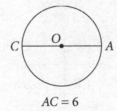

$$AC = 6$$

The **circumference** of a circle is the distance around it. It is equal to πd, or $2\pi r$. In this example, Circumference $= \pi d = 6\pi$.

The **area** of a circle equals π times the square of the radius, or πr^2. In this example, since AC is the diameter, $r = \dfrac{6}{2} = 3$, and area $= \pi r^2 = \pi(3^2) = 9\pi$.

COORDINATE GEOMETRY

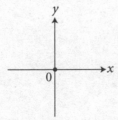

Coordinate geometry has to do with plotting points on a graph. The diagram above represents the coordinate axes—the perpendicular number lines in the coordinate plane. The horizontal line is called the x-axis. The vertical line is called the y-axis. In a coordinate plane, the point O at which the two axes intersect is called the **origin**, or $(0, 0)$.

The pair of numbers, written inside parentheses, specifies the location of a point in the coordinate plane. These are called coordinates. The first number is the *x*-coordinate, and the second number is the *y*-coordinate. The origin is the zero point of both axes, with coordinates $(0, 0)$.

Starting at the origin:

- To the right: *x* is positive.
- To the left: *x* is negative.
- Up: *y* is positive.
- Down: *y* is negative.
- The two axes divide the coordinate plane into four quadrants. When you know what quadrant a point lies in, you know the signs of its coordinates. A point in the upper left quadrant, for example, has a negative *x*-coordinate and a positive *y*-coordinate.

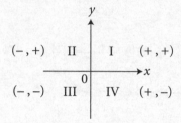

If you were asked the coordinates of a given point, you would start at the origin, count the number of units given to the right or left on the *x*-axis, and then do the same up or down on the *y*-axis.

If you had to plot given points, you would start at the origin, count the number of units given on the *x*-axis, and then on the *y*-axis. To plot $(2, -3)$, for example, you would count two units to the right along the *x*-axis, then three units down along the *y*-axis.

GEOMETRY PRACTICE SET

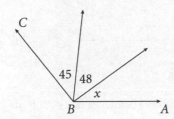

1. If the measure of angle ABC is 145 degrees, what is the value of x?

    (A) 39
    (B) 45
    (C) 52
    (D) 62

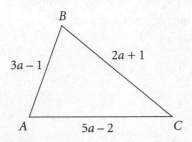

2. If the perimeter of triangle ABC is 28 meters, what is the number of meters in the length of AC?

    (A) 28
    (B) 13
    (C) 10
    (D) 12

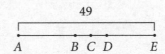

3. In the above diagram, $ABFG$ and $CDEF$ are rectangles, C bisects BF, and EF has a length of 2 cm. What is the area, in cm², of the entire figure?

    (A) 36
    (B) 32
    (C) 16
    (D) 72

4. In the figure above, AB is twice the length of BC, $BC = CD$, and DE is three times the length of CD. If $AE = 49$ cm, what is the length, in cm, of BD?

    (A) 14
    (B) 20
    (C) 22
    (D) 29

5. What is the radius of a circle whose circumference is 18π in?

    (A) 3 in
    (B) 6 in
    (C) 18 in
    (D) 9 in

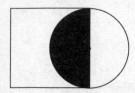

6. A square and a circle are drawn as shown above. The area of the square is 64 in^2. What is the area of the shaded region?

(A) 16π in^2

(B) 8π in^2

(C) 4π in^2

(D) 32π in2

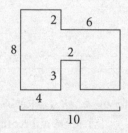

7. What is the area of the polygon above, in square units, if each corner of the polygon is a right angle?

(A) 40

(B) 62

(C) 68

(D) 74

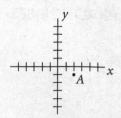

8. What are the coordinates of point A on the graph above?

(A) $(-1, 2)$

(B) $(2, -1)$

(C) $(-2, -1)$

(D) $(-2, 1)$

9. A bicycle rider travels 8 miles due north, then 6 miles due east. How many miles is she from her starting point?

(A) 16

(B) 12

(C) 10

(D) 14

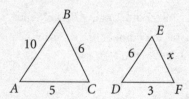

10. If triangle ABC is similar to triangle DEF, then $EF =$

(A) 6

(B) 3.6

(C) 4.1

(D) 5

ANSWERS AND EXPLANATIONS

1. C

This is a simple arithmetic problem if m∠ABC = 145 degrees, then x = 145 – (48 + 45), and x = 145 – 93 = 52 degrees.

2. B

The perimeter of triangle ABC is 28, so $AB + BC + AC$ = 28. Plug in the algebraic expression given for the length of each side in meters:

$$(3a – 1) + (2a + 1) + (5a – 2) = 28$$
$$10a – 2 = 28$$
$$10a = 30$$
$$a = 3$$

The length of AC is represented by the expression $5a – 2$, so $AC = 5(3) – 2 = 13$.

3. A

To find the area of the entire figure, determine the area of each rectangle and add these values together. $ABFG$ has an area of $8 \times 4 = 32$ square units.

$CDEF$ has a length of 2, and since C bisects BF which = 4, $CDEF$ also has a width of 2. In other words, it is a special type of rectangle, a square. If you eyeballed the diagram, rather than doing the math, you probably would not have arrived at the correct value. Remember, diagrams are not drawn to scale. The area of $CDEF$ then is $2^2 = 4$ square cm.

The area of the entire figure = 32 + 4 = 36 square cm.

4. A

Remember, don't rely on the diagrams, they are not drawn to scale. To solve this problem, set up an algebraic equation.

Let $BC = x$. AB is twice the length of BC, so it can be represented by $2x$. $BC = CD$, so $CD = x$. DE is three times the length of CD, or $3x$. Since $AE = 49$, $2x + x + x + 3x = 49$, $7x = 49$ and $x = 7$. BD is composed of segments BC and CD, so its length is $7 + 7 = 14$ units.

5. D

Circumference of a circle = $2\pi r$, where r is the radius of the circle. So, a circle with a circumference of 18π has a radius of $\frac{18\pi}{2\pi} = 9$ in.

6. B

The shaded region represents half the area of the circle. Find the length of the radius to determine this area. Notice that the diameter of the circle is equal to a side of the square. Since the area of the square is 64 in², it has a side length of 8 in. So, the diameter of the circle is 8, and its radius is 4. The area of a circle is πr^2, where r is the radius, so the area of this circle is $\pi(4)^2 = 16\pi$ in². This isn't the answer though; the shaded region is only half the circle, so its area is 8π in².

7. B

Think of the figure as a rectangle with two rectangular bites taken out of it. Sketch in lines to make one large rectangle as shown below.

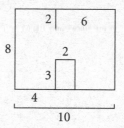

The area of a rectangle is length times width. If we call the length of the large rectangle 10, then its width is 8, so its area is $10 \times 8 = 80$ square units. The rectangle missing from the top right corner has dimensions of 6 and 2, so its area is $6 \times 2 = 12$ square units. The rectangle missing from the bottom has dimensions of 2 and 3, so its area is $2 \times 3 = 6$ square units. To find the area of the polygon, subtract the areas of the two missing shapes from the area of the large rectangle: $80 – (12 + 6) = 80 – 18 = 62$ square units, choice (B).

8. B

When giving coordinates, give the *x*-coordinate first, and then the *y*-coordinate second. Point *A* lies at 2 on the *x*-axis and –1 on the *y*-axis. Therefore, (2, –1) is correct.

9. C

This is a geometry word problem. If you draw the path with the directions provided, you'll see a right triangle. The question is asking you how many miles the rider is from her starting point, or the hypotenuse of the triangle. Use the formula $(\text{leg}_1)^2 + (\text{leg}_2)^2 = (\text{hypotenuse})^2$.

The legs are 8 and 6, so $8^2 + 6^2 = 64 + 36 = 100 = (\text{hypotenuse})^2$. $\sqrt{100} = 10$. The rider is 10 miles from her starting point.

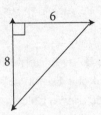

10. B

Since the triangles are similar, set up a proportion to solve for the unknown side.

$$\frac{10}{6} = \frac{6}{x}$$
$$10x = 36$$
$$x = \frac{36}{10} = 3.6$$

Tables, Charts, Graphs, and Maps

You are likely to see some type of table, chart, graph, or map on the COOP or HSPT; they will definitely appear on the TACHS. You will have to use information from these graphics to solve accompanying questions.

Keep in mind that no matter which type of graphic you see, labels or keys must be given to identify the material. By carefully reading the labels, we can understand what information is contained and in what manner it is organized. A table, chart, or graph is a visual way of organizing information.

In this chapter, we will review various types of tables, charts, and graphs and then give you a systematic approach to answering the questions that are associated with them. Even if you feel familiar with graphic representations, you should read the material below. Be sure to do the practice set at the end of the chapter.

LINE GRAPHS

A line graph presents information by plotting points on an *xy* coordinate system, then connecting them with a line. Because you can plot more than one line, a line graph is widely used to communicate relationships. Also, since the lines clearly indicate rising or decreasing trends, a line graph is a great way to show growth or decline trends.

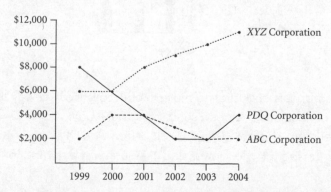

Notice that the previous graph is not titled. Charts, tables, and graphs may not have titles. However, we can use the information found on the *x*- and *y*-axes to decode or make sense of the graph. The *x*-axis is labeled 1999–2004. Therefore, each marking represents one year from 1999 to 2004. The *y*-axis is marked in units of increasing dollar value. Each unit going up the *y*-axis increases $2,000 dollars. The lines themselves are labeled *ABC* Corporation, *PDQ* Corporation, and *XYZ* Corporation. Therefore, we can see the dollar amount of each company at a particular point in time during the period of 1999–2004. A line connects these points to show an upward, or downward trend.

Though the individual charts may not be titled, the accompanying question will help you identify what the material is.

BAR GRAPHS

A bar graph is also called a histogram or histograph. In it, numerical values are shown in bars of varying length. This type of graph is also a good, clear way to show comparisons.

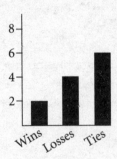

The bar graph above labels the various bars on the *x*-axis "wins," "losses," or "ties." The *y*-axis shows units of 2. This bar graph represents the numerical value of a team's wins, losses, and ties. See how far each vertical bar extends on the *y*-axis. The bar representing wins is at the 2 unit; the team has two wins. The bar representing losses is at 4 units; the team has four losses. The bar representing ties is at 6 units; the team has six ties.

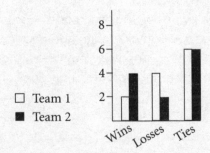

A bar graph has the added benefit of illustrating multiple comparisons in a way that is still visually clear. The previous bar graph includes a second set of bars. These bars, the shaded bars, represent the performance of another team. By placing the two sets of bars side by side, we can easily see that Team 2 won more games than Team 1, it lost fewer, and it tied the same number of games.

A bar graph can be vertical or horizontal. Decode it the same way you would a line graph, by reading the labels on the *x*- and *y*-axes which tell what the bars represent and the value of the units given.

PICTOGRAPHS

A pictograph uses simple drawings to depict quantities.

Each truck = 1,000 vehicles

Pictographs can make a point vividly, but they work best when a large number of items is being shown. The key at the bottom lets us know that each truck represents 1,000 vehicles. Imagine if we really wanted to draw all 1,000 of them!

TABLES

Tables compare information in rows and columns. Because information appears side by side, tables are a good way to present detailed information to compare.

	Mon	Tues	Wed	Thurs	Fri
New York	70°	72°	65°	71°	80°
Boston	65°	70°	60°	63°	72°
L.A.	81°	82°	85°	80°	80°
Miami	80°	85°	86°	81°	84°

Labels in the far left column and on the top row will identify the information in the table. The left column in the table above, for example, contains the names of cities. The top row is labeled with days of the week. Let's say you were looking for the temperature in New York on Thursday. You would find the row labeled New York and the column labeled Thursday. The box that aligns with these two axes gives you the temperature in New York on Thursday, 71 degrees.

Tables may also use pictures rather than numbers. Either way, when you are looking for information in a table, find the row corresponding to the information you are looking for. Then, read across and find the vertical column that corresponds to the second detail you are looking for. The box at which these details meet will give you your data.

PIE CHARTS

A pie chart is a circle cut into parts. You can think of it as showing the pieces of a pie or how the pie is divided. Thus, a pie chart is a good chart to use when showing the distribution of a whole, or into which parts a whole is divided. On a pie chart, the portions or pieces of the pie will be labeled. The labels will explain what the different sections represent and the percentage of the whole each section comprises.

NOTE: The whole pie always equals 100%. That does not mean that the numbers shown in a pie chart will equal 100. However, you should think of a pie chart as 100% with each section representing a part (percentage) of the whole.

The pie chart above shows the various after-school activities of students in a class. The whole pie represents the whole class. As the labels indicate, 40% of the students participate in sports, 40% participate in the drama club, and 20% participate in the band.

While pie charts are a great way to show how a whole is divided, they can be difficult to use if the pie is divided into sections that are too small. The following pie chart shows an example of when NOT to use a pie chart. It is meant to show the after-school activities of an entire class, but breaking the sections down into such small pieces makes the chart difficult to use.

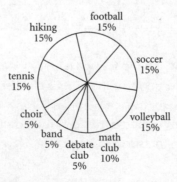

VENN DIAGRAMS

A Venn diagram uses circles to represent groups, but unlike a pie chart, a Venn diagram contains more than one intersecting circle. The place where the circles intersect shows elements or characteristics shared by the various wholes.

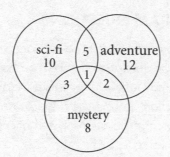

The Venn diagram above shows how many students in a class at Rosewood High read various types of fiction. The number 10 in the sci-fi circle indicates that ten students read only science fiction. Twelve students read only adventure novels. Eight students read only mysteries. Where the science fiction and adventure circles intersect, the number 5 indicates that five students read both science fiction and adventure novels. The number 3 where the mystery and science fiction circles intersect indicates that three students read both types of fiction.

MAPS

Don't worry, no one is going to ask you for complicated directions to the corner store. Reading maps on the tests will be relatively simple. Actually, maps may more likely resemble a coordinate graph than a road map. We will review coordinates first, and then provide some additional map basics just in case.

Coordinates

Coordinates are given according to x- and y-axes. The x-axis runs horizontally (across) and the y-axis runs vertically (up and down). The point where the axes meet is called the origin. Going right along the x-axis from the origin, numbers are positive and increase incrementally. Going left along the x-axis from the origin, numbers are negative and decrease incrementally. Going up along the y-axis from the origin, numbers are positive. Going down along the y-axis, numbers are negative. When giving coordinates, state the x-axis coordinate first and the y-axis coordinate second.

Reading Directions

Directions on a map are always as follows:

north

northwest northeast

west east

southwest southeast

south

HOW TO APPROACH DIAGRAM QUESTIONS

The tables, charts, and graphs you have just reviewed are valuable ways to organize information, which will help you in everyday life. But, remember we have a goal here—preparing for the COOP, TACHS, or HSPT. So, while you may take your time examining a table, chart, graph, or map you encounter in everyday life, it's important to approach these materials a little differently on test day. You have to stay on track and approach questions systematically to win the maximum number of points. The Kaplan Method will help you do that.

Kaplan's 3-Step Method for Diagram Questions

Step 1. Read the question.
Step 2. Decode the diagram.
Step 3. Find the answer.

Step 1—Read the Question

It may seem obvious, but the point here is not to spend any time examining the chart, graph, or table until you read the question. Think of the information in a diagram as detail questions on the Reading Comprehension section. It doesn't make sense to spend too much time reviewing all the details until you know what the questions are asking.

For example:

The diagram above shows the safety habits of a group of 60 skateboarders. How many of the group always wear their helmets?

An essential element of reading the question includes reading exactly what the diagram illustrates. In the example above, we are told that the pie chart shows the **safety habits** of a group of **60 skateboarders**. The size of the group is important information you may chose to circle or underline.

Naturally, the other important part of reading the question is determining what the question asks. This question asks how many of the group (the 60 total) always wear their helmets.

Step 2—Decode the Diagram

Now that you have read the question and know what you are looking for, refer to the diagram. Use the labels provided to decode it.

This pie chart is divided into sections, each labeled with a percent amount and titled *always wear helmet, often wear, wear infrequently, never wear.* Thus, the sections represent how often the group of 60 skateboarders wear their helmets.

Step 3—Find the Answer

Now that we know what we are looking for and what the diagram means, we can look for the relevant information within the diagram and do any calculations necessary. Remember we want to know how many of the group always wear their helmets. The diagram shows a section labeled 60% as always wearing their helmets. We need a number, so we must convert the 60% into a number of skateboarders. 60% of 60 = 0.60 x 60 = 36. Look for an answer choice that matches.

Let's use Kaplan's 3-Step Method to answer the question below.

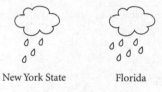

New York State   Florida

1 raindrop = 2 inches of rain

The diagram above shows the average annual rainfall of two states. What is the annual average rainfall in Florida?

Step 1—Read the Question

What is the question asking for? The annual average rainfall in Florida.

Step 2—Decode the Diagram

The information before the question explains that the diagram represents the average annual rainfall of two states. The key at the bottom of the diagram tells us that one raindrop represents two inches of rainfall. If you don't read the key, you won't arrive at the correct answer.

Step 3—Find the Answer

The question asks the annual average rainfall in Florida. There are six raindrops in the picture and we are told that each one represents two inches of rain. 6 x 2 = 12, so an average of 12 inches of rain fell in Florida. Look for the answer choice that matches.

The Best Way to Show Information

Some questions may ask you which is the best way to present information. Remember that certain types of tables, graphs, and charts lend themselves best to certain kinds of information.

Line Graphs: good for showing upward or downward trends over time
Bar Graphs: good for showing comparisons
Pie Charts: good for showing how a whole is divided into various parts
Venn Diagrams: good for showing how information intersects, or what is in common
Pictographs: good for large amounts, graphically showing large differences
Coordinate Graphs and Maps: good for showing location
Tables: good for large amounts of data and for comparison

Despite the pros and cons of various diagrams, the best way to present information is always the clearest and simplest way! When evaluating various diagrams and deciding which best presents certain information, be sure to look at the labels provided. A good diagram will be clearly labeled to help the reader decode its information.

Look at this example:

Which of the following diagrams is the best way to compare various types of tables, charts, and graphs?

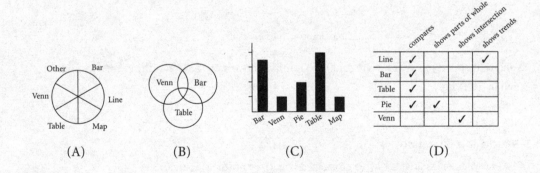

(A)   (B)   (C)   (D)

(A), though it divides the pie into parts, doesn't *compare* the various types of diagrams. It doesn't answer the question!

(B) shows various types of diagrams intersecting, but again, it doesn't do anything to *compare* them.

Though bar graphs can be a good way to illustrate comparisons, choice (C) is not a good one since the *y*-axis contains no information to help us decode the chart. Why are some bars higher than others? What value does the *y*-axis represent? We don't know. Therefore, it's not a good chart.

Choice (D) clearly labels the rows and columns of the table. The rows represent the various types of diagrams and the columns represent their characteristics. The checkmarks show in which area each diagram is successful. This is the best way to compare the various diagrams because it is clearest. (D) is the correct answer.

TABLES, CHARTS, GRAPHS, AND MAPS PRACTICE SET

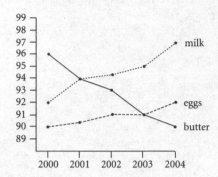

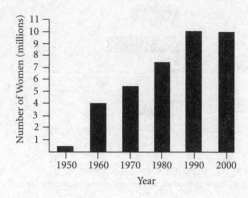

1. The graph above shows the price of milk and eggs between 2000–2004. What is the price of eggs in 2002?

    (A) 91 cents
    (B) 92 cents
    (C) 90 cents
    (D) 93 cents

2. What is the difference between the price of milk in 2004 and the price of milk in 2000?

    (A) 2 cents
    (B) 4 cents
    (C) 5 cents
    (D) 6 cents

3. The diagram above shows the number of women in the workplace in the years 1950–2000.

    Which year experienced the greatest increase of women in the workplace?

    (A) 1960
    (B) 1950
    (C) 2000
    (D) 2010

Answer question 4 based on the table below.

Price of Different Tickets on Different Airlines

	First Class	Business Class	Economy Class
Happy Air	$301	$252	$108
Jet Stream Airways	$309	$250	$99
Lucky Travel Airline	$357	$312	$89

4. How much does a business class ticket cost on Lucky Travel Airline?

    (A) $357
    (B) $312
    (C) $99
    (D) $108

5. Examine the graph and find the best answer.

    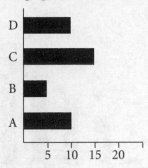

    (A) D plus A are greater than C plus B.

    (B) A plus B equals C.

    (C) A and D are less than C and A.

    (D) B is greater than A.

6. The pie chart below shows the lunch orders of a group of 150 junior high school students. How many students ordered lasagna?

    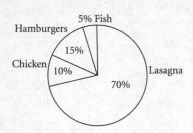

    (A) 70

    (B) 105

    (C) 100

    (D) 95

Answer question 7 based on the Venn diagram below, which shows three categories involving the children of Garden Village.

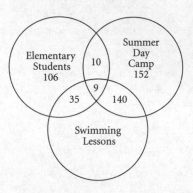

7. According to the diagram, how many children are attending summer day camp only?

    (A) 9

    (B) 10

    (C) 140

    (D) 152

8. The diagram below represents students who take the bus to school in three school districts.

    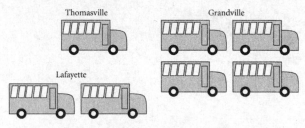

    Each bus = 54 students

    How many students take the bus in Grandville?

    (A) 54

    (B) 216

    (C) 200

    (D) 108

9. At what coordinates is the location of the rowboat?

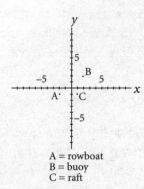

A = rowboat
B = buoy
C = raft

(A) (−2, −1)
(B) (2, 1)
(C) (−1, 2)
(D) (2, −1)

10. The map below shows a seating arrangement.

	A	B	C
1	Inessa	Tom	Geoff
2	Susan	Victoria	Don
3	Tori	Aarthi	Evan

Where is Tori seated?

(A) 1C
(B) 2B
(C) 2A
(D) 3A

ANSWERS AND EXPLANATIONS

1. A

Locate the line that shows the price of eggs, then find 2002 on the x-axis. Then, locate the coordinate on the y-axis, the price value where the line representing eggs is in 2002. It falls at 91 cents.

2. C

Locate the price of milk in 2000 on the y-axis. It is 92 cents. Then locate the price of milk in 2004. It is at 97 cents on the y-axis. The price of milk has gone up 5 cents.

3. A

The height at which the vertical bars reach on the y-axis represents the number of women in the workplace at a given year in millions. In order to find the year in which there was the greatest increase of women in the workplace, look for the greatest leap between the previous bar and the next. The bar at 1950 is at less than one million, while the bar at 1960 shows a dramatic rise to the four million mark. Therefore, the year 1960 experienced the greatest increase of women in the workplace. Choice (A) is the correct answer.

4. B

Find the row labeled Lucky Travel Airline. Read across until you reach the corresponding column labeled business class. The box that aligns with these two labels will give you the price of a business class ticket on Lucky Airlines. It is $312, choice (B).

5. B

Don't be put off by the fact that this bar graph is arranged horizontally. Read it as you would any other bar graph, identifying the values at which each bar falls. Bar A is at the 10 mark. Bar B is at the 5 mark. Bar C is at the 15 mark, and bar D is at the 10 mark. Add the various combinations in the answer choices until you arrive at the correct answer. A + B = C; 10 + 5 = 15.

6. B

First, find the percent of students in the pie chart who ordered lasagna: 70%. Since there are 150 students in the whole group, 70% of 150 ordered lasagna; 0.7 x 150 = 105.

7. D

Read the labels on the various circles that make up the Venn diagram. The one to the right is labeled Summer Day Camp. That entire circle comprises all the children who are attending summer day camp. The number in the portion of the circle that does not intersect with any other is 152. That is the number of children who are attending summer day camp only.

8. B

There are four buses under the label Grandville. The key indicates that each bus represents 54 students; 54 × 4 students take the bus to Grandville = 216 students.

9. A

The key indicates that point A represents the row boat. Locate point A on the graph, then note its coordinates, giving the x-coordinate first and the y-coordinate second. Point A, the rowboat, is at (−2, −1) on the graph.

10. D

Locate the name Tori on the chart. Note which row and column it falls under. It is in column A, row 3. Thus, answer choice (D) is the correct answer.

chapter thirteen

Quantitative Reasoning

The Quantitative Reasoning test on the COOP is different from mathematics sections you will see on other tests. It's intended to test your reasoning ability, rather than learned math skills, so it has several special question types. Though they might seem strange at first, the more you practice, the more comfortable you'll feel. Because you have to switch gears rapidly in the time you are allotted for this section, it is important to have a clear grasp of what each of the various question types requires you to do. We'll review each of them here and give you some techniques for answering these question types.

The 20 Quantitative Reasoning questions are made up of three question types. Since the COOP changes from year to year, the breakdown may be slightly different in the year that you take the exam. At the time of printing, the section breaks down as follows:

- Number relationships—questions 1–6
- Visual problems—questions 7–13
- Symbol relationships—questions 14–20

NUMBER RELATIONSHIPS

The instructions for number relationship questions instruct you to find the relationship between the two numbers in an expression. You'll see three expressions. Arrows point from a number on the left to a blank box, then to a number on the right. The final set in the column has a blank at the end. You have to decide what number should go in the blank.

$3 \rightarrow \square \rightarrow 7$ (A) 5

$5 \rightarrow \square \rightarrow 9$ (B) 6

$1 \rightarrow \square \rightarrow \_\_$ (C) 10

(D) 4

To find the answer, look at each expression and think about what operation was performed on the number on the left to arrive at the number on the right. Because it is possible for more than one relationship or operation to fit in the missing box, always be sure to test your assumption on all the examples given.

$$3 + 4 = 7$$
$$5 + 4 = 9$$

The pattern is +4. Therefore, to find the missing number, add 4 to 1; 1 + 4 = 5. The correct answer is choice (A), 5.

KAPLAN TIP

Be sure to work ACROSS from left to right, not up and down, when you are looking for the pattern.

Look at this example:

$$2 \rightarrow \boxed{} \rightarrow 4$$

$$3 \rightarrow \boxed{} \rightarrow 6$$

$$5 \rightarrow \boxed{} \rightarrow \underline{}$$

Look at the first row of numbers: 2 and 4. The operation being performed could be +2 or ×2. Note this, then look at the next row of numbers: 3 and 6; 3 × 2 = 6. The pattern is ×2, rather than +2. The number that belongs in the blank is 5 × 2, or 10.

When you approach number relationship questions, work through all the examples and predict the answer before reading the answer choices. This will help keep you from falling for trick answers or becoming confused.

VISUAL PROBLEMS

These problems ask you to look at a shaded shape and determine how much of the whole is shaded. Basically, they are asking you to express a fraction of a whole. The key to doing well on this question type is taking the time to actually count the shaded and unshaded sections that make up the whole.

Look at this example:

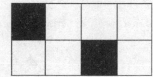

(A) $\dfrac{2}{6}$

(B) $\dfrac{1}{2}$

(C) $\dfrac{1}{4}$

(D) 2

The rectangle is sectioned into 8 equal squares. Two are shaded and 6 are not. In other words 2 out of 8 are shaded. This can be expressed as a fraction thus: $\dfrac{2}{8}$. Reduced, $\dfrac{2}{8} = \dfrac{1}{4}$. The correct answer is $\dfrac{1}{4}$, or choice (C).

Notice how the incorrect answers assume that you have made a mistake in counting either the total number of sections or the number of sections that are shaded. Choice (A) puts the shaded portion, 2, over the amount that are not shaded, 6, rather than the whole, which is 8.

You could rule out choice (B) since you can easily see that less than $\dfrac{1}{2}$ of the whole is shaded.

Choice (D) is incorrect because it fails to put the number of shaded squares as a numerator above the number of sections in the whole.

Sometimes in visual problems you may find that you will have to create lines to divide a whole into equal parts so that you can count them. Doing this will help you work quickly and accurately.

In the drawing above, the square is sectioned into four equal smaller squares. A triangular region of one of these squares is shaded. The triangular region is $\dfrac{1}{2}$ of one square. Because the other three square regions are not divided in this way, you may be tricked into counting the shaded portion or the whole incorrectly. To avoid this, divide the other three square regions in half as well.

By making all the sections the same, you can more easily count the sections that make up the whole: there are 8. How many are shaded? 1 of 8, or $\dfrac{1}{8}$.

SYMBOL RELATIONSHIPS

Symbol relationship questions use symbols or drawings of objects—such as cones or cubes—in place of numbers. A scale shows how many of each of the symbols equal one another.

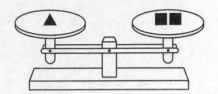

(A) ▲▲   ■

(B) ▲■   ▲■■■

(C) ▲▲■■   ▲▲▲

(D) ▲■■   ▲■

Because the scale is balanced by one cone on the left and two cubes on the right, we can read it as: 1 cone = 2 cubes.

Your job is to find the set of shapes from the answer choices that could also balance the scale. The easiest way to do this is to convert the symbols in each answer choice to either all cones or all cubes.

See how we've done this with the answer choices:

(A) ■■■■ (4)   1   4 cubes (1 cone = 2 cubes) ≠ 1 cube
    ▲▲   ■

(B) ■■ (2 + 1)   ■■ (2 + 2)   2 cubes (1 cone = 2 cubes) + 1 cube ≠
    ▲■   ▲■■   2 cubes (1 cone = 2 cubes) + 2 cubes

(C) ■■■■ (4 + 2) = ■■■■■■ (6)   4 cubes (1 cone = 2 cubes) + 2 cubes =
    ▲▲■■   ▲▲   6 cubes (1 cone = 2 cubes)

(D) ■■ (2 + 2)   ■■ (2 + 1)   2 cubes (1 cone = 2 cubes) + 2 cubes ≠
    ▲■■   ▲■   2 cubes (1 cone = 2 cubes) + 1 cube

It doesn't matter whether you make the answer choices all cones or all cubes, but it is important to be consistent. Here's an example where we've changed all the symbols to cones.

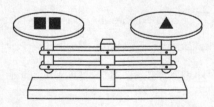

(A) 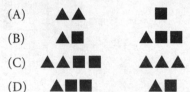 (2) = ■▲▲ (2)

(B) ■▲▲ (3)   ▲■■ (2)

(C) ▲ (1½)   ▲■■▲ (2½)

(D) ▲▲▲ (3½)   ▲ ▲ (2)
    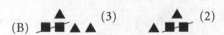

By changing all the cubes to cones, we realize:

A: 1 cone (2 cubes = 1 cone) + 1 cone = 2 cones. This is the correct answer.

B: 1 cone (2 cubes = 1 cone) + 2 cones ≠ 1 cone + 1 cone (2 cubes = 1 cone)

C: $\frac{1}{2}$ cone (if 2 cubes = 1 cone, then 1 cube = $\frac{1}{2}$ cone) + 1 cone ≠ 1 cone (2 cubes = 1 cone)

+ $\frac{1}{2}$ cone (1 cube = $\frac{1}{2}$ cone) + 1 cone

D: $\frac{1}{2}$ cone (2 cubes = 1 cone, 1 cube = $\frac{1}{2}$ cone) + 3 cones ≠ 2 cones (2 cubes = 1 cone)

This method will help you work through symbol relationship problems efficiently and accurately. No matter how simple a symbol relationship question may look, it is better to take the time and work through answer choices in this way; in the end you'll save time you otherwise may waste if you try to answer by eyeballing the scale and moving on to the answer choices without a clear plan of action.

QUANTITATIVE REASONING PRACTICE SET

Directions: For questions 1–4, find the relationship of the numbers in the left column to the numbers in the right column. Choose the number that should replace the blank.

1. 172 → ☐ → 167

    58 → ☐ → 53

    47 → ☐ → __

43	42	40	44
(A)	(B)	(C)	(D)

2. 20 → ☐ → 38

    10 → ☐ → 18

    9 → ☐ → __

22	18	16	20
(A)	(B)	(C)	(D)

3. 99 → ☐ → 91

    7 → ☐ → −1

    12 → ☐ → __

0	4	5	−2
(A)	(B)	(C)	(D)

4. 4 → ☐ → 12

    9 → ☐ → 27

    1 → ☐ → __

9	3	42	4
(A)	(B)	(C)	(D)

Directions: For questions 5–8, find the fraction of the grid that is shaded.

5.

(A) $\frac{1}{6}$

(B) $\frac{1}{4}$

(C) $\frac{1}{8}$

(D) $\frac{1}{10}$

6.

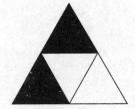

(A) $\frac{1}{4}$

(B) $\frac{2}{5}$

(C) $\frac{2}{3}$

(D) $\frac{1}{2}$

7.

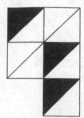

(A) $\frac{5}{10}$

(B) $\frac{3}{5}$

(C) $\frac{3}{10}$

(D) $\frac{4}{10}$

8.

(A) $\frac{1}{2}$

(B) $\frac{1}{50}$

(C) $\frac{10}{100}$

(D) $\frac{100}{100}$

Directions: For questions 9–10, the scale shows sets of shapes of equal weight. Find a pair of sets that would also balance the scale.

9.

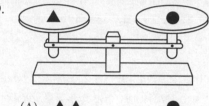

(A) ▲▲   ●

(B) ▲   ●●

(C) ▲▲▲   ●● ●●

(D) ▲▲▲   ●●●

10.

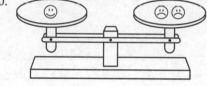

(A) ☺☺☹   ☹☹☹

(B) ☺☹☹   ☺☺

(C) ☺☹☹   ☺☺☺

(D) ☺☺☺   ☹☹☹☹

ANSWERS AND EXPLANATIONS

1. B

The number in the right column is 5 less than the number in the left hand column. The relationship is –5. The missing number = 47 – 5 = 42.

2. C

The number in the right column is 2 less than twice the number in the left hand column. The relationship is to multiply the term by 2, and then subtract 2. The missing number = (9 × 2) – 2 = 18 – 2 = 16.

3. B

The number in the right column is 8 less than the number in the left hand column. The relationship is –8. The missing number = 12 – 8 = 4.

4. B

The number in the right column is 3 times the number in the left column. In the final row, if 1 is the number on the left, then 3 is the number on the right.

5. C

Count the total pieces of the circle and count the number of pieces shaded. There are 8 pieces and 1 is shaded; 1 part of 8 is shaded, or $\frac{1}{8}$.

6. D

Count the total pieces of the triangle and count the number of pieces shaded. There are 4 pieces and 2 are shaded; 2 parts of 4 are shaded, or $\frac{2}{4}$, which reduces to $\frac{1}{2}$.

7. C

Count the total pieces of the diagram and count the number of pieces shaded. There are 10 pieces and 3 are shaded; 3 parts of 10 are shaded, or $\frac{3}{10}$.

8. A

Count the total pieces of the circle and count the number of pieces shaded. There are 2 pieces and 1 is shaded; 1 part of 2 is shaded, or $\frac{1}{2}$.

9. D

The diagram shows that one triangle equals one circle. Therefore, three triangles must equal three circles.

10. B

1 smile = 2 frowns; thus, 1 smile + 2 frowns = 2 smiles.

chapter fourteen

Reasoning Skills

Naturally, all question types on the COOP, TACHS, or HSPT require you to use your reasoning skills. Not only do you need to have a good command of mathematics, geometry, algebra, and verbal skills, you also need to be able to work through questions methodically.

We have covered nearly every question type in the previous chapters, but there are a few more question types we have yet to review. These questions fall outside or between the bounds of the subject areas we have covered already. These are Reasoning Skills questions.

Reasoning Skills questions include:

1. Sequence questions—on the COOP, in some TACHS Ability questions, and in the Mathematics section of the HSPT
2. Logic questions—on both the COOP and the HSPT
3. Essential element questions—on the COOP and in some TACHS Ability questions
4. Picture analogy questions—on the COOP only
5. Verbal sequence questions—on the COOP only
6. Ability questions—on the TACHS only

What do these six question types have in common? They each test your reasoning ability. You may find the question types challenging or strange at first. However, working through this chapter and the practice set at the end will help you become accustomed to them. Try to approach them as something fun, a puzzle that needs to be solved, or a code that needs to be cracked.

QUESTION TYPE 1—SEQUENCE

A sequence is a logical arrangement of objects, numbers, or letters.

Sequence questions, the first subtest on the COOP, are also similar to most of the TACHS Ability questions. You will also see one special type of sequence question, the number series question, on the Mathematics section of the HSPT.

Here are some examples of sequence questions:

			_____

·			⊢	⊤
(A)	(B)	(C)	(D)

aB	bC	dE	_____

(A) fG
(B) FG
(C) Gh
(D) eF

What is the next number in the following series:
44, 21, 20, 9, 8, …

(A) 6
(B) 4
(C) 3
(D) 5

Your job is to figure out the logic behind the arrangement of the items and select an answer choice that completes the sequence.

How do you do that?

Kaplan's 3-Step Method for Sequence Questions
Step 1. Examine the building blocks and define the sequence.
Step 2. Predict the answer.
Step 3. Select the answer choice that best fits your prediction.

Step 1—Examine the Building Blocks and Define the Sequence
Stay focused and remember that there always IS a relationship, an arrangement, a movement, or a progression of some sort between the items.

Figure out the progression by adding on one building block at a time.

1. Examine each building block by itself.
2. Examine the relationship or movement from one building block to the next.

Don't try to define the progression until you have worked through each of the building blocks given. Look at the first example question to see how this is done.

Sequence Type 1—Picture Sequence Questions

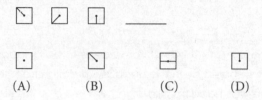

Look carefully at the first building block of the sequence:

Your definition doesn't have to be a complete sentence, just something to help you bring the picture into focus. Your definition might be "square with dot in center, line from dot to top corner." Now, look at the next building block of the sequence:

It's a "square with dot in center, line from dot to bottom corner." Now, define this as it relates to the first building block. The building blocks of the sequence are made up of a square with a dot in the center and a line drawn from that dot to a corner of the square.

But wait! If you try to define your pattern now, you will be in trouble. According to your definition, the third building block should also contain a square with a line drawn from a dot in the center to a corner of the square. However, that is not the case. What happened?

Don't give up on breaking the code, and don't define the code until you have reached the end of the items given. Look carefully at the third square. What can you say about it by itself? In the third building block of the pattern, the line drawn from the dot in the center of the square is drawn to the center of the base, NOT to a corner.

So, you have recognized several important things about the sequence.

- Each item has a square with a dot in the center.
- A line is drawn from the dot in the center to some point of the square's perimeter.
- In each subsequent building block of the pattern, the line is drawn to a different place than in the previous one.

By analyzing each building block of the pattern separately, and then comparing each block to the one that went before it, you defined the pattern.

Marking up the test booklet might help you do this more easily.

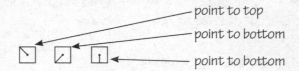

Step 2—Predict the Answer

If we were to continue the pattern, what would we have next? The next item needs to be a square with a point in the middle. The line drawn from the point should be in the opposite direction from the previous square. Since in the previous square the line was heading down, in this next one it needs to be heading up.

Now that you have a clear idea of what the correct answer should look like, you are ready for Step 3.

Step 3—Select the Answer Choice That Best Fits Your Prediction

Look at the answer choices again.

There it is. Choice (D) matches your prediction. It's the right answer. But ... what if no choice exactly matches your prediction? You have got to redefine, refocus, broaden, or narrow your prediction.

What if these were the answer choices?

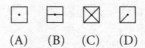

None of these choices has a line drawn from the dot, up. Choice (A) has a dot in the center but no line. In choice (B) the line is too long. Choice (C) has two lines that cross. However, the fourth one still does have a line drawn from the center dot of the square. The line, like those in the rest of the pattern is short. Choice (D) still best fits the prediction you made.

 KAPLAN TIP

Look out for common patterns. The direction of lines, shapes, sizes, shading, and more or less detail are often elements of picture sequence patterns.

Common Patterns to Look For

Doing well on picture sequence questions has a lot to do with your powers of observation. Take your time, focus, and look for the details that make one building block different from the next. Some common differences to watch out for are:

Direction of lines: Does one piece of the diagram point up, down, or sideways? Do pieces of the pattern point in opposite directions?

Shapes and size of shapes: Is the pattern made up of squares, circles, or other shapes? Do the shapes increase or decrease in size?

Shading: Are portions of the building blocks shaded? Is the shading increasing or decreasing as you progress through the sequence?

Increasing or decreasing detail: Does each subsequent building block have more or less detail than the one before it?

TACH3 "changes" questions offer two figures, the second a changed version of the first. A third figure is presented, and the answer choice will be a version of that figure that is changed in the same way as figure 2 was changed from figure 1.

Directions: The second figure shows a particular change from the first figure. The third figure, if changed in the same way, will become which of the answer choices?

(J)

(K)

(L)

(M)

(N)

(M) is the correct choice. Although only two figures are given to demonstrate the sequence, these questions test basically the same skills, and the same Kaplan Method applies. Take your time and work step-by-step.

Step 1: The first figure is an open triangle, the second is a black triangle with a small white triangle in the center. That's about all.

Step 2: So we can predict that the new figure, an open circle, will be changed to black with a small figure at its center. We don't know whether the small, inscribed figure will be a triangle, or whether a triangle was inscribed in a triangle but a circle will be inscribed in a circle.

Step 3: Only one choice fits our pattern, a black circle with a small white triangle in the center.

The common variations in these ability questions are similar to those in the picture sequence questions.

Sequence Type 2—Alphabet Sequence Questions

The same techniques you have just learned and practiced for picture sequence questions also apply to alphabet sequence questions. (We have called this question type alphabet sequence, but you might also see letters of the alphabet mixed in with numbers.)

Let's take the example from the beginning of this chapter to work through.

aB   bC   dE   _____

(A) fG
(B) FG
(C) Gh
(D) eF

Step 1—Examine the Building Blocks and Define the Sequence

Look carefully at the first building block of the sequence: aB. Define it. Your definition might be "lowercase letter, capital of next letter."

Look at the next building block of the sequence: bC. Again you have "lowercase letter, capital of next letter." Now, define this as it relates to the first building block. The first letter in the pair moved up one letter of the alphabet from *a* to *b*. The second letter also moved up a letter in the alphabet from *B* to *C*. It seems as though the building blocks of the sequence are made up of two letters, a lowercase letter, followed by a capital letter. And each subsequent pair begins with the second letter of the previous pair.

If you tried to define your pattern now though, you would be wrong. According to our definition, we expect the next pair to be cD. But the third building block is NOT cD, it is dE. Remember, don't define the code until you have reached the end of the three items given.

Okay, we have to look at the third item given, dE. What can we say about it by itself? Well, dE is made up of a lowercase letter followed by a capital of the next letter of the alphabet.

Now that we have defined the pair, see how it relates to the previous item, bC. Instead of the first letter being THE SAME as the second letter of the previous pair, it is the NEXT letter. The first letter doesn't start with a lowercase c, it starts with a d. The pattern then is: firstSECOND secondTHIRD fourthFIFTH, or two alike and one different.

Marking up the test booklet might help you do this more easily.

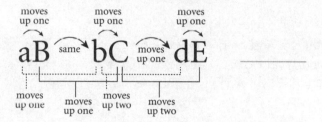

Step 2—Predict the Answer

If you continue the pattern, what would you have next?

The next pair needs to return to the "move up one" beginning of the pattern. Keep in mind that the pattern just completed itself with dE, so you know you need to return to the beginning of the formula—in which the first letter of the subsequent pair is the same as the second letter of the previous pair. dE should be followed by the next capital letter in the alphabet. So, you move from dE to eF.

Step 3—Select the Answer Choice That Best Fits Your Prediction

Of the choices provided, choice (D) fits your prediction.

(A) fG
(B) FG
(C) Gh
(D) eF

This was a not a particularly obvious sequence, but it does illustrate a couple of important points to remember when you approach alphabet sequence problems.

Look for Common Patterns

There is only so much the test makers can do with the letters of the alphabet.

Look out for movement or changes in:

1. **Letters going up or down:** Does the pattern move toward Z? As in PQR … or does it move toward A as in LKJIH?
2. **Lowercase vs. capital letters:** BdBB, BDbb, BDBb, etc.
3. **Patterns that skip letters:** A C E G (skips one letter) or A D G J (skips two), etc.
4. **Letters with numbers thrown in:** a1 b2 c3 $A^1B^2C^3$ AB3 BC2 CD1

Analyze these the way you would any other pattern: examine the details in the building blocks and look for changes as the sequence progresses.

Be Tenacious

Know that there IS a pattern. Analyze one building block at a time. Then, examine the movement from one block to another, trying to see what the difference between them is. Do this for every piece of the pattern. Use all the pieces given to you. Then, define the pattern.

Know Your Alphabet

It may seem obvious, but the only way to find the pattern in an alphabet item is to know the alphabet inside out. If you find yourself getting confused, or just don't see it, write out the alphabet at the top of your test booklet. There is nothing wrong with having a clear list to refer to.

If You Are Stumped, Eliminate Wrong Choices and Guess

Let's say you did your best to define the pattern, and you just aren't clear on what it is. Maybe in the previous example you recognized that each of the first letters of the pair started with a lowercase letter followed by a capital letter. But the difference between the second and third building block confused you.

Don't give up. Use the information to eliminate clearly incorrect choices. Remember, you know the next pair has to start with a lowercase letter.

aB   bC   dE   _____

(A) fG

(B) FG

(C) Gh

(D) eF

Right off the bat you can rule out (B) and (C) since they begin with capital letters. Take your best guess from the remaining choices. By eliminating two of the answer choices, you have greatly improved the odds of choosing the correct one.

Defining the building blocks of each pattern and examining the relationship between them is essential to solving sequence items. Let's practice a bit with both skills. Then, we will apply Kaplan's 3-Step Method.

Now that we have practiced with picture and letter sequences, there is one more type of sequence question to cover.

Sequence Type 3—Numerical Sequence/Series

On the COOP, numerical sequence items look like this:

37   11   2   6   10   8   12   ___

You will also see series questions on the Mathematics section of the HSPT. They are mixed in with the rest of the mathematical questions and they look like this:

What is the next number in the series: 2, 5, 8, 11…

On both tests, each question will be followed by four answer choices.

Though the question formats on each exam look slightly different, the idea is basically the same. You need to come up with a missing number using the pattern established by the numbers given. How do you do that?

Kaplan's 3-Step Method for Numerical Sequence and Series Questions

Step 1. Define the pattern.
Step 2. Predict the answer.
Step 3. Find an answer choice that fits your prediction.

Step 1—Define the Pattern

The nice thing about numerical sequence questions is that you already recognize the building blocks of the pattern—numbers. You know that in order to make a pattern from one building block—one number—to the next, some mathematical procedure had to be performed on the first number. It was either added to, subtracted from, multiplied by, or divided by some other number.

How do you find the operation that was performed to create the pattern? Compare each subsequent number to the one before it.

Let's see how this works, using the first example. The sequence given is:

3   7   11   2   6   10   8   12   ___

1. Compare the first and second numbers given. What is the relationship between 3 and 7? 7 is 4 more than 3. What operation has been performed to the first number? +4

2. Compare the second and third numbers: What is the relationship between 7 and 11? 11 is 4 more than 3. Aha! A pattern of +4 emerges.

But wait, you're not finished yet.

3. Verify your pattern by checking the second group given. Treat this set as a completely different entity. Examine it by itself, *not in relation to the first set!* That is, don't look for any connection between the 3 in the first set and the 2 in the second. This is not the way sequence items are set up.

Okay, look at 2, 6, and 10. Look at them with an open mind, and go through the comparison process once more.

1. Compare the first and second numbers given. What is the relationship between 2 and 6? 6 is 4 more than 2. What operation has been performed to the first number? +4

2. Compare the second and third number. What is the relationship between 6 and 10? 10 is 4 more than 6. Our pattern of +4 applies here as well.

Now, we can say with confidence that the pattern is +4. However, you must still check this out using the pieces of the third pattern given to you. What is the relationship between 8 and 12? 12 is 4 more than 8; +4 is indeed our pattern.

Step 2—Predict the Answer

Now that you have uncovered the pattern (+4), the operation that makes up the series, on to the missing number in the last set. $8 + 4 = 12$, and $12 + 4 = 16$. The next number in the set or series must be 16.

Step 3—Find an Answer Choice That Fits Your Prediction

Review the answer choices. Which one best fits your prediction?

3   7   11   2   6   10   8   12   ___

(A) 16
(B) 14
(C) 10
(D) 11

Choice (A) is the correct answer. You got it; fill in the answer bubble on your answer sheet and move on. There is no need to read through the rest of the answers and allow yourself to be distracted or confused by them.

On the other hand, *do* be careful when performing arithmetical operations. Use the blank space in your answer booklet to work through the equation. You don't want to rush, do the math incorrectly in your head, and accidentally come up with a wrong answer.

Common Patterns

Since only so many mathematical procedures can be performed with numbers, you will see certain common patterns on the COOP or HSPT. Being familiar with these should help you recognize the pattern more quickly: +, −, ×, or ÷.

Strange Patterns

A few additional mathematical operations that may lead to strange patterns are operations performed using the number 1, or the square root and square of a number.

1   1   1   2   4   8   3   9   ___

Can you figure out the pattern? Compare the first and second number in the first set; 1 and 1. These appear to be the same number. Hmm... This is strange. Compare the second and third number in the first set; 1 and 1. Again, these appear to be the same number. Could the pattern be made up of repeating numbers? Look at the next set given before you can determine your pattern. Compare the first and second number in the second set. 2 and 4; 2 + 2 is 4, or 2 × 2 is 4.

Compare the second and third number in the first set. 4 and 8; 8 is 4 plus 4, or 4 × 2. Since the pattern has to be the same, we look for some procedure the movements have in common. That is ×2. The pattern looks to be ×2.

Yet, a pattern of ×2 certainly didn't apply to the first grouping of the set. Move on to the third set and examine it for a pattern. Compare the first and second numbers in the second set; 3 and 9; 9 is the first number, 3, multiplied by itself.

This is an important clue that can help you refocus your understanding of the pattern; 3 was multiplied by itself. So was 2, the first number of the second set. Therefore, you can say that the pattern is the first number multiplied by itself. Second number, again, multiplied by the first. Now our 1, 1, 1 makes sense; 1 times itself is 1. Times itself again is still 1.

When the Blank Is in the Middle

Sometimes the missing number will be in the middle of a series, like this:

3   6   12   2   4   8   5   ___   20

(A) 10
(B) 12
(C) 8
(D) 2

The same rules apply. Compare the first and second numbers of the first pattern, 3 and 6; 6 is 3×2.

Compare the second and third numbers of the first pattern, 6 and 12; 12 is 6×2.

Compare the first and second numbers of the next pattern, 2 and 4; 4 is 2×2.

Compare the second and third numbers of the next pattern, 4 and 8; 8 is 4×2.

Apply the pattern to the missing number, and check it, working backward. $5 \times 2 = 10$. Does $10 \times 2 = 20$? Yes. The pattern is correct.

In fact, it doesn't matter where the missing number is in the pattern. Examine the building blocks of each complete pattern first. Find the relationship between each preceding number and the one that follows it. Apply that operation to the missing number.

Double Operation Patterns

Series questions may contain double operation patterns, where the pattern may seem to be more than one operation. This is where the importance of examining each subsequent step in the sequence is really essential. Look at this example:

What is the next number in the set 1, 2, 4, 5, 10, ...

Compare the first and second numbers, 1 to 2, and you realize that the second number is one more than the first. Write down +1. Compare 2 and 4 and you realize that 4 is the second number +2, or ×2. Could be either. Write both down.

At this point, your analytical ability and your patience really come into play. You might be asking yourself is the pattern +1, ×2, or +2? Rather than becoming frustrated, or annoyed, stay focused. Think of yourself as a detective. Your job is to remain skeptical and examine all the evidence before you jump to any conclusions.

Continue examining the series. The next number in the series is 5; 5 is one more than 4. Write down +1 again.

Don't stop yet. Use all the numbers given to you before you try to define the pattern. The next number in the series is 10; 10 is the previous number, 5, × 2. Look at all your observations. +1, ×2, +1, ×2.

Aha! The pattern is +1, ×2. What is the next number in the series? You just finished with ×2, the next procedure needs to be +1; 10 + 1 = 11. That's your answer.

Look Out for Combination Patterns

If the operation being performed isn't immediately obvious, suspect a combination pattern. Use the empty space in your test booklet to quickly write down relationships. This will help you stay focused, especially on series questions that use combination patterns.

Work Backward to Verify Missing Numbers in the Middle of a Sequence

Rather than finding the next number in a series, you may be asked to find a number missing from the middle of a series. In this case, you need to work backward.

What is the missing number in the set: 8, 10, ____, 8, 4, 6

Compare the first and second numbers: 10 is two more than 8. Write down +2.

The next number is missing, so move on and continue comparing numbers that are given to you.

Compare the fourth and fifth numbers in the set: 8 and 4; 4 is 8 – 4. Write down –4.

Compare the sixth and seventh numbers in the set: 4 and 6; 6 is two more than 4. Write down +2. So, the pattern is +2, –4, +2, –4.

The first and second numbers, 8 and 10, contain the +2, –4, +2, –4 element of the pattern; therefore, the next operation should be –4; 10 – 4 = 6. The missing number is 6. You got it.

QUESTION TYPE 2—LOGIC

You have worked through the various types of sequence questions and you are thinking methodically, skeptically, step-by-step. You are relying on evidence, rather than jumping to conclusions. These skills are essential in approaching our next question type—logic questions.

Logic questions are short statements that require you to reach a logical conclusion. You will find them mixed in with the rest of the Verbal Reasoning questions—synonyms, antonyms, analogies, and verbal classification—on the HSPT. On the COOP, these questions will appear on the Verbal Reasoning subtest, in a group by themselves.

On the HSPT, logic questions are followed by three choices. They are the only question type of the test with three rather than four choices. They look like this:

> Amy runs faster than Pete. Pete runs faster than Jack. Amy runs faster than Jack. If the first two statements are true, the third is
>
> (A) true
> (B) false
> (C) uncertain

On the COOP, logic questions are followed by four choices. The statements themselves may be two sentences, or they could be longer. Here's an example:

> The Grand Canyon is in Arizona. Mark has visited the Grand Canyon.
>
> (A) Mark has been in Arizona.
> (B) Mark is from Arizona.
> (C) Mark's family likes to take road trips.
> (D) The Grand Canyon is the largest canyon in the world.

Just the Facts

The key to solving logic questions is relying on the facts. Faulty logic and incorrect answer choices make use of unfounded assumptions.

Approach logic questions with...

Kaplan's 3-Step Method for Logic Questions

Step 1. Read the statement for facts.
Step 2. Think about what the facts *are* and *are not* telling you.
Step 3. Predict the correct answer choice.

Step 1—Read the Statement for Facts

Because a logical deduction is based on facts, not assumptions, it is important to be able to tell what elements of each logic statement are indeed FACTS.

A FACT is something that exists. A fact is real or true.

> Fact: The Grand Canyon is located in Arizona.
> Fact: Ann runs faster than Jack.
> Fact: The Declaration of Independence was signed in 1776.
> Opinions, desires, assumptions are NOT FACTS.

Now that we are clear on this, read the following statement and underline the facts.

> Katherine is the best violinist in the orchestra. Suzie plays cello.

You should have underlined both sentences. Both are statements of fact.

Step 2—Think About What The Facts *Are* and *Are Not* Telling You

What do the facts tell us?

- Katherine plays violin.
- Katherine is the best violin player in the orchestra.
- Suzie plays cello.

Notice also the information you are not given.

- Whether Suzie is a good cellist
- Whether Suzie and Katherine play together
- Whether Suzie and Katherine are friends, relatives, or even know each other

What else don't we know about Suzie and Katherine? We don't know what color hair they have, how old they are, or where they live … the list could go on and on.

If the example about Katherine and Suzie was a logic question on the HSPT, a third statement would follow the first two. The third statement tests your understanding of the first two. It would look like this:

> Katherine is the best violinist in the orchestra. Suzie plays cello. Katherine is a better musician than Suzie. If the first two statements are true, the third is

(A) true
(B) false
(C) uncertain

Notice that the previous example *does not* say that the third statement is true. Rather, it asks you to decide whether or not it could be true if the first two statements are true. In other words, take the first two statements as fact. Then, based on those facts, decide whether or not the third statement could be proven true or false. If you don't have enough information to go on, select choice (C), uncertain.

Step 3—Predict the Correct Answer Choice

We already figured out that all we know for certain is that Katherine plays violin the best, and Suzie plays cello.

So, do we have enough information to say whether or not Katherine is a better musician than Suzie? We don't! The answer is uncertain, choice (C).

Sometimes it can become difficult to see the connection between facts if a lot of information is given to you. Diagrams can help you visualize the connection, or the lack of one. For example:

> Bread is more expensive than rice, but less expensive than tuna. Rice is more expensive than beans, but less expensive than potatoes. Tuna is more expensive than rice. If the first two statements are true, the third is
>
> (A) true
> (B) false
> (C) uncertain

A question like this becomes a lot clearer if you plot it out. According to the first statement: bread > rice, and tuna > bread. Combine these two statements into one: tuna > bread > rice. According to the second statement: potatoes > rice > beans. Add this to the first statement and we see that: tuna > bread ≥ potatoes > rice > beans.

Notice how bread is greater than or equal to potatoes. Although you know that bread is more expensive than rice and potatoes are more expensive than rice, you don't know the value of these items in relation to one another.

Finally, in the third statement, you are told that tuna is more expensive than rice. Is that true? Based on the information in the first two statements, is tuna more expensive than rice?

> tuna > bread ≥ potatoes > rice > beans

Yes! It is. The third statement is true.

Now that we have a method in place for evaluating facts, let's examine some common logic questions and some important traps to avoid. To illustrate our point, we will draw examples from COOP format questions.

Logic Type 1—Category

One type of logic question might ask you to base your conclusion on whether or not an item fits into the category defined. Decide which one is correct based only on the information provided.

> Bees are attracted to bright flowers. Terry has a bouquet of yellow roses in a vase by her window.
>
> (A) Bees will fly into Terry's window.
> (B) Terry's favorite flowers are yellow roses.
> (C) Yellow roses are wildflowers.
> (D) Bees are attracted to yellow roses.

Remember our method. First read the statements and think about what the facts do and do not tell us.

The facts tell us:	They do not tell us:
• Bees are attracted to bright flowers.	• What color Terry's vase is
• Terry has a vase of yellow roses by her window.	• If the window is open
• Terry is a female; the pronoun *she* is used to describe her.	• What season it is
• Terry has a window.	• Whether or not there are bees outside of Terry's window
	• Where Terry lives

Which answer choice is the only conclusion we can make based just on the facts? Choice (D). Since yellow roses fall into the category of bright flowers, bees must be attracted to them.

Read each answer choice carefully before you select one based just on the facts given in the statements.

Logic Type 2—Cause/Effect

Another type of question you might see in the logic sections is cause and effect reasoning.

One thing and only one thing must be the cause of an effect in order for the cause/effect relationship to be logical. *Facts*, not feelings, have to bear out the cause/effect relationship.

Here's an example of a cause/effect question. Read the statements; think of what the facts do and do not tell us. Then evaluate each answer choice.

> Mr. Brown usually drinks coffee every morning. Today Mr. Brown hasn't had his coffee and he has a headache.
>
> (A) Mr. Brown is drinking tea instead of coffee.
> (B) Mr. Brown isn't feeling well.
> (C) Mr. Brown is quitting drinking coffee.
> (D) Coffee gives Mr. Brown a headache.

Can we say that Mr. Brown is drinking tea instead of coffee? Not based on the information given.

Can we say that Mr. Brown isn't feeling well? Yes, the facts state that he has a headache.

Can we say that Mr. Brown is quitting drinking coffee? Not based on the statements given. We were not told the reason he missed his morning cup. Maybe he was just running late.

Can we say coffee gives Mr. Brown a headache? Today he *hasn't* had his coffee and he *does have a headache*. This choice doesn't make sense.

The only choice we know is true based on the facts is (B), Mr. Brown isn't feeling well.

Logic Type 3—All/Some/Most

Solving this logic question type hinges on carefully attending to the use of the words *all*, *some*, or *most*. Here's an example:

> Most people require between seven and ten hours of sleep each night. Joe slept four hours last night.
>
> (A) Joe is sick.
> (B) Something was bothering Joe.
> (C) Joe has more energy than others.
> (D) Joe did not sleep much last night.

Examining the facts of the statement we know that *most people* require a certain number of hours sleep. *Most people* is not everyone. Some people require less sleep, and some people require more.

The fact that Joe slept four hours only proves that Joe slept little. It does not say anything about his energy as compared with others or the reason he slept so little or even that he is sick today. Here's another example:

> All yurps warble. Blue yurps fly. Blue yurps fly and warble. If the first two statements are true, the third is
>
> (A) true
> (B) false
> (C) uncertain

The first statement said that *all yurps warble*, the second that *blue yurps fly*. Therefore, the third statement *blue yurps fly and warble* must be true since the group of *all yurps* includes blue yurps. On a question like this, you might find it helpful to draw a diagram:

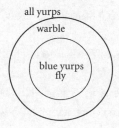

Four Traps to Avoid

Drawing sound logical conclusions depends on the facts and just the facts. Make sure you read and understand the facts before attempting to draw any conclusion. Quickly sketching a diagram may help you keep your facts straight. Know the limits of what the facts tell you and beware of these common traps.

Trap 1—Character Assumption

Don't select answer choices that make assumptions about a person or group not stated in the question.

> Thomas accepted a part-time job as a receptionist in the afternoons. Unfortunately, he lost the first telephone call that he tried to transfer to his boss. When the person called back and Thomas tried to transfer the call again, again he lost it and disconnected the caller.
>
> (A) Thomas's telephone is broken.
> (B) Thomas's boss will be angry with him.
> (C) Thomas is having trouble connecting calls.
> (D) Thomas should get another job.

The only thing we know for certain is that Thomas is having trouble connecting calls; he lost two of them. Thus, the answer is (C). We cannot speculate on the emotions of his boss, nor do we know whether or not his telephone is broken. Perhaps Thomas's performance will improve in time; he need not get another job yet.

Trap 2—Too Much Information

Some statements may deliberately try to throw you off the track by including too much information.

> The Dixon family eats dinner together three nights a week. On Monday night, Mrs. Dixon has pizza delivered from the Italian restaurant on Main Street. On Tuesday night, Joe Dixon makes hotdogs. On Wednesday night, the Dixons belong to a family bowling team.
>
> (A) The Dixons eat dinner together Monday, Tuesday, and Wednesday.
> (B) The Dixons are good bowlers.
> (C) Joe Dixon eats alone on Tuesday night.
> (D) There is an Italian restaurant on Main Street.

Despite all the information, we don't know which nights the Dixons eat together. Mrs. Dixon could eat the pizza all by herself. Joe Dixon, likewise, could be cooking for one. Do the Dixons eat at the bowling alley together on Wednesday? We don't know. Don't be distracted by the amount of information given. The only thing we know for sure is that (D) there is an Italian restaurant on Main Street. How do we know? It delivers pizza to Mrs. Dixon on Monday night!

Trap 3—No Relationship

This trap could also be called the "not enough information" trap. Although a lot of details are given, it is possible you still might not have enough information to draw a conclusion relating two distinct people or groups. Here's an example of a question that uses this trap.

> Danika is faster than Julio. Maribel is faster than Tanya. Danika is faster than Maribel. If the first two statements are true, the third is

    (A)   true

    (B)   false

    (C)   uncertain

Sketch a diagram to help you keep the facts straight. Remember, the first two statements are given, the third is in question.

The facts tell us: D > J, and M > T.

Notice that there is no relationship or point of comparison given between the two different pairs. Based only on the information provided, we can't say whether Danika is faster than Maribel. The third statement is (C), uncertain.

Trap 4—Using Previous Knowledge to Answer a Question

While it is important to rely on facts, you can rely only on the facts you are given in the question. For example, read the following question:

> Sacramento is in California. Albert has been to Sacramento.

    (A)   Sacramento is the capital of California.

    (B)   Albert has been to California.

    (C)   San Francisco is a city in California.

    (D)   Albert loved Sacramento.

You might be tempted to choose (A) or (C) because they are facts. However, although these statements are true, they cannot be determined based only on the information given in the first two statements. You should NOT use previous knowledge to answer these questions. Remember, they are testing your ability to reason. In this example, the correct answer is (B).

You will have a chance to practice with all these types of logic questions at the end of this chapter. We still have a few more Reasoning questions to review.

QUESTION TYPE 3—ESSENTIAL ELEMENT

Essential element questions appear on the COOP. The directions instruct you to find the essential element or necessary part of an underlined word. Each underlined word is followed by four answer choices. For example:

<u>cookie</u>

(A) sweet
(B) round
(C) chocolate
(D) snack

If you look at the answer choices, you will notice that all of them have something to do with a cookie. Remember, the question isn't asking which answer is vaguely related to the underlined word. The question is asking what is the *essential element* or *necessary part of* the underlined word. How do you approach this question type then?

Kaplan's 3-Step Method for Essential Element Questions

Step 1. Define the word or identify the common element.
Step 2. Find the answer choice that fits best.
Step 3. If no choice fits, think of other definitions for the word and go through the choices again.

Step 1—Define the Word or Identify the Common Element

The words in essential element questions will usually be words you know. Defining the word means asking yourself: "What makes a cookie a cookie?"

What is the one thing that makes a cookie a cookie and nothing else? *Cookies are sweet.*

Step 2—Find the Answer Choice That Fits Best

Now that you have a sense of what makes a cookie a cookie and nothing else, you are ready to look at the answer choices. Happily, choice (A) fits your definition.

Step 3—If No Choice Fits, Think of Other Definitions (or Common Elements) and Go Through the Choices Again

Let's try another example to illustrate Step 3.

<u>tool</u>

(A) hammer
(B) twist
(C) assist
(D) break

First, define what makes a tool a tool. Let's say the word *tool* immediately made you think of a crowbar, a screwdriver, or a wrench. If so, your definition of a tool: *it helps you open.*

You would go to the answer choices and look for the word *open.* However, *open* is not among the answer choices. Since no choice fits your definition, you would have to think of other definitions of the word.

We have to rethink what makes a tool a tool and nothing else. A hammer is a tool. So is a telephone. So is a car. Many, many things are tools. What do all of these things have in common? They *help people* accomplish tasks. So, our definition of the word tool becomes *something that helps.*

Go back to the answer choices and look for a choice that fits our refocused definition. Choice (C), *assist*, is closest to *help*. That's it!

Watch Out for Traps!

Wrong answers will be concerned with one part, one expression, one situation, or one possible use of the word in question, rather than what makes it what it is. Avoid this trap by zeroing in on what makes this thing unique. What does it do? What is it used for? What makes it special or different from anything else?

TACHS Ability "pattern" questions ask you to recognize a rule or principle shown in three figures. Your job is to analyze the pattern and select the choice that would continue the pattern.

Directions: The first three figures in each question are alike in certain ways. Choose the answer that goes with them.

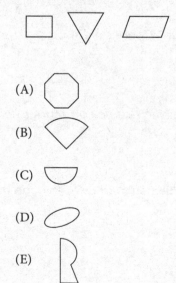

(A) is the correct answer choice. As you can see, these Ability questions are essential element questions using pictures instead of words. So apply the same steps.

Step 1: Though the three original figures are different shapes and have different internal angles, they are all made up of straight lines.

Step 2: Only choice (A) consists only of straight lines. The other choices all have at least one curved side.

No need for Step 3 in this case, but if your first attempt didn't eliminate all but one of the choices, you would go back and look for another essential element of the three figures and try again.

Common features to consider in these Ability questions are shape, shading, number of sides, lines, inscribed figures.

QUESTION TYPE 4—PICTURE ANALOGY

Twenty picture analogy questions make up the second subtest of the COOP. (You won't find these on the TACHS or HSPT.) They are just like verbal analogy questions, only instead of words, they give you pictures. If you haven't done so yet, be sure to work through the analogy section in the Verbal Skills chapter; it will help you understand how analogies work. All the techniques discussed apply to picture analogy questions as well.

A picture analogy question looks like this:

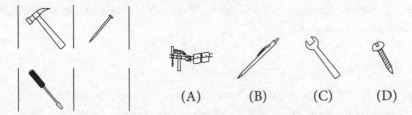

(A)   (B)   (C)   (D)

Your job is to find the item that creates the same relationship in the bottom row as the two pictures in the top row have.

Remember, time is of the essence. Don't waste time gazing at the pictures. DO look at them carefully, and make sure you are clear about what the picture represents. Naming the object to yourself, in your head, is a helpful way to keep focused. It is important to note exactly what the picture is and not embellish it, elaborate on it, or add anything to it that is not there.

Once you have noted what the picture is, you are ready to solve the picture analogy question. Work systematically using the Kaplan Method.

Kaplan's 3-Step Method for Picture Analogy Questions

Step 1. Build a bridge.

Step 2. Predict your answer choice and select an answer.

Step 3. Adjust your bridge if necessary.

Step 1—Build a Bridge

Your first job is to build a bridge or a link between the pictures in the question.

In the example, you have a hammer and a nail. How are these items connected? Well, you could say a hammer bangs a nail into place. That's your bridge.

Step 2—Predict Your Answer Choice and Select an Answer

Now we can use this bridge to predict an answer choice for the missing item. We said the first item, the hammer, bangs the second one into place. So ... we use this bridge in the bottom row: A screwdriver bangs a _____ into place. Well, a screwdriver doesn't bang anything, so right away we know we have to move to Step 3.

Step 3—Adjust Your Bridge if Necessary

Since our bridge was a bit too specific, let's adjust it. Rather than bang, lets say a hammer is used to put a nail in place. Apply the bridge on the bottom to predict the missing word. A screwdriver puts a screw in place.

Now that we have predicted an answer, screw, we can look for the best fit from among the answer choices. Choice (D) fits our prediction. We got it.

Remember these important things about picture analogy questions:

- Read picture analogies ACROSS, not up and down. Connect the items in the top row with a bridge. Then, think of an item that completes the same relationship with the item in the bottom row.
- In every analogy question, there is a strong, definite connection between the two items pictured.
- Try to build a bridge that relates the items to each other by definition.

Avoid the Traps!

Wrong answer choices will often remind you of something related to one of the items pictured. The best way to avoid trap answers is to build a strong, definite bridge. Review classic bridges in chapter 5.

QUESTION TYPE 5—VERBAL SEQUENCE

Verbal sequence questions look like this:

Choose the word that best fits in the blank provided.

warm   hot   _____

(A) scalding

(B) frozen

(C) tepid

(D) toasty

They could also look like this:

Words in the top row are related in some way. Words in the bottom row are related in the same way. Find the word that completes the bottom row.

major	significant	large
minor	trivial	

(A) essential

(B) mediocre

(C) small

(D) miniature

Your job is to find a word for the missing blank that completes the sequence.

As always, working methodically using Kaplan's 3-Step Method will help you hone in on the correct answer choice and avoid incorrect ones.

Kaplan's 3-Step Method for Verbal Sequence Questions

Step 1. Define the sequence.

Step 2. Predict the answer and select the answer choice that best fits.

Step 3. If necessary refocus. If no answer choice or more than one answer choice fits, think of other definitions for the sequence and go through the choices again.

Let's use the first example to demonstrate how this works. Here it is again:

warm   hot   _____

(A) scalding

(B) frozen

(C) tepid

(D) toasty

Step 1—Define the Sequence

To define the sequence, read each word given and notice the direction it is moving in. The second word, *hot*, is greater in temperature than *warm*. We can say the sequence is *getting hotter*.

Step 2—Predict the Answer and Select the Answer Choice That Best Fits

If the sequence is *getting hotter*, what should the next word be? Something that means hotter than hot. Don't worry about choosing a fancy word for your prediction. The important thing is to note that the next word in the sequence has to be very hot.

Now that you have made a prediction, look at the answer choices. Which one fits your prediction *very hot*? Choice (A), *scalding*, is the correct answer.

Step 3—If Necessary Refocus. If NO Answer Choice or More Than One Answer Choice Fits, Think of Other Definitions for the Sequence and Go through the Choices Again.

That example fit our prediction very well. What happens if that's not the case? Let's use a two-row verbal sequence question. Remember, the words in the bottom row have to be related in the same way as the words in the top row.

petal	flower	bouquet
mound	hill	

(A) valley
(B) ditch
(C) mountain
(D) cliff

Define the sequence. A petal is a small piece of a flower, a bouquet is a bunch of flowers. Let's define our sequence, as a *group of*.

Now predict an answer and select an answer choice. You need a word for the blank that completes the sequence below in the same way that the words on the top are related.

Is a hill a *group of* a mound? Not exactly, though hill is a bigger mound. If you continued with the definition *group of*, what could we predict would come next? Something that means a *group of hills*.

Yet, when you go to the answer choices, none of them means *group of hills*. Refocus your definition then. *Bigger* also worked, when you looked at the movement or progression between mound and hill. Try *bigger* in the top row and see if that works. Is a flower *bigger* than a petal? Yes. Is a bouquet *bigger* than a flower? Yes. *Bigger* works as a sequence.

Go back now and predict an answer choice using the sequence definition *bigger*. What's bigger than a hill? A mountain. Look at the answer choices; choice (C) fits your prediction. That's it!

Three Typical Verbal Sequences

Like analogies, there are typical relationships you will find again and again in verbal sequence questions. Being familiar with these will help you work through this question type at an improved pace.

Sequence 1—Degree of

One typical sequence will move from one degree to another. It will either get smaller or less in amount:

tiny	minute	miniscule
mansion	house	shack

Or larger or greater in amount:

large	great	grand
wordy	talkative	garrulous

Sequence 2—Members of a Group

In this type of sequence, the group or category is named.

flower   daisy   rose

The first word of the sequence tells what the group is, and the two words that follow are members of the group.

Sequence 3—Elements of an Unnamed Group

This type of sequence is not a sequence at all. Instead, the words are linked because they belong to the same, unnamed category. These can be tricky because the category is not immediately obvious. You have to figure out what it is.

star	planet	moon: Are all in the sky
winter	spring	summer: Are all seasons

If you are just not getting it...

Get Rid of Trick Answers

You can still improve your odds of choosing the correct answer by eliminating bad answer choices. This works especially well on two-line verbal sequence questions, where bad answer choices will usually relate to the top row rather than to the bottom.

Here's an example:

cleat	boot	slipper
uniform	coat	

(A) robe
(B) sandal
(C) heel
(D) vest

Let's say this question caused you difficulty, and you are running very low on time. Notice that two of the choices relate to shoes, the elements of the top row. These must be incorrect since we are looking to complete the bottom row. Eliminate them.

Now that you have narrowed down your choices to (A) *robe* and (D) *vest*, take your best guess based on the definition you came up with for your sequence.

Did you have trouble defining the sequence because you were uncertain about the meaning of the word *cleat*? Perhaps you guessed that it was a type of shoe because it is in a group with other things you put on your feet. Or maybe you took a hunch since you heard *cleat* in context of a soccer cleat.

In that case, you could say that the sequence moves from something you wear in sports, to something you wear in cold weather, to something you wear at home.

Backsolve

Since the items in a sequence must be related in a strong and definite way, the word that fills in the blank must have a strong, definite relationship to the word that precedes it.

Plug in answer choices and see if they have a strong relationship to the preceding word in the sequence. In the previous example, ask yourself:

- Could a robe be related to a coat? Yes. A robe is a casual coat.
- Could a sandal be related to a coat? No. Neither of these items help define the other.
- Could a heel be related to a coat? No. Neither of these items help define the other.
- Could a vest be related to a coat? No. Although a vest may go under a coat, neither or these items help define the other.

Choice (A) is the only one with a strong and definite relationship to the preceding word in the sequence. Select this answer choice.

Congratulations, COOP and HSPT test takers are done! We just have one question type to cover for the TACHS, then you will have a chance to practice all your skills.

QUESTION TYPE 6—ABILITY QUESTIONS

On the TACHS, the Ability section is intended to assess abstract reasoning ability. As you've seen, the skills used in COOP and HSPT sequence or essential element questions will work for the first two types of Ability questions, which we'll call "pattern" and "changes" questions.

A third type of Ability question shows directions for folding and punching holes in a piece of paper. The correct answer shows how the paper will look when unfolded.

Directions: For each question, you can see in the top row how a square piece of paper is folded and where holes are punched in it. From the bottom row, select the choice that shows how the paper will look when unfolded again.

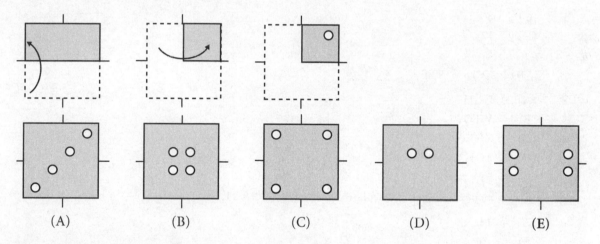

| (A) | (B) | (C) | (D) | (E) |

(C) is right. Once the paper is folded as shown, all four of the corners are together, so a hole punched there goes through all four corners, choice (C).

The general reasoning abilities you've developed with other question types will help. Take your time and work step-by-step. Think of what one level of unfolding will look like before considering the next unfolding. Use your scratch paper and draw the holes in the appropriate place as you think through each fold.

Congratulations!

We have covered a lot of ground in this chapter. Give yourself a big pat on the back for working through some difficult material.

Spend some time revisiting the questions in this chapter that you found most challenging. Review the Kaplan Method for these question types, and go through sample questions and answers again. With each new pass you will find that your pacing and facility will improve.

REASONING SKILLS PRACTICE SET

Directions: For questions 1–3, choose the element that would continue the pattern or sequence.

1. △○ ⊙□ ⊙△ _____

   △○   ⊡⊡   △⊙   □□
   (A)   (B)   (C)   (D)

2. 2   7   9   3   8   10   4 ___ 11
   (A)   6
   (B)   9
   (C)   8
   (D)   12

3. ZAB   XCD   VEF   _____
   (A)   UGH
   (B)   WFG
   (C)   YHI
   (D)   TGH

4. What is the next number in the following series: 9, 7, 10, 8, 11, …

   (A)   13
   (B)   10
   (C)   9
   (D)   11

Directions: For questions 5 and 6, look at the two pictures on top. Then, choose the picture that belongs in the space so that the bottom two pictures are related the same way that the top two are related.

5.

   (A)   (B)   (C)   (D)

6.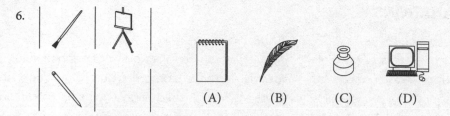

Directions: Read the statement in question 7. Based on the information in the statement, select the answer choice that is true.

7. The bus costs $1.50 for adults and is free for students traveling to school in the morning and returning home from school in the afternoon until 4 P.M. It is now 4:30 P.M. and Karen does not have enough money to take the bus.

   (A)   Karen usually gets home before 3 P.M.
   (B)   Karen is coming home late from school.
   (C)   Karen is a student.
   (D)   Karen has less than $1.50.

Directions: Read the statements and based on the information, select true, false, or uncertain.

8. Elissa has scored more baskets than Tina. Tina has scored more baskets than Gail. Elissa has scored more baskets than Gail. If the first two statements are true, the third is

   (A)   true
   (B)   false
   (C)   uncertain

Directions: For question 9, find the answer choice that names an essential element of the under-lined word.

9. <u>transportation</u>

   (A)   driving
   (B)   commuting
   (C)   sitting
   (D)   paying

Directions: For question 10, find the word that completes the bottom row of words so that it is related in the same way as the words in the top row.

10.
crayon	marker	pen
house	apartment	

   (A)   shutter
   (B)   door
   (C)   cabin
   (D)   cave

ANSWERS AND EXPLANATIONS

1. A

Examine the building blocks of each section that makes up the sequence. The first shape has a hole in the middle of it, and the second one is whole. Notice that the second shape is always different from the first. The shapes are either circles, squares, or triangles. Therefore, the next element in the pattern has to begin with a shape with a hole in it, followed by a circle, triangle, or square. Only choice (A) fits this pattern.

2. B

The pattern is +5, +2. The missing number must be 4 + 5 = 9.

3. D

The first letter of each sequence moves toward A, skipping a letter of the alphabet. Notice that we move from Z to X, having skipped Y. We move from X to V having skipped W. The second and third letters of each sequence move toward Z. AB, CD, EF. The next part of the sequence should move from V to T, skipping U and followed by GH. Writing down the alphabet somewhere in the blank margins of your test booklet would help you map out the sequence and see the skipped letters on a question like this one.

4. C

The pattern is −2, +3. Writing down the progression from one number to the next will help keep you focused and make sure that you don't accidentally perform the wrong operation next. The next number must be 11 − 2 = 9.

5. B

Make sure you are clear on what each picture represents. You have a broom, a dust pan, a mop, and a missing item. Build a bridge between *broom* and *dustpan*. You use a dustpan with a broom to clean. *Use with* is our bridge. Apply it to *mop* to predict an answer. You use a mop with a bucket to clean. Bucket is choice (B). Notice how the incorrect answers are related to cleaning, but do not have the relationship defined by our bridge.

6. A

We have a paintbrush, painter's canvas, and pen. Build a bridge between paintbrush and canvas. You use a paintbrush to perform a task (paint) on a canvas. What do you use with a pen to perform a task? The task is writing, so in order to write, you would also need a piece of paper. Which answer choice best fits our prediction? Choice (A), the notepad, is correct.

7. D

Although we are told the price of riding the bus for adults and students traveling to and from school, no mention is made of Karen's age. Even if Karen is a student, it is after 4 P.M., so she would have to pay $1.50 to ride the bus. All we can tell for certain is that Karen has less that $1.50.

8. A

Draw a diagram or write down the initials of each girl in order of baskets scored to help you see this more clearly.

E > T > G

Since the first two statements are true, the third is true as well according to the order given.

9. B

Before looking at the answer choices, ask yourself what makes this thing special. What defines it? Transportation is the act of *taking people from one place to another*. The answer choice that is closest to our definition is (B) which conveys the idea of traveling. Notice how the incorrect answer choices are things we might associate with transportation, such as driving in a car, sitting on a plane, or even paying a toll. However, they do not define what transportation is—getting from one place to another.

10. C

First, define the sequence in the top row. Crayon, marker, and pen are all types of writing implements. *Types of* is your sequence. Predict an answer choice for the missing element of the bottom row. Houses and apartments are types of homes. The missing word should be another type of home. Choice (C), *cabin*, is the closest to our prediction.

Section 4
Practice Tests

COOP Practice Test 1
Answer Sheet

Remove or photocopy this answer sheet and use it to complete the Practice Test.

Sequences

1. Ⓐ Ⓑ Ⓒ Ⓓ	5. Ⓐ Ⓑ Ⓒ Ⓓ	9. Ⓐ Ⓑ Ⓒ Ⓓ	13. Ⓐ Ⓑ Ⓒ Ⓓ	17. Ⓐ Ⓑ Ⓒ Ⓓ
2. Ⓕ Ⓖ Ⓗ Ⓙ	6. Ⓕ Ⓖ Ⓗ Ⓙ	10. Ⓕ Ⓖ Ⓗ Ⓙ	14. Ⓕ Ⓖ Ⓗ Ⓙ	18. Ⓕ Ⓖ Ⓗ Ⓙ
3. Ⓐ Ⓑ Ⓒ Ⓓ	7. Ⓐ Ⓑ Ⓒ Ⓓ	11. Ⓐ Ⓑ Ⓒ Ⓓ	15. Ⓐ Ⓑ Ⓒ Ⓓ	19. Ⓐ Ⓑ Ⓒ Ⓓ
4. Ⓕ Ⓖ Ⓗ Ⓙ	8. Ⓕ Ⓖ Ⓗ Ⓙ	12. Ⓕ Ⓖ Ⓗ Ⓙ	16. Ⓕ Ⓖ Ⓗ Ⓙ	20. Ⓕ Ⓖ Ⓗ Ⓙ

Analogies

1. Ⓐ Ⓑ Ⓒ Ⓓ	5. Ⓐ Ⓑ Ⓒ Ⓓ	9. Ⓐ Ⓑ Ⓒ Ⓓ	13. Ⓐ Ⓑ Ⓒ Ⓓ	17. Ⓐ Ⓑ Ⓒ Ⓓ
2. Ⓕ Ⓖ Ⓗ Ⓙ	6. Ⓕ Ⓖ Ⓗ Ⓙ	10. Ⓕ Ⓖ Ⓗ Ⓙ	14. Ⓕ Ⓖ Ⓗ Ⓙ	18. Ⓕ Ⓖ Ⓗ Ⓙ
3. Ⓐ Ⓑ Ⓒ Ⓓ	7. Ⓐ Ⓑ Ⓒ Ⓓ	11. Ⓐ Ⓑ Ⓒ Ⓓ	15. Ⓐ Ⓑ Ⓒ Ⓓ	19. Ⓐ Ⓑ Ⓒ Ⓓ
4. Ⓕ Ⓖ Ⓗ Ⓙ	8. Ⓕ Ⓖ Ⓗ Ⓙ	12. Ⓕ Ⓖ Ⓗ Ⓙ	16. Ⓕ Ⓖ Ⓗ Ⓙ	20. Ⓕ Ⓖ Ⓗ Ⓙ

Quantitative Reasoning

1. Ⓐ Ⓑ Ⓒ Ⓓ	5. Ⓐ Ⓑ Ⓒ Ⓓ	9. Ⓐ Ⓑ Ⓒ Ⓓ	13. Ⓐ Ⓑ Ⓒ Ⓓ	17. Ⓐ Ⓑ Ⓒ Ⓓ
2. Ⓕ Ⓖ Ⓗ Ⓙ	6. Ⓕ Ⓖ Ⓗ Ⓙ	10. Ⓕ Ⓖ Ⓗ Ⓙ	14. Ⓕ Ⓖ Ⓗ Ⓙ	18. Ⓕ Ⓖ Ⓗ Ⓙ
3. Ⓐ Ⓑ Ⓒ Ⓓ	7. Ⓐ Ⓑ Ⓒ Ⓓ	11. Ⓐ Ⓑ Ⓒ Ⓓ	15. Ⓐ Ⓑ Ⓒ Ⓓ	19. Ⓐ Ⓑ Ⓒ Ⓓ
4. Ⓕ Ⓖ Ⓗ Ⓙ	8. Ⓕ Ⓖ Ⓗ Ⓙ	12. Ⓕ Ⓖ Ⓗ Ⓙ	16. Ⓕ Ⓖ Ⓗ Ⓙ	20. Ⓕ Ⓖ Ⓗ Ⓙ

Verbal Reasoning—Words

1. Ⓐ Ⓑ Ⓒ Ⓓ	5. Ⓐ Ⓑ Ⓒ Ⓓ	9. Ⓐ Ⓑ Ⓒ Ⓓ	13. Ⓐ Ⓑ Ⓒ Ⓓ	17. Ⓐ Ⓑ Ⓒ Ⓓ
2. Ⓕ Ⓖ Ⓗ Ⓙ	6. Ⓕ Ⓖ Ⓗ Ⓙ	10. Ⓕ Ⓖ Ⓗ Ⓙ	14. Ⓕ Ⓖ Ⓗ Ⓙ	18. Ⓕ Ⓖ Ⓗ Ⓙ
3. Ⓐ Ⓑ Ⓒ Ⓓ	7. Ⓐ Ⓑ Ⓒ Ⓓ	11. Ⓐ Ⓑ Ⓒ Ⓓ	15. Ⓐ Ⓑ Ⓒ Ⓓ	19. Ⓐ Ⓑ Ⓒ Ⓓ
4. Ⓕ Ⓖ Ⓗ Ⓙ	8. Ⓕ Ⓖ Ⓗ Ⓙ	12. Ⓕ Ⓖ Ⓗ Ⓙ	16. Ⓕ Ⓖ Ⓗ Ⓙ	20. Ⓕ Ⓖ Ⓗ Ⓙ

Verbal Reasoning—Context

1. Ⓐ Ⓑ Ⓒ Ⓓ	5. Ⓐ Ⓑ Ⓒ Ⓓ	9. Ⓐ Ⓑ Ⓒ Ⓓ	13. Ⓐ Ⓑ Ⓒ Ⓓ	17. Ⓐ Ⓑ Ⓒ Ⓓ
2. Ⓕ Ⓖ Ⓗ Ⓙ	6. Ⓕ Ⓖ Ⓗ Ⓙ	10. Ⓕ Ⓖ Ⓗ Ⓙ	14. Ⓕ Ⓖ Ⓗ Ⓙ	18. Ⓕ Ⓖ Ⓗ Ⓙ
3. Ⓐ Ⓑ Ⓒ Ⓓ	7. Ⓐ Ⓑ Ⓒ Ⓓ	11. Ⓐ Ⓑ Ⓒ Ⓓ	15. Ⓐ Ⓑ Ⓒ Ⓓ	19. Ⓐ Ⓑ Ⓒ Ⓓ
4. Ⓕ Ⓖ Ⓗ Ⓙ	8. Ⓕ Ⓖ Ⓗ Ⓙ	12. Ⓕ Ⓖ Ⓗ Ⓙ	16. Ⓕ Ⓖ Ⓗ Ⓙ	20. Ⓕ Ⓖ Ⓗ Ⓙ

Reading and Language Arts

1. Ⓐ Ⓑ Ⓒ Ⓓ	9. Ⓐ Ⓑ Ⓒ Ⓓ	17. Ⓐ Ⓑ Ⓒ Ⓓ	25. Ⓐ Ⓑ Ⓒ Ⓓ	33. Ⓐ Ⓑ Ⓒ Ⓓ
2. Ⓕ Ⓖ Ⓗ Ⓙ	10. Ⓕ Ⓖ Ⓗ Ⓙ	18. Ⓕ Ⓖ Ⓗ Ⓙ	26. Ⓕ Ⓖ Ⓗ Ⓙ	34. Ⓕ Ⓖ Ⓗ Ⓙ
3. Ⓐ Ⓑ Ⓒ Ⓓ	11. Ⓐ Ⓑ Ⓒ Ⓓ	19. Ⓐ Ⓑ Ⓒ Ⓓ	27. Ⓐ Ⓑ Ⓒ Ⓓ	35. Ⓐ Ⓑ Ⓒ Ⓓ
4. Ⓕ Ⓖ Ⓗ Ⓙ	12. Ⓕ Ⓖ Ⓗ Ⓙ	20. Ⓕ Ⓖ Ⓗ Ⓙ	28. Ⓕ Ⓖ Ⓗ Ⓙ	36. Ⓕ Ⓖ Ⓗ Ⓙ
5. Ⓐ Ⓑ Ⓒ Ⓓ	13. Ⓐ Ⓑ Ⓒ Ⓓ	21. Ⓐ Ⓑ Ⓒ Ⓓ	29. Ⓐ Ⓑ Ⓒ Ⓓ	37. Ⓐ Ⓑ Ⓒ Ⓓ
6. Ⓕ Ⓖ Ⓗ Ⓙ	14. Ⓕ Ⓖ Ⓗ Ⓙ	22. Ⓕ Ⓖ Ⓗ Ⓙ	30. Ⓕ Ⓖ Ⓗ Ⓙ	38. Ⓕ Ⓖ Ⓗ Ⓙ
7. Ⓐ Ⓑ Ⓒ Ⓓ	15. Ⓐ Ⓑ Ⓒ Ⓓ	23. Ⓐ Ⓑ Ⓒ Ⓓ	31. Ⓐ Ⓑ Ⓒ Ⓓ	39. Ⓐ Ⓑ Ⓒ Ⓓ
8. Ⓕ Ⓖ Ⓗ Ⓙ	16. Ⓕ Ⓖ Ⓗ Ⓙ	24. Ⓕ Ⓖ Ⓗ Ⓙ	32. Ⓕ Ⓖ Ⓗ Ⓙ	40. Ⓕ Ⓖ Ⓗ Ⓙ

Mathematics

1. Ⓐ Ⓑ Ⓒ Ⓓ	9. Ⓐ Ⓑ Ⓒ Ⓓ	17. Ⓐ Ⓑ Ⓒ Ⓓ	25. Ⓐ Ⓑ Ⓒ Ⓓ	33. Ⓐ Ⓑ Ⓒ Ⓓ
2. Ⓕ Ⓖ Ⓗ Ⓙ	10. Ⓕ Ⓖ Ⓗ Ⓙ	18. Ⓕ Ⓖ Ⓗ Ⓙ	26. Ⓕ Ⓖ Ⓗ Ⓙ	34. Ⓕ Ⓖ Ⓗ Ⓙ
3. Ⓐ Ⓑ Ⓒ Ⓓ	11. Ⓐ Ⓑ Ⓒ Ⓓ	19. Ⓐ Ⓑ Ⓒ Ⓓ	27. Ⓐ Ⓑ Ⓒ Ⓓ	35. Ⓐ Ⓑ Ⓒ Ⓓ
4. Ⓕ Ⓖ Ⓗ Ⓙ	12. Ⓕ Ⓖ Ⓗ Ⓙ	20. Ⓕ Ⓖ Ⓗ Ⓙ	28. Ⓕ Ⓖ Ⓗ Ⓙ	36. Ⓕ Ⓖ Ⓗ Ⓙ
5. Ⓐ Ⓑ Ⓒ Ⓓ	13. Ⓐ Ⓑ Ⓒ Ⓓ	21. Ⓐ Ⓑ Ⓒ Ⓓ	29. Ⓐ Ⓑ Ⓒ Ⓓ	37. Ⓐ Ⓑ Ⓒ Ⓓ
6. Ⓕ Ⓖ Ⓗ Ⓙ	14. Ⓕ Ⓖ Ⓗ Ⓙ	22. Ⓕ Ⓖ Ⓗ Ⓙ	30. Ⓕ Ⓖ Ⓗ Ⓙ	38. Ⓕ Ⓖ Ⓗ Ⓙ
7. Ⓐ Ⓑ Ⓒ Ⓓ	15. Ⓐ Ⓑ Ⓒ Ⓓ	23. Ⓐ Ⓑ Ⓒ Ⓓ	31. Ⓐ Ⓑ Ⓒ Ⓓ	39. Ⓐ Ⓑ Ⓒ Ⓓ
8. Ⓕ Ⓖ Ⓗ Ⓙ	16. Ⓕ Ⓖ Ⓗ Ⓙ	24. Ⓕ Ⓖ Ⓗ Ⓙ	32. Ⓕ Ⓖ Ⓗ Ⓙ	40. Ⓕ Ⓖ Ⓗ Ⓙ

TEST 1: SEQUENCES

20 minutes

Directions: For questions 1–20, choose the answer that best continues the sequence.

1.  ↑↓↑↓ ↓↑↓↓ ↑↓↑↓ ___

   ↑↓↑↓   ↓↑↓↓   ↓↑↑↓   ↓↑↑↑
   (A)   (B)   (C)   (D)

2. 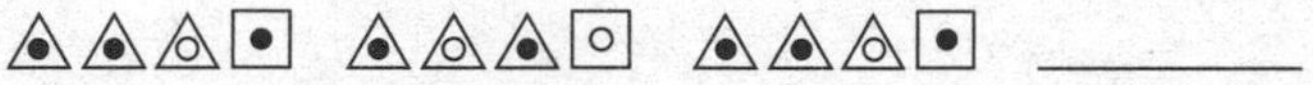 ▲▲Ⓐ▣ ▲▲Ⓐ▢ ▲▲Ⓐ▣ _____

   Ⓐ▲Ⓐ▢   ▲Ⓐ▣▲   ▲Ⓐ▣▢   ▲Ⓐ▲▣
     (F)   (G)   (H)   (J)

3.  ✕✕✕ ✕✕✕ ✕✕✕ ✕✕__

    ✕   ✕   ✕   ✕
   (A)   (B)   (C)   (D)

4.  ☆★★★ ★★★☆ ★★★☆ ☆★★__

    ☆   ★   ★   ☆
   (F)   (G)   (H)   (J)

5.  ⏢△ ⏢△ ⏢△___

   ⏢   ▽   △   ▱
   (A) (B) (C) (D)

6.

(F)   (G)   (H)   (J)

7. 2 5 10   3 7 21   4 9 ___

(A) 13
(B) 36
(C) 27
(D) 5

8. 1 2 6   3 6 18   5 10 ___

(F) 30
(G) 20
(H) 25
(J) 22

9. 100 10 7   64 8 5   49 7 ___

(A) 2
(B) 4
(C) 3
(D) 1

10. 64 51 13   52 40 12   33 22 ___

(F) 11
(G) 9
(H) 5
(J) 10

11. 2 8 0   4 16 8   7 28 ___

(A) 15
(B) 21
(C) 20
(D) 16

12. 6 7 9   8 9 11   12 13 ___

(F) 15
(G) 18
(H) 20
(J) 19

13. 72 67 65   87 82 80   91 86 ___

(A) 79
(B) 82
(C) 84
(D) 80

14. 100 90 25   80 70 20   40 30___

(F) 23
(G) 10
(H) 30
(J) 5

15. A1B0C1   A2B1C2 _____ A4B3C4

(A) A3B2C3
(B) A4B3C3
(C) A3B3C3
(D) A4B4C3

16. $X^1Y^9Z^2$ $X^2Y^7Z^4$ _____ $X^4Y^3Z^8$

(F) $X^3Y^2Z^6$
(G) $X^3Y^3Z^5$
(H) $X^1Y^3Z^4$
(J) $X^3Y^5Z^6$

17. lfg   mgh _____ oij

(A) hgm
(B) nhi
(C) ngh
(D) mhi

18. BxY   cXy   DxY   _____

    (F) ExY
    (G) eXy
    (H) exy
    (J) Dxy

20. ABE   BCF   CDG   _____

    (F) DFG
    (G) DEF
    (H) DFH
    (J) DEH

19. ZAB   YBC   _____   WDE

    (A) WDC
    (B) XCD
    (C) XAE
    (D) XCF

TEST 2: ANALOGIES

20 minutes

Directions: For questions 1–20, look at the two pictures on top. Then, choose the picture that belongs in the space so that the bottom two pictures are related the same way that the top two are related.

1.

    (A)   (B)   (C)   (D)

2.

    (F)   (G)   (H)   (J)

3.

    (A)   (B)   (C)   (D)

4.

(F) (G) (H) (J)

5.

(A) (B) (C) (D)

6.

(F) (G) (H) (J)

7.

(A) (B) (C) (D)

8.

(F) (G) (H) (J)

9.

(A) (B) (C) (D)

10.

(F)　(G)　(H)　(J)

11.

(A)　(B)　(C)　(D)

12.

(F)　(G)　(H)　(J)

13.

(A)　(B)　(C)　(D)

14.

(F)　(G)　(H)　(J)

15.

(A)　(B)　(C)　(D)

16.

(F) (G) (H) (J)

17.

(A) (B) (C) (D)

18.

(F) (G) (H) (J)

19.

(A) (B) (C) (D)

20.

(F) (G) (H) (J)

TEST 3: QUANTITATIVE REASONING

20 minutes

Directions: For questions 1–6, find the relationship of the numbers in the left column to the numbers in the right column. Choose the number that should replace the blank.

1.

3 → ☐ → 9

1 → ☐ → 7

2 → ☐ → —

5	4	8	9
(A)	(B)	(C)	(D)

2.

4 → ☐ → 6

1 → ☐ → 3

5 → ☐ → —

7	5	4	8
(F)	(G)	(H)	(J)

3.

$\frac{1}{2}$ → ☐ → $1\frac{1}{2}$

$\frac{1}{3}$ → ☐ → $1\frac{1}{3}$

2 → ☐ → —

3	$2\frac{1}{4}$	1	$1\frac{1}{2}$
(A)	(B)	(C)	(D)

4.

12 → ☐ → 3

20 → ☐ → 5

8 → ☐ → —

4	2	1	3
(F)	(G)	(H)	(J)

5.

9 → ☐ → 4

4 → ☐ → –1

10 → ☐ → —

–2	4	7	5
(A)	(B)	(C)	(D)

6.

0.5 → ☐ → 0.05

1.0 → ☐ → 0.1

10.0 → ☐ → —

1.0	10	100	0.01
(F)	(G)	(H)	(J)

Directions: For questions 7–13, find the fraction of the grid that is shaded.

7.

(A) $\dfrac{1}{4}$ (B) $\dfrac{1}{8}$ (C) $\dfrac{1}{6}$ (D) $\dfrac{1}{10}$

8.

(F) 2   (G) $\dfrac{1}{16}$ (H) $\dfrac{1}{8}$ (J) $\dfrac{2}{10}$

9.

(A) 1   (B) $\dfrac{1}{4}$ (C) $\dfrac{2}{1}$ (D) $\dfrac{1}{2}$

10.

(F) $\dfrac{1}{8}$ (G) $\dfrac{1}{2}$ (H) $\dfrac{2}{3}$ (J) $\dfrac{1}{4}$

11.

(A) $\dfrac{1}{8}$ (B) $\dfrac{1}{2}$ (C) $\dfrac{3}{8}$ (D) $\dfrac{1}{5}$

12.

(F) $\dfrac{1}{2}$ (G) $\dfrac{1}{3}$ (H) $\dfrac{1}{4}$ (J) $\dfrac{2}{7}$

13.

(A) 2   (B) $\dfrac{2}{3}$ (C) $\dfrac{1}{3}$ (D) $\dfrac{1}{2}$

Directions: For questions 14–20, the scale shows sets of shapes of equal weight. Find a pair of sets that would also balance the scale.

14.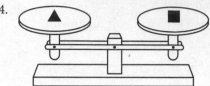

(F)   ▲   ▲■
(G)   ■   ▲▲
(H)   ▲▲   ■
(J)   ▲■   ▲■

15.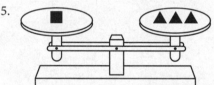

(A)   ▲▲▲   ■■■
(B)   ▲▲▲■   ▲▲▲▲▲▲▲
(C)   ▲▲■   ■■■■
(D)   ▲   ▲■

16.

(F)   ■■   ■▲
(G)   ▲▲■   ▲▲▲
(H)   ▲■   ■▲▲
(J)   ▲▲▲   ▲■

17.

(A) ▲▲   ■■▲
(B) ■■▲   ■■■■■■
(C) ■▲   ▲▲▲
(D) ▲   ■

19.

(A) ■▲▲   ■■
(B) ▲▲▲   ■■
(C) ■■▲   ▲▲■
(D) ▲   ■■

18.

(F) ■   ▲▲
(G) ■■   ■▲▲
(H) ■▲   ▲▲▲▲▲
(J) ■■   ■▲

20.

(F) ■■   ▲■■
(G) ■   ▲▲▲▲▲▲
(H) ▲▲   ▲■■■■
(J) ■■■   ▲■■

TEST 4: VERBAL REASONING—WORDS

20 minutes

Directions: For questions 1–9, find the word that names a necessary part of the underlined word.

1. cage

(A) captivity
(B) security
(C) display
(D) door

2. megaphone

(F) hearing
(G) understanding
(H) singing
(J) announcing

3. oven

(A) coal
(B) heat
(C) aroma
(D) food

4. carpet

(F) comfort
(G) pattern
(H) fringe
(J) thread

5. <u>concert</u>

    (A) stage
    (B) audience
    (C) seats
    (D) conductor

6. <u>trial</u>

    (F) objection
    (G) witness
    (H) verdict
    (J) courtroom

7. <u>message</u>

    (A) letter
    (B) writing
    (C) communication
    (D) telephone

8. <u>fish</u>

    (F) gills
    (G) ocean
    (H) lake
    (J) tail

9. <u>leash</u>

    (A) walk
    (B) control
    (C) drag
    (D) encircle

Directions: For questions 10–13, the words in the top row are related in some way. The words in the bottom row are related in the same way. Find the word that competes the bottom row of words.

10.

content	happy	ecstatic
ruffled	annoyed	

    (F) peaceful
    (G) agitated
    (H) controlled
    (J) emotional

11.

tree	trunk	leaf
flower	stem	

    (A) petal
    (B) branch
    (C) root
    (D) bouquet

12.

umbrella	rain-hat	galoshes
sunglasses	sun-hat	

    (F) parasol
    (G) nature
    (H) sandals
    (J) hammock

13.

daughter	mother	grandmother
	father	grandfather

    (A) brother
    (B) son
    (C) cousin
    (D) uncle

Directions: For questions 14–17, find the word that does *not* belong with the others.

14. Which word does *not* belong with the others?

    (F) bottle
    (G) diaper
    (H) crib
    (J) slide

15. Which word does *not* belong with the others?

    (A) rooster
    (B) mare
    (C) bull
    (D) stallion

16. Which word does *not* belong with the others?

    (F) data
    (G) evidence
    (H) opinion
    (J) fact

17. Which word does *not* belong with the others?

   (A) wink
   (B) grimace
   (C) frown
   (D) smile

Directions: For questions 18–20, find the word that is most like the underlined words.

18. <u>calm</u>   <u>peaceful</u>   <u>tranquil</u>

   (F) clean
   (G) boring
   (H) relaxing
   (J) restless

19. <u>moral</u>   <u>honest</u>   <u>loyal</u>

   (A) true
   (B) brave
   (C) verbose
   (D) durable

20. <u>tidy</u>   <u>neat</u>   <u>orderly</u>

   (F) cozy
   (G) disorderly
   (H) cute
   (J) spotless

TEST 5: VERBAL REASONING—CONTEXT

20 minutes

Directions: For questions 1–20, find the statement that is true according to the given information.

1. The Statue of Liberty is in New York City. Christine has climbed to the top of the Statue of Liberty.

   (A) Many tourists visit the Statue of Liberty.
   (B) The Statue of Liberty was a gift from the French.
   (C) Christine has been to New York City.
   (D) Christine is in good physical condition.

2. Marcia is older than Jan. Jan is 5 feet 2 inches tall.

   (F) Marcia is taller than Jan.
   (G) Jan is taller than Marcia.
   (H) Jan is younger than Marcia.
   (J) Marcia and Jan are sisters.

3. A slice of white bread is 100 calories a slice. A slice of wheat bread is 150 calories a slice.

   (A) Wheat bread is fattening and white bread is not.
   (B) White bread is tastier than wheat bread.
   (C) More people buy white bread than wheat bread.
   (D) There is more caloric energy in a slice of wheat bread than in a slice of white bread.

4. Jean sold six used cars in March. No one sold more cars than Jean in March.

   (F) Jean also sold the most cars in April.
   (G) Jean was employee of the month in March.
   (H) No one other than Jean sold cars in March.
   (J) Jean sold the most cars in March.

5. Dogs often bark to protect their territory from intruders. Fluffy the dog is inside the house barking.

   (A) Someone is threatening his owner.
   (B) Someone may be trying to break into Fluffy's owner's home.
   (C) Fluffy is too high strung.
   (D) Fluffy is tired of being locked up and he needs to go outside.

6. Lisa sent an email to her friend Amy. Amy hasn't written Lisa back yet.

   (F) Lisa hasn't received a reply from Amy yet.
   (G) Amy is too busy to write Lisa.
   (H) Lisa likes to write letters.
   (J) Amy is probably angry at Lisa.

7. Rare coins are worth a lot of money. Jim has a rare 1942 copper penny.

   (A) Jim collects coins.
   (B) Jim has a valuable coin.
   (C) Silver dollars are rare coins.
   (D) Copper pennies are no longer made.

8. Mercedes Brown lives at #2 Front Street. Yesterday she found a letter in her mailbox addressed to Mercedes Brow at #3 Front Street.

   (F) A woman with a similar name lives next door to Mercedes Brown.
   (G) The mail carrier made a mistake when he delivered the letter to Mercedes Brown.
   (H) The person addressing the letter probably made a mistake.
   (J) A woman with a similar name lived in Mercedes Brown's house before she did.

9. John's computer suddenly turns off. His lights, television, and radio are still running.

   (A) There is a blackout.
   (B) There is a problem with John's computer.
   (C) John's computer is unplugged.
   (D) John does not know how to use a computer.

10. Romero's offers a free pizza to any delivery customer who waits longer than 30 minutes to receive his or her order. Samina ordered a large pepperoni pizza from Romero's.

    (F) Samina is a customer of Romero's.
    (G) Samina likes pepperoni pizza.
    (H) Romero's always delivers on time.
    (J) Romero's is faster than the competitor.

11. Joseph would like to attend Minetta Music School. The school only accepts students who can read music.

    (A) Joseph is a talented musician.
    (B) Joseph must read music in order to attend Minetta Music School.
    (C) Joseph cannot read music.
    (D) Minetta Music School is the best in Joseph's town.

12. Polar bears live in Alaska. There are two polar bears at the Bronx Zoo in New York.

    (F) Polar bears also live in New York.
    (G) The polar bear at the zoo is unhappy.
    (H) It is too warm in New York for a polar bear.
    (J) Polar bears are threatened with extinction.

13. Maria lives in New Jersey. Monday through Friday she commutes to New York City for work. On Saturday and Sunday afternoon she pitches for a softball team. On Sunday evening she cooks dinner for the entire week.

    (A) Maria works in New York City five days a week.
    (B) Maria shares her cooking with players on her team.
    (C) Softball players are good cooks.
    (D) Maria has a microwave oven.

14. Zookeepers in Seattle brought a black bear from Kodiak Island to share a cage with another black bear. Yesterday, the black bear from Kodiak Island gave birth to a baby bear. Zookeepers were overjoyed and threw a little birthday party for the baby bear.

    (F) Black bears prefer salmon to birthday cake.
    (G) Zookeepers like to have birthday parties.
    (H) Black bears are friendly.
    (J) The bear from Kodiak Island is female.

15. Brandon was looking for his car keys all morning. He looked under the bed, in the kitchen cabinet, and in his coat pocket. Finally, he looked in the ignition of the car and shouted, "Aha!"

    (A) Brandon is always absentminded.
    (B) The lost keys were in the car.
    (C) Brandon left the car running.
    (D) Brandon was late to work.

16. Mr. Sloan wears reading glasses. He can't find his glasses.

    (F) Mr. Sloan likes to read.
    (G) He won't be able to find his glasses.
    (H) Mr. Sloan probably won't be able to read without his glasses.
    (J) Mr. Sloan reads the paper every morning.

17. On its way uptown, the local train stops every ten blocks, starting at 10th Street. The express train also starts at 10th Street, but after that it stops only at every other station. The #6 train is an express train.

    (A) The local train is very slow.
    (B) The #6 train does not stop at 10th Street.
    (C) The #6 train stops at 20th Street.
    (D) The #6 train is faster than the #5 train.

18. Lunch is served in the cafeteria Monday through Friday between 12 P.M. and 2 P.M. It is now 11:55 A.M. on Thursday.

    (F) Lunch is being served early today.
    (G) The cafeteria food is not good.
    (H) Lunch is served every day of the week.
    (J) Lunch will be served in five minutes.

19. You must be 16 years old to get a driver's permit. John's birthday is in March.

    (A) No one under the age of 16 is allowed to get a driver's permit.
    (B) John will apply for a driver's permit this year.
    (C) John is looking forward to driving.
    (D) All 16 year olds apply for driver's permits.

20. Mount Everest is the highest mountain in the world. Mount Everest is in Nepal.

    (F) Mount Everest is in the Himalayas.
    (G) The highest mountain in the world is in Nepal.
    (H) The Rocky Mountains are the highest mountain range in the United States.
    (J) Mount Everest is hard to climb.

TEST 6: READING AND LANGUAGE ARTS

40 minutes

Directions: Follow the directions for questions 1–40.

Read the following passage and answer questions 1–5.

It's a beautiful spring day. There has been a brief shower, and now, with the sun shining brightly again, a brilliant rainbow appears in the sky. It feels as though the entire world is celebrating the reappearance of the sun. Yet, there is a <u>precise</u> scientific reason why rainbows can only be seen on particular types of day, at particular times of day, and from particular vantage points. For example, have you ever noticed that the sun is always behind you when you face a rainbow? Or, have you noticed that when you face a rainbow the center of its arc is opposite the sun?

French philosopher and scientist Rene Descartes studied and discussed the basis for this marvelous phenomenon in 1637. Descartes reasoned that since rainbows only appear in the sky when there are drops of water illuminated by the sun, the rainbow must be caused by the way in which the rays of light act on water drops and pass from them to our eyes. As sunlight hits a raindrop it is refracted, or bent, by the drop in such a way that the light appears as a spectrum of colors. Traditionally, the rainbow is described as containing seven colors—red, orange, yellow, green, blue, indigo, and violet. In reality, the rainbow is a whole continuum of colors from red to violet, including colors on either end of the spectrum that the eye cannot even see.

The colors are only apparent, however, when the angle of reflection between the sun, the drop of water, and the observer's line of sight is an angle between 40 and 42 degrees. The lower the sun is in the sky, the higher the rainbow appears. As the sun rises higher, the rainbow appears lower, thus keeping the essential 40 to 42 degree angle. When the sun is more than 42 degrees above the horizon line, we can no longer see the rainbow, because the required angle is then over our heads.

1. The word <u>precise</u> most nearly means

   (A) true
   (B) exact
   (C) precious
   (D) difficult

2. Rainbows are caused by

   (F) light acting on water
   (G) the angle of the sun in the sky
   (H) warm air currents
   (J) a spectrum of colors

3. A rainbow is made up of

   (A) white light
   (B) a continuum of colors
   (C) seven colors
   (D) sunlight

4. Rainbows disappear when

   (F) the sun sets
   (G) you stand in front of them
   (H) the sun is higher than 42 degrees
   (J) the sun rises

5. In a rainbow, water drops affect light by

   (A) absorbing it
   (B) refracting it
   (C) making it visible
   (D) illustrating it

Here is a story a student wrote about seeing a rainbow one spring afternoon. There are a few mistakes that need correcting. Read the story, then answer questions 6–8.

(1) Yesterday afternoon was a sunny, Spring Day. (2) Janet and me were outside riding our bicycles around the block. (3) It began to rain. (4) Janet's mother called, "Come inside girls." (5) It only rained a few minutes. (6) So we kept riding. (7) When the rain finished, we looked up in the sky and saw the most beautifulest rainbow.

6. Which sentence contains a capitalization error?

(F) Sentence 1
(G) Sentence 2
(H) Sentence 3
(J) Sentence 4

7. Choose the best way to combine sentences 5 and 6.

(A) It only rained a few minutes and so we kept riding.
(B) It only rained a few minutes, and so we kept riding.
(C) It only rained a few minutes; so we kept riding.
(D) It only rained a few minutes so we kept riding.

8. Choose the best way to rewrite sentence 7.

(F) When the rain finished, we looked up in the sky and saw the more beautifuller rainbow.
(G) When the rain finished, we looked up in the sky and saw the beautifulest rainbow.
(H) When the rain finished, we looked up in the sky and saw the most beautiful rainbow.
(J) Best as is.

Read the following passage and answer questions 9–14.

The alarm clock rings, we rush out of bed, we throw on our clothes, maybe grab a quick breakfast, and run out the door. Maybe we get stuck in a traffic jam on our way to work or school. As we wait, trapped in the middle of a sea of automobiles, our pulse quickens, our breath grows shallow, we growl at the other drivers, who we blame for our predicament. This is a typical morning for many Americans. Not only is it stressful, it is also unhealthy.

The constant pressures of everyday life take a toll on the physical and mental well-being of millions of people each year. Medical research indicates that common illnesses such as high blood pressure, heart disease, stomach ulcers, and headaches are related to stress. Stress is also an underlying factor in emotional and behavioral problems including difficulty concentrating, aggressive behavior, and difficulty sleeping or eating. While these are the "positive" effects of stress, there are "negative" ones as well, which we often fail to link to their true cause. Instead of nervousness and aggression, people who manifest these reactions to stress find themselves lethargic, sleeping too much, overeating, or becoming anti-social.

What's the solution? Relax! It sounds simple, but many people find it incredibly difficult. True relaxation is more than getting away from the regular routine. It is the experience of finding peace of mind, self-awareness, and thoughtful reflection. Find small ways to build relaxation into your day-to-day routine. Exercise to relieve stress. Walk, bicycle, dance, or swim a little bit each day. For physically fit people, strenuous exercise, which allows them to work up a sweat, can give a tremendous feeling of relaxation when it is finished. The deep breathing necessitated by exercise can help calm the anxious body. Deep breathing in general is a great way to relax. Participate in creative activities such as painting, drawing, knitting, or cooking. Try some mental exercises to relieve stress, such as imagining a special place where you enjoy going. Most importantly, try to build relaxation into every day.

9. Relaxation is essential because it

   (A) keeps us physically fit
   (B) prevents us from becoming aggressive
   (C) helps us to lead healthy lives
   (D) is difficult to do

10. According to this article

   (F) people become aggressive under pressure
   (G) people don't eat enough breakfast
   (H) stress allows us to accomplish many things
   (J) stress may cause health problems

11. In this article, the term "negative" response to stress means

   (A) any bad reactions to stress
   (B) ulcers, headaches, high blood pressure
   (C) reactions that show low energy
   (D) emotional reactions

12. All of the following are mentioned as possible ways to relax EXCEPT

   (F) mental exercise
   (G) denying worries or concerns
   (H) physical movement
   (J) pursuing an artistic endeavor

13. Here are two sentences related to the passage:
   Regular exercise is a good way to stay healthy.
   Regular exercise can reduce blood pressure and help maintain a stable weight.
   Select the answer choice that best combines the two sentences into one.

   (A) There are two reasons why regular exercise is a good way to stay healthy; it can reduce blood pressure and help maintain a stable weight.
   (B) Regular exercise is a good way to stay healthy; it can reduce blood pressure and help maintain a stable weight.
   (C) Regular exercise can reduce blood pressure and help maintain a stable weight that is why it's a good way to stay healthy.
   (D) Regular exercise is a good way to stay healthy and it can reduce blood pressure and help maintain a stable weight.

14. Choose the sentence that would be the best conclusion to the article.

   (F) Relax, but don't fall asleep.
   (G) Remember, relaxation can help you stay in good shape.
   (H) Some athletes practice relaxation techniques before a competition.
   (J) Remember, it's essential to relax in order to be in good shape to meet the demands of a busy lifestyle.

Read the following passage and answer questions 15–18.

It was part of her nefarious plot! Of that I had no doubt. She would slowly deprive me of my delicious slumber until finally, exhausted, I gave in to her wretched demands. She could claw her way into my dreams, she could growl and complain, but no, I would not give in. I pulled the covers close over my head and rolled over. I was the stronger of we two. I was the determined one. I was the human, and she the beast. She must have understood my determination, for mercifully, the whining stopped. My breathing grew deeper and I returned to my wonderful sleep. Until moments later a crash awakened me. I bolted out of bed and there she was, in the kitchen guiltily lapping kitty treats off the floor. The mischievous beast had jumped onto the countertop and knocked the bag of food onto the floor. "Bad kitty!" I scolded, pushing her away from the mess of chow. But that sweet face, that little sandpaper tongue licking her chops somehow softened me.

15. Probably the next thing that will happen is that the author will

    (A) lock the kitten out of the bedroom
    (B) let the kitten eat the treats
    (C) bring the kitten to bed
    (D) go back to sleep

16. The action described in this selection could *not* be part of

    (F) a children's television show
    (G) a situation comedy
    (H) a digest magazine
    (J) a science fiction movie

17. The author's attitude toward the kitten is

    (A) reluctant indulgence
    (B) total animosity
    (C) patient resolve
    (D) complete annoyance

18. The reader is *not* told

    (F) the kitten's tactics
    (G) why the author is annoyed at the kitten
    (H) where the author got the kitten
    (J) what the kitten's plot is

Here is a story a student wrote about her own kittens. There are a few mistakes that need correcting. Read the story, then answer questions 19–21.

(1) I have three kittens named Orange, Apple, and Nana. (2) To take care of them is a lot of work. (3) I have to make sure they have water every day. (4) And food. (5) There's also cleaning their litter box.

19. Which is the best way to write sentence 1?

    (A) I have three kittens. And they are named Orange, Apple, and Nana.

    (B) I have three kittens. They are named Orange, Apple, and Nana.

    (C) Three kittens that I have are named Orange, Apple, and Nana.

    (D) Best as is.

20. What is the best way to combine sentences 3 and 4?

    (F) I have to make sure they have water and food every day.

    (G) Everyday, I am having to make sure they have water and food.

    (H) Having to make sure they have water and food every day.

    (J) Water and food every day is what I have to make sure they have.

21. Choose the best way to write sentence 5.

    (A) There is also the litter box to clean.

    (B) Cleaning the litter box there is also.

    (C) I also have to clean their litter box.

    (D) Best as is.

Read the following passage and answer questions 22–26.

When we think of elephants, we generally conjure images of Africa and India because that is where they live today. But in the recent past, elephants, or their close relative, the woolly mammoth, inhabited every continent except Australia and South America. Although most mammoths died out at least 10,000 years ago, some continued to populate Wrangel Island near Siberia until as recently as 4,000 years ago, around the same time as the construction of the Great Pyramid in Egypt. In the United States, woolly mammoth remains have been found in Wisconsin, Indiana, and Alaska.

Closely related to existing African and Asian species, the woolly mammoth most likely originated in Eurasia about a quarter of a million years ago. They migrated to the Americas over the Bering land bridge. Thanks to numerous cave paintings in Europe, and the discovery of well-preserved mammoth body parts in the permafrost of Alaska and Siberia, the mammoth's appearance is well-known today.

Mammoths stood 9 to 11 feet tall and weighed four to six tons. The great beasts were covered with long, shaggy hair and had a high, domed head, a hunched back, and long, twisted tusks. However, since the trunks were composed of soft tissue, they did not survive in fossil form. Scientists are convinced of the mammoth's appearance due to the cave paintings, and a large cavity in the skull of mammoth remains precisely where the trunks would have been. The great mammoths' skulls, with one massive opening, may have been the basis for the myth of the Cyclopes, the imaginary one-eyed giants. Perhaps ancient people, observing mammoth remains, mistook the trunk opening in the mammoth's skull for an eye socket.

22. Woolly mammoths came to the Americas from

    (F) India
    (G) Eurasia
    (H) Africa
    (J) Europe

23. We know the appearance of woolly mammoths because

    (A) legends have been passed down
    (B) paintings of thcm have been discovered
    (C) they resemble elephants in India
    (D) they disappcarcd during the ice age

24. Mammoths lived

    (F) during the time of the pharaohs of Egypt
    (G) until Alaska became a state
    (H) at the same time as the Cyclops
    (J) about a quarter of a century ago

25. Mammoth trunks are not found among their remains because

    (A) North American mammoths did not have trunks
    (B) they were carried away by ancient peoples
    (C) they were not fossilized
    (D) they were composed of bone

26. Compared with modern elephants, the mammoth

    (F) traveled longer distances
    (G) lived in warmer climates
    (H) had a longer trunk
    (J) had more natural habitats

Here is a paragraph related to the passage. Read thc paragraph, then answer questions 27–28.

The Asian elephant has a large domed head with small ears, an arched back, and a single finger-like protrusion at the tip of the trunk. An Asian elephant has five toes on the front feet and four toes on the back. The African elephant has a straight back, enormous ears, and two trunk "fingers" instead of one. African elephants live in family groups headed by a female cow. The African elephant has only four toes on the front feet and three on the back. African elephants are also much larger than Asian elephants.

27. Choose the best topic sentence for this paragraph.

    (A) Asian elephants are completely different than African elephants.
    (B) *Elephas maximus* is the species name for the Asian elephant.
    (C) Asian and African elephants have some noticeable differences.
    (D) Elephants can weigh between four and seven tons.

28. Which sentence does NOT belong in the paragraph?

    (F) African elephants are also much larger than Asian elephants.
    (G) The African elephant has a straight back, enormous ears, and two trunk "fingers" instead of one.
    (H) African elephants live in family groups headed by a female cow.
    (J) An Asian elephant has five toes on the front feet and four toes on the back.

Read the following passage and answer questions 29–35.

Today we planted the first seeds of our very own victory garden. How wonderful it felt to know that we were part of the effort, supporting our brave troops fighting overseas. Such a small step—this little garden of ours, but still it makes me proud that we are doing our part to help the American World War II effort against Hitler's tyranny and oppression. I can almost imagine that as our seeds take root and grow, so does democracy root out the evil weed spreading through Europe.

Meanwhile, George complains about the gasoline rationing. He hates not being able to drive that spiffy new car of his. I personally could never stand our little pleasure drives over the bumpy back roads and I find it no sacrifice at all to forgo a tank of gasoline if it will help the war effort. It is doing without silk stockings that bothers me. Though I am ashamed to admit it, I do love my little luxuries. And though I do admire our many "Rosie the Riveters" I myself can't imagine taking up work in a factory. Who knows, maybe I'd feel differently with my first paycheck in hand. But all that remains speculation, for now there are four little boys to feed, bathe, and tuck in for the night. When we receive next month's ration coupons, I plan to bake all manner of cakes. Until then, unfortunately the pantry is out of sugar and George has to make do with unsweetened coffee. Though the coffee too is almost finished and we most certainly will run out before the next book of ration coupons arrives.

29. This passage takes place during

   (A) futuristic times
   (B) the Korean War
   (C) World War II
   (D) World War I

30. George is most likely

   (F) the author's son
   (G) the author's husband
   (H) the author
   (J) a soldier

31. The author of this selection is most probably a

   (A) baker
   (B) "Rosie the Riveter"
   (C) homemaker
   (D) farmer

32. According to the passage, all of the following must be rationed EXCEPT

   (F) vegetables
   (G) sugar
   (H) gasoline
   (J) silk stockings

33. Why do you think the author felt her garden was helping the war effort?

   (A) It meant more canned food would be available for the troops.
   (B) She was going to send the food she grew to the troops in Europe.
   (C) She was earning money which she would give to support the soldiers.
   (D) By gardening, she was promoting peaceful activity.

34. Here are two sentences related to the passage:
Certain items such as metal, gasoline, and silk were not available.
They were needed for the war effort.
Select the answer choice that best combines the two sentences into one.

(F) Certain items such as metal, gasoline, and silk were not available and they were needed for the war effort.

(G) Metal, gasoline, and silk were not available and they were needed for the war effort.

(H) Certain items such as metal, gasoline, and silk were not available; they were needed for the war effort.

(J) Because they were needed for the war effort, certain items such as metal, gasoline, and silk were not available.

35. Choose the sentence that is written correctly.

(A) Many rationed items people were able to get on the black market.

(B) Although many items were rationed, people still managed to get them on the black market.

(C) Getting many items on the black market people managed although they were rationed.

(D) Although they were rationed, people still managed to get many items on the black market.

Read the following passage and answer questions 36–40.

The state lottery is unfair because it steals from the poor and gives to the rich. Every study available shows that the lottery is played more often by poor people than by rich people. Since the state takes a percentage of every dollar bet on the lottery, this amounts to a greater tax on poor people than on rich. We all know the odds of winning the lottery are horrendously bad. It is common knowledge that a person has more chance of being hit by lightning than winning the lottery. Thus, the lottery is nothing more than an elaborate excuse to separate a fool from his money. It is shameful that the government, whose function should be to protect the public good, administers and even advertises this sham. Let's say Joe Schmoe has the astoundingly good fortune to win a grand prize of a million dollars. Paid out over 20 years, this amounts to only $50,000 per year for 20 years. While Joe receives his annual $50,000, the balance of Joe's jackpot remains in the bank. The government collects on the interest, not Joe. Plus, Joe has to pay taxes on his winnings. Joe's relatives crawl out of the woodwork, looking for a piece of the pie. He argues with his family over how to spend his winnings. Or, he blows all the money living beyond his means and finds himself alone and miserable a year later. When you do the math, there is no question who the real winner of the lottery is.

36. According to the author, the main problem with the lottery is

    (F) winners often find they are unhappy a year later
    (G) it is unfair because it steals from the poor
    (H) the government taxes winnings
    (J) not enough people win

37. The author argues against

    (A) the happiness of the winners
    (B) government support of the lottery
    (C) using taxes to pay for public good
    (D) taxing a lottery winner's jackpot

38. The name *Joe Schmoe* is used to

    (F) make the reader jealous of one winner
    (G) make fun of people who play the lottery
    (H) give an example of a specific winner
    (J) represent the common man

39. In this selection, the author

    (A) illustrates why the lottery is unfair
    (B) tells people to stop buying lottery tickets
    (C) asks the government to ban the lottery
    (D) shows how the lottery fails to help education

40. According to the passage all of these are benefits to the government for lottery EXCEPT

    (F) collecting tax on winnings
    (G) keeping interest on winnings
    (H) paying out lump sum winnings
    (J) receiving tax on each ticket purchased

TEST 7: MATHEMATICS

40 minutes

Directions: For questions 1–40, read each problem and find the answer.

1. $3^3 \times 3^4 =$

    (A) 312
    (B) 3^7
    (C) $3 \times 3 \times 3 \times 3 \times 3 \times 3$
    (D) 1,260
    (E) None of these

2. $6.2 - 0.4 =$

    (F) 2.8
    (G) 6.5
    (H) 2.2
    (J) 5.8
    (K) None of these

3. 0.04% is equal to

    (A) 4
    (B) 40
    (C) $\frac{1}{4}$
    (D) $\frac{4}{10,000}$
    (E) None of these

4. $\frac{16}{35}$ is greater than

    (F) $\frac{7}{8}$
    (G) $\frac{5}{6}$
    (H) $\frac{12}{61}$
    (J) $\frac{43}{45}$
    (K) None of these

5. $0.875 - 0.625 =$

(A) 0.5

(B) 0.375

(C) 0.25

(D) 0.125

(E) None of these

6. $0.3 \times 19.95 =$

(F) 5.985

(G) 5.895

(H) 5.85

(J) .5895

(K) None of these

7. $-6(3 - 4 \times 3) =$

(A) −66

(B) −54

(C) −12

(D) 18

(E) None of these

8. $\dfrac{3}{4} + 7.55 =$

(F) 8.2

(G) 8.3

(H) 7.25

(J) 5.6

(K) None of these

9. Lisa's drive to work each day takes her 45 minutes. If she travels at an average speed of 60 miles per hour, how far is her home from her place of work?

(A) 450 miles

(B) 270 miles

(C) 2,700 miles

(D) 45 miles

10. In a recent board meeting, the executives of Company X decided that 10% of their operating budget should go to advertising, 50% to operating expenses, 25% to salaries, and the rest to developing new products. What fraction of the budget will be used for developing new products?

(F) $\dfrac{5}{100}$

(G) $\dfrac{3}{20}$

(H) $\dfrac{4}{10}$

(J) $\dfrac{1}{7}$

11. In the number 215,602 what is the value of the digit 1?

(A) 10,000

(B) 1,000

(C) 1

(D) 10

12. If a birthday cake is divided into five slices, one slice is what percent of the whole cake?

(F) 10%

(G) 2%

(H) 20%

(J) .2%

13. Alexis earns $350 a week as a salesperson, plus 6% commission on her sales. What will she earn this week if she has sold $2,500 worth of merchandise?

(A) $350

(B) $400

(C) $500

(D) $550

14. A health club has 5 treadmills, 12 stationary bi-cycles, and 4 stair-climbing machines. When $\frac{2}{3}$ of all the machines are occupied, how many people are using the machines?

    (F) 14
    (G) 12
    (H) 15
    (J) 7

15. Which of the following sets of numbers may be placed in the blank to make the statement below true?

    $5 > \underline{\quad} > 0$

    (A) {5, 4, 3, 2, 1, 0}
    (B) {5, 4, 3, 2, 1}
    (C) {4, 3, 2, 1}
    (D) {4, 3, 2, 1, 0}

16. One inch is what part of one yard?

    (F) $\frac{1}{12}$

    (G) $\frac{1}{100}$

    (H) $\frac{1}{3}$

    (J) $\frac{1}{36}$

17. A luncheonette serves 56 burgers a day. $\frac{7}{8}$ of these burgers are ordered with cheese. How many cheeseburgers are ordered?

    (A) 56
    (B) 49
    (C) 50
    (D) 42

18. Which of the following are the prime factors of 72?

    (F) $2^2, 3^3$
    (G) $2^3, 3^2$
    (H) 2, 3, 5
    (J) 2, 36

19. Complete the following statement:

    $2(5 \times \underline{\quad}) + 4 = 54$

    (A) 5
    (B) 6
    (C) 10
    (D) 4

20. Find the area of a triangle whose base is 12 inches and whose height is 5 inches.

    (F) 34 square inches
    (G) 60 square inches
    (H) 30 square inches
    (J) 36 square inches

21. Which of the following is equivalent to *five hundred fifty thousand sixty nine*?

    (A) 500,069
    (B) 550,069
    (C) 500,690
    (D) 55,690

22. A quadrilateral is ALWAYS a

    (F) four-sided polygon
    (G) polygon with four equal sides
    (H) five-sided polygon
    (J) polygon with four right angles

23. A clothing store made $120,650 in sales during the month of August. Two of its six salespeople made 50% of the sales. How much did the other four salespeople sell altogether?

    (A) $24,130
    (B) $60,325
    (C) $15,081
    (D) $25,300

24. The set of common factors for 50 and 250 is

    (F) {2, 5, 10, 25}
    (G) {2, 5, 10, 25, 50}
    (H) {2, 5, 10, 25, 50, 100}
    (J) {2, 5, 10, 20, 25, 50}

25. If $-1 < x < 2$, which of the following must NOT be true?

   (A) $x > -3$
   (B) $x = 0$
   (C) $x = 1$
   (D) $x > 2$

26. Which of these points on the number line represents 5×10^3?

A   B   C   D   E   F

0   500   5,000   25,000   50,000   100,000

   (F) Point E
   (G) Point B
   (H) Point C
   (J) Point F

27. If one glass of lemonade costs x dollars and y cents, what is the cost of three glasses of lemonade?

   (A) $3(x + y)$
   (B) $3x(y)$
   (C) $3x - 3y$
   (D) $3(xy)$

28. Ken and Keisha disagree about how to solve the problem below. Ken thinks that the first thing to do is add all the terms. Keisha thinks they should perform the operations within the parentheses first.
   $(8 + 5 + 4) \times (12 + 3 + 2)$

   (F) Only Ken is correct.
   (G) Only Keisha is correct.
   (H) They are both correct.
   (J) Neither Ken nor Keisha is correct.

29. An importer reasons that in order to make a profit on each item that she sells, she must mark it up to 200% of the original cost. If she imports a scarf for $6, including her shipping costs, how much must she sell it for in order to be profitable?

   (A) $12
   (B) $6
   (C) $9
   (D) $60

30. Which coordinates show most clearly the location of Rosewood City?

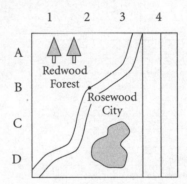

   (F) C3
   (G) B3
   (H) B2
   (J) C4

31. The product of a negative integer and a positive integer is

   (A) zero
   (B) negative
   (C) positive
   (D) 1

32. Reesa is deciding which telephone company offers her the best day, evening, and weekend rates. Which chart or graph below would be most helpful to her?

(F)

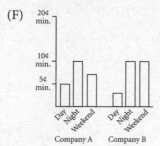

(G)

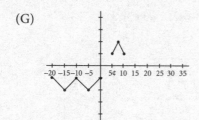

(H)

	Company A	Company B
Day	5¢	3¢
Night	10¢	10¢
Weekend	7¢	10¢

(J)

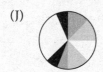

33. What is the circumference of the circle below?

2 units

(A) 16π units
(B) 4π units
(C) 8π units
(D) 6π units

34. A right angle measures

(F) 45 degrees
(G) 80 degrees
(H) 180 degrees
(J) 90 degrees

35. All of the following are quadrilaterals EXCEPT

(A) rhombus
(B) square
(C) rectangle
(D) pentagon

36. Mr. Strong took out a bank loan for $2,500 to repair his roof. The interest is 12%. What is the total amount he owes the bank?

(F) $3,000
(G) $2,600
(H) $2,800
(J) $300

37. If $x > -3$, and $y < 1$, and x and y are integers, then which of the following sets represents all values that would satisfy both x and y?

(A) {0, 1}
(B) {-2, -1, 0}
(C) {-1, 0, 1}
(D) {-2, -1, 0, 1}

38. What is the value of x if $2(3 + x) = 46$?

(F) 41
(G) 40
(H) 46
(J) 20

39. What are the coordinates of point *A* on the graph?

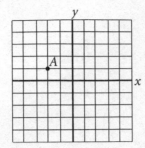

   (A) (2, –1)
   (B) (2, 1)
   (C) (–2, 1)
   (D) (1, –2)

40. A certain county experienced 39 inches of rainfall this year—12 more inches than last year. What is this year's monthly average rainfall?

   (F) $\dfrac{39}{12}$ inches

   (G) $39 - \dfrac{12}{12}$ inches

   (H) $39 + \dfrac{12}{12}$ inches

   (J) $\dfrac{12}{12}$ inches

ANSWERS AND EXPLANATIONS

Answer Key

Test 1: Sequences

1. D
2. J
3. C
4. J
5. A
6. H
7. B
8. F
9. B
10. F
11. C
12. F
13. C
14. G
15. A
16. J
17. B
18. G
19. B
20. J

Test 2: Analogies

1. D
2. G
3. D
4. G
5. B
6. F
7. C
8. G
9. A
10. G
11. B
12. H
13. A

14. J
15. B
16. H
17. A
18. H
19. D
20. G

Test 3: Quantitative Reasoning

1. C
2. F
3. A
4. G
5. D
6. F
7. B
8. H
9. D
10. G
11. C
12. H
13. D
14. J
15. B
16. J
17. A
18. H
19. A
20. H

Test 4: Verbal Reasoning—Words

1. A
2. F
3. B
4. J

5. B
6. H
7. C
8. F
9. B
10. G
11. A
12. F
13. B
14. J
15. B
16. H
17. A
18. H
19. A
20. J

Test 5: Verbal Reasoning—Context

1. C
2. H
3. D
4. J
5. B
6. F
7. B
8. H
9. B
10. F
11. B
12. F
13. A
14. J
15. B
16. H
17. B

18. J
19. A
20. G

Test 6: Reading and Language Arts

1. B
2. F
3. B
4. H
5. B
6. F
7. D
8. H
9. C
10. J
11. C
12. G
13. B
14. J
15. B
16. J
17. A
18. H
19. B
20. F
21. C
22. G
23. B
24. F

25. C
26. J
27. C
28. H
29. C
30. G
31. C
32. F
33. A
34. J
35. B
36. G
37. B
38. J
39. A
40. H

Test 7: Mathematics

1. B
2. J
3. D
4. H
5. C
6. F
7. E
8. G
9. D
10. G
11. A
12. H

13. C
14. F
15. C
16. J
17. B
18. G
19. A
20. H
21. B
22. F
23. B
24. G
25. D
26. H
27. A
28. H
29. A
30. H
31. B
32. H
33. B
34. J
35. D
36. H
37. B
38. J
39. C
40. F

Test 1: Sequences

1. D

Each set is made up of four arrows. The first, second, and fourth arrow alternate between pointing up or down. The third arrow always points up. The next set should start with an arrow pointing down, followed by one pointing up, the third arrow always points up, and the fourth should point up.

2. J

The pattern is made up of three triangles and a square. The first triangle always has a solid dot in the center, though the second and third triangle alternate between having a solid or an empty dot in the middle. The square also alternates between having a solid or empty dot in the center. Therefore, the next set should include a triangle with a solid dot, a triangle with an open dot, a triangle with a solid dot, and a square with an open dot.

3. C

Each set is made up of three Xs. In the first set, two small vs are inside the vertex of each of the Xs. In the second set, a third v is added to all the Xs. In the next set, a third v is added to the Xs. In the last set, another detail is added; the ends of the Xs are now arrows. Since in all three sets each X has the same amount of detail, the missing X in the last set should also have arrow points on the ends of the rays of the X and should have four vs inside the vertex of the X like the other Xs in its set.

4. J

The sets are made up of four stars; two are filled in and two are not. The missing star in the last set should be empty so that the balance of two filled in and two empty remains the same. There is no reason to believe the star would be only partially filled in.

5. A

The elements in each set are either the bottom part of a triangle, the mid-section of a triangle, or the top section of a triangle. The only answer choice that has one of these elements is choice (A).

6. H

Each set is made up of two "houses." One points up, the next points down. In each subsequent set, the second house gains a detail that was present previously in the first house. Therefore, the missing house should point down (as the second one always does), and it should gain the shading in the top triangle that the first house had in the preceding set.

7. B

The first two numbers of each set are multiplied to get the third number of each set. For example, $2 \times 5 = 10$, $3 \times 7 = 21$, and finally $4 \times 9 = 36$.

8. F

In each set, the first number is multiplied by 2 to obtain the second number, and the second number is multiplied by 3 to obtain the third number; $10 \times 3 = 30$.

9. B

In each set, the second number is the square root of the first number, and the third number is that square root minus 3; $7 - 3 = 4$.

10. F

In this sequence, the third number in each set is the difference between the first and second number in each set. For example, $64 - 51 = 13$, $52 - 40 = 12$, and $33 - 22 = 11$.

11. C

In each set, the first number is multiplied by 4 to obtain the second number, and the second number is reduced by 8 to obtain the third number; $28 - 8 = 20$.

12. F

In each set, the second number is 1 more than the first number, and the third number is 2 more than the second number; $13 + 2 = 15$.

13. C

In each set, the difference between the first two numbers is 5 and the difference between the second and third number is 2; $86 - 2 = 84$.

14. G

In each set, the second number is 10 less than the first number, and the third number is $\frac{1}{4}$ of the first number.

15. A

Note the pattern as shown below.

A1B0C1   A2B1C2   A3B2C3   A4B3C4

In other words, B is 1 behind A and C.

16. J

As you move from left to right, the superscript of X is increased by 1; the superscript of Y is decreased by 2 and the superscript of Z is increased by 2.

$X^1Y^9Z^2$ $X^2Y^7Z^4$ $X^3Y^5Z^6$ $X^4Y^3Z^8$

17. B

The first letter of each set goes up by one letter: l, m, n, o. The last two letters are also increased by one letter, but the last letter is repeated: fg, gh, hi, ij. So the missing set is nhi.

18. G

Notice that in the first and third sets, the first letter is capitalized, the second letter is lowercase, and the last letter is capitalized. In the second set, the first letter is lowercase, the second letter is capitalized, and the last letter is also lowercase. The last two letters are always x and y, and the first letter increases by one letter: b, c, d. So, to follow the pattern, you are looking for a set beginning with a lowercase e, followed by a capital X, followed by a lowercase y. The correct answer is choice (G).

19. B

As we move from left to right, the first letters are arranged in decreasing alphabetical order, and the second letters and third letters are arranged in increasing alphabetical order.

ZAB   YBC   XCD   WDE

20. J

Note the pattern of the first and second letter of each group: AB, BC, CD, DE. Also note the pattern of the third letter of each group: E, F, G, H.

ABE   BCF   CDG   DEH

Test 2: Analogies

1.   D

A car travels on a road. A boat travels on water.

2.   G

A rectangle is an elongated version of a square. An oval is an elongated version of a circle.

3.   D

An umbrella protects against the rain. Sunglasses protect against the sun.

4.   G

A flower is displayed in a vase. A photo is displayed in a picture frame.

5. B

A parachute is used to escape from an airplane. A lifeboat is used to escape from a boat.

6. F

A computer is the modern version of a feather pen; they are both used to write. A cell phone is the modern version of a regular phone.

7. C

A sweater is worn in winter; a T-shirt is worn in summer. Long pants are worn in winter; shorts are worn in summer.

8. G

An apple grows on a tree. A carrot grows in the ground.

9. A

Scissors are used to cut paper. A saw is used to cut wood.

10. G

A bear eats fish. A giraffe eats foliage.

11. B

A playpen is an enclosure that holds a baby. A fishbowl is an enclosure that holds a goldfish.

12. H

Clothes are kept in a dresser. Papers are kept in a file cabinet.

13. A

A slice of cake is a portion of the whole cake. A slice of bread is a portion of the whole loaf.

14. J

Boots protect the feet. A helmet protects the head.

15. B

A bridle and saddle are used to control a horse, and a collar and leash are used to control a dog.

16. H

A chicken produces eggs. A cow produces milk.

17. A

An acorn grows into a tree. A seed grows into a flower.

18. H

A flag is a symbol of a country. A dove is a symbol of peace.

19. D

A teddy bear is a toy figure of a real bear. A toy truck is a smaller figure of a real 18-wheeler truck.

20. G

A fork and knife are both implements used to eat. A hoe and trowel are both implements used to garden.

Test 3: Quantitative Reasoning

1. C

Figure out what operation is being done to the number in the left column. What is done to 3 to make it 9? 6 is added. What is done to 1 to make it 7? 6 is added. The pattern is +6; 2 + 6 = 8, choice (C).

2. F

In this set, 2 is added to 4 to make 6; 2 is added to 1 to make 3. The pattern is +2; 5 + 2 = 7, choice (F).

3. A

1 is added to $\frac{1}{2}$ to make $1\frac{1}{2}$. 1 is added to $\frac{1}{3}$ to make $1\frac{1}{3}$. The pattern is +1. 2 + 1 = 3, choice (A).

4. G

What is done to 12 to make 3? It is divided by 4. What is done to 20 to make 5? It is divided by 4. The pattern is ÷4. 8 ÷ 4 = 2.

5. D

First, figure out what operation is being performed to the number on the left; $9 - 5 = 4$; $4 - 5 = -1$. The operation is -5; $10 - 5 = 5$.

6. F

Each number on the left is divided by 10 to arrive at the number on the right. Therefore, 0.5 divided by 10 = 0.05; 1.0 divided by 10 = 0.1; 10 divided by 10 = 1.

7. B

There are 4 equal segments. If you were to divide each of these 4 segments with a diagonal line you would have 8 segments making up the whole.

Count the shaded segments. There is 1. The fraction of the grid that is shaded is $\frac{1}{8}$.

8. H

There are 16 squares and 2 are shaded; $\frac{2}{16}$ reduces to $\frac{1}{8}$.

9. D

There are 4 sections and 2 are shaded. That is 2 parts out of 4, or $\frac{2}{4}$, which reduces to $\frac{1}{2}$.

10. G

There are 4 parts and 2 are shaded. That is 2 parts out of 4, or $\frac{2}{4}$, which reduces to $\frac{1}{2}$.

11. C

Count the number of triangular sections. There are 8 triangular sections and 3 of these 8 sections are shaded. The answer is $\frac{3}{8}$.

12. H

There are 8 sections and 2 are shaded; $\frac{2}{8}$ reduces to $\frac{1}{4}$.

13. D

There are 4 sections and 2 are shaded. That is 2 parts out of 4, or $\frac{2}{4}$, which reduces to $\frac{1}{2}$.

14. J

Use the information to evaluate each answer choice. You are told that 1 cone is equal to 1 cube. Therefore:

F: 1 cone ≠ 1 cone + 1 cone (remember, the cube equals 1 cone)

G: 1 cone (1 cube = 1 cone) ≠ 2 cones

H: 2 cones ≠ 1 cone (remember, 1 cube is equal to 1 cone)

J: 1 cone + 1 cone (1 cube = 1 cone) = 1 cone + 1 cone (the cube = a cone)

15. B

One cube is equal to three cones. Convert the answer choices to either all cones or all cubes to more readily see the equation.

A: 3 cones ≠ 9 cones (since each cube equals 3 cones and there are 3 cubes)

B: 3 cones + 3 cones (the cube) = 6 cones

C: 2 cones + 3 cones (since the cube equals 3 cones) ≠ 12 cones (since each cube equals 3 cones)

D: 1 cone ≠ 4 cones (1 cone + 1 cube which equals 3 cones)

16. J

2 cones = 1 cube. Convert the answer choices to either all cones or all cubes to more readily see the equation.

F: 4 cones (the 2 cubes) ≠ 3 cones (1 cube = 2 cones + 1 more cone)

G: 2 cones + 2 cones (the cube) ≠ 3 cones

H: 1 cone + 2 cones (the cube) ≠ 4 cones (1 cube = 2 cones + 2 more cones)

J: 3 cones = 1 cone + 2 cones (1 cube = 2 cones)

17. A

1 cone = 2 cubes. Convert the answer choices to either all cones or all cubes to more readily see the equation.

A: 2 cones = 1 cone (the two cubes) + 1 cone

B: 1 cone (the 2 cubes) + 1 cone ≠ 3 cones (the 6 cubes)

C: $\frac{1}{2}$ cone (1 cube) + 1 cone ≠ 3 cones

D: 1 cone ≠ $\frac{1}{2}$ cone (the 1 cube)

18. H

3 cones = 1 cube. Convert the answer choices to either all cones or all cubes to more readily see the equation.

F: 3 cones (1 cube) ≠ 2 cones

G: 6 cones (2 cubes) ≠ 3 cones (1 cube) + 2 cones

H: 3 cones (1 cube) + 1 cone = 4 cones

J: 6 cones (2 cubes) ≠ 3 cones (1 cube) + 1 cone

19. A

3 cones = 1 cube. Convert the answer choices to either all cones or all cubes to more readily see the equation.

A: 2 cones (the 1 cube) + 2 cones = 4 cones (the 2 cubes)

B: 3 cones ≠ 4 cones (the 2 cubes)

C: 4 cones (the 2 cubes) + 1 cone ≠ 2 cones + 2 cones (the 1 cube)

D: 2 cones ≠ 4 cones (the 2 cubes)

20. H

4 cubes = 1 cone. Convert the answer choices to either all cones or all cubes to more readily see the equation.

F: $\frac{1}{2}$ cone (the 2 cubes) ≠ 1 cone + $\frac{1}{2}$ cone (the 2 cubes)

G: $\frac{1}{4}$ cone (the 1 cube) ≠ 5 cones

H: 2 cones = 1 cone + 1 cone (the 4 cubes)

J: $\frac{3}{4}$ cone (the 3 cubes) ≠ 1 cone + $\frac{1}{2}$ cone (the 2 cubes)

Test 4: Verbal Reasoning—Words

1. A

A cage is intended for captivity, not security or display. Although it may have a door, the essential element is that it keeps something or someone inside.

2. F

A megaphone amplifies the speaker's voice so that it may be heard more readily.

3. B

While food is cooked in an oven a pleasant aroma may result, but the essential element of an oven is that it cooks food because it contains heat.

4. J

A carpet is woven of thread. Although it may have fringe, or a pattern, or provide comfort, a carpet must be woven of thread.

5. B

A concert is given to an audience. It may take place without a stage, seats, or a conductor, but there must be a group of people to hear a concert.

6. H

A trial reveals guilt or innocence; it must result in a verdict regardless of whether or not there is a witness, or an objection, or an actual courtroom.

7. C

A message is a communication between two people. It can take any form—a letter, a telephone conversation, or an email. However, the essential idea is to communicate something.

8. F

A fish is unique because it has gills and can breathe in water. Though it has a tail, so do other animals. The essential element of a fish is its ability to live and breathe in water which gills allow it to do. A fish can live in a lake, ocean, pond, or river, so these are not essential elements.

9. B

A leash's function is to control. Though it does encircle an animal's neck, the essential thing about a leash is that it is used to control, not to drag or walk, an animal.

10. G

This relationship is one of degree. The items above the line are increasingly joyful; those below the line are increasingly bothered.

11. A

The items above the line are parts of a tree, and they are moving from general (tree) to specific (leaf). The items below the line are parts of a flower. They are moving from general (flower) to specific (petal).

12. F

The items above the line are all related to protection from rain. Those below the line are all related to protection from sun.

13. B

The items above the line express increasing age in family generations. The items below the line show the same relationship. Therefore, the correct answer is *son*.

14. J

The items in (F), (G), and (H) are all related to babies. A slide is used by children at a playground.

15. B

A mare is a female animal (a female horse). Roosters, bulls, and stallions are all male.

16. H

Data, evidence, and fact are all indisputable truths; an opinion is not.

17. A

Grimace, frown, and smile are facial expressions of the mouth. A wink is a facial expression of the eye.

18. H

Before looking at the answer choices, think about what the three words have in common. All three are adjectives with the same meaning—they all mean calm. Now look at the answer choices for a word that is most similar to *calm*. The most similar word is *relaxing*.

19. A

The three words have to do with good moral character and mean honest or trustworthy. Now evaluate the answer choices. Is *true* trustworthy? Yes it is. This is the correct answer. But be sure to look at all the other choices to make sure you have selected the best one. Is *brave* trustworthy? No, it is not. Is *verbose* trustworthy? It is not (it means wordy). If you don't know the meaning of the word, leave it in. Is *durable* trustworthy? No, it is not. It is long lasting. You now must choose between (A) and (C)—a word you know is correct and one you may not be sure of. Choose the word you know is correct—*true*.

20. J

Before looking at the answer choices, think about what the three words have in common. All three are adjectives with the same meaning—they all mean clean. Now look at the answer choices for a word that is most similar to *clean*. The most similar word is *spotless*.

Test 5: Verbal Reasoning—Context

1. C

The only thing known for certain is that Christine has been to New York City. Although (A) and (B) may be true, there is nothing in the two statements to support either of these conclusions. There is no way to verify choice (D).

2. H

Based on the two statements, the only one of these answer choices that we can conclude is correct is that Jan is younger than Marcia (since Marcia is older than Jan). No mention is made of Marcia's height, so rule out choices (F) and (G). We also do not know if the girls are sisters.

3. D

Based on the two statements, the only one of these answer choices that is correct is that wheat bread contains more caloric energy (50 calories more) than white bread. There is no point of comparison to allow us to judge whether either of these types of bread is fattening. We also have no information on people's buying habits. Choice (B) is an opinion, unsupported by the facts stated.

4. J

Based only on the information given, you do not know if Jean sold the most cars in April, nor if she was employee of the month. Although no one sold more cars than Jean, you do not know for certain that no one else sold a car. The only statement that is true based solely on the passage is that Jean sold the most cars in March.

5. B

The key here is the word *often* in the first statement and *may* in choice (B). There are many reasons dogs bark; the first statement offers one. Someone could be threatening Fluffy's owner, but this sentence is not tempered with *may* or *might be*. Choices (C) and (D), though possibly true, do not relate to the information given in the statements. Remember, you are choosing the statement that is true according to the information given.

6. F

Based on the two statements, the only thing we know for sure is that Amy hasn't written Lisa back yet (since Lisa hasn't received a reply). We do not know why Amy hasn't written back, only that she hasn't.

We also cannot say based only on the information given whether or not Lisa likes to write letters.

7. B

Since Jim has a rare coin and rare coins are worth a lot of money, Jim has a valuable coin. Based on the information given, we cannot say with certainty whether or not Jim collects coins. Regardless of whether or not it is true, the information in (C) and (D) is not related to the information given and is incorrect.

8. H

It is most reasonable to assume that the person addressing the letter probably made a mistake since the details are so similar to Mercedes Brown's real name and address. The mail carrier probably also made this reasonable assumption.

9. B

Based on the information given, the only thing we know for sure is that there is a problem with John's computer. Although being unplugged may be a reason for the problem, we do not have the information to arrive at this conclusion. (If the statement included the phrase *probably unplugged* this would be a stronger answer choice.) There is clearly not a blackout since the other electric appliances are working. We cannot make a judgment about John's ability based solely on the information given.

10. F

Based on the information given, the only thing known for sure is that Samina is a customer of Romero's. The statements do not tell us whether Samina herself likes pepperoni pizza—she may have ordered it for her family or friends. Although Romero's offers a free pizza to customers who wait longer than 30 minutes to receive their order, we do not know how often Romero's delivers late or how they compare to the competition.

11. B

Based on the information given, all that we know is that Minetta Music School requires its students to read music. We do not know whether it is the best school in town. Think about what information we have on Joseph. We do not know whether or not he is a talented musician, or whether he reads music at all. All we know is that Joseph *would like to attend*. The sentence tells us that he does not yet attend. If Joseph would like to attend the school, based on the school's requirements, he must read music.

12. F

Based only on the information given, we know that polar bears also live in New York. Based on the statements, we can say that polar bears live in New York. Choice (G) is a value judgment that we cannot affirm based only on the statements. Choice (H) must not be true, since there are polar bears in New York. Choice (J) depends on outside information to draw a conclusion, and remember, you are only allowed to use the statements given to come to a conclusion.

13. A

The only thing we can be sure of is that Maria works five days a week in New York City. We do not know whether she shares the food she cooks with her team or if she is a good cook. We also do not know if she has a microwave.

14. J

The black bear from Kodiak Island gave birth; therefore, she must be female. Although the zookeepers were happy and threw a party, we cannot generalize that they like to have parties. The paragraph gives no information about what black bears eat or if they are friendly.

15. B

The car keys must have been in the ignition, since when Brandon finally looked there he shouted,

"Aha!" Keys can be in an ignition while the car is off; therefore, we cannot assume that the car was running. We do not know if Brandon is always absentminded or if he was late to work that morning.

16. H

Based only on the information, the only statement that you can verify is that Mr. Sloan probably won't be able to read without his glasses. He has glasses for reading, so you can assume that he probably needs them in order to read. The other statements might be true, but you do not know for certain based on the information provided.

17. B

Express trains skip every other station. That is, they start at 10th Street, skip 20th Street, go to 30th Street, skip 40th Street, etc. The #6 train is an express, so it follows this pattern. That makes choice (B) correct, but choice (C) incorrect. We do not know the relative speed of the local train since it is not mentioned, nor do we know how slow the local train is.

18. J

Before looking at the answer choices, think about what the information does and does not tell you. You know that it is 11:55 A.M., five minutes to 12 on Thursday. Lunch is served Monday through Friday between 12 P.M. and 2 P.M. Eliminate choice (F); nothing is said about lunch being served early. Choice (G) is a guess; no information is given about the quality of the food. Choice (H) is wrong because lunch is only served Monday through Friday.

19. A

The statements tell how old one must be in order to drive and tell us when John's birthday is. They say nothing about how old John is and whether or not he can, can't, or would like to drive. Based on the information given, all we can conclude is that no one under the age of 16 may get a permit. You can eliminate choices (B) and (C)—we do not know these details about John. You can also eliminate choice (D) because it is a sweeping generalization. We cannot say that all 16 year olds apply for driver's permits.

20. G

If Mount Everest is the highest mountain in the world and it is in Nepal, the highest mountain in the world is in Nepal. Though (F) and (H) and (J) are true, remember that you are asked to draw a conclusion based *only* on the information given.

Test 6: Reading and Language Arts

1. B

You should use context clues to answer this question. The passage says there is a *precise scientific reason why rainbows can only be seen. Precise* is describing the scientific reason. Is a scientific reason sharp? Or exact? Or precious? Or difficult? The word *exact* makes the most sense in the context of this passage.

2. F

For the answer, see paragraph 2, sentence 2: *...the rainbow must be caused by the way in which the rays of light act on water drops and pass from them to our eyes.*

3. B

To find the correct answer, see the last sentence of paragraph 2.

4. H

When the sun is more than 42 degrees above the horizon line, we can no longer see the rainbow, because the required angle is now over our heads. See the last sentence of the passage.

5. B

This is a detail question. Paragraph 2, sentence 3 says: *As sunlight hits a raindrop it is refracted, or bent, by the drop in such a way that the light appears as a spectrum of colors.*

6. F

Sentence 1 contains the capitalization error. *Spring Day* does not need to be capitalized.

7. D

These sentences can be combined by simply adding the conjunction *so.* The word *and* in choice (A) is not necessary.

8. H

Most beautifulest is incorrect. The correct superlative is *most beautiful.*

9. C

Relaxation is important for mental and physical well-being. That is, it is an essential element of a healthy life.

10. J

Although some people may become aggressive under pressure, others do not. Choice (G) is also a generalization and may not be true of all people. The fact that stress allows us to accomplish things is not mentioned. A main idea of the article is that stress may cause health problems.

11. C

Reread the section where the term "negative" is used. It refers to reactions that do not demonstrate high energy such as sleeping too much or withdrawing socially.

12. G

Paragraph 3 mentions all of the answer choices except denying worries or concerns.

13. B

Since the second sentence supports the main idea of the first, the best way to combine these sentences is to arrange for it to follow the first. Choice (A) accomplishes this, but *there are two reasons why* is unnecessarily wordy. Choices (C) and (D) are also too wordy.

14. J

The best conclusion sums up ideas presented in the entire article. Choice (J) accomplishes this. Choice (F) introduces a new idea. Choice (G) adds to one detail discussed in the third paragraph rather than the article as a whole. Choice (H) introduces a new idea.

15. B

The kitten just knocked the bag of treats off the counter. The next logical thing to happen would be related to the treats; the author will probably let the kitten eat them.

16. J

The selection is a humorous story. The only medium that would not contain this type of story is a science fiction movie, since science fiction is about the future.

17. A

The author initially describes the kitten as an enemy and a monster, but his or her tone is humorous. In truth, the author loves the kitten and indulges it, as we see from his or her reaction at the end of the story when the author writes about *that sweet little face*.

18. H

Through the course of the selection we learn that the kitten is trying to get kitten treats. That is her plot. Her tactics have been to whine, growl, and otherwise wake the author. Thus, the author is annoyed. The only thing we don't know is where the author got the kitten.

19. B

The sentence is unclear. It implies the three kittens all have one name. Breaking the information into two sentences makes it more clear. Choice (A) does this as well, but it is incorrect to start a sentence with the conjunction *and*.

20. F

The best way to combine these sentences is to add the conjunction *and*. There is no reason to change every tense or make the structure of the sentence more complicated.

21. C

This sentence extends the idea that the writer has a lot of responsibilities. Using the subject pronoun *I* and an active verb makes this idea clearer.

22. G

This is a detail question. The answer is located in the second paragraph.

23. B

Paragraph 2 explains that we know how mammoths looked thanks to cave paintings and the discovery of mammoth remains.

24. F

Mammoths lived a quarter of a million years ago. (Not a quarter of a century.) They inhabited some parts of Siberia until as recently as 4,000 years ago. That means they would have existed during the time of the Egyptian pharaohs. The Cyclops was an imaginary beast. Alaska became a state in modern times.

25. C

Paragraph 3, sentence 3 explains that the mammoth's trunk was composed of soft tissue and was not fossilized. That is, it decomposed and was not preserved.

26. J

The woolly mammoth inhabited five continents, while the elephant's only natural habitats are in India and Africa. Although we are told that the mammoth migrated over the Bering land bridge, no mention is made of the distance either animal traveled. Relative trunk size is not mentioned either. Mammoths were found in Siberia, which is colder than Africa, ruling out choice (G).

27. C
The paragraph gives some details about Asian and African elephants for the purpose of comparison. A good topic sentence should introduce this idea. Choice (A), although it contains the idea of comparison, is not the best choice because it states that the two species are *completely different*, which is not correct based on the information in the paragraph.

28. H
The information about family groups is not related to the rest of the paragraph, which discusses details about the physical characteristics of African and Asian elephants.

29. C
The author mentions Hitler. This is related to World War II.

30. G
From the author's tone it seems that George is the author's husband. We know that the author is a woman because she mentions wearing silk stockings. We have no clues that George is younger than she, and thus her son, since George owns a car (which he misses being able to drive), and she does not include him when talking about the boys she must feed, bathe, and tuck in for the night.

31. C
Although she mentions baking, there is no reason to believe that is her occupation. And, though she writes that she admires the "Rosie the Riveters," she goes on to say that she is not among them. She does discuss needing to care for four children, which implies that she is a homemaker. She only planted the garden that particular day, which does not make her a full-time farmer.

32. F
The author mentions not being able to drive because her family cannot receive gasoline; thus, it must be rationed. Likewise, she is waiting for her ration book in order to buy more sugar. She misses silk stockings because they are not available and must be rationed. The only thing not mentioned as rationed is vegetables.

33. A
The author discusses her garden and rationing in the same passage. Therefore, the garden and rationing are related. America was undergoing a period of increased demand because of the war effort. Therefore, supplies that might normally be available for civilians were needed for the troops. By growing her own food, she ensures that supplies of canned food would be available for the troops.

34. J
These two sentences are related by cause/effect. Therefore, the best way to combine them expresses this relationship. Only choice (J), which contains the word *because*, makes clear the cause/effect.

35. B
This sentence expresses the idea clearly and correctly using the conjunction *although* to show how the clauses related to one another. Choice (D) also uses *although*, but the way the sentence is constructed it conveys that people were rationed rather than the items.

36. G
The main problem is expressed in the introductory sentence: *The state lottery is unfair because it steals from the poor and gives to the rich.*

37. B

Although the author does not feel that playing the lottery is a good choice, his or her main argument concerns government support of the lottery. The author is not opposed to using taxes to pay for public works, nor does he or she argue whether or not it is fair to tax a winner's jackpot.

38. J

Though the author uses Joe as one example of a winner, the term *Joe Schmoe* refers to the common Joe, the common man on the street. The description of what happens to Joe after he wins does not inspire the reader's jealousy. Despite the silly sound of Joe's name, the term is not used to make fun of people who play the lottery.

39. A

The author makes the main point that the lottery is unfair and then goes on to illustrate why. He or she does not tell people to stop buying lottery tickets. Although the author does argue against government involvement, nowhere is a ban mentioned. Nor is the connection made between the lottery and education.

40. H

The passage does not mention paying out lump sum winnings. It does, however, explain that the lottery takes a tax on each ticket purchased, that it taxes winnings, and that it benefits by collecting interest on portions of jackpots held in the bank for winners who only receive a portion of their winnings annually.

Test 7: Mathematics

1. B

When multiplying numbers to a power, add the powers. Thus, $3^3 \times 3^4 = 3^7$.

2. J

Line up the decimal points and subtract:

$$
\begin{array}{r}
6.2 \\
-0.4 \\
\hline
5.8
\end{array}
$$

3. D

A percent is a part of 100. Thus, 0.04% is $\frac{0.04}{100}$, or $\frac{4}{10,000}$.

4. H

Notice that $\frac{16}{35}$ is just slightly greater than $\frac{16}{32}$, or $\frac{1}{2}$. Answers (F) and (G) are (J) are far greater than $\frac{1}{2}$.

5. C

Subtract the decimals and you get 0.25, choice (C).

6. F

Be careful when you multiply decimals that you put the decimal in the correct place; $0.3 \times 19.95 = 5.985$.

7. E

According to the order of operations, start in the parentheses. Perform multiplication before subtraction: –6(3 –12). After the subtraction: –6(–9). Since a negative times a negative is a positive, the answer is 54. Because that is not one of the answer choices, the correct answer is (E).

8. G

First, change the fraction to a decimal; $\frac{3}{4} = 0.75$. Now, add the two decimals: 0.75 + 7.55 = 8.3.

9. D

Distance = Rate × Time; 60 mph × $\frac{3}{4}$ hour = 45 miles.

10. G

First, total the percent going to everything but new products: $10 + 50 + 25 = 85$.

$100\% - 85\% = 15\%$ left over for developing new products. To express this as a fraction of the whole budget, write $\frac{15}{100}$, which reduces to $\frac{3}{20}$.

11. A

The 1 is in the ten thousand's place.

12. H

One slice out of five can be written as $\frac{1}{5}$, which is equal to 20%.

13. C

$0.06 \times 2{,}500 = 150 + 350$ (her salary) $= 500$

14. F

First, determine the total number of machines: $5 + 12 + 4 = 21$.

$$21 \times \frac{2}{3} = \frac{42}{3} = 14 \text{ people using the machines.}$$

15. C

The statement reads: $5 > \underline{\hspace{1cm}} > 0$. Thus, the numbers that may be placed in the blank must be less than 5 but greater than 0; 4, 3, 2, 1 are less than 5 but greater than 0.

16. J

A yard is 3 feet. One foot is 12 inches; 1 yard = 36 inches. Thus, 1 inch = $\frac{1}{36}$ of a yard.

17. B

$$56 \times \frac{7}{8} = 49$$

18. G

A prime number is a whole number whose only factors are 1 and itself. The prime factors of 72 are the prime numbers whose product is equal to 72; 2 and 3 are both prime numbers, and $2^3 = 8$ and $3^2 = 9$. Since the product of 8 and 9 is 72, choice (G) is the answer.

19. A

Let x equal the unknown number.

$$2(5x) + 4 = 54$$
$$10x + 4 = 54$$
$$10x = 50$$
$$x = 5$$

20. H

The formula for area of a triangle is: $A = \frac{1}{2}bh$.

$$A = \frac{1}{2}(12 \times 5) = \frac{1}{2}(60) = 30 \text{ square inches}$$

21. B

five hundred thousand	500,000
fifty thousand	50,000
sixty-nine	69
	550,069

22. F

A quadrilateral is always polygon with four sides.

23. B

First, find how much money the two top salesmen made.

50% of $120{,}650 = .50 \times 120{,}650 = \$60{,}325$

Since 50% is half of the total sales, the other four sales people together made $60,325.

24. G

50 and 250 are both divisible by the factors 2, 5, 10, 25, and 50.

25. D

The sentence states that x is greater than –1 but less than 2. Only choice (D) does not support this range of numbers, since if x is greater than 2 it will not be contained in the interval.

26. H

$5 \times 10^3 = 5 \times (10 \times 10 \times 10) = 5 \times 1,000 = 5,000$

27. A

One glass of lemonade = x dollars + y cents. Three glasses = $3(x + y)$.

28. H

In this case, both Ken and Keisha are essentially saying the same thing. Ken wants to add the terms in parentheses; Keisha also wants to perform the operations within the parentheses first. This is the correct order of operations.

29. A

100% equals 1 whole; 200% = 2 wholes; $6 × 2 = $12.

30. H

Rosewood City is horizontally across from the section labeled B and below the section labeled 2. Therefore, it falls under coordinates B2.

31. B

A negative integer times a positive one results in a negative integer.

32. H

The table demonstrates most clearly the various rates the phone companies offer.

33. B

Circumference = diameter × π
diameter = 2 × radius = 2 × 2 = 4
circumference = 4π units

34. J

A right angle measures 90 degrees.

35. D

A quadrilateral has four sides; a pentagon has five sides.

36. H

Add the interest to the original loan amount.
$2500 × 0.12 = $300
$300 + $2,500 = $2,800 total

37. B

Organize these two sentences in ascending value.
$x > –3$; $x = –2, –1, 0$, and all positive integers.
$y < 1$; $y = 0, –1, –2$, and all negative integers.
Therefore, the set of numbers in common with both x and y is {–2, –1, 0}.

38. J

Solve for x.
$$2(3 + x) = 46$$
$$6 + 2x = 46$$
$$2x = 46 – 6$$
$$2x = 40$$
$$x = 20$$

39. C

When plotting points on a coordinate graph, list the x-axis first and the y-axis second. In order to get to the indicated point on the graph, move two units over to the left on the x-axis and then one unit up parallel to the y-axis. This gives the coordinates of (–2, 1).

40. F

The comparison to last year is irrelevant in determining this year's monthly average.

The average = $\dfrac{\text{number of inches total}}{\text{months}} = \dfrac{39}{12}$

COOP Practice Test 2
Answer Sheet

Remove or photocopy this answer sheet and use it to complete the Practice Test.

Sequences

1. Ⓐ Ⓑ Ⓒ Ⓓ	5. Ⓐ Ⓑ Ⓒ Ⓓ	9. Ⓐ Ⓑ Ⓒ Ⓓ	13. Ⓐ Ⓑ Ⓒ Ⓓ	17. Ⓐ Ⓑ Ⓒ Ⓓ
2. Ⓕ Ⓖ Ⓗ Ⓙ	6. Ⓕ Ⓖ Ⓗ Ⓙ	10. Ⓕ Ⓖ Ⓗ Ⓙ	14. Ⓕ Ⓖ Ⓗ Ⓙ	18. Ⓕ Ⓖ Ⓗ Ⓙ
3. Ⓐ Ⓑ Ⓒ Ⓓ	7. Ⓐ Ⓑ Ⓒ Ⓓ	11. Ⓐ Ⓑ Ⓒ Ⓓ	15. Ⓐ Ⓑ Ⓒ Ⓓ	19. Ⓐ Ⓑ Ⓒ Ⓓ
4. Ⓕ Ⓖ Ⓗ Ⓙ	8. Ⓕ Ⓖ Ⓗ Ⓙ	12. Ⓕ Ⓖ Ⓗ Ⓙ	16. Ⓕ Ⓖ Ⓗ Ⓙ	20. Ⓕ Ⓖ Ⓗ Ⓙ

Analogies

1. Ⓐ Ⓑ Ⓒ Ⓓ	5. Ⓐ Ⓑ Ⓒ Ⓓ	9. Ⓐ Ⓑ Ⓒ Ⓓ	13. Ⓐ Ⓑ Ⓒ Ⓓ	17. Ⓐ Ⓑ Ⓒ Ⓓ
2. Ⓕ Ⓖ Ⓗ Ⓙ	6. Ⓕ Ⓖ Ⓗ Ⓙ	10. Ⓕ Ⓖ Ⓗ Ⓙ	14. Ⓕ Ⓖ Ⓗ Ⓙ	18. Ⓕ Ⓖ Ⓗ Ⓙ
3. Ⓐ Ⓑ Ⓒ Ⓓ	7. Ⓐ Ⓑ Ⓒ Ⓓ	11. Ⓐ Ⓑ Ⓒ Ⓓ	15. Ⓐ Ⓑ Ⓒ Ⓓ	19. Ⓐ Ⓑ Ⓒ Ⓓ
4. Ⓕ Ⓖ Ⓗ Ⓙ	8. Ⓕ Ⓖ Ⓗ Ⓙ	12. Ⓕ Ⓖ Ⓗ Ⓙ	16. Ⓕ Ⓖ Ⓗ Ⓙ	20. Ⓕ Ⓖ Ⓗ Ⓙ

Quantitative Reasoning

1. Ⓐ Ⓑ Ⓒ Ⓓ	5. Ⓐ Ⓑ Ⓒ Ⓓ	9. Ⓐ Ⓑ Ⓒ Ⓓ	13. Ⓐ Ⓑ Ⓒ Ⓓ	17. Ⓐ Ⓑ Ⓒ Ⓓ
2. Ⓕ Ⓖ Ⓗ Ⓙ	6. Ⓕ Ⓖ Ⓗ Ⓙ	10. Ⓕ Ⓖ Ⓗ Ⓙ	14. Ⓕ Ⓖ Ⓗ Ⓙ	18. Ⓕ Ⓖ Ⓗ Ⓙ
3. Ⓐ Ⓑ Ⓒ Ⓓ	7. Ⓐ Ⓑ Ⓒ Ⓓ	11. Ⓐ Ⓑ Ⓒ Ⓓ	15. Ⓐ Ⓑ Ⓒ Ⓓ	19. Ⓐ Ⓑ Ⓒ Ⓓ
4. Ⓕ Ⓖ Ⓗ Ⓙ	8. Ⓕ Ⓖ Ⓗ Ⓙ	12. Ⓕ Ⓖ Ⓗ Ⓙ	16. Ⓕ Ⓖ Ⓗ Ⓙ	20. Ⓕ Ⓖ Ⓗ Ⓙ

Verbal Reasoning—Words

1. Ⓐ Ⓑ Ⓒ Ⓓ	5. Ⓐ Ⓑ Ⓒ Ⓓ	9. Ⓐ Ⓑ Ⓒ Ⓓ	13. Ⓐ Ⓑ Ⓒ Ⓓ	17. Ⓐ Ⓑ Ⓒ Ⓓ
2. Ⓕ Ⓖ Ⓗ Ⓙ	6. Ⓕ Ⓖ Ⓗ Ⓙ	10. Ⓕ Ⓖ Ⓗ Ⓙ	14. Ⓕ Ⓖ Ⓗ Ⓙ	18. Ⓕ Ⓖ Ⓗ Ⓙ
3. Ⓐ Ⓑ Ⓒ Ⓓ	7. Ⓐ Ⓑ Ⓒ Ⓓ	11. Ⓐ Ⓑ Ⓒ Ⓓ	15. Ⓐ Ⓑ Ⓒ Ⓓ	19. Ⓐ Ⓑ Ⓒ Ⓓ
4. Ⓕ Ⓖ Ⓗ Ⓙ	8. Ⓕ Ⓖ Ⓗ Ⓙ	12. Ⓕ Ⓖ Ⓗ Ⓙ	16. Ⓕ Ⓖ Ⓗ Ⓙ	20. Ⓕ Ⓖ Ⓗ Ⓙ

Verbal Reasoning—Context

1. Ⓐ Ⓑ Ⓒ Ⓓ	5. Ⓐ Ⓑ Ⓒ Ⓓ	9. Ⓐ Ⓑ Ⓒ Ⓓ	13. Ⓐ Ⓑ Ⓒ Ⓓ	17. Ⓐ Ⓑ Ⓒ Ⓓ
2. Ⓕ Ⓖ Ⓗ Ⓙ	6. Ⓕ Ⓖ Ⓗ Ⓙ	10. Ⓕ Ⓖ Ⓗ Ⓙ	14. Ⓕ Ⓖ Ⓗ Ⓙ	18. Ⓕ Ⓖ Ⓗ Ⓙ
3. Ⓐ Ⓑ Ⓒ Ⓓ	7. Ⓐ Ⓑ Ⓒ Ⓓ	11. Ⓐ Ⓑ Ⓒ Ⓓ	15. Ⓐ Ⓑ Ⓒ Ⓓ	19. Ⓐ Ⓑ Ⓒ Ⓓ
4. Ⓕ Ⓖ Ⓗ Ⓙ	8. Ⓕ Ⓖ Ⓗ Ⓙ	12. Ⓕ Ⓖ Ⓗ Ⓙ	16. Ⓕ Ⓖ Ⓗ Ⓙ	20. Ⓕ Ⓖ Ⓗ Ⓙ

Reading and Language Arts

1. Ⓐ Ⓑ Ⓒ Ⓓ	9. Ⓐ Ⓑ Ⓒ Ⓓ	17. Ⓐ Ⓑ Ⓒ Ⓓ	25. Ⓐ Ⓑ Ⓒ Ⓓ	33. Ⓐ Ⓑ Ⓒ Ⓓ
2. Ⓕ Ⓖ Ⓗ Ⓙ	10. Ⓕ Ⓖ Ⓗ Ⓙ	18. Ⓕ Ⓖ Ⓗ Ⓙ	26. Ⓕ Ⓖ Ⓗ Ⓙ	34. Ⓕ Ⓖ Ⓗ Ⓙ
3. Ⓐ Ⓑ Ⓒ Ⓓ	11. Ⓐ Ⓑ Ⓒ Ⓓ	19. Ⓐ Ⓑ Ⓒ Ⓓ	27. Ⓐ Ⓑ Ⓒ Ⓓ	35. Ⓐ Ⓑ Ⓒ Ⓓ
4. Ⓕ Ⓖ Ⓗ Ⓙ	12. Ⓕ Ⓖ Ⓗ Ⓙ	20. Ⓕ Ⓖ Ⓗ Ⓙ	28. Ⓕ Ⓖ Ⓗ Ⓙ	36. Ⓕ Ⓖ Ⓗ Ⓙ
5. Ⓐ Ⓑ Ⓒ Ⓓ	13. Ⓐ Ⓑ Ⓒ Ⓓ	21. Ⓐ Ⓑ Ⓒ Ⓓ	29. Ⓐ Ⓑ Ⓒ Ⓓ	37. Ⓐ Ⓑ Ⓒ Ⓓ
6. Ⓕ Ⓖ Ⓗ Ⓙ	14. Ⓕ Ⓖ Ⓗ Ⓙ	22. Ⓕ Ⓖ Ⓗ Ⓙ	30. Ⓕ Ⓖ Ⓗ Ⓙ	38. Ⓕ Ⓖ Ⓗ Ⓙ
7. Ⓐ Ⓑ Ⓒ Ⓓ	15. Ⓐ Ⓑ Ⓒ Ⓓ	23. Ⓐ Ⓑ Ⓒ Ⓓ	31. Ⓐ Ⓑ Ⓒ Ⓓ	39. Ⓐ Ⓑ Ⓒ Ⓓ
8. Ⓕ Ⓖ Ⓗ Ⓙ	16. Ⓕ Ⓖ Ⓗ Ⓙ	24. Ⓕ Ⓖ Ⓗ Ⓙ	32. Ⓕ Ⓖ Ⓗ Ⓙ	40. Ⓕ Ⓖ Ⓗ Ⓙ

Mathematics Concepts and Applications

1. Ⓐ Ⓑ Ⓒ Ⓓ Ⓔ	9. Ⓐ Ⓑ Ⓒ Ⓓ	17. Ⓐ Ⓑ Ⓒ Ⓓ	25. Ⓐ Ⓑ Ⓒ Ⓓ	33. Ⓐ Ⓑ Ⓒ Ⓓ
2. Ⓕ Ⓖ Ⓗ Ⓙ Ⓚ	10. Ⓕ Ⓖ Ⓗ Ⓙ	18. Ⓕ Ⓖ Ⓗ Ⓙ	26. Ⓕ Ⓖ Ⓗ Ⓙ	34. Ⓕ Ⓖ Ⓗ Ⓙ
3. Ⓐ Ⓑ Ⓒ Ⓓ Ⓔ	11. Ⓐ Ⓑ Ⓒ Ⓓ	19. Ⓐ Ⓑ Ⓒ Ⓓ	27. Ⓐ Ⓑ Ⓒ Ⓓ	35. Ⓐ Ⓑ Ⓒ Ⓓ
4. Ⓕ Ⓖ Ⓗ Ⓙ Ⓚ	12. Ⓕ Ⓖ Ⓗ Ⓙ	20. Ⓕ Ⓖ Ⓗ Ⓙ	28. Ⓕ Ⓖ Ⓗ Ⓙ	36. Ⓕ Ⓖ Ⓗ Ⓙ
5. Ⓐ Ⓑ Ⓒ Ⓓ Ⓔ	13. Ⓐ Ⓑ Ⓒ Ⓓ	21. Ⓐ Ⓑ Ⓒ Ⓓ	29. Ⓐ Ⓑ Ⓒ Ⓓ	37. Ⓐ Ⓑ Ⓒ Ⓓ
6. Ⓕ Ⓖ Ⓗ Ⓙ Ⓚ	14. Ⓕ Ⓖ Ⓗ Ⓙ	22. Ⓕ Ⓖ Ⓗ Ⓙ	30. Ⓕ Ⓖ Ⓗ Ⓙ	38. Ⓕ Ⓖ Ⓗ Ⓙ
7. Ⓐ Ⓑ Ⓒ Ⓓ Ⓔ	15. Ⓐ Ⓑ Ⓒ Ⓓ	23. Ⓐ Ⓑ Ⓒ Ⓓ	31. Ⓐ Ⓑ Ⓒ Ⓓ	39. Ⓐ Ⓑ Ⓒ Ⓓ
8. Ⓕ Ⓖ Ⓗ Ⓙ Ⓚ	16. Ⓕ Ⓖ Ⓗ Ⓙ	24. Ⓕ Ⓖ Ⓗ Ⓙ	32. Ⓕ Ⓖ Ⓗ Ⓙ	40. Ⓕ Ⓖ Ⓗ Ⓙ

TEST 1: SEQUENCES

20 minutes

Directions: For questions 1–20, choose the answer that best continues the sequence.

1.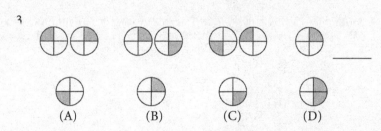

    (A)   (B)   (C)   (D)

2.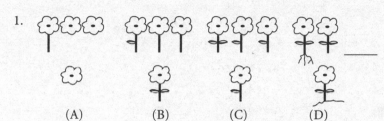

    (F)   (G)   (H)   (J)

3.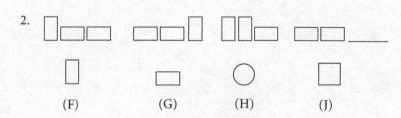

    (A)   (B)   (C)   (D)

4. Ab AA Ac   Ad AA Ae   Af AA Ag   Ah _____ Ai

    AA   Ai   Aj   Ak

    (F)   (G)   (H)   (J)

5.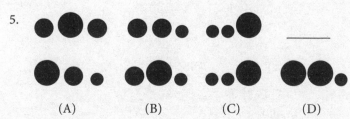

    (A)   (B)   (C)   (D)

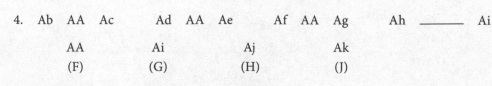

COOP Practice Test 2

6.

(F)   (G)   (H)   (J)

7. 5 14 23   15 24 33   27 36 ____

   (A) 38
   (B) 45
   (C) 42
   (D) 44

8. 55 51 47   43 39 35   81 ____ 73

   (F) 75
   (G) 79
   (H) 77
   (J) 78

9. 27 9 3   63 21 7   ____ 18 6

   (A) 54
   (B) 24
   (C) 42
   (D) 25

10. 15 23 18   27 35 30   62 ____ 65

   (F) 84
   (G) 82
   (H) 80
   (J) 70

11. 5 20 10   8 32 16   7 28 ____

   (A) 10
   (B) 12
   (C) 20
   (D) 14

12. 6 7 13   9 7 16   8 ____ 15

   (F) 7
   (G) 10
   (H) 9
   (J) 13

13. 1 1 1   3 9 27   2 ____ 8

   (A) 6
   (B) 4
   (C) 5
   (D) 1

14. $A_6B_5C_4$ $A_5B_4C_3$ $A_4B_3C_2$ ____

   (F) $A_4B_3C_2$
   (G) $A_3B_2C_1$
   (H) $A_5B_3C_2$
   (J) $A_4B_3C_3$

15. $2X^1Y_5$ $2X^2Y_4$ $2X^3Y_3$ ____

   (A) $2X_4Y_2$
   (B) $2X^3Y_3$
   (C) $2X^4Y_2$
   (D) $2X^4Y_1$

16. $A^1B^1C^2$ $B^2B^3C^3$ ____ $D^4B^7C^5$

   (F) $C^3B^5C^4$
   (G) $C^3B^3C^5$
   (H) $C^3B^4B^3C^4$
   (J) $C^3B^4C^6$

17. BOB   MOM   ____   PIP

   (A) POP
   (B) MOP
   (C) BOP
   (D) BIP

18. CDAI   FGEO   HJUA   ____

   (F) IJKO
   (G) KJEA
   (H) JKOP
   (J) KLOA

19. Yxx   Wvv   _____   Srr

    (A) Zyy

    (B) Qrr

    (C) Utt

    (D) Tuu

20. AABA   BACB   CADC   _____

    (F) ACAE

    (G) ACDC

    (H) DAED

    (J) DADE

TEST 2: ANALOGIES

20 minutes

Directions: For questions 1–20, look at the two pictures in the top boxes. Then, choose the picture that belongs in the empty box so that the bottom two pictures are related the same way that the top two are related.

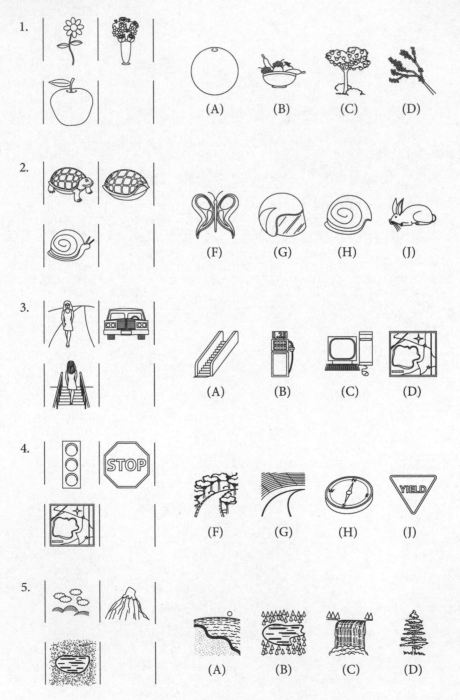

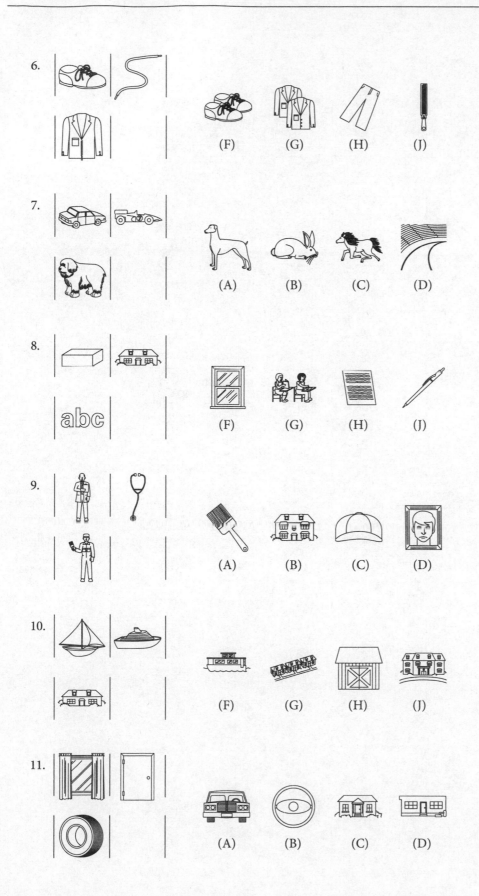

6.

(F) (G) (H) (J)

7.

(A) (B) (C) (D)

8.

(F) (G) (H) (J)

9.

(A) (B) (C) (D)

10.

(F) (G) (H) (J)

11.

(A) (B) (C) (D)

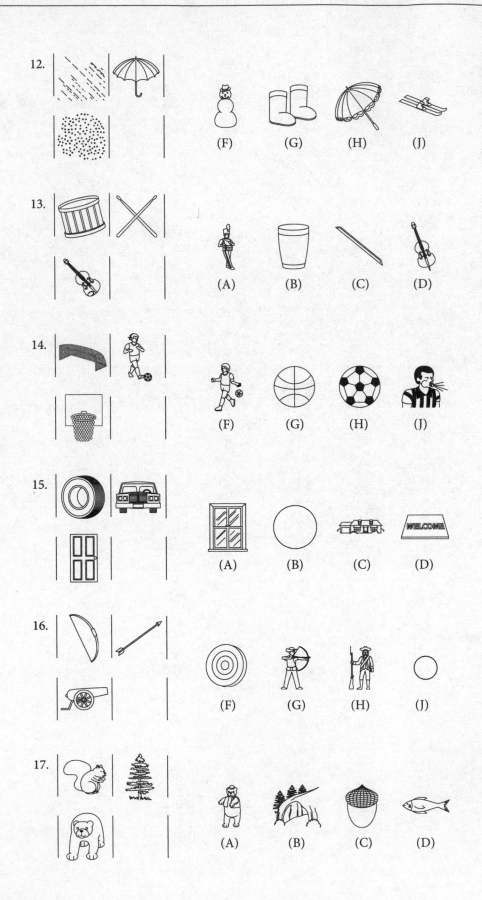

12.

(F) (G) (H) (J)

13.

(A) (B) (C) (D)

14.

(F) (G) (H) (J)

15.

(A) (B) (C) (D)

16.

(F) (G) (H) (J)

17.

(A) (B) (C) (D)

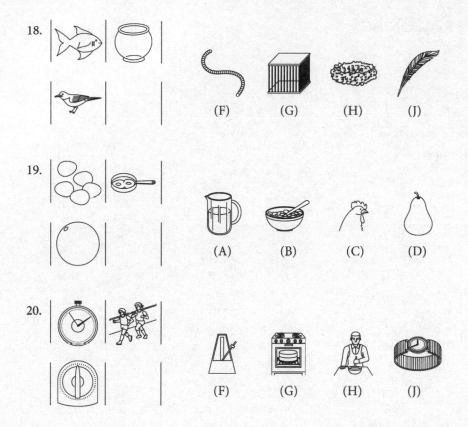

TEST 3: QUANTITATIVE REASONING

20 minutes

Directions: For questions 1–6, find the relationship of the numbers in the left column to the numbers in the right column. Choose the number that should replace the blank.

1. $2 \rightarrow \square \rightarrow 12$

   $1 \rightarrow \square \rightarrow 6$

   $3 \rightarrow \square \rightarrow$ ____

4	18	9	24
(A)	(B)	(C)	(D)

2. $15 \rightarrow \square \rightarrow 8$

   $16 \rightarrow \square \rightarrow 9$

   $11 \rightarrow \square \rightarrow$ ____

3	10	12	4
(F)	(G)	(H)	(J)

3. $12 \rightarrow \square \rightarrow 19$

   $2 \rightarrow \square \rightarrow 9$

   $5 \rightarrow \square \rightarrow$ ____

12	15	13	10
(A)	(B)	(C)	(D)

4. $\frac{1}{3} \rightarrow \square \rightarrow \frac{4}{3}$

   $\frac{1}{4} \rightarrow \square \rightarrow \frac{5}{4}$

   $\frac{1}{5} \rightarrow \square \rightarrow$ ____

$\frac{5}{5}$	1	$\frac{6}{5}$	$\frac{7}{5}$
(F)	(G)	(H)	(J)

5. $2 \rightarrow \square \rightarrow 1$

   $1 \rightarrow \square \rightarrow 0$

   $3 \rightarrow \square \rightarrow$ ____

2	$\frac{1}{3}$	1	-1
(A)	(B)	(C)	(D)

6. $17 \rightarrow \square \rightarrow 22$

   $9 \rightarrow \square \rightarrow 14$

   $3 \rightarrow \square \rightarrow$ ____

9	6	8	10
(F)	(G)	(H)	(J)

Directions: For questions 7–13, find the fraction of the grid that is shaded.

7.

(A) $\frac{1}{2}$ (B) $\frac{1}{4}$ (C) $\frac{1}{8}$ (D) $\frac{1}{16}$

8.

(F) 2   (G) $\frac{1}{6}$ (H) $\frac{2}{3}$ (J) $\frac{1}{3}$

9.

(A) $\frac{1}{2}$ (B) $\frac{1}{5}$ (C) 5   (D) $\frac{5}{12}$

10.

(F) $\frac{1}{4}$ (G) 12   (H) $\frac{2}{9}$ (J) $\frac{2}{7}$

11.

(A) $\frac{3}{8}$ (B) $\frac{1}{3}$ (C) $\frac{1}{4}$ (D) $\frac{1}{2}$

12.

(F) $\frac{1}{3}$ (G) $\frac{1}{12}$ (H) $\frac{3}{10}$ (J) $\frac{1}{4}$

13.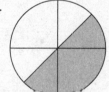

(A) $\frac{1}{4}$ (B) $\frac{1}{3}$ (C) $\frac{1}{2}$ (D) $\frac{2}{3}$

Directions: For questions 14–20, the scale shows sets of shapes of equal weight. Find a pair of sets that would also balance the scale.

14.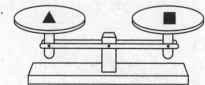

(F) ▲   ▲▲

(G) ▲■   ■▲

(H) ■▲   ■

(J) ▲▲■   ■

15.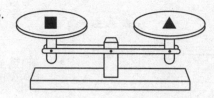

(A) ▲   ▲■

(B) ▲■   ▲▲

(C) ■▲   ■

(D) ▲▲   ■

16.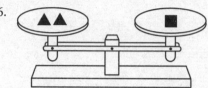

(F) ■▲   ▲▲■

(G) ■■   ▲▲

(H) ▲   ■■

(J) ▲▲■   ▲▲▲

17.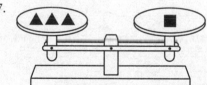

(A) ■▲▲▲   ■■

(B) ■■   ▲▲▲▲▲

(C) ■■▲   ▲▲■

(D) ▲   ■■

18.

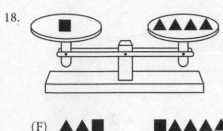

(F)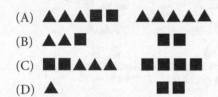

(G)

(H)

(J)

19.

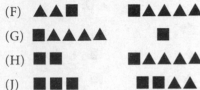

(A)

(B)

(C)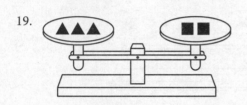

(D)

20.

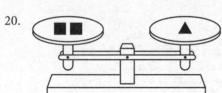

(F)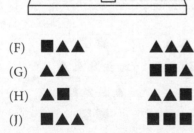

(G)

(H)

(J)

TEST 4: VERBAL REASONING—WORDS

20 minutes

Directions: For questions 1–9, find the word that names a necessary part of the underlined word.

1. <u>wedding</u>

   (A) invitation
   (B) party
   (C) dress
   (D) bride

2. <u>controversy</u>

   (F) disagreement
   (G) aggression
   (H) truce
   (J) resolution

3. <u>drum</u>

   (A) cymbals
   (B) sticks
   (C) rhythm
   (D) rhyme

4. <u>agriculture</u>

   (F) seasons
   (G) livestock
   (H) garden
   (J) crops

5. <u>candidate</u>

   (A) politics
   (B) choice
   (C) freedom
   (D) poll

6. <u>optimist</u>

    (F) joy
    (G) love
    (H) hope
    (J) emotion

7. <u>flower</u>

    (A) garden
    (B) petal
    (C) daisy
    (D) bee

8. <u>guitar</u>

    (F) strings
    (G) concert
    (H) electric
    (J) bass

9. <u>ticket</u>

    (A) window
    (B) stadium
    (C) expense
    (D) entry

Directions: For questions 10–13, the words in the top row are related in some way. The words in the bottom row are related in the same way. Find the word that competes the bottom row of words.

10. drizzle   rain   downpour

    warm   hot

    (F) scorching
    (G) sun
    (H) tepid
    (J) heat

11. car   truck   motorcycle

    jet   hot air balloon

    (A) helicopter
    (B) scooter
    (C) horse
    (D) sky

12. word   sentence   paragraph

    chapter   book

    (F) magazine
    (G) title
    (H) series
    (J) author

13. snail   worm   turtle

    cheetah   greyhound

    (A) horse
    (B) race
    (C) snake
    (D) spots

Directions: For questions 14–17, find the word that does not belong with the others.

14. Which word does *not* belong with the others?

    (F) approve
    (G) scorn
    (H) condemn
    (J) mock

15. Which word does *not* belong with the others?

    (A) license
    (B) visa
    (C) permit
    (D) regulation

16. Which word does *not* belong with the others?

    (F) kick
    (G) draw
    (H) bounce
    (J) throw

17. Which word does *not* belong with the others?

    (A) nose
    (B) aroma
    (C) odor
    (D) scent

Directions: For questions 18–20, find the word that is most like the underlined words.

18. land   earth   dirt

    (F) soil
    (G) island
    (H) muddy
    (J) garden

19. exercise   sports   workout

    (A) athletics
    (B) gym
    (C) tennis
    (D) sweat

20. work   job   occupation

    (F) employment
    (G) boss
    (H) salary
    (J) promotion

TEST 5: VERBAL REASONING— CONTEXT

20 minutes

Directions: For questions 1–20, find the statement that is true according to the given information.

1. Cherry trees bloom in the spring. The cherry tree in Alonso's backyard is blooming.

    (A) Alonso has a cherry tree in his yard.
    (B) It is March.
    (C) It is not April.
    (D) Alonso lives in the country.

2. Today is a windy day. Sailboats need wind in order to move.

    (F) It is fall.
    (G) It is November.
    (H) Today is a good day to sail.
    (J) It is easy to sail.

3. "Hola" means hello in Spanish. Marco just told Lena "hello" in French.

    (A) Marco speaks French well.
    (B) Marco probably did not say "hola."
    (C) Lena speaks French.
    (D) Marco does not speak Spanish.

4. At an auction, the highest bidder wins the item. Rachel bid $100 on an antique chair.

    (F) Someone will probably outbid Rachel.
    (G) Rachel is the auctioneer.
    (H) Rachel will win the chair.
    (J) Rachel is at an auction.

5. Mr. and Mrs. Bowden have a two-year-old son and a five-year-old daughter. Clarissa is eight years old.

   (A) Clarissa is not Mr. and Mrs. Bowden's daughter.
   (B) Clarissa is Mr. and Mrs. Bowden's niece.
   (C) Clarissa is younger than Mr. and Mrs. Bowden's daughter.
   (D) Clarissa lives next door to the Bowdens.

6. There is a tasty smell coming from the kitchen. David is in the kitchen.

   (F) David is baking cookies.
   (G) Something is in the oven.
   (H) David is making a sandwich.
   (J) Someone is in the kitchen.

7. The flowers in the front yard need to be watered twice a day. The flowers in the front yard are wilting.

   (A) The flowers need more water.
   (B) Someone is watering the flowers too much.
   (C) The flowers are not healthy.
   (D) There are flowers in the backyard.

8. Adina is watching television. She is smiling.

   (F) Adina is probably happy.
   (G) Adina loves to watch television.
   (H) Adina is watching a comedy.
   (J) Adina is sitting down.

9. A cookie is missing from Sarah's cookie jar. Seung Hee loves cookies.

   (A) Seung Hee took the missing cookie.
   (B) The cookie jar is easy to open.
   (C) Sarah bakes cookies.
   (D) Sarah keeps cookies in a cookie jar.

10. Suzie received ten Valentine's Day cards. One card was signed "from your secret admirer."

    (F) Suzie's secret admirer sent her only one card.
    (G) Suzie sent a card to her secret admirer.
    (H) Suzie received fewer than a dozen Valentine's Day cards.
    (J) Suzie's secret admirer is in her class.

11. All soldiers in boot camp must be able to run the camp's obstacle course. Elise is in boot camp.

    (A) Elise is in good physical condition.
    (B) Elise is able to run the camp's obstacle course.
    (C) Elise is stronger than the men in boot camp.
    (D) Elise is a drill sergeant.

12. Hope and Joey went fishing. Hope caught three fish and Joey caught five.

    (F) Joey is a better fisher than Hope.
    (G) Hope used different bait than Joey.
    (H) Hope and Joey are best friends.
    (J) Hope caught fewer fish than Joey.

13. Babies cry if they are tired or hungry. Baby X is crying. Her parents just fed her.

    (A) Baby X doesn't like to eat.
    (B) Baby X does not sleep enough at night.
    (C) Baby X is confusing her parents.
    (D) Baby X needs to take a nap.

14. The Bailer family lives in an apartment complex with a swimming pool and a communal tennis court. The tennis court can get very crowded on Saturdays, and they must make a reservation if they want to play.

    (F) The Bailers like to swim.
    (G) The Bailers do not live in a house.
    (H) The people in the complex are good tennis players.
    (J) Everyone likes to play tennis.

15. Bobby Lee tried out for the fall production and won the lead role. In the spring he only landed a bit part. Bobby Lee is joining the town football league in the summer.

    (A) Bobby Lee has given up acting.
    (B) Bobby Lee is a better actor than football player.
    (C) Bobby Lee's acting is improving.
    (D) Bobby Lee enjoys various activities.

16. Karl and Karla Cooper watch television in the evenings. Karl sits on the sofa and changes channels frequently. Karla sits in the armchair and does the crossword puzzle.

    (F) Karla Cooper is good at the crossword puzzle.
    (G) Karla Cooper would like to watch just one show.
    (H) Karl Cooper does not like to watch only one show.
    (J) Karl and Karla Cooper are married.

17. Rene's grandmother calls her every Sunday from Paris. Rene is always happy to hear from her grandmother.

    (A) Rene has a good relationship with her grandmother.
    (B) Rene understands French.
    (C) Rene has been to Paris.
    (D) Rene's grandmother speaks French.

18. The special of the day at Kelly's Diner is fried chicken. All the employees at Kelly's can eat the special of the day for free.

    (F) All the employees at Kelly's will eat fried chicken.
    (G) The cooks cannot eat fried chicken for free today.
    (H) The employees at Kelly's do not have to pay for the special of the day.
    (J) The employees at Kelly's love fried chicken.

19. Jason is taking a ferry to New Hope Island. The ferry ride to New Hope Island takes one hour.

    (A) Jason cannot swim to New Hope Island.
    (B) Jason likes the ferry ride.
    (C) Jason will be at New Hope Island in an hour.
    (D) New Hope Island is an hour ferry ride from shore.

20. There is a "buy one get one free" sale at Shoe Shack. Sam left Shoe Shack with two pairs of sneakers.

    (F) Sam should get two more pairs of sneakers for free.
    (G) Sam always buys his sneakers at Shoe Shack.
    (H) Shoe Shack has the best deal in town.
    (J) Sam only paid for one pair of sneakers.

TEST 6: READING AND LANGUAGE ARTS

40 minutes

Directions: Follow the directions for questions 1–40.

Read the following passage and answer questions 1–4.

Say the word "Dada." It may sound like gibberish, baby talk, or just plain nonsense. That's what the creators of the Dada art movement wanted. The ideas these artists put forth and the artwork they created intentionally mocked mature, rational culture. In reaction to the brutality of World War I, the Dadaists rejected the values that they believed led to the war—nationalism, militarism, and rational philosophy. Instead they stressed child like creativity and the triumph of life in the face of war and destruction.

The Dadaists did not acquire their name until 1916, but the work of several artists years earlier sparked the spirit of the movement. In 1913, French artist Marcel Duchamp made the first of his *ready-mades*, in which he selected everyday objects, such as a bicycle wheel or a toilet seat, and raised them to the status of art by signing them and exhibiting them in art galleries. Duchamp also had the gall to take the world famous Leonardo da Vinci painting, the *Mona Lisa*, and draw a moustache on Mona Lisa's face. He then declared the painting his own. Every musician today who "samples" tunes from other sources owes a debt of gratitude to Marcel Duchamp.

The artist Francis Picabia was also an important "father" of the Dada movement. Working in New York City in 1915, Picabia created playful paintings, drawings, and sculptures that depicted human figures in the form of machines—a joking stab at new technology. Picabia and Duchamp's work drew the attention of a small but active circle of American patrons, writers, and artists who helped them gain notoriety.

The official—if Dadaism can be called official—launch of Dada took place in 1916 with the opening of the nightclub the Cabaret Voltaire in Zurich, Switzerland. As a neutral country, Switzerland attracted artists and intellectuals opposed to the war. The exact genesis of the name Dada is debated, but Romanian-born French poet, Tristan Tzara claims to have created it. Some argue that Dada means rocking horse in French but Tzara proclaimed "Dada means nothing!" arguing for the absurdity of the movement and its art.

1. According to this article

    (A) the Dadaists were children
    (B) Dadaists were reacting to the war
    (C) Dadaists were not good artists
    (D) Dadaism was started by Marcel Duchamp

2. All of the following were mentioned as qualities of Dadaism EXCEPT

    (F) love of nonsense
    (G) making fun of rational thought
    (H) joking about technology
    (J) patriotic demonstrations

3. Dadaism officially began

    (A) when Cabaret Voltaire opened in Zurich
    (B) when Marcel Duchamp began to create ready-mades
    (C) when World War I began
    (D) when Tristan Tzara declared "Dada means nothing!"

4. Duchamp probably drew a moustache on the *Mona Lisa*

    (F) because he didn't like the painting
    (G) to insult the original artist
    (H) to mock the establishment
    (J) to make himself famous

Here is a paragraph a student wrote about the Dada movement. There are a few mistakes that need correcting. Read the story, then answer questions 5–7.

(1) The Dada art movement was an interesting, exciting, and original movement. (2) It was also very creative. (3) These artists believed it was important not to take life too seriously. (4) They thought that War was caused by too much seriousness and since they were against War, they wanted to act differently. (5) They behaved childish and made childish artwork.

5. Which is the best way to combine sentences 1 and 2?

    (A) The Dada art movement was an interesting, exciting, and original, and creative movement.
    (B) The Dada art movement was an interesting, exciting, original movement and it was also very creative.
    (C) The Dada art movement was an interesting, exciting, and original and creative movement.
    (D) The Dada art movement was interesting, exciting, original, and creative.

6. Which sentence contains a capitalization error?

    (F) Sentence 1
    (G) Sentence 2
    (H) Sentence 3
    (J) Sentence 4

7. Which is the best way to write sentence 5?

    (A) They behaved childish and childishly made artwork.
    (B) They were behaving childish and were making childish artwork.
    (C) They behaved childishly and made childish artwork.
    (D) Best as is.

Read the following passage and answer questions 8–13.

"A rose by any other name would smell as sweet," said Shakespeare's Romeo to Juliet. Meaning, he would love her no matter what her name was. Juliet was still Juliet to Romeo no matter whether she was a Capulet (from the enemy family), a Montague, or a Smith.

But, is Romeo's declaration true? Would a rose by any other name smell as sweet? Linguists have been asking this question for many years. They wonder does someone or something's name contribute to how we see that person or thing? If Juliet were called Barney, would Romeo still feel romantic about her? If a rose were called a stinkweed, would we still consider it beautiful and fragrant? What if we called the rose George? Or, what if we used the word *kurchup* to signify a rose? Is it still a rose?

The French linguist Ferdinand Saussure said no. In a series of lectures Saussure delivered in 1910, he rejected the idea that words have a relationship to real, concrete objects. Words, according to Saussure, exist in relation to one another. A rose is a rose because it is **not** a daisy, a violet, a peony, or an ant. Words, or the sounds we make that become words, are randomly selected and take on meaning only because we give them meaning. This theory makes sense when you realize that the word for rose is different in many of the world's hundreds of languages. The group of sounds that make up the word rose have come to mean that particular flower because we all have agreed to let them mean that thing. The words that make up a language come about because they are mutually agreed on by a group, rather than from any special character of the object they describe.

8. A good title for this selection would be

   (F) Romeo and Juliet
   (G) All about Roses
   (H) A Theory of Language
   (J) Shakespeare's Drama

9. The author's tone in this selection is

   (A) enthusiastic
   (B) biased
   (C) matter-of-fact
   (D) poetic

10. The author uses questions in this selection to

   (F) inspire the reader to think about a complicated idea
   (G) show that no one has answers to these difficult questions
   (H) prove that Saussure had answers to all these questions
   (J) demonstrate that Shakespeare is confusing

11. Which of the following BEST demonstrates Saussure's theory?

   (A) one person making up his own word to describe a flower
   (B) a group of people agreeing to call a flower a *blurp*
   (C) a pet owner naming her cat Mittens
   (D) a flower having a different name in ten different languages

12. Here are two sentences related to the passage:

    Saussure was a French linguist.
    Saussure changed the way people thought about language.

    Select the answer choice that best combines the two sentences into one.

    (F) Saussure was a French linguist and he changed the way people thought about language.

    (G) Saussure was a French linguist, which changed people's thinking about language.

    (H) Saussure, a French linguist, changed the way people thought about language.

    (J) Saussure changed the way people thought about language, and was a French linguist.

13. Choose the sentence that is written correctly.

    (A) Linguists study the origins, evolution, and roots of languages.

    (B) Linguists are people whom are skilled in languages.

    (C) Saussure discussed many new ideas when he lectures in 1910.

    (D) Speaking many languages, are necessary to a linguist.

Read the following passage and answer questions 14–16.

It's 9 o'clock on a dark, moonlit night and you're rowing a boat over the calm waters of a bay. You slip your oar into the water and notice a curious thing. A glowing green light shines from the waters below. You raise your oar out of the water and the light vanishes. What is this strange phenomenon? The glow you're seeing is caused by a bioluminescent creature, an animal able to emit its own light. Many marine animals possess this amazing quality—from microscopic bacteria to the five-meter-long 'Megamouth' shark.

Despite their tremendous diversity, all bioluminescent organisms create light by the same process. Bioluminescence occurs as a result of a chemical reaction between a protein (luciferin) and an enzyme (luciferase) in the presence of oxygen. If you've ever accidentally touched a lightbulb when it's on, you know that most light sources give off a lot of heat. This reduces the amount of free energy that can be converted into light. Another source of energy loss is the production of sound—think of the humming noise that same lightbulb makes. Bioluminescence however is almost 100% efficient. Practically all of the energy generated by the luciferin-luciferase reaction is converted into light without being lost in heat or sound production. Bioluminescence is amazingly a 'cold fire.'

14. Bioluminescent organisms create light by

    (F) a chemical reaction
    (G) converting free energy into light
    (H) producing sound
    (J) touching other organisms

15. Bioluminescent light differs from other light sources because

    (A) it takes place in the presence of oxygen
    (B) it loses heat in light production
    (C) it is more efficient
    (D) it is a type of fire

16. According to the passage, all of the following are true of bioluminescent creatures EXCEPT

    (F) there are a wide variety of bioluminescent creatures
    (G) all bioluminescent creatures make light the same way
    (H) many bioluminescent creatures are marine animals
    (J) it may be painful to touch a bioluminescent creature

Here is a paragraph related to the passage. Read the paragraph, then answer questions 17–18.

The first category of bioluminescent creatures includes animals equipped with 'photophores.' These are organs similar to eye structures located deep within the skin. In photophores, light is produced by specialized cells and reflected through a lens or clear outer covering. The second category of bioluminescent animal uses the luminosity of bacteria that live within it. The host cannot control the amount of light produced by the bacteria, so those organisms with bacterial symbionts have developed some interesting ways to "turn out the light" when necessary.

17. Choose the best topic sentence for this paragraph.

    (A) Bioluminescent creatures can be classified into two basic categories.
    (B) Bioluminescent creatures often use their light to stun or confuse predators.
    (C) Some bioluminescent creatures are photophores.
    (D) Many deep-sea creatures migrate toward the surface nightly, following their prey.

18. What might you expect the next paragraph to be about?

    (F) how symbionts get inside the host animal
    (G) how bioluminescence can help an animal
    (H) some ways bioluminescent animals can control their symbionts
    (J) why host organisms may need to "turn out the light"

Read the following passage and answer questions 19–22.

As the saying goes, Rome wasn't built in a day. Writing a top-notch essay takes time, planning, and careful revision. In order to revise, you must first have something down on paper. Many students feel that this is the most difficult part of the composition process. When faced with an assignment, they suffer from writer's block.

Brainstorming is often a helpful way to overcome writer's block. Sit quietly somewhere with a piece of blank paper and your chosen topic. Jot down all the things that occur to you on that topic. For example, if you were writing an essay about horses, you might jot down *fast, beautiful, Arabian Stallion, work horses*, or anything else that jars your imagination. Once you have some ideas down on paper, you can begin to organize them.

19. You might expect the next paragraph to be about

    (A) organizing your essay
    (B) the topic sentence
    (C) overcoming writer's block
    (D) work horses

20. Where would you most likely find this selection?

    (F) a teacher's edition of an English textbook
    (G) a book about horses
    (H) a manual for students
    (J) a magazine for poets

21. The saying *Rome wasn't built in a day* is intended to do all of the following EXCEPT

    (A) encourage students
    (B) tell the reader to study Romans
    (C) create interest in the passage
    (D) introduce the topic

22. A good title for this passage would be

    (F) An Essay about Horses
    (G) Things Take Time
    (H) How to Write an Essay
    (J) Overcoming Writer's Block

Here is part of an essay a student contributed to the school magazine. There are a few mistakes that need correcting. Read the story, then answer questions 23–26.

(1) Some of the people don't like to write papers. (2) I do. (3) I enjoy putting my ideas down on paper and to share them with my audience. (4) I never have a problem with writer's block because I think of my writing as a conversation I am having with my reader. (5) If you imagine someone reading what you write, you wouldn't have any problem coming up with ideas.

23. Which is the best way to write sentence 1?

    (A) Some of the people doesn't like to write papers.
    (B) Some people don't like to write papers.
    (C) Some people doesn't like to write papers.
    (D) Best as is.

24. What would be the best way to combine sentences 1 and 2?

    (F) I do like to write papers, unlike those people.
    (G) Some people don't like to write papers, but I do.
    (H) Some of the people don't like to write papers. But I do.
    (J) Writing papers is not liked by other people except for me.

25. Which is the best way to write sentence 3?

    (A) I am enjoying putting my ideas down on paper and to share them with my audience.
    (B) I enjoy to put my ideas down on paper and to share them with my audience.
    (C) I enjoy putting my ideas down on paper and sharing them with my audience.
    (D) Best as is.

26. Which is the best way to write sentence 5?

    (F) If you could imagine that someone is reading what you write, you wouldn't have any problem coming up with ideas.
    (G) If you imagine someone reading what you write, then you wouldn't have any problem to come up with ideas.
    (H) If you imagine someone reading what you write, you won't have any problem coming up with ideas.
    (J) Best as is.

Read the following passage and answer questions 27–33.

By the late 1800s, many native peoples were being pushed off their lands to make way for American expansionism. There were numerous battles of resistance, and many brave tribal leaders led the fight to keep their ancestral homes. Chief Joseph of the Nez Perce, a peaceful nation that spread from Idaho to Northern Washington, was one such leader. He became well known for his courageous resistance and his eloquent speeches.

Chief Joseph, known by his people as In-mut-too-yah-lat-lat (Thunder coming up over the land from the water), assumed the role of tribal leader from his father, Old Joseph. Old Joseph was on friendly terms with the American government and had signed a treaty that allowed his people to retain much of their land.

In 1863 however, following the discovery of gold in Nez Perce territory, the federal government took back almost 6 million acres of territory. Old Joseph argued that his people had never agreed to this second treaty and he refused to move them.

A showdown over the second "non-treaty" came after Old Joseph died in 1871 and the young Chief Joseph assumed his place. Chief Joseph resisted all efforts to relocate his people to a small reservation in Idaho. The Nez Perce tribe was terribly outnumbered though.

After months of fighting and forced marches, many of the Nez Perce were sent to a reservation in what is now Oklahoma. Many died from malaria and starvation. Chief Joseph tried every possible appeal to the federal authorities to return the Nez Perce to their land. He explained, "All men were made brothers. The earth is the mother of all people, and all people should have equal rights upon it. You might as well expect the rivers to run backward as that any man who was born free should be contented when penned up and denied liberty to go where he pleases." Despite his appeals, Chief Joseph was sent to a reservation in Washington where, according to the reservation doctor, he later died of a broken heart.

27. A showdown between the federal authorities and the Nez Perce began

   (A) when Old Joseph died
   (B) when gold was discovered in Nez Perce territory
   (C) when Chief Joseph refused to move his people
   (D) in 1871

28. The federal government probably wanted to move the Nez Perce

   (F) so they could take possession of gold-rich lands
   (G) to protect the Nez Perce from gold diggers
   (H) to teach them how to farm on settled land
   (J) to punish Chief Joseph for resisting

29. Chief Joseph was different from his father because

   (A) he was an eloquent speaker
   (B) he was a more courageous hunter
   (C) he helped his people move to new land
   (D) he led his people in battle against the government

30. Chief Joseph probably died of a broken heart because

   (F) he missed his father
   (G) he missed his freedom
   (H) he was wounded in battle
   (J) he was upset about losing the gold

31. The author includes the quote at the end of the passage to show

   (A) why Chief Joseph died
   (B) what a good speaker Chief Joseph was
   (C) how Chief Joseph felt about the U.S. government
   (D) what a good leader Chief Joseph was

32. Choose the sentence that is written correctly.

   (F) Chief Joseph appealed to the U.S. government and asking to stay on his land.
   (G) If he would of moved his people, the government wouldn't have fought the Nez Perce.
   (H) When gold was discovered on Nez Perce land, the government broke its treaty.
   (J) In Oklahoma, was the Nez Perce reservation.

33. Here are two sentences related to the passage:

   Chief Joseph was a courageous leader.
   Chief Joseph fought for the rights of his people.

   Select the answer choice that best combines the two sentences into one.

   (A) Chief Joseph was a courageous leader who fought for the rights of his people.
   (B) Chief Joseph was a courageous leader and he also fought for the rights of his people.
   (C) Chief Joseph, a courageous leader, was fighting for the rights of his people.
   (D) Chief Joseph was a courageous leader; who fought for the rights of his people.

Read the following passage and answer questions 34–37.

Sight, taste, touch, hearing, and sight—these are the five senses we all know about. But did you know that some creatures have a sixth sense? What is this sixth sense and what animal possesses it? The shark, the most efficient hunter on Earth, is endowed with a sensitivity to electric fields that help it to pinpoint any animal, even in dark waters.

Special receptors located around the shark's head and snout enable it to detect the electric vibrations that all animals, even human beings, give off. This sense works best at close range and helps the shark zero in on its prey. However, the shark cannot tell the difference between electrical signals given off by animals, and those made by objects such as metal and wire. This is why sharks may sometimes attack boats, docks, or underwater divers in steel cages. The shark's amazing sensory system has earned it the nickname the perfect predator. However, only a few shark species are dangerous to humans. Most sharks shy away from people and avoid large animals whenever possible.

34. This passage is mostly about

    (F) how sharks hunt
    (G) the five senses
    (H) why sharks attack people
    (J) the shark's special sense

35. As it is used in the passage, *efficient* most nearly means

    (A) capable
    (B) slow
    (C) unskilled
    (D) sensitive

36. All of the following are true of the shark's sixth sense EXCEPT

    (F) it helps the shark detect electric vibrations
    (G) it works best at far range
    (H) it cannot tell the difference between certain types of vibrations
    (J) it helps the shark find its prey

37. According to this passage, sharks may attack divers in steel cages because

    (A) the divers are in their territory
    (B) they mistake the diver for a boat
    (C) they think the cage is an animal
    (D) the cage is vibrating

Here is a story a student wrote about seeing a shark and other animals at an aquarium. There are a few mistakes that need correcting. Read the story, then answer questions 38–40.

(1) Every saturday my family tries to do something special. (2) Last week we visited a museum. (3) This weekend, we went to Sea Life Park. (4) Swimming around in the tanks, I saw lots of fish. (5) There was even a bottlenose shark. (6) He was pretty scary looking but we were behind the glass. (7) You're not supposed to tap on the glass but somebody next to us did anyway.

38. Which sentence contains a capitalization error?

    (F) Sentence 1
    (G) Sentence 2
    (H) Sentence 3
    (J) Sentence 5

39. Which sentence does not belong within this paragraph?

    (A) Sentence 1
    (B) Sentence 2
    (C) Sentence 5
    (D) Sentence 7

40. Which of the following is the best way to rewrite sentence 4?

    (F) I saw lots of fish swimming around in the tanks.
    (G) Swimming around in the tanks; I saw lots of fish.
    (H) Swimming around in the tanks there were lots of fish that I saw.
    (J) Best as is.

TEST 7: MATHEMATICS CONCEPTS AND APPLICATIONS

40 minutes

Directions: For questions 1–40, read each problem and find the answer.

1. $4(-4) - 3 =$

    (A) -16
    (B) -19
    (C) -3
    (D) 48
    (E) None of these

2. $\dfrac{15 \times 7 \times 3}{9 \times 5 \times 2} =$

    (F) $\dfrac{2}{7}$
    (G) $\dfrac{3}{5}$
    (H) 7
    (J) $7\dfrac{1}{2}$
    (K) None of these

3. $-2^3(1 - 2)^3 + (-2)^3 =$

    (A) -12
    (B) -4
    (C) 0
    (D) 4
    (E) None of these

4. $\sqrt{1500} =$

   (F) $10 + \sqrt{15}$

   (G) $10\sqrt{15}$

   (H) 25

   (J) $100 + \sqrt{15}$

   (K) None of these

5. $4^2 \times 4^3 =$

   (A) 120

   (B) 4^6

   (C) $4 \times 4 \times 4 \times 4 \times 4$

   (D) 4×8

   (E) None of these

6. $13.254 - 1.04 =$

   (F) 12.251

   (G) 13.214

   (H) 12.214

   (J) 13.114

   (K) None of these

7. $6\% =$

   (A) $\dfrac{60}{100}$

   (B) $\dfrac{6}{100}$

   (C) 6

   (D) $\dfrac{1}{6}$

   (E) None of these

8. The number 100,000 is equivalent to

   (F) 10^6

   (G) 10^4

   (H) 10^5

   (J) 10^3

   (K) None of these

9. In the number 328,567 what is the value of the digit 8?

   (A) 8,000

   (B) 8

   (C) 80,000

   (D) 80

10. In a recent poll, 10% of voters were in favor of a new bill, 42% were against it, and 18% were undecided. The rest did not vote. What is the ratio of voters to non-voters?

    (F) $\dfrac{7}{3}$

    (G) 70%

    (H) $\dfrac{7}{100}$

    (J) $\dfrac{3}{7}$

11. Which of the following represents $\{2, 3, 5, 6, 7\} \cap \{3, 4, 5, 8, 10\}$?

    (A) $\{2, 3, 4, 5\}$

    (B) $\{3, 4, 5\}$

    (C) $\{3, 5\}$

    (D) $\{3\}$

12. An office contains 40 cubicles. When the cubicles are $\dfrac{1}{5}$ full, how many cubicles are full?

    (F) 8

    (G) 9

    (H) $\dfrac{1}{8}$

    (J) $\dfrac{1}{9}$

13. A centimeter is what part of a meter?

    (A) $\dfrac{1}{10}$

    (B) $\dfrac{1}{1000}$

    (C) $\dfrac{1}{100}$

    (D) $\dfrac{1}{12}$

14. The express train travels from Boston to New York City in three hours. Boston and New York City are 216 miles apart. How fast does the train travel?

    (F) 120 mph
    (G) 72 mph
    (H) 642 mph
    (J) 64 mph

15. Which of the following shows all integer values that may replace the blank to make the statement true?

    7 > _____ > 4

    (A) 5
    (B) 7, 6, 5, 4
    (C) 6, 5, 4
    (D) 6, 5

16. Which of the following represents {5, 6, 8, 9, 10} ∩ {3, 4, 8, 9}?

    (F) {8, 9, 10}
    (G) {8}
    (H) {3, 8}
    (J) {8, 9}

17. What are the prime factors of 230?

    (A) 2, 5, 10
    (B) 2, 5, 23
    (C) 10, 23
    (D) 2, 3, 4

18. If a pizza is cut into nine equal pieces and Joe eats $\dfrac{2}{3}$ of the pie, approximately what percent did Joe eat?

    (F) 30%
    (G) 40%
    (H) 60%
    (J) 67%

19. Carpet salespeople at Cover Up Carpets do not earn a base salary. Instead, they receive a commission of 7.5% on all of their sales. How many dollars worth of carpets will Max have to sell if he wants to bring home $600 a week?

    (A) $900
    (B) $1,200
    (C) $8,000
    (D) $7,000

20. Which of the following is equivalent to "three million, one hundred and seventy eight thousand, forty two"?

    (F) 3,100,742
    (G) 3,178,042
    (H) 3,170,842
    (J) 3,078,420

21. An equilateral triangle has

    (A) three equal angles
    (B) one right angle
    (C) two equal sides and one right angle
    (D) angles that each equal 80 degrees

22. The set of all common factors of 62 and 84 is

    (F) {2, 3, 6, 8}
    (G) {2, 3, 4, 8}
    (H) {2, 3}
    (J) {2}

23. A group of eight girl guides raised $590 for their group by selling cookies. Three of the guides collectively raised 90% of the money. How much did the other five girls raise together?

    (A) $590
    (B) $49
    (C) $59
    (D) $159

24. Children play in a rectangular sandbox that is 3 feet wide by 16 feet long. What is the perimeter of the sandbox?

    (F) 19 feet
    (G) 48 feet
    (H) 24 feet
    (J) 38 feet

25. Check-It-Out Motors charged Mr. Franco $97 to replace a faulty part in his car, plus $42 per hour for each hour that a mechanic worked on his car. The total charge was $230. About how long did the mechanic work on Mr. Franco's car?

    (A) 1 hour
    (B) 2 hours
    (C) 3 hours
    (D) 4 hours

26. Find the area of the triangle below.

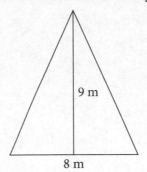

9 m

8 m

    (F) 36 m^2
    (G) 30 m^2
    (H) 72 m^2
    (J) 35 m^2

27. Complete the following statement:

$$7(2 \times \text{\_\_\_\_}) + 6 = 4{,}206$$

    (A) 3,000
    (B) 30 × 10
    (C) 3 × 10^2
    (D) 3 × 10^3

The salespeople at Sit Down Furniture Store had their best month of sales ever. The chart below shows the dollar amount each salesperson sold of each item. Answer questions 28–30 based on the chart.

	Chairs	Sofas	Ottomans	Sofa and loveseat sets
John	$400	$10,330	$0	$4,050
Marina	$1,800	$6,800	$400	$7,620
Leslie	$200	$5,450	$150	$9,170
Total	$2,400	$22,580	$550	$20,840

28. If 20 sofas were sold, what was the average price of each sofa?

    (F) $1,000
    (G) $1,240
    (H) $1,128
    (J) $1,129

29. What percentage of chair sales was Marina responsible for?

    (A) 66%
    (B) 33%
    (C) 75%
    (D) 80%

30. The manager of Sit Down Furniture Store is designing a graph to show the fraction of total sales revenues that were made on each item that the store sells. Which of these is the best graph for him to use?

    (F)

    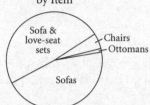

    (G)

    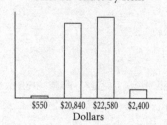

    (H)

    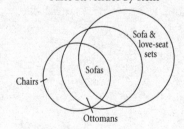

    (J)

    Sales Revenues by Item

Chairs	Ottomans	Sofas	Sets

31. Which of these points on the number line represents 4×10^4?

A	B	C	D
400	4,000	40,000	400,000

   (A)   Point A
   (B)   Point B
   (C)   Point C
   (D)   Point D

32. 1.6 kilometers equals approximately 1 mile. If a charity walkathon is 18 kilometers, about how many miles is it?

   (F)   18
   (G)   10
   (H)   12
   (J)   11

33. A 20-ounce bottle of soda costs x cents while a 12-ounce can of the same soda costs 10 cents less. What is the cost of two cans of soda?

   (A) $2x - 10$
   (B) $2(x - 10)$
   (C) $2(x + 10)$
   (D) $2x - 2(x - 10)$

34. If $-4 < x < -2$, which of the following could be a value of x?

   (F)   1
   (G) -1
   (H) -3
   (J) -4

35. A football team won 22 games and tied 2. This was 60% of its season. How many games did the team lose?

   (A)   12
   (B)   10
   (C)   6
   (D)   16

36. In which case are the numbers arranged in ascending order with the smallest value listed first?

   (F)   40%, 0.04, $\dfrac{1}{2}$

   (G) $\dfrac{3}{100}, \dfrac{1}{3}, \dfrac{2}{3}$

   (H) $\dfrac{1}{5}$, 0.22, 2%

   (J)   0.4, 20%, 30%

37. Which of the following is an example of the distributive property of multiplication over addition?

   (A) $a(b + c) = ab + ac$
   (B) $a(b + c) = abc$
   (C) $a(bc) = \dfrac{a}{bc}$
   (D) $a(b - c) = ab + ac$

38. David has $200 to spend on new winter clothes. However there is 8% sales tax on items costing $100 or more. Which combination of items below allows him to buy the greatest number of items without going over his $200 limit?

   (F) $60 shoes, $42 sweater, $10 shirt, $100 boots
   (G) $100 boots, $20 sweater, $50 shirt
   (H) $110 coat, $40 pants, $50 sweater
   (J) $12 socks, $100 coat, $85 suit

39. The gym teacher at Hollingsworth High wants to show her principal a graph illustrating that students who choose to play on varsity football often join other varsity teams as well. Which of the graphs below best achieves that goal?

    (A)

    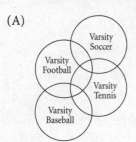

    (B)

    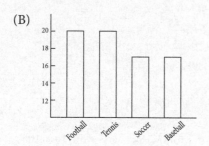

    (C)

    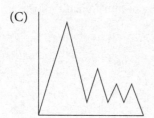

    (D)

    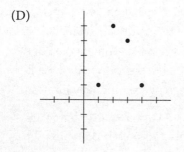

40. What is the circumference of the wheel whose spoke is 15 inches long?

    (F) 30π in

    (G) 15π in

    (H) 7.5π in

    (J) 225π in

ANSWERS AND EXPLANATIONS

Answer Key

Test 1: Sequences
1. B
2. F
3. C
4. F
5. D
6. J
7. B
8. H
9. A
10. J
11. D
12. F
13. B
14. G
15. C
16. F
17. A
18. J
19. C
20. H

Test 2: Analogies
1. B
2. H
3. A
4. H
5. B
6. J
7. A
8. H
9. A
10. J
11. B
12. G
13. C
14. F

15. C
16. J
17. B
18. G
19. C
20. G

Test 3: Quantitative Reasoning
1. B
2. J
3. A
4. H
5. A
6. H
7. A
8. J
9. A
10. F
11. C
12. F
13. C
14. G
15. B
16. J
17. A
18. H
19. A
20. G

Test 4: Verbal Reasoning— Words
1. D
2. F
3. C
4. J
5. B
6. H

7. B
8. F
9. D
10. F
11. A
12. H
13. A
14. F
15. D
16. G
17. A
18. F
19. A
20. F

Test 5: Verbal Reasoning— Context
1. A
2. H
3. B
4. J
5. A
6. J
7. C
8. F
9. D
10. H
11. B
12. J
13. D
14. G
15. D
16. H
17. A
18. H
19. D
20. J

Test 6: Reading and Language Arts

1. B
2. J
3. A
4. H
5. D
6. J
7. C
8. H
9. C
10. F
11. B
12. H
13. A
14. F
15. C
16. J
17. A
18. H
19. A
20. H
21. B
22. H
23. B
24. G
25. C
26. H
27. C
28. F
29. D
30. G
31. B
32. H
33. A
34. J
35. A
36. G
37. C
38. F
39. D
40. F

Test 7: Mathematics Concepts and Applications

1. B
2. K
3. C
4. G
5. C
6. H
7. B
8. H
9. A
10. F
11. C
12. F
13. C
14. G
15. D
16. J
17. B
18. J
19. C
20. G
21. A
22. J
23. C
24. J
25. C
26. F
27. C
28. J
29. C
30. F
31. C
32. J
33. B
34. H
35. D
36. G
37. A
38. G
39. A
40. F

Test 1: Sequences

1. B

In each set of the pattern, the first flower has more detail than the second two. The second two flowers are the same. The missing flower should be the same as the one in the middle and have a stem and two leaves.

2. F

Each set of the pattern contains three rectangles, either on their side (horizontal) or standing up (vertical). Two are of the same orientation, the third is of another. Since in the last set two rectangles are already horizontal, the third should be vertical. There is no reason to believe the missing shape should be anything other than a rectangle.

3. C

Notice how the shading is moving clockwise from its position in the first circle of each set to the second circle of each set. Therefore, the missing circle should be shaded in the quadrant below where the shading is located in the first circle. There is no reason to believe that two segments of the circle should be shaded.

4. F

Look at the sequence and see what is missing. Every set has "AA" in the middle. That is what is missing from the last set.

5. D

Each set is made up of three circles. They are either small, medium, or large. Notice that the size of the last circle in each set dictates the number of circles of that particular size in the next set. In the first set a medium size circle is last. There are two medium size circles in the next set, followed by a small circle. The small circle is the last element of this second set. Therefore, there are two small circles in the third set. These are followed by a large circle. Therefore, there should be two large circles in the missing set. These may be followed by a circle of any size. Only choice (D) has the two large circles necessary to begin the set.

6. J

Each set is made up of a square, a rectangle, and a triangle. When the square is shaded, the triangle points up. When the square is not shaded, it points down. The number of lines in the rectangle has no bearing on this. So, since the square is not shaded in the last set, the missing triangle must point down. Only choice (J) has the downward pointing triangle.

7. B

The pattern in this series is +9. Within each set, each number is 9 more than the preceding number; $36 + 9 = 45$.

8. H

The pattern in this series is –4. Thus, from the first number in the last set, we subtract 4; $81 - 4 = 77$.

9. A

The pattern in this series is ÷3. Since we know this, multiply the second number in the last set by 3 to arrive at the missing first number; $18 \times 3 = 54$.

10. J

Within each set the pattern is +8, –5. Thus, the middle number must be 8 more than the preceding one; $62 + 8 = 70$.

11. D

The pattern is ×4, ÷2. Divide 28 by 2 to arrive at the next number in the sequence.

12. F

The pattern in this series is that the number 7 in the middle remains constant.

13. B

If the first set doesn't help you recognize the sequence, look at the second set. It has a number (3), its square (3 × 3 = 9), and its cube (3 × 3 × 3 = 27). So, you are looking for the square of 2, or 2 × 2. The answer is 4.

14. G

Isolate the subscript and the letters in order to see the pattern more readily.

The subscripts are decreasing, while the letters are always A, B, and C.

15. C

The numeral 2 remains the same in each set. Each number always has an X and a Y attached. The Xs have superscripts, the Ys have subscripts. The superscripts attached to the Xs are increasing, while the subscripts attached to the Ys are decreasing.

16. F

As we move from left to right, the first letter ascends alphabetically: A, B, __, D. The second letters are always B and C. The superscript attached to the first letter is increased by 1; the superscript B is increased by 2 and the superscript C is increased by 1.

17. A

The series consists of palindromes—words that are the same spelled backwards and forwards. Only POP is a palindrome.

18. J

The pattern consists of two consonants and two vowels. The consonants are two letters of the alphabet in ascending order. The vowels are random. Thus, the next part of the series must be KLOA.

19. C

The pattern is a capitalized letter, followed by the lowercase of the previous letter listed twice. What comes before the letter v? The next set should begin with a capital U and be followed by tt.

20. H

Note that in each set, the first and last letter are the same and are increasing, AA, BB, CC...Therefore, the missing sequence should begin and end with the letter D. Next, you should focus on the two letters in the middle of each set. The letters in the middle are always A followed by an increasing letter in the alphabet, for example, AB, AC, AD. Its middle letters should be A and E. So, the next set should be DAED.

Test 2: Analogies

1. B

The bouquet is a combination of various flowers. The bowl of fruit is a combination of various fruits.

2. H

A turtle is protected by its shell. A snail is protected by its shell.

3. A

A car helps the woman travel more easily. The escalator helps the woman go up more easily.

4. H

Both the traffic light and the stop sign serve the same function: they instruct people how to drive. Both the map and compass serve the same function: they help people find their way.

5. B

The mountain is a larger version of the hill. The lake is a larger version of the pond.

6. J

The lace is used to close the shoe. The zipper is used to close the jacket.

7. A

A race car is a fast car. A greyhound is a fast dog.

8. H

Bricks make up a house. The letters of the alphabet make up a letter.

9. A

The stethoscope is a tool of the doctor. The paint-brush is a tool of the painter.

10. J

The yacht is a luxurious boat. The mansion is a luxurious house.

11. B

The window and door are parts of a house. The tire and steering wheel are parts of a car.

12. G

The umbrella protects against the rain. The snow boots protect against the snow.

13. C

Drumsticks are used to play a drum. A bow is used to play a violin.

14. F

The soccer player's goal is to shoot a goal. The basketball player's goal is to shoot a hoop.

15. C

A tire is a component of a car. A door is a component of a house.

16. J

An arrow is shot from a bow. A cannon ball is shot from a cannon.

17. B

A squirrel lives in a tree. A bear lives in a cave.

18. G

A goldfish is kept in a fishbowl. A bird is kept in a cage.

19. A

Eggs are used to make sunny-side-up eggs. Oranges are used to make orange juice.

20. G

The stopwatch times a race. The egg timer times a cake baking.

Test 3: Quantitative Reasoning

1. B

First, determine what operation is being performed to the number on the left; 2 is multiplied by 6 to make 12; 1 is multiplied by 6 to make 6; $3 \times 6 = 18$, choice (B).

2. J

First, figure out the pattern; $15 - 7 = 8$; $16 - 7 = 9$. The pattern is -7; $11 - 7 = 4$, choice (J).

3. A

What operation is done to 12 to make 19? Seven is added. What is done to 2 to make 9? Seven is added. Add 7 to 5; the result is 12, choice (A).

4. H

What is done to $\frac{1}{3}$ to make $\frac{4}{3}$? One, or $\frac{3}{3}$, is added.

What is done to $\frac{1}{4}$ to make $\frac{5}{4}$? One, or $\frac{4}{4}$, is added.

Add 1, or $\frac{5}{5}$, to $\frac{1}{5}$ and the result is $\frac{6}{5}$, choice (H).

5. A

What operation is performed to 2 to arrive at 1? One is subtracted; 1 – 1 = 0; 3 – 1 = 2, choice (A).

6. H

First, determine the pattern. What is done to 17 to arrive at 22? 5 is added; 9 + 5 = 14. The pattern is +5; 3 + 5 = 8, choice (H).

7. A

There are two rectangles. If you were to divide the rectangles into triangular sections,

there would be eight equal sections. four of these are shaded; $\frac{4}{8} = \frac{1}{2}$.

8. J

Count the number of segments that make up the whole. There are six segments and two of these are shaded. $\frac{2}{6}$ reduces to $\frac{1}{3}$.

9. A

Count the number of segments that make up the whole. There are ten segments and five of these are shaded. Turn this into a fraction to determine the amount of the whole that is shaded; $\frac{5}{10}$ reduces to $\frac{1}{2}$.

10. F

The square is made up of four equal segments; one of these is shaded, or $\frac{1}{4}$.

11. C

Count the number of segments that make up the whole. There are four; one of these is shaded, or $\frac{1}{4}$.

12. F

There are 6 rectangular segments that make up the whole. Draw a diagonal line down each segment to divide it in half, and you have 12 equal segments.

Count the number of triangular segments that are shaded; there are four, or $\frac{4}{12}$, which reduces to $\frac{1}{3}$.

13. C

There are four equal segments that make up the whole circle. Draw a diagonal line through each segment to divide it in half, and you have eight equal segments.

Count the number of segments that are shaded; there are four, or $\frac{4}{8}$, which reduces to $\frac{1}{2}$.

14. G

Although it might be tempting, don't try to solve these by eyeballing the scales. Even on these simpler ones, it is a bad habit to get into. Instead, use the information to evaluate each answer choice. This is easiest if you convert all the choices to either cones or cubes.

You are told that one cone is equal to one cube. Therefore:

F: 1 cone ≠ 2 cones

G: 1 cone + 1 cone (1 cube = 1 cone) does equal 1 cone + 1 cone (1 cube = 1 cone). This is the correct answer.

H: 2 cones ≠ 1 cone (1 cube = 1 cone)

J: 2 cones + 1 cone (1 cube = 1 cone) ≠1 cone (1 cube = 1 cone)

15. B

1 cube = 1 cone. Convert the answer choices to either all cones or all cubes to more readily see the equation.

A: 1 cone ≠ 1 cone + 1 cone (1 cube = 1 cone)

B: 1 cone + 1 cone (the cube) = 2 cones. This is the correct answer.

C: 1 cone + 1 cone (the cube) ≠ 1 cone (the cube)

D: 2 cones ≠ 1 cone (the cube)

16. J

2 cones = 1 cube. Convert the answer choices to either all cones or all cubes to more readily see the equation.

F: 2 cones (1 cube = 2 cones) + 1 cone ≠
2 cones + 2 cones (1 cube = 2 cones)

G: 4 cones (1 cube = 2 cones) ≠ 3 cones

H: 1 cone ≠ 4 cones (1 cube = 2 cones)

J: 2 cones + 2 cones (1 cube = 2 cones) =
4 cones. This is the correct answer.

17. A

3 cones = 1 cube. Convert the answer choices to either all cones or all cubes to more readily see the equation.

A: 3 cones (1 cube = 3 cones) + 3 cones = 6 cones
(1 cube = 3 cones). This is the correct answer.

B: 6 cones (1 cube = 3 cones) ≠ 5 cones

C: 6 cones (1 cube = 3 cones) + 1 cone ≠ 3 cones +
3 cones

D: 1 cone ≠ 6 cones (1 cube = 3 cones)

18. H

1 cube = 4 cones. Convert the answer choices to either all cones or all cubes to more readily see the equation.

F: 4 cones (1 cube = 4 cones) + 2 cones ≠ 4 cones
(1 cube = 4 cones) + 4 cones

G: 4 cones (1 cube = 4 cones) + 4 cones ≠ 4 cones

H: 8 cones (1 cube = 4 cones) = 4 cones (1 cube =
4 cones) + 4 cones. This is the correct answer.

J: 12 cones (1 cube = 4 cones) ≠ 10 cones (1 cube =
4 cones) + 2 cones

19. C

3 cones = 2 cubes. Convert the answer choices to either all cones or all cubes to more readily see the equation.

A: 3 cones + 3 cones (2 cubes = 3 cones) ≠ 5 cones

B: 2 cones + $1\frac{1}{2}$ cones (2 cubes = 3 cones) ≠
3 cones

C: 3 cones + 3 cones = 6 cones. This is the correct answer.

D: 1 cone ≠ 3 cones. This is one of the rare answer choices you could have eliminated just by looking at, since the scale in the question indicated that it takes 3 cones to balance 2 cubes.

20. G

The scale indicates that 2 cubes = 1 cone. Convert all the answer choices to cones to more easily evaluate them.

F: $\frac{1}{2}$ cone (2 cubes = 1 cone) + 2 cones ≠
3 cones

G: 2 cones = 1 cone (2 cubes = 1 cone) + 1 cone

H: 1 cone + $\frac{1}{2}$ cone (if 2 cubes = 1 cone, then
1 cube must equal $\frac{1}{2}$ cone) ≠ 2 cones + $\frac{1}{2}$ cone
(1 cube = $\frac{1}{2}$ cone)

J: $\frac{1}{2}$ cone (if 2 cubes = 1 cone, then 1 cube must
equal $\frac{1}{2}$ cone) + 2 cones ≠ $1\frac{1}{2}$ cones

Test 4: Verbal Reasoning—Words

1. D

In order for there to be a wedding, there must be a bride (and groom). The other elements are not necessary elements.

2. F

A controversy is a hotly debated topic. There must be two sides in a controversy, which disagree. Truce, resolution, and aggression are not the essential elements of controversy.

3. C

A drum provides rhythm. Cymbals and (drum) sticks are used as rhythmic instruments though they do not convey the essential element of what a drum is. Rhyme is not an essential element of a drum.

4. J

The intention of agriculture is to grow crops. A garden may grow crops or flowers. Livestock are animals on a farm. Seasons, though necessary to farming, do not convey the essential element of producing food to eat.

5. B

A candidate is chosen, which necessitates choice. A poll asks public opinion. Politics is related, but not the essential element of a candidate. Freedom reminds us of democracy, but again is not the essential element of the word *candidate*.

6. H

An optimist is full of hope; that is what defines him or her.

7. B

What makes a flower a flower? It has petals. It need not be in a garden, so you can eliminate (A). There are many types of flowers, so you can eliminate (C). A bee, though related to the idea of flowers and gardens, is a distracter and not the essential element of what defines a flower.

8. F

Before looking at the answer choices, think about what defines a guitar. It is a musical instrument with strings. Choice (F) fits this definition. You don't have to play guitar at a concert. A guitar doesn't have to be electric. A bass, though a related instrument, does not name an essential element of a guitar.

9. D

A ticket gains you admittance to someplace. Look for the answer choice that has to do with gaining admittance. Window, stadium, and expense are not essential elements that define what a ticket is. The ticket may or may not be purchased at a window. It may be used to enter a stadium or a train. It may or may not be an expense. Maybe it is free. Only choice (D) defines the purpose of a ticket.

10. F

The words in the top row are increasing in degree. For example, a downpour is more severe than a drizzle. So, you are looking for something that is more severe than warm. The best choice is scorching.

11. A

The words in the top row are all types of vehicles on land. The words in the bottom row are all types of vehicles for the air. Only a helicopter is a type of airborne vehicle.

12. H

Items above and below the line are ordered in increasingly larger sizes.

13. A

The items above the line are slow animals; those below the line are fast.

14. F

Approve is the opposite of the other words, which are all verbs meaning to criticize or judge in a negative manner.

15. D

A regulation is a rule, while the other choices are all grants of permission.

16. G

Kick, bounce, and throw are all actions that can be performed on a ball. Draw is not.

17. A

Although you need a nose to smell, it does not belong in this list. The words aroma, odor, and scent are other ways of referring to a smell.

18. F

The underlined words are all ways of referring to dirt, or the soil. Don't be tempted by choice (J), garden. Although a garden does have dirt in it, it is not the closest in meaning to the underlined words.

19. A

The underlined words all have to do with physical activity. Although these may take place in a gym, a gym is not the same as a physical activity. You may have been tempted to choose (C) tennis, but that is too specific to be the correct answer.

20. F

You are looking for a word that is similar in meaning to a job or work. Although choices (G), (H), and (J) are tempting, the correct answer is employment.

Test 5: Verbal Reasoning—Context

1. A

Read the statements carefully and think about what they tell you: cherry trees bloom in spring. Alonso has a blooming cherry tree in his backyard. Also consider what the statements **do not** tell you: which month it is, where Alonso lives, how old Alonso is, or anything else about Alonso or his yard. Now, read each answer choice carefully. The only one that is true based solely on the information given is (A).

2. H

Read the statements and consider the facts. It is windy and sailboats need wind. What conclusion can you draw? Will it be possible to sail today? Yes.

That's all the statements help you conclude. They say nothing about the time of year or how easy or difficult it is to sail.

3. B

What do we know based on the statements? "Hola" means hello in Spanish. Fact: Marco told Lena "hello" in French. What can we conclude? Marco speaks at least one word of French (he said "hello" in French). What don't we know? What that word for "hello" is in French. (Remember, you cannot apply any outside knowledge, you can only use the statements given to draw a conclusion.) We also don't know whether or not Marco knows any other words in French or any other languages. We also don't know whether Lena understands Marco or not. Eliminate choices (A), (C), and (D). Choice (B) is the best answer choice. Since Marco did not say hello in Spanish (he said hello in French), it is safe to assume he *probably did not say "hola."*

4. J

Based on the two statements, the only thing we can conclude for certain is that Rachel is attending an auction. Therefore, we do not know whether or not she will be outbid and win or lose the chair. She is *not* the auctioneer because she is bidding.

5. A

The two statements tell about Mr. and Mrs. Bowden's children (who are two and five). Clarissa is eight years old. She cannot be one of the Bowden's children—that's clear. We are not told whether she is another member of the family (a niece or a cousin) or what if any relationship she has to them. Don't be led astray just because the two statements are next to one another. They are unrelated facts.

6. J

Based on the statements given, all that we know is that David is in the kitchen. We do not know (based only on the statements) what the nice smell is, what is being cooked or baked, or who is making it.

7. C

The flowers need water twice a day and they are wilting. Why are they wilting? We don't know why based on the statements. Maybe they are getting too much water or too little. Or maybe they need more sun or less. The only conclusion we can draw is that the flowers are not healthy. We are not told whether or not there are also flowers in the backyard.

8. F

Based on the statements given, we can conclude that Adina is probably happy—smiling is a generally accepted sign of happiness. We do not know why she is smiling or whether or not it is related to the program she is watching. We do not know whether she likes to watch television or whether she is watching sitting, standing, or lying down.

9. D

Someone took a cookie from the cookie jar—we do not know who. Although Seung Hee loves cookies, there is no evidence to lead us to the conclusion that she took the missing cookie—no cookie crumbs on her face, for example. We do not know whether the cookie jar was easy or difficult to break into and open, or that Sarah bakes cookies. We do know that Sarah has a cookie jar and keeps cookies in it.

10. H

Suzie received ten cards and one was signed by a secret admirer. Did he send any of the other nine? Perhaps. Perhaps she also unknowingly sent one to him, not realizing that this person was her secret admirer. Based on the information stated, we can only conclude that Suzie received fewer than a dozen Valentine's Day cards. No mention is given of whether or not Suzie is a schoolgirl or whether the cards were from classmates; therefore, we can't determine whether the admirer is in her class.

11. B

Elise is in boot camp and the first statements says that all soldiers in boot camp must be able to run the camp's obstacle course. Therefore, you can conclude that Elise is able to run the course. You cannot conclude for certain that the other statements are true.

12. J

The statements only tell us that Joey caught more fish than Hope. We do not know whether this is because of talent or luck or the quality of their bait, hooks, or style. The only certain thing is that Hope caught fewer fish than Joey. (The fact that they went fishing does not make them best friends or even friends at all.)

13. D

We are told that babies cry if they are tired or hungry. Baby X is crying but she was just fed. Therefore, she must be tired (in need of a nap).

14. G

The only thing we know for certain is that the Bailers live in an apartment complex. Although we are told many details about their apartment complex, we do not know if they like to swim. Nor can we make a generalization about whether everyone likes to play tennis. We only know that they do not live in a house.

15. D

Bobby Lee has acted, and now he is joining the football league. He must enjoy various activities. We do not know from the passage whether or not he will continue to act next year, or which activity he is better at. Nor do we know why he won the lead role and then later a bit part; we cannot assume that his acting is improving nor getting worse.

16. H

The only thing we can be sure of is that Karl Cooper does not like to watch only one show because he changes channels frequently. We know that Karla does the crossword puzzle, but not whether she is good at it. Nor do we know whether or not she would like to watch just one show. Furthermore, we are not told whether or not Karl and Karla are married; they could be brother and sister.

17. A

We are told that Rene is happy to hear from her grandmother; thus, you can say that the two have a good relationship.

18. H

The statements tell us that today's special at Kelly's Diner is fried chicken and that all of the employees at the diner can eat the special (fried chicken) for free. That is, they do not have to pay if they order the special. However, the statements do not tell us if all the employees will eat fried chicken or even if they like the fried chicken.

19. D

Think of what the information does and does not tell you. We know where Jason is and where he is going. We know how long the complete ferry ride takes, but not how long Jason's been on the ferry so far or whether or not he likes the ferry. We also are not told about his swimming abilities. Only choice (D) is correct based on the limited information given.

20. J

The sale is *buy one get one free*. So, for every pair he buys, Sam gets one free—that means if he left the store with two pairs, he only paid for one. This is the only thing that is true based on the information given.

Test 6: Reading and Language Arts

1. B

Dadaism, although preferring childish style, was not a movement of children. Paragraph 1 states the *Dadaists rejected the values that they believe led to the war.* The passage does not comment as to whether or not they were good artists. The movement was not actually started by Duchamp, but sparked by his work. Be sure to take notes in the margins and jot down the main idea of each paragraph to help you locate information later.

2. J

The passage mentions all of the qualities of the Dada movement except patriotism. Paragraph 1 states that the Dadaists rejected nationalism and militarism, or patriotism.

3. A

This is a detail question. Paragraph 4 begins with the following sentence: *The official—if Dadaism can be called official—launch of Dada took place in 1916 with the opening of the nightclub the Cabaret Voltaire in Zurich, Switzerland.* While you read, be sure to underline or circle important information in the passage as well as jot down the main idea of paragraphs in the margins to help you locate the information you need to answer questions later.

4. H

This is an inference question. Based on what the passage stated about Dada goals of making fun of established culture, this is the best answer choice. Although Duchamp started working before the Dada movement officially began, we know that Dadaists admired him. Therefore, it makes sense that his style and message were the same as those of the Dadaists.

5. D

Simplest is best. Choice (D) combines the sentences concisely by adding one more adjectives to the list.

Choices (A) and (C) contain a redundant *and*. Choice (B) is a run-on sentence.

6. J

In sentence 4, *war* should not be capitalized because it is not naming a specific war, such as World War II. In sentence 1, *Dada* should be capitalized since it is the name of the movement. Sentences 2 and 3 are correct; they do not contain any proper nouns to capitalize.

7. C

After the verb *behaved* the adverb *childishly* should be used. The simplest way to fix this error is exhibited in choice (C). There is no reason to change the verb tense.

8. H

The title of the selection should reflect the main idea discussed in the selection. Because the selection is mainly about one theory of language, choice (H) is the best answer. Choice (G) is too vague, and choices (J) and (F) are details within the selection, but not the main idea of the selection.

9. C

The author states opinions and presents theories in a matter-of-fact manner. Although the author says that Saussure's theories make sense, she does not write in a biased manner, nor does she gush enthusiastically. There is no poetic language used in this selection.

10. F

The questions are a device intended to get the reader to think about the ideas presented in the article. The questions are answered, which eliminates choice (G). Although Saussure does have answers to the questions, they are not included to prove that. Though the questions do show that the topic is complicated, they are not included to demonstrate that the issue is confusing.

11. B

According to the Saussure, *the words that make up a language come about because they are mutually agreed on by a group ...* Putting ideas from the passage into your own words will help you arrive at the answer more readily. Make a habit of paraphrasing and jotting down ideas in the margin of each reading.

12. H

The modifying clause *a French linguist* correctly sets off additional information about Saussure. Choice (F) is a run-on sentence. Choice (G) incorrectly uses *which* rather than *who* to describe a person, and it includes an unnecessary comma. Choice (J) also contains an unnecessary comma and does not succinctly combine the two sentences.

13. A

Choice (A) correctly lists items, separating them with a comma. Choice (B) uses *whom* incorrectly; it should be the subject pronoun *who*. Choice (C) contains an incorrect verb tense—*lectures* should be *lectured* since it is in the past.

14. F

This is a detail question. To answer this question, locate and reread the part of the passage that discusses how bioluminescent organisms create light. The beginning of paragraph 2 clearly states that *bioluminescence occurs as a result of a chemical reaction between a protein (luciferin) and an enzyme (luciferase) in the presence of oxygen.*

15. C

Paragraph 2 explains how bioluminescence differs from other light sources: *Bioluminescence however is almost 100% efficient.* Circle key words like *however, although, despite* when reading. They indicate a change of direction and may help you locate important information within a passage that is asked about. Choice (B) is not true of bioluminescence. Choices (A) and (D), though correct, are details taken out of context and not the reason biolumi-nescent light differs from other light sources.

16. J

The passage discussed the diversity of biolumi-nescent creatures, that many of them are marine animals, and that they all make light the same way. Nothing was stated in the passage about whether or not touching these creatures would be painful. Be sure to circle important key words while you are reading. *Marine animals, diversity*, and *same process* would be important words to circle. Doing this can help you focus on the information and locate details more readily later.

17. A

A good topic sentence should introduce the ideas to be discussed in the paragraph. Since the paragraph is about two different categories of bioluminescent creatures, choice (A) is the best choice. Choices (B) and (D) are unrelated to the paragraph. Choice (C) introduces the idea of photophores, but not the other category of biolumi-nescent creatures also discussed in the paragraph.

18. H

The ideas within a well-organized essay should flow logically from one to the next. Since the last idea developed in the preceding paragraph claimed that *organisms with bacterial symbionts have developed some interesting ways to "turn out the light" when necessary*, you would expect a discussion of these techniques to follow. While (F), (G), and (J) may be interesting ideas to discuss, they wouldn't logically follow the idea that symbionts have interesting ways to turn out the light.

19. A

The paragraph ends *once you have some ideas down on paper, you can begin to organize them.* Therefore, the logical continuation would be a paragraph about organizing. Writer's block was already dealt with. The passage is not about horses.

And while the topic sentence is an important element of essay writing, it wouldn't flow smoothly to discuss it next, after the introduction of the topic of organization.

20. H

This paragraph is about essay writing and would be most helpful to students who need to write essays. Therefore, you could expect to find it in a student's manual.

21. B

This saying is intended to create an interesting introduction to the passage. It also means that doing something well takes time. Therefore, it is used here to encourage students who may struggle with writing.

22. H

A title should let the reader know what the piece is generally about. This piece is a guide about how to write an essay. The part about horses is meant to serve as an example and is not the main idea of the essay. The part about overcoming writer's block is just one element of the essay, not the whole process. The quote about time is an introduction to the idea that writing a good essay takes time, but again, it is not the main idea of the paragraph.

23. B

The subject of the sentence should be *some people* not some of the *people*. It should have the plural verb *don't*.

24. G

Choices (F) and (J) are unclear. *But I do* is not correct as a sentence, so choice (G) is the best way to combine the two sentences.

25. C

Parallelism demands that the verbs be in the same tense. Because the correct idiom is *enjoy putting*, the verbs must be *putting* and *sharing*.

26. H

Before reading the answer choices, reread the sentence in question. Look carefully at the placement of commas, verb agreement, and verb tense. Identify the error before reading the answer choices to avoid becoming confused by them. The correct modal of the verb after an *if* clause is the future *won't*. If you imagine … you *won't* have any problem.

27. C

This is a detail question. Reread the order of events described after the word *showdown*. Be sure to read a few sentences before and after the key word so as not to take details out of context. The passage explains that the showdown came after Old Joseph died and Chief Joseph refused to relocate his people.

28. F

This is an inference question. The passage explains that the government broke its original treaty once gold was discovered in Nez Perce territory. Thus, it makes sense that the federal government wanted to move the tribe in order to take possession of the gold-rich lands.

29. D

The passage does not go into detail about the character of Old Joseph. However, it does say that Old Joseph was on good terms with the U.S. government. Chief Joseph was different because he led his people in battle against the federal government in order to try to keep the land.

30. G

The quotation at the end of the passage shows how much Chief Joseph valued his freedom. He died on the reservation, without his freedom.

31. B

The introductory paragraph of the passage indicates that Chief Joseph was known for being a brave leader and an *eloquent* speaker. Even if you did not know what *eloquent* means, you could guess that it was something positive, since the passage has a positive tone about Chief Joseph. Therefore, the quote is included to prove that Chief Joseph was a good speaker. Although the quote mentions freedom and may explain indirectly why he died and how he felt about the government, it is used as a device to back up the initial claim about his speaking ability. Because it does not mention how this speech motivated people, it does not show what a good leader he was.

32. H

Read each answer choice carefully, looking for common errors. You can expect to find mistakes in comma usage, subject-verb agreement, and verb tense. Choice (F) has a problem with verb tense—since the first verb is *appealed*, a simple past tense verb, the second verb should also be simple past—*asked* rather than *asking*. Choice (G) has a mistake in usage. The correct phrase is *would have* not *would of*. Choice (H) correctly uses a comma to separate an adverbial clause from the main clause. Choice (J) incorrectly inserts a comma where none is necessary. It is also a convoluted sentence and would be more clearly stated as: *The Nez Perce reservation was in Oklahoma.*

33. A

The best answer choice is clearest and most succinct—that is, it doesn't add unnecessary words. Choice (A) combines the sentences with an adjective phrase describing Chief Joseph. Choice (B) is not incorrect, but rather more wordy than necessary—it is not the best choice. Choice (C) unnecessarily changes verb tense and alters the meaning of the sentences. However, setting the adjective phrase between commas is correct. Choice (D) would be correct (though not the best and simplest way to combine the two sentences) if the semicolon were followed by *he* rather than *who*. As is, the *who* makes the sentence unclear.

34. J

The first and last sentences of the first paragraph are the best place to look for the main topic of the passage. They discuss the shark's special abilities. Choices (G) and (H) are details taken out of context from the passage. Choice (F) is incorrect since the passage is not about how sharks hunt, but rather about one of their particular skills.

35. A

Reread the sentences in and around where the word *efficient* is found. They describe how the shark is a good hunter, able to find it's prey. *Efficient* must be a positive word, having to do with ability. *Capable* is the best answer choice. However, even if you are unsure of the answer, you can use word charge to help you eliminate poor answer choices. *Slow* and *unskilled* are both negative—eliminate these. *Sensitive* is taken out of context and is meant to mislead you since the following phrase discusses the shark's sensitivity. However, the sensitivity is just one more detail that makes the shark an *efficient* or capable hunter.

36 G

Underlining or circling important information in the passage will help you answer this type of question more easily. You should have circled *sixth sense* and then the phrase that defines it as an ability to detect electric vibrations. The details within the passage explain that it works best *at close range*. The passage also explains that sharks cannot distinguish between vibrations given off by humans or those by electrical fences. However, this is one of the abilities that makes the shark a great hunter.

37. C

Reread the section that explains why sharks attack steel cages. It explains that sharks cannot tell the difference between vibrations made by metal and those made by animals. They attack the cage not because it is vibrating (choice D), but because they mistakenly think the cage is an animal, or possible prey. Choice (A) is not mentioned in the pas-

sage, and choice (B) is an incorrect paraphrase of details in the passage.

38. F

Capitalize proper names, days of the week, months, and holidays. *Saturday* must be capitalized in sentence 1.

39. D

All the sentences in a well-written paragraph should concern the same topic or theme. This sentence does not follow the topic of Sea Life Park.

40. F

Because of the dangling modifier, the original sentence implies that the writer was actually swimming around in the tanks. Choice (F) makes the subject of the sentence clear and uses a simple verb. Choice (G) is not correct because the first phrase is not a complete sentence; it lacks a pronoun. Who was swimming around in the tanks? Choice (H) is a run-on sentence.

Test 7: Mathematics Concepts and Applications

1. B

Remember the order of operations: PEMDAS. In this equation, you should complete the multiplication first; $4 \times -4 = -16$. Now, you need to subtract 3 from -16; $-16 - 3 = -19$.

2. K

Before you do the multiplication, see which common factors in the numerator and denominator can be canceled. Cancelling a 3 from the 3 in the numerator and the 9 in the denominator leaves $\frac{15 \times 7 \times 1}{3 \times 5 \times 2}$. Cancelling a 5 from the 15 in the numerator and the 5 in the denominator leaves $\frac{3 \times 7 \times 1}{3 \times 1 \times 2}$. Cancelling the 3 in the numerator and the 3 in the denominator leaves $\frac{7 \times 1}{1 \times 2} = \frac{7}{2} = 3\frac{1}{2}$. Because this is not one of the choices, the answer is (K).

3. C

A negative number raised to an odd power is negative. Using PEMDAS:

$-2^3(1-2)^3 + (-2)^3$

$\quad = -2^3(-1)^3 + (-2)^3$

$\quad = -8(-1) + (-8)$

$\quad = 8 + (-8)$

$\quad = 8 - 8$

$\quad = 0$

4. G

To simplify the square root of a large number, break the number down into two or more factors and write the number as the product of the square roots of those factors. This is especially useful when one of the factors is a perfect square. In this case, break 1,500 down into two factors; 1,500 = 15 × 100, and 100 is a perfect square. So, 1,500 = $\sqrt{100 \times 15} = \sqrt{100} \times \sqrt{15} = 10\sqrt{15}$.

5. C

$4^2 = 4 \times 4$, and $4^3 = 4 \times 4 \times 4$.
Thus, $4^2 \times 4^3 = 4 \times 4 \times 4 \times 4 \times 4$.

6. H

Line up the decimal points and subtract:

$$\begin{array}{r} 13.254 \\ -1.040 \\ \hline 12.214 \end{array}$$

7. B

A percent is a part of 100. Thus, 6% is equivalent to $\frac{6}{100}$.

8. H

$10^1 = 10$, $10^2 = 100$, $10^3 = 1,000$, $10^4 = 10,000$, $10^5 = 100,000$

9. A

The eight is in the thousand's place, so the value is 8,000.

10. F

First, find the total the percentage of voters: 10 + 42 + 18 = 70%. Of 100% of the people polled, 70% voted and 30% did not. The ratio of voters to non-voters is $\frac{70}{30}$, which reduces to $\frac{7}{3}$.

11. C

The symbol ∩ represents intersection. The intersection of two sets consists of the elements that are common to both sets; 3 and 5 are common elements of both sets.

12. F

$40 \times \frac{1}{5} = 8$ cubicles are full.

13. C

One hundred centimeters make up one meter. Thus, one centimeter is $\frac{1}{100}$ of a meter.

14. G

Rate × Time = Distance. Since we are looking for rate, we use the equation:

Rate = $\dfrac{\text{Distance}}{\text{Time}}$

Rate = $\dfrac{216}{3}$ = 72 miles per hour

15. D

The sentence reads: 7 > ____ > 4. Thus, the numbers that may be placed in the blank must be less than 7 but greater than 4; 6 and 5 are less than 7 but greater than 4.

16. J

The symbol ∩ represents intersection. The intersection of two sets consists of the elements that are common to both sets; 8 and 9 are common elements of both sets.

17. B

2, 5, and 23 are prime numbers and are also factors of 230.

18. J

$\frac{2}{3}$ = 0.6666 … = 67%. Note that you didn't need the information about the nine slices.

19. C

You can set this up as an algebraic equation. Let x be the amount Max needs to sell.

$x(0.075) = 600$

$x = \frac{600}{0.075} = 8,000$

20. G

Convert each part of the number:

three million	3,000,000
one hundred seventy eight thousand	178,000
forty two	42
	3,178,042

21. A

An equilateral triangle has equal sides and equal angles. The angles in a triangle have a sum of 180 degrees. Therefore, each angle in an equilateral triangle would equal 60 degrees.

22. J

The only factor common to both 62 and 84 is 2.

23. C

First, find how much money the three guides raised.
90% × (590) = 0.9 × 590 = $531

Subtract that amount from the whole to determine how much the other five girls raised.
590 – 531= $59

24. J

Perimeter = width × 2 + length × 2
(3 × 2) + (16 × 2) = 6 + 32 = 38 feet

25. C

Subtract $97 for the part from the total 230 to find the charge for the labor; 230 – 97 = 133. The problem then asks you to estimate *about how many hours* the mechanic worked on the car. Start your estima-tion by multiplying 42 × 2 = 84; 133 is 49 more than 84, so the mechanic definitely worked more than two hours. Try 42 × 3 = 136. Since 136 is only 3 dollars more than 133, we know that the mechanic worked about three hours.

26. F

The formula for area of a triangle is: A = $\frac{1}{2}$ bh.
$\frac{1}{2}$ (8 × 9) = $\frac{1}{2}$ (72) = 36 m²

27. C

Let x equal the unknown number.

$7(2x) + 6 = 4,206$
$14x + 6 = 4,206$
$14x = 4,200$
$\frac{4,200}{14} = 300$ or 3×10^2

28. J

Average = $\frac{\text{total amount}}{\text{number of items}}$

$\frac{\$22,580}{20} = \$1,129$

29. C

The total amount of chair sales = 2,400. Marina sold 1,800. You can express this as a ratio: $\frac{1,800}{2,400} = \frac{3}{4}$; $\frac{3}{4}$ = 75%.

30. F

The manager wants to show the fraction of total sales revenue that each item brought in. The clearest way to demonstrate this needs to show parts of a whole. A pie chart does this best since it clearly shows parts of a whole. The bar graph allows you to compare the revenues of each item, but doesn't allow you to compare them to the whole amount. Choice (H) is confusing and indecipherable. Choice (J) does represent how many of the items were sold, but it is not clear how many each star stands for—there's no key.

31. C

$4 \times 10^4 = 4 \times (10 \times 10 \times 10 \times 10) = 4 \times 10,000 = 40,000$.

32. J

1.6 kilometers = 1 mile

Divide the number of kilometers by 1.6 to find the number of miles.

$\dfrac{18 \text{ kilometers}}{1.6} = 11.25$. Round off to 11 miles for the closest approximation.

33. B

One can of soda costs 10 cents less than a bottle which costs x cents.

One can = $x - 10$; two cans = $2(x - 10)$.

34. H

The sentence states that x is greater than −4, but less than −2. Only choice (H) supports this.

35. D

$0.60x = 24$; $x = 40$ games total in the season. If the team won and tied 24 games out of 40 total, they lost 16.

36. G

By writing all the numbers as decimals, we can more readily compare.

F: 0.4, 0.04, 0.5—the smallest one is not first.
G: 0.03, 0.33, 0.66—the smallest one is first. This is the correct answer.
H: 0.2, 0.22, 0.02—the smallest one is not first.
J: 0.4, 0.2, 0.3—the smallest one is not first.

37. A

The distributive property of multiplication over addition states that when multiplying a value that is a quantity, the multiplier is distributed to each number in the parentheses.

38. G

Add each combination of items, don't forget to add sales tax to each item costing $100 or more.

Boots = 100 + 100(0.08) = 100 + 8 = $108
Sweater = 20 + 20(0.08) = 20 + 1.60 = $21.60
Shirt = 50 + 50 (0.08) = 50 + 4 = $54
This results in a total of $108 + $21.60 + $54 = $183.60.
All answer choices but (G) put David over $200.

39. A

The Venn diagram achieves the gym teacher's goal; it shows an intersection between the students who play football and other varsity sports. None of the other charts show the intersection. Choice (B) is a good way to show how many students play each sport. Notice that choice (C) is unclear—there is no label on either axis to explain what the peaks and lows on the chart are. Choice (D) is also unclear. A coordinate graph would be best to map points in a quadrant, such as to show where things are located on a map.

40. F

Circumference = π × diameter

Diameter = 2 × radius = 2 × 15 = 30; C = 30π inches

HSPT Practice Test 1
Answer Sheet

Remove or photocopy this answer sheet and use it to complete the Practice Test.

Verbal Skills

1. A B C D	13. A B C D	25. A B C D	37. A B C D	49. A B C D
2. A B C D	14. A B C D	26. A B C D	38. A B C D	50. A B C D
3. A B C D	15. A B C D	27. A B C D	39. A B C D	51. A B C D
4. A B C D	16. A B C D	28. A B C D	40. A B C D	52. A B C D
5. A B C D	17. A B C D	29. A B C D	41. A B C D	53. A B C D
6. A B C D	18. A B C D	30. A B C D	42. A B C D	54. A B C D
7. A B C D	19. A B C D	31. A B C D	43. A B C D	55. A B C D
8. A B C D	20. A B C D	32. A B C D	44. A B C D	56. A B C D
9. A B C D	21. A B C D	33. A B C D	45. A B C D	57. A B C D
10. A B C D	22. A B C D	34. A B C D	46. A B C D	58. A B C D
11. A B C D	23. A B C D	35. A B C D	47. A B C D	59. A B C D
12. A B C D	24. A B C D	36. A B C D	48. A B C D	60. A B C D

Quantitative Skills

61. A B C D	72. A B C D	83. A B C D	93. A B C D	103. A B C D
62. A B C D	73. A B C D	84. A B C D	94. A B C D	104. A B C D
63. A B C D	74. A B C D	85. A B C D	95. A B C D	105. A B C D
64. A B C D	75. A B C D	86. A B C D	96. A B C D	106. A B C D
65. A B C D	76. A B C D	87. A B C D	97. A B C D	107. A B C D
66. A B C D	77. A B C D	88. A B C D	98. A B C D	108. A B C D
67. A B C D	78. A B C D	89. A B C D	99. A B C D	109. A B C D
68. A B C D	79. A B C D	90. A B C D	100. A B C D	110. A B C D
69. A B C D	80. A B C D	91. A B C D	101. A B C D	111. A B C D
70. A B C D	81. A B C D	92. A B C D	102. A B C D	112. A B C D
71. A B C D	82. A B C D			

Reading

113. Ⓐ Ⓑ Ⓒ Ⓓ   126. Ⓐ Ⓑ Ⓒ Ⓓ   139. Ⓐ Ⓑ Ⓒ Ⓓ   152. Ⓐ Ⓑ Ⓒ Ⓓ   165. Ⓐ Ⓑ Ⓒ Ⓓ
114. Ⓐ Ⓑ Ⓒ Ⓓ   127. Ⓐ Ⓑ Ⓒ Ⓓ   140. Ⓐ Ⓑ Ⓒ Ⓓ   153. Ⓐ Ⓑ Ⓒ Ⓓ   166. Ⓐ Ⓑ Ⓒ Ⓓ
115. Ⓐ Ⓑ Ⓒ Ⓓ   128. Ⓐ Ⓑ Ⓒ Ⓓ   141. Ⓐ Ⓑ Ⓒ Ⓓ   154. Ⓐ Ⓑ Ⓒ Ⓓ   167. Ⓐ Ⓑ Ⓒ Ⓓ
116. Ⓐ Ⓑ Ⓒ Ⓓ   129. Ⓐ Ⓑ Ⓒ Ⓓ   142. Ⓐ Ⓑ Ⓒ Ⓓ   155. Ⓐ Ⓑ Ⓒ Ⓓ   168. Ⓐ Ⓑ Ⓒ Ⓓ
117. Ⓐ Ⓑ Ⓒ Ⓓ   130. Ⓐ Ⓑ Ⓒ Ⓓ   143. Ⓐ Ⓑ Ⓒ Ⓓ   156. Ⓐ Ⓑ Ⓒ Ⓓ   169. Ⓐ Ⓑ Ⓒ Ⓓ
118. Ⓐ Ⓑ Ⓒ Ⓓ   131. Ⓐ Ⓑ Ⓒ Ⓓ   144. Ⓐ Ⓑ Ⓒ Ⓓ   157. Ⓐ Ⓑ Ⓒ Ⓓ   170. Ⓐ Ⓑ Ⓒ Ⓓ
119. Ⓐ Ⓑ Ⓒ Ⓓ   132. Ⓐ Ⓑ Ⓒ Ⓓ   145. Ⓐ Ⓑ Ⓒ Ⓓ   158. Ⓐ Ⓑ Ⓒ Ⓓ   171. Ⓐ Ⓑ Ⓒ Ⓓ
120. Ⓐ Ⓑ Ⓒ Ⓓ   133. Ⓐ Ⓑ Ⓒ Ⓓ   146. Ⓐ Ⓑ Ⓒ Ⓓ   159. Ⓐ Ⓑ Ⓒ Ⓓ   172. Ⓐ Ⓑ Ⓒ Ⓓ
121. Ⓐ Ⓑ Ⓒ Ⓓ   134. Ⓐ Ⓑ Ⓒ Ⓓ   147. Ⓐ Ⓑ Ⓒ Ⓓ   160. Ⓐ Ⓑ Ⓒ Ⓓ   173. Ⓐ Ⓑ Ⓒ Ⓓ
122. Ⓐ Ⓑ Ⓒ Ⓓ   135. Ⓐ Ⓑ Ⓒ Ⓓ   148. Ⓐ Ⓑ Ⓒ Ⓓ   161. Ⓐ Ⓑ Ⓒ Ⓓ   174. Ⓐ Ⓑ Ⓒ Ⓓ
123. Ⓐ Ⓑ Ⓒ Ⓓ   136. Ⓐ Ⓑ Ⓒ Ⓓ   149. Ⓐ Ⓑ Ⓒ Ⓓ   162. Ⓐ Ⓑ Ⓒ Ⓓ
124. Ⓐ Ⓑ Ⓒ Ⓓ   137. Ⓐ Ⓑ Ⓒ Ⓓ   150. Ⓐ Ⓑ Ⓒ Ⓓ   163. Ⓐ Ⓑ Ⓒ Ⓓ
125. Ⓐ Ⓑ Ⓒ Ⓓ   138. Ⓐ Ⓑ Ⓒ Ⓓ   151. Ⓐ Ⓑ Ⓒ Ⓓ   164. Ⓐ Ⓑ Ⓒ Ⓓ

Mathematics

175. Ⓐ Ⓑ Ⓒ Ⓓ   188. Ⓐ Ⓑ Ⓒ Ⓓ   201. Ⓐ Ⓑ Ⓒ Ⓓ   214. Ⓐ Ⓑ Ⓒ Ⓓ   227. Ⓐ Ⓑ Ⓒ Ⓓ
176. Ⓐ Ⓑ Ⓒ Ⓓ   189. Ⓐ Ⓑ Ⓒ Ⓓ   202. Ⓐ Ⓑ Ⓒ Ⓓ   215. Ⓐ Ⓑ Ⓒ Ⓓ   228. Ⓐ Ⓑ Ⓒ Ⓓ
177. Ⓐ Ⓑ Ⓒ Ⓓ   190. Ⓐ Ⓑ Ⓒ Ⓓ   203. Ⓐ Ⓑ Ⓒ Ⓓ   216. Ⓐ Ⓑ Ⓒ Ⓓ   229. Ⓐ Ⓑ Ⓒ Ⓓ
178. Ⓐ Ⓑ Ⓒ Ⓓ   191. Ⓐ Ⓑ Ⓒ Ⓓ   204. Ⓐ Ⓑ Ⓒ Ⓓ   217. Ⓐ Ⓑ Ⓒ Ⓓ   230. Ⓐ Ⓑ Ⓒ Ⓓ
179. Ⓐ Ⓑ Ⓒ Ⓓ   192. Ⓐ Ⓑ Ⓒ Ⓓ   205. Ⓐ Ⓑ Ⓒ Ⓓ   218. Ⓐ Ⓑ Ⓒ Ⓓ   231. Ⓐ Ⓑ Ⓒ Ⓓ
180. Ⓐ Ⓑ Ⓒ Ⓓ   193. Ⓐ Ⓑ Ⓒ Ⓓ   206. Ⓐ Ⓑ Ⓒ Ⓓ   219. Ⓐ Ⓑ Ⓒ Ⓓ   232. Ⓐ Ⓑ Ⓒ Ⓓ
181. Ⓐ Ⓑ Ⓒ Ⓓ   194. Ⓐ Ⓑ Ⓒ Ⓓ   207. Ⓐ Ⓑ Ⓒ Ⓓ   220. Ⓐ Ⓑ Ⓒ Ⓓ   233. Ⓐ Ⓑ Ⓒ Ⓓ
182. Ⓐ Ⓑ Ⓒ Ⓓ   195. Ⓐ Ⓑ Ⓒ Ⓓ   208. Ⓐ Ⓑ Ⓒ Ⓓ   221. Ⓐ Ⓑ Ⓒ Ⓓ   234. Ⓐ Ⓑ Ⓒ Ⓓ
183. Ⓐ Ⓑ Ⓒ Ⓓ   196. Ⓐ Ⓑ Ⓒ Ⓓ   209. Ⓐ Ⓑ Ⓒ Ⓓ   222. Ⓐ Ⓑ Ⓒ Ⓓ   235. Ⓐ Ⓑ Ⓒ Ⓓ
184. Ⓐ Ⓑ Ⓒ Ⓓ   197. Ⓐ Ⓑ Ⓒ Ⓓ   210. Ⓐ Ⓑ Ⓒ Ⓓ   223. Ⓐ Ⓑ Ⓒ Ⓓ   236. Ⓐ Ⓑ Ⓒ Ⓓ
185. Ⓐ Ⓑ Ⓒ Ⓓ   198. Ⓐ Ⓑ Ⓒ Ⓓ   211. Ⓐ Ⓑ Ⓒ Ⓓ   224. Ⓐ Ⓑ Ⓒ Ⓓ   237. Ⓐ Ⓑ Ⓒ Ⓓ
186. Ⓐ Ⓑ Ⓒ Ⓓ   199. Ⓐ Ⓑ Ⓒ Ⓓ   212. Ⓐ Ⓑ Ⓒ Ⓓ   225. Ⓐ Ⓑ Ⓒ Ⓓ   238. Ⓐ Ⓑ Ⓒ Ⓓ
187. Ⓐ Ⓑ Ⓒ Ⓓ   200. Ⓐ Ⓑ Ⓒ Ⓓ   213. Ⓐ Ⓑ Ⓒ Ⓓ   226. Ⓐ Ⓑ Ⓒ Ⓓ

Language

239. Ⓐ Ⓑ Ⓒ Ⓓ
240. Ⓐ Ⓑ Ⓒ Ⓓ
241. Ⓐ Ⓑ Ⓒ Ⓓ
242. Ⓐ Ⓑ Ⓒ Ⓓ
243. Ⓐ Ⓑ Ⓒ Ⓓ
244. Ⓐ Ⓑ Ⓒ Ⓓ
245. Ⓐ Ⓑ Ⓒ Ⓓ
246. Ⓐ Ⓑ Ⓒ Ⓓ
247. Ⓐ Ⓑ Ⓒ Ⓓ
248. Ⓐ Ⓑ Ⓒ Ⓓ
249. Ⓐ Ⓑ Ⓒ Ⓓ
250. Ⓐ Ⓑ Ⓒ Ⓓ

251. Ⓐ Ⓑ Ⓒ Ⓓ
252. Ⓐ Ⓑ Ⓒ Ⓓ
253. Ⓐ Ⓑ Ⓒ Ⓓ
254. Ⓐ Ⓑ Ⓒ Ⓓ
255. Ⓐ Ⓑ Ⓒ Ⓓ
256. Ⓐ Ⓑ Ⓒ Ⓓ
257. Ⓐ Ⓑ Ⓒ Ⓓ
258. Ⓐ Ⓑ Ⓒ Ⓓ
259. Ⓐ Ⓑ Ⓒ Ⓓ
260. Ⓐ Ⓑ Ⓒ Ⓓ
261. Ⓐ Ⓑ Ⓒ Ⓓ
262. Ⓐ Ⓑ Ⓒ Ⓓ

263. Ⓐ Ⓑ Ⓒ Ⓓ
264. Ⓐ Ⓑ Ⓒ Ⓓ
265. Ⓐ Ⓑ Ⓒ Ⓓ
266. Ⓐ Ⓑ Ⓒ Ⓓ
267. Ⓐ Ⓑ Ⓒ Ⓓ
268. Ⓐ Ⓑ Ⓒ Ⓓ
269. Ⓐ Ⓑ Ⓒ Ⓓ
270. Ⓐ Ⓑ Ⓒ Ⓓ
271. Ⓐ Ⓑ Ⓒ Ⓓ
272. Ⓐ Ⓑ Ⓒ Ⓓ
273. Ⓐ Ⓑ Ⓒ Ⓓ
274. Ⓐ Ⓑ Ⓒ Ⓓ

275. Ⓐ Ⓑ Ⓒ Ⓓ
276. Ⓐ Ⓑ Ⓒ Ⓓ
277. Ⓐ Ⓑ Ⓒ Ⓓ
278. Ⓐ Ⓑ Ⓒ Ⓓ
279. Ⓐ Ⓑ Ⓒ Ⓓ
280. Ⓐ Ⓑ Ⓒ Ⓓ
281. Ⓐ Ⓑ Ⓒ Ⓓ
282. Ⓐ Ⓑ Ⓒ Ⓓ
283. Ⓐ Ⓑ Ⓒ Ⓓ
284. Ⓐ Ⓑ Ⓒ Ⓓ
285. Ⓐ Ⓑ Ⓒ Ⓓ
286. Ⓐ Ⓑ Ⓒ Ⓓ

287. Ⓐ Ⓑ Ⓒ Ⓓ
288. Ⓐ Ⓑ Ⓒ Ⓓ
289. Ⓐ Ⓑ Ⓒ Ⓓ
290. Ⓐ Ⓑ Ⓒ Ⓓ
291. Ⓐ Ⓑ Ⓒ Ⓓ
292. Ⓐ Ⓑ Ⓒ Ⓓ
293. Ⓐ Ⓑ Ⓒ Ⓓ
294. Ⓐ Ⓑ Ⓒ Ⓓ
295. Ⓐ Ⓑ Ⓒ Ⓓ
296. Ⓐ Ⓑ Ⓒ Ⓓ
297. Ⓐ Ⓑ Ⓒ Ⓓ
298. Ⓐ Ⓑ Ⓒ Ⓓ

VERBAL SKILLS

16 minutes

Directions: For questions 1–60, choose the best answer.

1. Which word does *not* belong with the others?

    (A) argue
    (B) debate
    (C) angry
    (D) disagree

2. Which word does *not* belong with the others?

    (A) hopeful
    (B) optimistic
    (C) cordial
    (D) confident

3. Giant is to large as miniature is to

    (A) small
    (B) size
    (C) big
    (D) cute

4. Allan lives closer to the bus stop than Mark. Pat lives closer to the bus stop than Allan. Pat lives farther from the bus stop than Mark. If the first two statements are true, the third is

    (A) true
    (B) false
    (C) uncertain

5. Permit most nearly means

    (A) forgive
    (B) allow
    (C) forbid
    (D) give

6. Ink is to pen as paint is to

(A) brush
(B) bucket
(C) wall
(D) painter

7. Which word does *not* belong with the others?

(A) event
(B) affair
(C) occasion
(D) accident

8. Lake is to water as glacier is to

(A) ice
(B) snow
(C) mountain
(D) cold

9. Which word does *not* belong with the others?

(A) weather
(B) rain
(C) snow
(D) fog

10. A spider is a(n)

(A) feline
(B) reptile
(C) arachnid
(D) phobia

11. Conceited most nearly means

(A) arrogant
(B) inferior
(C) worthy
(D) hardworking

12. Button is to jacket as lace is to

(A) shoe
(B) zipper
(C) sweater
(D) foot

13. Water is to flower as birdseed is to

(A) garden
(B) fertilizer
(C) plant
(D) bird

14. Optimist is to hope as sage is to

(A) creativity
(B) fear
(C) talent
(D) wisdom

15. Christine is shorter than Louise. Louise is shorter than Joon. Christine is shorter than Joon. If the first two statements are true, the third is

(A) true
(B) false
(C) uncertain

16. An abridged book is

(A) short
(B) difficult
(C) thick
(D) published

17. Complex most nearly means

(A) intricate
(B) simple
(C) delicate
(D) double

18. Corrode most nearly means

(A) destroy
(B) rusty
(C) dishonest
(D) cheat

19. Ring is to bell as knock is to

    (A) door
    (B) alarm
    (C) hammer
    (D) ring

20. Actors is to director as players is to

    (A) coach
    (B) team
    (C) soccer
    (D) fan

21. Variation most nearly means

    (A) comparison
    (B) classification
    (C) support
    (D) difference

22. Frank is more outgoing than Joe. Joe is more outgoing than Rob. Rob is more outgoing than Frank. If the first two statements are true, the third is

    (A) true
    (B) false
    (C) uncertain

23. A <u>postponed</u> appointment

    (A) necessary
    (B) long
    (C) late
    (D) delayed

24. A is longer than B. B is longer than C. C is longer than D. If the first two statements are true, the third is

    (A) true
    (B) false
    (C) uncertain

25. A <u>unanimous</u> vote

    (A) complete
    (B) correct
    (C) undisputed
    (D) controversial

26. A <u>practical</u> person

    (A) normal
    (B) kind
    (C) sensible
    (D) silly

27. Which word does *not* belong with the others?

    (A) assembly
    (B) team
    (C) choir
    (D) director

28. Abandon most nearly means

    (A) adopt
    (B) realize
    (C) leave
    (D) litter

29. A <u>dynamic</u> speaker

    (A) energetic
    (B) loud
    (C) unstoppable
    (D) timid

30. A <u>penniless</u> person

    (A) thoughtless
    (B) poor
    (C) unkind
    D) helpful

31. Folder is to paper as drawer is to

    (A) clothes
    (B) lamp
    (C) furniture
    (D) desk

32. Which word does *not* belong with the others?

    (A) hearing
    (B) sight
    (C) touch
    (D) sense

33. All googles are moogles. No googles wear glasses. No moogles wear glasses. If the first two statements are true, the third statement is

    (A) true
    (B) false
    (C) uncertain

34. Which word does *not* belong with the others?

    (A) coin
    (B) bill
    (C) check
    (D) money

35. Reduce means the *opposite* of

    (A) enlarge
    (B) relate
    (C) allot
    (D) react

36. Ladle is to soup as shovel is to

    (A) garage
    (B) hole
    (C) sand
    (D) beach

37. Disperse means the *opposite* of

    (A) gather
    (B) display
    (C) reverse
    (D) handle

38. Hiking trail L is longer than hiking trail K. Trail K is longer than trail J. Trail L is longer than trail J. If the first two statements are true, the third is

    (A) true
    (B) false
    (C) uncertain

39. Hamper means the *opposite* of

    (A) relax
    (B) hinder
    (C) seize
    (D) assist

40. Aptitude means the *opposite* of

    (A) inability
    (B) height
    (C) peak
    (D) talent

41. Agenda is to meeting as program is to

    (A) television
    (B) plan
    (C) play
    (D) detail

42. Which word does *not* belong with the others?

    (A) hood
    (B) trunk
    (C) wheel
    (D) car

43. Sturdy means the *opposite* of

    (A) flimsy
    (B) stout
    (C) slender
    (D) solid

44. Gullible means the *opposite* of

    (A) dirty
    (B) cosmopolitan
    (C) incredulous
    (D) immaculate

45. Which word does *not* belong with the others?

    (A) gaunt
    (B) thin
    (C) svelte
    (D) rotund

46. Which word does *not* belong with the others?

    (A) pail
    (B) bucket
    (C) container
    (D) rag

47. Genuine most nearly means

    (A) real
    (B) friendly
    (C) original
    (D) intelligent

48. Content is the *opposite* of

    (A) restless
    (B) happy
    (C) argumentative
    (D) static

49. Magazines are longer than catalogues but not as long as books. Dictionaries are longer than magazines but not as long as encyclopedias. Magazines are the shortest of the types of writing. If the first two statements are true, the third is

    (A) true
    (B) false
    (C) uncertain

50. Which word does *not* belong with the others?

    (A) canoe
    (B) yacht
    (C) kayak
    (D) submarine

51. Replenish is the *opposite* of

    (A) reward
    (B) supply
    (C) increase
    (D) deplete

52. Fatima blocks more goals than Maria. Maria blocks more goals than Ellen. Jaylene blocks more goals than Ellen. If the first two statements are true, the third is

    (A) true
    (B) false
    (C) uncertain

53. Enlist is the *opposite* of

    (A) join
    (B) quit
    (C) enter
    (D) elect

54. Which word does *not* belong with the others?

    (A) fragile
    (B) breakable
    (C) brittle
    (D) robust

55. The individual pizza is smaller than the small pizza. The regular pizza is larger than the small pizza but not as big as the jumbo. The jumbo is not as big as the small pizza. If the first two statements are true, the third is

    (A) true
    (B) false
    (C) uncertain

56. Which word does *not* belong with the others?

    (A) cup
    (B) mug
    (C) saucer
    (D) glass

57. Renovate most nearly means

    (A) build
    (B) renew
    (C) create
    (D) remove

58. Which word does *not* belong with the others?

    (A) diamond
    (B) ruby
    (C) sapphire
    (D) gem

59. Which word does *not* belong with the others?

    (A) pacific
    (B) lively
    (C) playful
    (D) spirited

60. Mr. Thomas has more grandchildren than Mr. Blake. Mr. Smith has more grandchildren than Mr. Walter, but not as many as Mr. Thomas. Mr. Blake has the most grandchildren. If the first two statements are true, the third is

    (A) true
    (B) false
    (C) uncertain

QUANTITATIVE SKILLS

30 minutes

Directions: For questions 61–112, choose the best answer.

61. What number is 7 more than 10% of 100?

    (A) 10
    (B) 17
    (C) 3
    (D) 18

62. What is the next number in the following series: 21, 27, 33, ...

    (A) 37
    (B) 35
    (C) 39
    (D) 36

63. What is the next number in the following series: 51, 46, 41, 36, ...

    (A) 28
    (B) 29
    (C) 32
    (D) 31

64. Examine (a), (b), and (c) and select the correct answer.
    (a) two nickels
    (b) two quarters
    (c) two pennies and one dime

    (A) (a) plus (c) is greater than (b).
    (B) (b) is equal to (a).
    (C) (a) is more than (c).
    (D) (b) minus (a) is greater than (c).

65. Examine (a), (b), and (c) and select the correct answer.

    (a) .75

    (b) $\frac{5}{8}$ .6. ...

    (c) 0.26×3.4

    (A) (a) plus (b) is less than (c).
    (B) (a) is greater than (c).
    (C) (a) is equal to (b).
    (D) (c) is greater than (b).

66. What number is the cube of 4 divided by 8?

    (A) 64
    (B) 24
    (C) 3
    (D) 8

67. What number is $\frac{1}{2}$ of the average of 12, 8, 15, 6, and 29?

    (A) 7
    (B) 14
    (C) 70
    (D) 9

68. Examine (a), (b), and (c) and select the correct answer.

    (a)   (b)   (c)

    (A) (a) is shaded more than (b).
    (B) (a) and (b) are equally shaded and both are shaded more than (c).
    (C) (c) is shaded more than (a) and shaded less than (b).
    (D) (a), (b), and (c) are equally shaded.

69. What is the missing number in the following series: 88, 85, ___, 79, 76

    (A) 84
    (B) 82
    (C) 78
    (D) 81

70. Examine (a), (b), and (c) and select the correct answer.

    (a) 20% of 60
    (b) 60% of 20
    (c) 60% of 20%

    (A) (b) is greater than (a) or (c).
    (B) (a), (b), and (c) are equal.
    (C) (a) is greater than (c).
    (D) (b) is equal to (c) and smaller than (a).

71. What is the next number in the following series: 240, 120, 60, 30, ...

    (A) 20
    (B) 10
    (C) 15
    (D) 12

72. What are the next three numbers in the following series: 1, 7, 5, 6, ...

    (A) 12, 10, 11
    (B) 13, 11, 12
    (C) 12, 9, 10
    (D) 14, 11, 12

73. What number subtracted from 62 leaves 3 more than $\frac{3}{5}$ of 75?

    (A) 48
    (B) 41
    (C) 45
    (D) 14

74. What number is 8 more than $\frac{3}{4}$ of 24?

    (A) 12
    (B) 18
    (C) 22
    (D) 26

75. Examine (a), (b), and (c) and select the correct answer.

    (a) $(2 \times 7) - 4$
    (b) $(5 \times 6) + 1$
    (c) $(6 \times 6) - 15$

    (A) (c) is greater than (b).
    (B) (b) is less than (a) and (c).
    (C) (a) plus (c) is equal to (b).
    (D) (a) is greater than (c) and less than (b).

76. What is the next number in the following series: 228, 236, 244, 252, ...

    (A) 260
    (B) 262
    (C) 258
    (D) 256

77. Examine (a), (b), and (c) and select the correct answer.

    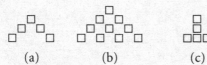

    (a)   (b)   (c)

    (A) (a) has more squares than (c).
    (B) (a) and (b) each have more squares than (c).
    (C) (b) and (c) each have more squares than (a).
    (D) (a) and (c) each have fewer squares than (b).

78. Examine (a), (b), and (c) and select the correct answer.

    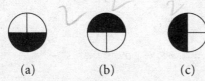

    (a)   (b)   (c)

    (A) (a) is more shaded than (b).
    (B) (a) and (b) are equally shaded, and each are less shaded than (c).
    (C) (b) is more shaded than (c) and less shaded than (a).
    (D) (a), (b), and (c) are equally shaded.

79. What is the next number in the following series: 110, 105, 101, 98, 96, ...

    (A) 95
    (B) 96
    (C) 94
    (D) 91

80. What number divided by 6 is $\frac{1}{5}$ of 80?

    (A) 420
    (B) 96
    (C) 16
    (D) 300

81. What is the next number in the following series: 6, X, 14, ...

    (A) IV
    (B) XVIII
    (C) IX
    (D) 18

82. Examine (a), (b), and (c) and select the correct answer.

    (a) $\frac{1}{3}$ of 9
    (b) $\frac{2}{3}$ of 12
    (c) $\frac{2}{5}$ of 15

    (A) (b) and (c) are equal.
    (B) (a) and (b) are each greater than (c).
    (C) (c) is greater than (a).
    (D) (a), (b), and (c) are equal.

83. $\frac{1}{2}$ of what number is 5 times 4?

    (A) 20
    (B) 22
    (C) 40
    (D) 41

84. Examine (a), (b), and (c) and select the correct answer.

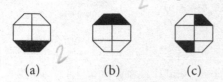

(a)   (b)   (c)

(A) (a) is shaded less than (b).
(B) (b) is shaded more than (c) and less than (a).
(C) (a), (b), and (c) are equally shaded.
(D) (c) is less shaded than (a).

85. What number added to 7 is 2 times the product of 5 and 3?

(A) 29
(B) 14
(C) 15
(D) 23

86. What is the next number in the following series: 17, 13, 16, 12, …

(A) 15
(B) 16
(C) 13
(D) 17

87. Examine (a), (b), and (c) and select the correct answer.
(a) 25%
(b) $\frac{1}{4}$
(c) 0.25

(A) (a) is greater than (b) which is greater than (c).
(B) (a), (b), and (c) are equal.
(C) (c) is greater than (b) but less than (a).
(D) (a) and (b) are each more than (c).

88. $\frac{2}{5}$ of what number is 2 times 20?

(A) 10
(B) 6
(C) 40
(D) 100

89. What is the missing number in the following series: 1, 5, 3, ___, 13, …

(A) 12
(B) 15
(C) 4
(D) 6

90. What is the next number in the following series: 6, 11, 12, 13, 18, 19, 20, …

(A) 23
(B) 24
(C) 25
(D) 26

91. Examine the square ABCD and select the correct answer.

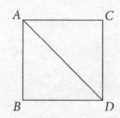

(A) AB is greater than AC.
(B) AC and AB are each less than AD.
(C) AC is greater than AB.
(D) AB is equal to AC plus CD.

92. What number multiplied by 6 is 2 less than 20?

(A) 18
(B) 3
(C) 24
(D) 12

93. What is the missing number in the following series: 12, 24, 25, 50, ___, 102, …

(A) 51
(B) 52
(C) 74
(D) 54

94. Examine (a), (b), and (c) and select the correct answer.

    (a) $(15 \div 3) \times 2$
    (b) $(3 \div 1) \times 2$
    (c) $(25 \div 5) \times 2$

    (A) (a) and (c) are equal.
    (B) (a) is greater than (b) and less than (c).
    (C) (b) and (c) are equal to (a).
    (D) (b) is less than (c) but greater than (a).

95. What are the next two numbers in the following series: 75, 77, 74, 76, 73, ...

    (A) 71, 74
    (B) 74, 75
    (C) 75, 72
    (D) 76, 73

96. Examine the cube and select the correct answer.

    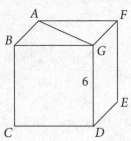

    (A) $AG < AB$
    (B) $AB + BG < AG$
    (C) $AG > DE$
    (D) $CG > AG$

97. What number divided by 6 leaves 3 more than 9?

    (A) 72
    (B) 12
    (C) 9
    (D) 3

98. Examine (a), (b), and (c). If both a and b are greater than zero, select the correct answer.

    (a) $6(a + b)$
    (b) $6a + 6b$
    (c) $6(a + b) + b$

    (A) (a) and (b) are greater than (c).
    (B) (b) and (c) are equal to (a).
    (C) (c) is greater than (a) and (b), which are equal.
    (D) (a), (b), and (c) are equal.

99. What is the next number in the following series: 2, 5, 10, 13, 26, ...

    (A) 29
    (B) 28
    (C) 42
    (D) 52

100. What number subtracted from 12 leaves $\frac{1}{5}$ of 40?

    (A) 4
    (B) 6
    (C) 12
    (D) 7

101. What is the next term in the following series: A2, b4, C6, d8, ...

    (A) F10
    (B) e9
    (C) E8
    (D) E10

102. Examine the bar graph and select the correct answer.

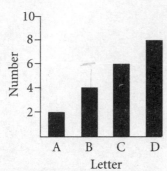

(A) Height of A plus height of B is equal to height of D.
(B) Height of C minus height of A equals height of B.
(C) Height of D is less than height of A but more than height of C.
(D) Height of A minus height of B equals height of C plus height of D.

103. What number is 7 less than $\frac{2}{3}$ of 15?

(A) 3
(B) 7
(C) 10
(D) 2

104. What is the next number in the following series: 3, 12, 4, 16, 8, …

(A) 32
(B) 8
(C) 60
(D) 12

105. Examine (a), (b), and (c) and select the correct answer.
(a) 2 squared
(b) 3 cubed
(c) 4 cubed

(A) (c) > (a) > (b)
(B) (a) > (b) > (c)
(C) (b) > (a) > (c)
(D) (c) > (b) > (a)

106. What is the next number in the following series: $9, 7\frac{3}{4}, 6\frac{1}{2}, 5\frac{1}{4}, …$

(A) $3\frac{1}{2}$
(B) $4\frac{1}{4}$
(C) 4
(D) $\frac{1}{4}$

107. What number is 6 times $\frac{1}{4}$ of 60?

(A) 80
(B) 15
(C) 90
(D) 300

108. What are the next three numbers in the following series: 15, 16, 19, 17, 18, 21, 19, …

(A) 20, 23, 22
(B) 21, 24, 22
(C) 21, 19, 18
(D) 20, 23, 21

109. $\frac{1}{8}$ of what number and added to 6 is 2 times 7?

(A) 14
(B) 16
(C) 8
(D) 64

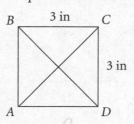

110. Examine the square and select the correct answer.

(A) The area of triangle *ABC* is greater than the area of triangle *ABD*.
(B) The area of the square is 9 inches.
(C) The perimeter of the square is 12 inches.
(D) The perimeter of triangle *ABC* is equal to the perimeter of the square.

111. What number is 8 more than $\frac{4}{5}$ of 10?

   (A) 18
   (B) 16
   (C) 40
   (D) 14

112. What number is 4 less than 3 cubed?

   (A) 27
   (B) 23
   (C) 22
   (D) 31

READING

Questions 113–174

25 minutes

Comprehension

Directions: Read the passages and answer questions 113–152.

Read the following passage and answer questions 113–122.

Insects can be classified into fourteen separate groupings, or orders. Butterflies and moths belong to the Lepidoptera order. Lepidoptera means "scale wings," from the Greek words "lepido" which means "scales" and "ptera" which means "wing."

Lepidoptera is one of the largest and most <u>diverse</u> insect orders. The only order with more different species is Coleoptera, that of beetles. So far, scientists have observed approximately 150,000 different species of butterflies and moths. Each species is distinguished by the <u>unique</u> arrangement, color, and pattern of its scales. Worldwide, there are about 28,000 butterfly species. The rest of the species comprising Lepidoptera are species of moths. Though butterflies and moths both have scaled wings, there are some important differences between them. Butterflies are <u>distinguished</u> by their brightly colored wings. Moth's wings are usually less bright. Butterflies are usually active during the day, while moths are active at night. A butterfly's antennae are swollen at the tip, while a moth's antennae are feathery.

113. The largest order of insects is

   (A) Lepidoptera
   (B) Butterfly
   (C) Moth
   (D) Coleoptera

114. How many insect orders are there?

   (A) 2
   (B) 14
   (C) 3
   (D) 150

115. Which of the following is true?

    (A) Butterflies and moths belong to different orders.
    (B) Butterflies and moths are both Lepidoptera.
    (C) Butterflies are insects, while moths are not.
    (D) Butterflies fly faster than other Lepidoptera.

116. You would expect to find the kind of information in this passage in

    (A) a scientific journal
    (B) a social studies text
    (C) neither of these
    (D) both of these

117. According to the passage, how many species of butterflies are there worldwide?

    (A) 14
    (B) 28
    (C) 28,000
    (D) 150,000

118. As used in the passage, the word <u>diverse</u> most nearly means

    (A) multiple
    (B) flying
    (C) winged
    (D) varied

119. Which of the following is true?

    (A) Scientists know the exact number of Lepidoptera species.
    (B) Scientists have not identified all Lepidoptera.
    (C) Scientists have already observed all Lepidoptera species.
    (D) Scientists are debating how to classify butterflies and moths.

120. In comparing butterflies and moths, you would find that butterflies

    (A) are more friendly
    (B) are not attracted to sunlight
    (C) are more colorful
    (D) are more aggressive

121. As used in the passage, the word <u>distinguished</u> most nearly means

    (A) recognizable
    (B) respectable
    (C) similar
    (D) organized

122. As used in the passage, the word <u>unique</u> most nearly means

    (A) lonely
    (B) different
    (C) beautiful
    (D) order

Read the following passage and answer questions 123–132.

The man catches a glimpse of a redcoat emerging from the woods. His heart beats faster as first one British soldier steps into the open, then another, then another. Soon, a line of redcoats fills the field. They far outnumber the man's own regiment. Surely, the rebel soldiers will be defeated. A general gives the command, and the man lowers his musket to aim. So do his comrades, standing beside him.

A sharp crackle rips through the quiet morning air. It is the first gunshot of the battle. In moments, the battlefield is crackling with the sound of bullets. A pungent aroma fills the air. The man's eyes <u>smart</u> and his vision dims from the thick cloud of gun smoke. His comrade beside him falls wounded.

But the man is only feigning injury. He will lie on the field until smoke clears and the war reenactment is finished. Then, he will get up, dust himself off, and join the rest of the soldiers for a picnic. This is not a real skirmish, but rather a carefully planned and orchestrated recreation of a revolutionary war battle. The redcoats and the rebels are members of a club, who reenact the battles of the Revolutionary War each Fourth of July.

Reenactors feel that demonstrating what the War for Independence was really like is not only an enjoyable way to spend a morning, but also a way to bring history alive.

123. The first two paragraphs of this passage de-
     scribe a battle's

     (A) sights and sounds
     (B) soldiers and commanders
     (C) weapons and soldiers
     (D) costumes and actors

124. As used in the passage, the word skirmish most
     nearly means

     (A) picnic
     (B) battle
     (C) soldier
     (D) wound

125. The author of this passage is most likely a

     (A) historian
     (B) reenactor
     (C) redcoat
     (D) soldier

126. The battle the man was reenacting was probably

     (A) won by the British
     (B) won by the rebels
     (C) the final battle of the war
     (D) a secret attack

127. According to this passage, why did the rebel
     soldier lower his musket?

     (A) He was afraid.
     (B) His general gave an order.
     (C) The British began to fire.
     (D) His friend was injured.

128. The man's heart beat when the British took the
     field because he was

     (A) motivated
     (B) afraid
     (C) surprised
     (D) elated

129. As used in the passage, the word smart most
     nearly means

     (A) intelligent
     (B) see
     (C) hurt
     (D) fog

130. According to this passage, reenactors enjoy

     (A) fighting
     (B) history
     (C) picnics
     (D) skirmishes

131. A good title for this passage would be

    (A) History Comes Alive
    (B) A Fallen Soldier
    (C) Muskets Ready
    (D) The War for Independence

132. According to this passage, which word would most nearly describe reenacting?

    (A) courageous
    (B) rebellious
    (C) studious
    (D) fun

Read the following passage and answer questions 133–142.

A garbage dump is a place for things we consider useless, but garbage dumps can provide a useful source of energy.

Garbage dumps, also called landfills, give off a small amount of energy. Wastes in the dump, such as apple cores, egg shells, and banana peels create methane gas as they <u>decompose</u>. At large dumps, the methane gas is burned, in order to prevent a hazardous gas buildup. Although landfill gas is generally a pollutant, it can also be a valuable source of fuel. Methane is the same gas sold by natural gas utility companies. At garbage dumps, the methane is either sold to commercial industries or collected and used to power electric generators.

Depending on the size and age of the landfill, a <u>significant</u> amount of energy can be collected. For example, a five-megawatt generator could produce 42 million kilowatt-hours per year. That's enough electricity to supply about 3,200 homes with power.

There's an added benefit of recovering methane gas from garbage dumps too. Methane that is released directly into the atmosphere can contribute to global warming. So you see, there's treasure in the trash.

133. The creation of methane gas in a garbage dump is caused by

    (A) pollution
    (B) fires
    (C) electricity
    (D) decomposition

134. Although the author of this passage describes garbage dumps as a place for things we consider useless, her feeling toward garbage dumps is one of

    (A) appreciation
    (B) affection
    (C) sarcasm
    (D) disgust

135. Which of the following is true?

    (A) Garbage dumps are clean.
    (B) Garbage dumps produce electricity.
    (C) Garbage dumps can be useful.
    (D) Garbage dumps power automobiles.

136. According to this passage, a five-megawatt generator can power

    (A) thousands of homes
    (B) a small city
    (C) a large factory
    (D) 42 garbage dumps

137. As used in the passage, the word <u>significant</u> most nearly means

   (A) sizable
   (B) polluted
   (C) electric
   (D) small

138. Methane gas is

   (A) dirty
   (B) natural
   (C) useless
   (D) dangerous

139. A good title for this passage might be

   (A) Don't Throw It Away
   (B) How to Recycle
   (C) Treasure in the Trash
   (D) The Science of Decomposition

140. This passage implies that an added benefit of recovering methane gas from garbage dumps is that it

   (A) prevents the contribution to global warming
   (B) supplies all our electricity
   (C) decreases the amount of trash we throw away
   (D) provides an endless supply of power

141. As used in the passage, the word <u>decompose</u> most nearly means

   (A) smell
   (B) rot
   (C) burn
   (D) build

142. Based on the passage, it could be said that garbage dumps cause the

   (A) decomposition of minerals
   (B) reduction of global warming
   (C) pollution of the oceans
   (D) production of methane

Read the following passage and answer questions 143–148.

The practice of bloodletting, misguided by modern standards, was a popular cure of medieval medicine. During medieval times, the body was viewed as part of the larger universe. People believed that the four elements of nature—earth, air, water, and fire—were related to four elements in the human body. Those elements were, <u>respectively</u>, black bile, blood, phlegm, and yellow bile. Medieval doctors believed that illness was caused by an <u>imbalance</u> of one of these four elements. For example, too much black bile could be the cause of a sad person's melancholy. These disease-causing imbalances were commonly treated with herbal remedies, meditation, and bloodletting.

Specialized medical books of the day, called leech books, contained description of various ailments and methods for treating them. These antique physician's desk references detailed where to apply bloodsucking leeches to a patient, or how much blood to drain from an individual to cure him or her. For despite the dangers obvious to us now, medieval doctors and barbers believed they were helping their patients by causing them to bleed.

As modern doctors know, draining a person's blood does not have restorative powers. In spite of that, bloodletting persisted as a common cure well into the 18th century. In fact, George Washington, the father of the United States, eventually died as a result of improper bloodletting intended to cure him of a common cold.

143. This passage was probably printed in

(A) a medical journal
(B) a history book
(C) a letter to a friend
(D) an instructional booklet

144. According to this passage, the technique of bloodletting is

(A) successful as a cure
(B) still in practice
(C) unused in current times
(D) the beginning of modern medicine

145. With which of the following would the author of this passage most likely agree?

(A) Medieval medicine is unparalleled.
(B) George Washington was murdered.
(C) Modern doctors are more aware of the causes of diseases.
(D) Leeches are extinct.

146. According to the passage, which group had members that practiced bloodletting?

(A) herbalists
(B) midwives
(C) politicians
(D) barbers

147. This passage calls bloodletting *misguided*. Which of these would also be misguided?

(A) Wearing small shoes to keep your feet from growing
(B) Drinking tea to cure a sore throat
(C) Washing your hands to prevent spreading germs
(D) Saying "good luck," to someone about to compete in a race

148. It is implied that modern doctors think bloodletting is

(A) harmless
(B) common
(C) curative
(D) unsafe

Read the following passage and answer questions 149–152.

Almost everyone enjoys hearing some kind of live music. But few of us realize the complex process that goes into designing the acoustics of concert and lecture halls. In the design of any building where the audibility of sound is a major consideration, architects have to carefully match the space and materials they use to the intended purpose of the venue. One problem is that the intensity of sound may build too quickly in an enclosed space. Another problem is that only part of the sound we hear in any large room or auditorium comes directly from the source. Much of it reaches us a fraction of a second later after it has been reflected off the walls, ceiling, and floor as reverberated sound. How much each room reverberates depends upon both its size and the ability of its contents to absorb sound. Too little reverberation can make music sound thin and weak; too much reverberation can blur the listener's sense of where one note stops and the next begins.

Consequently, the most important factor in acoustic design is the time it takes for these reverberations to die down altogether, called the reverberation time.

149. Which of the following is the main topic of this passage?

(A) the challenges of an architect's job
(B) the differences between speech and music
(C) the experience of hearing live music
(D) the role of reverberation in acoustic design

150. The passage suggests that the *complex process* of acoustic design is

(A) not widely appreciated by the public
(B) really a matter of listener sensitivity
(C) an engineer's problem, not an architect's
(D) most difficult in concert hall construction

151. According to the passage, too little reverberation in a concert hall can result in

(A) a rapid increase in the volume of sound
(B) the blurring of details in a piece of music
(C) a quiet and insubstantial quality of sound
(D) confusion among a listening audience

152. Which of the following does the author regard as the most significant consideration in the design of a concert hall?

(A) an appreciation for music
(B) an understanding of reverberation time
(C) the choice of building materials
(D) the purpose of the venue

Vocabulary

Directions: For questions 153–174, choose the word that is closest in meaning to the underlined word.

153. To <u>predict</u> the future

(A) change
(B) prevent
(C) foretell
(D) control

154. <u>Mutual</u> respect

(A) strong
(B) understandable
(C) common
(D) lost

155. A <u>gap</u> in logic

(A) break
(B) mistake
(C) theory
(D) grab

156. A <u>frank</u> response

(A) honest
(B) masculine
(C) cold
(D) lengthy

157. To <u>allege</u>

(A) allow
(B) arrest
(C) imply
(D) inspect

158. An important <u>consequence</u>

(A) coincidence
(B) effect
(C) circumstance
(D) point

159. To <u>confine</u>

   (A) restrict
   (B) reduce
   (C) separate
   (D) polish

160. To <u>delete</u> information

   (A) add
   (B) erase
   (C) edit
   (D) avoid

161. A <u>glossy</u> brochure

   (A) influential
   (B) glib
   (C) interesting
   (D) shiny

162. An <u>outrageous</u> remark

   (A) extraordinary
   (B) false
   (C) political
   (D) respectful

163. A <u>sophisticated</u> woman

   (A) learned
   (B) cosmopolitan
   (C) fashionable
   (D) wealthy

164. An interesting <u>proposal</u>

   (A) engagement
   (B) invention
   (C) suggestion
   (D) result

165. A <u>radical</u> idea

   (A) subversive
   (B) superb
   (C) novel
   (D) scientific

166. To <u>interrogate</u> a prisoner

   (A) interrupt
   (B) release
   (C) question
   (D) inspect

167. A <u>plausible</u> theory

   (A) proven
   (B) economic
   (C) extensive
   (D) valid

168. Public <u>access</u>

   (A) park
   (B) tax
   (C) entrance
   (D) ramp

169. To <u>compose</u>

   (A) write
   (B) review
   (C) erase
   (D) send

170. An <u>ostentatious</u> person

   (A) skillful
   (B) conspicuous
   (C) bossy
   (D) humble

171. An <u>essential</u> element

   (A) necessary
   (B) elementary
   (C) elated
   (D) pure

172. A challenging <u>obstacle</u>

   (A) exam
   (B) track
   (C) difficulty
   (D) task

173. a <u>precise</u> instrument

    (A) musical
    (B) complicated
    (C) accurate
    (D) automotive

174. a <u>gracious</u> host

    (A) forgetful
    (B) unwelcome
    (C) useful
    (D) warm

MATHEMATICS

45 minutes

Directions: For questions 175–238, choose the best answer.

Concepts

175. Which of the following is *not* a type of triangle?

    (A) isosceles
    (B) equilateral
    (C) obtuse
    (D) rhomboid

176. $\{1, 6, 11, 16\} \cap \{1, 2, 6, 10, 14\} =$

    (A) $\{1, 6\}$
    (B) $\{1, 2, 6\}$
    (C) $\{1, 2, 3, 4\}$
    (D) $\{6, 12, 14\}$

177. To the nearest tenth, 75.891 is written

    (A) 75.8
    (B) 75.9
    (C) 75
    (D) 75.91

178. Simplify: $3(-3)^2$

    (A) 9
    (B) 27
    (C) 18
    (D) 12

179. As a fraction, 0.12 can be written as

    (A) $\dfrac{1}{12}$
    (B) $\dfrac{12}{100}$
    (C) $\dfrac{1}{10}$
    (D) $\dfrac{100}{12}$

180. The measure of the angle labeled x is

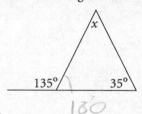

    (A) 65°
    (B) 35°
    (C) 100°
    (D) 95°

181. To multiply a number by 1,000, move the decimal point

    (A) two places to the right
    (B) three places to the right
    (C) three places to the left
    (D) four places to the right

182. Which of the following is a pair of consecutive numbers?

    (A) 4, 5
    (B) −4, +4
    (C) 3, 6
    (D) $\dfrac{1}{3}, \dfrac{3}{1}$

183. The diameter of this circle is

(A) 4π m
(B) 4 m
(C) 8 m
(D) 2π m

184. One centimeter is equal to how many meters?

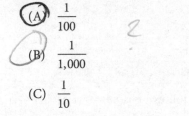

(A) $\dfrac{1}{100}$

(B) $\dfrac{1}{1,000}$

(C) $\dfrac{1}{10}$

(D) $\dfrac{1}{10,000}$

185. How many integers are between $\dfrac{25}{3}$ and 12.3?

(A) 12
(B) 3
(C) 5
(D) 4

186. Which of the following is always true?

(A) Adding two negative numbers results in a positive number.
(B) Multiplying one negative and one positive number results in a positive number.
(C) Multiplying one negative and one positive number results in a negative number.
(D) Subtracting a negative from a positive number results in zero.

187. The square root of 122 is between

(A) 11 and 12
(B) 12 and 13
(C) 100 and 130
(D) 120 and 130

188. Which of these statements is true?

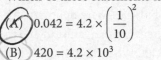

(A) $0.042 = 4.2 \times \left(\dfrac{1}{10}\right)^2$

(B) $420 = 4.2 \times 10^3$

(C) $0.42 = 4.2 \times 10$

(D) $4{,}200 = 4.2 \times 10^4$

189. Two numbers are in the ratio 3:1. The sum of the two numbers is 52. What is the larger number?

(A) 39
(B) 52
(C) 13
(D) 3

190. Which of the following fractions has a value between $\dfrac{1}{5}$ and $\dfrac{4}{9}$?

(A) $\dfrac{1}{8}$

(B) $\dfrac{3}{5}$

(C) $\dfrac{2}{3}$

(D) $\dfrac{1}{3}$

191. If the measure of angle $AOB = 60$ degrees, what fractional part of the circle shown below is shaded?

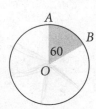

(A) $\dfrac{1}{6}$

(B) $\dfrac{1}{5}$

(C) $\dfrac{1}{3}$

(D) $\dfrac{2}{10}$

192. A recent poll showed that 42% of people polled favored a new bill, 28% were opposed to it, 20% were neither for nor against it, and the rest did not vote at all. What fractional part of the whole did not vote at all?

    (A) $\dfrac{1}{9}$

    (B) $\dfrac{9}{10}$

    (C) $\dfrac{1}{10}$

    (D) $\dfrac{2}{10}$

193. One week, a child spent 40% of her allowance on soft drinks. If her allowance is $5, how much did she spend on soft drinks?

    (A) $4
    (B) $1.20
    (C) $20
    (D) $2

194. Which of the following is *not* a type of quadrilateral?

    (A) trapezoid
    (B) parallelogram
    (C) square
    (D) Pythagorean

195. If triangle *ADE* is similar to triangle *ABC*, which of the following proportions is true?

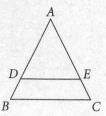

    (A) $\dfrac{AD}{AB} = \dfrac{DE}{BC}$

    (B) $\dfrac{AD}{AE} = \dfrac{AB}{AD}$

    (C) $\dfrac{AB}{BC} = \dfrac{AC}{EC}$

    (D) $\dfrac{DB}{DE} = \dfrac{AD}{EC}$

196. Which of the following is *not* a prime factor of 30?

    (A) 7
    (B) 3
    (C) 2
    (D) 5

197. The least common multiple of 3 and 4 is

    (A) 12
    (B) 6
    (C) 4
    (D) 3

198. Which of the following is an example of the associative property of addition?

    (A) $\dfrac{2}{3} + \dfrac{1}{3} + 3 = 2\left(\dfrac{1}{3} + \dfrac{2}{3}\right)$

    (B) $\dfrac{1}{3} + \dfrac{1}{2} + \dfrac{1}{4} = 1$

    (C) $\left(\dfrac{1}{3} + \dfrac{2}{3}\right) + 3 = \dfrac{1}{3} + \left(\dfrac{2}{3} + 3\right)$

    (D) $\dfrac{2}{3} + \dfrac{1}{3} = 3\dfrac{1}{3}$

Problem Solving

199. Solve the following equation for x:

    $12 + 3x = x + 40$

    (A) 4
    (B) 14
    (C) 28
    (D) 12

200. An artist bought five tubes of paint at $2.25 each and three paintbrushes at $4.30 each. How much did she spend?

    (A) 24.35
    (B) 25.00
    (C) 24.25
    (D) 24.15

201. Find the difference between $2\frac{1}{3}$ and $1\frac{1}{4}$.

    (A) $1\frac{1}{3}$

    (B) $1\frac{1}{2}$

    (C) $\frac{3}{4}$

    (D) $1\frac{1}{12}$

202. Mr. Brown paid $850 for bus tickets this year. Approximately how much did he pay, on the average, each month?

    (A) $70.80
    (B) $70.08
    (C) $85.00
    (D) $75.00

203. $1\frac{1}{2} \times 2\frac{1}{4} \times \frac{2}{3} =$

    (A) $5\frac{2}{8}$

    (B) $2\frac{1}{4}$

    (C) $2\frac{1}{2}$

    (D) 3

204. Simplify: $-5 + 6 + (-4) + (-8) =$

    (A) -8
    (B) -9
    (C) -17
    (D) -11

205. Ruth has saved $3 less than two times the amount Mona has. If Mona has $102, how much does Ruth have?

    (A) $35
    (B) $201
    (C) $99
    (D) $45

206. The formula $F = \frac{9}{5}C + 32$ converts temperature from Centigrade to Fahrenheit. What is the Fahrenheit temperature equivalent to 5 degrees Centigrade?

    (A) 32
    (B) 40
    (C) 41
    (D) 37

207. Solve: $9 + (-3) + 4 + (-5) =$

    (A) 6
    (B) 5
    (C) 12
    (D) 13

208. If the sum of two numbers is *a* and one of the numbers is 4, then two times the other number is

  (A) $2(a \times 4)$
  (B) $2(a + 4)$
  (C) $2a$
  (D) $2(a - 4)$

209. If a man can mow 3 acres in an hour, how many acres can he mow in 12 hours?

  (A) 36 acres
  (B) 12 acres
  (C) 6 acres
  (D) 38 acres

210. Martin has $4 less than two times the amount his sister has. If his sister has $36, how much does Martin have?

  (A) $66
  (B) $32
  (C) $68
  (D) $72

211. A deli charges $2 per pound for items on its salad bar. What is the cost of a salad that weighs one pound two ounces?

  (A) $2.75
  (B) $2.25
  (C) $2.50
  (D) $3.00

212. If $a + 4 = b + 6$, then

  (A) $a < b$
  (B) $a = b$
  (C) $a > b$
  (D) $a = 2b$

213. If $3a - 2 > 10$, then a^2 must be

  (A) more than 16
  (B) less than 16
  (C) less than 10
  (D) equal to 16

214. In one year, Mrs. Daly paid $35.50 interest on a loan that had a 5% simple interest rate. How much did she borrow?

  (A) $177.50
  (B) $7,100.00
  (C) $700.00
  (D) $710.00

215. Find the value of $x^3 + 3y + 2$, if $x = 3$ and $y = \frac{1}{2}$.

  (A) 20
  (B) 30
  (C) $30\frac{1}{2}$
  (D) $12\frac{1}{2}$

216. What is the volume of this rectangular solid?

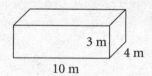

10 m, 3 m, 4 m

  (A) 37 m^3
  (B) 74 m^3
  (C) 240 m^3
  (D) 120 m^3

217. Suzanne would like to put wall-to-wall carpeting in her living room. At $4 a square foot, how much will it cost her to carpet a room that measures 12 ft by 15 ft?

  (A) $240
  (B) $720
  (C) $170
  (D) $108

218. If the 6% tax on a pair of roller blades was $4.50, how much were the Rollerblades, not including tax?

  (A) $65
  (B) $75
  (C) $80
  (D) $85

219. If $X = 2$, $Y = 3$, and $Z = 4$, then $2XYZ =$

    (A) 48
    (B) 24
    (C) 11
    (D) 96

220. $5.31\overline{)2.7633}$ is approximately

    (A) .31
    (B) 31
    (C) 52
    (D) .52

221. $42.13 \times .082 =$

    (A) 34.5466
    (B) 345.466
    (C) .345466
    (D) 3.45466

222. If $2x - 7 > 9$, then x^2 must be greater than

    (A) 16
    (B) 64
    (C) 8
    (D) 7

223. $0.354 + 7.9 + 2.03 =$

    (A) 9.444
    (B) 9.284
    (C) 10.284
    (D) 8.457

224. If $8x + 2 = 3x + 5$, then $x =$

    (A) $\dfrac{3}{5}$

    (B) $\dfrac{3}{4}$

    (C) $\dfrac{2}{5}$

    (D) $\dfrac{1}{6}$

225. A soccer player scores four goals in 10 games played. How many goals will she score in 15 games if she continues to score at the same rate?

    (A) 5
    (B) 7
    (C) 6
    (D) 4.5

226. If x is an even integer and $-1 > x > -4$, what is the value of x?

    (A) -2
    (B) 0
    (C) -1
    (D) 4

227. What is the value of a in the equation $3a - 6 = b$, if $b = 18$?

    (A) 4
    (B) 6
    (C) 8
    (D) 10

228. If it costs $22.75 to dry-clean seven shirts, how much will it cost to dry-clean four shirts at the same price?

    (A) $9.75
    (B) $6.50
    (C) $13.00
    (D) $13.50

229. Ellen earns $30 a week babysitting. She puts 20% of everything she earns in a bank account earmarked for college. How much does she put in her college savings account each month?

    (A) $240
    (B) $24
    (C) $6
    (D) $60

230. $534 \times 32 =$

   (A) 17,088
   (B) 17,188
   (C) 17,988
   (D) 18,088

231. If $\sqrt{a+6} = 12$, then $a =$

   (A) 136
   (B) 132
   (C) 138
   (D) 116

232. What is the area of the figure shown in the diagram?

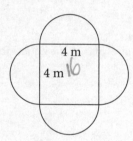

   (A) $(16 + 8\pi)\ \text{m}^2$
   (B) $(16 + 64\pi)\ \text{m}^2$
   (C) $(16 + 16\pi)\ \text{m}^2$
   (D) $(16 + 4\pi)\ \text{m}^2$

233. If $\frac{3}{4}x = 30$, find the value of $\frac{5}{8}x$.

   (A) 90
   (B) 25
   (C) 120
   (D) 40

234. A supervisor earns $25 an hour more than her coworker. The two, working together, earn $600 for an eight-hour work day. How much does the supervisor earn per hour?

   (A) $36
   (B) $500
   (C) $400
   (D) $50

235. The ratio of $\frac{2}{3}$ to $\frac{3}{8}$ is

   (A) $\frac{2}{1}$
   (B) $\frac{3}{1}$
   (C) $\frac{16}{3}$
   (D) $\frac{16}{9}$

236. Mark has saved three times as much money as his younger brother. If Mark gives his brother $10, the two will have equal amounts of money. How much money did Mark save?

   (A) $30
   (B) $5
   (C) $15
   (D) $20

237. If $6 > y > 3$ and y is an odd integer, then $y =$

   (A) 6
   (B) 5
   (C) 3
   (D) 7

238. If the square root of $a + 12 = 7$, then $a =$

   (A) 36
   (B) 7
   (C) 47
   (D) 37

LANGUAGE

Usage
Questions 239–298

25 minutes

Directions: For questions 239–278, choose the sentence that contains an error in punctuation, capitalization, or usage. If there is no error, select choice (D).

239. (A) Suzie said, "I'm going to the store."
     (B) The president gave a speech last night.
     (C) Martina arrived on Tuesday February 8.
     (D) No mistake.

240. (A) What time is it?
     (B) Independence day is July 4.
     (C) Howard's aunt is 50 years old.
     (D) No mistake.

241. (A) We hope to visit the Museum of history.
     (B) Dave takes the bus every morning.
     (C) The teacher asked Jane to close the window.
     (D) No mistake.

242. (A) We watched *Treasure Island* yesterday afternoon.
     (B) My sister told me, "Mail the letter."
     (C) Where is the bus stop? Jose asked.
     (D) No mistake.

243. (A) You may have dessert after you eat your dinner.
     (B) Please carry these books for me.
     (C) Bob and Aarthi are the best singers in the choir.
     (D) No mistake.

244. (A) Miss Larson asked us to remain seated.
     (B) One of the puppies is smaller than the others.
     (C) Jerry and me will stay after school.
     (D) No mistake.

245. (A) Copenhagen is in Denmark.
     (B) Teresa asked, "Would you like a soda?"
     (C) May you pass the salt?
     (D) No mistake.

246. (A) Carol asked, "How are you feeling?"
     (B) The flock of birds was singing this morning.
     (C) San Diego is a beautiful city.
     (D) No mistake.

247. (A) Who is going to bring cups to the picnic?
     (B) Did you request two tickets?
     (C) The girl threw the ball.
     (D) No mistake.

248. (A) I told them I was going to be late.
     (B) You and I are in the class government.
     (C) Hello, Nancy said, how are you?
     (D) No mistake.

249. (A) The Girl Scouts are hiking in the mountains.
     (B) Their going to the beach this afternoon.
     (C) Dr. Hysmith gave a lecture at the university.
     (D) No mistake.

250. (A) Alex said, "I'm getting bored."
     (B) May I go out?
     (C) What will happen next, I wonder?
     (D) No mistake.

251. (A) I prefer apples to pears; they are sweeter.
     (B) Janet asked if she might play with the puppy.
     (C) The program begins at 8:00, right?
     (D) No mistake.

252. (A) Don't lay down on the sofa.
     (B) Have you met the new coach?
     (C) Winter recess starts on Thursday.
     (D) No mistake.

253. (A) Jamal exclaimed, "That's a great book!"
     (B) How much is your monthly bus pass?
     (C) Who's shoe is this?
     (D) No mistake.

254. (A) Kevin is the oldest person in our class.
     (B) The duty was given to Frank and I.
     (C) Let's visit the museum on our field trip.
     (D) No mistake.

255. (A) Lisa's grandparents live in Alabama.
     (B) George remarked, "she is the best player on the team."
     (C) The Redwood Forest is a beautiful place to visit.
     (D) No mistake.

256. (A) My mother is a lawyer.
     (B) What time did Roberto leave?
     (C) How are you feeling today.
     (D) No mistake.

257. (A) The Browns bought a new car.
     (B) How old is your cousin Mark?
     (C) The dog lied down in the corner.
     (D) No mistake.

258. (A) The teacher asked we to bring our projects home.
     (B) Did you notice the flowers blooming in the yard?
     (C) How long have you been working in the garage?
     (D) No mistake.

259. (A) Amy said, "I love reading to my little sister."
     (B) Cats sometimes catch mice.
     (C) It was the first time he had ever went horseback riding.
     (D) No mistake.

260. (A) Mayor Rivera has an office near the park.
     (B) Laura, please keep your dog on a leash.
     (C) Uncle Dan told us to wait in the car.
     (D) No mistake.

261. (A) There is a bicycle path along the river.
     (B) Everyone did their homework.
     (C) Veronica will join the Navy in November.
     (D) No mistake.

262. (A) We're all going to the Rocky Mountains this summer.
     (B) Have you ever seen the sunset?
     (C) Helen asked, "What are we having for dinner?"
     (D) No mistake.

263. (A) When the show was over, everyone leaves.
     (B) Our neighbor helped us shovel the driveway.
     (C) It's time for the show to start.
     (D) No mistake.

264. (A) Neither Kate nor Rachel has walked the dog.
     (B) You should of brought your lunch.
     (C) I have many more books than you.
     (D) No mistake.

265. (A) Jane asked, "How much did you pay for that pen?"
     (B) The womens' notebooks are on the table.
     (C) The sun rose at 5:00 this morning.
     (D) No mistake.

266. (A) The football players wear uniforms.
     (B) Mrs. Kahn is learning the children to swim.
     (C) I am glad that you're feeling better.
     (D) No mistake.

267. (A) Thomas is attending the University of california.
     (B) Ellen asked me to help her with her errands.
     (C) Everyone wants her drawing to win the prize.
     (D) No mistake.

268. (A) David didn't know whether he should call his mother or his father.
     (B) Dad put to much detergent in the washing machine.
     (C) If I wanted to go, I would have bought a ticket.
     (D) No mistake.

269. (A) Charles asked Greg and me to play catch with him.
     (B) When we go camping, we can see the Big Dipper.
     (C) Dinner is ready, but the children are not home yet.
     (D) No mistake.

270. (A) When will the cake be ready?
     (B) Before the blizzard stopped, our car was covered in snow.
     (C) Christine and me are skateboarding in the park.
     (D) No mistake.

271. (A) The baby is drinking her milk now.
     (B) If you would like to go, please tell me.
     (C) Shawn ran home quick.
     (D) No mistake.

272. (A) May I open my presents now?
     (B) Actually, Jim doesn't like to go to the beach.
     (C) I can't do nothing about it now.
     (D) No mistake.

273. (A) There are too many people on the subway.
     (B) Nelson is more talkative than Ramon.
     (C) The concert is Saturday, May 5.
     (D) No mistake.

274. (A) If you would like to go, please let me know.
     (B) Pamela is the faster of the three athletes.
     (C) I do not agree that Mike is stronger.
     (D) No mistake.

275. (A) When the bell rings, please turn off the oven.
     (B) Most cats like to drink milk.
     (C) He has fewer money than his brother.
     (D) No mistake.

276. (A) Herself has gone to the library.
     (B) Kim has more toys than Fran.
     (C) Joseph will leave for West Point tomorrow.
     (D) No mistake.

277. (A) We arrived on time at grand central station in New York City.
     (B) There is a spot on the glass.
     (C) My sister-in-law is coming to visit this week.
     (D) No mistake.

278. (A) The dog growled angrily at the letter carrier.
     (B) Alice said; "Let's all watch the movie tonight."
     (C) They would have waited, if they had known you were coming.
     (D) No mistake.

Spelling

Directions: For questions 279–288, choose the sentence that contains a spelling error. If there is no error, select choice (D).

279. (A) Our school cafateria always opens at 8:00 in the morning.
     (B) His proposal for a new park was very interesting.
     (C) The secretary typed very quickly.
     (D) No mistake.

280. (A) She described the circus in great detail.
     (B) Please turn in your composition on time.
     (C) If you work efficiently, you will finish on time.
     (D) No mistake.

281. (A) Do not criticize what you do not understand.
     (B) We waited impatiently for an answer.
     (C) The plane departed at 9:00.
     (D) No mistake.

282. (A) I think that author is a genius.
     (B) Dr. Alvarez is very successful.
     (C) The jury promised not to be prejediced.
     (D) No mistake.

283. (A) I wish it were possible to live forever.
     (B) Turn in your assignment imediately.
     (C) We visit the lake frequently.
     (D) No mistake.

284. (A) The art exhibition is downtown.
     (B) Each player has a specific role.
     (C) Tom and Sam argued about the election.
     (D) No mistake.

285. (A) The nurse said Mary is running a temperture.
     (B) General Radisson is the commander.
     (C) The tickets are inexpensive.
     (D) No mistake.

286. (A) I hope the delivery will arrive by noon.
     (B) Do you recognize that girl?
     (C) The sports arena is gigantic.
     (D) No mistake.

287. (A) The submarine rose to the surfice.
     (B) Oil is a natural resource.
     (C) The scientist examined the data.
     (D) No mistake.

288. (A) Please try not to interupt me when I'm speaking.
     (B) Are you sure this information is accurate?
     (C) This knitting pattern is very complicated.
     (D) No mistake.

Composition

Directions: For questions 289–298, follow the directions for each question.

289. Choose the best word to join the thoughts together.
     I would like to take a walk; _____ I'm afraid it is going to rain.

     (A) however,
     (B) moreover,
     (C) also,
     (D) none of these

290. Choose the words that best complete the following sentence.
     The museum's new exhibit is_____

     (A) a display dating back from the 12th century of antique armor.
     (B) from the 12th century of display of antique armor dating back to then.
     (C) dating back from the 12th century a display of antique armor.
     (D) a display of antique armor dating back from the 12th century.

291. Choose the group of words that best completes the sentence.
When we have enough time, _____

   (A) swimming is what we do.
   (B) we like to swim.
   (C) we are swimming.
   (D) to swim is what we like.

292. Which of these best fits under the topic "Bicycle Maintenance"?

   (A) You should care for your bicycle if you want it to perform at its best.
   (B) Henry Ford's first invention was a bicycle with an engine.
   (C) It is easiest to change bicycle gears when you are pedaling.
   (D) none of these

293. Choose the word to begin the following sentence.
_____ some feel that the high cost of space exploration is not worth the expense, others argue that it is an important expression of humankind's desire for knowledge.

   (A) However,
   (B) Importantly,
   (C) Therefore,
   (D) Although

294. Which of these expresses the idea most clearly?

   (A) Before leaving the house, we must turn off the lights.
   (B) Leaving the house, first we must turn off the lights.
   (C) To turn off the lights before leaving the house.
   (D) Turning off the lights before leaving the house is what we must do.

295. Choose the best word or words to join the thoughts together.
Skiing is not an easy sport; _____ it requires skill, dexterity, and talent.

   (A) but also
   (B) in addition
   (C) and moreover
   (D) none of these

296. Which sentence does *not* belong in the paragraph?
   (1) Though his brother liked to sleep late, Tom preferred to wake early. (2) He enjoyed the quiet calm of early morning. (3) He would often slip downstairs while the rest of the family was sleeping, stretch out on the sofa, and stare out the window while the sun came up. (4) Sometimes, he would make pancakes for dinner.

   (A) sentence 1
   (B) sentence 2
   (C) sentence 3
   (D) sentence 4

297. Which topic is best for a one paragraph theme?

   (A) The Politics of Western Africa
   (B) How to Make a Great Cup of Tea
   (C) Flowers of North America
   (D) none of these

298. Where should the following sentence be placed in the paragraph below?
These lava spills, in addition to volcanic eruptions, may have together killed off the dinosaurs.
   (1) Scientists have long argued over the causes leading to the extinction of the dinosaurs. (2) One common view holds that a combination of catastrophic events doomed the dinosaurs. (3) For example, a meteor shower hitting the Earth could have cracked the Earth's crust and allowed molten lava to spill across the land.

   (A) between sentences 1 and 2
   (B) between sentences 2 and 3
   (C) before sentence 1
   (D) after sentence 3

ANSWERS AND EXPLANATIONS

Answer Key

VERBAL SKILLS

1. C
2. C
3. A
4. B
5. B
6. A
7. D
8. A
9. A
10. C
11. A
12. A
13. D
14. D
15. A
16. A
17. A
18. A
19. A
20. A
21. D
22. B
23. D
24. C
25. C
26. C
27. D
28. C
29. A
30. B
31. A
32. D
33. C
34. D
35. A
36. C
37. A
38. A

39. D
40. A
41. C
42. D
43. A
44. C
45. D
46. D
47. A
48. A
49. B
50. D
51. D
52. C
53. B
54. D
55. B
56. C
57. B
58. D
59. A
60. B

QUANTITATIVE SKILLS

61. B
62. C
63. D
64. D
65. D
66. D
67. A
68. A
69. B
70. C
71. C
72. A
73. D
74. D

75. C
76. A
77. D
78. D
79. A
80. B
81. B
82. C
83. C
84. C
85. D
86. A
87. B
88. D
89. B
90. C
91. B
92. B
93. A
94. A
95. C
96. C
97. A
98. C
99. A
100. A
101. D
102. B
103. A
104. A
105. D
106. C
107. C
108. D
109. D
110. C
111. B
112. B

READING
Comprehension

113. D
114. B
115. B
116. A
117. C
118. D
119. B
120. C
121. A
122. B
123. A
124. B
125. B
126. A
127. B
128. B
129. C
130. B
131. A
132. D
133. D
134. A
135. C
136. A
137. A
138. B
139. C
140. A
141. B
142. D
143. B
144. C
145. C
146. D
147. A
148. D
149. D
150. A
151. C
152. B

Vocabulary

153. C
154. C
155. A
156. A
157. C
158. B
159. A
160. B
161. D
162. A
163. B
164. C
165. A
166. C
167. D
168. C
169. A
170. B
171. A
172. C
173. C
174. D

MATHEMATICS
Concepts

175. D
176. A
177. B
178. B
179. B
180. C
181. B
182. A
183. B
184. A
185. D
186. C
187. A
188. A
189. A
190. D

191. A
192. C
193. D
194. D
195. A
196. A
197. A
198. C

Problem Solving

199. B
200. D
201. D
202. A
203. B
204. D
205. B
206. C
207. B
208. D
209. A
210. C
211. B
212. C
213. A
214. D
215. C
216. D
217. B
218. B
219. A
220. D
221. D
222. B
223. C
224. A
225. C
226. A
227. C
228. C
229. B
230. A

231. C
232. A
233. B
234. D
235. D
236. A
237. B
238. D

LANGUAGE
Usage
239. C
240. B
241. A
242. C
243. D
244. C
245. C
246. D
247. D
248. C
249. B
250. D
251. D
252. A
253. C

254. B
255. B
256. C
257. C
258. A
259. C
260. D
261. D
262. D
263. A
264. B
265. B
266. B
267. A
268. B
269. D
270. C
271. C
272. C
273. D
274. B
275. C
276. A
277. A
278. B

Spelling
279. A
280. B
281. D
282. C
283. B
284. B
285. A
286. D
287. A
288. A

Composition
289. A
290. D
291. B
292. A
293. D
294. A
295. D
296. D
297. B
298. D

Verbal Skills

1. C

Angry is an emotion. The other choices are verbs with similar meanings.

2. C

Hopeful, optimistic, and *confident* are synonyms. *Cordial* means gracious or friendly.

3. A

Giant means extremely large, *miniature* means extremely small.

4. B

Because the first two statements are true and Pat lives closer to the bus stop than Allan, Pat cannot live farther from the bus stop than Mark.

5. B

To permit means to give permission or to allow.

6. A

Create a bridge to link the first pair of words, then use it to think of the missing word in the second pair. A pen is a tool that uses ink. What is a tool that uses paint? A paintbrush. Look at the answer choices. Choice (A), *brush,* fits.

7. D

While all four terms are occurrences, *accident* is the only term that means an unfortunate or unforeseen occurrence. *Event, affair,* and *occasion* are planned occurrences.

8. A

A lake is made up of water, and a glacier is made up of ice.

9. A

Weather is the general classification. The other choices are specific types of weather.

10. C

A spider is an arachnid. Even if you are not familiar with the term *arachnid,* you could make an intelligent guess by eliminating the other answer choices. Is a spider a feline? Well, a feline is a cat, so the answer would be no. Is a spider a reptile? Snakes and lizards are reptiles, but not spiders, so this can be eliminated. Is a spider a phobia? A phobia is a huge fear. You might have a huge fear of spiders, but a spider itself is not a phobia. So, the only answer left is (C), *arachnid.*

11. A

Conceited means proud in an unfriendly manner, so *arrogant* is the correct answer.

12. A

A button is used to close a jacket, and a lace is used to close or secure a shoe.

13. D

Water feeds a flower and birdseed feeds a bird.

14. D

Optimistic means full of hope; *sage* means full of wisdom.

15. A

From the first two statements it is certain that Christine is shorter than Joon.

16. A

Abridged means shortened, so an abridged book is short.

17. A

Complex means intricate or complicated.

18. A

Although *rusty* is an adjective you might use to describe corrosion, *corrode* most nearly means destroy.

19. A

We ring a bell to attract attention and we knock on a door to attract attention.

20. A

Actors are led by a director and players are led by a coach.

21. D

A variation is a difference or a slightly modified or changed version. Though variations can be used for the purpose of comparison, *comparison* doesn't define as closely what a variation is. Remember, you're looking for the word that is closest in meaning to the word in the question. *Classification* is a distracter meant to trick you by including the *-tion* from *variation*.

22. B

The first two statements indicate that Frank is the most outgoing. Therefore, the third statement is false.

23. D

Postponed means moved to a later time, so a postponed appointment is delayed.

24. C

There is no way to know for certain if C is longer than D.

25. C

A unanimous vote is one that is completely agreed upon, or undisputed.

26. C

A practical person is sensible.

27. D

A director is one individual; the other choices are groups.

28. C

To abandon means to leave.

29. A

A dynamic speaker is full of life, or energetic.

30. B

A penniless person is without a penny, or poor.

31. A

A folder holds papers, and a drawer holds clothes.

32. D

Sense is the general classification. The other choices are examples of senses.

33. C

All *googles* are *moogles*, but not all *moogles* must be *googles*, so some *moogles* might wear glasses.

34. D

Money is the general classification. The other choices are types of money.

35. A

To reduce means to lessen or decrease; the opposite is enlarge.

36. C

A ladle is used for soup; a shovel is used for sand.

37. A

To disperse means to scatter; the opposite is *gather*.

38. A

Because the first two statements are true and hiking trail L is longer than K and K is longer than J, L is longer than J as well.

39. D

To hamper means hinder or interfere with; the opposite is *assist*.

40. A

Aptitude is ability; the opposite is *inability*.

41. C

An agenda creates a plan for a meeting, and a program creates a plan for a play.

42. D

Car is the general classification. The other choices are parts of a car.

43. A

Sturdy means strong; the opposite is *flimsy*.

44. C

Gullible means naïve or easily deceived; the opposite is *incredulous*.

45. D

Rotund means round; the other choices are synonyms for *thin*.

46. D

A rag is not a type of container.

47. A

Genuine means real.

48. A

Content means satisfied or happy; the opposite is *restless*.

49. B

Because the first two statements are true and magazines are longer than catalogues, magazines cannot be the shortest of the types of writing.

50. D

All the other choices are types of boats, a submarine is different from a boat.

51. D

To replenish means to provide more; the opposite is *deplete*.

52. C

While the first two statements are true, they do not provide any information about Jaylene. Therefore, we cannot be certain whether she blocks more goals than Ellen or not.

53. B

To enlist means to join; the opposite is resign, or *quit*.

54. D

Robust is strong or sturdy; all the other choices are synonyms for *breakable*.

55. B

Because the first two statements are true and the small pizza is not as big as the jumbo, the third statement must be false.

56. C

A saucer is a plate; all the other choices are types of drink containers.

57. B

To renovate means to renew.

58. D

Gem is the general classification; all the other choices are types of gems.

59. A

Pacific means calm; the other words are all synonyms for *energetic*.

60. B

Because the first two statements are true and Mr. Thomas has more grandchildren than Mr. Blake, the third statement must be false.

Quantitative Skills

61. B

Begin by finding 10% of 100: .10 × 100 = 10. Then, add 7: 10 + 7 = 17.

62. C

The pattern in this series is made by adding 6 to each number; 33 + 6 = 39.

63. D

The pattern in this series is made by subtracting 5 from each number; 36 − 5 = 31.

64. D

Determine the amount of money for (a), (b), and (c). Then, calculate each answer choice to see which is correct. (a) is 10 cents, (b) is 50 cents, and (c) is 12 cents.

(A) (10 cents) plus (12 cents) is greater than (50 cents) is incorrect.

(B) (50 cents) is equal to (10 cents) is incorrect.

(C) (10 cents) is more than (12 cents) is incorrect.

(D) (50 cents) minus (10 cents) is greater than (12 cents) is correct.

65. D

5 divided by 8 (b) equals .625; .26 × 3.4 (c) equals .884. Clearly, .884 (c) is greater than either (a) or (b), so answer (D) is correct. And (c) is less than (a) plus (b), which is why answer (A) is incorrect.

66. D

The cube of 4 is 64; 64 ÷ 8 = 8.

67. A

The sum of 12 + 8 + 15 + 6 + 29 = 70; 70 ÷ 5 = 14; $\frac{1}{2}$ of 14 = 7.

68. A

Count the number of small triangles shaded within each larger triangle and compare each choice. (a) only has two sections shaded and (b) only has one.

69. B

The pattern in this series is to subtract 3 from each term. 85 − 3 = 82.

70. C

Determine the amounts for (a), (b), and (c) and test each alternative to see which is correct. (a) 20% of 60 is 12, (b) 60% of 20 is 12, (c) 60% of 20% is .12.

(A) 12 is greater than 12 or .12 is not correct.

(B) 12, 12, and .12 are equal is not correct.

(C) 12 is greater than .12 is correct.

(D) 12 is equal to .12 and smaller than 12 is not correct.

71. C

The pattern in this series is to take $\frac{1}{2}$ of the previous term to get the next. One-half of 30 is 15.

72. A

The pattern in this series is +6, −2, +1, and so on.

73. D

Start this problem from the end and work backward.

First find $\frac{3}{5}$ of 75:

$$\frac{3}{5} \times \frac{75}{1} = 45$$

But remember, we need 3 more than 45, or 45 + 3 = 48.

So what number subtracted from 62 equals 48? The quickest way to find out: subtract 48 from 62, and see what you get. 62 − 48 = 14.

Or, plug in each answer choice to see which one is correct.

Does 62 − 48 = 48? NO

Does 62 − 41 = 48? NO

Does 62 − 45 = 48? NO

Does 62 − 14 = 48? YES

74. D

Begin with $\frac{3}{4}$ of 24: $\frac{3}{4} \times \frac{24}{1} = 18$. Then, $8 + 18 = 26$.

75. C

First, determine the amounts of (a), (b), and (c). Then, test each alternative to see which is true. Remember to do the operations within the parentheses first. (a) is 10, (b) is 31, (c) is 21.

(A) 21 is greater than 31 is incorrect.

(B) 31 is less than 10 and 21 is incorrect.

(C) 10 plus 21 is equal to 31 is correct.

(D) 10 is greater than 21 and less than 31 is incorrect.

76. A

The pattern in the series is made by adding 8 to each number; $252 + 8 = 260$.

77. D

Count the squares in (a), (b), and (c). Then, test each alternative to see which is true. (a) and (c) each have 5 squares and (b) has 10.

78. D

Determine how much of each figure is shaded. Then, test each alternative to see which is true. Each circle has two equally sized sections shaded, so they are shaded equally.

79. A

The pattern in this series is −5, −4, −3, −2, and so on. Therefore, $96 − 1 = 95$.

80. B

Determine $\frac{1}{5}$ of 80: $\frac{1}{5} \times \frac{80}{1} = 16$. Multiply this result by 6 to find the answer: $16 \times 6 = 96$.

81. B

The pattern in this series is +4, with the result alternately expressed in Arabic, then in Roman numerals; $14 + 4 = 18$, or XVIII in Roman numerals.

82. C

Determine the amounts for (a), (b), and (c). Test each alternative to find the one that is true. (a) is 3, (b) is 8, (c) is 6.

(A) 8 and 6 are equal is incorrect.

(B) 3 and 8 are each greater than 6 is incorrect.

(C) 6 is greater than 3 is correct.

(D) 3, 8, and 6 are equal is incorrect.

83. C

First, find $5 \times 4 = 20$; 20 is one-half of what number? Double the result to find the answer: $20 \times 2 = 40$.

84. C

Each box has two trapezoidal sections shaded. Therefore, only (C) can be true.

85. D

First, determine the product of 5 and 3: $5 \times 3 = 15$, and $2 \times 15 = 30$.

Now, you need to find out which number plus 7 equals 30.

$$30 = x + 7$$
$$30 − 7 = 23$$

86. A

The pattern in this series is −4, +3, −4, +3, and so on. Therefore, the next term is $12 + 3 = 15$.

87. B

You can change (a), (b), and (c) so that they are all in the same form—either all fractions, decimals, or percents. However, knowing common decimal, fraction, and percent equivalents will help you do questions like these with greater ease. (a), (b), and (c) are all equal.

(A) 25% is greater than $\frac{1}{4}$ which is greater than 0.25 is incorrect.

(B) 25%, $\frac{1}{4}$, and 0.25 are equal is correct.

(C) 0.25 is greater than $\frac{1}{4}$ but less than 25% is incorrect.

(D) 25% and $\frac{1}{4}$ are each more than 0.25 is incorrect.

88. D

You can figure out this problem with algebra. First, translate the sentence into an equation.

$$\frac{2}{5} \times x = 2 \times 20$$

$$\frac{2}{5} \times x = 40$$

$$x = \frac{40}{1} \times \frac{5}{2}$$

$$x = 100$$

Another method is to plug in the answer choices to see which one works.

$$\frac{2}{5} = \frac{40}{x}$$

$$\frac{2}{5} = \frac{40}{100}$$

89. B

The pattern in this series is ×5, −2, ×5, −2, and so on. Therefore, the next term is 3 × 5 = 15.

90. C

The pattern in this series is +5, +1, +1, +5, +1, +1, and so on. Therefore, the next term is 20 + 5 = 25.

91. B

The line drawn from point *A* to point *D* divides this square into two right triangles. One of which is triangle *ABC*. In this right triangle, *AB* and *AC* are legs and *AD* is the hypotenuse. The length of the hypotenuse will always be the longest side of a right triangle, so the length of *AD* is greater than both *AB* and *AC*.

92. B

Begin by subtracting 2 from 20. This number divided by 6 will provide the answer.

20 − 2 = 18

18 ÷ 6 = 3

93. A

The pattern in this series is ×2, +1, ×2, +1, and so on. Therefore, the missing term is 50 + 1 = 51.

94. A

Determine the amounts for (a), (b), and (c), then choose the best alternative. Be sure to do the operations in parentheses first. (a) is 10, (b) is 6, and (c) is 10. Therefore, (a) and (c) are equal.

95. C

The pattern in this series is +2, −3, +2, −3, and so on. Therefore, the next two terms will be 73 + 2 = 75 and 75 − 3 = 72.

96. C

Because the figure is a cube, all edges and sides are equal. When a diagonal line is drawn across one side like *AG*, it forms a hypotenuse of a right triangle whose length is longer than the length of either of its sides. Because the sides of the cube are all equal, *AG* must also be longer than *DE*.

97. A

This can be done with algebra. If *Z* is the number you're looking for:

$$Z \div 6 = 3 + 9$$

$$Z \div 6 = 12$$

$$Z = 12 \times 6$$

$$Z = 72$$

98. C

Perform multiplication as indicated to arrive at these values:

(a) $6a + 6b$

(b) $6a + 6b$

(c) $6a + 6b + b = 6a + 7b$

It can now be seen that (a) and (b) are equal and that (c) is greater than both of them. Therefore, (C) is the best answer if *a* and *b* are greater than zero.

99. A

The pattern in this series is +3, ×2, +3, ×2, and so on. Therefore, the next term is 26 + 3 = 29.

100. A

To begin, find $\frac{1}{5}$ of 40. This is the same as 40 divided by 5, which equals 8. If a is the number you are looking for:

$$12 - a = 8$$
$$a = 4$$

101. D

The pattern for the letters in this series is made by using sequential letters in the alphabet, alternately uppercase or lowercase. The pattern for the numbers is made by using +2, +2, and so on. Therefore, the next term is E10.

102. B

Determine the values for each section of the chart. A = 2, B = 4, C = 6, and D = 8. Then, choose the correct alternative. Since 6 – 2 = 4 is true, the answer is choice (B).

103. A

This can be set up as an algebraic equation. If b is the number you are looking for:

$$b = \frac{2}{3}(15) - 7$$
$$b = \frac{30}{3} - 7$$
$$b = 10 - 7$$
$$b = 3$$

104. A

The pattern in this series is: ×4, –8, ×4, –8, and so on. Therefore, the next term is 8 × 4 = 32.

105. D

Determine the amounts for (a), (b), and (c). Then, decide which alternative is true.

(a) $2 \times 2 = 4$
(b) $3 \times 3 \times 3 = 27$
(c) $4 \times 4 \times 4 = 64$

Therefore, (c) > (b) > (a).

106. C

The pattern is made by subtracting $1\frac{1}{4}$ from each number.
Therefore, the next term is $5\frac{1}{4} - 1\frac{1}{4} = 4$.

107. C

First, figure out $\frac{1}{4}$ of 60. This number multiplied by 6 will provide the answer.

$$\frac{1}{4} \times 60 = \frac{60}{4} = 15$$
$$15 \times 6 = 90$$

108. D

The pattern in this series is +1, +3, –2, +1, +3, –2, and so on. Therefore, the next three terms are 19 + 1 = 20, 20 + 3 = 23, and 23 – 2 = 21.

109. D

This can be set up as an algebraic equation. If y is the number you are looking for:

$$6 + \frac{1}{8}y = 2 \times 7$$
$$6 + \frac{1}{8}y = 14$$
$$\frac{1}{8}y = 14 - 6$$
$$\frac{1}{8}y = 8$$
$$y = 8 \times 8$$
$$y = 64$$

110. C

Test each alternative to find the correct one. To find the perimeter, add the length of all four sides. Since the figure is a square, each of the sides measure 3 inches; 3 + 3 + 3 + 3 = 12 inches. Note the area of the square is 9 square inches, not 9 inches as choice (B) says.

111. B

This can be set up as an algebraic equation. If z is the number you are looking for:

$$z = 8 + \frac{4}{5} \times 10$$
$$z = 8 + \frac{40}{5}$$
$$z = 8 + 8$$
$$z = 16$$

112. B

First, find the cube of 3, and then subtract 4 from the result.

$$3 \times 3 \times 3 = 27 - 4 = 23$$

READING

Comprehension

113. D

Paragraph 2 begins with the sentences, *Lepidoptera is one of the largest and most diverse insect orders. The only order with more different species is Coleoptera.* Therefore, the answer is (D).

114. B

You might have missed this detail from the first sentence that states that *insects can be classified into fourteen separate groupings.* Therefore, choice (B) is the answer.

115. B

Skim the passage for any mention of butterflies and moths to answer this question. The second sentence states, *Butterflies and moths belong to the Lepidoptera order.*

116. A

Because of the nature of the information, this passage would most likely be found in a scientific journal.

117. C

This is a detail question. Find and reread the sentence in the passage with the key words *butterfly species* and *worldwide.* It states that there are 28,000 species.

118. D

Diverse most nearly means varied. Read the context or sentences in and around where the word is found. They discuss difference, which is an important clue in decoding the word's meaning. *Flying* and *winged* are trick answers because although they have to do with butterflies, they do not define diverse. *Multiple* means many and does not really imply difference.

119. B

This is an inferential question. Though not specifically stated, the answer can be assumed based on the words *so far* in sentence 6.

120. C

The word *comparing* is a clue that you are looking for a difference. The end of the passage discusses the *important differences.* One of these differences is that butterflies have *brightly colored wings.*

121. A

In this passage, *distinguished* means recognizable. If you don't know the answer, try using each of the answer choices in the sentence: are butterflies recognizable by their wings? Are they respectable by their wings? Are they similar by their wings? Are they organized by their wings? The best choice is (A).

122. B

Although each species may be beautiful, in this passage, *unique* most nearly means different.

123. A

The question directs you to the first two paragraphs of the passage. If you skim them, you will notice words such as *glimpse, aroma,* and *crackling.* These words describe sights and sounds of the battle. This answer can be verified by eliminating choices (B), (C), and (D). The commanders, weapons, and costumes are not described in detail.

124. B

If you don't know what *skirmish* means, read the sentence in which it is used to understand the context. The sentence states that it is not *a skirmish, but rather…a battle.* The word *battle* is used to replace *skirmish,* so choice (B) is the answer.

125. B

Think about who might be writing this passage. Because there aren't many historical facts, you can eliminate choice (A). Choices (C) and (D) are not likely authors based on the information written in the passage, and the tone of the passage. Therefore, choice (B) is the best answer.

126. A

This question is asking you to make an inference, or guess, about the passage. In other words, the answer isn't stated directly in the passage. If you read the first paragraph again, it mentions that the British *far outnumber the man's own regiment.* Therefore, the battle was probably won by the British.

127. B

Reread the part of the passage that mentions lowering a musket. This information is found at the end of the first paragraph, and states: *A general gives the command, and the man lowers his musket to aim.* Therefore, choice (B) is the correct answer.

128. B

The man was most likely afraid when he saw the number of opposing troops.

129. C

Always read the context in which a word is used so that you don't choose the most obvious answer. In this case, you may think *smart* means intelligent. It does, but that is not its meaning in this passage. The sentence says, *the man's eyes smart and his vision dims.* Now you may be tempted to choose *fog,* because the man's vision is dimmed. However, the correct choice is (C); to smart also means to hurt.

130. B

The end of the passage talks about the reenactors, so you should read this part again. The last sentence says that *reenactors feel that demonstrating what the War for Independence was really like* [is] *a way to bring history alive.* Therefore, choice (B) is the best answer.

131. A

Though the author mentions these other elements, the general topic is making history come alive through reenacting battles.

132. D

According to the last paragraph, reenactors enjoy what they do.

133. D

Skim the passage for any mention of methane gas. The second paragraph states that *wastes in the dump…create methane gas when they decompose.* Therefore, *decomposition* is the best answer.

134. A

If you are not sure of the answer, skim over the passage and think of the overall tone the author uses in this passage. Nothing in the passage conveys her affection for the dump, and the passage is matter-of-fact, not sarcastic. Although you might be tempted to choose *disgust,* because of the subject matter, that is not the author's tone. The author appreciates the usefulness of garbage dumps.

135. C

There is nothing in the passage that suggests that garbage dumps are clean or that they power automobiles, so eliminate choices (A) and (D). Choice (B) is a distracter, the passage says that *methane gas* (not garbage dumps) is *used to power electric generators*, so the answer is (C).

136. A

Since this is a detail question, you should look for the part of the passage that discusses the five-megawatt generator. The passage states: *A five-megawatt generator could produce 42 million kilowatt-hours per year* [which is] *enough electricity to supply about 3,200 homes with power.*

137. A

Significant most nearly means sizable. You can test the meaning of the word by replacing the word *significant* with the answer choices. Only (A) makes sense in the context of the passage.

138. B

You may think you know the answer without referring to the passage. However, you should check your answer in the passage. The end of paragraph 2 says that *methane is the same gas sold by natural gas utility companies.* This supports answer choice (B).

139. C

This answer is supported by the last sentence of the passage. It says, *there's treasure in the trash.*

140. A

The last paragraph says: *Methane that is released directly into the atmosphere can contribute to global warming.* Therefore, an added benefit of recovering methane gas from garbage dumps is that it prevents the contribution to global warming.

141. B

Careful, choice (A) is a distracter. Although something that is decomposing might smell, *decompose* most nearly means rot.

142. D

The main topic of the passage is that garbage dumps produce methane. Therefore, the best answer is (D).

143. B

Because this passage does not contain any instructions or excessive medical detail, you can eliminate choices (A) and (D). It is also unlikely that this is a letter to a friend, so you can eliminate choice (C). Therefore, the answer is choice (B).

144. C

You should refer back to the passage if you don't know the answer. The first sentence says that bloodletting is *misguided by modern standards,* and the end of the passage states: *as modern doctors know,* [bloodletting] *does not have restorative powers.* The best answer is (C).

145. C

There is nothing in the passage to support choices (A), (B), and (D), so you can eliminate them. The passage does support choice (C), so it is the correct answer.

146. D

This is a detail question, the only group mentioned in the passage are barbers. Reread the end of the second paragraph, which mentions that *medieval doctors and barbers believed they were helping their patients by causing them to bleed.*

147. A

The question is testing your vocabulary. *Misguided* means using poor judgment, therefore wearing small shoes to keep your feet from growing is also using poor judgment.

148. D

This is an inference question. It is never stated in the passage that modern doctors think that bloodletting is unsafe, however the passage does say that doctors know that *draining a person's blood does not have restorative powers.*

149. D

The middle of the passage focuses on reverberation, which the author describes as the *most important factor in acoustic design* at the end of the passage.

150. A

Choice (A) is the correct answer because the author says that *few of us realize the complex process that goes into designing the acoustics of concert and lecture halls.*

151. C

According to the passage, *too little reverberation can make sound thin and weak.*

152. B

The final sentence of the passage says that *the most important factor in acoustic design is the reverberation time,* which makes (B) correct.

Vocabulary

153. C

To predict means to tell in advance, or foretell.

154. C

Mutual means exchanged, given and received, or common.

155. A

A gap is a hole, opening, or break.

156. A

Frank means clear, plain, or honest.

157. C

To allege means to assert without proof, or to imply.

158. B

A consequence is an outcome, a result, or an effect.

159. A

To confine means to imprison, to shut in, or to restrict.

160. B

To delete means to remove, to cancel, or to erase.

161. D

Glossy means slick, smooth, or shiny.

162. A

Outrageous means beyond reason, extravagant, extraordinary.

163. B

Sophisticated means worldly, refined, or cosmopolitan. *Learned* means educated, which is not the same thing. Although we may think that sophisticated women are fashionable, this does not define sophisticated. The word *wealthy* is often associated with the word *sophisticated,* but it does not define the word.

164. C

A proposal is an idea, a plan, or a suggestion.

165. A

Radical means extreme, revolutionary, or subversive.

166. C

To interrogate means to examine, to ask, or to question.

167. D

Plausible means acceptable, credible, or valid.

168. C

Access means acceptance, admission, or entrance.

169. A

To compose means to create, to author, or to write.

170. B

Ostentatious means conspicuous or showy.

171. A

Essential means vital, required, or necessary.

172. C

An obstacle is a block, a barrier, or a difficulty.

173. C

Precise means accurate.

174. D

Gracious means warm as in friendly, not warm as in temperature.

MATHEMATICS

Concepts

175. D

A *rhomboid* is a type of quadrilateral; it has four sides, not three as in a triangle.

176. A

The symbol in the question stands for intersection. The intersection of two or more sets is the set of elements they share in common. In this case, the common elements are 1 and 6.

177. B

This problem requires you to round off the given number to the place one digit to the right of the decimal point, the tenth's column. Since the number in the hundredth's place is 9, round up to 75.9.

178. B

Start with the operations in the parentheses first:

$(-3)^2 = -3 \times -3 = 9$

Then, continue with the operations outside the parentheses:

$3 \times 9 = 27$

179. B

The digit farthest to the right is in the hundredth's place. This means $0.12 = \frac{12}{100}$.

180. C

A straight line represents a straight angle of 180 degrees. An angle of 135 is given, so the measure of the interior angle must be 45 to complete the line. $180 - 135 = 45$. Knowing that all the angles in a triangle added together equal 180 degrees:

$$m \angle x + 45 + 35 = 180$$
$$m \angle x = 180 - 80 = 100$$

181. B

When multiplying a number by 10, 100, 1,000, etc., move the decimal point one place to the right for each zero in the multiplier. In this example, 1,000 has three zeros, so the decimal point would be moved three places to the right.

182. A

Consecutive numbers are numbers that follow one after another, in order.

183. B

The formula for finding the diameter of a circle is two times the radius; $2 \times 2 = 4$ m.

184. A

100 centimeters = 1 meter. Each centimeter is $\frac{1}{100}$ of a meter.

185. D

State $\dfrac{25}{3}$ as a decimal number.

$\dfrac{25}{3} \approx 8.3$.

An integer is a whole number. Between 8.3 and 12.3, there are four whole numbers {9, 10, 11, and 12}.

186. C

To figure out whether your product is positive or negative, count the number of negatives you had to start. If you had an odd number of negatives, the product is negative.

187. A

$11^2 = 121$; $12^2 = 144$. Therefore, the square root of 122 is between 11 and 12.

188. A

When working with scientific notation, the exponent represents the number of places to move the decimal point in the multiplier. If the base of the exponent is 10, the decimal point moves to the right. If it is $\dfrac{1}{10}$, the decimal point moves to the left.

189. A

Since the ratio is 3:1, let $3x$ = the larger number and $1x$ = the smaller number.

$$3x + 1x = 52$$
$$4x = 52$$
$$x = \dfrac{52}{4}$$

$x = 13$, which is the smaller number.
So, $3(13) = 39$, which is the larger number.

190. D

To make the comparison more readily, we convert the fractions to decimals:

$\dfrac{1}{5} = 0.20$, $\dfrac{4}{9} = 0.44$

Since $\dfrac{1}{3}$ has a value of 0.33, $\dfrac{1}{3}$ has a value between $\dfrac{1}{5}$ and $\dfrac{4}{9}$.

191. A

The sector AOB (which is shaded) is 60 degrees out of a total of 360 degrees, $\dfrac{60}{360}$ or $\dfrac{1}{6}$ of the circle.

192. C

$42 + 28 + 20 = 90\%$ voted.

$100 - 90 = 10$, so $\dfrac{10}{100}$ or $\dfrac{1}{10}$ did not vote.

193. D

$40\% = 0.4$; $0.4\,(5) = \$2$

194. D

Pythagorean refers to a formula used in geometry to find the unknown length of a right triangle's side.

195. A

Since triangles ABC and ADE are similar, their corresponding sides are in proportion.

If we separate the two triangles, we can see the proportion readily:

$$\dfrac{AD}{AB} = \dfrac{DE}{BC}$$

196. A

Prime factorization is factoring a number to the point where all factors are prime. $30 = 10 \times 3 = 5 \times 2 \times 3$. Seven is not a prime factor of 30.

197. A

The least common multiple is the smallest number divisible by both given numbers.

198. C

The associative property of addition means that you may group the numbers to be added in different ways and still achieve the same result.

Problem Solving

199. B

$$12 + 3x = x + 40$$
$$2x = 40 - 12$$
$$2x = 28$$
$$x = 14$$

200. D

tubes of paint	$11.25 (5 × $2.25)
paintbrushes	$12.90 (3 × $4.30)
total	$24.15

201. D

$$2\frac{1}{3} = \frac{7}{3}, \; 1\frac{1}{4} = \frac{5}{4}$$

$$\frac{7}{3} - \frac{5}{4} = \frac{7(4)}{12} - \frac{5(3)}{12}$$

$$\frac{28}{12} - \frac{15}{12} = \frac{13}{12} = 1\frac{1}{12}$$

202. A

$$\frac{\$850}{12} \approx 70.8333 \approx \$70.80.$$

203. B

$$1\frac{1}{2} = \frac{3}{2}, \; 2\frac{1}{4} = \frac{9}{4}$$

$$\frac{3}{2} \times \frac{9}{4} \times \frac{2}{3} = \frac{9}{4} = 2\frac{1}{4}$$

204. D

$$(-5) + (-4) + (-8) = -17$$
$$+6 + (-17) = -11$$

205. B

First, multiply $102 by 2 to get $204. Then subtract 3 from 204 to get $201.

206. C

Replace the C in the equation with 5 and solve:

$$F = \frac{9}{5}(5) + 32 = 9 + 32 = 41.$$

207. B

First, add all the positive numbers, then add the negative numbers. Then, combine the results.

$9 + 4 = 13, (-3) + (-5) = -8$

$13 + (-8) = 5$

208. D

If the sum of the two numbers is a and one of the numbers is 4, then the other number is $a - 4$. Two times the other number is $2(a - 4)$.

209. A

This problem is done by ratios:

$$\frac{3}{1} = \frac{x}{12}$$
$$x = 12 \times 3$$
$$x = 36$$
$$36 = x$$

210. C

First, multiply 2 by 36 to get 72. Then subtract 4 from 72 to get an answer of $68.

211. B

1 pound 2 ounces = $1\frac{2}{16}$, or $\frac{18}{16}$

$$\frac{18}{16} \times \$2.00 = \$2.25$$

212. C

We may write the given equation, $a + 4 = b + 6$, as $a - b = 6 - 4$, or $a - b = 2$. This tells us that a is 2 more than b, or $a > b$.

213. A

$$3a - 2 > 10$$
$$3a > 12$$
$$a > 4$$

If $a > 4$, then $a^2 > 16$.

214. D

This can be set up as an algebraic equation. If x is the amount Mrs. Daly borrowed:

$$5\%(x) = \$35.50$$

$$x = \frac{35.50}{0.05} = \$710$$

215. C

$$3^3 + 3\left(\frac{1}{2}\right) + 2 = 27 + 1\frac{1}{2} + 2 = 30\frac{1}{2}$$

216. D

Volume = length × width × height

Volume = $10 \times 4 \times 3 = 120$ m^3

217. B

First, find the area of the room. Multiply the area by $4 to arrive at the cost.

Area = $12 \times 15 = 180$ square feet

$180 \times \$4 = \$720$

218. B

This can be set up as an algebraic equation. If y equals the price of the Rollerblades is z, 6% of z equals $4.50 or $0.06z = 4.50$.

$$z = \frac{4.50}{0.06} = \$75$$

219. A

Replace the letters in the problem with the numbers given. $2XYZ = 2(2)(3)(4) = 48$.

220. D

$$5.31\overline{)2.7633}$$

First, move the decimal points

$$
\begin{array}{r}
.52 \\
531\overline{)276.33} \\
\underline{265.5} \\
10.83 \\
\underline{10.62}
\end{array}
$$

221. D

Remember that the number of decimal places to the right of the decimal point in the answer should equal the total number of places to the right of the decimal points in the two factors being multiplied; in this case 5.

$$
\begin{array}{r}
42.13 \\
\times\ 0.082 \\
\hline
8426 \\
\underline{337040} \\
3.45466
\end{array}
$$

222. B

$$
\begin{aligned}
2x - 7 &> 9 \\
2x &> 9 + 7 \\
2x &> 16 \\
x &> 8
\end{aligned}
$$

If $x > 8$, then $x^2 > 8^2$, and $x^2 > 64$.

223. C

When adding decimal numbers, line up the decimal points.

$$
\begin{array}{r}
0.354 \\
7.9 \\
\underline{2.03} \\
10.284
\end{array}
$$

224. A

$$
\begin{aligned}
8x + 2 &= 3x + 5 \\
5x &= 3 \\
x &= \frac{3}{5}
\end{aligned}
$$

225. C

Let x = the number of goals in 15 games. We set up the proportion:

$$
\begin{aligned}
\frac{4}{10} &= \frac{x}{15} \\
4(15) &= x(10) \\
60 &= 10x \\
\frac{60}{10} &= 6
\end{aligned}
$$

226. A

The only even integer less than -1, but greater than -4, is -2.

227. C

Plug in 18 for b in the equation:

$3a - 6 = 18$

Isolate a on one side of the equation:

$3a = 18 + 6$

$3a = 24$

Divide both sides by 3 to find the value of a: $a = 8$.

228. C

$22.75 \div 7 = 3.25$; $3.25 \times 4 = 13.00$

229. B

$30 × 0.20 = $6 per week. Multiply that $6 by 4 (since there are 4 weeks in a month) for a total of $24 per month.

230. A

$$
\begin{array}{r}
534 \\
\times\ 32 \\
\hline
1068 \\
\underline{16{,}020} \\
17{,}088
\end{array}
$$

231. C

If we square both sides of the equation, we have:

$$a + 6 = 12^2$$
$$a + 6 = 144$$
$$a = 138$$

232. A

The area of the square is length × width or $4 \times 4 = 16$ m^2. The area of the semicircles on each side = $\frac{1}{2}$(radius)$^2 \times \pi$, or $\frac{1}{2}(2)^2 \times \pi = 2\pi$. However, since there are four semicircles, the area of all of them put together = $2\pi + 2\pi + 2\pi + 2\pi = 8\pi$ m^2. Therefore, the area of the whole figure is $(16 + 8\pi)$m^2.

233. B

$\frac{3}{4}x = 30$. Multiply both sides of the equation by the reciprocal to obtain:

$$x = 30 \times \frac{4}{3} = \frac{120}{3} = 40$$

The value of $\frac{5}{8}x = \frac{5}{8}(40) = 25$.

234. D

Let x = the coworker's hourly wage.

And $x + 25$ = the supervisor's wage.

$$8x + 8(x + 25) = 600$$
$$16x + 200 = 600$$
$$16x = 600 - 200 = 400$$

$\frac{400}{16} = 25$. The coworker earns $25, and the supervisor earns $25 + $25 = $50 per hour.

235. D

$$\frac{2}{3} : \frac{3}{8} = \frac{2}{3} \div \frac{3}{8} = \frac{2}{3} \times \frac{8}{3} = \frac{16}{9}$$

236. A

Let x = the amount of money Mark's younger brother has.

$$3x - 10 = x + 10$$
$$2x = 20$$
$$x = 10$$

Mark saved three times much as his brother; therefore, Mark saved 3(10) = $30.

237. B

Since in the given inequality $6 > y > 3$, y must be an odd number integer, it must be 5, since that is the only odd number integer greater than 3 but less than 6.

238. D

Begin solving this equation by squaring both sides:

$$a + 12 = 7^2$$
$$a + 12 = 7(7) = 49$$
$$a = 49 - 12$$
$$a = 37$$

LANGUAGE

Usage

239. C

There should be a comma after *Tuesday*.

240. B

Day should be capitalized.

241. A

History should be capitalized.

242. C

There should be quotations before *where* and after the question mark.

243. D

There are no mistakes.

244. C

Me should be *I* since it is a subject in this sentence.

245. C

It is not standard English to use *may* to ask the question *May you pass the salt?* The word *may* asks permission, so it should not be used in this question.

246. D

There are no mistakes.

247. D

There are no mistakes.

248. C

There should be quotation marks in this sentence to show that what Nancy said is a direct quote.

249. B

The word *their* is incorrect in this context. The word should be *they're* (they are).

250. D

There are no mistakes.

251. D

There are no mistakes.

252. A

The word *lay* is incorrect in this context. The word should be *lie*.

253. C

The word *who's* (who is) is incorrect in this context. The word should be *whose*.

254. B

The object of he preposition *to* is Frank and *me*.

255. B

The word *she* should be capitalized.

256. C

This is a question, so it should end with a question mark, not a period.

257. C

The past tense of the verb to *lie* is *lay*.

258. A

The word *we* is incorrect in this sentence. The word *us* should be used.

259. C

The tense is incorrect. The last part of the sentence should read *ever gone horseback riding*.

260. D

There are no mistakes.

261. D

There are no mistakes.

262. D

There are no mistakes.

263. A

There is a shift in verb tense in this sentence. It shifts from the past tense (*the show was over*) to the present tense (*everyone leaves*). Both verbs should be in the same tense.

264. B

The word *of* is incorrect in this context. The word should be *have*.

265. B

The apostrophe in *women's* should be placed before the s since *women* is a plural word.

266. B

The word *learning* is incorrect in this sentence. The word should be *teaching*.

267. A

California should be capitalized.

268. B

The preposition *to* is incorrect in this context. The word should be *too*.

269. D

There are no mistakes.

270. C

The object *me* is incorrect in this context. The correct pronoun is *I* since it is a subject.

271. C

Quick should be *quickly* since it is an adverb, describing how Shawn ran.

272. C

Using double negatives is incorrect. The sentence should be: *I can do nothing*, OR *I can't do anything*.

273. D

There are no mistakes.

274. B

Because there are three athletes mentioned, the superlative *fastest* (not the comparative *faster*) is required.

275. C

Money is a singular noun and can't be counted, so the word *less* should replace *fewer* to make the sentence grammatically correct.

276. A

The subject and verb of the sentence should be *she has*.

277. A

Grand, Central, and *Station* should be capitalized.

278. B

There should be a comma after *said*, not a semicolon.

Spelling

279. A

The correct spelling is *cafeteria*.

280. B

The correct spelling is *composition*.

281. D

There are no mistakes.

282. C

The correct spelling is *prejudiced*.

283. B

The correct spelling is *immediately*.

284. B

The correct spelling is *specific*.

285. A

The correct spelling is *temperature*.

286. D

There are no mistakes.

287. A

The correct spelling is *surface*.

288. A

The correct spelling is *interrupt*.

Composition

289. A

The word *however* indicates the contrasting relationship of the two clauses.

290. D

The phrase *display of antique armor* should come immediately after the verb *is* in order to make the sentence as clear as possible. The phrase *dating back from the 12th century* describes the armor and should come after it.

291. B

The subject *we* must follow the introductory phrase, and since the phrase does not indicate a present continuous form, choice (C) is incorrect.

292. A

Caring for your bicycle fits under the topic of bicycle maintenance.

293. D

The two clauses contradict one another, so *although* is the best answer choice.

294. A

The first sentence is the most clear and correct way of expressing the idea.

295. D

The second clause stands independently. No linking words are necessary.

296. D

Sentences 1, 2, and 3 are about Tom's enjoyment of the early morning. Sentence 4 talks about what he likes to cook and, therefore, does not belong in the paragraph.

297. B

This topic is simple enough to be dealt with in a brief theme.

298. D

The given sentence should be after sentence 3 because it ties together the idea that a combination of events led to the extinction of the dinosaurs.

VERBAL SKILLS

16 minutes

Directions: For questions 1–60, choose the best answer.

1. Which word does *not* belong with the others?

   (A) lenient
   (B) light
   (C) mild
   (D) severe

2. Christine runs faster than Joanne. Joanne runs faster than Katie. Christine runs faster than Katie. If the first two statements are true, the third is

   (A) true
   (B) false
   (C) uncertain

3. Abundant is the *opposite* of

   (A) scarce
   (B) lush
   (C) collect
   (D) loyal

4. Shell is to egg as peel is to

   (A) rind
   (B) orange
   (C) omelet
   (D) helmet

5. If Mr. Johnson is not at work, he is at home. If Mr. Johnson is not at home, he is at the golf club. If Mr. Johnson is not at the golf club, he must be at home. If the first two statements are true, the third is

   (A) true
   (B) false
   (C) uncertain

6. Endorse most nearly means

   (A) approve
   (B) check
   (C) wear
   (D) beg

7. Which word does *not* belong with the others?

   (A) expand
   (B) reduce
   (C) summarize
   (D) abbreviate

8. Hank has hit more home runs than Peter. Peter has hit more home runs than Joe. Hank has hit fewer home runs than Joe. If the first two statements are true, the third is

   (A) true
   (B) false
   (C) uncertain

9. Claw is to eagle as paw is to

    (A) bird
    (B) nest
    (C) hunt
    (D) lion

10. Fiction means the *opposite* of

    (A) imaginary
    (B) science
    (C) fact
    (C) invention

11. Territory most nearly means

    (A) land
    (B) border
    (C) capital
    (D) home

12. Impose means most nearly

    (A) question
    (B) interrupt
    (C) imply
    (D) force

13. Which word does *not* belong with the others?

    (A) diplomat
    (B) ambassador
    (C) representative
    (D) spy

14. Paddle is to canoe as pedal is to

    (A) road
    (B) bicycle
    (C) gear
    (D) engine

15. Infinite most nearly means

    (A) unending
    (B) miniscule
    (C) complex
    (D) undiscovered

16. Which word does *not* belong with the others?

    (A) kitchen
    (B) basement
    (C) attic
    (D) lot

17. Steak is more expensive than hamburger but less expensive than lobster. Chicken is more expensive than hamburger but less expensive than swordfish. Of all the foods mentioned, hamburger is the least expensive. If the first two statements are true, the third is

    (A) true
    (B) false
    (C) uncertain

18. Average is the *opposite* of

    (A) outstanding
    (B) individual
    (C) medium
    (D) general

19. Saw is to cut as handle is to

    (A) door
    (B) jar
    (C) open
    (D) tool

20. Mandate most nearly means

    (A) speak
    (B) command
    (C) vote
    (D) council

21. Embellish most nearly means

    (A) wipe out
    (B) embroider
    (C) polish
    (D) adorn

22. Wary means the *opposite* of

    (A) forgetful
    (B) wise
    (C) hopeful
    (D) careless

23. Serene most nearly means

    (A) mermaid
    (B) serious
    (C) peaceful
    (D) dangerous

24. Which word does not belong with the others?

    (A) solemn
    (B) elated
    (C) serious
    (D) grave

25. Small is to minute as large is to

    (A) toy
    (B) miniature
    (C) big
    (D) colossal

26. Acquainted most nearly means

    (A) familiar
    (B) distant
    (C) friendly
    (D) unknown

27. Which word does *not* belong with the others?

    (A) remote
    (B) distant
    (C) beside
    (D) far

28. Colleague most nearly means

    (A) coworker
    (B) manager
    (C) friend
    (D) university

29. Wolf Lake is larger than Rosebud Lake. Rosebud Lake is smaller than Beaver Lake. Wolf Lake is larger than Beaver Lake. If the first two statements are true, the third is

    (A) true
    (B) false
    (C) uncertain

30. The radioactive half-life of ement A is longer than the radioactive half-life of element B. The half-life of element C is longer than the half-life of element D. The half-life of element A is longer than the half-life of element D. If the first two statements are true, the third is

    (A) true
    (B) false
    (C) uncertain

31. Underhanded most nearly means

    (A) easier
    (B) sneaky
    (C) graceful
    (D) lucky

32. Which word does *not* belong with the others?

    (A) choose
    (B) punish
    (C) sentence
    (D) condemn

33. Which word does *not* belong with the others?

    (A) condone
    (B) excuse
    (C) condemn
    (D) pardon

34. Praise is to admiration as insult is to

    (A) injury
    (B) contempt
    (C) annoy
    (D) barb

35. All mammals give birth to live young. All kangaroos are mammals. All kangaroos do not give birth to live young. If the first two statements are true, the third is

    K=M M=LY

    (A) true
    (B) false
    (C) uncertain

36. Fortuitous most nearly means

    (A) hazardous
    (B) circular
    (C) lucky
    (D) safe

37. Ambivalent most nearly means

    (A) emotional
    (B) fair
    (C) ambidextrous
    (D) uncertain

38. Which word does *not* belong with the others?

    (A) letter
    (B) magazine
    (C) newspaper
    (D) tabloid

39. All X is Y. No Z is X. No Z is Y. If the first two statements are true, the third is

    X=Y
    Z≠X
    Z

    (A) true
    (B) false
    (C) uncertain

    orge is to signature as counterfeit is to

    create
    ke
    ney

41. Which word does *not* belong with the others?

    (A) detain
    (B) enlist
    (C) enroll
    (D) register

42. Renowned most nearly means

    (A) worldly
    (B) secretive
    (C) novel
    (D) famed

43. Implicit most nearly means

    (A) fake
    (B) inferred
    (C) stated
    (D) granted

44. Fool is to wisdom as pauper is to

    (A) humor
    (B) knowledge
    (C) grace
    (D) riches

45. Ingenious most nearly means

    (A) dull
    (B) clever
    (C) silly
    (D) unworthy

46. Which word does *not* belong with the others?

    (A) fool
    (B) mimic
    (C) jester
    (D) clown

47. Bombastic most nearly means

    (A) explosion
    (B) sturdy
    (C) overblown
    (D) refined

48. All myops are nearsighted. Lester is a myop. Lester is nearsighted. If the first two statements are true, the third is

    (A) true
    (B) false
    (C) uncertain

49. Which word does *not* belong with the others?

    (A) school
    (B) herd
    (C) pack
    (D) cub

50. Warrant is to search as visa is to

    (A) right
    (B) license
    (C) travel
    (D) charge

51. Sedentary means the *opposite* of

    (A) optimistic
    (B) calm
    (C) active
    (D) loyal

52. Which word does *not* belong with the others?

    (A) suit
    (B) shoe
    (C) hat
    (D) wardrobe

53. Rudimentary is the *opposite* of

    (A) advanced
    (B) polite
    (C) regulated
    (D) essential

54. Which word does *not* belong with the others?

    (A) fasten
    (B) tie
    (C) secure
    (D) unleash

55. Which word does *not* belong with the others?

    (A) battle
    (B) victory
    (C) win
    (D) triumph

56. Malevolent means most nearly

    (A) evil
    (B) smelly
    (C) bossy
    (D) kind

57. Which word does *not* belong with the others?

    (A) stage
    (B) actors
    (C) play
    (D) ticket

58. Chapter is to book as section is to

    (A) title
    (B) newspaper
    (C) heading
    (D) contents

59. City A is south of City B. City C is north of City D, but south of City A. City B is south of City D. If the first two statements are true, the third is

    (A) true
    (B) false
    (C) uncertain

60. Transient means most nearly

    (A) transparent
    (B) fixed
    (C) temporary
    (D) electric

QUANTITATIVE SKILLS

30 minutes

Directions: For questions 61–112, choose the best answer.

61. If three times a number is $34\frac{1}{2}$, then half the number is

    (A) $5\frac{1}{4}$

    (B) 11

    (C) $11\frac{1}{2}$

    (D) $5\frac{3}{4}$

62. What is the next number in the following series: 2, 5, 8, 11, …

    (A) 14
    (B) 13
    (C) 12
    (D) 15

63. In the figure below, if A > B > C, which of the following is correct?

    (A) A < C
    (B) A > C
    (C) A = B + C
    (D) B > A

64. What is the next number in the following series: 54, 49, 44, 39, …

    (A) 40
    (B) 35
    (C) 34
    (D) 36

65. When a number is subtracted from 36, the result is 4 more than the product of 5 and 6. What is the number?

    (A) 2
    (B) 4
    (C) 3
    (D) 5

66. In the diagram below, A, B, and C represent the angles of an equilateral triangle. Which of the following must be true?

    (A) A < B
    (B) A = B + C
    (C) A − B = C
    (D) A + B > C

67. Examine (a), (b), (c), and (d) and select the correct answer.

    (a) 0.33

    (b) $\frac{2}{3}$

    (c) 33%

    (d) 0.3

    (A) (d) is equal to (b).
    (B) (c) is greater than (a).
    (C) (b) is greater than (a).
    (D) Of the numbers given, (d) is greatest.

68. What is the missing number in the following series: 61, 57, 53, ___, 45

(A) 50
(B) 49
(C) 48
(D) 51

69. On a menu, each item from column A costs $2.25, each item from column B costs $4.50, and each item from column C costs $5.25.

Terry ordered four items from column A and one from column C.

John ordered two items from column A and two from column C.

Maria ordered one item from column A, one from column B, and one from column C.

Which of the following is correct?

(A) Maria's meal cost more than Terry's but less than John's.
(B) Terry's, John's, and Maria's meals all cost the same.
(C) Terry's meal cost more than John's meal and also cost more than Maria's meal.
(D) John's meal cost more than Terry's meal.

70. Examine (a), (b), and (c) and select the correct answer.

(a) 11 – (6 + 3)
(b) (8 – 2) – 3
(c) 12 – (5 – 4)

(A) (a) + (b) = (c)
(B) (c) – (b) < (a)
(C) (b) > (c)
(D) (c) > (a) + (b)

71. In the figure below, lines A and B intersect in the center of circle O.

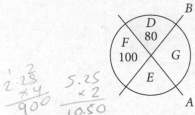

Which of the following must be correct?

(A) measure of angle D > measure of angle E
(B) measure of angle D = measure of angle E
(C) measure of angle D > measure of angle F
(D) measure of angle D + measure of angle E = measure of angle F + measure of angle G

72. Examine (a), (b), and (c) and select the correct answer.

(a) 50% of 20
(b) 30% of 90
(c) 25% of 80

(A) 2(a) = (b)
(B) (b) – (a) = (c)
(C) (a) + (c) – (b)
(D) 2(a) = (c)

73. What is the next number in the following series: 15, 12, 17, 14, 19, …

(A) 14
(B) 13
(C) 16
(D) 15

74. If $\frac{3}{5}$ of a number is 6 less than 15, the number is

(A) 15
(B) 45
(C) 30
(D) 50

75. What percentage of the figure below is shaded?

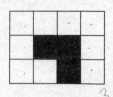

(A) 33%

(B) 30%

(C) 25%

(D) 20%

76. If $\frac{1}{3}$ of a number is 2 more than $\frac{1}{4}$ of the same number, what is the number?

(A) 20

(B) 24

(C) 12

(D) 48

77. The number of fourths in $\frac{7}{8}$ is

(A) $3\frac{1}{2}$

(B) 8

(C) 28

(D) 14

78. A grocer purchased three super-sized cartons of eggs. A super-sized carton has four rows with 12 spaces for eggs in each row. He wants to repackage these in regular cartons that have two rows with six spaces for eggs in each row. How many regular cartons will he need?

(A) 4

(B) 3

(C) 6

(D) 12

79. What number represents the cube of 4 divided by 4?

(A) 16

(B) 64

(C) 12

(D) 32

80. What is the next number in the following series: 48, 24, 12, 6, ...

(A) 1

(B) 2

(C) 3

(D) 4

81. Triangle *ABC* is a right triangle. The measure of angle *BAL* is

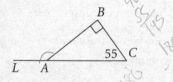

(A) 145°

(B) 45°

(C) 90°

(D) 75°

82. What fraction divided by $\frac{1}{5}$ is equal to $\frac{7}{8}$?

(A) $\frac{1}{6}$

(B) $\frac{7}{40}$

(C) $\frac{7}{45}$

(D) $\frac{35}{8}$

83. What is the next number in the following series: 1, 2, 4, 7, ...

(A) 14

(B) 9

(C) 10

(D) 11

84. What is the circumference of the circle below?

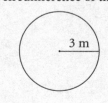

(A) 3π m

(B) 4π m

(C) 6π m

(D) 9π m

85. The circle below is divided into eight equal sectors. What portion of the circle is shaded?

(A) $\frac{1}{3}$

(B) $\frac{1}{2}$

(C) $\frac{1}{4}$

(D) $\frac{2}{4}$

86. Which of the following is correct?

(A) $\frac{1}{5} > \frac{1}{3} > \frac{2}{3}$

(B) $\frac{1}{5} > \frac{2}{3} > \frac{1}{3}$

(C) $\frac{2}{3} > \frac{1}{3} > \frac{1}{5}$

(D) $\frac{2}{3} = \frac{1}{5} + \frac{1}{3}$

87. By how much does the average of 15, 24, 32, and 13 exceed 9?

(A) 12

(B) 9

(C) 16

(D) 8

88. What is the next number in the following series: 1, 4, 5, 8, 9, 12, ...

(A) 15

(B) 11

(C) 14

(D) 13

89. If $a = 3^2$, $b = 2 \times 2^2$, and $c = 3 \times 2^3$, which of the following is true?

(A) $a < b$

(B) $c > a + b$

(C) $a + b > c$

(D) $a + b + c > 100$

90. When a number is increased by 50% of itself, the result is 30. What is that number?

(A) 15

(B) 20

(C) 40

(D) 30

91. What is the missing number in the following series: 3, 2, 4, 3, 6, ___, 10, 9

(A) 5

(B) 12

(C) 3

(D) 8

92. What number is 12 more than the result of 4^3 divided by 4?

(A) 26

(B) 28

(C) 16

(D) 30

93. The number of eighths in 10 is

(A) 80

(B) 8

(C) 16

(D) 12

94. What is the next number in the following series: 1, 4, 2, 8, 3, 12, 4, ...

(A) 10

(B) 5

(C) 16

(D) 18

95. Examine (a), (b), and (c) and select the correct answer.

    (a) $31 - 2 \times 7$
    (b) $5 \times 4 - 8$
    (c) $7 + 6 - 2$

    (A) $(c) - (b) = (a)$
    (B) $(b) + (c) = (a)$
    (C) $(a) > (b) + (c)$
    (D) $(a) > (b)$

96. Line *BD* bisects right angle *B* and right angle *D* in square *ABCD* below. *E* is the midpoint of line *BD*. What portion of the square is shaded?

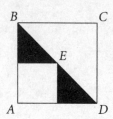

    (A) $\frac{1}{2}$

    (B) $\frac{1}{4}$

    (C) $\frac{1}{8}$

    (D) $\frac{1}{6}$

97. What is the next number in the following series: XI, 9, VII, 5, …

    (A) 3
    (B) III
    (C) V
    (D) X

98. When a number is divided by 4, the quotient is 3 and the remainder is 1. What is the number?

    (A) 11
    (B) 12
    (C) 13
    (D) 14

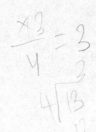

99. Examine (a), (b), and (c) and select the correct answer.

    (a) $(5 + 1)^2$
    (b) $3^2 + 2^2$
    (c) $25 - 2 \times 3$

    (A) $(a) + (b) > (c)$
    (B) $(c) > (a) + (b)$
    (C) $(c) = (a) + (b)$
    (D) $(b) > (a) + (c)$

100. 15% of a school's student body rides a bicycle to school. If every student who rides chained his or her bicycle outside the school, and the number of bicycles chained outside the school is 12, what is the total number of students in the school?

    (A) 120
    (B) 800
    (C) 80
    (D) 1,200

101. The sum of $\frac{3}{4}$ and $\frac{5}{6}$ is greater than $\frac{1}{2}$ by

    (A) $\frac{13}{12}$

    (B) $\frac{6}{14}$

    (C) $\frac{7}{8}$

    (D) $\frac{7}{14}$

102. $33\frac{1}{3}$ percent of a number is 15. What is the reciprocal of the number?

    (A) $\frac{1}{5}$

    (B) 5

    (C) 45

    (D) $\frac{1}{45}$

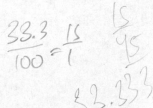

103. What is the next number in the following series:

5, 10, 8, 7, 12, 10, 9, ...

(A) 7

(B) 8

(C) 11

(D) 14

104. Examine the graph and select the correct answer.

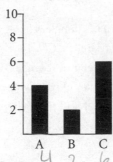

(A) A + C = B

(B) B + A = C

(C) B + C = A

(D) C > A + B

105. Examine the triangle and select the correct answer.

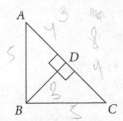

(A) AB is greater than AD.

(B) AD and DB are greater than AB and BC.

(C) AB is equal to AC.

(D) DC is equal to BC.

106. Examine (a), (b), and (c).

(a) $3\frac{1}{2}\%$

(b) $3\frac{1}{2}$

(c) 0.33

Which of the following is correct?

(A) (b) > (a) + (c)

(B) (a) > (b)

(C) (a) = (b)

(D) (a) = (c)

107. $\frac{2}{3}$ of what number added to 8 is 4 times 10?

(A) 45

(B) 96

(C) 48

(D) 32

108. What is the next number in the following series: $8, 6\frac{1}{2}, 5, 3\frac{1}{2}, ...$

(A) 1

(B) $1\frac{1}{2}$

(C) 2

(D) $2\frac{1}{4}$

109. What is the next number in the following series: 2, 4, 3, 6, 5, 10, ...

(A) 7

(B) 8

(C) 9

(D) 5

110. What is the next term in the following series: Z1, Y2, X3, W4, ...

(A) V3

(B) X3

(C) X5

(D) V5

111. What number is 8 less than 3 cubed?

    (A) 18

    (B) 27

    (C) 19

    (D) 20

112. Examine the parallelogram and select the correct answer.

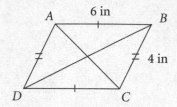

    (A)   The perimeter of the parallelogram is 10 inches.

    (B)   The area of triangle *ABD* is greater than the area of triangle *ACD*.

    (C)   The perimeter of triangle *BDA* is equal to the perimeter of parallelogram *ABCD*.

    (D)   The perimeter of parallelogram *ABCD* is 20 inches.

READING

Questions 113–174

25 minutes

Comprehension

Directions: Read the passages and answer questions 113–152.

Read the following passage and answer questions 113–120.

In April 1861, when the Sixth Massachusetts Regiment arrived in Washington, D.C., without their baggage, one energetic woman set to work, supplying their needs. Clara Barton responded by supplying old sheets for towels and handkerchiefs, and cooking for the troops. Thus began an incredible career as a patriot and humanitarian.

After the battle of Bull Run, Barton was deeply affected by tales of shortages of supplies in the field. So, she advertised for <u>provisions</u> in a local newspaper. The public responded by sending huge amounts, and Barton established an agency to distribute them.

In 1862, the government granted Barton permission to <u>accompany</u> sick and wounded soldiers from the battlefield. Barton gave her sympathetic aid to many. After the war, she supervised a federal search for missing soldiers, eventually heading the Missing Soldiers Office. Barton was the first woman to run a government bureau. In her role, she tracked down information on nearly 22,000 soldiers before the office was closed in 1868.

From 1869 and 1873, Barton lived in Europe, where she worked with the International Red Cross distributing supplies in France and Germany during the Franco-Prussian War. She returned home in 1873 with Germany's Iron Cross for outstanding military service. She also returned with the goal of creating the Red Cross in the United States. She <u>campaigned</u> tirelessly for its establishment, educating the public through brochures and lobbying cabinet heads and Congress. Her efforts paid off, and in 1881, the National Society of the Red Cross was organized with a grant from John D. Rockefeller. The Red Cross's national headquarters were established in Washington, D.C., one block from the White House.

113. Barton began her career as a nurse in

    (A) Washington, D.C.
    (B) France
    (C) Germany
    (D) Massachusetts

114. As used in the passage, the word <u>accompany</u> most nearly means

    (A) care for
    (B) go with
    (C) befriend
    (D) cure

115. The best title for this selection would be

    (A) Women of the Red Cross
    (B) Battles of the Civil War
    (C) Nursing Wounded Soldiers
    (D) A Career of Caring

116. Clara volunteered to help soldiers because

    (A) she was well paid
    (B) she was a school teacher
    (C) she wanted to lessen their suffering
    (D) she wanted to stop the war

117. As used in the passage, the word <u>provisions</u> most nearly means

    (A) nurses
    (B) soldiers
    (C) supplies
    (D) towels

118. Clara won a medal for

    (A) being a good soldier
    (B) aiding soldiers during the Franco-Prussian War
    (C) helping to locate missing soldiers
    (D) establishing the Red Cross

119. As used in the passage, the word <u>campaigned</u> most nearly means

    (A) volunteered to help
    (B) argued with politicians
    (C) fought for recognition
    (D) ran for office

120. The author implies that it is patriotic to

    (A) help one's fellow countrymen
    (B) become a nurse
    (C) join the Red Cross
    (D) travel in Europe

Read the following passage and answer questions 121–125.

Since the invention of Henry Ford's first Model T, the automobile has had an enormous <u>impact</u> on life in the United States. What was once a novel form of transportation has become the source of two of the most powerful global industries: petroleum and automobiles. Highways criss-cross our landscape, and automobile ownership is at an astounding high. On average, we find three passenger vehicles for every four Americans. But the American love affair with the automobile carries a high price.

Almost all automobiles in the United States are powered by the combustion of petroleum. While these vehicles help make our lives easier, the combustion of fossil fuels is an environmental hazard. Car emissions are a leading cause of global warming—the gradual increase of our Earth's temperature. Yet, people seem to accept the sacrifices that owning a car requires. We continue to buy more cars and bigger cars. The United States leads the world in car ownership, at about 0.8 cars per capita. Meanwhile, American motor vehicles consume more than 150 billion gallons of petroleum per year. The manufacture and use of gasoline for consumer vehicles cause more environmental damage than any other single consumer spending category. Environmental hazards could be considered a speed bump on the road of modern convenience.

121. The main idea of this passage is that

    (A) Henry Ford changed the face of America
    (B) every step forward comes with a price
    (C) the automobile causes global warming
    (D) highways have taken the place of parks

122. As used in the passage, the word <u>impact</u> most nearly means

    (A) effect
    (B) damage
    (C) strike
    (D) benefit

123. The author of this passage

    (A) uses foreshadowing
    (B) discusses historical facts
    (C) includes statistics
    (D) uses quotations

124. Why did the author choose to begin by mentioning the Model T?

    (A) She wanted the reader to think about how cars have changed our lives.
    (B) She wanted the reader to realize how much cars have changed the environment.
    (C) She wanted the passage to be humorous in tone.
    (D) The Model T was the first car to be mass-produced.

125. In the last sentence of paragraph 1, what is the author really trying to say about *the American love affair with the automobile carr[ying] a high price*?

    (A) that cars are expensive in the United States
    (B) that the large number of cars in the United States will have a negative effect on the environment
    (C) that everyone in the United States can afford to buy a car
    (D) that Americans love to pay a lot of money for things

Read the following passage and answer questions 126–132.

The first amendment to the Bill of Rights states, "Congress shall make no law … abridging the freedom of speech…" This amendment was passed to protect our right to express our opinions without fear. Yet we must stop using the first amendment as a justification to say whatever we want, whenever we want. No speech is "free" when it has detrimental effects on the well-being of others, the protection of our privacy, the safety of our borders, or the quality of our thinking.

While censorship is not the way of this land, we must take into account the effect of musical lyrics that influence young listeners. How often do we find ourselves singing a tune or repeating a phrase from a song instinctively, without stopping to ponder the meaning of the words? When those words are <u>demeaning</u> to any group of people or when they incite violence, we are unknowingly repeating phrases of hate. How long does it take until those phrases become worn into our patterns of thought and we find ourselves believing the words we mindlessly hummed?

126. The best title for this selection would be

   (A) The Bill of Rights
   (B) Think about What You Say
   (C) The First Amendment
   (D) Ban Bad Music

127. As used in the passage, the word <u>demeaning</u> most nearly means

   (A) distasteful
   (B) complimentary
   (C) insulting
   (D) delightful

128. The author implies that the most important aim of the right to free speech is

   (A) the ability to disagree with Congress
   (B) the ability to say whatever you want when- ever you want
   (C) the right to express our opinions freely
   (D) the right to listen to violent music

129. The author attempts to persuade the reader with

   (A) statistics
   (B) impassioned generalizations
   (C) historical quotations
   (D) anecdotes and examples

130. Phrases become *worn into our patterns of thought* when

   (A) we repeat them again and again
   (B) we listen to music
   (C) we agree with them
   (D) we think about them

131. According to the author, speech is not free when it

   (A) must be purchased
   (B) is ugly
   (C) is censored
   (D) harms others

132. This passage is most likely from a(n)

   (A) speech given to a radio station
   (B) textbook on the Constitution
   (C) magazine article on American music
   (D) editorial in a school newspaper

Read the following passage and answer questions 133–140.

Throughout the history of humankind, people have wondered why children take after one parent or another. Yet it was research into plant biology that ultimately helped answer questions about human genetics. In the 1860s, a little known Central European monk named Gregor Mendel discovered the secrets of <u>heredity</u> through his observations growing pea plants. By selectively growing common pea plants over many generations, Mendel discovered that particular characteristics showed up in the off-spring pea plants again and again. For example, Mendel found that pea flowers are either purple or white; they are never a blend of these colors. In all, Mendel found seven traits could be <u>readily</u> observed in only one of two forms. These traits included flower color, flower position, stem length, seed shape, seed color, pod shape, and pod color. This observation was in direct contrast to the theorists of the day, who believed that traits blended from generation to generation. In cross-pollinating plants, or breeding plants with different traits, Mendel found that the first generation always exhibited only one trait. For example, a short plant and a tall plant would only yield tall plants. However, the second generation would yield three tall and one short plants—a 3 to 1 ratio.

Observing many pea plants over many generations, Mendel concluded three important things. First, that traits were passed on to offspring un-changed. Second, that an individual inherits traits from each parent. And third, that even though a trait may not show up in one individual, it could still be passed on to the next generation. These three observations were enormously important in helping understand human heredity.

133. Which of the following definitions of <u>heredity</u> best fits its use in this selection?

(A) genetics
(B) inherited wealth
(C) inherited personality
(D) plant biology

134. The title that best fits this selection is

(A) Nature Not Nurture
(B) Peas in a Pod
(C) Observing Life
(D) It's All in the Genes

135. The number of traits Mendel observed in pea plants is

(A) three
(B) seven
(C) four
(D) innumerable

136. Which of the following is most likely true of Gregor Mendel?

(A) He was impatient.
(B) He was lonely.
(C) He was systematic.
(D) He was friendly with Charles Darwin.

137. Which of the following is true of traits?

 (A) They blend from one generation to the next.
 (B) They appear unchanged from one generation to the next.
 (C) If they appear in one generation, they are never seen again.
 (D) They are cross-pollinated.

138. Mendel's system of research was based on

 (A) Central European education
 (B) writings of his fellow monks
 (C) existing theories
 (D) careful observation

139. Within any offspring

 (A) traits can be inherited from either parent
 (B) traits can be inherited from the father only
 (C) traits can be inherited from the mother only
 (D) traits appear the same way in each generation

140. As used in the passage, the word underline{readily} most nearly means

 (A) scientifically
 (B) understandably
 (C) easily
 (D) surprisingly

Read the following passage and answer questions 141–146.

The dictionary tells us that the root of the word *communicate* comes from the Latin verb *comunicare*: to make common, to make known, to be connected, to have an interchange of thoughts, ideas, and feelings. underline{Genuine} communication is more than an exchange of words; it is the process of sharing meaning. This act of sharing underline{naturally} involves two individuals—the one sending the message and the one receiving it. The ability to share your ideas effectively requires not only that you present an idea, but also that you make sure your intended message is interpreted correctly by the receiver. In order to minimize any misunderstanding, you must pay careful attention to the words you choose, your body language, and your tone of voice. Research shows that people pay more attention to tone of voice and body language than they do to the actual words used in a message. In other words, if your behaviors transmit one message and your words transmit another, the listener will pay more attention to the behaviors.

141. The best title for this selection would be

 (A) How to Be a Good Listener
 (B) Sending Messages
 (C) Effective Communication
 (D) Body Language

142. As used in the passage, the word underline{genuine} most nearly means

 (A) real
 (B) intelligent
 (C) extraordinary
 (D) spontaneous

143. Communication takes place when

 (A) two people understand one another
 (B) one person talks, and one person listens
 (C) two people talk with one another
 (D) two people speak the same language

144. Which of the following is stressed in this passage as an advantage of choosing your words carefully?

 (A) influencing others
 (B) communicating more often
 (C) making people pay attention
 (D) eliminating any misunderstanding

145. This passage most likely was printed in a

    (A) manual on how to run effective meetings
    (B) treatise on effective management
    (C) textbook on linguistics
    (D) social studies textbook

146. As used in the passage, the word <u>naturally</u> most nearly means

    (A) accidentally
    (B) purely
    (C) organically
    (D) obviously

Read the following passage and answer questions 147–152.

Throughout the first few decades of American diplomacy, the first and foremost principle of American foreign <u>policy</u> was isolationism. As laid out by George Washington in his speech of 1796, isolationism meant that the United States should form no permanent alliance and should forge "as little political connection as possible" with foreign powers. However, this policy applied only to diplomatic relations, since trade with other nations was an essential element of the American economy.

In the early 1800s, the United States expanded its isolationist policies to the entire Western Hemisphere. President Monroe, in his now famous address to Congress, stated that the United States would stay out of European affairs, and that in turn, Europe should not intervene in <u>affairs</u> of the Americas. This policy, known as the Monroe Doctrine, was designed to signal a clear break between the New World and the Old. However, it was also used to assert American influence in Latin America.

147. The best title for this selection would be

    (A) President Monroe
    (B) American Diplomacy Past and Present
    (C) Evolution of the Monroe Doctrine
    (D) American Neutrality

148. As used in the passage, the word <u>policy</u> most nearly means

    (A) guiding principles
    (B) strict regulations
    (C) exact measurements
    (D) political arguments

149. In the 1800s, isolationism came to mean

    (A) the refusal of the United States to trade with other nations
    (B) the influence of the United States over the Western Hemisphere
    (C) interference in European affairs
    (D) a break between the United States and Latin America

150. Isolationism does *not* mean

    (A) reluctance to form permanent alliances
    (B) minimizing political affiliations
    (C) American refusal to side with any one European nation
    (D) banning of all trade

151. Comparing the two paragraphs, we can say that

    (A) the first paragraph contains more statistics than the second
    (B) the second provides examples of ideas discussed in the first
    (C) the second shows a shift in the definition of isolationism
    (D) the second paragraph completely disagrees with the first

152. As used in the passage, the word <u>affairs</u> most nearly means

    (A) festivities
    (B) wars
    (C) meetings
    (D) business

Vocabulary

Directions: For questions 153–174, choose the word that is closest in meaning to the underlined word.

153. To <u>apprehend</u> a criminal

    (A) catch
    (B) understand
    (C) view
    (D) approach

154. To <u>secure</u> an agreement

    (A) break
    (B) protect
    (C) end
    (D) obtain

155. <u>Blatant</u> disrespect

    (A) angry
    (B) unfair
    (C) youthful
    (D) obvious

156. <u>Excessive</u> spending

    (A) exact
    (B) enormous
    (C) successful
    (D) necessary

157. An <u>unassailable</u> fortress

    (A) impenetrable
    (B) unprotected
    (C) undefeated
    (D) ancient

158. An added <u>incentive</u>

    (A) profit
    (B) rebate
    (C) motivation
    (D) demand

159. A <u>scowling</u> face

    (A) pale
    (B) ruddy
    (C) beautiful
    (D) frowning

160. An <u>ulterior</u> motive

    (A) concealed
    (B) alternate
    (C) unwise
    (D) ultimate

161. To <u>aggravate</u> one's mother

    (A) bother
    (B) embrace
    (C) boss
    (D) discuss

162. An <u>executive</u> decision

    (A) governing
    (B) friendly
    (C) stern
    (D) serious

163. To <u>contemplate</u> an idea

    (A) judge
    (B) consider
    (C) punish
    (D) decide

164. An <u>efficient</u> worker

    (A) expensive
    (B) shoddy
    (C) outgoing
    (D) capable

165. An <u>unprecedented</u> ruling

    (A) strict
    (B) extraordinary
    (C) unanimous
    (D) orderly

166. A <u>verbatim</u> quote

    (A) brief
    (B) historical
    (C) wordy
    (D) exact

167. To <u>resolve</u> an argument

    (A) settle
    (B) break
    (C) win
    (D) avoid

168. <u>Subordinate</u> rank

    (A) high
    (B) military
    (C) inferior
    (D) organized

169. A <u>perilous</u> journey

    (A) lengthy
    (B) hazardous
    (C) solitary
    (D) adventurous

170. To <u>refrain</u> from eating

    (A) cease
    (B) return
    (C) sing
    (D) resolve

171. A <u>dilapidated</u> building

    (A) luxurious
    (B) overrated
    (C) decayed
    (D) renovated

172. A <u>prevailing</u> theory

    (A) proven
    (B) dominant
    (C) technical
    (D) antiquated

173. To <u>found</u> a business

    (A) lead
    (B) tax
    (C) discover
    (D) begin

174. A <u>credible</u> witness

    (A) trustworthy
    (B) legal
    (C) unbelievable
    (D) experienced

MATHEMATICS

45 minutes

Directions: For questions 175–238, choose the best answer.

Concepts

175. Which of the following is *not* a type of angle?

    (A) obtuse
    (B) acute
    (C) isosceles
    (D) right

176. $\{4, 5, 7, 9, 11\} \cap \{5, 7, 10, 11\} =$

    (A) $\{4, 5, 7, 9\}$
    (B) $\{3, 6, 9, 12\}$
    (C) $\{5, 7, 11\}$
    (D) $\{5, 6, 7, 11\}$

177. What is 83.456 rounded to the nearest tenth?

    (A) 83
    (B) 83.45
    (C) 83.5
    (D) 83.46

178. Simplify: $2(-3)^3 =$

    (A) –52
    (B) –54
    (C) –27
    (D) –44

179. As a fraction, 0.45 equals

    (A) $\frac{45}{1,000}$
    (B) $\frac{100}{45}$
    (C) $\frac{9}{20}$
    (D) $\frac{1}{2}$

180. The measure of angle A is

    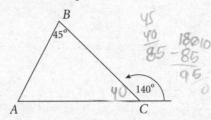

    (A) 95°
    (B) 90°
    (C) 85°
    (D) 80°

181. To divide a number by 100, move the decimal point

    (A) two places to the right
    (B) three places to the right
    (C) two places to the left
    (D) four places to the right

182. Which of the following is a pair of reciprocals?

    (A) $(4 \times 2), (2 \times 1)$
    (B) $2\frac{1}{2}, \frac{2}{5}$
    (C) 24, 42
    (D) $0.25, \frac{1}{4}$

183. The area of this circle is

    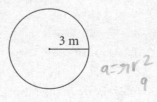

    (A) 3π m²
    (B) 9π m²
    (C) 6π m²
    (D) 12π m²

184. The ratio of 36 inches to two yards is equivalent to

    (A) 1 to 2
    (B) 2 to 1
    (C) 3 to 2
    (D) 1 to 3

185. How many integers are between $\frac{17}{2}$ and 9.5?

    (A) 1
    (B) 2
    (C) 12
    (D) 0

186. Which of the following is true?

    (A) $\frac{a+b+a}{b} = a(b+a)$
    (B) $a(b+c) = ab + ac$
    (C) $a + b + b2 = ab(b)$
    (D) $2a + 2b + 2c = 2(abc)$

187. Which of the following numbers is an example of a perfect square?

    (A) 12
    (B) 24
    (C) 32
    (D) 81

188. Which of these is correctly written in scientific notation?

    (A) $345 \times \left(\frac{1}{10}\right)^3 = 345,000$
    (B) $3.45 \times 10^2 = 345$
    (C) $0.345 \times 10^4 = 345$
    (D) $0.0345 \times 10^3 = 345$

189. Two integers are in the ratio 5:7. The sum of the two integers is 36. What is the larger integer?

    (A) 36
    (B) 15
    (C) 21
    (D) 7

190. The exact number of hundreds in 8,675 is

    (A) 875
    (B) 8675
    (C) 86.75
    (D) 0.8675

191. A luncheonette serves lemonade in eight-ounce glasses. How many servings can be obtained from two gallons of lemonade?

    (A) 32
    (B) 128
    (C) 256
    (D) 64

192. At a school bake sale, the marching band sold two more brownies than cupcakes. In total, the marching band sold 30 items. How many cupcakes did they sell?

    (A) 14
    (B) 28
    (C) 15
    (D) 10

193. What is the measure in degrees of each acute angle in an isosceles right triangle?

    (A) 50
    (B) 90
    (C) 36
    (D) 45

194. The formula for the area of a rectangle is

    (A) $A = (\text{length})(\text{width})$
    (B) $A = \frac{1}{2}(\text{base})(\text{height})$
    (C) $A = (\text{diameter})(\pi)$
    (D) $A = (\text{width})(\text{base})(\text{height})$

195. If triangle *DCE* is similar to triangle *ABC*, the length of *AB* is

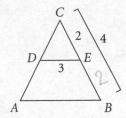

(A) 6 units

(B) 12 units

(C) 5 units

(D) 4 units

196. The prime factorization of 16 is

(A) 4^3

(B) 4×4

(C) 2×4

(D) $2 \times 2 \times 2 \times 2$

197. The lowest common denominator of $\frac{1}{3}$ and $\frac{2}{9}$ is

(A) 15

(B) 9

(C) 2

(D) 3

198. Which of the following is *not* equivalent to $75\frac{1}{2}\%$?

(A) $\frac{151}{200}$

(B) 75.5

(C) $\frac{75.5}{100}$

(D) 0.755

Problem Solving

199. Find the difference between $3\frac{1}{4}$ and $1\frac{1}{5}$.

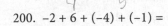

(A) $2\frac{1}{20}$

(B) $2\frac{1}{4}$

(C) $2\frac{1}{6}$

(D) $1\frac{1}{2}$

200. $-2 + 6 + (-4) + (-1) =$

(A) -3

(B) -4

(C) -7

(D) -1

201. A family went to the amusement park and bought 10 ride tickets for the Ferris wheel at $3.25 each and four tickets for the roller coaster at $2.75 each. How much did they spend?

(A) $31.50

(B) $31.25

(C) $43.50

(D) $43.25

202. Find the product: $1\frac{1}{5} \times 2\frac{1}{4} \times 1\frac{1}{3} =$

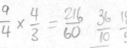

(A) $3\frac{3}{5}$

(B) 3

(C) $3\frac{4}{5}$

(D) 4

203. If a building has a shadow 12 feet long when a 3-foot tall child has a shadow 1 foot long, what is the height of the building?

(A) 36 feet

(B) 12 feet

(C) 34 feet

(D) 4 feet

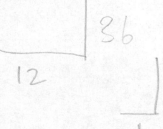

204. Solve for x in the following equation:

$10 + 2x = x + 14$

(A) 4
(B) 14
(C) 10
(D) 8

205. Mrs. Young drove 1,250 miles last week. Approximately how much, on average, did she drive each day for the seven days?

(A) 205
(B) 105
(C) 125
(D) 179

206. If the 8% tax on a new car was $1,600, how much was the car, not including tax?

(A) $30,000
(B) $2,000
(C) $20,000
(D) $25,000

207. Martin has $4 less than two times the amount his sister has. If his sister has $36, how much does Martin have?

(A) $36
(B) $72
(C) $68
(D) $34

208. If $2a + 3 > 9$, then a^2 must be

(A) equal to 6
(B) less than 9
(C) greater than 9
(D) equal to 9

209. A salesman earns 5% commission on every piece of furniture he sells. If he sells four sofas at $1,200 each, what is his commission?

(A) $280
(B) $2,400
(C) $120
(D) $240

210. If 20 is added to an integer and the result is $\frac{3}{2}$ of the integer, what is the integer?

(A) 30
(B) 15
(C) 20
(D) 40

211. Solve: $1\frac{1}{2} + 2\frac{1}{3} + 2\frac{1}{4} =$

(A) $6\frac{1}{12}$
(B) $5\frac{1}{12}$
(C) $6\frac{1}{2}$
(D) $7\frac{7}{12}$

212. If the sum of two numbers is x and one of the numbers is 5, then three times the other number is

(A) $3(x - 5)$
(B) $3(x + 5)$
(C) $3x + 5$
(D) $3x(5)$

213. The fancy chocolate shop charges $2 per ounce of chocolate. What is the cost of a gift box with one pound, four ounces of chocolate?

(A) $40
(B) $4
(C) $8
(D) $6

214. If $x + 5 = y + 10$, then

(A) $x > y$
(B) $x = y$
(C) $x < y$
(D) $x = y - 5$

215. Find the value of $3x^2 + 2y - 1$, if $x = \frac{1}{3}$ and $y = 2$.

    (A) $3\frac{1}{9}$

    (B) $3\frac{1}{3}$

    (C) $5\frac{1}{6}$

    (D) 30

216. The Smiths paid $420 interest on a loan that had a 6% simple interest rate. How much did they borrow?

    (A) $7,000

    (B) $8,000

    (C) $700

    (D) $800

217. What is the volume of this cube solid?

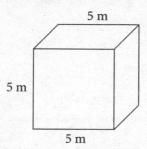

5 m

5 m

5 m

    (A) 125 m³

    (B) 250 m³

    (C) 500 m³

    (D) 150 m³

218. How many strips of paper 1 inch wide by $1\frac{1}{3}$ inches long can be cut from a sheet of paper 1 inch wide by $4\frac{1}{4}$ inches long?

    (A) $5\frac{2}{3}$

    (B) $5\frac{1}{3}$

    (C) 4

    (D) $3\frac{3}{16}$

219. $3.22\overline{)1.5232}$ is approximately

    (A) 0.57

    (B) 0.47

    (C) 47

    (D) 57

220. If P% of 60 is 12, then P =

    (A) 20

    (B) 200

    (C) 66

    (D) 60

221. $233.5 \times 0.051 =$

    (A) 1.19085

    (B) 11.9085

    (C) 0.119085

    (D) 119.085

222. $0.784 + 8.2 + 0.31 =$

    (A) 9.294

    (B) 16.35

    (C) 11.914

    (D) 12.084

223. If the tax rate is $3.72 per $100, how much are the taxes on a home valued at $500,000?

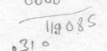

    (A) $1,750

    (B) $1,860

    (C) $18,600

    (D) $17,500

224. If $5x - 8 > 2$, then

    (A) $x^3 > 8$

    (B) $x^3 > 16$

    (C) $x^3 > 9$

    (D) $x^3 > 7$

225. Mr. Battle earns $36,000 annually. He puts 5% of his salary in a savings account toward his retirement. How much does Mr. Battle save for retirement each month?

    (A) $150

    (B) $180

    (C) $1,800

    (D) $1,500

226. Given the series: 23.01, 23.04, 23.07, 23.10, …
What number should come next?

(A) 24.02

(B) 23.13

(C) 25.01

(D) 24.01

227. Solve: $726 \times 19 =$

(A) 13,794

(B) 12,794

(C) 14,794

(D) 13,804

228. What is the area of the figure shown in the diagram?

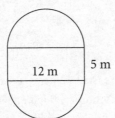

(A) $(60 + \frac{3}{2}\pi)$ m^2

(B) $(60 + 9\pi)$ m^2

(C) $(60 + 3\pi)$ m^2

(D) $(60 + 36\pi)$ m^2

229. Solve for x: $\left(\frac{2}{3} + \frac{2}{5}\right) - \left(\frac{1}{3} + \frac{1}{10}\right) = x$

(A) $\frac{1}{6}$

(B) $\frac{6}{5}$

(C) $\frac{5}{6}$

(D) $\frac{19}{30}$

230. The product of 8 and 9 is 12 more than x. What is x?

(A) 50

(B) 69

(C) 68

(D) 60

231. $ABCD$ is a rectangle in which $AD = 9$ inches and $DC = 15$ inches. What is the area, in square inches, of the rectangle?

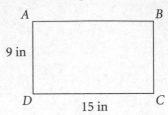

(A) 135

(B) 144

(C) 120

(D) 108

232. The ratio of $\frac{1}{3}$ to $\frac{5}{9}$ is equivalent to

(A) $\frac{5}{3}$

(B) $\frac{3}{5}$

(C) $\frac{5}{27}$

(D) $\frac{5}{18}$

233. If the square root of $y - 3$ is equal to 2, then $y =$

(A) 7

(B) 4

(C) 9

(D) 8

234. A ladder is extended to a length of ten feet and is leaning against the side of a house. If the base of the ladder is six feet from the house, how high up the house does the ladder reach?

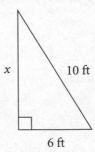

(A) 12 ft

(B) 10 ft

(C) 6 ft

(D) 8 ft

235. Which number is a multiple of 60?

    (A) 213
    (B) 350
    (C) 540
    (D) 1,060

236. On a cross-country tour, Rosemarie drove 60 miles in one day—which was 40% of her planned mileage for that day. How many more miles did Rosemarie plan to drive that day?

    (A) 70
    (B) 90
    (C) 60
    (D) 150

237. The measure of two acute angles of a right triangle is in a ratio of 2:1. The measure of the larger acute angle is

    (A) 35
    (B) 50
    (C) 60
    (D) 30

238. Solve for x: $.8x + 5.5 = 9.7$

    (A) 5
    (B) 5.25
    (C) 5.50
    (D) 0.52

LANGUAGE

25 minutes

Usage

Directions: For questions 239–278, choose the sentence that contains an error in punctuation, capitalization, or usage. If there is no error, select choice (D).

239. (A) It's been a very cold winter.
     (B) The Tigers won a victory over the falcons.
     (C) Why don't you bring your sister to the party?
     (D) No mistake.

240. (A) I had never been on a roller coaster before.
     (B) The students took off they're coats.
     (C) Marjorie asked, "Who is the fastest runner on the team?"
     (D) No mistake.

241. (A) Safety is our primary concern.
     (B) We should of voted in the election.
     (C) How often have you been to Los Angeles?
     (D) No mistake.

242. (A) Aunt Edith bought a new tractor.
     (B) They won't allow dogs in the store.
     (C) The Hudson River is a great place to sail.
     (D) No mistake.

243. (A) Neither Alice and John liked the book.
     (B) I prefer chocolate ice cream.
     (C) Maria, please sit down.
     (D) No mistake.

244. (A) She is a Professor at the college.
     (B) Veronica promised to visit this afternoon.
     (C) If you're ready, please let me know.
     (D) No mistake.

245. (A) There aren't any peaches left.
     (B) A swan lives by the community pond.
     (C) I looked, but I couldn't find the book nowhere.
     (D) No mistake.

246. (A) We still haven't agreed on a solution.
     (B) The situation will affect everyone.
     (C) If you finish quick, we will have time to go to the store.
     (D) No mistake.

247. (A) I wish you could have seen her reaction.
     (B) She lended her book to Thomas.
     (C) Doesn't she want to join us?
     (D) No mistake.

248. (A) He hung the clothes on the clothesline.
     (B) The faucet has been leaking for days.
     (C) I've been studying Spanish for five years.
     (D) No mistake.

249. (A) I believe you are the first to arrive.
     (B) That there boy lost his eyeglasses.
     (C) Which jacket belongs to Sally?
     (D) No mistake.

250. (A) If she had known there would be cake,
          Rachel would of come.
     (B) It's a long way from Boston to New York City.
     (C) Joseph and I are renting a canoe.
     (D) No mistake.

251. (A) Would you like a piece of pie?
     (B) My favorite season is summer.
     (C) The lion got a thorn in it's paw.
     (D) No mistake.

252. (A) The book was wrote by Jim.
     (B) The office will be closed on Memorial Day.
     (C) I saw the movie that you recommended.
     (D) No mistake.

253. (A) Who's coat is this?
     (B) Give the pen and paper to us.
     (C) We can take care of the mistake ourselves.
     (D) No mistake.

254. (A) Don't forget to wear your helmet.
     (B) The plants have grown since you watered
          them.
     (C) I hope you return back the library books on
          time.
     (D) No mistake.

255. (A) We go to school every day accept Saturday
          and Sunday.
     (B) Don't forget to study your lesson.
     (C) Carlos is teaching his brother how to spell.
     (D) No mistake.

256. (A) If you feel tired, why don't you lie down?
     (B) Actually, I'd rather not go.
     (C) Lisa asked, "Did you keep your receipt?"
     (D) No mistake.

257. (A) The policeman is controlling traffic.
     (B) We had never went bowling before.
     (C) That's a great kick!
     (D) No mistake.

258. (A) Each of the books is interesting.
     (B) We eat turkey on Thanksgiving.
     (C) Barb and me are going to play tennis.
     (D) No mistake.

259. (A) What is the capital of Illinois?
     (B) Which house is Mary's?
     (C) We telephoned her and Carol.
     (D) No mistake.

260. (A) Can you lift that heavy chair?
     (B) Aunt Charlene brought us each a present.
     (C) John plays the saxophone as well as Christo-
          pher does.
     (D) No mistake.

261. (A) Can I watch television tonight?
     (B) Please help me clean up.
     (C) George asked us all to come to his game.
     (D) No mistake.

262. (A) Donald told us to turn right from the corner.
     (B) "Hey," said Karen, "do you want to ride
          bicycles?"
     (C) It's a lovely day, isn't it?
     (D) No mistake.

263. (A) Have you seen Anthonys golf clubs?
     (B) I'd like to practice two or three hours a day.
     (C) The coach asked the team to take their uniforms home.
     (D) No mistake.

264. (A) We don't owe them nothing.
     (B) I would rather go to the beach than to the movies.
     (C) John enjoys reading novels.
     (D) No mistake.

265. (A) It is important to exercise daily.
     (B) She wouldn't of come if she knew he would be there.
     (C) Is it time to leave yet?
     (D) No mistake.

266. (A) Mary is taller then Pete.
     (B) Most people have some artistic talent.
     (C) How many apples are in the carton?
     (D) No mistake.

267. (A) How often does Jack bake?
     (B) Daniel and his friend John have made the Dean's List.
     (C) Its too late to begin the project now.
     (D) No mistake.

268. (A) I just called to say hello.
     (B) Patricia's mother will drive.
     (C) Why you don't come with us?
     (D) No mistake.

269. (A) Let's go to the store after lunch.
     (B) Why do you think she cancelled the meeting?
     (C) You and me are best friends.
     (D) No mistake.

270. (A) Us students must organize a petition.
     (B) I'll let you know what time the game begins.
     (C) Our whole band played well yesterday.
     (D) No mistake.

271. (A) Drive slow in the center of town.
     (B) Harry apologized for his mistake.
     (C) This kind of behavior is unacceptable.
     (D) No mistake.

272. (A) The men's room is down the hall to the left.
     (B) My sisters and I all share a room.
     (C) I've bought a new folder for my homework.
     (D) No mistake.

273. (A) Clarence graduated at the head of his class.
     (B) You should have spoken to your mother.
     (C) The Great Lakes are in the northern United States.
     (D) No mistake.

274. (A) The commander issued an order.
     (B) Would you please pass the salt?
     (C) Jim please set the table.
     (D) No mistake.

275. (A) Can you describe what happened?
     (B) Marie Curie was a brilliant scientist.
     (C) I didn't see nothing.
     (D) No mistake.

276. (A) I'm relieved that no one was hurt.
     (B) If you have a question, raise your hand.
     (C) Frank throws as well as her does.
     (D) No mistake.

277. (A) We have more cousins than you.
     (B) Sit down immediately!
     (C) Dad's going to cook dinner tonight.
     (D) No mistake.

278. (A) When she was finished the crowd applauded.
     (B) The baby is sleeping soundly.
     (C) Will you be joining us this evening?
     (D) No mistake.

Spelling

Directions: For questions 279–288, choose the sentence that contains a spelling error. If there is no error, select choice (D).

279. (A) Emily telephoned recently.
     (B) Did you recieve instructions?
     (C) Everyone except Claire will come.
     (D) No mistake.

280. (A) Please disregard my previous message.
     (B) Dad apologized for blaming Tim.
     (C) The principle patrolled the corridors of the school.
     (D) No mistake.

281. (A) The substitute teacher is very nice.
     (B) That was a terrific show.
     (C) I am going to cancel my subscription.
     (D) No mistake.

282. (A) What time will the room be availible?
     (B) Smoking is not allowed in public places.
     (C) We used various fruits in the salad.
     (D) No mistake.

283. (A) She gave me many encouraging words.
     (B) It is important to coopurate with the rest of the team.
     (C) Kate is concerned about her younger cousin.
     (D) No mistake.

284. (A) Martin pretended not to recognize me at the party.
     (B) We were disappointed that the show was mediocer.
     (C) I'm sure you are capable of completing the task.
     (D) No mistake.

285. (A) The doctor prescribed cough medicine.
     (B) Please complete the questionaire.
     (C) No one can predict the future.
     (D) No mistake.

286. (A) The hole is not noticeable.
     (B) We will conduct a formal inquiry.
     (C) Dana is an excelent athlete.
     (D) No mistake.

287. (A) We refered her to the proper authorities.
     (B) Everyone sympathized with the main character.
     (C) Forgive me, I bumped into you by accident.
     (D) No mistake.

288. (A) The audiance was amazed.
     (B) Whether or not you agree, I like this book very much.
     (C) Everyone except Mary attended the lecture.
     (D) No mistake.

Composition

Directions: For questions 289–298, follow the directions for each question.

289. Choose the word that is a clear connective to complete the sentence.

     The blizzard raged outside; _____ we remained cautiously at home, sitting rapt by the fire.

     (A) in addition,
     (B) for example,
     (C) therefore,
     (D) none of these

290. Choose the group of words that best completes the sentence.

     Before planting the seeds, _____ .

     (A) watering the ground well was what Bob did
     (B) Bob first watered the ground
     (C) the ground was well watered, Bob made sure
     (D) water the ground was first for Bob

291. Choose the group of words that best completes the sentence.

    Most athletes find that it is essential
    _____ .

    (A) daily practicing
    (B) for practicing daily
    (C) to practice daily
    (D) daily to practice

292. Which choice most clearly expresses the intended meaning?

    (A) The violin was played by the musician beautifully.
    (B) The musician played her violin beautifully.
    (C) The violin played by the musician was beautiful.
    (D) The musician's violin, when played, played beautifully.

293. Which choice most clearly expresses the intended meaning?

    (A) After playing all afternoon, the hammock looked inviting.
    (B) The hammock looked inviting after playing all afternoon.
    (C) Playing all afternoon, the hammock looked inviting.
    (D) After we played all afternoon, the hammock looked inviting.

294. Which of the following pairs of sentences fits best under this topic sentence?

    John Wayne is best known for his cowboy roles in films of the Wild West.

    (A) His portrayal of tough but fair cowboys won him a place in America's heart. He has become a symbol of our national spirit.
    (B) His incredible career spanned 50 years. He acted in more than 200 films.
    (C) There are not many cowboys around anymore. Nonetheless, kids still enjoy wearing cowboy costumes for Halloween.
    (D) His heroism was notable not only on screen, but in his life as well. He was a model of character for a generation.

295. Which of the following expresses the idea most clearly?

    (A) The 7 A.M. bus she took in order to arrive at work on time.
    (B) She took the 7 A.M. bus in order to arrive at work on time.
    (C) In order to arrive at work on time, the 7 A.M. bus she took.
    (D) The 7 A.M. bus she took, and she arrived at work on time.

296. Which of these best fits under the topic "Protecting Our Natural Resources"?

    (A) The National Parks system was created by Theodore Roosevelt to ensure that Americans could enjoy nature for generations to come.
    (B) It is important to regulate the high cost of petroleum.
    (C) Many zoos feature exhibits that allow the animals space to roam.
    (D) Uranium is an important source of energy.

297. Choose the best word or words to join the thoughts together.

     In the North, textile mills and other industrial plants fueled the economy; _____ agriculture was the staple of the economy in the South.

     (A) therefore,
     (B) in contrast,
     (C) moreover,
     (D) none of these

298. Which of the following sentences best creates an element of foreshadowing?

     (A) The foghorn's deep and spine-tingling sound cut through the night as the ship approached Thunder Bay.
     (B) In the end, detectives determined that the watch had been stolen by the butler.
     (C) Mosquitoes are the most misunderstood members of the insect world.
     (D) The people of this enchanted isle lived isolated from the woes of modern society.

ANSWERS AND EXPLANATIONS

Answer Key

VERBAL SKILLS

1.	D
2.	A
3.	A
4.	B
5.	C
6.	A
7.	A
8.	B
9.	D
10.	C
11.	A
12.	D
13.	D
14.	B
15.	A
16.	D
17.	A
18.	A
19.	C
20.	B
21.	D
22.	D
23.	C
24.	B
25.	D
26.	A
27.	C
28.	A
29.	C
30.	C
31.	B
32.	A
33.	C
34.	B
35.	B
36.	C
37.	D

38.	A
39.	C
40.	C
41.	A
42.	D
43.	B
44.	D
45.	B
46.	B
47.	C
48.	A
49.	D
50.	C
51.	C
52.	D
53.	A
54.	D
55.	A
56.	A
57.	D
58.	B
59.	B
60.	C

QUANTITATIVE SKILLS

61.	D
62.	A
63.	B
64.	C
65.	A
66.	D
67.	C
68.	B
69.	D
70.	D
71.	B
72.	D
73.	C

74.	A
75.	C
76.	B
77.	A
78.	D
79.	A
80.	C
81.	A
82.	B
83.	D
84.	C
85.	C
86.	C
87.	A
88.	D
89.	B
90.	B
91.	A
92.	B
93.	A
94.	C
95.	D
96.	B
97.	B
98.	C
99.	A
100.	C
101.	A
102.	D
103.	D
104.	B
105.	A
106.	A
107.	C
108.	C
109.	C
110.	D
111.	C
112.	D

READING
Comprehension
113. **A**
114. **B**
115. **D**
116. **C**
117. **C**
118. **B**
119. **C**
120. **A**
121. **B**
122. **A**
123. **C**
124. **A**
125. **B**
126. **B**
127. **C**
128. **C**
129. **B**
130. **A**
131. **D**
132. **A**
133. **A**
134. **D**
135. **B**
136. **C**
137. **B**
138. **D**
139. **A**
140. **C**
141. **C**
142. **A**
143. **A**
144. **D**
145. **A**
146. **D**
147. **C**
148. **A**
149. **B**
150. **D**
151. **C**
152. **D**

Vocabulary
153. **A**
154. **D**
155. **D**
156. **B**
157. **A**
158. **C**
159. **D**
160. **A**
161. **A**
162. **A**
163. **B**
164. **D**
165. **B**
166. **D**
167. **A**
168. **C**
169. **B**
170. **A**
171. **C**
172. **B**
173. **D**
174. **A**

MATHEMATICS
Concepts
175. **C**
176. **C**
177. **C**
178. **B**
179. **C**
180. **A**
181. **C**
182. **B**
183. **B**
184. **A**
185. **A**
186. **B**
187. **D**
188. **B**
189. **C**
190. **C**

191. **A**
192. **A**
193. **D**
194. **A**
195. **A**
196. **D**
197. **B**
198. **B**

Problem Solving
199. **A**
200. **D**
201. **C**
202. **A**
203. **A**
204. **A**
205. **D**
206. **C**
207. **C**
208. **C**
209. **D**
210. **D**
211. **A**
212. **A**
213. **A**
214. **A**
215. **B**
216. **A**
217. **A**
218. **D**
219. **B**
220. **A**
221. **B**
222. **A**
223. **C**
224. **A**
225. **A**
226. **B**
227. **A**
228. **D**
229. **D**
230. **D**

231. **A**
232. **B**
233. **A**
234. **D**
235. **C**
236. **B**
237. **C**
238. **B**

LANGUAGE
Usage
239. **B**
240. **B**
241. **B**
242. **D**
243. **A**
244. **A**
245. **C**
246. **C**
247. **B**
248. **D**
249. **B**
250. **A**
251. **C**
252. **A**
253. **A**

254. **C**
255. **A**
256. **D**
257. **B**
258. **C**
259. **D**
260. **D**
261. **A**
262. **A**
263. **A**
264. **A**
265. **B**
266. **A**
267. **C**
268. **C**
269. **C**
270. **A**
271. **A**
272. **D**
273. **D**
274. **C**
275. **C**
276. **C**
277. **D**
278. **A**

Spelling
279. **B**
280. **C**
281. **D**
282. **A**
283. **B**
284. **B**
285. **B**
286. **C**
287. **A**
288. **A**

Composition
289. **C**
290. **B**
291. **C**
292. **B**
293. **D**
294. **A**
295. **B**
296. **A**
297. **B**
298. **A**

Verbal Skills

1. D

Severe means the opposite of the other choices, which are all synonyms for *easygoing*.

2. A

In terms of speed, the order is Christine, Joanne, Katie, so (A) is true.

3. A

Abundant means plenty, so the opposite is *scarce*.

4. B

A shell surrounds and protects an egg; a peel surrounds and protects an orange.

5. C

We are not told where Mr. Johnson would be if he were not at the golf club.

6. A

To endorse most nearly means approve.

7. A

To expand means to grow.

8. B

The order from most home runs to least according to the first two statements is: Hank, Peter, Joe. Therefore, Hank has hit the most home runs.

9. D

A claw is the foot of an eagle, while a paw is the foot of a lion.

10. C

Fiction means made up, so the opposite is *fact*.

11. A

Territory most nearly means land.

12. D

To force most nearly means to impose.

13. D

A spy seeks out hidden information; the other choices are all examples of people who represent a country or region.

14. B

A paddle makes a canoe move, and a pedal makes a bicycle move.

15. A

Unending fits the definition of infinite. While something that's infinite may also be complex and undiscovered, those are not actual synonyms of infinite.

16. D

A lot is an empty space; the other choices are spaces found in a house.

17. A

Hamburger is named as the least expensive food in both statements.

18. A

Average means typical or medium; *outstanding* is atypical or superb.

19. C

A saw is used to cut, and a handle is used to open.

20. B

Mandate means command or decree. It may be used as a noun or as a verb. For example: *Before the city council voted to mandate 'no parking' rules, many citizens spoke out against the mandate.*

21. D

To embellish most nearly means to adorn. To em-broider would be one way to embellish something, but embroider is too specific to be a close synonym for embellish.

22. D

Wary means careful; the opposite is *careless*.

23. C

Serene means peaceful.

24. B

Elated means happy; solemn, serious, and grave are synonyms that mean the opposite of happy.

25. D

This is a degree relationship. *Minute* means extremely small, and *colossal* means extremely large.

26. A

Only the word *familiar* fits the definition of the word *acquainted*.

27. C

Beside means close to. All the other choices are synonyms of *far*.

28. A

A colleague is a coworker.

29. C

We have no information regarding the size relation-ship between Wolf Lake and Beaver Lake.

30. C

There is no information comparing the half-lives of elements A and D.

31. B

Underhanded means sneaky.

32. A

The word *choose* is unlike the other choices, which are all synonyms for *punish*.

33. C

To condemn means to judge. The other answer choices all mean to overlook or to excuse.

34. B

Praise is an expression of admiration, while *insult* is an expression of contempt.

35. B

Since the first two statements are true, and kanga-roos are mammals, kangaroos must give birth to live young.

36. C

Fortuitous means lucky or fortunate.

37. D

Ambivalent means having mixed feelings or being uncertain.

38. A

The word *letter* does not belong with the other choices, which are examples of published writing.

39. C

The key word is *all*. All *X* is *Y* doesn't mean all *Y* is *X*, so some *Z* could be *Y*.

40. C

One forges a signature, and one counterfeits money.

41. A

To detain means to keep back, while all the other choices mean to enter.

42. D

Renowned means well-known or famed.

43. B

Implicit means implied or inferred.

44. D

A fool lacks wisdom and a pauper lacks riches.

45. B

Ingenious means clever.

46. B

A mimic imitates. The other choices are synonyms for clown.

47. C

Bombastic means loud, exaggerated, or overblown.

48. A

The key word is *all*. Since Lester is a myop and all myops are nearsighted, Lester must be nearsighted.

49. D

A cub is a young animal. All the other choices are names of groups of animals.

50. C

A warrant grants permission to search, while a visa grants permission to travel.

51. C

Sedentary means seated or inactive; the opposite is *active*.

52. D

Wardrobe is the general classification; all the other choices are types of clothing.

53. A

Rudimentary means basic; the opposite is *advanced*.

54. D

The word *unleash* is the opposite of the other choices.

55. A

Although a battle may result in success, the other words are synonyms for *success*.

56. A

Malevolent means evil.

57. D

Although a ticket may be needed to watch a play, the other words are all elements of a theatrical performance.

58. B

A chapter is a piece of a book, a section is a piece of a newspaper.

59. B

According to the first two statements, the order of cities from north to south is B, A, C, D. Therefore, the third statement is false.

60. C

Transient means passing or temporary.

QUANTITATIVE SKILLS

61. D

Let x = the number

$$3x = 34\frac{1}{2} = \frac{69}{2}$$

$$x = \frac{69}{2} \div 3 = 11\frac{1}{2}$$

Half the number $= \frac{1}{2} \times 11\frac{1}{2} = \frac{1}{2} \times \frac{23}{2} = \frac{23}{4} = 5\frac{3}{4}$.

62. A

The pattern in the series is +3. Therefore, the next term is 11 + 3 = 14.

63. B

If A > B > C, A must also be greater than C.

64. C

The pattern in the series is –5; 39 – 5 = 34.

65. A

The product of 5 and 6 is 5 × 6 = 30.

The product plus 4 = 30 + 4 = 34.

$36 - x = 34$

$x = 36 - 34 = 2$

66. D

Since all three angles in an equilateral triangle are equal (each angle is 60 degrees), A + B must be greater than C.

67. C

Calculate the value of each number as a decimal to readily compare them.

(A) = 0.33, (B) = 0.66, (C) = 0.33, (D) = 0.30. We see, therefore, that (B) has the greatest value.

68. B

The pattern is –4; 53 – 4 = 49.

69. D

Terry's meal cost 4(2.25) + 5.25 = $14.25.

John's meal cost 2(2.25) + 2(5.25) = $15.00.

Maria's meal cost 2.25 + 4.50 + 5.25 = $12.00.

70. D

Calculate the value of each answer choice, performing the operation within the parentheses first.

(a) 11 – (6 + 3) = 11 – 9 = 2
(b) (8 – 2) – 3 = 6 – 3 = 3
(c) 12 – (5 – 4) = 12 – 1 = 11

Then, plug in the numbers to the equation in each answer choice to arrive at the correct equation; 11 > 2 + 3.

71. B

Since the vertical angles formed by two intersecting lines are equal, and a circle totals 360 degrees: angles D and E each equal 80 degrees, and angles F and G each equal 100 degrees. Therefore, the only correct answer is (B).

72. D

(a) = 0.50 × 20 = 10

(b) = 0.30 × 90 = 27

(c) = 0.25 × 80 = 20

The correct choice is (D) because 2(a) = 20 = (c).

73. C

The pattern in the series is –3, +5, –3, +5, –3, and so on. Therefore, the next number is 19 – 3 = 16.

74. A

6 less than 15 = 15 – 6 = 9

Let x = the number:

$\frac{3}{5}x = 9$

$3x = 9 \times 5 = 45$

$x - \frac{45}{3} = 15$

75. C

Count the shaded boxes; 3 of 12 are shaded.

$\frac{3}{12} = \frac{x}{100}$

$12x = 300$

$x = 25$

Expressed as a percent, $\frac{25}{100} = 0.25$, or 25%.

76. B

Let x = the number:

$\frac{1}{3}x = 2 + \frac{1}{4}x$

$\frac{x}{3} = 2 + \frac{x}{4}$

If we multiply both sides of the equation by 12, we have:

$$4x = 24 + 3x$$
$$4x - 3x = 24$$
$$x = 24$$

77. A

$$\frac{7}{8} \div \frac{1}{4} = \frac{7}{8} \times \frac{4}{1} = \frac{28}{8} = 3\frac{4}{8}$$ or reduced, $3\frac{1}{2}$.

Another way to approach this problem is with cross multiplication:

$$\frac{7}{8} = \frac{x}{4}$$

$$\frac{8x}{8} = \frac{28}{8}$$

$$x = \frac{7}{2} = 3\frac{1}{2}$$

78. D

The grocer will need 12 cartons.

He has: 3 super-sized cartons.

Each holds 4 rows × 12 spaces = 48 eggs.

A regular carton holds = 2 rows × 6 spaces = 12 eggs.

$\frac{48}{12}$ = 4 cartons × 3 super-sized cartons = 12 cartons total.

79. A

Let x = the number:

$$x = \frac{4^3}{4} = \frac{4 \times 4 \times 4}{4} = \frac{16 \times 4}{4} = 16$$

80. C

Each successive number in the series is obtained by dividing the preceding number by 2. In this case, $6 \div 2 = 3$.

81. A

The angles of a triangle total 180 degrees. Two angles are given: 90 and 55.

$$180 = 90 + 55 + A$$
$$180 = 145 + A$$
$$180 - 145 = A$$
$$A = 35$$

Furthermore, a straight line represents a straight angle of 180 degrees. Since the measure of angle A = 35 degrees, angle *BAL* must measure 145 degrees, since 35 + 145 = 180.

82. B

Let x = the unknown fraction:

$$x \div \frac{1}{5} = \frac{7}{8}$$

$$x \times 5 = \frac{7}{8}$$

$$5x = \frac{7}{8}$$

$$x = \frac{7}{8} \div 5 = \frac{7}{8} \times \frac{1}{5} = \frac{7}{40}$$

83. D

The pattern is +1, +2, +3, and so on. The subsequent number in the series should be 7 + 4 = 11.

84. C

The equation for circumference = diameter × π.

Since the radius of the circle is 3 m, the diameter = 6 m; therefore, the circumference is 6π m.

85. C

Of eight sectors, two are shaded: $\frac{2}{8} = \frac{1}{4}$.

86. C

By writing each fraction as a decimal, we can readily compare.

$$\frac{1}{5} = 0.20, \quad \frac{1}{3} = 0.33, \quad \frac{2}{3} = 0.66$$

Since 0.66 > 0.33 > 0.20, (C) is the correct answer.

87. A

The average of 15, 24, 32, and 13 = the sum of these numbers, divided by 4.

$$84 \div 4 = 21$$
$$21 - 9 = 12$$

88. D

The pattern is $+3, +1, +3, +1$. Thus, $12 + 1 = 13$.

89. B

$a = 3^2 = 3 \times 3 = 9$

$b = 2 \times 2^2 = 2 \times (2 \times 2) = 2(4) = 8$

$c = 3 \times 2^3 = 3 \times 2 \times 2 \times 2 = 3 \times 8 = 24$

(B) is the correct answer since $24 > 8 + 9$.

90. B

Let x = the number:

$$30 = x + x(0.50)$$
$$30 = 1.5x$$
$$30 \div 1.5 = 300 \div 15 = 20$$

91. A

The pattern is to subtract 1 from the preceding number, and then double the result; $6 - 1 = 5$.

92. B

$$\frac{4^3}{4} = 4^2 = 16$$
$$16 + 12 = 28$$

93. A

$$10 \div \frac{1}{8} = 10 \times \frac{8}{1} = 80$$

94. C

In moving from left to right in the series, we note that the odd-numbered terms follow the counting numbers: 1, 2, 3. Each even-numbered term is 4 more than the preceding number: 4, 8, 12. In this case, the even-numbered term following 12 is $12 + 4 = 16$.

95. D

Find the values of each answer choice and compare. Remember in order of operations, multiplication comes before addition or subtraction.

(a) $31 - 2 \times 7 = 31 - 14 = 17$

(b) $5 \times 4 - 8 = 20 - 8 = 12$

(c) $7 + 6 - 2 = 13 - 2 = 11$

We can therefore see that (a) is greater than (b).

96. B

Since the square is bisected into two equal triangles, and E is the midpoint of line BD, $\frac{1}{2}$ of one triangle is shaded, or $\frac{1}{4}$ of the square is shaded.

97. B

The pattern alternates Roman numerals and Arabic numerals. Each subsequent number is two less than the preceding number. $5 - 2 = 3$. This should be expressed as a Roman numeral.

98. C

Let x = the number:

$$\frac{x}{4} = 3\frac{1}{4}$$
$$x = 3 \times 4 + 1 = 13$$

99. A

Calculate the value of each answer choice.

(a) $(5 + 1)^2 = 6^2 = 6 \times 6 = 36$

(b) $3^2 + 2^2 = 3 \times 3 + 2 \times 2 = 9 + 4 = 13$

(c) $25 - 2 \times 3 = 25 - 6 = 19$

100. C

Let x = the number of students:

$0.15x = 12$

$$x = \frac{12}{0.15} = \frac{1,200}{15} = 80$$

101. A

$$\frac{3}{4} + \frac{5}{6} = \frac{3 \times 6}{24} + \frac{5 \times 4}{24} = \frac{18}{24} + \frac{20}{24} = \frac{38}{24} = 1\frac{14}{24}$$

Compare $\frac{38}{24}$ to $\frac{1}{2}$: $\left(\frac{1}{2} = \frac{12}{24}\right)$.

$\frac{38}{24} - \frac{12}{24} = \frac{26}{24}$. Reducing: $\frac{26}{24} = \frac{13}{12}$.

102. D

Let x = the number. Recall that $33\frac{1}{3}$% of a number is equal to $\frac{1}{3}$ of the number.

$\frac{1}{3}x = 15$

$x = 15 \times 3 = 45$

The reciprocal of 45 is $\frac{1}{45}$.

103. D

The pattern is +5, –2, –1, +5, –2, –1, and so on. Therefore, add 5 to get the next value in the pattern: 9 + 5 = 14.

104. B

Determine the values for each bar in the graph using the number scale to the left. Then, choose the correct alternative. B + A = 2 + 4 = 6 = C.

105. A

AB must be greater than *AD* since it is the hypotenuse of a right triangle. The hypotenuse is the longest side of a right triangle.

106. A

Write each number as a decimal to readily compare.

(a) $3\frac{1}{2}$% = 0.035

(b) $3\frac{1}{2}$ = 3.50

(c) 0.33 = 0.33

Therefore, we see that (b) > (a) + (c).

3.5 > 0.035 + 0.33

3.5 > 0.365

107. C

Let x = the number:

$\frac{2}{3}x + 8 = 40$

$\frac{2}{3}x = 40 - 8 = 32$

$x = 32 \times \frac{3}{2} = \frac{96}{2} = 48$

108. C

The pattern is $-1\frac{1}{2}$ from each term in the series.

Therefore, $3\frac{1}{2} - 1\frac{1}{2} = 2$.

109. C

The pattern is ×2, –1, and so on. Therefore, 10 – 1 = 9.

110. D

The pattern works backward from end to beginning in the alphabet. Each letter is paired with a subsequent integer, working forward from 1. The letter before W is V; the next number after 4 is 5.

111. C

Let x = the number:

$x = 3^3 - 8$

$x = 3 \times 3 \times 3 - 8$

$x = 9 \times 3 - 8$

$x = 27 - 8 = 19$

112. D

Test each of the alternatives to find the true one. To find the perimeter, add the length of all sides; 6 + 4 + 6 + 4 = 20 inches.

READING

Comprehension

113. A

Although you might be tempted to choose (D) because it is mentioned first in the passage, you need to read carefully. The first sentence says that Clara Barton started her work in Washington, D.C.

114. B

In this passage, the word *accompany* means go with.

115. D

Choices (A), (B), and (C) are not correct because they are too general. The passage only discusses the career of Clara Barton, so (D) is the best choice.

116. C

There is nothing in the passage to support choices (A), (B), or (D). We can infer that Clara volunteered to help because she felt compassion for the soldiers.

117. C

The second paragraph tells how there were *shortages of supplies* and Clara *advertised for provisions*. Therefore, *supplies* is a synonym for *provisions*.

118. B

Although it is not clearly written that the Iron Cross is a medal, you can infer that from the context in the fourth paragraph. Locate the sentence about the Iron Cross. It says *she returned home... with Germany's Iron Cross for outstanding military service*. Although it doesn't directly say that it was for aiding soldiers during the war, the other choices are not supported by the passage.

119. C

Read the sentence in which the word *campaigned* is used. The sentence mentions that she worked at *educating the public...and lobbying cabinet heads*. Although you may be tempted to choose (B) and (D), they are not closest in meaning to how the word is used in the passage.

120. A

This is an inference question. If you read the last sentence in paragraph 1, the word *patriot* is used to describe Clara Barton after discussing how she helped other people. Therefore, (A) is the best choice.

121. B

Choices (A), (C), and (D) are supporting the main idea that our love affair with automobiles, a step forward, comes with a price.

122. A

Even if you know the meaning of the word, you should refer its context to confirm your choice. In this passage, *impact* means effect.

123. C

Choices (A) and (D) are incorrect because there is no use of foreshadowing or quotations. Choice (B) is incorrect because the historical fact is only an introduction to the topic.

124. A

By mentioning the Model T, the author shows that automobiles were not always part of our lives; they are an invention that changed our lives.

125. B

You need to understand the context of this statement in the passage. The author is not talking about the financial cost of automobiles, but rather about the environmental cost. Therefore, the best answer is (B).

126. B

The author is arguing for more careful use of the right to free speech; therefore, (B) is the best choice.

127. C

Even if you know the meaning of the word, you should check its context in the passage. In this passage, *demeaning* means insulting.

128. C

This is an inference question. Although the author never explicitly states the most important aim, the second sentence of the passage gives us a clue. The author says freedom of speech *protect*[s] our *right to express opinions without fear*.

129. B

There are no statistics, quotations, or anecdotes (stories) offered. The argument is based on the author's impassioned opinions.

130. A

You need to understand the context of this quote. If you reread the second paragraph, the author asks, *How often do we find ourselves...repeating a phrase...without stopping to ponder the meaning of the words?* Choice (A) is the best answer.

131. D

The word *free* is used in quotations in the first paragraph to show that speech is not free if it is harmful to any group.

132. A

Because the passage discusses musical lyrics, this selection was most likely intended as a speech to a radio station.

133. A

This selection discusses inherited traits, or genetics.

134. D

This selection discusses Gregor Mendel's study of how traits are inherited. It concludes that traits are passed on through genes. Therefore, choice (D) is the best title for the passage.

135. B

This is a detail question. Look for the part of the passage that discusses traits. The first paragraph includes the sentence that gives the answer: *In all, Mendel found seven traits that could be readily observed in only one of two forms.*

136. C

Mendel must have been systematic in his approach, to achieve the results that he did over time.

137. B

This is another detail question. Paragraph 2 gives the answer: *Traits* [are] *passed on to offspring unchanged.*

138. D

The selection explains that Mendel did his research by breeding and observing pea plants over many generations.

139. A

The second paragraph says *that an individual inherits traits from each parent.* Therefore, choice (A) is the best answer.

140. C

Readily means easily. Mendel could *easily* see these traits and study them.

141. C

There is nothing in the passage that supports choices (A), (B), and (D). The passage is mostly about effective communication.

142. A

Even if you know the meaning of the word, you should refer to its context in the passage. In this example, *genuine* means real.

143. A

According to the passage, two people must understand one another for communication to have taken place.

144. D

The passage discusses effective communication. The sentence that mentions minimizing misunderstanding supports choice (D).

145. A

Since this passage discusses communication, it would be helpful information in a manual on effective meetings.

146. D

The word *naturally* here is used to mean obviously; it *obviously* takes two people to share something—in this case, a message.

147. C

This passage discusses how interpretation of the Monroe Doctrine has evolved or changed.

148. A

Based on the context of the word, *policy* means guiding principles.

149. B

This is a detail question. You see that the 1800s are mentioned in paragraph 2. The first sentence in that paragraph states: *In the early 1800s, the United States expanded its isolationist policies to the entire Western Hemisphere.* This supports answer choice (B).

150. D

The answer to this question might not be obvious. If you skim the passage again for information about isolationism, you will notice that the last sentence in paragraph 1 states that isolationism *applied only to diplomatic relations, since trade with other nations was an essential element of the American economy.*

151. C

The second paragraph expands on the idea of the Monroe Doctrine and explains how it has shifted in meaning.

152. D

You need to understand how the word is used in context. In this passage, *affairs* most nearly means business.

Vocabulary

153. A

To apprehend means to nab, to grab, or to catch.

154. D

To secure means to obtain or to acquire.

155. D

Blatant means apparent, showy, or obvious.

156. B

Excessive means exaggerated, needless, or enormous.

157. A

Unassailable means safe, secure, or impenetrable.

158. C

Incentive means stimulus, encouragement, or motivation.

159. D

Scowling means unhappy or frowning.

160. A

Ulterior means covert or concealed.

161. A

To aggravate means to annoy, to irritate, or to bother.

162. A

Executive means controlling or governing.

163. B

To contemplate means to think, to speculate, or to consider.

164. D

Efficient means effective, competent, or capable.

165. B

Unprecedented means unheard of, exceptional, or extraordinary.

166. D

Verbatim means word for word or exact.

167. A

To resolve means to solve, to decide, or to settle.

168. C

Subordinate means lowly or inferior.

169. B

Perilous means dangerous, difficult, or hazardous.

170. A

To refrain means to abstain, to avoid, or to cease.

171. C

Dilapidated means crumbling, damaged, or decayed.

172. B

Prevailing means dominant, popular, or current.

173. D

To found means to create, to initiate, or to begin.

174. A

Credible means reliable, believable, or trustworthy.

MATHEMATICS

Concepts

175. C

There is no such thing as an isosceles angle.

176. C

The symbol stands for intersection. The intersection of two or more sets is the set of elements they share in common. In this case, the common elements are 5, 7, and 11.

177. C

This problem requires you to round off the given number to the place one digit to the right of the decimal point, the tenth's column. Since the number in the hundredth's place is 5, round to 83.5.

178. B

Start with the operations in the parentheses first:
$(-3)^3 = -3 \times -3 \times -3 = -27$

Then, continue with the operations outside the parentheses:

$2 \times (-27) = -54$

179. C

$0.45 = \dfrac{45}{100}$; $\dfrac{45}{100}$ can then be reduced to $\dfrac{9}{20}$.

180. A

A straight line represents a straight angle of 180 degrees. An angle of 140 degrees is given, so the measure of angle C must be 40 degrees to complete the line. Knowing that all the angles in a triangle added together equal 180 degrees:

$m\angle A + m\angle B + m\angle C = 180$
$m\angle A + 45 + 40 = 180$
$m\angle A = 180 - 85; m\angle A = 95$ degrees

181. C

When dividing a number by 10, 100, 1,000, etc., move the decimal point one place to the left for each zero in the divisor. In this example, 100 has two zeros, so the decimal point would be moved two places to the left.

182. B

The reciprocal of a fraction is the fraction with the numerator and denominator switched. Change $2\dfrac{1}{2}$ to an improper fraction; $\dfrac{5}{2}$ is the reciprocal of $\dfrac{2}{5}$.

183. B

The formula for finding the area of a circle is π × the radius squared. The radius is 3, so $3^2 = 9$; the area is 9π m^2.

184. A

The components of this problem must be stated in the same units. Therefore, 36 inches = 1 yard. So, the ratio is 36:72, or 1:2 simplified.

185. A

State $\dfrac{17}{2}$ as a decimal number:

$\dfrac{17}{2} = 8.5$

Between 8.5 and 9.5 there is only one integer; the number 9.

186. B

This is an example of the distributive property of multiplication over addition.

187. D

A perfect square is a number whose factors multiplied by themselves equal the number. In this case, the perfect square is 81 since $9 \times 9 = 81$.

188. B

When working with scientific notation, the exponent represents the number of places to move the decimal point in the multiplier. If the base of the exponent is 10, the decimal point moves to the right. If it is $\frac{1}{10}$, the decimal point moves to the left.

189. C

The easiest way to approach this problem is to add multiples of 5 and 7 until you find a pair of multiples that equals 36.

$5 + 7 \neq 36$.	Try again.
$10 + 14 \neq 36$.	Try again.
$15 + 21 = 36$.	And what is the larger of these two multiples? 21.

190. C

To find the exact number of hundreds in 8,675, we must divide by 100.

$8{,}675 \div 100 = 86.75$

191. A

1 quart = 32 fluid ounces
1 gallon = 4 quarts
$4 \times 32 = 128$ fluid ounces
$2 \times 128 = 256$ ounces
$256 \div 8 = 32$

192. A

Let x = number of cupcakes sold and $x + 2$ = the number of brownies.

$$x + x + 2 = 30$$
$$2x + 2 = 30$$
$$2x = 28$$
$$x = 14$$

193. D

Together, all the angles in a triangle add up to 180. A right angle is 90 degrees, so the sum of the remaining angles must also be 90 degrees. Since the triangle is isosceles, the two acute angles must be equal to one another.

$\frac{90}{2} = 45$ degrees

194. A

The area of a rectangle is determined by multiplying its length times its width.

195. A

The two triangles are similar. Therefore, we can solve this problem by ratios. Let x = the base *AB*:

$$3:2 = x:4$$
$$\frac{3}{2} = \frac{x}{4}$$
$$12 = 2x$$
6 units = x

196. D

Prime factorization is factoring a number to the point where all factors are prime numbers.

$16 = 4 \times 4$
$16 = 2 \times 2 \times 2 \times 2$

197. B

The lowest common denominator is the least number that is a product of both denominators. In this case, 9 is the lowest number both denominators can factor into.

198. B

For (B) to be equal, it would need the percent symbol after it.

Problem Solving

199. A

$$\frac{13}{4} - \frac{6}{5} = \frac{65}{20} - \frac{24}{20} = \frac{41}{20} = 2\frac{1}{20}$$

200. D

$$(-2) + (-4) + (-1) = -7$$
$$+6 + (-7) = -1$$

201. C

tickets for the Ferris wheel	$32.50 (10 × $3.25)
tickets for the roller coaster	$11.00 (4 × $2.75)
total	$43.50

202. A

$$1\frac{1}{5} = \frac{6}{5}, 2\frac{1}{4} = \frac{9}{4}, 1\frac{1}{3} = \frac{4}{3}$$

$$\frac{6}{5} \times \frac{9}{4} \times \frac{4}{3} = \frac{54}{15} = 3\frac{9}{15} = 3\frac{3}{5}$$

203. A

This problem is done by ratios:

$$\frac{x}{3} = \frac{12}{1}$$

$$36 \text{ ft} = x$$

204. A

$$10 + 2x = x + 14$$
$$x = 14 - 10$$
$$x = 4$$

205. D

$$\frac{1,250}{7} \approx 178.57 \approx 179 \text{ miles}$$

206. C

This can be set up as an algebraic equation. If y equals the price of the car, 8% of y equals 1,600, or $0.08y = 1,600 y = \frac{1,600}{0.08} = 20,000$.

207. C

First, multiply $36 × 2 = $72. Then subtract 4 from $72 to get $68.

208. C

$$2a + 3 > 9$$
$$2a > 6$$
$$a > 3$$

If $a > 3$, then $a^2 > 9$.

209. D

$$0.05(\$1,200 \times 4) = 0.05(\$4,800) = \$240$$

210. D

Solve this as an algebraic equation with x as the unknown integer.

$$x + 20 = x\left(\frac{3}{2}\right)$$

$$20 = \frac{3}{2}x - x$$

$$20 = \frac{3}{2}x - \frac{2}{2}x = \frac{1}{2}x$$

$$20 \times 2 = x$$

$$40 = x$$

211. A

Convert the mixed numbers into improper fractions. Then, find the common denominator and add:

$$\frac{3}{2} + \frac{7}{3} + \frac{9}{4} = \frac{18}{12} + \frac{28}{12} + \frac{27}{12} = \frac{73}{12} = 6\frac{1}{12}$$

212. A

If the sum of the two numbers is x, and one of the numbers is 5, then the other number is $x - 5$. Three times the other number is $3(x - 5)$.

213. A

1 pound = 16 ounces; 1 pound 4 ounces = 20 ounces.

$$20 \times \$2 = \$40$$

214. A

We may write the given equation, $x + 5 = y + 10$, as $x - y = 10 - 5$ or $x - y = 5$. Therefore, $x > y$.

215. B

$3\left(\dfrac{1}{3}\right)^2 + 2(2) - 1$, if $x = \dfrac{1}{3}$ and $y = 2$.

$3\left(\dfrac{1}{9}\right) + 4 - 1$

$\dfrac{3}{9} + 3 = 3\dfrac{1}{3}$

216. A

This can be set up as an algebraic equation. It x is the amount the Smiths borrowed, then:

$6\%(x) = 420$

$x = \dfrac{420}{0.06} = \$7{,}000$

217. A

Volume = length × width × height

Volume = 5 × 5 × 5 = 125 m³

218. D

Convert the mixed numbers into improper fractions. Then divide the total length of the paper by the length into which it must be cut.

$\dfrac{17}{4} \div \dfrac{4}{3} = \dfrac{17}{4} \times \dfrac{3}{4} = \dfrac{51}{16} = 3\dfrac{3}{16}$

219. B

First, move the decimal points in order to divide by a whole number. Then, carry out the division.

```
       0.47
 322)152.32
      128 8
       23 52
```

220. A

P% of 60 is 12.

vP% = 0.20

P = 20

221. B

Remember that the number of decimal places to the right of the decimal point in the answer should equal the total number of places to the right of the decimal points in the two factors being multiplied; in this case 4.

```
   233.5
 ×0.051
   2335
 116750
 11.9085
```

222. A

When adding decimal numbers, line up the decimal points.

```
  0.784
  8.2
+ 0.31
  9.294
```

223. C

First, determine how many times \$500,000 can be divided by 100; 500,000 ÷ 100 = 5,000. Then multiply by 3.72 since that is the amount due per hundred; 5,000 × 3.72 = \$18,600.

224. A

$5x - 8 > 2$

$5x > 10$

$x > 2$

If $x > 2$, $x^3 > 2^3$; thus, $x^3 > 8$.

225. A

0.05 of 36,000 = 1,800 saved per year. Divide 1,800 by 12 to arrive at how much Mr. Battle saves each month; $\dfrac{1{,}800}{12} = 150$.

226. B

The pattern is made by adding 0.03 to each number.

227. A

$$
\begin{array}{r}
726 \\
\times\ 19 \\
\hline
6{,}534 \\
7{,}260 \\
\hline
13{,}794
\end{array}
$$

228. D

The area of the rectangle is length × width, or $5 \times 12 = 60$ m².

The area of the semicircles on each side = $\frac{1}{2}$ (radius)² × π, or $\frac{1}{2}(6)^2 \times \pi = 18\pi$ m². However, since there are two semicircles, the area of both of them put together = 36π m². Therefore, the area of the whole figure = $(60 + 36\pi)$ m².

229. D

Rename the fractions with a common denominator, then do the operations in parentheses first.

$$\left(\frac{2}{3}+\frac{2}{5}\right) - \left(\frac{1}{3}+\frac{1}{10}\right)$$

$$\left(\frac{20}{30}+\frac{12}{30}\right) - \left(\frac{10}{30}+\frac{3}{30}\right)$$

$$\frac{32}{30} - \frac{13}{30} = \frac{19}{30}$$

230. D

First, translate into an equation, and then solve.

$8 \times 9 = x + 12$

$72 = x + 12$

$60 = x$

231. A

The formula for area is length × width; $9 \times 15 = 135$ square inches.

232. B

The ratio of $\frac{1}{3}$ to $\frac{5}{9} = \frac{1}{3} \div \frac{5}{9} = \frac{1}{3} \times \frac{9}{5} = \frac{9}{15} = \frac{3}{5}$.

233. A

If we square both sides of the equation, we have

$y - 3 = 2^2$

$y - 3 = 4$

$\quad y = 7$

234. D

Since this is a right triangle, you can use the Pythagorean theorem to solve this problem.

$x^2 + 6^2 = 10^2$

$x^2 + 6^2 = 100$

$\quad x^2 = 100 - 36 = 64$

$\quad x = 8$

235. C

A number that is a multiple of 60 must be both a multiple of 10 and a multiple of 6. A number that is a multiple of 10 ends in a 0, so you can eliminate (A). A multiple of 6 meets the requirements for multiples of 2 and 3. Choices (B), (C), and (D) are all divisible by 2. The one that is divisible by 3 is the correct answer.

236. B

Let x = the total number of miles planned for that day.

$0.40x = 60$

$\quad x = \dfrac{60}{0.4} = 150$

Of that 150 planned miles, Rosemarie has already driven 60. Therefore, the number of miles she has left to drive to reach her total planned miles = $150 - 60 = 90$ miles.

237. C

All the angles in a triangle = 180. We know that one angle of this triangle is right, or 90 degrees. The remaining angles must therefore = 90 degrees (for a total of 180 degrees). Since the ratio is 2:1, set up the equation:

$$2x + 1x = 90$$
$$3x = 90$$
$$x = 30$$

Therefore, the larger angle is 2(30) = 60 degrees, and the smaller is 30 degrees.

238. B

Multiply both sides of the equation by 10 to make it more manageable.

$$8x + 55 = 97$$
$$8x = 97 - 55$$
$$8x = 42$$
$$x = \frac{42}{8} = 5.25$$

LANGUAGE

Usage

239. B

The name of the team, the *Falcons*, should be capitalized. While you might have been on the lookout for incorrect contractions, *it's* in choice (A) is the correct contraction for *it has*, and *don't* in choice (B) is used correctly as well.

240. B

They're is the subject/verb *they are*. *Their* is the possessive.

241. B

The correct verb is *should have*, not *should of*.

242. D

There are no mistakes.

243. A

The correct phrase is *neither...nor*.

244. A

Professor does not need to be capitalized since it is a general job classification, not a title.

245. C

The double negative is incorrect. The correct usage would be *couldn't find the book anywhere*.

246. C

Quick should be *quickly* as it is an adverb, describing the verb *finish*.

247. B

The past tense of to *lend* is *lent*.

248. D

There are no mistakes.

249. B

That means the one there; the word *there* is not needed.

250. A

The correct verbal phrase is *would have come*.

251. C

It's is the contraction for *it is*. *Its* is the possessive which should be used here.

252. A

Was wrote is incorrect. The correct passive verb is *was written*.

253. A

Who's is incorrect; it is the contraction of *who is*. The correct word here should be *whose*.

254. C

Return back is incorrect; it is repetitive to *return back*.

255. A

Accept means *welcome* or *receive*; in this case, the word should be *except*.

256. D

There are no mistakes.

257. B

The correct verbal phrase is *had never gone*.

258. C

Barb and me should be *Barb and I* since the pronoun is a subject. If you thought that choice (A) should use the plural verb *are* instead of the singular verb *is*, look again at the sentence and see that the verb is correctly paired with the singular noun *each*.

259. D

There are no mistakes.

260. D

There are no mistakes.

261. A

Can refers to ability. The correct word here should be *may*.

262. A

The correct prepositional phrase is *to turn right at the corner*.

263. A

There should be an apostrophe in *Anthonys* to show possession.

264. A

The double negative, *don't...nothing*, is incorrect. The correct wording should be *don't owe anything* or *we owe nothing*.

265. B

The word *of* is incorrect. The correct word should be *have*.

266. A

Then is incorrect. The correct word should be *than*.

267. C

Its is incorrect. The contraction *it's (it is)* should be used here.

268. C

The word order *you don't* is incorrect. When asking a question, the correct word order is *don't you*.

269. C

Me is incorrect; the subject pronoun is *I*.

270. A

If we omit the word *students* we see that *we*, the subject form of the pronoun, is required: *We students must...*

271. A

The adverb *slowly* is required.

272. D

There are no mistakes.

273. D

There are no mistakes.

274. C

A noun in a direct address should be followed by a comma: *Jim, please set the table*.

275. C

The double negative is incorrect. The sentence should read: *I didn't see anything*.

276. C

Her is incorrect. The sentence should read: *Frank throws as well as she does*.

277. D

There are no mistakes.

278. A

A comma is needed between the clauses: *When she was finished, the crowd applauded.*

Spelling

279. B

The correct spelling is *receive*. The spelling rule is *i* before *e*, except after *c*.

280. C

Principle is incorrect. Remember, the princi*pal* is your *pal*.

281. D

There are no mistakes.

282. A

The correct spelling is *available*.

283. B

The correct spelling is *cooperate*.

284. B

The correct spelling is *mediocre*.

285. B

The correct spelling is *questionnaire*.

286. C

The correct spelling is *excellent*.

287. A

The correct spelling is *referred*.

288. A

The correct spelling is *audience*.

Composition

289. C

The connective must convey the idea of the blizzard being the reason we remained inside.

290. B

The subject *Bob* must follow the introductory phrase.

291. C

The infinitive *to practice* should not be split.

292. B

The sentence needs to imply that the musician is playing the violin. Therefore, choice (B) is correct.

293. D

Choices (A), (B), and (C) are incorrect because they imply that the hammock had been playing. (D) is the only choice that makes it clear that we were the ones who were playing, not the hammock.

294. A

Tough cowboys are roles in Wild West films. These are part of the American spirit.

295. B

The second clause offers the reason why she took the 7 A.M. bus.

296. A

The creation of the National Park system fits under the topic of protecting natural resources.

297. B

The second clause provides a contrasting statement.

298. A

The foreshadowing is based on the sense of doom that the sound of the foghorn invokes.

TACHS Practice Test
Answer Sheet

Remove or photocopy this answer sheet and use it to complete the Practice Test.

Reading Part 1

1. Ⓐ Ⓑ Ⓒ Ⓓ   5. Ⓐ Ⓑ Ⓒ Ⓓ   9. Ⓐ Ⓑ Ⓒ Ⓓ   13. Ⓐ Ⓑ Ⓒ Ⓓ   17. Ⓐ Ⓑ Ⓒ Ⓓ
2. Ⓙ Ⓚ Ⓛ Ⓜ   6. Ⓙ Ⓚ Ⓛ Ⓜ   10. Ⓙ Ⓚ Ⓛ Ⓜ   14. Ⓙ Ⓚ Ⓛ Ⓜ   18. Ⓙ Ⓚ Ⓛ Ⓜ
3. Ⓐ Ⓑ Ⓒ Ⓓ   7. Ⓐ Ⓑ Ⓒ Ⓓ   11. Ⓐ Ⓑ Ⓒ Ⓓ   15. Ⓐ Ⓑ Ⓒ Ⓓ   19. Ⓐ Ⓑ Ⓒ Ⓓ
4. Ⓙ Ⓚ Ⓛ Ⓜ   8. Ⓙ Ⓚ Ⓛ Ⓜ   12. Ⓙ Ⓚ Ⓛ Ⓜ   16. Ⓙ Ⓚ Ⓛ Ⓜ   20. Ⓙ Ⓚ Ⓛ Ⓜ

Reading Part 2

21. Ⓐ Ⓑ Ⓒ Ⓓ   27. Ⓐ Ⓑ Ⓒ Ⓓ   33. Ⓐ Ⓑ Ⓒ Ⓓ   39. Ⓐ Ⓑ Ⓒ Ⓓ   45. Ⓐ Ⓑ Ⓒ Ⓓ
22. Ⓙ Ⓚ Ⓛ Ⓜ   28. Ⓙ Ⓚ Ⓛ Ⓜ   34. Ⓙ Ⓚ Ⓛ Ⓜ   40. Ⓙ Ⓚ Ⓛ Ⓜ   46. Ⓙ Ⓚ Ⓛ Ⓜ
23. Ⓐ Ⓑ Ⓒ Ⓓ   29. Ⓐ Ⓑ Ⓒ Ⓓ   35. Ⓐ Ⓑ Ⓒ Ⓓ   41. Ⓐ Ⓑ Ⓒ Ⓓ   47. Ⓐ Ⓑ Ⓒ Ⓓ
24. Ⓙ Ⓚ Ⓛ Ⓜ   30. Ⓙ Ⓚ Ⓛ Ⓜ   36. Ⓙ Ⓚ Ⓛ Ⓜ   42. Ⓙ Ⓚ Ⓛ Ⓜ   48. Ⓙ Ⓚ Ⓛ Ⓜ
25. Ⓐ Ⓑ Ⓒ Ⓓ   31. Ⓐ Ⓑ Ⓒ Ⓓ   37. Ⓐ Ⓑ Ⓒ Ⓓ   43. Ⓐ Ⓑ Ⓒ Ⓓ   49. Ⓐ Ⓑ Ⓒ Ⓓ
26. Ⓙ Ⓚ Ⓛ Ⓜ   32. Ⓙ Ⓚ Ⓛ Ⓜ   38. Ⓙ Ⓚ Ⓛ Ⓜ   44. Ⓙ Ⓚ Ⓛ Ⓜ   50. Ⓙ Ⓚ Ⓛ Ⓜ

Language Part 1

1. Ⓐ Ⓑ Ⓒ Ⓓ   9. Ⓐ Ⓑ Ⓒ Ⓓ   17. Ⓐ Ⓑ Ⓒ Ⓓ   25. Ⓐ Ⓑ Ⓒ Ⓓ   33. Ⓐ Ⓑ Ⓒ Ⓓ
2. Ⓙ Ⓚ Ⓛ Ⓜ   10. Ⓙ Ⓚ Ⓛ Ⓜ   18. Ⓙ Ⓚ Ⓛ Ⓜ   26. Ⓙ Ⓚ Ⓛ Ⓜ   34. Ⓙ Ⓚ Ⓛ Ⓜ
3. Ⓐ Ⓑ Ⓒ Ⓓ   11. Ⓐ Ⓑ Ⓒ Ⓓ   19. Ⓐ Ⓑ Ⓒ Ⓓ   27. Ⓐ Ⓑ Ⓒ Ⓓ   35. Ⓐ Ⓑ Ⓒ Ⓓ
4. Ⓙ Ⓚ Ⓛ Ⓜ   12. Ⓙ Ⓚ Ⓛ Ⓜ   20. Ⓙ Ⓚ Ⓛ Ⓜ   28. Ⓙ Ⓚ Ⓛ Ⓜ   36. Ⓙ Ⓚ Ⓛ Ⓜ
5. Ⓐ Ⓑ Ⓒ Ⓓ   13. Ⓐ Ⓑ Ⓒ Ⓓ   21. Ⓐ Ⓑ Ⓒ Ⓓ   29. Ⓐ Ⓑ Ⓒ Ⓓ   37. Ⓐ Ⓑ Ⓒ Ⓓ
6. Ⓙ Ⓚ Ⓛ Ⓜ   14. Ⓙ Ⓚ Ⓛ Ⓜ   22. Ⓙ Ⓚ Ⓛ Ⓜ   30. Ⓙ Ⓚ Ⓛ Ⓜ   38. Ⓙ Ⓚ Ⓛ Ⓜ
7. Ⓐ Ⓑ Ⓒ Ⓓ   15. Ⓐ Ⓑ Ⓒ Ⓓ   23. Ⓐ Ⓑ Ⓒ Ⓓ   31. Ⓐ Ⓑ Ⓒ Ⓓ   39. Ⓐ Ⓑ Ⓒ Ⓓ
8. Ⓙ Ⓚ Ⓛ Ⓜ   16. Ⓙ Ⓚ Ⓛ Ⓜ   24. Ⓙ Ⓚ Ⓛ Ⓜ   32. Ⓙ Ⓚ Ⓛ Ⓜ   40. Ⓙ Ⓚ Ⓛ Ⓜ

Language Part 2

41. Ⓐ Ⓑ Ⓒ Ⓓ   43. Ⓐ Ⓑ Ⓒ Ⓓ   45. Ⓐ Ⓑ Ⓒ Ⓓ   47. Ⓐ Ⓑ Ⓒ Ⓓ   49. Ⓐ Ⓑ Ⓒ Ⓓ
42. Ⓙ Ⓚ Ⓛ Ⓜ   44. Ⓙ Ⓚ Ⓛ Ⓜ   46. Ⓙ Ⓚ Ⓛ Ⓜ   48. Ⓙ Ⓚ Ⓛ Ⓜ   50. Ⓙ Ⓚ Ⓛ Ⓜ

Math Part 1

1. Ⓐ Ⓑ Ⓒ Ⓓ   8. Ⓙ Ⓚ Ⓛ Ⓜ   15. Ⓐ Ⓑ Ⓒ Ⓓ   21. Ⓐ Ⓑ Ⓒ Ⓓ   27. Ⓐ Ⓑ Ⓒ Ⓓ
2. Ⓙ Ⓚ Ⓛ Ⓜ   9. Ⓐ Ⓑ Ⓒ Ⓓ   16. Ⓙ Ⓚ Ⓛ Ⓜ   22. Ⓙ Ⓚ Ⓛ Ⓜ   28. Ⓙ Ⓚ Ⓛ Ⓜ
3. Ⓐ Ⓑ Ⓒ Ⓓ   10. Ⓙ Ⓚ Ⓛ Ⓜ   17. Ⓐ Ⓑ Ⓒ Ⓓ   23. Ⓐ Ⓑ Ⓒ Ⓓ   29. Ⓐ Ⓑ Ⓒ Ⓓ
4. Ⓙ Ⓚ Ⓛ Ⓜ   11. Ⓐ Ⓑ Ⓒ Ⓓ   18. Ⓙ Ⓚ Ⓛ Ⓜ   24. Ⓙ Ⓚ Ⓛ Ⓜ   30. Ⓙ Ⓚ Ⓛ Ⓜ
5. Ⓐ Ⓑ Ⓒ Ⓓ   12. Ⓙ Ⓚ Ⓛ Ⓜ   19. Ⓐ Ⓑ Ⓒ Ⓓ   25. Ⓐ Ⓑ Ⓒ Ⓓ   31. Ⓐ Ⓑ Ⓒ Ⓓ
6. Ⓙ Ⓚ Ⓛ Ⓜ   13. Ⓐ Ⓑ Ⓒ Ⓓ   20. Ⓙ Ⓚ Ⓛ Ⓜ   26. Ⓙ Ⓚ Ⓛ Ⓜ   32. Ⓙ Ⓚ Ⓛ Ⓜ
7. Ⓐ Ⓑ Ⓒ Ⓓ   14. Ⓙ Ⓚ Ⓛ Ⓜ

Math Part 2

33. Ⓐ Ⓑ Ⓒ Ⓓ   37. Ⓐ Ⓑ Ⓒ Ⓓ   41. Ⓐ Ⓑ Ⓒ Ⓓ   45. Ⓐ Ⓑ Ⓒ Ⓓ   48. Ⓙ Ⓚ Ⓛ Ⓜ
34. Ⓙ Ⓚ Ⓛ Ⓜ   38. Ⓙ Ⓚ Ⓛ Ⓜ   42. Ⓙ Ⓚ Ⓛ Ⓜ   46. Ⓙ Ⓚ Ⓛ Ⓜ   49. Ⓐ Ⓑ Ⓒ Ⓓ
35. Ⓐ Ⓑ Ⓒ Ⓓ   39. Ⓐ Ⓑ Ⓒ Ⓓ   43. Ⓐ Ⓑ Ⓒ Ⓓ   47. Ⓐ Ⓑ Ⓒ Ⓓ   50. Ⓙ Ⓚ Ⓛ Ⓜ
36. Ⓙ Ⓚ Ⓛ Ⓜ   40. Ⓙ Ⓚ Ⓛ Ⓜ   44. Ⓙ Ⓚ Ⓛ Ⓜ

Ability Part 1

1. Ⓐ Ⓑ Ⓒ Ⓓ Ⓔ   11. Ⓐ Ⓑ Ⓒ Ⓓ Ⓔ   21. Ⓐ Ⓑ Ⓒ Ⓓ Ⓔ   31. Ⓐ Ⓑ Ⓒ Ⓓ Ⓔ
2. Ⓙ Ⓚ Ⓛ Ⓜ Ⓝ   12. Ⓙ Ⓚ Ⓛ Ⓜ Ⓝ   22. Ⓙ Ⓚ Ⓛ Ⓜ Ⓝ   32. Ⓙ Ⓚ Ⓛ Ⓜ Ⓝ
3. Ⓐ Ⓑ Ⓒ Ⓓ Ⓔ   13. Ⓐ Ⓑ Ⓒ Ⓓ Ⓔ   23. Ⓐ Ⓑ Ⓒ Ⓓ Ⓔ   33. Ⓐ Ⓑ Ⓒ Ⓓ Ⓔ
4. Ⓙ Ⓚ Ⓛ Ⓜ Ⓝ   14. Ⓙ Ⓚ Ⓛ Ⓜ Ⓝ   24. Ⓙ Ⓚ Ⓛ Ⓜ Ⓝ   34. Ⓙ Ⓚ Ⓛ Ⓜ Ⓝ
5. Ⓐ Ⓑ Ⓒ Ⓓ Ⓔ   15. Ⓐ Ⓑ Ⓒ Ⓓ Ⓔ   25. Ⓐ Ⓑ Ⓒ Ⓓ Ⓔ   35. Ⓐ Ⓑ Ⓒ Ⓓ Ⓔ
6. Ⓙ Ⓚ Ⓛ Ⓜ Ⓝ   16. Ⓙ Ⓚ Ⓛ Ⓜ Ⓝ   26. Ⓙ Ⓚ Ⓛ Ⓜ Ⓝ   36. Ⓙ Ⓚ Ⓛ Ⓜ Ⓝ
7. Ⓐ Ⓑ Ⓒ Ⓓ Ⓔ   17. Ⓐ Ⓑ Ⓒ Ⓓ Ⓔ   27. Ⓐ Ⓑ Ⓒ Ⓓ Ⓔ   37. Ⓐ Ⓑ Ⓒ Ⓓ Ⓔ
8. Ⓙ Ⓚ Ⓛ Ⓜ Ⓝ   18. Ⓙ Ⓚ Ⓛ Ⓜ Ⓝ   28. Ⓙ Ⓚ Ⓛ Ⓜ Ⓝ   38. Ⓙ Ⓚ Ⓛ Ⓜ Ⓝ
9. Ⓐ Ⓑ Ⓒ Ⓓ Ⓔ   19. Ⓐ Ⓑ Ⓒ Ⓓ Ⓔ   29. Ⓐ Ⓑ Ⓒ Ⓓ Ⓔ   39. Ⓐ Ⓑ Ⓒ Ⓓ Ⓔ
10. Ⓙ Ⓚ Ⓛ Ⓜ Ⓝ   20. Ⓙ Ⓚ Ⓛ Ⓜ Ⓝ   30. Ⓙ Ⓚ Ⓛ Ⓜ Ⓝ   40. Ⓙ Ⓚ Ⓛ Ⓜ Ⓝ

Ability Part 2

41. Ⓐ Ⓑ Ⓒ Ⓓ Ⓔ   44. Ⓙ Ⓚ Ⓛ Ⓜ Ⓝ   47. Ⓐ Ⓑ Ⓒ Ⓓ Ⓔ   49. Ⓐ Ⓑ Ⓒ Ⓓ Ⓔ
42. Ⓙ Ⓚ Ⓛ Ⓜ Ⓝ   45. Ⓐ Ⓑ Ⓒ Ⓓ Ⓔ   48. Ⓙ Ⓚ Ⓛ Ⓜ Ⓝ   50. Ⓙ Ⓚ Ⓛ Ⓜ Ⓝ
43. Ⓐ Ⓑ Ⓒ Ⓓ Ⓔ   46. Ⓙ Ⓚ Ⓛ Ⓜ Ⓝ

READING PART 1

10 minutes

Directions: This section is about the meaning of words. For each question, decide which choice has most nearly the same meaning as the underlined word or words given. Fill in the corresponding letter on your answer sheet.

1. A <u>sojourn</u>

   (A) sad story
   (B) temporary stay
   (C) tall building
   (D) steep mountain

2. A level <u>terrain</u>

   (J) locomotive
   (K) body of water
   (L) discovery
   (M) tract of land

3. A <u>savvy</u> shopper

   (A) bored
   (B) clueless
   (C) extravagant
   (D) knowledgeable

4. To <u>peruse</u> a book

   (J) write
   (K) buy
   (L) read
   (M) borrow

5. To walk <u>gingerly</u>

   (A) quickly
   (B) carefully
   (C) barefoot
   (D) recklessly

6. <u>Tactile</u> sensitivity

   (J) odor
   (K) touch
   (L) light
   (M) sound

7. <u>Ambiguous</u> directions

   (A) easy to follow
   (B) unclear
   (C) lengthy
   (D) concise

8. He acted <u>gamely</u>

   (J) bravely
   (K) athletic
   (L) angry
   (M) ghastly

9. A <u>vessel</u> is

   (A) a ship
   (B) a vase
   (C) an artery
   (D) all of the above

10. To give <u>solace</u>

    (J) advice
    (K) comfort
    (L) gifts
    (M) knowledge

11. Ocean <u>swells</u>

    (A) shore
    (B) waves
    (C) seaweed
    (D) shells

12. To suddenly <u>inundate</u>

    (J) overwhelm
    (K) flood
    (L) submerge
    (M) all of the above

13. A <u>musty</u> attic

    (A) cluttered
    (B) stale
    (C) cold
    (D) large

14. To speak with <u>candor</u>

    (J) honesty
    (K) a deep voice
    (L) deception
    (M) malice

15. A <u>profusion</u> of flowers

    (A) abundance
    (B) garden
    (C) painting
    (D) display

16. To feel <u>trepidation</u>

    (J) joy
    (K) fear
    (L) confidence
    (M) sorrow

17. A <u>luminous</u> moon

    (A) full
    (B) shining
    (C) new
    (D) eclipsed

18. To work <u>diligently</u>

    (J) carelessly
    (K) unwillingly
    (L) with effort
    (M) too quickly

19. To <u>whet</u> your appetite

    (A) stimulate
    (B) decrease
    (C) suppress
    (D) ignore

20. To <u>collate</u> papers

    (J) correct
    (K) copy
    (L) arrange in order
    (M) staple

READING PART 2

25 minutes

Directions: Read the passages below and the questions relating to them. Choose the best answer from among the four given for each question, and mark the corresponding space on your answer sheet.

Read the following passage and answer questions 21–25.

Penguins are relatively small aquatic birds with short legs. Although they have feathers and wings like other birds, penguins are unable to fly. Their wings are stiff fin-like flippers they use for swimming. While swimming, penguins use their feet and tails as rudders. When it comes to walking, penguins are all thumbs. Their short legs make it troublesome for them to walk. As a result, penguins prefer sliding down hills of snow on their stomachs to get around.

Penguins live together in large colonies called rookeries in the cold seas of the Southern Hemisphere. They are well adapted to this environment. They have three layers of short thick feathers and are insulated from freezing waters by a large layer of fat underneath their feathers. They molt their water repellant feathers in huge patches once a year and develop new feathers. Penguins remain at sea for weeks at a time hunting for food. The waters of the Southern Hemisphere provide the fish, squid, shrimp, and krill that comprise the two pounds of food penguins eat each day.

21. Penguins molt their feathers. This means they

   (A) wash them
   (B) shed them
   (C) ruffle them
   (D) dry them

22. Penguins are well adapted to their cold environment because

   (J) they cannot fly
   (K) they have an insulating layer of fat
   (L) they are aquatic birds
   (M) they have short legs

23. Penguins use their feet and tails as <u>rudders</u>. This would help them

   (A) dive
   (B) eat
   (C) steer
   (D) stop

24. What is a good topic sentence for this passage?

   (J) Penguins are fun to watch.
   (K) Penguins are intelligent birds.
   (L) Penguins are interesting birds.
   (M) Penguins live in the Southern Hemisphere.

25. What does the statement "penguins are all thumbs" mean in this passage?

   (A) Penguins use their thumbs to walk.
   (B) Penguins are not able to walk.
   (C) Penguins have a difficult time walking.
   (D) None of the above.

Read the following passage and answer questions 26–30.

Wetlands, known as swamps, marshes, and bogs, are areas covered by water at least part of the year. They're relatively common in tropical areas and are found on every continent except Antarctica. Wetlands are some of the most fertile and productive ecosystems on the planet. They are overflowing with plant, fish, insect, and animal life. Wetlands can be thought of as "biological supermarkets." They provide generous amounts of food that attract many animal species. In addition to food, many species of birds and mammals rely on wetlands for water and shelter. Wetlands control water cycles by absorbing floodwater. They filter pollution from the water that passes through them.

Previously, wetlands were erroneously considered wastelands and breeding grounds for pesky insects. Nearly all the wetlands in the United States were filled in or drained for building and farming. Today, however, we realize their importance. We know wetlands provide fish and wildlife habitats, store floodwaters, and help maintain surface water during dry periods. Destroying wetlands in the United States and some other parts of the world is now illegal.

26. Wetlands are important because they

    (J) control water cycles
    (K) store floodwaters
    (L) provide fish and wildlife habitats
    (M) all of the above

27. Wetlands control water cycles by

    (A) filtering polluted water
    (B) absorbing floodwater
    (C) maintaining surface water
    (D) providing habitats for fish

28. According to the passage, wetlands are "biological supermarkets" means

    (J) they provide scientists with many species to study
    (K) they have been filled in to build supermarkets
    (L) they provide generous amounts of food that attract many species
    (M) you can buy water and fish from wetland areas

29. The author would most likely support

    (A) more laws to protect wetlands
    (B) using wetlands to farm
    (C) filling in wetlands to provide land to build
    (D) the notion that wetlands are wastelands

30. Based on the passage, why do you think wetlands are not found in Antarctica?

    (J) Antarctica is surrounded by salt water.
    (K) There are no fish in Antarctica.
    (L) Antarctic temperatures are too cold.
    (M) There are no plants in Antarctica.

Read the following passage and answer questions 31–35.

When Franklin D. Roosevelt became president of the United States in 1932, his wife Eleanor became First Lady. Unlike previous First Ladies, Eleanor Roosevelt played a major, if unofficial, role in the president's administration. She was a visible, politically involved wife who shunned the accepted notion that the primary responsibility of a First Lady was to be a hostess at the White House. While traveling extensively and keeping informed of public sentiment, Eleanor served as the eyes and ears of the president. She provided the president with extremely useful firsthand information. She traveled to hospitals, slums, industrial plants, and coal mining towns to understand the American people. Upon her return from these travels, she urged her husband to alleviate the problems of the underprivileged. Eleanor is credited with many humanitarian projects that include nursery schools and slum clearance. She also found time to speak out for the rights of African-Americans and women during a time when few people cared about these issues. After her husband died, Eleanor continued her great humanitarian efforts with an appointment to the United Nations.

31. According to the passage, Eleanor Roosevelt was a great

    (A) speaker
    (B) hostess
    (C) politician
    (D) humanitarian

32. Eleanor being the "eyes and ears" of the president meant

    (J) the president had sight and hearing problems
    (K) the president did not want contact with people
    (L) the president relied on his wife to bring him firsthand information
    (M) the president was unable to travel

33. The passage mainly deals with

    (A) President Roosevelt's administration
    (B) Eleanor Roosevelt's many accomplishments
    (C) Eleanor Roosevelt's travels
    (D) Eleanor Roosevelt's job at the U.N.

34. After the death of her husband, Eleanor

    (J) continued public speaking
    (K) traveled across the country
    (L) continued her humanitarian efforts
    (M) became a recluse

35. When Eleanor shunned the accepted notion of a First Lady as hostess, she

    (A) enjoyed the notion
    (B) misunderstood the notion
    (C) avoided the notion
    (D) none of the above

Read the following passage and answer questions 36–40.

Computers are electronic machines for storing and retrieving information and performing calculations. One of the main reasons for using a computer is that it can perform certain functions faster than the human brain. Computers have revolutionized everyday life in the United States. The U.S. government uses computers to increase the efficiency of law enforcement and tax collections. Sophisticated military and space instruments depend on computerized speed and accuracy. In health and medicine, computers aid in diagnosis and regulate complex medical equipment. Communications equipment and automobiles depend on computer technology. However, technological improvements in business and industry have caused complications in the workplace. The use of automation and robotics in factories has reduced employment, especially in the automotive, steel, and mining industries. Constantly changing technology has also forced employers to modernize their facilities to keep up with foreign competition and increased the need for computer literacy among workers. Another negative consequence of the computer age is our loss of individual privacy. Computers have increased the capacity of government and others to obtain our personal information.

36. Which statement would a proponent of computers agree with?

   (J) Computers ensure that more workers must be computer literate.

   (K) Computers process information faster than the human brain.

   (L) Computers reduce unemployment.

   (M) Computers help to eliminate our individual privacy.

37. According to the passage, the use of automation has

   (A) increased profits for business

   (B) created new jobs for workers

   (C) increased unemployment

   (D) all of the above

38. Employers modernize their facilities to

   (J) increase their workforce

   (K) improve conditions for their workers

   (L) increase automation

   (M) keep up with foreign competition

39. One of the main reasons we should use a computer is that

   (A) it enables us to be computer literate

   (B) it can perform some functions faster than our brain

   (C) it can store our personal information

   (D) it can protect our individual privacy

40. The author's intent in writing this passage was

   (J) to extol the impact of computers

   (K) to negate the importance of computers

   (L) to explain the consequences of computer technology

   (M) to explain how computers make our lives easier

Read the following passage and answer questions 41–45.

Swedish inventor Alfred Nobel was born into a family that had gained wealth producing inventions that were useful to the art of making war. Carrying on the family tradition of perfecting explosives, Alfred Nobel executed dangerous experiments. In 1864, a tragic accident with unstable nitroglycerin destroyed the Nobel laboratory in Stockholm. As a result, several people, including Alfred's youngest brother, were killed. Nobel was deeply shocked but not deterred by this event. He continued his work on a floating barge in the middle of a lake. It was here that Nobel made one of his most important discoveries. In 1867, Nobel patented an invention that he named dynamite and it helped him accrue a massive fortune. While dynamite proved beneficial to industry, it was also capable of causing death and destruction. It is said that guilt over the suffering caused by his invention prompted Alfred to will much of his fortune to create the Nobel Prizes. These are awards given each year to those who benefit humanity and promote world peace.

41. The author wrote this passage to

   (A) entertain
   (B) persuade
   (C) inform
   (D) theorize

42. According to the passage, Nobel might have started the Nobel Prizes

   (J) to encourage inventors
   (K) to alleviate his conscience
   (L) to gain popularity
   (M) to promote his business

43. Nobel's 1864 experiment was inherently dangerous because

   (A) his laboratory was ill-equipped
   (B) it involved an unstable element
   (C) it killed his brother
   (D) it was performed on a floating barge

44. We learn from the passage that Nobel perfected explosives

   (J) to carry on the family tradition
   (K) to invent dynamite
   (L) to increase his fortune
   (M) to benefit humanity

45. Based on the passage, Nobel would want to be remembered for

   (A) his invention of dynamite
   (B) his wealth
   (C) his legacy of the Nobel Prizes
   (D) none of the above

Read the following passage and answer questions 46–50.

U.S. Food and Drug Administration fish sniffers have the sense to stop bad seafood. They guard America's coastal borders with their sense of smell. There are about two dozen or so FDA sensory specialists whose job it is to sniff out bad seafood before it reaches America's consumer market. They practice their craft from seven mega-labs scattered throughout the country. While sticking your nose into raw fish might not be appealing to most people, it is an important task that serves an important purpose. Sensory specialists attempt to detect spoiled, diseased, or tainted seafood before it can find its way to American dinner tables. In addition to smelling fish, the sensory inspectors also rely on their senses of touch, sight, and taste. They closely scrutinize types of seafood products that may be toxic to humans. These trained professionals can tell, through the nose and otherwise, if a certain piece of fish is fresh, questionable, or definitely spoiled and unsafe to eat. In addition to relying on experience, sensory specialists attend workshops to access their sensory abilities.

46. The author wrote this passage to

   (J) warn the reader
   (K) chastise the reader
   (L) explain how to do something
   (M) none of the above

47. To determine if seafood is bad, fish sniffers rely on

   (A) their olfactory sense
   (B) experience
   (C) their sense of taste
   (D) all of the above

48. In the passage, the word scrutinize means to

   (J) sniff
   (K) taste
   (L) question
   (M) examine

49. The main function of a sensory specialist is to

   (A) protect the fish industry in America
   (B) reassure Americans that fish is safe
   (C) keep their sensory abilities sharp
   (D) prevent tainted seafood from entering the consumer market

50. According to the passage, FDA sensory specialists guard

   (J) our fish consumption
   (K) our coastal borders
   (L) the fishing industry
   (M) mega-labs

LANGUAGE PART 1

23 minutes

Directions: This is a test of how well you can find errors in a piece of writing. The directions below tell what type of mistake may be present. If no mistake is made, choose the last answer.

Directions: Look for <u>punctuation</u> mistakes.

1. (A) The winter in upstate New York is
   (B) cold and snowy. However the summer
   (C) is warm and sunny.
   (D) *(No mistakes)*

2. (J) Everyone at school was happy
   (K) because the girls soccer team won
   (L) a championship game.
   (M) *(No mistakes)*

3. (A) Birds flock to the feeders in our yard
   (B) every winter. Is it because they know we
   (C) will always feed them.
   (D) *(No mistakes)*

4. (J) Its been an extremely busy week at work.
   (K) We are all looking forward to relaxing and
   (L) enjoying our days off this weekend.
   (M) *(No mistakes)*

5. (A) There are many activities that my
   (B) family enjoys doing together. We enjoy
   (C) biking camping, and exercising together.
   (D) *(No mistakes)*

6. (J) The union demonstrators demanded the
   (K) following-better working conditions, an
   (L) increase in salary, and better medical coverage.
   (M) *(No mistakes)*

7. (A) My neighbor's horse must be loose
   (B) again. I just heard my neighbor yelling,
   (C) Blondie, come back!
   (D) *(No mistakes)*

8. (J) Henry wanted to know why many
   (K) elementary schools don't have
   (L) language programs?
   (M) *(No mistakes)*

9. (A) Dr Martin Luther King, Jr., had a
   (B) mission to change the world through
   (C) nonviolent social action.
   (D) *(No mistakes)*

10. (J) Misty bolted away during a
    (K) thunderstorm and we searched everywhere
    (L) until we found her.
    (M) *(No mistakes)*

Directions: Look for mistakes in <u>spelling</u>.

11. (A) My neice Christine possesses many
    (B) wonderful qualities and is loved by
    (C) everyone who knows her.
    (D) *(No mistakes)*

12. (J) The class voted unanimously to
    (K) cancel the reciteal at school because
    (L) of the impending storm.
    (M) *(No mistakes)*

13. (A) To save additional animals from
    (B) dieing, we must all learn more about
    (C) endangered species.
    (D) *(No mistakes)*

14. (J)   The small child felt panicy when
    (K)   he looked around and realized he
    (L)   was hopelessly lost.
    (M)   *(No mistakes)*

15. (A)   Puppys need large amounts of
    (B)   love, attention, and training if they are
    (C)   to become good pets.
    (D)   *(No mistakes)*

16. (J)   Clara Barton, who founded the American
    (K)   Red Cross, is remembered for her careing
    (L)   ways and determination to help others.
    (M)   *(No mistakes)*

17. (A)   The couragous actions of the
    (B)   firemen saved the frightened residents
    (C)   and their home.
    (D)   *(No mistakes)*

18. (J)   Although Jamie was hungry, he decided
    (K)   that niether of his choices for lunch would
    (L)   satisfy him.
    (M)   *(No mistakes)*

19. (A)   The local shelter recently asked for
    (B)   additional donations because they had not
    (C)   recieved many items they needed.
    (D)   *(No mistakes)*

20. (J)   Wild turkies seem to know when
    (K)   Thanksgiving is approaching, and
    (L)   they disappear deep into the woods.
    (M)   *(No mistakes)*

Directions: Look for capitalization mistakes.

21. (A)   Audubon's collection of American bird
    (B)   drawings was compiled into his book called
    (C)   *The birds of America.*
    (D)   *(No mistakes)*

22. (J)   George Washington cried, "what brave
    (K)   fellows I must this day lose!" when he
    (L)   realized his troops were outnumbered.
    (M)   *(No mistakes)*

23. (A)   As temperatures begin to plummet
    (B)   in November, we know that Winter
    (C)   is upon us.
    (D)   *(No mistakes)*

24. (J)   In 1950, Mother Teresa founded a group,
    (K)   The Missionaries of charity, to help
    (L)   her work with the poor people of India.
    (M)   *(No mistakes)*

25. (A)   Mother was smiling because
    (B)   dad and I finished reading a series
    (C)   of books together.
    (D)   *(No mistakes)*

26. (J)   Mount McKinley, the highest peak
    (K)   in the United States, is located in Mount
    (L)   McKinley national park in Alaska.
    (M)   *(No mistakes)*

27. (A)   In honor of arbor day, our town
    (B)   planted ten trees to beautify and
    (C)   protect our local environment.
    (D)   *(No mistakes)*

28. (J)   In 1886, the unveiling of the
    (K)   Statue of Liberty was accompanied by
    (L)   a parade that started on fifth avenue.
    (M)   *(No mistakes)*

29. (A)   John D. Rockefeller, jr., was
    (B)   particularly well known for buying land
    (C)   to build national parks.
    (D)   *(No mistakes)*

30. (J)   although he is most remembered for
    (K)   the invention of the lightbulb, Thomas
    (L)   Edison patented more than 1,093 inventions.
    (M)   *(No mistakes)*

Directions: Look for <u>usage</u> mistakes.

31. (A) Diversity of trees, shrubs,
    (B) and other plants offer good
    (C) habitation for birds.
    (D) *(No mistakes)*

32. (J) The judges of the local pet
    (K) competition had to choose between
    (L) the remaining four cats.
    (M) *(No mistakes)*

33. (A) The new gardening catalog
    (B) we received offers alot of new
    (C) plant and vegetable varieties.
    (D) *(No mistakes)*

34. (J) Dedicated athletes must practice
    (K) most every day to keep themselves
    (L) physically fit.
    (M) *(No mistakes)*

35. (A) We stopped to ask for directions
    (B) because we did not know where
    (C) the Grand Canyon was.
    (D) *(No mistakes)*

36. (J) Because the annual average rainfall
    (K) is about 80 inches in Ireland, it is wise
    (L) to carry a umbrella when visiting there.
    (M) *(No mistakes)*

37. (A) If you travel further inland from the
    (B) coast of Antarctica, you will find only tiny
    (C) creatures such as fleas and mites.
    (D) *(No mistakes)*

38. (J) We were definitely prepared for
    (K) our rainy camping trip because we
    (L) bought rain gear with us.
    (M) *(No mistakes)*

39. (A) I drank a gallon of water
    (B) almost after the marathon race
    (C) because I was so thirsty.
    (D) *(No mistakes)*

40. (J) Everyone expressed they're differing
    (K) opinions in a very friendly manner
    (L) at the town meeting.
    (M) *(No mistakes)*

LANGUAGE PART 2

7 minutes

Directions: For questions 41–42, choose the best answer based on the following paragraph:

[1]North America is the third largest of Earth's seven continents. [2]The different people of North America almost represent every country, race, and culture in the world. [3]This massive continent also has many different climates and weather conditions. [4]Northern areas of the continent tend to be colder because they receive less direct sunlight. [5]The southern parts of the continent are located near the equator and have a tropical climate. [6]From the tropics to the Arctic Circle, each part of North America also has its own unique variety of animals. [7]Walruses, seals, and polar bears

are found in the far north while monkeys and parrots live in the tropical areas of Central America. [8]Its variety of human races, climates, and animals make North America one of the most exciting and diverse places in the world.

41. Where should the word "almost" be placed in sentence 2?

    (A) after represent

    (B) before different

    (C) after culture

    (D) no change

42. Which word is not correct in sentence 8?

    (J) Its

    (K) most

    (L) make

    (M) one

Directions: For questions 43–44, choose the best answer based on the following paragraph:

[1]Creating a friendly environment for birds is not very difficult. [2]With a few alterations, your backyard can become a bird sanctuary for all your feathered friends. [3]A garden, filled with a mixture of plants that birds like to eat, was a necessity. [4]This mixture should include plants that produce flowers, seeds, and berries. [5]Birds also need plants that provide shelter. [6]They need a safe haven from predators and harsh weather. [7]You should also provide a source of water for birds to bathe in and drink. [8]As you may see, there are many ways to provide a friendly environment for birds.

43. In sentence 3, which word is in the wrong tense?

    (A) filled

    (B) like

    (C) eat

    (D) was

44. Which word in sentence 8 should be replaced?

    (J) may

    (K) there

    (L) are

    (M) no change

Directions: For questions 45–47, choose the best answer based on the following paragraph:

[1]Games have been played for centuries all over the world. [2]Each country has their own traditional games that have been passed from generation to generation. [3]A game played in remote areas of the world can be very similar to one found in developed cities. [4]The need for people to entertain themselves is the principle reason for the invention of games. [5]For outdoor recreation, people enjoy physical activities that include challenges and competition. [6]Indoor games such as cards, board games, and computer games are also very popular. [7]Although the types of games can be different from county to country. [8]People all over the world share the same desire to have fun.

45. Sentence 2 has

   (A) a verb not in agreement with its subject
   (B) a pronoun not in agreement with the noun it refers to
   (C) a verb in the wrong tense
   (D) an incomplete sentence

46. In sentence 4, which word is used incorrectly?

   (J) principle
   (K) themselves
   (L) invention
   (M) to

47. Sentence 7 in this paragraph

   (A) is a run-on sentence
   (B) has a misspelled word
   (C) is an incomplete sentence
   (D) needs no correction

Directions: For questions 48–50, choose the best answer based on the following paragraph:

[1]Rain forests account for only too percent of the earth's surface, but they are vital habitats.[2]Located around the equator, their climate is hot and wet year-round. [3]The combination of high humidity and heavy rainfall produces abundant plant and animal life. [4]The rain forest provides food, fine woods, minerals, and medicine. [5]However, these treasures of the rain forest are disappearing quickly. [6]Each day, large numbers of rain forest acres are being destroyed by farms, gold mines, roads, and greed. [7]Today, we must carefully nurtured the rain forest if we expect to utilize its resources in the future.

48. Which word in sentence 1 is incorrect?

   (A) for
   (B) only
   (C) too
   (D) earth's

49. What is the adverb in sentence 5?

   (J) quickly
   (K) these
   (L) of
   (M) are

50. In sentence 7, which word is in the wrong tense?

   (A) find
   (B) nurtured
   (C) while
   (D) using

MATH PART 1

33 minutes

Directions: Choose the best answer from the four given for each problem.

1. 1.90 written as a fraction is _____?

   (A) $1\frac{9}{100}$

   (B) $\frac{1}{90}$

   (C) $1\frac{1}{10}$

   (D) $1\frac{9}{10}$

2. Based on the table, how many more ships did England have than Portugal from 1600–1700?

   Number of Ships Sailing to Asia
   from European Countries, 1500–1800

	1500–99	1600–1700	1701–1800
Portugal	706	371	196
Netherlands	65	1,770	2,950
England	—	811	1,865
France	—	155	1,300

   (J) 440 ships
   (K) 1,399 ships
   (L) 1,669 ships
   (M) Cannot be determined.

3. $\frac{5}{6} \div \frac{11}{12}$ is equal to _____?

   (A) $\frac{10}{11}$

   (B) $\frac{1}{12}$

   (C) $\frac{21}{12}$

   (D) $\frac{55}{72}$

4. Which of the following is <u>not</u> a prime number?

   (J) 29
   (K) 43
   (L) 57
   (M) 71

5. The least common denominator of $\frac{1}{5}$, $\frac{5}{6}$, and $\frac{1}{3}$ is _____?

   (A) 6
   (B) 12
   (C) 30
   (D) 60

6. Amanda uses three rolls of yarn to make one scarf. If she already has four rolls, how many more rolls must she buy in order to make a total of three scarves?

   (J) 3
   (K) 4
   (L) 5
   (M) 9

7. Based on the following chart, how much less revenue does worker B earn than worker D?

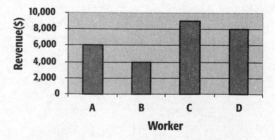

   Revenue per Worker

   (A) $1,000
   (B) $2,000
   (C) $3,000
   (D) $4,000

8. A bookstore just received a shipment of 126 new books that need to be displayed. If each shelf holds 9 books, how many shelves are needed in order to display all of the books?

   (J) 9 shelves
   (K) 14 shelves
   (L) 16 shelves
   (M) 32 shelves

9. $13^2 =$

   (A) 26
   (B) 52
   (C) 166
   (D) 169

10. Mary works at a fruit smoothie stand. How much will it cost for a large peach smoothie with calcium and protein supplements?

Smoothie Flavors	Small	Large	Each Supplement $0.55 Extra
Strawberry-Banana	2.65	3.75	Calcium
Peach	2.85	3.95	Protein
Blueberry	2.75	3.85	Vitamin C

   (J) $3.95
   (K) $4.50
   (L) $4.85
   (M) $5.05

11. What is the greatest common factor of 18 and 24?

   (A) 3
   (B) 6
   (C) 8
   (D) 24

12. What is the decimal equivalent of $\frac{5}{8}$?

   (J) 0.58
   (K) 0.6
   (L) 0.625
   (M) 1.6

13. Three different homeroom classes (A, B, and C) kept track of the total amount of outside reading books the students in each class completed each month. What is the only month in which Class B read more books than Class A?

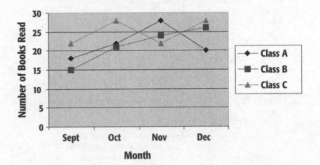

   (A) September
   (B) October
   (C) November
   (D) December

14. 15% =

   (J) $\frac{3}{20}$

   (K) $\frac{3}{5}$

   (L) $\frac{7}{20}$

   (M) $\frac{1}{5}$

15. Anna earns $40 for babysitting one night. If $5 of her total is tip, how much did Anna earn per hour if she worked 5 hours?

   (A) $6
   (B) $7
   (C) $8
   (D) $9

16. Brian decided to give his younger brother 30% of his allowance this week for helping him with his chores. If Brian ends up giving his brother $5.55, how much was his allowance for the week?

    (J) $7.22
    (K) $16.65
    (L) $18.50
    (M) $25.55

17. Mike, Maria, A.J., and Clare divided up their assigned project according to the chart. What fraction of the total project were Maria and A.J. responsible for?

	Portion of Assignment
Mike	0.10
Maria	0.25
A.J.	0.05
Clare	0.60

    (A) $\frac{1}{4}$

    (B) $\frac{7}{20}$

    (C) $\frac{3}{10}$

    (D) $\frac{3}{4}$

18. $1 - (-4) =$

    (J) −5
    (K) 5
    (L) −3
    (M) 3

19. Michael wants to bike over to his friend's house. He decides to take a shortcut through the park, which is 346 yards less than if he did not take the shortcut. If the distance from his house to his friend's house is 1,120 yards using the shortcut, what is the distance without using the shortcut?

    (A) 774 yards
    (B) 1,466 yards
    (C) 1,812 yards
    (D) 2,586 yards

20. The following table shows the scores of 40 students on a science test. Which is a correct histogram of the data?

Scores	Number of Students
51–60	2
61–70	5
71–80	12
81–90	15
91–100	6

(J)

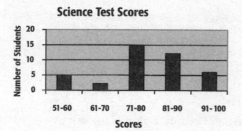

(K)

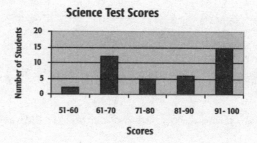

(L)

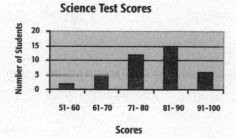

(M)

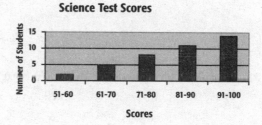

21. 0.000045 written in scientific notation is _____?

(A) 4.5×10^{-5}

(B) 4.5×10^{5}

(C) 45×10^{-6}

(D) 4.5×10^{-4}

22. Alexandra bought two books at the bookstore. One book cost $8.95 and the other was unmarked. If the total price came to $22.45, how much did the second book cost? (Assume there is no sales tax.)

(J) $13.50

(K) $14.40

(L) $14.50

(M) $31.40

23. For his science project, Chip decided to test how well plants grew with fertilizer. He started off by planting seeds in three different pots and labeling each of the plants. Plant A had no fertilizer. Plant B had the recommended amount of fertilizer. Plant C had four times the recommended amount of fertilizer. For ten consecutive days he measured the height of each plant in centimeters. The following table shows his results. Which plant grew the most from Day 7 to Day 9?

Day	1	2	3	4	5	6	7	8	9	10
Plant A (height in cm)	0	1	2	2	3	4	7	9	12	14
Plant B (height in cm)	0	1	2	4	7	10	12	14	15	16
Plant C (height in cm)	0	0	1	1	2	3	4	4	5	5

(A) Plant A
(B) Plant B
(C) Plant C
(D) Cannot be determined from this data.

24. Jaime always puts $\frac{3}{4}$ of her weekly allowance into her savings account and uses the rest as her spending money. If she earned $18 this week for her allowance, how much money will be for spending?

(J) $4.50
(K) $6.00
(L) $3.00
(M) $13.50

25. The stacked bar graph shows the percentage of people in each age group for five different countries. What two countries have the smallest percentage of their population in the 65+ age group? (*Source: CIA World Factbook, 2004*)

Age Stucture of Various Countries

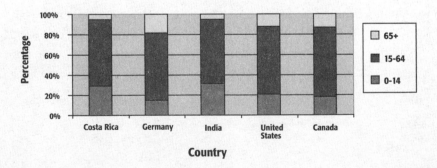

(A) Germany and Canada
(B) Costa Rica and India
(C) United States and Canada
(D) Costa Rica and United States

26. Joe works at a store which is currently having a sale where every frame is 30% off. A customer wants to purchase a frame that was originally priced at $24.90. How much is the new sale price?

    (J) $7.47
    (K) $8.30
    (L) $16.60
    (M) $17.43

27. The graph below shows oil production and oil consumption for five different countries. Which two countries consume more than they produce? *(Source: CIA World Factbook, 2004)*

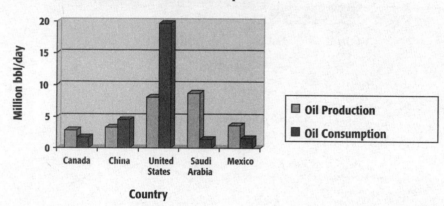

Oil Production and Consumption

    (A) China and United States
    (B) Canada and China
    (C) United States and Saudi Arabia
    (D) Mexico and Canada

28. If peaches are on sale for $1.25 per pound, how much will 2.4 pounds cost?

    (J) $2.00
    (K) $2.40
    (L) $3.00
    (M) $3.25

29. Jordan wanted to keep track of how many points he scored during his final basketball game of the season. After each quarter, he recorded how many points he had earned. How many more points did Jordan earn in the second quarter than in the first and third quarters combined?

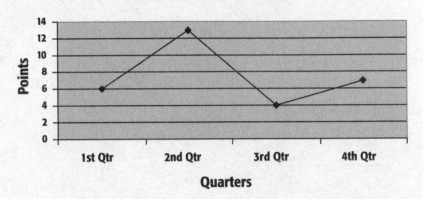

Jordan's Basketball Score

(A) 7
(B) 9
(C) 2
(D) 3

30. Based on the following table, what is the total percentage of young children and adults who are allergic to peanuts?

Prevalence of Food Allergies in the United States

Food	Young Children	Adults
Milk	2.5%	0.3%
Egg	1.3%	0.2%
Peanut	0.8%	0.6%
Tree nuts	0.2%	0.5%
Fish	0.1%	0.4%
Shellfish	0.1%	2.0%
Overall	6%	3.7%

(J) 0.8%
(K) 0.6%
(L) 1.4%
(M) 9.7%

31. Based on the following chart of exchange rates, if Tony had one unit of currency from each country, which is worth the most in U.S. dollars?

Currency	The foreign value equivalent of $1
Australia	1.2842
Britain	0.5416
India	45.420
Euro	0.7840

(A) Australia

(B) Britain

(C) India

(D) Euro

32. Martin decided to study for his math test by doing practice problems. If each problem takes him the same amount of time, and he finished 105 problems between the hours of 2 P.M. and 5 P.M., how many problems did he finish per hour?

(J) 35

(K) 21

(L) 52.5

(M) 33

MATH PART 2

7 minutes

Directions: For questions 33–50, estimate the answer; no scratch work is allowed. Do not try to calculate exact answers.

33. The closest estimate of 661 + 382 is _____ .

(A) 800

(B) 900

(C) 1,100

(D) 1,300

34. The closest estimate of 539 ÷ 6 is _____ .

(J) 9

(K) 90

(L) 900

(M) 9,000

35. The closest estimate of 25,840 – 16,109 is _____ .

(A) 900

(B) 9,000

(C) 1,000

(D) 10,000

36. The closest estimate of 6.44 × 11.38 is _____ .

(J) 66

(K) 72

(L) 77

(M) 84

37. The number 8.542 rounded to the nearest tenths place is _____ .

(A) 8.0

(B) 8.5

(C) 8.54

(D) 9.0

38. The closest estimate of $20.00 – $13.28 is _____ .

(J) $7.00

(K) $6.00

(L) $5.00

(M) $4.00

39. The closest estimate of 23 + 25 + 32 is _____ .

(A) 60

(B) 70

(C) 80

(D) 90

40. The closest estimate of 99 × 72 is _____.

    (J) 70
    (K) 700
    (L) 7,000
    (M) 70,000

41. The number 612.786 rounded to the nearest
    hundredths place is _____.

    (A) 600.000
    (B) 613.000
    (C) 612.800
    (D) 612.790

42. The closest estimate of 7,372 − 2,938 is _____.

    (J) 2,000
    (K) 3,000
    (L) 4,000
    (M) 5,000

43. Rounding to the nearest dollar, the closest
    estimate of $3.75 + $4.50 + $1.75 is _____.

    (A) $8.00
    (B) $9.00
    (C) $10.00
    (D) $11.00

44. The number 5,609 rounded to the nearest
    hundreds place is _____.

    (J) 6,000
    (K) 5,600
    (L) 5,700
    (M) 5,610

45. The closest estimate of 23,522 ÷ 3 is _____.

    (A) 8
    (B) 80
    (C) 800
    (D) 8,000

46. The closest estimate of 15.87 − 5.38 is _____.

    (J) 9
    (K) 10
    (L) 11
    (M) 12

47. The closest estimate of 523 × 563 is _____.

    (A) 25,000
    (B) 30,000
    (C) 250,000
    (D) 300,000

48. Round 25.006 to the nearest tenths place.

    (J) 30.000
    (K) 25.000
    (L) 25.100
    (M) 25.010

49. The cost of Maggie's book with tax is $8.72. If
    she gives the cashier a 20 dollar bill, what is the
    closest estimate of the amount of change that she
    should receive?

    (A) $11.00
    (B) $12.00
    (C) $13.00
    (D) $14.00

50. The closest estimate of (289 + 850) ÷ 40 is _____.

    (J) 25
    (K) 30
    (L) 250
    (M) 300

ABILITY PART 1

25 minutes

Directions: For each question, the three figures in the question are alike in some way. Select the answer choice that shares that similarity.

| | (A) | (B) | (C) | (D) | (E) |

1.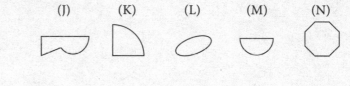

| | (J) | (K) | (L) | (M) | (N) |

2.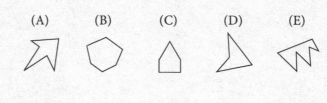

| | (A) | (B) | (C) | (D) | (E) |

3.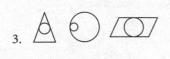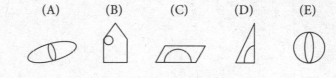

| | (J) | (K) | (L) | (M) | (N) |

4.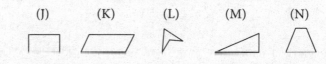

| | (A) | (B) | (C) | (D) | (E) |

5.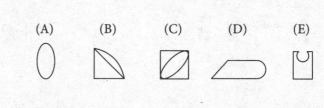

| | (J) | (K) | (L) | (M) | (N) |

6.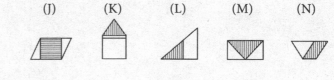

7.
(A) (B) (C) (D) (E)

8.
(J) (K) (L) (M) (N)

9.
(A) (B) (C) (D) (E)

10.
(J) (K) (L) (M) (N)

11.
(A) (B) (C) (D) (E)

12.
(J) (K) (L) (M) (N)

13.
(A) (B) (C) (D) (E)

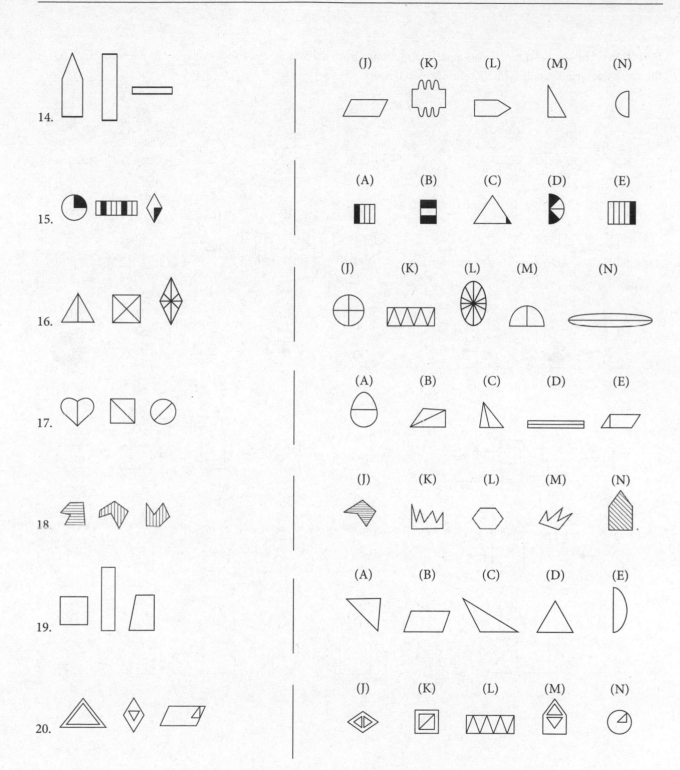

14.

(J)   (K)   (L)   (M)   (N)

15.

(A)   (B)   (C)   (D)   (E)

16.

(J)   (K)   (L)   (M)   (N)

17.

(A)   (B)   (C)   (D)   (E)

18.

(J)   (K)   (L)   (M)   (N)

19.

(A)   (B)   (C)   (D)   (E)

20.

(J)   (K)   (L)   (M)   (N)

Directions: The second figure shows a particular change from the first figure. The third figure, if changed in the same way, will become which of the answer choices?

| | (A) | (B) | (C) | (D) | (E) |

21. 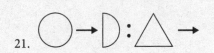   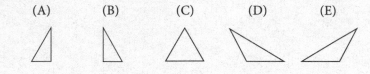

| | (J) | (K) | (L) | (M) | (N) |

22. 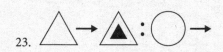   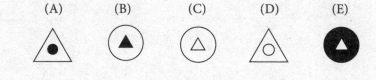

| | (A) | (B) | (C) | (D) | (E) |

23.    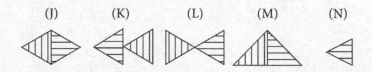

| | (J) | (K) | (L) | (M) | (N) |

24. 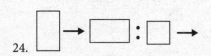   

| | (A) | (B) | (C) | (D) | (E) |

25. 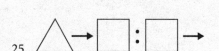

| | (J) | (K) | (L) | (M) | (N) |

26. 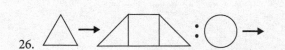 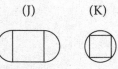

27.

(A) (B) (C) (D) (E)

28.

(J) (K) (L) (M) (N)

29.

(A) (B) (C) (D) (E)

30.

(J) (K) (L) (M) (N)

31.

(A) (B) (C) (D) (E)

32.

(J) (K) (L) (M) (N)

33.

(A) (B) (C) (D) (E)

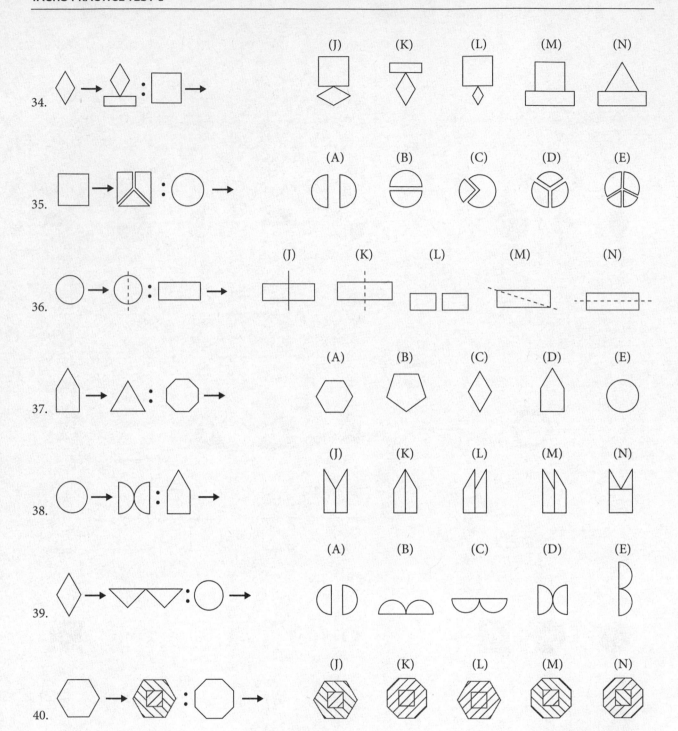

ABILITY PART 2
7 minutes

Directions: The second figure shows a particular change from the first figure. Which answer choice shows the figure that would result if the same change is made to the third figure?

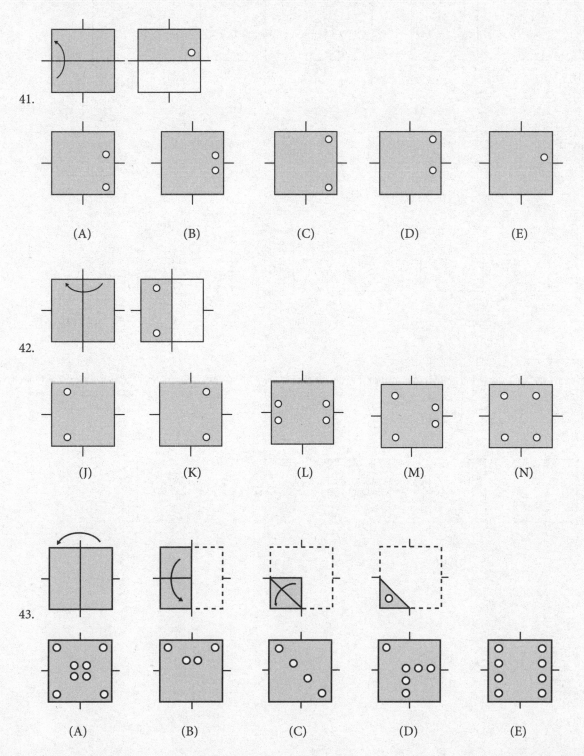

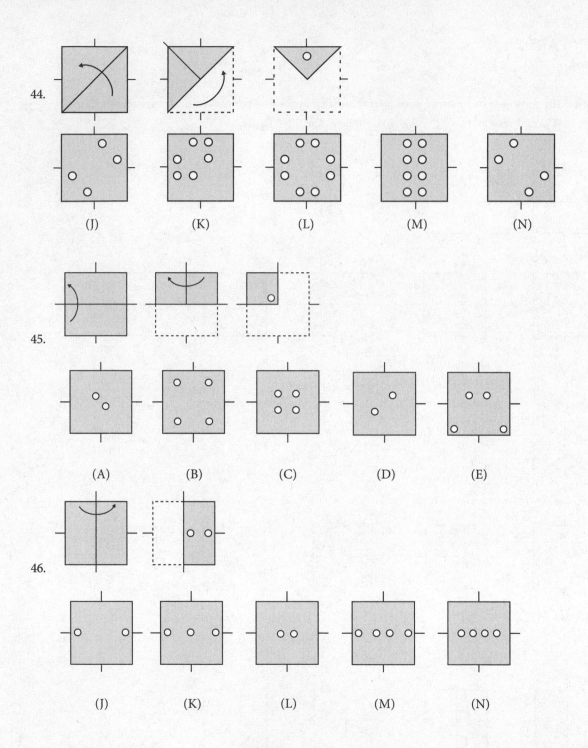

44.

(J)   (K)   (L)   (M)   (N)

45.

(A)   (B)   (C)   (D)   (E)

46.

(J)   (K)   (L)   (M)   (N)

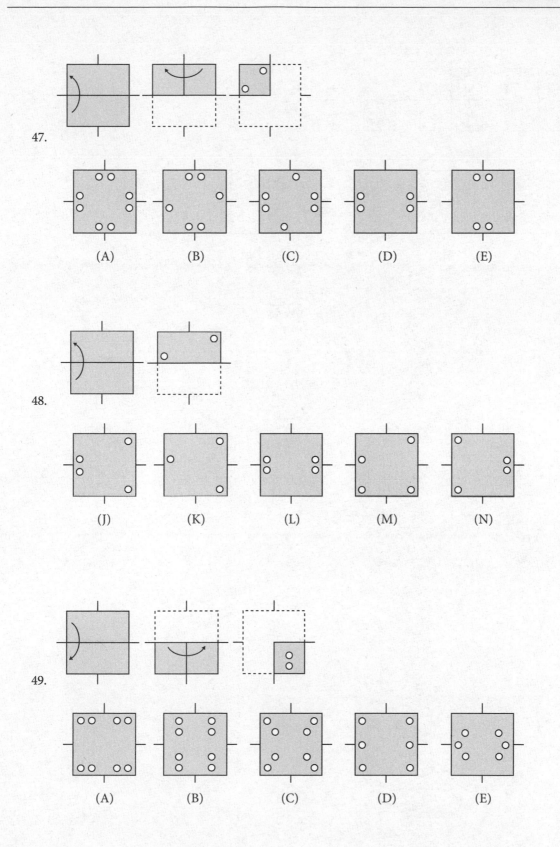

47.

(A)   (B)   (C)   (D)   (E)

48.

(J)   (K)   (L)   (M)   (N)

49.

(A)   (B)   (C)   (D)   (E)

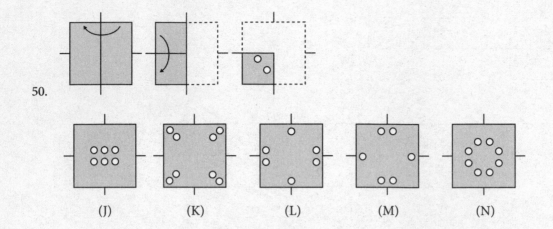

50.

ANSWERS AND EXPLANATIONS

Answer Key

READING

Part 1

1. B
2. M
3. D
4. L
5. B
6. K
7. B
8. J
9. D
10. K
11. B
12. M
13. B
14. J
15. A
16. K
17. B
18. L
19. A
20. L

Part 2

21. B
22. K
23. C
24. L
25. C
26. M
27. B
28. L
29. A
30. L
31. D
32. L
33. B
34. L
35. C
36. K
37. C
38. M
39. B
40. L
41. C
42. K
43. B
44. J
45. C
46. M
47. D
48. M
49. D
50. K

LANGUAGE

Part 1

Punctuation

1. B
2. K
3. C
4. J
5. C
6. K
7. C
8. L
9. A
10. K

Spelling

11. A
12. K
13. B
14. J
15. A
16. K

17. A
18. K
19. C
20. J

Capitalization

21. C
22. J
23. B
24. K
25. B
26. L
27. A
28. L
29. A
30. J

Usage

31. B
32. K
33. B
34. K
35. C
36. L
37. A
38. L
39. B
40. J

Part 2

41. A
42. L
43. D
44. J
45. B
46. J
47. C
48. C

49. **J**
50. **B**

MATH

Part 1
1. **D**
2. **J**
3. **A**
4. **L**
5. **C**
6. **L**
7. **D**
8. **K**
9. **D**
10. **M**
11. **B**
12. **L**
13. **D**
14. **J**
15. **B**
16. **L**
17. **C**
18. **K**
19. **B**
20. **L**
21. **A**
22. **J**
23. **A**
24. **J**
25. **B**
26. **M**
27. **A**
28. **L**
29. **D**
30. **L**
31. **B**
32. **J**

Part 2
33. **C**
34. **K**
35. **D**
36. **J**
37. **B**
38. **J**
39. **C**
40. **L**
41. **D**
42. **L**
43. **D**
44. **K**
45. **D**
46. **L**
47. **D**
48. **K**
49. **A**
50. **K**

ABILITY

Part 1
1. **C**
2. **N**
3. **B**
4. **J**
5. **D**
6. **L**
7. **E**
8. **K**
9. **D**
10. **K**
11. **C**
12. **J**
13. **E**
14. **K**
15. **A**
16. **K**

17. **D**
18. **L**
19. **A**
20. **N**
21. **B**
22. **L**
23. **B**
24. **N**
25. **D**
26. **J**
27. **E**
28. **M**
29. **B**
30. **K**
31. **A**
32. **N**
33. **C**
34. **M**
35. **D**
36. **K**
37. **A**
38. **J**
39. **C**
40. **M**

Part 2
41. **B**
42. **N**
43. **A**
44. **J**
45. **C**
46. **M**
47. **A**
48. **J**
49. **B**
50. **N**

Reading

Part 1

1. B

The answer must contain the word *temporary*. A sojourn is a temporary stay and is sometimes used to describe a short trip. Tall buildings (C), steep mountains (D), and a sad story (A) do not reflect the meaning of sojourn.

2. M

The root *terra* always refers to land. This eliminates *body of water* (K) and *discovery* (L). If the word *terrain* is read incorrectly as *train*, *locomotive* (J) might be chosen.

3. D

Savvy means to understand or have knowledge of. *Clueless* (B) is opposite in meaning. *Extravagant* (C) means wasteful, and a savvy shopper would not waste money or be bored (A).

4. L

The answer must contain the words *read* or *examine*. If you misread *peruse* as *purchase*, then *buy* (K) might be chosen. *Write* (J) and *borrow* (M) should be easily eliminated as choices.

5. B

The word *gingerly* means cautiously or carefully. *Recklessly* (D) would be the opposite. If you are walking quickly (A) or barefoot (C), you would not be walking cautiously or carefully.

6. K

Tactile refers to the sense of touch. An odor (J) relates to the sense of smell. A person could have sensitivity to light (L), sound (M), or odor and this could be misleading if you do not know that *tactile* pertains only to touch.

7. B

Ambiguous means unclear in meaning or confusing, so this would eliminate (A). Directions may be concise (D), meaning brief and compact, but this is an opposite meaning. Directions may be lengthy, but that doesn't capture the negative meaning.

8. J

Gamely means bravely or with spirit. This eliminates *angry* (L) and *ghastly* (M), which means horrible. If you don't know the meaning of *gamely*, you may choose *athletic* because athletes play games, but this is incorrect.

9. D

A vessel can be a ship (A) for traveling on water, a vase (B) or hollow object to hold water, or an artery (C) or vein to carry fluid in the body (you've heard of "blood vessels"). So all of the above (D) is the correct answer.

10. K

Solace is comfort or consolation. You can give advice (J), gifts (L), or knowledge (M) to someone, but comfort is the only choice for solace.

11. B

Ocean swells are long waves that move without breaking. *Shore* (A), *seaweed* (C), and *shells* (D) all have to do with the ocean, but only waves are referred to as swells. Since *swell* means to grow in size, waves would be a good choice by process of elimination.

12. M

Inundate means to overwhelm (J), flood (K), and submerge (L), so (M) is the correct answer. It is used frequently when referring to water flooding, submerging, or overwhelming an area. All the choices are rather similar in meaning, so this is a clue that they are all correct.

13. B

Musty means having a stale or moldy odor. Attics can be the other choices, but *musty* is not another word for cluttered (A), cold (C), or large (D).

14. J

Candor is sincerity or honesty. *Deception* (L) would be the opposite in meaning. *Malice* (M) is a desire to harm so this is incorrect. *A deep voice* (K) should be easily eliminated.

15. A

Profusion means abundance or a great quantity of. *Garden* (B) may seem like a good choice because a garden contains flowers. *Painting* (C) and *display* (D) are also words that are associated with flowers, so this may be confusing if you do not know the actual meaning of profusion.

16. K

Trepidation is defined as fear, alarm, or nervous apprehension. *Confidence* (L) would be the opposite in meaning. *Joy* (J) and *sorrow* (M) are opposites of each other and emotions we can feel, but they do not describe trepidation.

17. B

Luminous means shining or full of light. The other choices all describe phases of the moon. Only *shining* (B) describes luminous.

18. L

If you work diligently, you work with effort and persistence. *Carelessly* (J), *unwillingly* (K), and *too quickly* (M) are all similar in that they would not describe good work habits. *With effort* (L) is different from the other choices and is the correct one.

19. A

Whet means to stimulate or sharpen. *Decrease* (B), *suppress* (C), and *ignore* (D) are similar words, as they would all have a negative effect on appetite. *Stimulate* is the word that has a totally different

meaning from the other choices, and this is a hint that it is the correct one.

20. L

Collate means to arrange in numerical order, so (L) is the best choice. *Copy* (K), *correct* (J), and *staple* (M) are all things you can do with papers, so you need to know that collate has to do with numerical order.

Part 2

21. B

The definition of *molt* is "to cast or shed the feathers, skin, or the like," so *shed* is the best answer. A and D are not good choices because the passage states that a penguin's feathers are waterproof so they should not need to wash and dry them. Choice C is also not correct. When a bird ruffles his feathers, it means he erects them in anger.

22. K

Penguins are well adapted to a cold environment because they have a layer of fat under their feathers that insulates them, as described in the second paragraph. This would help to keep them warm. The facts that they cannot fly (choice J) and have short legs (choice M) have no bearing on their ability to live in a cold environment. Being an aquatic bird (choice L) means that penguins spend time in water but does not necessarily mean cold water.

23. C

A rudder is the part of a ship or airplane that allows them to be steered. It follows that penguins would use their feet and tails to steer if they used them as rudders. The other choices of *dive* (choice A), *eat* (choice B), or *stop* (choice D) are incorrect because they do not reflect the purpose of a rudder.

24. L

A good topic sentence will state the main idea of a passage or the general idea that the author is trying to express. This passage contains more than one interesting fact about penguins. Penguins may be fun to watch (choice J), but the author does not mention this in the passage. The passage contains factual information. Penguins may be intelligent birds (choice K), but this is a statement of opinion and it is not explored in the passage. Penguins do live in the Southern Hemisphere (choice M), but this would not be a good topic sentence because it is only one fact mentioned in the passage and it was not the main idea.

25. C

"All thumbs" is an idiom, or an expression that doesn't mean exactly what the words say. If you are "all thumbs" you will have difficulty doing tasks. The passage mentions that penguins have difficulty walking because of their short legs. Choice A is not a good choice because the passage does not mention penguins having thumbs. The passage states that penguins are not able to fly but they do walk, so (B) is not a good choice.

26. M

According to the passage, wetlands are important because they control water cycles (J), store flood-waters (K), and provide fish and wildlife habitats (L). The main idea of the passage is to describe all the benefits of the wetlands.

27. B

Although wetlands do filter polluted water (A), maintain surface water (C), and provide habitats for fish (choice D), it is specifically stated in the passage that "wetlands control water cycles by absorbing floodwater."

28. L

Although scientists studying wetlands may consider them a biological supermarket (J), the question begins with "According to the passage," which suggests that the answer will be found directly in the passage. In the passage, the sentence

immediately following the "biological supermarket" description clearly states that wetlands provide generous amounts of food that attract many animal species. Although wetlands have been filled in for building, the idea that some of this land might have been used to build supermarkets (K) does not support the meaning of "biological supermarkets" as described in the passage. The passage does not even mention buying fish or water from wetlands (M).

29. A

The author would most likely support more laws to protect wetlands based on the sentence in the passage stating "Today, however, we realize their importance." The author wrote the passage to inform us of the benefits of wetlands. Therefore, the author would not support using wetlands to farm (B) or filling in the wetlands to build (C) because both these choices would eliminate wetlands. The author also does not consider the wetlands to be wastelands (D) based on the statement in the passage that says "wetlands were erroneously considered wastelands." This means it was an error to consider them as wastelands.

30. L

In order to answer this question, you do not need much prior knowledge about the continent of Antarctica. The question begins with "Based on the passage," suggesting that the answer will be found in the passage itself. The second sentence mentions that wetlands are relatively common in tropical areas, and this suggests a warm and humid environment. Temperatures in Antarctica would be too cold to support any of the conditions necessary for a wetland. The passage does not give details describing wetlands as either salt or freshwater (J). The existence of fish (K) or plants (M) would not be good choices because they represent only two components that are necessary to sustain a wetland.

31. D

It is mentioned more than once that Eleanor was concerned with humanitarian efforts. Although she spoke out for rights, the passage does not state that she was a great speaker (choice A). (B) is not a good choice because the passage mentions that Eleanor shunned the notion of being a hostess. (C) is also not a good choice because the passage states that Eleanor was a politically involved wife. It does not state that she was a politician.

32. L

Serving as the "eyes and ears" of the president is an expression that means Eleanor was able to see and hear things in her travels that enabled her to give firsthand information to the president. It was almost as though he had made the trips himself. It does not mean that the president had any sight or hearing problems (J). The passage does not contain any information about the president not wanting contact with people (K) or about his being unable to travel (M).

33. B

While the passage does mention President Roosevelt's administration (choice A), the majority of the passage is devoted to Eleanor's accomplishments during this administration. It focuses on her efforts to help people and how she went about this. Although the passage mentions that Eleanor traveled extensively, her travels were not what the passage was mainly about (choice C). Eleanor's appointment to the U.N. (choice D) was mentioned only briefly in the passage and was not what the passage "mainly dealt with."

34. L

The last line of the passage tells us that Eleanor continued her humanitarian efforts after her husband died, with an appointment to the UN. There is no mention of public speaking (choice J) or traveling (choice K) after her husband died. Accepting an appointment to the U.N. would definitely eliminate the possibility that Eleanor was a recluse (choice M) since this would mean that she lived in seclusion.

35. C

To shun something means to avoid it. Eleanor Roosevelt avoided being a hostess for the White House by becoming politically involved in the administration of her husband. She did not enjoy (choice A) or misunderstand (choice B) the role of hostess. Eleanor Roosevelt, we learn from the passage, was far too busy traveling and helping the American people to be entertaining guests at the White House.

36. K

A proponent of computers would argue in favor of them. The fact that computers can process information faster than the human brain would support an argument in favor of them. (J) is not a good choice because ensuring that more workers are computer literate is actually a drawback to industry, as it would increases the need for training. (L) states that computers reduce unemployment. This is not the case according to the passage, as computers have reduced employment. This means that they have increased unemployment. Reducing employment would definitely not provide a good argument in favor of computers. (M) indicates that computers have helped to eliminate our individual privacy. As most people are concerned with their privacy, eliminating it would not serve as a good argument for a proponent of computers.

37. C

The passage clearly states that the use of automation has reduced employment in certain industries. The passage does not mention anything about a profit increase for business (A). Although you may assume that the need for less workers would increase profits, it is not mentioned in the passage and the question specifically begins with "According to the passage." (B) is wrong because automation has eliminated jobs—not created them. (D) would not be a good choice because "all of the above" would mean that the other choices were all correct.

38. M

The passage states that employers modernize their facilities to keep up with foreign competition. They have been forced to do so by constantly changing technology. Increasing their workforce (J) is not the reason stated in the passage. Although modernizing their facilities might improve conditions for employees (K), it is not the reason given in the passage. Increasing automation (L) is also not a good answer because it is not given as a reason for modernizing facilities in the passage. The question did not ask your opinion or suggest that you use your own judgment, so you must rely on information in the passage.

39. B

The question asks for one of the main reasons we should use a computer, and this is stated clearly in the second sentence of the passage. A computer can perform some functions faster than a human brain. Computers may enable us to be computer literate (A), but this is not the main reason stated in the passage. The storage of personal information (C) is a function of a computer but not a good choice for the answer to this question. The passage states that the obtaining of our personal information by others reduces our individual privacy. This would definitely not be the main reason for using a computer. Since computers reduce our personal privacy, (D) is not a good choice for an answer, as it indicates that computers protect our privacy.

40. L

The author of the passage explains the consequences, both positive and negative, of computers in our lives. The author does not only extol their impact (J) because this means to praise them. The author also does not just negate the importance of computers (K). This choice would mean the author denied the importance of computers. Although the author does explain how computers may make our lives easier (M), it is clear from the passage that this is not the author's only intent. The author attempts to explain both the positive and the negative impact of computers on our lives.

41. C

The author wrote this to inform the reader. The passage contains factual information about Nobel, his invention of dynamite, and the effect it had on his life. (A) would not be a good answer because the subject matter of the passage is serious and there is really nothing entertaining about dynamite or the fact that Nobel might have suffered guilt because of his invention. The author was presenting facts and did not attempt to influence or persuade the reader with any opinions, so (B) should be eliminated. Although the passage does contain a theory or possible explanation for the Nobel Prizes, this was only one part of the passage. Theorizing (choice D) is not the author's main intent.

42. K

Out of the choices given, this is the best one. The second to last sentence in the passage states that it is said Nobels guilt prompted him to will much of his fortune to create the Nobel Prizes. This would mean that he was trying to alleviate or make it easier to live with his conscience. (J) states that Nobel was trying to encourage investors and this does not make any sense. The Nobel Prizes were to be given after Nobel's death and this would not influence any investors. If Nobel had been concerned with gaining popularity (choice L), he would have started the Nobel Prizes while he was still alive so this is not a good choice. It is clear from the passage that Nobel wanted the prizes to be given after his death to those who benefited humanity and promoted world peace. He was not attempting to promote his business (choice M) in any way.

43. B

Nobel's 1864 experiment was inherently dangerous because of the use of an unstable element. The word *inherently* suggests that the danger was permanent and always present. All of Nobel's experiments were dangerous because he worked with an unstable element. Although the experiment did kill Nobel's brother (choice C), his death was a result of the experiment and not a permanent danger. An ill-equipped lab (choice A) did not present the inherent danger—the passage tells us that it was a tragic accident with unstable glycerin. The 1864 experiment could not have been performed on the floating lab (choice D) because Nobel utilized this lab after the tragic accident of 1864.

44. J

Nobel perfected explosives to carry on a family tradition. This is clearly stated in the second sentence. Nobel did invent dynamite (choice K), but the question begins with "we learn from the passage" so the answer will be in the passage. The question is not asking us to give the outcome of his perfecting explosives. Increasing Nobel's fortune (choice L) was also an outcome of his perfecting explosives but not the reason given in the passage to explain why he did it. Nobel was carrying on a family tradition and not looking to benefit humanity (choice M).

45. C

The passage tells us that it was said Nobel suffered guilt over the suffering caused by his invention. This prompted him to will much of his fortune to the creation of the Nobel Prizes. If he suffered guilt over his creation of dynamite, it would follow that he would not want to be remembered for just that (choice A). Also, based on the passage, it is unlikely that Nobel would want to be remembered for the wealth (choice B) he accumulated since he was giving it away in his will.

46. M

Based on the passage, the author did not write the passage for any of the choices given. There was no warning (choice J) to the reader. The passage actually reassures the reader that sensory specialists are keeping contaminated fish from reaching American dinner tables. The author also did not chastise the reader (choice K) as this means the author would have inflicted punishment on the reader. The author was also not explaining how to do anything (L) because the passage did not provide any instructions to the reader.

47. D

Sensory specialists or fish sniffers rely on their olfactory sense which is their sense of smell. The passage states that they also rely on their senses of touch, sight, and taste in addition to relying on experience.

48. M

To scrutinize means to examine closely. Sensory specialists do sniff (choice J) and taste (choice K) fish, but these choices do not reflect the meaning of *scrutinize* in the passage. It would be impossible for a sensory specialist to question (choice L) fish.

49. D

According to the passage, the main function of sensory specialists is to prevent bad fish from entering the consumer market. They try to sniff out bad fish before it reaches us. Sensory specialists are trying to protect the American consumer and not the fish industry, so (A) is not a correct choice. It is reassuring to the American public (choice B) to know that sensory specialists are protecting us, but it is not their main function. Although it makes sense that sensory specialists would likely try to keep their sensory abilities sharp, this would help them with their job and is not their main function.

50. K

The second sentence in the passage tells us that FDA fish sniffers guard our coastal borders. They protect our consumption of fish (J), but the passage does not say they guard it. According to the passage, sensory specialists can be considered to be investigating the fish industry and not guarding it (L). They probably take good care of their mega-labs, but the passage also does not mention them guarding their mega-labs (M).

LANGUAGE

Part 1
Punctuation

1. B

There should be a comma after *However* since it is an introductory word that comes before the main part of the sentence.

2. K

An apostrophe is added at the end of plural words to show possession. An apostrophe is needed after the *s* in *girls* (girls').

3. C

There should be a question mark after *them*. The second sentence is asking a question.

4. J

Its is a contraction for *it has* in this sentence and should be spelled *it's*.

5. C

There should be a comma after the word *biking*. A comma is used to separate words that are part of a list of three or more items.

6. K

A colon (:), not a hyphen, is used to introduce a list in a sentence.

7. C

Quotation marks are used to set off a speaker's exact words. They enclose a direct quotation. It should be "Blondie, come back!"

8. L

A period—not a question mark—is used, even though the sentence contains an indirect question.

9. A

A period is used after an abbreviation that shortens a word. Dr. is an abbreviation for Doctor.

10. K

This is a compound sentence made up of two independent sentences connected by *and*. A comma is always used before the connecting word in a compound sentence, so there should be a comma before *and*.

Spelling

11. A

Neice is spelled *niece*. Words having the sound of long *e* are commonly spelled with *ie* following all letters except *c*.

12. K

Reciteal should be spelled *recital*. The root word is *recite* and a silent *e* is dropped at the end of a word before a suffix beginning with a vowel (such as *al*) is added.

13. B

Words ending in final *ie* (die) change to *y* before adding *ing*. The correct spelling is *dying*.

14. J

Panicy should be spelled *panicky*. Before adding *y* to words ending in *c*, a *k* is added to keep the hard sound of the *c*.

15. A

The plural of words ending in *y* following a consonant are formed by dropping the *y* and adding *ies*. *Puppys* should be spelled *puppies*.

16. K

Careing should be spelled *caring*. Silent *e* (in *care*) should be dropped before adding an ending that begins with a vowel (such as *ed* or *ing*).

17. A

Words ending in *ge* (courage) retain the silent *e* before a suffix beginning with *a* or *o*. The correct spelling is *courageous*.

18. K

Neither, *either*, *their*, *height*, and *weird* are all exceptions to the *i* before *e* spelling rule.

19. C

I before *e* except after *c* in a word such as *received*.

20. J

Turkies should be spelled *turkeys*. The plural of nouns that end in *y* following a vowel are formed by adding *s*.

Capitalization

21. C

The first, last, and all important words in a book title should be capitalized. The *b* in *birds* should be a capital.

22. J

The first word of a direct quotation must be capitalized. *What* should be capitalized in (J).

23. B

Months of the year are capitalized, but seasons of the year (like *winter*) are not capitalized unless they are part of a proper name.

24. K

Charity should be capitalized. All important words in the names of organizations and groups should be capitalized.

25. B

Dad should be capitalized in this sentence because it is a proper noun that names a specific person.

26. L

All important words in the names of specific public areas such as "Mount McKinley National Park" should be capitalized. If the sentence was referring to national parks in general and not a specific park, no capitalization would be needed.

27. A

"Arbor Day" should be capitalized. All holidays must be capitalized.

28. L

You should capitalize the names of all streets, roads, and highways, so *fifth* and *avenue* should both be capitalized in this sentence.

29. A

All titles (such as *jr.*) that are used with names must be capitalized. The name in Sentence A should have been written "John D. Rockefeller, Jr." with all capitals.

30. J

The first word in every sentence must be capitalized, so *although* should begin with a capital.

Usage

31. B

A noun must agree with its verb in number. The noun in this sentence is *diversity* and it is a singular noun. The singular verb *offers* should be used to agree with *diversity*.

32. K

Between should be *among*. *Between* is used when comparing two people or things. *Among* is used to indicate more than two people or things and should be used when referring to the four cats.

33. B

A lot should always be written as two words. It is used to mean many. *Alot* is not a word.

34. K

Most should be replaced with *almost*. *Practice* is the word being described in this sentence, and it should be followed by the adverb *almost* which means *nearly*. *Most* is defined as "greatest in number" and does not fit in the context of this sentence.

35. C

Was is incorrect and should be replaced with *is*. The Grand Canyon exists in the present and *was* is a verb in the past tense.

36. L

A should be replaced with *an* before *umbrella*. *An* is used before words beginning with vowels such as *umbrella*.

37. A

Farther indicates physical distance and should replace *further*. The word *further* should only be used to refer to additional time or amount. This sentence refers to traveling a physical distance.

38. L

Bought is the past participle of *buy* and is not correct in this sentence. *Brought* should have been used since it is the past participle of *bring*. You would *bring* rain gear with you and not *buy* it with you.

39. B

The word *almost* should be placed before "a gallon." A modifier, such as *almost*, must be placed in a position that makes it clear which word it modifies. In this sentence, *almost* seems to be describing *after* instead of *gallon*.

40. J

"They're" should be spelled "their." These two words sound alike but have different meanings. "They're" is a contraction for "they are" while "their" is the possessive form of they and means "belonging to them." In this sentence, "their" is referring to the opinions that belong to everyone.

Part 2

41. A

Almost is a modifier and should be placed before the word it modifies, which is *every* in this sentence. The people do not "almost represent"; they represent "almost every country."

42. L

A noun should agree with its verb in number. *Variety*, the noun in this sentence, is singular and requires the singular verb *makes*. (He makes; they make.)

43. D

Was (D) is a verb in the past tense and should be replaced with *is*. The author is describing actions that the reader can take in the present or future to create a sanctuary. Using *was* indicates that the action happened in the past.

44. J

The word *may* (J) should be replaced with *can*. The word *may* should only be used to convey permission. The sentence is referring to an ability to see and not a permission to see. The word *can* is used to indicate ability.

45. B

The pronoun *their* is plural, but the noun it refers to, *country*, is singular.

46. J

Principle should be *principal. Principle* can be used only as a noun and means *a rule* or general truth. *Principal* can be a noun or an adjective. As an adjective, principal means *first* or *highest* and is the correct usage in this sentence.

47. C

Sentence 7 is an incomplete sentence. Although it has a noun and verb, it does not express a complete thought.

48. C

Too means more than enough, very, or also. The number two should be used for a percent.

49. J

An adverb is a word that describes a verb and tells how and why an action is done. *Quickly* (adverb) tells how the rain forests are disappearing (verb) in the sentence.

50. B

Nurtured is in the past tense, which means the action happened in the past. The sentence is stating what we must do today, so *nurture* should be used.

MATH

Part 1

1. D

The number 1.90 involves a whole number, which is the 1 to the left of the decimal. This means that the answer will be a mixed number—a whole number plus a fraction. The fraction is the number to the right of the decimal, 9. Since the 9 is in the tenth's place, the fraction would be $\frac{9}{10}$. The whole number plus the fraction is $1\frac{9}{10}$.

2. J

Look in the middle column which represents the dates 1600–1700 and find the appropriate row to match each country. There were 811 ships in England during this time period and 371 in Portugal. 811 – 371 = 440 ships (J). (K) is the difference between the Netherlands and Portugal during this time. (L) is the difference between England and Portugal from 1701–1800.

3. A

To divide fractions, invert the second fraction $\left(\frac{11}{12}\right)$ and multiply the fractions together. Multiply the two numerators, and then multiply the two denominators. Place the product of the numerators over the product of the denominators and simplify the fraction. In this problem, the fraction is simplified by dividing both the numerator and denominator by 6.

$$\frac{5}{6} \times \frac{12}{11} = \frac{60}{66} \div \frac{6}{6} = \frac{10}{11}$$

(B) is found by subtracting the two fractions instead of dividing. (C) comes from adding the two fractions. (D) comes from multiplying the two fractions.

4. L

A prime number is a positive integer that has exactly two positive integer factors, 1 and itself. (J), (K), and (M) are all prime numbers because each one can only be divided by 1 and itself. (L) is the only choice that is NOT a prime number. 57 has four positive integer factors: 1, 3, 19, and 57.

5. C

The least common denominator (LCD) of two or more non zero denominators is the smallest whole number that is divisible by each of the denominators. For this problem, the denominators of $\frac{1}{5}, \frac{5}{6}$, and $\frac{1}{3}$ are 5, 6, and 3, respectively. Go through the multiples of the largest number, 6, until there is a number that is also divisible by 5 and 3.

Multiples of 6 = 6, 12, 18, 24, 30 (C). 30 is divisible by 3, 5, and 6. Answers (A) and (B) are common denominators of $\frac{5}{6}$ and $\frac{1}{3}$, but not $\frac{1}{5}$ because they are not divisible by 5. (D) is a common denominator of all three fractions, but it is not the lowest value.

6. L

The first step is to figure out how many rolls of yarn Amanda will need to make three scarves (n).

$$n = (3)\ (3) = 9 \text{ rolls}$$

Next, subtract the four rolls of yarn that she already has. 9 – 4 = 5 rolls (L).

7. D

According to the graph, worker D earns $8,000 and worker B earns $4,000. Subtract $4,000 from $8,000 to get the difference.

$$\begin{array}{r} \$8,000 \\ -\ 4,000 \\ \hline \$4,000 \end{array}$$

(A) is the difference between workers C and D. (B) is the difference between workers A and B or D and A. (C) is the difference between workers C and A.

8. K

If n = the number of shelves, then 9 (the number of books on each shelf) times n = 126 (the number of total books) or $9n = 126$. Solve this equation by dividing both sides by 9. $n = 126 \div 9 = 14$ (K).

9. D

$13^2 = 13 \times 13$

$$\begin{array}{r} 13 \\ \times\ 13 \\ \hline 169 \end{array}$$

A common mistake might be to add 13 + 13 (A). Errors in multiplication could lead to (B) and (C).

10. M

Look at the table to find the corresponding price for a large peach smoothie ($3.95). Each supplement costs $0.55 extra. Since Mary got two supplements (calcium and protein), $0.55 + 0.55 = $1.10. Add everything together to get the total, $3.95 + $1.10 = $5.05 (M). (J) is the price of a small peach smoothie with two supplements. (K) is the price of a large peach smoothie and only one supplement. (L) is the price of a large strawberry-banana smoothie with two supplements.

11. B

The greatest common factor of two or more whole numbers is the largest whole number that divides evenly into each of the numbers. List all of the numbers that are factors of 18 and 24, and look for the largest number that they have in common.

18: 1, 2, 3, 6, 9, 18
24: 1, 2, 3, 4, 6, 8, 12, 24

Therefore, the greatest common factor is 6 (B). (A) is a common factor of both, but is not the greatest. (C) and (D) are only factors of 24, not 18.

12. L

In order to convert the fraction to a decimal, divide the numerator by the dominator.

$$8\overline{)5.000}\ \ ^{0.625}$$

13. D

The first step is to recognize which line belongs to the corresponding class based on the legend to the right of the graph. Looking at Class A and Class B, it is clear that the line for Class A is above the line for Class B in all months but December.

14. J

To change a percentage to a fraction, divide it by 100 and reduce the fraction. $\frac{15}{100} \div \frac{5}{5} = \frac{3}{20}$

15. B

The first step is to figure out how much Anna earned without the tip (n). $n + \$5 = \$40$. Subtract 5 from both sides to get $n = 40 - 5$. $n = \$35$. Next, figure out how much Anna earned per hour by dividing n by the number of hours she worked (5 hours) $n/5 = 35$ hours/5 hours $= 7$. Therefore, Anna earned $\$7$/hr. (B). You would get (C) if you forgot to subtract the tip and (D) if you added the tip instead of subtracting it.

16. L

Let n represent Brian's weekly allowance. Therefore, $(30\%)n = \$5.55$ (30% of his weekly allowance is $5.55). Divide both sides by 30% to get $n = \$5.55 \div 30\%$. To solve this, convert 30% to a decimal by moving the decimal two places to the left (0.30). You can simplify the numbers 5.55 and 0.30 by shifting each decimal one place to the right which is equivalent to multiplying both by 10. This should make the division easier.

$$3\overline{)5{,}550} \quad 1{,}850$$

If you multiply instead of divide, and misplace the decimal, you get (K). If you multiply instead of divide and add this to the brother's pay, you get (J).

17. C

First, add up the portion that Maria and A.J. are responsible for in order to find their sub total. $0.25 + 0.05 = 0.30$. Then convert this into a fraction by placing 3 over 10 (since the 3 falls in the tenth's place, which is one place to the right of the decimal). The answer is $\frac{3}{10}$ because this fraction cannot be reduced any more. (A) is the fraction that only Maria has to do. (B) is the fraction that Mike and Maria have to do. (D) is the fraction that Mike, A.J., and Clare have to do.

18. K

In order to subtract integers, remember to "add the opposite." In other words, first change the subtraction sign, to an addition sign and then switch the integer to its opposite sign (if it is negative, change it to positive and visa versa). In this problem, the (−4) would become (+4), which is simply, 4. $1 + 4 = 5$ (K). (J) would be the answer for (−1) + (−4) or (−1) − 4. (L) would be the answer for 1 − 4 or 1 + (−4). (M) would be the answer for (−1) + 4 or (−1) − (−4).

19. B

If $n =$ the non-shortcut distance, then $n - 346 = 1{,}120$. Add 346 to both sides to get $n = 1{,}120$ yards + 346 yards.

$$\begin{array}{r} 1{,}120 \\ + 346 \\ \hline 1{,}466 \text{ yards.} \end{array}$$

You would get (A) if you subtracted 364 instead of adding it.

20. L

When converting a data table to a graph, keep in mind which variables are on each axis. In this case, the scores are on the x-axis (horizontal) and the number of students is on the y-axis (vertical). You can always plot the numbers in order to see which graph is accurate, but a quicker way would be to look at the overall trends. Based on the data, we would expect a bell shaped curve with the peak being around the 81–90 area (15 students) and dropping for both the low and high scores. The only graph that fits this description is (L). (J) and (K) have a more random dispersion, and (M) trends upward with the peak at the highest score (91–100).

21. A

Scientific notation is a way to handle large numbers. The exponent of 10 is the number of places the decimal point must be shifted to write the number in long form. A positive exponent signifies that the decimal point is shifted that number of places to the right. A negative exponent shows that the decimal point is shifted that number of places to the left. In this problem, move the decimal to the right in order to satisfy the condition of having one non zero digit to the left of the decimal (4.5). The decimal point needs to be moved 5 places to the right in order to get there. Since it is being moved to the right, the power will be negative, 4.5×10^{-5} (A). (B) written in long form would be 450,000. (C) is incorrect since there is more than one digit to the left of the decimal. (D) written in long form would be 0.00045.

22. J

If n = the cost of the second book, then $\$8.95 + n = \$22.45$. Subtract $\$8.95$ from both sides to get $n = \$22.45 - \$8.95$.

$$\begin{array}{r} 22.45 \\ -8.95 \\ \hline 13.50 \end{array}$$

23. A

Look at the values of each plant on Day 7 and Day 9. Find the differences and compare to see which plant grew the most during this time.

Day 9 – Day 7 height

Plant A   12 cm – 7 cm = **5 cm**

Plant B   15 cm – 12 cm = 3 cm

Plant C   5 cm – 4 cm = 1 cm

24. J

If x = the amount of money for her savings account, then $\left(\dfrac{3}{4}\right)\$18 = x$.

$$\frac{3}{4} \times \frac{18}{1} = \frac{54}{4} = \text{(Reduce this fraction)} \quad \frac{54}{4} \div \frac{2}{2} = \frac{27}{2} =$$

$\$13.50 = x$

Let n = the amount of money for spending. $x + n = \$18$. $\$13.50 + n = \$18$. Subtract $\$13.50$ from both sides to get $n = \$18.00 - 13.50$.

$$\begin{array}{r} 18.00 \\ -13.50 \\ \hline 4.50 \end{array}$$

Another way to solve this problem would be to subtract $\dfrac{3}{4}$ from 1 in order to find the fraction of money that is spending money. $1 - \dfrac{3}{4} = \dfrac{1}{4}$. Therefore, $\left(\dfrac{1}{4}\right)$ $\$18 = n$. $\dfrac{18}{4} \div \dfrac{2}{2} = \dfrac{9}{2} = \$4.50$

25. B

Look at the legend to the right of the graph to see which part of the stacked bar represents the 65+ age group. 0–14 is on the bottom, 15–64 is in the middle, and 65+ is on the top. Looking at only the top section of each bar, it is clear that Costa Rica and India have the smallest percentages (B). Germany and Canada (A) have the smallest percentages of the 0–14 age group.

26. M

Figure out how much 30% is of $\$24.90$ by converting the percentage to a decimal and then multiplying the two numbers. $\$24.90 \times 0.30 = \$7.47$—this is (J), which is not the final answer. In order to find the new price, subtract the 30% savings ($\$7.47$) from the original price ($\$24.90$). $\$24.90 - \$7.47 = \$17.43$ (M).

27. A

Based on the legend, oil production is represented by the bar on the left within each country subgroup, and oil consumption is represented by the bar on the right. The only two countries in which oil consumption is greater than oil production (the right bar is greater than the left bar) are China and the United States (A).

28. L

Multiply the total weight (2.4 lb) and the sale cost ($\$1.25$) to get the total price. 2.4 lb $\times$ $\$1.25$/lb = $\$3.00$

29. D

Figure out how many points Jordan made in the first and third quarters by finding the y-axis value that corresponds with the x-axis. first quarter = 6 points. third quarter = 4 points. 6 + 4 = 10 points. second quarter = 13 points (the data point is located between the 12 and 14). 13 – 10 = 3 point difference (D). (A) is the difference between the second and first quarters. (B) is the difference between the second and third quarters.

30. L

Use the table to find the row for peanut allergy and the corresponding percentage of afflicted young children (0.8%) and adults (0.6%). Add these two values together to find the answer. 0.8% + 0.6% = 1.4% (L). (J) is only the percentage of young children who have peanut allergies. (K) represents the amount of adults who have peanut allergies. (M) is the overall percentage of young children and adults with the allergies listed.

31. B

One unit of the British currency would be worth the most in U.S. dollars. This is determined by looking for the lowest value in the chart. For example, it takes approximately 45 Indian units to equal $1. Therefore, 1 Indian unit would only be worth a small fraction of a dollar (1/45th). On the other hand, 1 British pound is worth almost $2. 1 pound × $1/0.5 pounds = $2. (Divide 1 by 0.5).

32. J

Figure out how many hours Martin worked. 2 P.M. to 5 P.M. = 3 hours. If n = the number of problems per hour, then $3n = 105$. $n = \dfrac{105}{3}$

$3\overline{)105}$ $\overset{35}{}$ $50n$ = 35 problems/hour (J). Errors in calculating the time would lead to variable answers such as (K) which uses 5 hours and (L) which uses 2 hours.

Part 2

33. C

In order to estimate the sum of two numbers, round each number and then add the rounded numbers. In this problem, it is easiest to round to the nearest hundreds place (6̲61). In the number 661, the digit to the right of the hundreds place is 6 (66̲1), and therefore, the number is rounded up to 700. If the digit to

the right of the hundreds place were 0–4, the number would be rounded down to 600. In the number 382, the digit to the right of the hundreds place is 8 (38̲2). Again, this digit is greater than or equal to 5, and the number is rounded up to 400. 700 + 400 = 1,100 (C). If the number(s) were rounded down instead of up, the answer would be wrong. 600 + 300 = 900 (B).

34. K

It is important to initially figure out a number close to 539 that can easily be divided by 6. 6 × 9 = 54, and therefore, it is easiest to round 539 to 540 in order to get a number without any remainder. If you set up the long division, you will see that 6 goes into 540 90 times (K).

$6\overline{)540}$ $\overset{90}{}$

Common mistakes might be forgetting the extra zero (J) or adding too many (L and M).

35. D

Round to the nearest thousands place by rounding 25,8̲40 up to 26,000 (8 ≥ 5, so round up) and 16,1̲09 to 16,000 (1 < 5, so round down). 26,000 – 16,000 = 10,000 (D). Errors made when rounding one or both numbers would give variable answers such as 25,000 – 16,000 = 9,000 (B).

36. J

Round to the nearest whole number. Both 6.4̲4 and 11.3̲8 have digits to the right of the decimal that are < 5 which means the whole numbers will not be rounded up. 6 × 11 = 66 (A). Errors in rounding one or both of the numbers would give variable answers: 6 × 12 = 72 (K), 7 × 11 = 77 (L), and 7 × 12 = 84 (M).

37. B

The tenths place is the first number to the right of the decimal which in this case is 5 (8.5̲42). In order to round to this place, look at the digit to the right (4). This number is less than 5, so the number is rounded down to 8.500 or 8.5 (B). (A) is incorrectly rounded down to the ones place. (C) is rounded to the nearest hundredths place. (D) is rounded to the ones place.

38. J

Round $13.28 to the nearest whole dollar. The number 2 is directly to the right of the decimal point. This number is less than 5, and therefore, the dollar amount is rounded down to $13.00. $20.00 – $13.00 = $7.00 (J). Incorrect rounding would lead to variable answers such as $20.00 – $14.00 (rounding up instead of down) = $6.00 (K).

39. C

Estimate the total by first rounding each of the numbers to the nearest tens place. 23 becomes 20 (3 < 5), 25 is rounded up to 30 (5 ≥ 5), and 32 becomes 30 (2 < 5). Then add the rounded numbers together. 20 + 30 + 30 = 80 (C). Any mistake in rounding the number(s) could lead to an incorrect answer.

40. L

First, round each number. In the number 99, the second 9 determines whether to round up or down. Since 9 is ≥ 5, the number is rounded up which changes the first 9 to 10. Therefore, 99 rounds up to become 100. 72 rounds down to become 70 (2 < 5). Multiply these two numbers together, making sure to keep track of the zeros: 100 × 70 = 7,000. An error in rounding up to 100, or with the zeros when multiplying, would lead to incorrect answers.

41. D

The hundredths place is the second number to the right of the decimal. Do not get confused with the hundreds place, which is three places to the left of the decimal. In this case, the hundredths place is occupied by the 8 (612.786). The number to the right of the hundredths place is a 6, which is ≥ 5 and means we round the number up to 612.790 (D). (A) is rounded to the nearest hundreds place. (B) is rounded to the nearest whole number, or ones place. (C) is rounded to the nearest tenths place.

42. L

Before subtracting, round each number to the nearest thousand. Look at the number directly to the right of the thousands place in order to determine whether to round up or not. For the number 7,372, the 3 is less than 5 and the number is rounded down to 7,000. For the number 2,938, the 9 is greater than 5 and the number is rounded up to 3,000. 7,000 – 3,000 = 4,000 (L). Errors in rounding one or both numbers would result in variable answers such as 7,000 – 2,000 = 5,000 (M).

43. D

Round each amount to the nearest dollar by looking at the digit to the right of the decimal in order to determine whether to round up or down. $3.75 is rounded up to $4.00 (7 ≥ 5), $4.50 is rounded up to $5.00 (5 ≥ 5), and $1.75 is rounded up to $2.00 (7 ≥ 5). Add the three rounded numbers together to get the estimated total. $4.00 + $5.00 + 2.00 = $11.00 (D). An error in rounding the number(s) would result in an incorrect total estimate. $3.00 + $4.00 + $1.00 = $8.00 (A). $4.00 + $4.00 + $1.00 = $9.00 (B). $4.00 + $4.00 + $2.00 = $10.00 (C).

44. K

The hundreds place is located three places to the left of the decimal. In the number 5,609, the decimal is not shown since it is a whole number, but is actually located after the 9 (5,609 = 5,609.00). The number in the hundreds place is the 6 (5,609). Look at the number directly to the right in order to determine whether to round up or down. In this case, the number is 0 and the number is rounded down to 5,600 (K). (J) is rounded to the nearest thousands place. (L) is incorrectly rounded up. (M) is rounded to the nearest tens place.

45. D

Round 23,522 to the nearest thousand. Look at the place to the right of the thousands place in order to determine whether to round up or down. In this case, we look at the 5 (23,522). Since this number is at least 5, round up to get 24,000. Divide this number by 3 to get 8,000, choice (D).

$$3 \overline{)24{,}000} = 8{,}000$$

46. L

Round each number to the nearest whole number by looking at the digit to the right of the decimal in order to determine whether to round up or down. 15.87 rounds up to become 16.00, and 5.38 rounds down to become 5.00. Subtract the rounded numbers. 16 − 5 = 11 (L)

47. D

Start by rounding each number to the nearest hundred. 523 rounds down to 500 (2 < 5), and 563 rounds up to become 600 (6 ≥ 5). Multiply the two rounded numbers, paying close attention to the zeros.

$$\begin{array}{r} 500 \\ \times\ 600 \\ \hline 300{,}000 \end{array}$$

48. K

The tenths place is the first place to the right of the decimal (25.006). The number to the right of the tenths place is zero, and therefore, the tenths place digit does not change. The answer is 25.000 (K). (J) is rounded to the tens place. (L) is incorrectly rounded. (M) is rounded to the hundredths place.

49. A

The first step is to round the cost to the nearest dollar. $8.72 rounds up to become $9.00. Then subtract this rounded amount from $20.00. $20.00 − $9.00 = $11.00 (A).

50. K

This is a multi-step problem. The first step is to add the two numbers that are in parentheses. Round both numbers to the nearest hundreds place: 289 rounds up to become 300. 850 rounds up to become 900. 300 + 900 = 1,200. The next step is to

divide this number by 40, paying close attention to the number of zeros.

$$40 \overline{)1{,}200} = 30$$

ABILITY

Part 1

1. C

All figures have five sides. The only answer choice with five sides is (C).

2. N

All of the original figures are made of straight lines. The only answer choice with no curved sides is (N).

3. B

All figures have a circle inscribed within. The only answer choice with a complete circle inscribed within is (B).

4. J

All figures have no acute angles. The only answer choice with no acute angles is (J).

5. D

All figures have a semicircle as one side. The only answer choice with a semicircle as one side is (D).

6. L

All figures have only vertical stripes. Don't be distracted by choices (M) and (N). Although they have vertical stripes, they also have at least one diagonal stripe. The correct answer is (L).

7. E

All figures have eight sides. The only answer choice with eight sides is (E).

8. K

All figures have no straight sides. The only answer choice with no straight side is (K).

9. D

All figures have only diagonal stripes. Although the first and third figures in the question have their own shapes inscribed within, that is not what all three figures have in common. Choice (D) is the correct answer.

10. K

All figures have their own shape inscribed within. Because the stripes on the figures in the question go in different directions, you can eliminate that as what the figures have in common.

11. C

All figures are flat on top. The only answer choice that is flat on top is (C).

12. J

All figures are 50% shaded. The only answer choice that is 50% shaded is (J).

13. E

All figures have a triangular base. The only answer choice that has a triangular base is (E).

14. K

All figures have vertical parallel sides. The only answer choice with vertical parallel sides is (K).

15. A

All figures are 25% shaded. The only answer choice that is 25% shaded is (A).

16. K

All figures are composed of triangles. The only answer choice that is composed of triangles is (K).

17. D

All figures are bisected, making two symmetrical shapes. The only answer choice that is bisected into two symmetrical shapes is (D).

18. L

All figures have six sides. Because the stripes on the figures in the question go in different directions, you can eliminate that as what the figures have in common. The only answer choice that has six sides is (L).

19. A

All figures have at least one right angle. The only answer choice that has at least one right angle is (A).

20. N

All figures have only one triangle inscribed within. The only answer choice with only one triangle inscribed within is (N). Note that each of the original figures is also straight-sided; if only one of the answer choices was straight-sided, that could be the correct answer. If more than one answer choice shares a quality, that can't be the one being tested.

21. B

The change shown is that only the right half of the figure remains.

22. L

The change shown is that the figure is faced with a figure with horizontal lines. Although you might be tempted to select the other choices, only (L) shows the same change that is displayed in the question. Choices (J), (K), and (M) change the direction of the first triangle.

23. B

The change shown is that the figure is inscribed by a solid triangle. The missing figure must be a circle, so you can eliminate choices (A) and (D). The only circle that is inscribed with a solid triangle is (B).

24. N

The change shown is that the figure is rotated 90 degrees to the right. This is tricky. Because a square has equal sides, when it is rotated 90 degrees, it looks the same as the square in the question.

25. D

The change shown is that the number of lines comprising the figures is increased by one. You may be tempted by choice (A), but that is a distracter. It would make the question like a mirror (triangle, square, square, triangle), but to answer the question, you must address the change that is made in the question.

26. J

The change shown is that the figure is split in half by a square.

27. E

The change shown is that the figures are stacked on top of each other (they are mirror images across a horizontal line). Only choice (E) reflects this change.

28. M

The change shown is that 25% less of the figure is shaded.

29. B

The change shown is that the figure is bisected diagonally and is shaded by diagonal lines on top. Only choice (B) reflects this change.

30. K

The change shown is that the outside rim of the figure becomes solid. Don't be tempted by choice (L); too much of the figure is shaded.

31. A

The change shown is that the figure is divided into quarters. Only choice (A) reflects this change.

32. N

The change shown is that the solid figure is inscribed by an unshaded figure. Be careful of the distracters. You are looking for a square that is completely shaded except for a smaller, unshaded shape inscribed within.

33. C

The change shown is that the figure is rotated 180 degrees. This might not be easy to visualize, but if you rotated the triangle in the question 180 degrees, it would look like choice (C).

34. M

The change shown is that the figure is set on a rectangular base. The only choice that shows a square on a rectangular base is choice (M).

35. D

The change shown is that the figure is split into three pieces.

36. K

The change shown is that a dashed line marks the vertical bisection of the figure. Choice (J) is a distracter. Even though it shows the vertical bisection of the shape, it is done with a solid, not dashed, line.

37. A

The change shown is that the number of sides making up the figures is decreased by two. The pentagon becomes a triangle, and the octagon becomes a hexagon.

38. J

The change shown is that the whole figure becomes two back-to-back halves. Only choice (J) shows the same change.

39. C

The change shown is that the figure is "split open." It is bisected vertically and each half is rotated 90 degrees.

40. M

The change shown is that the figure is inscribed with a square with diagonal lines going in the opposite direction from the lines in the outer figure. This is a tricky question. First, you are looking for an octagon, so you should delete choices (J) and (L), which are both hexagons. The only choice that reflects the same change that is found in the question is choice (M).

[No further explanation is possible for questions 41–50.]

TACHS Practice Test
Answer Sheet

Remove or photocopy this answer sheet and use it to complete the Practice Test.

Reading Part 1

1. Ⓐ Ⓑ Ⓒ Ⓓ	5. Ⓐ Ⓑ Ⓒ Ⓓ	9. Ⓐ Ⓑ Ⓒ Ⓓ	13. Ⓐ Ⓑ Ⓒ Ⓓ	17. Ⓐ Ⓑ Ⓒ Ⓓ
2. Ⓙ Ⓚ Ⓛ Ⓜ	6. Ⓙ Ⓚ Ⓛ Ⓜ	10. Ⓙ Ⓚ Ⓛ Ⓜ	14. Ⓙ Ⓚ Ⓛ Ⓜ	18. Ⓙ Ⓚ Ⓛ Ⓜ
3. Ⓐ Ⓑ Ⓒ Ⓓ	7. Ⓐ Ⓑ Ⓒ Ⓓ	11. Ⓐ Ⓑ Ⓒ Ⓓ	15. Ⓐ Ⓑ Ⓒ Ⓓ	19. Ⓐ Ⓑ Ⓒ Ⓓ
4. Ⓙ Ⓚ Ⓛ Ⓜ	8. Ⓙ Ⓚ Ⓛ Ⓜ	12. Ⓙ Ⓚ Ⓛ Ⓜ	16. Ⓙ Ⓚ Ⓛ Ⓜ	20. Ⓙ Ⓚ Ⓛ Ⓜ

Reading Part 2

21. Ⓐ Ⓑ Ⓒ Ⓓ	27. Ⓐ Ⓑ Ⓒ Ⓓ	33. Ⓐ Ⓑ Ⓒ Ⓓ	39. Ⓐ Ⓑ Ⓒ Ⓓ	45. Ⓐ Ⓑ Ⓒ Ⓓ
22. Ⓙ Ⓚ Ⓛ Ⓜ	28. Ⓙ Ⓚ Ⓛ Ⓜ	34. Ⓙ Ⓚ Ⓛ Ⓜ	40. Ⓙ Ⓚ Ⓛ Ⓜ	46. Ⓙ Ⓚ Ⓛ Ⓜ
23. Ⓐ Ⓑ Ⓒ Ⓓ	29. Ⓐ Ⓑ Ⓒ Ⓓ	35. Ⓐ Ⓑ Ⓒ Ⓓ	41. Ⓐ Ⓑ Ⓒ Ⓓ	47. Ⓐ Ⓑ Ⓒ Ⓓ
24. Ⓙ Ⓚ Ⓛ Ⓜ	30. Ⓙ Ⓚ Ⓛ Ⓜ	36. Ⓙ Ⓚ Ⓛ Ⓜ	42. Ⓙ Ⓚ Ⓛ Ⓜ	48. Ⓙ Ⓚ Ⓛ Ⓜ
25. Ⓐ Ⓑ Ⓒ Ⓓ	31. Ⓐ Ⓑ Ⓒ Ⓓ	37. Ⓐ Ⓑ Ⓒ Ⓓ	43. Ⓐ Ⓑ Ⓒ Ⓓ	49. Ⓐ Ⓑ Ⓒ Ⓓ
26. Ⓙ Ⓚ Ⓛ Ⓜ	32. Ⓙ Ⓚ Ⓛ Ⓜ	38. Ⓙ Ⓚ Ⓛ Ⓜ	44. Ⓙ Ⓚ Ⓛ Ⓜ	50. Ⓙ Ⓚ Ⓛ Ⓜ

Language Part 1

1. Ⓐ Ⓑ Ⓒ Ⓓ	9. Ⓐ Ⓑ Ⓒ Ⓓ	17. Ⓐ Ⓑ Ⓒ Ⓓ	25. Ⓐ Ⓑ Ⓒ Ⓓ	33. Ⓐ Ⓑ Ⓒ Ⓓ
2. Ⓙ Ⓚ Ⓛ Ⓜ	10. Ⓙ Ⓚ Ⓛ Ⓜ	18. Ⓙ Ⓚ Ⓛ Ⓜ	26. Ⓙ Ⓚ Ⓛ Ⓜ	34. Ⓙ Ⓚ Ⓛ Ⓜ
3. Ⓐ Ⓑ Ⓒ Ⓓ	11. Ⓐ Ⓑ Ⓒ Ⓓ	19. Ⓐ Ⓑ Ⓒ Ⓓ	27. Ⓐ Ⓑ Ⓒ Ⓓ	35. Ⓐ Ⓑ Ⓒ Ⓓ
4. Ⓙ Ⓚ Ⓛ Ⓜ	12. Ⓙ Ⓚ Ⓛ Ⓜ	20. Ⓙ Ⓚ Ⓛ Ⓜ	28. Ⓙ Ⓚ Ⓛ Ⓜ	36. Ⓙ Ⓚ Ⓛ Ⓜ
5. Ⓐ Ⓑ Ⓒ Ⓓ	13. Ⓐ Ⓑ Ⓒ Ⓓ	21. Ⓐ Ⓑ Ⓒ Ⓓ	29. Ⓐ Ⓑ Ⓒ Ⓓ	37. Ⓐ Ⓑ Ⓒ Ⓓ
6. Ⓙ Ⓚ Ⓛ Ⓜ	14. Ⓙ Ⓚ Ⓛ Ⓜ	22. Ⓙ Ⓚ Ⓛ Ⓜ	30. Ⓙ Ⓚ Ⓛ Ⓜ	38. Ⓙ Ⓚ Ⓛ Ⓜ
7. Ⓐ Ⓑ Ⓒ Ⓓ	15. Ⓐ Ⓑ Ⓒ Ⓓ	23. Ⓐ Ⓑ Ⓒ Ⓓ	31. Ⓐ Ⓑ Ⓒ Ⓓ	39. Ⓐ Ⓑ Ⓒ Ⓓ
8. Ⓙ Ⓚ Ⓛ Ⓜ	16. Ⓙ Ⓚ Ⓛ Ⓜ	24. Ⓙ Ⓚ Ⓛ Ⓜ	32. Ⓙ Ⓚ Ⓛ Ⓜ	40. Ⓙ Ⓚ Ⓛ Ⓜ

Language Part 2

41. Ⓐ Ⓑ Ⓒ Ⓓ	43. Ⓐ Ⓑ Ⓒ Ⓓ	45. Ⓐ Ⓑ Ⓒ Ⓓ	47. Ⓐ Ⓑ Ⓒ Ⓓ	49. Ⓐ Ⓑ Ⓒ Ⓓ
42. Ⓙ Ⓚ Ⓛ Ⓜ	44. Ⓙ Ⓚ Ⓛ Ⓜ	46. Ⓙ Ⓚ Ⓛ Ⓜ	48. Ⓙ Ⓚ Ⓛ Ⓜ	50. Ⓙ Ⓚ Ⓛ Ⓜ

Math Part 1

1. Ⓐ Ⓑ Ⓒ Ⓓ	8. Ⓙ Ⓚ Ⓛ Ⓜ	15. Ⓐ Ⓑ Ⓒ Ⓓ	21. Ⓐ Ⓑ Ⓒ Ⓓ	27. Ⓐ Ⓑ Ⓒ Ⓓ
2. Ⓙ Ⓚ Ⓛ Ⓜ	9. Ⓐ Ⓑ Ⓒ Ⓓ	16. Ⓙ Ⓚ Ⓛ Ⓜ	22. Ⓙ Ⓚ Ⓛ Ⓜ	28. Ⓙ Ⓚ Ⓛ Ⓜ
3. Ⓐ Ⓑ Ⓒ Ⓓ	10. Ⓙ Ⓚ Ⓛ Ⓜ	17. Ⓐ Ⓑ Ⓒ Ⓓ	23. Ⓐ Ⓑ Ⓒ Ⓓ	29. Ⓐ Ⓑ Ⓒ Ⓓ
4. Ⓙ Ⓚ Ⓛ Ⓜ	11. Ⓐ Ⓑ Ⓒ Ⓓ	18. Ⓙ Ⓚ Ⓛ Ⓜ	24. Ⓙ Ⓚ Ⓛ Ⓜ	30. Ⓙ Ⓚ Ⓛ Ⓜ
5. Ⓐ Ⓑ Ⓒ Ⓓ	12. Ⓙ Ⓚ Ⓛ Ⓜ	19. Ⓐ Ⓑ Ⓒ Ⓓ	25. Ⓐ Ⓑ Ⓒ Ⓓ	31. Ⓐ Ⓑ Ⓒ Ⓓ
6. Ⓙ Ⓚ Ⓛ Ⓜ	13. Ⓐ Ⓑ Ⓒ Ⓓ	20. Ⓙ Ⓚ Ⓛ Ⓜ	26. Ⓙ Ⓚ Ⓛ Ⓜ	32. Ⓙ Ⓚ Ⓛ Ⓜ
7. Ⓐ Ⓑ Ⓒ Ⓓ	14. Ⓙ Ⓚ Ⓛ Ⓜ			

Math Part 2

33. Ⓐ Ⓑ Ⓒ Ⓓ	37. Ⓐ Ⓑ Ⓒ Ⓓ	41. Ⓐ Ⓑ Ⓒ Ⓓ	45. Ⓐ Ⓑ Ⓒ Ⓓ	48. Ⓙ Ⓚ Ⓛ Ⓜ
34. Ⓙ Ⓚ Ⓛ Ⓜ	38. Ⓙ Ⓚ Ⓛ Ⓜ	42. Ⓙ Ⓚ Ⓛ Ⓜ	46. Ⓙ Ⓚ Ⓛ Ⓜ	49. Ⓐ Ⓑ Ⓒ Ⓓ
35. Ⓐ Ⓑ Ⓒ Ⓓ	39. Ⓐ Ⓑ Ⓒ Ⓓ	43. Ⓐ Ⓑ Ⓒ Ⓓ	47. Ⓐ Ⓑ Ⓒ Ⓓ	50. Ⓙ Ⓚ Ⓛ Ⓜ
36. Ⓙ Ⓚ Ⓛ Ⓜ	40. Ⓙ Ⓚ Ⓛ Ⓜ	44. Ⓙ Ⓚ Ⓛ Ⓜ		

Ability Part 1

1. Ⓐ Ⓑ Ⓒ Ⓓ Ⓔ	11. Ⓐ Ⓑ Ⓒ Ⓓ Ⓔ	21. Ⓐ Ⓑ Ⓒ Ⓓ Ⓔ	31. Ⓐ Ⓑ Ⓒ Ⓓ Ⓔ
2. Ⓙ Ⓚ Ⓛ Ⓜ Ⓝ	12. Ⓙ Ⓚ Ⓛ Ⓜ Ⓝ	22. Ⓙ Ⓚ Ⓛ Ⓜ Ⓝ	32. Ⓙ Ⓚ Ⓛ Ⓜ Ⓝ
3. Ⓐ Ⓑ Ⓒ Ⓓ Ⓔ	13. Ⓐ Ⓑ Ⓒ Ⓓ Ⓔ	23. Ⓐ Ⓑ Ⓒ Ⓓ Ⓔ	33. Ⓐ Ⓑ Ⓒ Ⓓ Ⓔ
4. Ⓙ Ⓚ Ⓛ Ⓜ Ⓝ	14. Ⓙ Ⓚ Ⓛ Ⓜ Ⓝ	24. Ⓙ Ⓚ Ⓛ Ⓜ Ⓝ	34. Ⓙ Ⓚ Ⓛ Ⓜ Ⓝ
5. Ⓐ Ⓑ Ⓒ Ⓓ Ⓔ	15. Ⓐ Ⓑ Ⓒ Ⓓ Ⓔ	25. Ⓐ Ⓑ Ⓒ Ⓓ Ⓔ	35. Ⓐ Ⓑ Ⓒ Ⓓ Ⓔ
6. Ⓙ Ⓚ Ⓛ Ⓜ Ⓝ	16. Ⓙ Ⓚ Ⓛ Ⓜ Ⓝ	26. Ⓙ Ⓚ Ⓛ Ⓜ Ⓝ	
7. Ⓐ Ⓑ Ⓒ Ⓓ Ⓔ	17. Ⓐ Ⓑ Ⓒ Ⓓ Ⓔ	27. Ⓐ Ⓑ Ⓒ Ⓓ Ⓔ	
8. Ⓙ Ⓚ Ⓛ Ⓜ Ⓝ	18. Ⓙ Ⓚ Ⓛ Ⓜ Ⓝ	28. Ⓙ Ⓚ Ⓛ Ⓜ Ⓝ	
9. Ⓐ Ⓑ Ⓒ Ⓓ Ⓔ	19. Ⓐ Ⓑ Ⓒ Ⓓ Ⓔ	29. Ⓐ Ⓑ Ⓒ Ⓓ Ⓔ	
10. Ⓙ Ⓚ Ⓛ Ⓜ Ⓝ	20. Ⓙ Ⓚ Ⓛ Ⓜ Ⓝ	30. Ⓙ Ⓚ Ⓛ Ⓜ Ⓝ	

Ability Part 2

36. Ⓙ Ⓚ Ⓛ Ⓜ Ⓝ	40. Ⓙ Ⓚ Ⓛ Ⓜ Ⓝ	44. Ⓙ Ⓚ Ⓛ Ⓜ Ⓝ	48. Ⓙ Ⓚ Ⓛ Ⓜ Ⓝ
37. Ⓐ Ⓑ Ⓒ Ⓓ Ⓔ	41. Ⓐ Ⓑ Ⓒ Ⓓ Ⓔ	45. Ⓐ Ⓑ Ⓒ Ⓓ Ⓔ	49. Ⓐ Ⓑ Ⓒ Ⓓ Ⓔ
38. Ⓙ Ⓚ Ⓛ Ⓜ Ⓝ	42. Ⓙ Ⓚ Ⓛ Ⓜ Ⓝ	46. Ⓙ Ⓚ Ⓛ Ⓜ Ⓝ	50. Ⓙ Ⓚ Ⓛ Ⓜ Ⓝ
39. Ⓐ Ⓑ Ⓒ Ⓓ Ⓔ	43. Ⓐ Ⓑ Ⓒ Ⓓ Ⓔ	47. Ⓐ Ⓑ Ⓒ Ⓓ Ⓔ	

READING PART 1

10 minutes

Directions: This section is about the meaning of words. For each question, decide which choice has most nearly the same meaning as the underlined word or words given. Fill in the corresponding letter on your answer sheet.

1. <u>Ominous</u> clouds

   (A) fair-weather
   (B) unusual
   (C) threatening
   (D) beautiful

2. Foreign <u>currency</u>

   (J) countries
   (K) money
   (L) travel
   (M) customs

3. To <u>vent</u> emotions

   (A) express
   (B) control
   (C) suppress
   (D) deny

4. A <u>vague</u> idea

   (J) intelligent
   (K) plain
   (L) clear
   (M) uncertain

5. He climbed <u>aloft</u>

   (A) down
   (B) upward
   (C) slowly
   (D) carefully

6. A <u>concise</u> report

   (J) brief
   (K) lengthy
   (L) book
   (M) business

7. To exercise <u>vigorously</u>

   (A) daily
   (B) alone
   (C) energetically
   (D) occasionally

8. An art <u>replica</u>

   (J) reproduction
   (K) course
   (L) museum
   (M) antique

9. Team wins <u>consistently</u>

   (A) constantly
   (B) continually
   (C) all the time
   (D) all of the above

10. To <u>shun</u> responsibility

    (J) avoid
    (K) accept
    (L) delegate
    (M) claim

11. A <u>credible</u> source

    (A) unknown
    (B) informed
    (C) reliable
    (D) unwilling

12. Take <u>precise</u> measurements

    (J) estimated
    (K) exact
    (L) careless
    (M) incorrect

13. To <u>heed</u> advice

    (A) consider
    (B) disregard
    (C) ignore
    (D) give

14. Band played with <u>fervor</u>

    (J) instruments
    (K) fear
    (L) difficulty
    (M) enthusiasm

15. To <u>tend</u> a garden

    (A) plan
    (B) dig in
    (C) plant
    (D) care for

16. A <u>stationary</u> train

    (J) motionless
    (K) speeding
    (L) paper
    (M) passenger

17. A <u>practical</u> solution

    (A) difficult
    (B) useful
    (C) complicated
    (D) simple

18. To be <u>punctual</u>

    (J) on time
    (K) late
    (L) tardy
    (M) absent

19. Start an <u>altercation</u>

    (A) project
    (B) journey
    (C) quarrel
    (D) change

20. <u>Ponder</u> choices

    (J) decide recklessly
    (K) consider carefully
    (L) choose quickly
    (M) avoid making

READING PART 2

25 minutes

Directions: Read the passages below and the questions relating to them. Choose the best answer from among the four given for each question, and mark the corresponding space on your answer sheet.

Read the following passage and answer questions 21–25.

About 5,000 years ago, the Egyptian invention of papyrus, paper like material made from an aquatic plant of the same name, revolutionized writing. The tall aquatic reed that produced the paper originated in Egypt and grew abundantly along the banks of the Nile River. Reaching heights from 11 to 25 feet, papyrus was fully utilized by ancient Egyptians. Thick stems of the plant were bound together for rafts. Its outer bark was woven into cloth, mats, shoes, and sails. Inside its thick stems was the spongelike, woody pith material that became paper. Egyptians sliced this pith into thin strips and placed them side by side in layers. The layers were then beaten to create thin sheets which were sun-dried, polished, and perfect for writing. The sheets of papyrus were glued together to form long scrolls that could be rolled for storage. Thousands of ancient papyri have been discovered and carefully excavated during archaeological digs in Egypt. It is believed the warm, dry climate of this country allowed these precious documents to survive.

21. Which of the following choices does not describe papyrus?

(A) an aquatic plant
(B) a short reed like plant
(C) a paper like material to write on
(D) a plant used to make sails and cloth

22. Based on the passage, ancient papyrus documents have survived because they were

(J) well-preserved by the Egyptians
(K) excavated carefully
(L) in a warm, dry climate
(M) glued together

23. The plural of papyrus is

(A) papyrus
(B) papyri
(C) papyruses
(D) none of the above

24. The author indicates that papyrus was

(J) exploited by ancient Egyptians
(K) scarce 5,000 years ago
(L) found growing in the deserts of Egypt
(M) a fragile plant

25. Who would most likely excavate ancient documents?

(A) a meteorologist
(B) a biologist
(C) a psychologist
(D) an archaeologist

Read the following passage and answer questions 26–30.

The most intelligent of all domestic animals, a cat can make an invaluable addition to any home. These feline creatures of beauty and independence are unique and worthy of our deepest affection. Cats are self-reliant, easy to house break, and naturally keep themselves clean. The addition of a cat to any household can have a life long impact on family members. This is especially true for children who are allowed to adopt a pet cat. In addition to supplying companionship, cats can furnish children with important lessons about life. The primary example of this would be the lesson of responsibility. Although children might not be able to accept complete responsibility for a cat, they will learn that a pet requires food, water, exercise, and love. Children can gain satisfaction from helping another living being and learn the importance of providing care for their cat. In addition, cat ownership can provide children with the equally important virtues of patience and gentleness. These are life long lessons and virtues that children will remember as adults.

26. What is the first important lesson that children who own cats will learn?

    (J) companionship
    (K) satisfaction
    (L) patience
    (M) responsibility

27. In the passage, the word domestic means

    (A) intelligent
    (B) clean
    (C) tame
    (D) independent

28. Which of the following was not mentioned as a reason to own a cat?

    (J) easy to house break
    (K) naturally clean
    (L) self-reliant
    (M) affectionate

29. A good title for this passage would be

    (A) Children Need Canine Pets
    (B) The Requirements of Cat Ownership
    (C) The Rewards of Feline Ownership
    (D) Cats Are Clean

30. According to the passage, children who own cats gain satisfaction from

    (J) assisting another living being
    (K) learning responsibility
    (L) owning an intelligent animal
    (M) supplying companionship

Read the following passage and answer questions 31–35.

No two snowflakes are exactly alike. This important discovery was made by Wilson "Snowflake" Bentley who was born on February 9, 1865, in Vermont. Living on a farm where the annual snowfall was 120 inches suited Bentley because he loved nature and snowflakes. He discovered, under a microscope, that every snow crystal was a masterpiece of design that was never repeated. It saddened Bentley to realize the beauty of a snowflake was lost forever when it melted. The intricate patterns he saw could not be saved or shared with others. This prompted him to draw the snowflakes he studied under his microscope, but they always melted before he could finish. When he was seventeen, Bentley received a camera with its own microscope and was finally able to photograph snowflakes to share with the world. For years he developed his technique of micro-photography and recorded the infinite number of snowflake designs he discovered. He spent his life preserving snowflake images and gathered his best photographs in a book named *Snow Crystals*.

31. It suited Bentley to live on a farm in Vermont. This means

    (A) he disliked living there
    (B) it was agreeable to him
    (C) he was not satisfied
    (D) he made his own clothes

32. Why was it difficult for Bentley to draw snowflakes?

    (J) he was not artistic
    (K) they melted before he could finish
    (L) the patterns were too difficult
    (M) he needed a better microscope

33. Why did Bentley try to draw snowflakes?

    (A) he loved nature
    (B) to prove they were all different
    (C) to save and share them
    (D) he was writing a book

34. Bentley first studied snowflakes with a

    (J) magnifying glass
    (K) telescope
    (L) camera
    (M) microscope

35. What is a good topic sentence for this passage?

    (A) Wilson Bentley was the first person to photograph snowflakes.
    (B) Snowflakes are unique.
    (C) Wilson Bentley spent his life studying snowflakes.
    (D) Wilson Bentley loved nature.

Read the following passage and answer questions 36–40.

Hurricanes are whirling storms of wind and rain and the most power-ful storms on Earth. Whether called typhoons in the western Pacific or cyclones in the Indian Ocean, these unpredictable storms, forming over the oceans in tropical regions, cause widespread destruction. Since hur-ricanes gather heat and energy through contact with warm ocean waters, they are limited to these tropical areas for development. The process starts with warm air rising and taking water from the ocean. Cool air rushes in to take the place of the rising warm air, and the same process of air warm-ing, rising, and picking up water continues. Winds begin to swirl around and huge thunderclouds build up which form a system of wind and tor-rential rains that can measure hundreds of miles across! The hurricane winds whirl around the eye, or center, of the storm which remains oddly calm, with little wind and no rain. As a hurricane moves onto land, heavy rain, strong winds, and huge waves, called the storm surge, wreak havoc and destruction.

36. According to the author, hurricanes need contact with tropical oceans to collect

   (J) tropical air
   (K) thunderclouds
   (L) water and energy
   (M) heat and energy

37. Hurricanes in the Indian Ocean are called

   (A) hurricanes
   (B) cyclones
   (C) typhoons
   (D) tornadoes

38. The eye of a hurricane

   (J) causes the most destruction
   (K) contains whirling winds
   (L) causes a storm surge
   (M) has little wind and no rain

39. The hurricane process starts with

   (A) warm air rising
   (B) cool air rushing in
   (C) current changes
   (D) cloud formation

40. Based on the passage, a hurricane that encounters cold water will probably

   (J) increase in size
   (K) have a larger storm surge
   (L) weaken in strength
   (M) none of the above

Read the following passage and answer questions 41–45.

Little is known about Henry Hudson's life. From his maps and journals, we know he was a skilled English navigator with remarkable abilities to map unknown territories. He made four important voyages of exploration while attempting to find an Arctic route to Asia. His first two attempts at success were thwarted by ice packs. In 1609, sailing for the Dutch, he encountered ice again and turned his ship west across the Atlantic Ocean. He sailed up what came to be called the Hudson River before realizing it wasn't the water route he was seeking. Although he failed again at finding a northern passage to Asia, Hudson had become the first European to explore this mighty river. He established Dutch claims to the area around the river and opened our country to Dutch colonization. Still looking for a passage to Asia, Hudson's failed fourth voyage was unfortunately his last. He sailed to what is now Hudson Bay in Canada, where his crew mutinied and cast him adrift. He was never seen again.

41. Hudson's first two voyages failed due to

    (A) stormy seas
    (B) poor navigation
    (C) ice packs
    (D) mutiny

42. The author's intent in writing this passage was to

    (J) provide details about Hudson's life
    (K) criticize Hudson's failed attempts
    (L) explain the importance of Hudson's voyages
    (M) indicate how the Artic route to Asia was discovered

43. Hudson's crew <u>mutinied</u>. This means they

    (A) overthrew his command
    (B) questioned his navigational skills
    (C) sided with Hudson against others
    (D) made claims on land they explored

44. On his third voyage, Hudson was attempting to

    (J) find an Arctic route for the English
    (K) explore North America for the Dutch
    (L) discover an Arctic route for the Dutch
    (M) establish Dutch claims in North America

45. We know Hudson was a skilled navigator from his

    (A) maps and journals
    (B) crew members
    (C) life history
    (D) English documents

Read the following passage and answer questions 46–50.

The Chinese New Year is celebrated on the first day of the first moon of the lunar calendar. It may occur as early as January 21 and as late as February 19. At one time it took 15 full days to welcome the New Year properly, but now the celebration lasts for only a few days. However, preparation for this event takes much longer! Weeks in advance every house is swept and cleaned. Doors and gates are painted in bright red—the color that symbolizes happiness to the Chinese. Inscriptions of fortune and happiness are written on red paper and attached to doors. Gifts are wrapped in red paper and all the candles used on this holiday are red. Lanterns are made, and new clothes are bought or made for family members. New shoes are especially important; tradition states that it is bad luck to step on the ground in old shoes on New Year's Day. Finally, when all the preparations are complete, the celebrating begins!

46. Which is not mentioned as a preparation for the Chinese New Year?

   (J) painting doors and gates
   (K) wrapping gifts
   (L) eating a special meal
   (M) buying new clothes

47. The celebration of Chinese New Year now lasts

   (A) for only a few days
   (B) a full 15 days
   (C) for weeks
   (D) one day

48. The date for the Chinese New Year is determined by

   (J) tradition
   (K) weather
   (L) convenience
   (M) lunar calendar

49. To the Chinese, red is a symbol of

   (A) good fortune
   (B) happiness
   (C) bad luck
   (D) cleanliness

50. The author wrote this passage to

   (J) entertain
   (K) criticize
   (L) persuade
   (M) express an opinion

LANGUAGE PART 1

23 minutes

Directions: This is a test of how well you can find errors in a piece of writing. The directions below tell what type of mistake may be present. If no mistake is made, choose the last answer.

Directions: Look for mistakes in <u>spelling</u>.

1. (A) pattern
    (B) gentle
    (C) cement
    (D) rotten
    (E) *(No mistakes)*

2. (J) special
    (K) frieght
    (L) recline
    (M) address
    (N) *(No mistakes)*

3. (A) followed
    (B) journal
    (C) safety
    (D) cansel
    (E) *(No mistakes)*

4. (J) practic
    (K) faint
    (L) barrier
    (M) seasons
    (N) *(No mistakes)*

5. (A) cracker
    (B) removeable
    (C) seriously
    (D) addresses
    (E) *(No mistakes)*

6. (J) nervous
    (K) pioneer
    (L) evening
    (M) churchs
    (N) *(No mistakes)*

7. (A) effort
    (B) gatherng
    (C) quarrel
    (D) orbit
    (E) *(No mistakes)*

8. (J) hourly
    (K) liberty
    (L) janitor
    (M) youthfull
    (N) *(No mistakes)*

9. (A) measure
    (B) daughter
    (C) orchard
    (D) imform
    (E) *(No mistakes)*

10. (J) fantacy
    (K) support
    (L) business
    (M) parachute
    (N) *(No mistakes)*

Directions: Look for mistakes in <u>capitalization</u>.

11. (A) Today our Teacher announced that
    (B) Mayor Anderson would be coming to
    (C) speak to our class next week.
    (D) *(No mistakes)*

12. (J)   Darryl's mother had no idea
    (K)   that the song "Happy birthday"
    (L)   was written in the state of Kentucky.
    (D)   *(No mistakes)*

13. (A)   The planet jupiter is only one
    (B)   of several planets made of gas
    (C)   in our solar system.
    (D)   *(No mistakes)*

14. (J)   In 1863, during the Civil war,
    (K)   Abraham Lincoln made
    (L)   Thanksgiving a national holiday.
    (M)   *(No mistakes)*

15. (A)   Right before Labor Day,
    (B)   we have plans to visit my
    (C)   grandfather in the south.
    (D)   *(No mistakes)*

16. (J)   Lily handed out fliers for
    (K)   her father's campaign, and made
    (L)   sure to say, "don't forget to vote!"
    (M)   *(No mistakes)*

17. (A)   The Golden Gate Bridge was
    (B)   the longest suspension Bridge
    (C)   in the world for 27 years.
    (D)   *(No mistakes)*

18. (J)   Women got the right to
    (K)   vote on May 19, 1919, when
    (L)   the 19th amendment was passed.
    (M)   *(No mistakes)*

19. (A)   When my mother was little,
    (B)   she used to fish in a River
    (C)   that ran past the back of her home.
    (D)   *(No mistakes)*

20. (J)   After consulting with his counselor,
    (K)   Carlos decided to register for
    (L)   cooking, geography, french, and P.E.
    (M)   *(No mistakes)*

Directions: Look for mistakes in <u>punctuation</u>.

21. (A)   When you go camping,
    (B)   its a good idea to take along
    (C)   a compass and a first aid kit.
    (D)   *(No mistakes)*

22. (J)   There are not as many
    (K)   brine shrimp in the Great
    (L)   Salt Lake as there used to be?
    (M)   *(No mistakes)*

23. (A)   "Don't forget to write
    (B)   a thank-you note to your
    (C)   grandmother," my father said.
    (D)   *(No mistakes)*

24. (J)   I was surprised when Liz
    (K)   told me that her family was
    (L)   moving to Tucson Arizona.
    (M)   *(No mistakes)*

25. (A)   While we were eating:
    (B)   a raccoon came into our
    (C)   backyard and startled Brian.
    (D)   *(No mistakes)*

26. (J)   Constellations can be defined
    (K)   as patterns of stars named
    (L)   for a people animals, or objects.
    (M)   *(No mistakes)*

27. (A)   Vincent Van Gogh was a famous
    (B)   Dutch painter; who had very little
    (C)   success during his lifetime.
    (D)   *(No mistakes)*

28. (J)   Our teacher announced
    (K)   "Please put your pencils
    (L)   away and close your books."
    (M)   *(No mistakes)*

29. (A) For the dinner, we needed
    (B) salad and bread, we also
    (C) needed juice and a dessert.
    (D) *(No mistakes)*

30. (J) O. Henry's story, The
    (K) Gift of the Magi," is a good
    (L) illustration of irony.
    (M) *(No mistakes)*

In questions 31 through 35, look for any mistakes
in <u>usage and expression</u>.

31. (A) The coach let Brittany play for two quarters
        of the game.
    (B) Brittany got tired, so she laid down on the
        court.
    (C) Her coach came over to see if she had been
        hurt.
    (D) *(No mistakes)*

32. (J) Jackson got a letter from Carlos in Peru.
    (K) Inside, Jackson found photos of Carlos and
        his pet dog.
    (L) Carlos wrote that he is doing very good in
        school.
    (M) *(No mistakes)*

33. (A) Mosquitoes usually live near still water, like
        ponds.
    (B) These insects feed mainly on the juices from
        plants.
    (C) But females have to draw blood in order to
        nourish its eggs.
    (D) *(No mistakes)*

34. (J) Most high schools offer drivers' education
        courses.
    (K) Students learn about traffic laws and safety
        on the road.
    (L) Many students go on to take and pass the test
        for a learner's permit.
    (M) *(No mistakes)*

35. (A) The neighbors paid my sister and I for do-
        ing odd jobs for them.
    (B) After a year of saving, we were able to buy
        our mountain bikes.
    (C) Now other kids in our neighborhood want to
        get mountain bikes.
    (D) *(No mistakes)*

In questions 36 through 40, choose the <u>best</u> way
of expressing the idea.

36. (J) I need to pick a book for my book report,
        which is due in two weeks.
    (K) My book report is due in two weeks, I need
        to pick a book.
    (L) Due in two weeks, I need to pick a book for
        my book report.
    (M) Due in two weeks, a book needs to be picked
        for my report.

37. (A) Amelia Earhart saw her first plane at a state
        fair, she was ten.
    (B) At age ten, at a state fair was when Amelia
        Earhart saw her first plane.
    (C) At age ten, Amelia Earhart saw her first plane
        at a state fair.
    (D) At a state fair was when Amelia Earhart saw
        her first plane at age ten.

38. (J) Lamar had a solo in the choir's Christmas
        concert. He was prepared.
    (K) Lamar was prepared for his solo in the choir's
        concert for Christmas.
    (L) Prepared for his solo, Lamar was singing in
        the choir's Christmas concert.
    (M) Lamar was prepared for his solo in the choir's
        Christmas concert.

39. (A) Wildfires destroy millions of acres of land: in this country every summer.

    (B) Every summer, wildfires destroy, in this country, millions of acres of land.

    (C) Wildfires destroy millions of acres of land in this country every summer.

    (D) Millions of acres of land in this country every summer wildfires destroy.

40. (J) Finally, Ashley's parents said that she could have her party at the pool.

    (K) Finally, she could have her party at the pool Ashley's parents said.

    (L) Ashley's parents said; that she could have her party at the pool, finally.

    (M) Finally, Ashley's parents said: that she could have her party at the pool.

LANGUAGE PART 2

7 minutes

Directions: For questions 41 and 42, choose the <u>best</u> answer based on the following paragraph.

[1]Many urban apartment dwellers who want fresh produce plant gardens in containers. [2]These people don't have backyards. [3]Plants grown in containers capture the sun from fire escapes, terraces, or balconies. [4]Vegetables that grow well in containers include carrots, cucumbers, tomatoes, and squash. [5]Some people even grow salad gardens, <u>in that they</u> consist of lettuce and herbs, like chives or basil. [6]These plants are decorative and they are also functional. [7]Fruit can also be grown in containers. [8]Strawberry and blueberry plants both grow well in containers. [9]But fruit plants, like all container plants, must be regularly watered, because their roots can't stretch in search of moisture.

41. What is the <u>best</u> way to write the underlined part of sentence 5?

    (A) and
    (B) they
    (C) which
    (D) *(No change)*

42. Which sentence should be left out of this paragraph?

    (J) Sentence 1
    (K) Sentence 2
    (L) Sentence 7
    (M) Sentence 8

Directions: For questions 43 and 44, choose the <u>best</u> answer based on the following paragraph.

> [1]Brandon's class was going to learn a dance in celebration of Cinco de Mayo and will perform the dance in front of the entire school. [2]Parents were planning to bring traditional Mexican food for a party to be held in the classroom. [3]After the first practice, Brandon found the dance very difficult. [4]So the teacher worked with Brandon, showing him how to move his feet quickly in a pattern. [5]Brandon's feet kept getting tangled up with each other, and at the same time, he had to keep a large sombrero on his head. [6]After much practice, Brandon remembered the pattern and his feet did, too. [7]He looked forward to the performance.

43. In sentence 1, which word is the wrong tense?

    (A) learn
    (B) perform
    (C) was
    (D) will

44. Which change should be made in sentence 4?

    (J) Change *so* to *however*
    (K) Change *him* to *her*
    (L) Change *quickly* to *quick*
    (M) *(No change)*

Directions: For questions 45 through 47, choose the <u>best</u> answer based on the following paragraph.

> [1]Over summer vacation, Kenya fractured her leg in two places during a ski trip. [2]She wondered if she would be able to play soccer when it started again in the fall. [3]Kenya had been playing soccer since kindergarten. [4]Her cast had just been removed. [5]Although the doctor said she could play sports again, Kenya's leg still felt sore. [6]She was also afraid of injuring it again. [7]Kenya's father made sure the coach understood this when Kenya arrived for practice the first day. [8]Kenya sat on the bench and watched her teammates play. [9]Once the ball went out of bounds and headed write toward her. [10]Unable to stop herself, Kenya put out her leg and kicked it!

45. What is the <u>best</u> way to combine sentences 4 and 5?

    (A) Since the doctor said she could play sports again, because her cast had just been removed, Kenya's leg still felt sore.
    (B) Her cast had just been removed, and although the doctor said she could play sports again, Kenya's leg still felt sore.
    (C) Her cast had just been removed, although the doctor said she could play sports again, Kenya's leg still felt sore.
    (D) Although the doctor said she could play sports again, her cast had just been removed, since Kenya's leg still felt sore.

46. Which sentence should be left out of this paragraph?

    (J) Sentence 2
    (K) Sentence 3
    (L) Sentence 8
    (M) Sentence 10

47. In sentence 9, which word is used incorrectly?

    (A) once
    (B) bounds
    (C) write
    (D) toward

Directions: For questions 48 through 50, choose the best answer based on the following paragraph.

[1]In times and places, where no money existed, people used the barter system. [2]The barter system worked best in rural areas where people produced goods that could be traded with others. [3]Here, people obtained what they needed not with money, but by bartering or trading things they grew or made. [4]For example, a farmer who needed a coat might offer to trade some of his wheat for a coat made by a local tailor. [5]Hopefully, the tailor would need wheat at that moment. [6]If not, the farmer would have to find another tailor or offer something else, like wool from his sheep. [7]The barter system does not work if people have nothing to trade.

48. Which change should be made in sentence 1?

    (J) Delete the comma after *places*.

    (K) Change *where* to *when*.

    (L) Change *in* to *wherein*.

    (M) *(No change)*

49. What is the best way to write the underlined part of sentence 3?

    (A) For this reason

    (B) In this system

    (C) In one example

    (D) *(No change)*

50. Which sentence could best be added after sentence 7?

    (J) Many goods were traded in this system, including vegetables.

    (K) For this reason, most people make their own money from jobs.

    (L) It is interesting to read about how people lived long ago.

    (M) For this reason, most communities no longer use the barter system.

MATH PART 1

33 minutes

Directions: Choose the best answer from the four given for each problem.

1. $4^2 - 3(5)$

    (A) −7
    (B) 1
    (C) 25
    (D) 65

2. Steve's ice cream stand conducted a survey of favorite ice cream toppings. The table shows the results of the survey. If Steve decides to sell only the three most popular toppings based on this survey, what will they be?

Toppings	Hot Fudge	Caramel	Peanut Butter	Butterscotch	Strawberry	Raspberry
Frequency	29	20	16	18	12	5

    (J) Hot Fudge, Caramel, and Peanut Butter
    (K) Butterscotch, Strawberry, and Raspberry
    (L) Hot Fudge, Caramel, and Butterscotch
    (M) Peanut Butter, Strawberry, and Raspberry

3. Melissa saved 20% of her first paycheck. If she saved $40, how much was her first paycheck?

    (A) $48
    (B) $60
    (C) $80
    (D) $200

4. $\dfrac{3}{4} + \dfrac{1}{6}$

    (J) $\dfrac{1}{3}$

    (K) $\dfrac{2}{5}$

    (L) $\dfrac{7}{12}$

    (M) $\dfrac{11}{12}$

5. Which of the following is <u>not</u> prime?

    (A) 13
    (B) 23
    (C) 51
    (D) 97

6. The following graph shows how many shoes of each color were sold at Sherry's Shoes. What percent of the shoes sold were black?

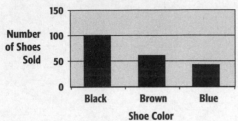

Shoes Sold at Sherry's Shoes

(J) 25%
(K) 50%
(L) 75%
(M) 100%

7. Evan had $9.63 left after he spent $21.25. How much money did he have originally?

(A) $11.62
(B) $21.25
(C) $24.67
(D) $30.88

8. In a high school, the tenth, eleventh, and twelfth grade classes kept track of the total amount of funds they raised each month. During which month did the tenth grade class raise more money than the eleventh and twelfth grade classes combined?

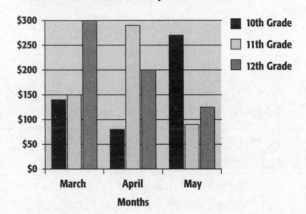

Amount of Funds Raised by Three Classes

(J) March
(K) April
(L) May
(M) Cannot be determined

9. Thirty-five students decided to use the bus for their transportation from school to summer camp. The bus ride costs $9 per student. How much money will the driver collect?

(A) $26
(B) $44
(C) $270
(D) $315

10. Renee's mom placed the following 16 baked goods on a tray. She said Renee could select one. Renee likes them all and selects with her eyes closed. What is the probability Renee selected a frosted brownie?

Baked Goods	Plain	Frosted
Cookie	4	1
Brownie	2	6
Cupcake	0	3

(J) $\dfrac{1}{8}$

(K) $\dfrac{3}{8}$

(L) $\dfrac{7}{16}$

(M) $\dfrac{5}{8}$

11. Madeline orders one plain pizza and one pizza with pepperoni, sausage, and mushrooms. A pizza costs $12 plus $1 per topping. How much will the pizza cost?

(A) $24

(B) $25

(C) $26

(D) $27

12. Mike divided his monthly expenses according to the chart. What fraction of his expenses goes toward rent and food?

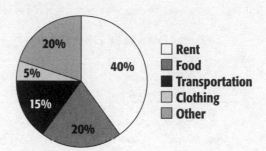

(J) $\dfrac{1}{5}$

(K) $\dfrac{2}{5}$

(L) $\dfrac{3}{5}$

(M) $\dfrac{4}{5}$

13. The perimeter of the pentagon is 22 meters. If x is the missing length of one side, find the value of x.

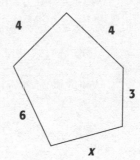

(A) 5

(B) 6

(C) 7

(D) 8

14. The fifth grade class at Morgan's Elementary ran a one-mile race in September, January, and June. Which student showed the overall most improvement over the course of the school year?

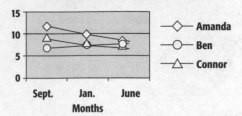

Minutes Taken to Run One Mile

(J) Amanda
(K) Ben
(L) Connor
(M) Cannot be determined

15. What is the greatest common factor of 45, 75, and 105?

(A) 5
(B) 15
(C) 25
(D) 45

16. $(-6)(3)(-2) =$

(J) −36
(K) −9
(L) 9
(M) 36

17. Ms. Harvey gave away six cases of bottled water during the school field days. Each case contains 24 bottles. How many bottles of water did she give away?

(A) 18
(B) 30
(C) 144
(D) 180

18. If a can of soup costs $0.89, how much will 100 cans of soup cost?

(J) $1.89
(K) $8.90
(L) $89.00
(M) $890.00

19. Corey orders a tossed salad with a side order each of French fries and fruit salad. How much will the meal cost?

Main Course	Price	Side Orders (Each Side Order $1.25 Extra)
Hamburger	$2.25	Macaroni & Cheese
Chicken Sandwich	$2.50	French Fries
Bowl of Soup	$3.00	Fruit Salad
Tossed Salad	$2.60	Apple Sauce

(A) $2.60
(B) $4.75
(C) $5.00
(D) $5.10

20. If $x + 16 = -64$, what is the value of x?

(J) −80
(K) −48
(L) 48
(M) 80

21. How many more United States presidents were named James than William?

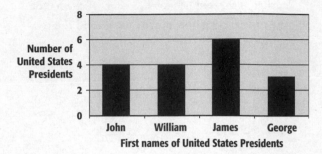

(A) 1

(B) 2

(C) 4

(D) 6

22. The varsity baseball team won $\frac{3}{4}$ of their games. They played 20 games. How many games did they win?

(J) 12

(K) 13

(L) 14

(M) 15

23. Arrange the following three fractions in order from least to greatest: $\frac{3}{5}$, $\frac{2}{7}$, and $\frac{1}{2}$

(A) $\frac{2}{7}$, $\frac{1}{2}$, and $\frac{3}{5}$

(B) $\frac{1}{2}$, $\frac{2}{7}$, and $\frac{3}{5}$

(C) $\frac{2}{7}$, $\frac{3}{5}$, and $\frac{1}{2}$

(D) $\frac{1}{2}$, $\frac{3}{5}$, and $\frac{2}{7}$

24. Brandon has $851.63 in his savings account. He deposits $43.50. How much will he have in his account after the deposit?

(J) $800.00

(K) $809.13

(L) $894.00

(M) $895.13

Use the following table for questions 25 and 26.

	Mercury	Venus	Earth	Mars
Average Distance from the Sun in Miles	36×10^6	67×10^6	93×10^6	141×10^6
Revolution in Earth-Days	88 days	224.7 days	365.26 days	687 days

25. According to the table, how much closer to the sun is the Earth than Mars?

(A) 48 miles

(B) 234 miles

(C) 48,000,000 miles

(D) 234,000,000 miles

26. According to the table, how many earth-days will it take for Mercury to complete two revolutions?

(J) 176

(K) 449.4

(L) 730.5

(M) 1,374

27. What fraction of students chose pepperoni as their favorite pizza topping?

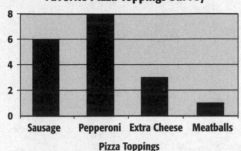

Favorite Pizza Toppings Survey

(A) $\dfrac{1}{3}$

(B) $\dfrac{4}{9}$

(C) $\dfrac{4}{5}$

(D) $\dfrac{8}{9}$

28. In a right triangle ABC, $m\angle A = 90°$, AB = 3, and AC = 4. Find BC.

(J) 3

(K) 4

(L) 5

(M) 6

29. $\dfrac{5}{8} \div \dfrac{3}{4} =$

(A) $\dfrac{5}{24}$

(B) $\dfrac{15}{32}$

(C) $\dfrac{5}{6}$

(D) $\dfrac{20}{21}$

30. Maureen went shopping for clothes during no-tax week. She bought two pairs of pants for $16 each and three shirts for $15 each. If she hands the cashier $80, how much change will she receive?

(J) $3

(K) $5

(L) $18

(M) $49

31. The table below shows the position, number of employees in each position, and annual salaries for employees in each position at The Kent and Bart Factory. How much money does the company spend annually on salaries for the president and vice presidents combined?

Position	Number of Employees	Annual Salary Each
President	1	$200,000
Vice President	3	$120,000
Sales Person	17	$60,000
Clerical Person	8	$25,000

(A) $120,000

(B) $200,000

(C) $320,000

(D) $560,000

32. Evaluate $|x| + 2y$, if $x = -4$ and $y = 3$.

(J) 2

(K) 6

(L) 7

(M) 10

MATH PART 2

7 minutes

Directions: For questions 33–50, <u>estimate</u> the answer; no scratch work is allowed. Do <u>not</u> try to calculate exact answers.

33. The closest estimate of 523 + 389 is ____.

   (A) 800
   (B) 900
   (C) 1,000
   (D) 1,100

34. The closest estimate of 9,032 – 6,312 is ____.

   (J) 1,000
   (K) 2,000
   (L) 3,000
   (M) 4,000

35. The closest estimate of 4,326 ÷ 62 is ____.

   (A) 7
   (B) 70
   (C) 700
   (D) 7,000

36. The closest estimate of 61 + 58 + 62 + 56 is ____.

   (J) 180
   (K) 200
   (L) 220
   (M) 240

37. The closest estimate of 7.21 × 9.74 is ____.

   (A) 63
   (B) 70
   (C) 80
   (D) 85

38. The closest estimate of $14.75 – $4.03 is ____.

   (J) $10.00
   (K) $11.00
   (L) $19.00
   (M) $21.00

39. The number 16.8236 rounded to the nearest hundredth's place is ____.

   (A) 16.8
   (B) 16.9
   (C) 16.82
   (D) 17.0

40. The closest estimate of 10.8 × 99.9 is ____.

   (J) 990
   (K) 1,000
   (L) 1,100
   (M) 11,000

41. The number 16,348.351 rounded to the nearest tenth's place is ____.

   (A) 16,348
   (B) 16,348.3
   (C) 16,348.35
   (D) 16,348.4

42. The number 6,295 rounded to the nearest thousand is ____.

   (J) 6,000
   (K) 6,200
   (L) 6,300
   (M) 7,000

43. The number 234.567 rounded to the nearest whole number is _____.

    (A) 234
    (B) 234.57
    (C) 234.6
    (D) 235

44. If a rocket travels at about 16,200 m/h and an airplane travels at about 387 m/h, the rocket travels approximately how many times faster than the airplane?

    (J) 30
    (K) 40
    (L) 50
    (M) 60

45. The number 3,630 rounded to the nearest hundred is _____.

    (A) 3,000
    (B) 3,600
    (C) 3,700
    (D) 4,000

46. The closest estimate of 21(3 + 6) is _____.

    (J) 100
    (K) 200
    (L) 300
    (M) 400

47. If Theresa works for 11 hours at $7.10 per hour, which is the closest estimate of the amount of money she will make during that 11 hour shift?

    (A) $70.00
    (B) $77.00
    (C) $88.00
    (D) $99.00

48. If you need to buy five jars of apple sauce at $1.12 and two pounds of cucumbers at $0.93 per pound, which is the closest estimate for the amount of money you should take to the store?

    (J) $5.00
    (K) $6.00
    (L) $8.00
    (M) $9.00

49. Last week the mileage on your car was 23,321. This week the mileage is 23,492. Which is the closest estimate for the number of miles driven during that time?

    (A) 200
    (B) 250
    (C) 300
    (D) 350

50. The closest estimate of (5,021 − 4,158) ÷ 10 is _____.

    (J) 25
    (K) 50
    (L) 75
    (M) 100

ABILITY PART 1

25 minutes

Directions: For each question, the three figures in the question are alike in some way. Select the answer choice that shares that similarity.

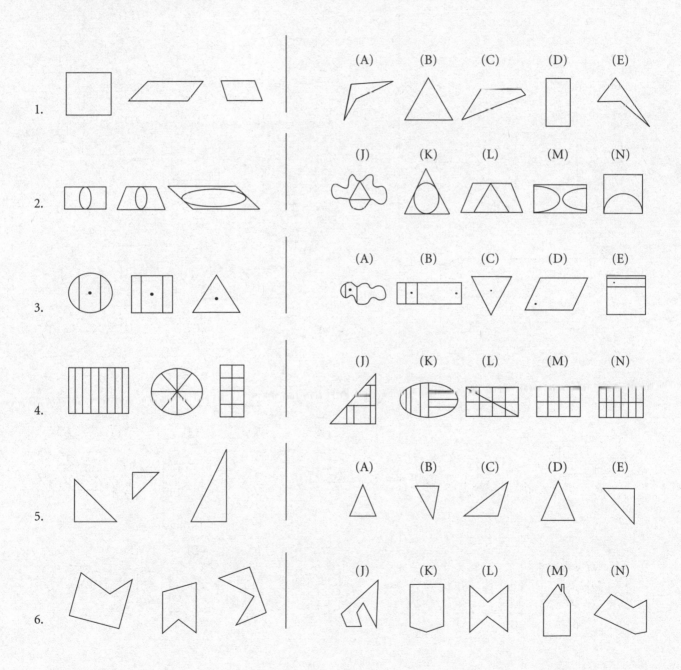

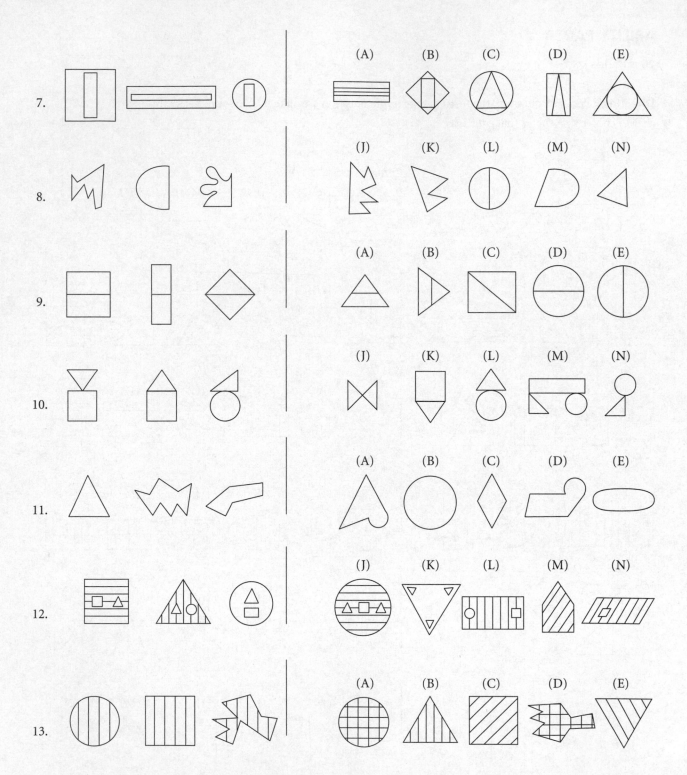

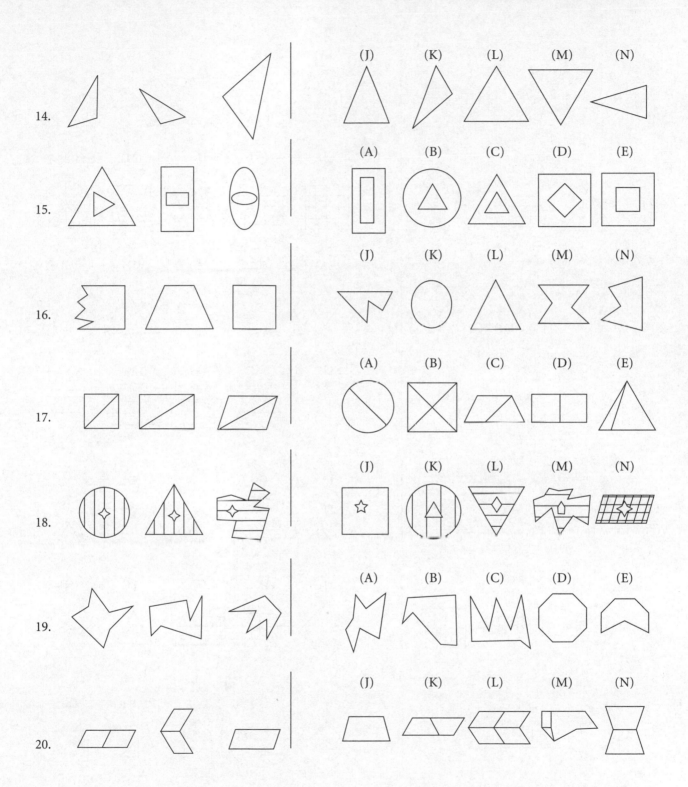

14.

(J) (K) (L) (M) (N)

15.

(A) (B) (C) (D) (E)

16.

(J) (K) (L) (M) (N)

17.

(A) (B) (C) (D) (E)

18.

(J) (K) (L) (M) (N)

19.

(A) (B) (C) (D) (E)

20.

(J) (K) (L) (M) (N)

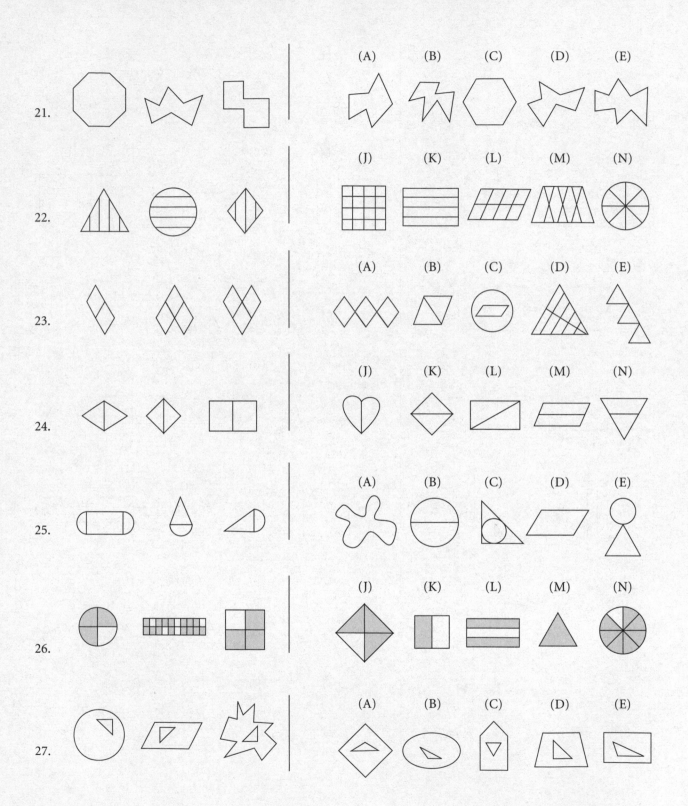

21.

(A) (B) (C) (D) (E)

22.

(J) (K) (L) (M) (N)

23.

(A) (B) (C) (D) (E)

24.

(J) (K) (L) (M) (N)

25.

(A) (B) (C) (D) (E)

26.

(J) (K) (L) (M) (N)

27.

(A) (B) (C) (D) (E)

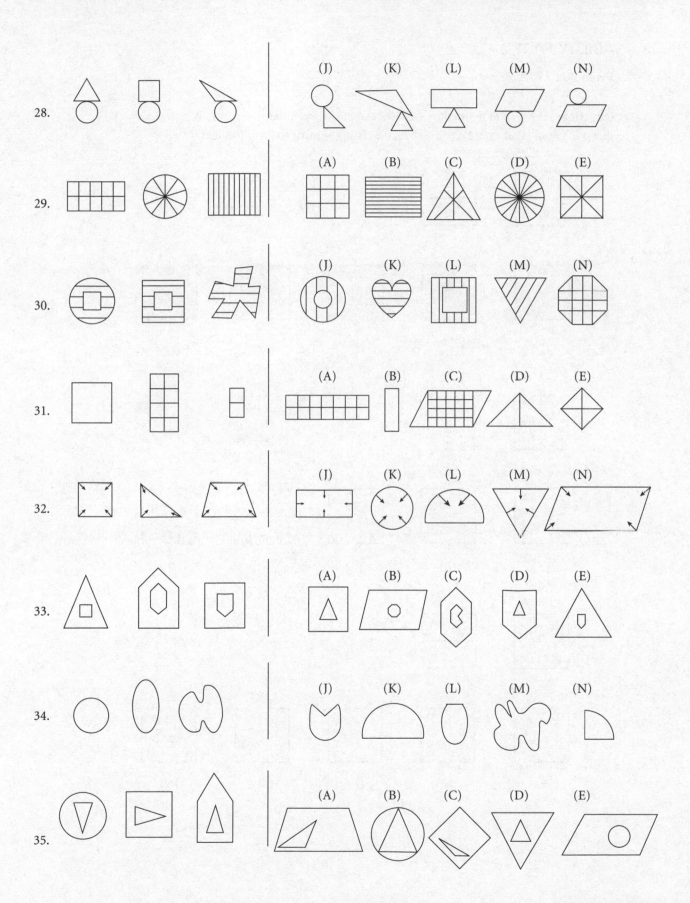

ABILITY PART 2

7 minutes

Directions: The second figure shows a particular change from the first figure. Which answer choice shows the figure that would result if the same change is made to the third figure?

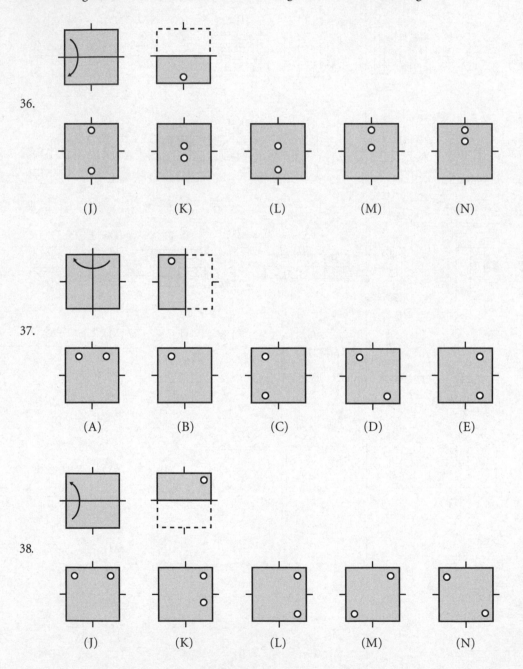

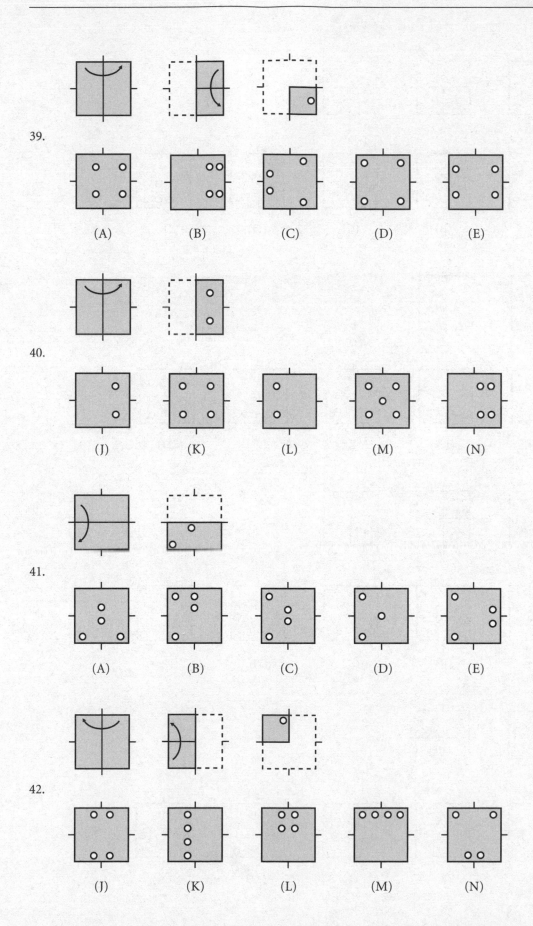

39.

(A)   (B)   (C)   (D)   (E)

40.

(J)   (K)   (L)   (M)   (N)

41.

(A)   (B)   (C)   (D)   (E)

42.

(J)   (K)   (L)   (M)   (N)

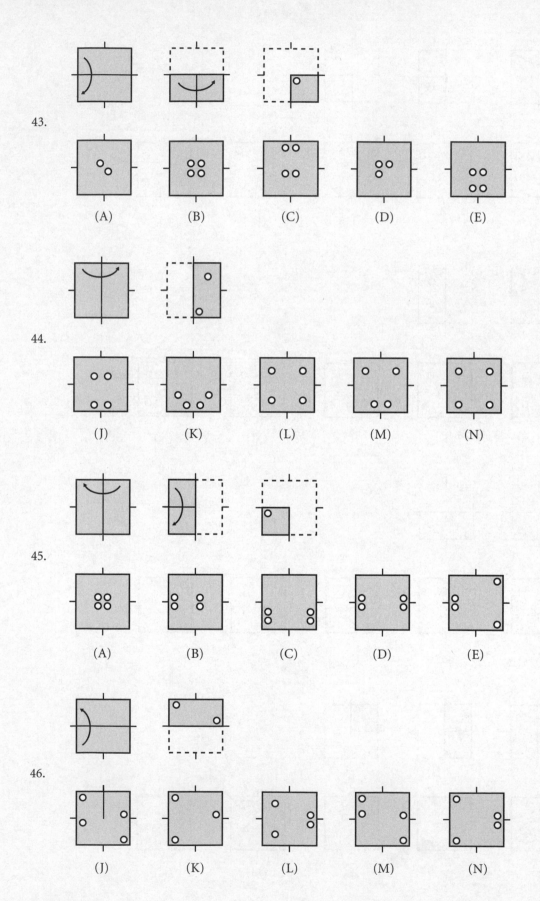

43.

(A) (B) (C) (D) (E)

44.

(J) (K) (L) (M) (N)

45.

(A) (B) (C) (D) (E)

46.

(J) (K) (L) (M) (N)

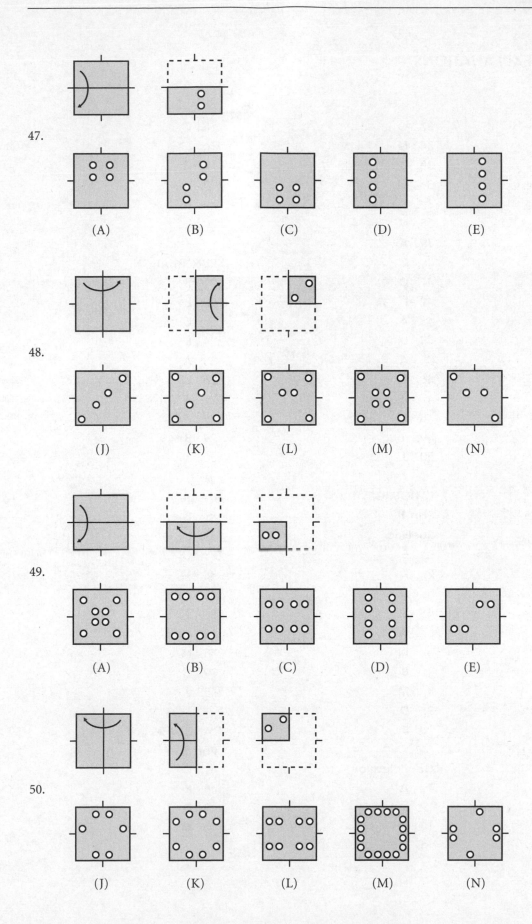

47.

(A)　(B)　(C)　(D)　(E)

48.

(J)　(K)　(L)　(M)　(N)

49.

(A)　(B)　(C)　(D)　(E)

50.

(J)　(K)　(L)　(M)　(N)

ANSWERS AND EXPLANATIONS

Answer Key

READING

Part 1

1. C
2. K
3. A
4. M
5. B
6. J
7. C
8. J
9. D
10. J
11. C
12. K
13. A
14. M
15. D
16. J
17. B
18. J
19. C
20. K

READING

Part 2

21. B
22. L
23. B
24. J
25. D
26. M
27. C
28. M
29. C
30. J
31. B
32. K

33. C
34. M
35. C
36. M
37. B
38. M
39. A
40. L
41. C
42. L
43. A
44. L
45. A
46. L
47. A
48. M
49. B
50. J

LANGUAGE

Part 1

Spelling

1. E
2. K
3. D
4. J
5. B
6. M
7. B
8. M
9. D
10. J

Capitalization

11. A
12. K
13. A
14. J

15. C
16. L
17. B
18. L
19. B
20. L

PUNCTUATION

21. B
22. L
23. D
24. L
25. A
26. L
27. B
28. J
29. B
30. J

Usage

31. B
32. L
33. C
34. M
35. A
36. J
37. C
38. M
39. C
40. J

LANGUAGE

Part 2

41. C
42. K
43. D
44. M

45. **B**
46. **K**
47. **C**
48. **J**
49. **B**
50. **M**

MATH
Part 1
1. **B**
2. **L**
3. **D**
4. **M**
5. **C**
6. **K**
7. **D**
8. **L**
9. **D**
10. **K**
11. **D**
12. **L**
13. **A**
14. **J**
15. **B**
16. **M**
17. **C**
18. **L**
19. **D**
20. **J**
21. **B**
22. **M**
23. **A**
24. **M**
25. **C**
26. **J**
27. **B**
28. **L**
29. **C**
30. **J**
31. **D**
32. **M**

MATH
Part 2
33. **B**
34. **L**
35. **B**
36. **M**
37. **B**
38. **K**
39. **C**
40. **L**
41. **D**
42. **J**
43. **D**
44. **K**
45. **B**
46. **K**
47. **B**
48. **L**
49. **A**
50. **M**

ABILITY
Part 1
1. **D**
2. **K**
3. **C**
4. **M**
5. **E**
6. **K**
7. **B**
8. **N**
9. **D**
10. **L**
11. **C**
12. **L**
13. **B**
14. **K**
15. **E**
16. **M**
17. **A**
18. **N**

19. **E**
20. **L**
21. **D**
22. **K**
23. **A**
24. **J**
25. **B**
26. **J**
27. **D**
28. **M**
29. **B**
30. **K**
31. **A**
32. **N**
33. **C**
34. **M**
35. **D**

ABILITY
Part 2
36. **J**
37. **A**
38. **L**
39. **E**
40. **K**
41. **C**
42. **J**
43. **B**
44. **M**
45. **D**
46. **N**
47. **E**
48. **M**
49. **C**
50. **K**

READING PART 1

1. C

The answer must contain the words *threatening* or *menacing* and would refer to storm clouds. Clouds may be fair-weather (A), unusual (B), or beautiful (D) but these do not describe *ominous*.

2. K

Currency is money in circulation. Countries (J), travel (L), and *customs* (M) are frequently used terms, so they might be confusing if you do not know the actual meaning of *currency*.

3. A

Vent means to give expression to or relieve. *Control* (B), *suppress* (C), which means to keep from being revealed, and *deny* (D), which means to refuse to recognize, are all different in meaning from *vent*.

4. M

Vague means uncertain or not clear, so this would eliminate *plain* (K) and *clear* (L) as correct choices. An idea that was vague or uncertain would also not be considered intelligent (J).

5. B

The word *aloft* means high up or upward (B). This eliminates *down* (A) as a choice since it is opposite in meaning. If you are climbing aloft you may climb slowly (C) or carefully (D), but neither of these choices mean *upward*.

6. J

A concise report would be brief (J), or short. *Lengthy* (K) is opposite in meaning. A book report (L) or a business report (M) could be concise, and these choices would be misleading if you do not know that *concise* is not a type of report.

7. C

Vigorously means energetically (C) or forcefully. *Daily* (A) and *occasionally* (D) refer to how often you can exercise. You may also exercise alone (B), but this does not mean *vigorously*.

8. J

A replica is a copy or a reproduction. *Course* (K), *museum* (L), and *antique* (M) are all words that might be associated with art, but *reproduction* is the only choice for replica.

9. D

Consistently means constantly (A), continually (B), unchanging, and all the time (C), so all of the above (D) is the correct choice. All the choices are very similar in meaning and this is a clue they are all correct.

10. J

Shun means to avoid or keep away from. *Accept* (K) and *claim* (M) are similar in definition and mean the opposite of shun. To delegate (L) responsibility would be to entrust it to another person, which is not the same as avoiding it.

11. C

The answer should contain the word *reliable* or *believable*. An informed (B) source might be credible, but this choice is not the best definition for *credible*. *Unknown* (A) and *unwilling* (D) do not reflect the meaning of *credible*.

12. K

Precise means exact or definite. *Estimated* (J), which means nearly exact, *incorrect* (M), and *careless* (L) are all similar in that they do not describe measurements that would be exact or definite.

13. A

Heed means to pay attention to or consider. *Disregard* (B) and *ignore* (C) are similar in meaning and are opposites of *heed*. You would not give (D) advice if you were just considering it.

14. M

Fervor is defined as enthusiasm (M) or intensity of feeling. It is understood that a band would need instruments (J) in order to play, but *fervor* is not another word for instruments. *Fear* (K) and *difficulty* (L) both describe negative conditions, and similar choices can be eliminated.

15. D

Tend means to look after, watch over, or care for. All the other choices are things you might do for a garden as you tend it, but only *care for* (D) means the same as *tend*.

16. J

Stationary means motionless or not moving. This eliminates *speeding* (K) and *passenger* (M) as choices. You might chose *paper* (L) as the answer if you mistake *stationary* for *stationery*, which is writing paper and envelopes.

17. B

Practical is defined as useful (B) or based on experience. *Difficult* (A), *complicated* (C), and *simple* (D) are all words that can describe a solution, but only *useful* describes the word *practical*.

18. J

Punctual is defined as prompt or on time (J). Late (K) and *tardy* (L), which means late or slow, are both opposites of *punctual*. You could not be on time if you were absent (M) and stayed away.

19. C

An altercation is defined as a noisy quarrel (C) or dispute. Project (A) and journey (B) are things you can start, but neither word means *altercation*. If only the beginning of the word *altercation* is recognized, *change* (D) might seem like a good choice since *alter* means to change.

20. K

Ponder means to consider carefully (K) or think over. To decide recklessly (J) or choose quickly (L) would be the opposite of considering carefully. If you avoid making (M) choices, there would be no need to ponder them.

READING PART 2

21. B

Papyrus is not a short reed like plant. The passage states it is a tall plant that grows from 11 to 25 feet. Papyrus is an aquatic plant (A), and it was used to make sails and cloth (D). A paper like material to write on might be confusing if the first sentence of the passage is not read carefully. It states that papyrus is a paper-like material that is made from a plant with the same name. Both the plant and the paper are called papyrus.

22. L

The last sentence of the passage clearly states it is believed the warm, dry climate (L) of Egypt allowed these documents to survive. The passage does mention that sheets of papyrus were glued together (M) and excavated carefully (K), but these were not given as reasons for their survival. The passage does not mention the Egyptians preserving the documents.

23. B

Plural means more than one. The passage states that thousands of papyri have been discovered, so *papyri* (B) is the plural of *papyrus*. *Papyruses* (C) may seem like a good choice since we usually add an *s* or *es* to words to make them plural.

24. J

Exploited (J) means to utilize fully, and the passage states that papyrus was fully utilized by the Egyptians. The passage also states that papyrus grew abundantly which means in great amounts, so it would not be scarce (K), or not abundant.

An aquatic plant grows on or in the water (along the banks of the Nile) and not in the desert (L). Papyrus could not have been a fragile or weak plant (M) since its stems were used to make rafts.

25. D

An archaeologist (D) studies the remains of ancient times, and the passage mentions that papyri were carefully excavated during archaeological digs. A biologist (B) studies living organisms, a psychologist (C) studies human behavior, and a meteorologist (A) studies weather conditions.

26. M

The author states the primary example of important lessons for children is the lesson of responsibility (M). *Primary* means occurring first in sequence or importance, so *responsibility* is correct. The passage indicates that cats supply companionship (J) and children gain satisfaction (K), but these are not lessons. *Patience* (L) is mentioned as a virtue and not a lesson.

27. C

Domestic, when referring to animals, means tame (C) or gentle. *Domestic*, when used as a noun, means a household servant, so *clean* (B) might seem like a good choice but is incorrect in this case. *Intelligent* (A) or smart and *independent* (D) should be easily eliminated since they don't mean *domestic*.

28. M

The author states that cats are worthy of our affection, but it does not specifically state that cats are affectionate (M). All the other choices were mentioned as reasons to add a cat to your household, and the question asks about what was not mentioned.

29. C

A good title will express the main idea of the passage. Choice (A) can be eliminated immediately if you know *canine* refers to dogs and they are not mentioned. The passage also does not mention the requirements (B) or demands of owning a cat. It mainly deals with rewards (C) or life lessons children receive. The fact that cats are clean (D) was mentioned in the passage but was not the main idea.

30. J

It is stated in the passage that children gain satisfaction from helping another living being. *Assisting* means the same as helping, so assisting another living being (J) is the best choice. Responsibility is mentioned as a lesson children learn (K), but it is not stated as the reason children gain satisfaction. Owning an intelligent animal (L) might seem like a good choice but "according to the passage," cat intelligence does not bring satisfaction to children. Supplying companionship (M) can be easily eliminated since the passage states that cats, not children, supply companionship.

31. B

Living on a farm with snow suited Bentley because he loved nature and snowflakes. If you are suited to something, it is agreeable (B) or pleasing to you. Bentley would not dislike living there (A) or not be satisfied (C) living there if he loved nature and snowflakes. He made his own clothes (D) might be misleading if you do not read the sentence in context and realize that the word *suited* does not refer to a suit of clothes.

32. K

The author tells us the snowflakes always melted before Bentley could finish drawing them (K). This eliminates all the other choices. We do not know if Bentley was artistic (J) or whether he needed a better microscope (M). The patterns were too difficult (L) might seem like a good choice since difficult patterns would take time to draw. However, (K) is a better choice since it was clearly stated in the passage as a reason.

33. C

Bentley was saddened because the intricate snow-flake patterns he saw could not be saved or shared (C), and this prompted him to draw them. Bentley loved nature (A), but it was more important to him to share its beauty. The author does not mention that Bentley was trying to prove (B) that the snow-flakes were different. The author mentions Bentley gathered his best photographs, not his drawings, for the book, so choice (D) can be eliminated.

34. M

The passage first mentions that Bentley used a microscope (M) to study snowflakes. A magnifying glass (J) and a telescope (K) are never mentioned and can be eliminated as choices. Although Bentley did use a camera (L) with a microscope to photograph snowflakes later on, his first instrument was a microscope.

35. C

A good topic sentence will state the main idea of a passage. It expresses the major thought that all other sentences in the passage prove. The main idea of this passage was that Wilson Bentley spent his life studying snowflakes (C). We learn from the passage that he studied snowflakes under a microscope, drew them, photographed them, and wrote a book about them. Although Bentley photographed snowflakes (A), we do not know if he was the first person to do this. We also learn Bentley loved nature (D), but this is just one fact about him and not the main idea.

36. M

To answer this question correctly, you need to know that *collect* is another word for *gather* and tropical oceans have warm water to answer this question correctly. The author states, in the third sentence, that hurricanes gather heat and energy (M) through contact with warm ocean waters.

37. B

The second sentence clearly states that hurricanes are called cyclones (B) in the Indian Ocean. Typhoons (C) might be chosen if the sentence is not read carefully. Hurricanes (A) and tornadoes (which form on land) (D) should be easily eliminated.

38. M

The eye of a hurricane is oddly calm with little wind and no rain (M). For this reason, it would not cause the most destruction (J) or a storm surge (L). The whirling winds (K) are around the eye and not contained in it.

39. A

The hurricane process starts with warm air rising (A) and taking water from the ocean, according to the author. Cool air rushing in (B) occurs next but is not the start of the process. Current changes (C) were not mentioned. Cloud formation (D) might be chosen, but thunderclouds build up later in the hurricane process.

40. L

Hurricanes need heat and energy. Cold water would absorb the hurricane's heat and the hurricane would weaken in strength (L). The passage stressed that hurricanes form in tropical regions, so you should be able to reason that cold water would not increase the size (J) or cause a larger storm surge (K).

41. C

Thwart means to prevent from taking place and the passage states that the success of his first two voyages was thwarted by ice packs (C). Mutiny (D) is mentioned in the passage but only for the fourth voyage. Poor navigation (B) and stormy seas (A) aren't mentioned.

42. L

The author states that Hudson made four important voyages of exploration (L) and proceeds to explain their impact. He could not provide details about Hudson's life (J) since little is known about it. There was no criticism of Hudson (K), and he never discovered an Arctic route to Asia (M).

43. A

Mutiny is the revolt or overthrow of authority. The crew overthrew Hudson's command (A). If the crew had questions about Hudson's navigational skills (B), this might lead to a mutiny but does not describe the word *mutinied*. Siding with Hudson (C) and making claims on land (D) don't reflect the meaning of *mutinied*.

44. L

Hudson was attempting to discover an Arctic route to Asia on all four of his voyages. This is stated in the third sentence of the passage. Finding an Arctic passage for the English (J) might seem correct, but his third voyage was for the Dutch. Exploring North America and establishing Dutch claims (M) were outcomes but not the purpose of the third voyage.

45. A

The second sentence states that we know he was a skilled navigator from his maps and journals (A). None of the other choices make sense.

46. L

Painted doors and gates (J), wrapped gifts (K), and new clothes (M) are all mentioned. Special meals (L) is not.

47. A

The word *now* is important in this question because the celebration now lasts for only a few days (A). If not read carefully, a full 15 days (B) might be chosen. Preparation, not celebration, takes weeks (C). One day (D) should be easily eliminated.

48. M

The first sentence indicates it is the lunar calendar (M). *Tradition* (J) might seem like a good choice but is only mentioned in connection with buying new shoes. *Convenience* (L) and *weather* (K) do not make sense in context.

49. B

Red is a symbol of happiness (B). *Good fortune* (A) might be chosen because inscriptions of good fortune are written on red paper. *Bad luck* (C) is the opposite, and *cleanliness* (D) should be easily eliminated.

50. J

Entertain (J) should be chosen by process of elimination. The author was not criticizing (K), expressing his opinion (L), or trying to persuade (M) the reader.

LANGUAGE PART 1

Spelling

1. E

There are no spelling mistakes in this question.

2. K

Frieght should be spelled *freight*. In cases where the word rhymes with *ay*, the *i* before *e* rule does not apply.

3. D

Often a *c* sounds soft, like an *s*. In this case, *cansel* should be spelled *cancel*.

4. J

Practic should be spelled *practice*. The silent *e*'s job is to change the sound of the vowel it follows. In this case, the *e* makes the *c* sound soft, like an *s*.

5. B

Since the suffix *able* begins with a vowel, the silent *e* is dropped. *Removeable* should be spelled *removable*.

6. M

Churchs should be spelled *churches*. Nouns ending in *ch* are made plural with an *es* added at the end, rather than just an *s*.

7. B

The common suffix *ing* needs an *i* to be correct. *Gatherng* should be spelled *gathering*.

8. M

When the word *full* is attached as a suffix to a root word, one of the *ls* must be dropped. *Youthfull* should be spelled *youthful*.

9. D

Inform is spelled with an *n* in its prefix, instead of an *m*. Be careful of consonants, in this case *n* and *m*, which sound very similar.

10. J

Fantacy should be spelled *fantasy.*.

Capitalization

11. A

Since *teacher* is a common noun, it is not capitalized. A teacher's name, however, would be capitalized. The first word in every sentence must be capitalized, so *today* should begin with a capital.

12. K

The word *birthday* in the title "Happy Birthday" should be capitalized. Every important word in titles of songs, books, movies, etc., should be capitalized.

13. A

All names, including the names of planets, are capitalized. The name of the planet Jupiter should be capitalized.

14. J

The Civil War is considered a proper noun because it is a specific historical event. Every major word in proper nouns is capitalized.

15. C

South should be capitalized in this sentence because it is a proper noun that names a specific geographic region in a country.

16. L

Capitalize the first word of a new sentence within quotation marks. In this case, the word *don't* should be capitalized.

17. B

Common nouns like *bridge* that stand alone are not capitalized. When *bridge* follows a name like Golden Gate, then it is capitalized.

18. L

You should capitalize nouns that appear in titles. *Amendment* should be capitalized, as it is the title of a specific amendment to the Constitution.

19. B

A common noun like *river* is not capitalized, unless it follows a specific name of a river, for example, Colorado River.

20. L

Names of school subjects are capitalized if they are names of languages. *French* should be capitalized.

Punctuation

21. B

Contractions like *it's* need an apostrophe to indicate that one word is acting like two words. In this case, *it's* means *it is*.

22. L

This sentence should end with a period instead of a question mark. If the first two words of this sentence had been switched, the sentence would have been a question.

23. D

There are no mistakes in this sentence. Keep in mind that the exact words of a speaker should be placed within quotation marks.

24. L

When the name of a city appears next to its state, it must be separated with a comma.

25. A

Colons only follow independent clauses, not dependent clauses. In this case, a comma should be used and not a colon.

26. L

Separate each item in a series with a comma. In this case, a comma should be placed after *people*.

27. B

A semicolon is used to separate closely related sentences. What follows the semicolon here is not a complete sentence.

28. J

Put a comma after the word that precedes the exact words within quotation marks of the speaker. A comma should be placed after *announced*.

29. B

Separate two complete sentences with a period, or in some cases, a semicolon. In this case, place a period after *bread*, and capitalize *we*.

30. J

Set off titles of short stories, songs, etc., with quotation marks. In this case, the opening quote is missing before *The* in this story's title.

Usage

31. B

The past-tense form of *lie* (meaning "to recline") is *lay*. In this sentence, *laid* should be changed to *lay*.

32. L

Good should be replaced with the adverb *well*. Since *good* is an adjective, it does not correctly modify the verb *doing*.

33. C

Since *females* is a plural noun, the pronoun that refers back to it also has to be plural. *Its* should be changed to *their*.

34. M

All the sentences are correct. Make sure that, as you move from sentence to sentence, the verb tenses remain the same. In this case, the passage is written in the present tense.

35. A

I is incorrect and should be replaced with *me*. Because the pronoun here functions as a direct object, it has to be an objective pronoun, like *me*. *I* is a subjective pronoun.

36. J

The other three sentences exhibit the following problems in the order in which they appear: run-on sentence, misplaced modifier, and awkward diction stemming from an unnecessary use of the passive voice.

37. C

Choice (A) is a run-on sentence; the comma should be replaced with a period. The other two sentences are awkwardly structured and that makes understanding the meaning of the sentences difficult.

38. M

While the first two sentences are technically correct, they are not the best, most clear ways of expressing the idea. In the third sentence, the most important point—that Lamar feels prepared for his solo—appears only as a dependent clause. This sentence structure muddies the point of the sentence.

39. C

Sentence (A) has an incorrect use of a colon that interrupts its meaning and flow. Sentence (B) is broken up awkwardly with prepositional phrases that also interrupt the sentence's flow. The last sentence is difficult to read because the parts of speech appear in an unusual and very awkward order.

40. J

In sentence (K), it is not clear to whom the pronoun *she* refers. In sentence (L), a semicolon is misused, and in sentence (M), a colon has been incorrectly used. In these two cases, the punctuation gets in the way of both of the sentences' meanings.

LANGUAGE PART 2

41. C

The underlined prepositional phrase makes the sentence wordy and very awkward. This phrase needs to be replaced with the non restrictive relative pronoun *which*, in for order the sentence to be clear and grammatically correct.

42. K

Sentence 1 is the topic sentence for the paragraph and should not be removed. Sentences 7 and 8 also provide more details that support the topic sentence. Sentence 2 is the best answer, as it provides information that is already implied in the topic sentence.

43. D

Will (D) is incorrect because it is in the future tense. The other verb choices are in the past tense, which fits with the rest of the paragraph.

44. M

The sentence is correct. No changes should be made. *However* doesn't link the sentence meaningfully to the sentence before. The pronoun *him* refers to Brandon. *Her* would be incorrect, as the teacher wouldn't show the dance step to herself. *Quickly* is an adverb, which correctly modifies *move*. Substituting it with the adjective *quick* would be grammatically incorrect.

45. B

Choice (A) is incorrect: it implies that the reason Kenya's leg is still sore is because her cast has just been removed. Choice (C) doesn't work because more than a mere comma is needed to adequately connect the two sentences. Choice (D) is incorrect because switching the basic order of the sentences confuses the meaning of this part of the paragraph.

46. K

Sentence 2 is needed because knowing Kenya's thoughts on her ability to play is essential to the paragraph. Sentences 8 and 10 describe actions that are necessary to the paragraph's overall meaning.

47. C

Write and *right* are homonyms, so it is easy to get confused. The verb *write* makes no sense in the sentence and should be substituted for the adverb *right*, which shows the direction the ball is heading.

48. J

The comma after *places* is unnecessary. In general, when you have questions about comma placement, read the sentence aloud. Notice where you naturally pause or where the meaning could be improved by putting in or taking out a comma.

49. B

"In this system" is the best of the three prepositional phrases. It makes the most sense, in that it refers back to the main topic of the paragraph.

50. M

This sentence is the best conclusion for the paragraph. Choice (L) is too general a conclusion. The other two sentences seem out of place as the last sentence of the paragraph: choice (J) is too detailed; and choice (K) could be a good topic sentence for another paragraph in a longer essay on the barter system.

MATH PART 1

1. B

Remember order of operations (PEMDAS): first: Parentheses; second: Exponents; third: Multiplication/Division; fourth: Addition/Subtraction.

Since there is nothing to do within parentheses, compute 4^2 first: $4^2 - 3(5) = 16 - 3(5)$

The next step is multiplication and division: $16 - 3(5) = 16 - 15$

The last step is subtraction: $16 - 15 = 1$

If you chose (A), you thought 4^2 meant 4×2. If you chose (D), you subtracted before you multiplied. (C) contains both of the errors made in (A) and (D).

2. L

Steve will sell the three most popular toppings. Based on this survey, the most popular toppings are hot fudge (29 people), caramel (20 people), and butterscotch (18 people).

(J) includes peanut butter (16 people) instead of butterscotch.

3. D

Let n represent Melissa's first paycheck. Since 20% of her paycheck is $40, $(20\%)n = 40$, or $0.20n = 40$. Divide both sides by 0.20 to get $n = 40 \div 0.20$. To make the division process easier, you can simplify the numbers by shifting each decimal one place to the right which is equivalent to multiplying both by 10.

$40 \div 0.20 = 400 \div 2 =$

$$2\overline{)400} \quad \frac{200}{}$$

That's (D). If you multiply instead of divide and misplace the decimal, you get (C).

4. M

For addition and subtraction of fractions, find the least common denominator (LCD).

The denominators in this problem are 4 and 6. Go through the multiples of the largest number (6) until there is a number that is also divisible by 4. The first multiple of 6 that is also a multiple of 4 is 12. Since the LCD is 12, multiply the numerator and denominator of $\frac{3}{4}$ by 3, and multiply the numerator and denominator of $\frac{1}{6}$ by 2.

$$\frac{3}{4} + \frac{1}{6} = \frac{3(3)}{4(3)} + \frac{1(2)}{6(2)} = \frac{9}{12} + \frac{2}{12} = \frac{11}{12}$$

5. C

A prime number is a positive integer that has exactly two positive integer factors, 1 and itself. (A), (B), and (D) are all prime numbers because each one can only be divided by 1 and itself. (C) is the only choice that is not prime (it's composite). 51 has four positive integer factors: 1, 3, 17, and 51.

6. K

First write a ratio that will compare the number of black shoes sold to the total number of shoes sold.

$$\frac{\text{The number of black shoes sold}}{\text{Total number of shoes sold}} = \frac{100}{200}$$

To convert the fraction $\frac{100}{200}$ to a percent, remember that a percent is a ratio that compares a number to 100.

Since $\frac{100}{200} = \frac{50}{100}$, that means 50 black shoes were sold per 100 shoes sold.

$$\frac{50}{100} = 50\%$$

7. D

Evan had $9.63 after he spent $21.25. Let n = the amount he had originally.

Then, the amount he had originally minus the amount he spent equals the amount he has left. $n - 21.25 = 9.63$. Add 21.25 to both sides to get $n = 9.63 + 21.25$.

$$\begin{array}{r} 9.63 \\ + 21.25 \\ \hline 30.88 \end{array}$$

If you subtract $9.63 from $21.25 instead of add, you get (A).

8. L

In the month of May, the 10th grade class raised approximately $270, the 11th grade raised approximately $90, and the 12th grade raised approximately $125. The 11th and 12th grade classes combined raised $215 ($90 + $125). Since $270 is more than $215, the 10th grade class raised more than the 11th and 12th grades combined. (J) is the month when the 12th grade class raised more than the 10th and 11th grades classes combined. (K) is the month when the 11th grade class raised more than the 10th and 12th grade classes combined.

9. D

Let n represent the amount the driver collected. $n = (9.00)(35) = 9(35)$

$$\begin{array}{r} 35 \\ \times 9 \\ \hline 315 \end{array}$$

10. K

The probability Renee selected a frosted brownie:

$$\frac{\text{Number of frosted brownies}}{\text{Total number of baked goods}} = \frac{6}{16} = \frac{3}{8}$$

11. D

The cost of one plain pizza is $12. The cost of one pizza with pepperoni, sausage, and mushrooms is $12 + $1 + $1 + $1 = $15. The total cost equals the cost of the plain pizza plus the cost of the pizza with the three toppings.

$$\begin{array}{r} \$12 \\ + \$15 \\ \hline \$27 \end{array}$$

12. L

40% of Mike's monthly expenses go toward rent. 20% goes toward food.

40% + 20% = 60% for rent and food.

$$60\% = \frac{60}{100}$$

Divide numerator and denominator by 10 to get $\frac{60}{100} = \frac{6}{10}$.

Divide numerator and denominator by 2 to get $\frac{6}{10} = \frac{3}{5}$.

13. A

The perimeter of a closed figure is the distance around it. Since the figure is a pentagon (5-sided polygon), $P = s_1 + s_2 + s_3 + s_4 + s_5$.

Using substitution, $22 = x + 6 + 4 + 4 + 3$.

$$22 = x + 17$$
$$x = 5$$

14. J

The question asked which student showed the most improvement. Be careful. Since the chart shows the number of minutes it takes each student to run one mile, the students show improvement by taking less time to run the mile (improvement when the line goes downward as it goes to the right). Amanda ran the mile in approximately 12 minutes in September and 8.5 minutes in June. She improved by 3.5 minutes (12 − 8.5). Connor ran the mile in approximately 9 minutes in September and 7 minutes in June. Connor improved by 2 minutes (9 − 7). It took Ben more time to run one mile as the year progressed, so he did not improve his time.

15. B

The greatest common factor (GCF) of two or more whole numbers is the largest whole number that divides evenly into each of the numbers. List all of the numbers that are factors of 45, 75, and 105, and look for the largest factor they have in common.

$$45: 1, 3, 5, 9, 15, 45$$
$$75: 1, 3, 5, 15, 25, 75$$
$$105: 1, 5, 7, 15, 21, 105$$

Therefore, the greatest common factor is 15 (B). (A) is a common factor of all three, but not the greatest common factor. (C) is a factor of 75 only. (D) is a factor of 45 only.

16. M

Remember:

The product of two integers with the same sign is positive.

The product of two integers with different signs is negative.

$$(-6)(3)(-2) = (-18)(-2) = 36$$

17. C

The total number of bottles = number of cases × number of bottles in each case.

If n = the number of bottles of water, then $n = 6 \times 24$.

$$\begin{array}{r} 24 \\ \times 6 \\ \hline 144 \end{array}$$

18. L

The total cost = the cost per can × the number of cans.

If n = the total cost, $n = 0.89 \times 100$.

$$\begin{array}{r} 100 \\ \times 0.89 \\ \hline 89.00 \end{array}$$

19. D

Look at the table to find the corresponding price for tossed salad ($2.60). Since each side order costs $1.25 extra and Corey got two side orders (French fries and fruit salad), $1.25 + $1.25 = $2.50. Add everything together to get the total, $2.60 + $2.50 = $5.10.

20. J

Isolate x by subtracting 16 from both sides of the equation.

$$\begin{array}{r} x + 16 = -64 \\ -16 \quad -16 \\ \hline x = -80 \end{array}$$

21. B

According to the chart, there were six presidents named James and four presidents named William. $6 - 4 = 2$

22. M

If the varsity team won $\frac{3}{4}$ of their games, they won $\frac{3}{4}$ of 20 games. *Of* means multiply.

$$\frac{3}{4} \times 20 = \frac{3}{4} \times \frac{20}{1}$$

Cancel the 4s in the numerator and denominator.

$$\frac{3}{4} \times \frac{20}{1} = \frac{3}{1(4)} \times \frac{5(4)}{1} = \frac{3}{1} \times \frac{5}{1} = \frac{15}{1} = 15$$

23. A

One way to answer this question is to convert each fraction to a decimal and then compare them. However, that work is not necessary. Since one of the fractions is $\frac{1}{2}$, let's compare the other two to $\frac{1}{2}$.

$\frac{2}{7}$: Imagine cutting a candy bar into 7 equal pieces. If you eat 2 of the pieces, you ate less than $\frac{1}{2}$ of the candy bar. Consequently, $\frac{2}{7}$ is less than $\frac{1}{2}$.

$\frac{3}{5}$: Imagine cutting a candy bar into 5 equal pieces. If you eat 3 of the pieces, you ate more than $\frac{1}{2}$ of the candy bar. Consequently, $\frac{3}{5}$ is more than $\frac{1}{2}$.

In order from least to greatest: $\frac{2}{7}$, $\frac{1}{2}$, and $\frac{3}{5}$.

24. M

The amount Brandon has in his account after the deposit is equal to the amount Brandon had originally plus the amount Brandon added to the account.

If n = the amount Brandon has in his account after the deposit, n = \$851.63 + \$43.50.

$$\begin{array}{r} \$851.63 \\ + \ \$43.50 \\ \hline \$895.13 \end{array}$$

25. C

Look in the row which represents the average distance from the sun and find the appropriate column to match each planet. The distance from Earth to the sun is 93×10^6. The distance from Mars

to the sun is 141×10^6. To find out how much closer Earth is to the sun use subtraction.

$$141 \times 10^6 = 141{,}000{,}000$$
$$93 \times 10^6 = 93{,}000{,}000$$
$$141{,}000{,}000 - 93{,}000{,}000 = 48{,}000{,}000$$

26. J

Look in the column that represents Mercury and the row that represents the number of earth-days it takes to make one complete revolution. It takes Mercury 88 days to make one complete revolution. Consequently, it takes 2(88) = 176 days to complete two revolutions.

27. B

The fraction of students who chose pepperoni as their favorite topping is:

$$\frac{\text{The number of students who chose pepperoni}}{\text{The total number of students surveyed}} =$$

$$\frac{8}{6+8+3+1} = \frac{8}{18} = \frac{4}{9}$$

28. L

Start by drawing the triangle.

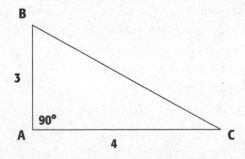

Since triangle ABC is a right triangle, use the Pythagorean theorem.

$c^2 = a^2 + b^2$, where c is the hypotenuse and a and b are the legs

$c^2 = 3^2 + 4^2$

$c^2 = 9 + 16$

$c^2 = 25$

$c = \sqrt{25}$

$c = 5$

29. C

To divide fractions, invert the second fraction $\left(\dfrac{3}{4}\right)$, cancel common factors between numerators and denominators, and multiply the fractions together.

$$\frac{5}{8} \div \frac{3}{4} = \frac{5}{8} \times \frac{4}{3} = \frac{5}{2(4)} \times \frac{1(4)}{3} = \frac{5}{2} \times \frac{1}{3} = \frac{5}{6}$$

30. J

First find out how much the two pairs of pants and three shirts cost.

2(cost of each pair of pants) + 3(cost of each shirt) = 2($16) + 3($15) = $32 + $45 = $77

Maureen's change = amount handed to cashier – cost of two pairs of pants and three shirts.

Maureen's change = $80 – $77 = $3

If Maureen had bought one pair of pants and one shirt, the answer would be (M).

31. D

According to the table, the company employs one president who makes $200,000 annually and three vice presidents who make $120,000 annually.

$200,000 + 3($120,000) = $200,000 + $360,000 = $560,000

32. M

The absolute value of a number is the distance it is from zero on the number line.

Since –4 is 4 units from 0, | –4 | = 4.

Use substitution.

$$|x| + 2y = |-4| + 2(3) = 4 + 6 = 10$$

MATH PART 2

33. B

In order to estimate the sum of two numbers, round each number and then add the rounded numbers. In this problem, since all answers are in hundreds, round to the nearest hundreds place.

In the number 543, the digit to the right of the hundreds place is 4 (5$\underline{4}$3). Since 4 is less than 5,

the number is rounded down to 500. If the digit to the right of the hundreds place had been greater than or equal to 5, the number would have been rounded up to 600. In the number 389, the digit to the right of the hundreds place is 8 (3$\underline{8}$9), and therefore the number is rounded up to 400.

500 + 400 = 900

34. L

Round to the nearest thousands place by rounding 9,$\underline{0}$32 down to 9,000 since 0 < 5, and 6,$\underline{3}$12 down to 6,000 since 3 < 5. 9,000 – 6,000 = 3,000 (L).

35. B

First, round the divisor down to become 60. Replace 4,326 with 4,200 because 4,200 can easily be divided by 60 since 6 × 7 = 42.

$$60\overline{)4{,}200} \;\; 70$$

Common mistakes might be forgetting the extra zero (A) or adding too many (C) and (D).

36. M

All four numbers can be rounded to 60, so the sum of the numbers is 60 + 60 + 60 + 60 = 240 or 4 × 60 = 240.

37. B

Round 7.21 to the nearest whole number. 7.21 will round down to 7 because the digit to the right of the ones place (2) is less than 5. 9.74 will round up to become 10 because the digit to the right of the ones place (7) is greater than 5. 7 × 10 = 70 (B). Errors in rounding one or both of the numbers would give variable answers: 7 × 9 = 63 (A) and 8 × 10 = 80 (C).

38. K

Round $14.75 to the nearest dollar. Since 7 is directly to the right of the decimal point and is more than 5, the dollar amount is rounded up to $15.00. Round $4.03 to the nearest dollar. Since 0 is directly to the right of the decimal point and is less than 5, the dollar amount is rounded down to $4.00. $15.00 – $4.00 = $11.00 (K). Incorrect rounding would lead to variable answers such as $14.00 – $4.00 = $10.00 (J).

39. C
The hundredths place is the second digit to the right of the decimal, which in this case is 2 (16.8236). In order to round to this place, look at the digit to the right of it (3). Since 3 < 5, the number will be rounded down to 16.8200, or 16.82 (C). (A) is correctly rounding to the nearest tenth. (B) is incorrectly rounding to the nearest tenth. (D) is correctly rounding to the nearest whole number.

40. L
Round to the nearest whole number. Both 10.8 and 99.9 have digits to the right of the decimal that are greater than 5, so both numbers are rounded up. 11 × 100 = 1,100 (L). Errors in rounding one or both numbers would lead to variable answers: 99 × 10 = 990 (J) and 100 × 10 = 1,000 (K). An error with the decimal point would lead to (M) 11,000.

41. D
The tenths place is the first digit to the right of the decimal, which in this case is 3 (16,348.351). In order to round to this place, look at the digit to the right of it (5). Since 5 ≥ 5, the number will be rounded up to 16,348.400 or 16,348.4 (D). (A) is correctly rounding to the nearest whole number. (B) is incorrectly rounding to the nearest tenth. (C) is correctly rounding to the nearest hundredth.

42. J
Round to the nearest thousands place by rounding 6,295 down to 6,000 since 2 < 5. (K) is incorrectly rounding to the nearest hundred. (L) is rounding to the nearest hundred. (M) is incorrectly rounding to the nearest thousand.

43. D
The ones place is the first digit to the left of the decimal, which in this case is 4 (234.567). In order to round to this place, look at the digit to the right (5). Since 5 ≥ 5, the number will be rounded up to 235.000, or 235 (D). (A) is incorrectly rounding to the nearest whole number. (B) is correctly rounding to the nearest hundredth. (C) is correctly rounding to the nearest tenth.

44. K
This problem will require division of the rocket's speed by the airplane's speed. Keep this in mind when rounding both numbers. The first step is to round the rocket's speed to the nearest thousand. Since the number to the right of the thousands place is 2, round 16,200 down to 16,000. The airplane's speed should be rounded to the nearest hundred. Since the number to the right of the hundreds place is 8, round 387 up to 400.

$$400\overline{)16{,}000}^{40}$$

45. B
The hundreds place is the third digit to the left of the decimal, which in this case is 6 (3,630). In order to round to this place, look at the digit to the right (3). Since 3 < 5, the number will be rounded down to 3,600 (B). (A) is incorrectly rounding to the nearest thousand. (C) is incorrectly rounding to the nearest hundred. (D) is correctly rounding to the nearest thousand.

46. K
This is a multi-step problem. The first step is to add the numbers in the parentheses. The problem becomes 21(9). 21 rounds down to become 20. 9 rounds up to become 10. Then multiply. 20(10) = 200, so choice (K) is correct.

47. B

The first step is to round $7.10 down to become $7.00 since 1 < 5. Then multiply the rounded amount by 11 since Theresa worked for 11 hours. 11($7.00) = $77.00, so choice (B) is correct.

48. L

First find the cost of five jars of apple sauce. $1.12 rounded to the nearest dollar becomes $1.00. Then multiply this rounded amount by 5. 5($1.00) = $5.00. Next, find the cost of the two pounds of cucumbers. $0.93 rounds up to become $1.00. 2($1.00) = $2.00. Add the two amounts together to get $7.00 ($5.00 + $2.00). However, the question asks for an estimate of the amount of money you should take with you to pay for these goods. Since $1.12 was rounded down and then multiplied by 5, $7.00 is actually a bit below the real answer. $7.00 is not enough to pay for these goods, so $8.00 is the better answer. Choice (L) is the correct answer.

49. A

The first step is to round last week's mileage to the nearest hundred. 23,321 will round down to become 23,300. The second step is to round this week's mileage to the nearest hundred. 23,492 will round up to become 23,500. Then subtract these rounded amounts. 23,500 − 23,300 = 200, so choice (A) is correct.

50. M

This is a multi-step problem. The first step is to round the numbers in parentheses to the nearest thousand. 5,021 is rounded down to become 5,000. 4,158 will round down to become 4,000. Subtract the rounded amounts. 5,000 − 4,000 = 1,000. The next step is to divide this number by 10.

$$10\overline{)1{,}000} = 100$$

Choice (M) is the correct answer.

ABILITY PART 1

Common

1. D

All figures are parallelograms. Note that some answer choices have four sides, but they are not parallellograms.

2. K

All figures are inscribed with an oval. The external shape is irrelevant.

3. C

All figures show the center of the figure. The vertical lines in the first two figures are irrelevant. You are looking for a figure whose center is shown. The only figure matching this description is choice (C).

4. M

All figures are marked in eight equal pieces. Do not be distracted by choices (J) and (K). Although they are cut into eight pieces, they are not equal.

5. E

All figures are right triangles. The size of the triangles is irrelevant. Instead, the correct answer must have an angle of 90 degrees. Only choice (E) is a right triangle.

6. K

All figures have five sides. Only choice (K) has five sides.

7. B

All figures are inscribed with one rectangle. Do not be distracted by choice (A), which is a figure inscribed by two rectangles.

8. N

All figures are flat on the right side. Only choice (N) is flat on the right side.

9. D

All figures are bisected horizontally. Do not be distracted by choice (A). Although the triangle has a horizontal line through it, the triangle was not bisected into two equal parts.

10. L

All figures have a triangle on top. Only choice (L) matches this description.

11. C

All figures are created with only straight lines. Only choice (C) matches this description.

12. L

All figures are inscribed with two shapes. The vertical and horizontal stripes are not what the figures have in common. Only choice (L) is correct.

13. B

All figures are designed with vertical lines. Only choice (B) matches this description.

14. K

All figures are scalene triangles. Only choice (K) matches this description.

15. E

All figures are inscribed with a smaller version of their own shapes rotated 90 degrees clockwise. Do not be distracted by choice (D) which shows a square with an inscribed square that has been rotated only 45 degrees clockwise. Because a square has four equal sides, when it is rotated 90 degrees clockwise it looks the same as the original square.

16. M

All figures have a parallel top and base.

17. A

All figures show one diagonal bisector. Do not be distracted by choice (B), which shows both diagonal bisectors, nor by choices (C) and (E), which show diagonal lines, but not diagonal bisectors.

18. N

All figures are inscribed with a four-pointed star. The stripes are not what the figures have in common, so you should only be looking for a shape inscribed by a four-pointed star. Only choice (N) matches this description.

19. E

All figures have seven sides. Only choice (E) matches this description.

20. L

All figures are composed of at least one parallelogram and no other shape. Only choice (L) matches this description.

21. D

All figures have eight sides. It might help to count the number of sides in each answer choice. Only choice (D) has eight sides.

22. K

All figures are decorated only with parallel lines. Note that the lines may be vertical or horizontal, but they must be parallel. Only choice (K) matches this description.

23. A

All figures are composed of diamond shapes. Do not be distracted by choice (B), which is two triangles forming a diamond. The figure must be composed of diamond shapes.

24. J

All figures are bisected vertically. Do not be distracted by choice (K) which is bisected horizontally.

25. B

All figures contain a semi circle. Choice (B) is a circle which contains two semi circles, therefore it is the correct answer.

26. J

All figures are 75% shaded. Only choice (J) is 75% shaded.

27. D

All figures are inscribed by right triangles. The external shape is irrelevant. You are looking for an answer choice with a right triangle inscribed within. Only choice (D) matches this description.

28. M

All figures have a circle at the base. Do not be distracted by choices (J) and (N), which contain circles. The circle must be at the base. Only choice (M) matches this description.

29. B

All figures are marked into ten equal pieces. Only choice (B) matches this description.

30. K

All figures are decorated only by horizontal lines. The inscribed shapes are distracters. Only choice (K) is decorated by horizontal lines only.

31. A

All figures are composed of only one or more squares. Only choice (A) matches this description.

32. N

All figures have rays from the vertices of the shape. Do not be distracted by choices (J), (K), (L), or (M). Although there are rays, they are not extending from any vertices of the figures.

33. C

All figures are inscribed with a shape comprised of one more side than the original. Choice (C) shows a six-sided figure inscribed with a seven-sided figure. Therefore, choice (C) is the correct answer.

34. M

All figures are created without straight lines. Only choice (M) matches this description.

35. D

All figures contain isoceles triangles within. You are looking for an answer choice that has an isosceles triangle within. Only choice (E) matches this description.

[No further explanation is possible for questions 36–50]

Design for Shopping

Design for Shopping

New Retail Interiors

By Sara Manuelli

ABBEVILLE PRESS   NEW YORK   LONDON

First published in the United States of America in 2006 by Abbeville Press,
137 Varick Street, New York, NY 10013

First published in Great Britain in 2006 by Laurence King Publishing Ltd,
71 Great Russell Street, London, WC1B 3BP

Printed in China

First Edition
10 9 8 7 6 5 4 3 2 1

ISBN-13: 978-0-7892-0898-9
ISBN-10: 0-7892-0898-9

Library of Congress Cataloging-in-Publication Data

Manuelli, Sara.
    Design for shopping : new retail interiors / by Sara Manuelli.—1st ed.
        p. cm.
Includes index.
ISBN 0-7892-0898-9 (alk. paper)
1. Store decoration—History—21st century. 2. Interior architecture—History—
21st century. I. Title.

    NK2195.S89M36 2006
    725'.21—dc22
                        2006006119

Project managed by Lara Maiklem
Designed by John Round Design
Jacket design by Misha Beletsky

Cover image: Alexander McQueen, NY (photo: Eric Laignel)

For bulk and premium sales and for text adoption procedures, write to Customer
Service Manager, Abbeville Press, 137 Varick Street, New York, NY 10013 or call
1-800-ARTBOOK.

CONTENTS

INTRODUCTION

THE WAY WE SHOP TODAY

The market has traditionally been the place for the exchange of goods and has defined the relationship between the retailer and the consumer. Mass culture and globalization resulted in the evolution of the marketplace into a wondrous array of subtle formats. Today, the digital technology revolution and the impact of saturated markets have altered it even further. What was once the marketplace has now evolved into a zone of experience and lifestyle, and shopping has changed with it. The basic behavioural patterns of consumer activity have now taken on a social and cultural complexity. Commodity has become increasingly substituted or incorporated into services; retail is gradually morphing into leisure; and art has been installed to elevate the purchasing act – as if by purifying the shopping experience, one could forget the very principles of commodity and the capital it is based upon.

As the culture of consumerism has advanced, the complexity of consumer thinking has been analyzed and revealed. It is clear that prominent in the psychology of the consumer are desire, longing and daydreaming. Sociologist and author Colin Campbell noted that people have a self-indulgence to desire, which he coined 'modern autonomous imaginative hedonism' (*Romantic Ethic and the Spirit of Modern Consumerism*, 1987). Paul Ginsborg, author and historian, also writes that 'The visible practice of consumption becomes just a small part of a complex model of individual hedonism, most of which takes place in the imagination of the consumer' (*Berlusconi, Television, Power and Patrimony*, 2004). The retail machine supports this theory by continuing to form a pathway for the shopper to this world of consumer hedonism. We can see in the sales of the Apple iPod, Nokia N-Gage, Nintendo Gameboy and the

Sony PSP that personal immersion is a consumable aspect of dreaming and imagination.

In this immersive world, brand alone is no longer the single inducement. Retailers have progressed to the creation of complex environments that can provoke an emotional response from their customers. The post-shopping age has created a whole set of challenges for retailers and designers. Epicenters, guerilla retailing, brand architecture and sensory environments are just of some of the new buzzwords being used. Brands like Bulgari, Gucci and Salvatore Ferragamo have expanded their retail businesses into branded hotels and bars. The distinction between buying and living is becoming strategically indistinguishable. These days, good-looking retail space is no longer enough. The post-shopping consumer expects to be engaged and entertained. The drive to create an unforgettable shopping experience, conducted in an amazing environment, has to be tempered by the need to pace the shopper and is underpinned by improving the customer's experience and service.

Retailers, architects and designers are constantly looking for ways of maximizing retail space. Fashion seems particularly drawn to the visual clout that architects can bring – the creative constructions of architects can add longevity and respectability to the otherwise ephemeral world of fashion. In the 1980s, Esprit owner, Doug Tompkins, commissioned Norman Foster, Ettore Sottsass, and Shiro Kuramata to design several stores. Rei Kawakubo, founder of Comme des Garçons, soon followed in 1983 with a New York store designed with Takao Kawasaki and a series of commissions with Future Systems). In 1986 came John Pawson's minimalist temple for Calvin Klein, in the 1990s Giorgio Armani's worldwide stores designed by Claudio

1 Bulgari Hotel, Milan.

2 Café Gucci, Milan

3 The Continentale, one of five Ferragamo-owned hotels in Florence.

1

2

3

Silvestrin, and the Noughties saw the Prada Epicenters by Rem Koolhaas and Herzog & de Meuron.

Some British grocers have also – albeit more rarely – sought architectural assistance. In the UK, for example, the 1988 Sainsbury's store in London's Camden Town, by Nicholas Grimshaw and Partners, and the 1999 'environmentally responsible' Greenwich branch of Sainsbury's, by Paul Hinkin of Chetwood Associates. Elsewhere in Europe the Austrian, family-run supermarket chain, MPreis, has 120 stores, dotted around the country. Over the past 15 years commissions for these have been given to up-and-coming architects. Before this relatively recent vogue for architecturally designed stores, however, other great architects had also ventured into retail design. At the end of the nineteenth century, Louis H Sullivan designed the Carson Pirie Scott and Company building in Chicago, Carlo Scarpa created the Venice Olivetti showroom in 1958 and in 1964 Hans Hollein designed the Retti Candles Shop in Vienna – this is to name but a few.

Yet even a high-profile architect cannot always supply the necessary transformation for a company's retail ambitions. In February 2004, Marks & Spencer opened its first Lifestore in Gateshead, Newcastle, UK, dedicated to selling the company's homeware range of products. In March 2003, Marks & Spencer lured Vittorio Radice from the London-based department store Selfridges to be the executive director of the new Marks & Spencer Home business. While at Selfridges he had established a notion of 'shopping as theatre' and had masterminded the store's expansion, first to Manchester and then to Birmingham in the landmark Future Systems building (pages 78–81) that turned the brand into a powerful shopping destination.

At Marks & Spencer, Radice repeated the process by commissioning John Pawson to design and build a full-size house inside the Gateshead location. The different rooms inside the house – styled by head of in-store visual merchandising Ilse Crawford – conveyed the new Marks & Spencer direction. At the back of the house, a dramatic staircase rose through a double height space to three rooms above. However, six months later, a board reshuffle, a change of management style and lucklustre sales resulted in the closure of Lifestore, and all future plans to open further stores were cancelled.

NEW APPROACHES

For top-end fashion labels, retail kudos is measured in buildings, megastores and epicenters. Luxury goods are now sold in modern cathedrals to consumerism – spaces that move large amounts of capital, selling famous label garments and even larger amounts of accessories. From the display of technology in the Prada epicenters (pages 38–43), to the commissioning of high-profile architects and the use of art installations, all of these are devices that aim to elevate the act of purchase into something resembling a ritual. More and more retail environments are appropriating terms and experience models of leisure places like spas, hotels, museums. It is not enough to just install a café; a store must now become a retreat, an escape, and also a destination.

There is a curatorial approach to the selection of merchandise, evident in concept stores like Colette in Paris, Corso Como in Milan and Dover Street Market in London (pages 174–177). Furniture showrooms, home furnishing stores, even top end grocery formats like the Sainsbury's

4 Esprit, London, by Foster and Partners.

5 Comme des Garçons, New York, by Future Systems.

6 Calvin Klein, New York, by John Pawson.

7 Giorgio Armani, Hong Kong, by Claudio Silvestrin.

4

5

6

7

8

9

Market in London, instil a value that promises a better, stylish and more healthy lifestyle. Some, like fashion designer Giorgio Armani, have taken the 'holistic vision' idea even further and used shopping as way to develop property sites in rundown areas of the city. In Milan, Italy, Armani acquired a Nestlé factory and commissioned architect Tadao Ando to transform the whole area (near Porta Genova) into a fashion space, theatre and gallery centre. Similarly, in Shanghai, China, he has opened a multi-concept store of 1,100 square metres (11,840 square feet), designed by Claudio Silvestrin, Doriana and Massimiliano Fuksas.

In a contrasting approach to building shopping empires, a consumer backlash has manifested itself most vehemently in the anti-globalization demonstrations of the early Noughties. At a micro level, consumer patterns, arguably influenced by a 'No Logo' approach, are changing. Freegan, Dumpster Diving, Recycle This! Food not Bombs are just some of the groups that have sprung up in favour of recycling, low consumption levels and freedom from brand domination. These groups often subsist as marginal counter cultures that abstain from buying and spending and contrast traditional shopping with alternative forms of consumption. Freegans, for example, obtain their food from supermarket refuse bins – often still packaged and in fresh condition – while Dumpster Diving practitioners delight in recycling objects from the bins of luxury apartment blocks.

In retail, the term 'guerrilla architecture' is being increasingly borrowed to denote a low-cost, provisional space arranged for shopping. In design terms it manifests itself as a more transient, light, portable, industrial chic approach, as opposed to the permanent, sleek detailing of the 'white box' of the 1980s and 1990s. Brands like Camper

(pages 100–101), Levi's, Comme des Garçons and Umbro are all employing these tactics as a marketing tool to sell more clothes and as a way out of long and expensive leases and high-cost buildings. Paradoxically, the first official spate of 'guerrilla stores' came from Comme des Garçons, the brand that first promoted the marriage between retail and high profile architects. However, guerilla architecture has very little reference to the anti-establishment antics of architectural groups involved in urban interventions, art installations and public art. As journalist Elaine Knutt wrote in the architectural magazine *Icon* (issue 020), 'It's hard to imagine anyone breaking the law for the sake of selling a Kangol hat or Comme des Garçons perfume: for these brands guerrilla retailing is more about finding an alternative channel for communicating with customers… Guerrilla retailing isn't so much a retail revolution, as a turn of the fashion wheel.'

NEW SCENARIOS
Unsurprisingly, it is in cities such as Berlin and Tokyo that we find some of the most interesting examples of contemporary retail design. Berlin, after a period spent as a giant construction site, is now gathering momentum as a city with unlimited potential, even though it lacks a prominent city centre and many parts of the city are still being rediscovered. Rents and property prices are low, making Berlin one of the cheaper European cities to live and generate business in. The mood here is very much 'self-made' with a younger generation of architects, designers and independent retailers taking control of disused spaces for innovative store concepts. The attitude that formed much of the city's nightlife in the early 1990s,

8 Armani Headquarters and Theatre, Milan, by Tadao Ando.

9 Carson, Pirie, Scott & Co., Chicago, by Louis H. Sullivan.

10

11

12

when clubs with a limited life span would spring up in warehouses, is now extending to retail. Comme des Garçons' first guerrilla store was in Berlin, because it arguably drew inspiration from the inhabitants' anti-monetary approach to retail. Concepts like BLESS (pages 102–105) and smart-travelling store (pages 154–157) are both valid examples of how low budget can breed creativity.

At the opposite end of the spectrum lies Tokyo with its conspicuous consumption and Western brand fetishes. Areas like Omotesando Avenue are where luxury names rush to open gleaming 'boutique palazzos' – usually high-rise buildings designed by renowned architects. The Dior building by SANAA, Tod's building by Toyo Ito and Prada's epicenter by Herzog & de Meuron, are not only valid examples of commercial architecture, but also reveal an increased tendency towards focusing on the façade of the building, in same cases leaving the interiors to shop fitters and designers. In a city of such building density and high property prices, a stunning 'outside' is often more powerful in terms of brand awareness than a very expensive advertising campaign.

'The "boutique palazzo" syndrome does run rampant through our profession, the thinking being that the façade is urban, the street the stage and the brand leveraged by the sophistication and expense that goes into the public "face" of the retail design,' says Hani Rashid of American architecture firm Asymptote. 'But while on streets like Madison Avenue, Via Monte Napoleone and Rodeo Drive that strategy is all-important, the strategy for newer, establishing brands might very well be the opposite. The interior experience is what makes the brand memorable and establishes it as sophisticated, fresh and fashionable,

and it is here that architects need to pay much closer attention to the actual experience as opposed to the image.'

TAILORING FOR DIFFERENT MIND SETS

As free location becomes scarce and rents rise, retailers are pushed into finding other ways of picking customers with new format strategies, locations and services. 'You need to tailor your offer to location as well as to different mind-sets,' says Rune Gustafson, senior partner at brand strategy and design group Lippincott Mercer. 'You might well have the same demographic profiles, but customers' needs change constantly. So you segment the customers by attitude and develop both different products and different retail formats.'

According to Gustafson, with people constantly pressed for time it is not only important to satisfy certain needs fairly quickly, but also to be able to tap in the 'share of purse', i.e. the need for different purchases at different moments. The UK-based, high-street chain-store chemist Boots, for example, has opened in London's Holborn area a store that can fulfil the high traffic flow of the area. In this particular store, basket sizes are smaller and the emphasis is on toiletries and health and beauty brands for the local office workers. As supermarkets are taking an increasing proportion of consumer's spending, they are keen to tap into other markets beyond groceries. They are bidding for the housewife's household budget, money left over from the weekly shop to invest in, for example, some clothes. 'People make trade-offs in budgets,' says Gustafson, 'and retailers are keen to have a piece of the pie.'

The installation of in-store technology should ideally be fitted because of need, rather than just the desire for high-tech gimmicks. In 2002, Sainsbury's opened a pilot

10 Olivetti showroom, Venice, by Carlo Scarpa.

11 Marks & Spencer Lifestore, Gateshead, UK, by John Pawson.

12 Colette, Paris.

store for time-pressured families in Hazel Grove near Stockport, UK. The store was driven by technology-enabling services and worked closely with the retail design group 20/20 on customer focus groups. The 'bottoms up' approach delivered a 3,700 square metre (39,830 square foot) store with a number of discrete areas, each including elements of new technology. A vending machine stocking 150 products, including milk and bread, proved popular among night-shift workers. A trial 'Pocket shopper' device was also installed that used a key fob to scan the bar codes on products so that they could then be used to print a shopping list, either to use in-store or to upload onto a computer to order online from home. Three interactive displays for children, devised in partnership with the Science Museum in London, were visited by over 23,000 people in the first 12 weeks of opening and proved to be a very successful marriage between technology, retail and play.

The boundaries between retail and leisure 'mind-sets' are also creating interesting concepts. After becoming firmly established in department stores, cafés are now springing up in bookstores. Brands like Starbucks are installing CD burners in their coffee bars and even publishing their own music CDs, in a bid to establish a 'theme'.

'With the advent of brands like H&M, Zara and Mango we have witnessed a formidable process of democratization of fashion,' adds Gustafson. Here, store formats and shop-fitting elements are kept simple and flexible, while the emphasis is on procuring the customer a 'fast fashion fix' with an average of 16 collections per year. Buying cheaper items is considered 'smart', even for those who can afford expensive clothing, and there is a tangible shift from luxury stores to more bargain-priced discount chains.

From railway stations to airports and petrol forecourts, travel locations are ripe with retail potential. 'Because people spend a huge amount of time in airports and stations, it is important that retailers manage this time in a reassuring way,' says Gustafson. The Sainsbury's branch in London's Paddington Station, for example, has a TV screen inside with the trains' departures times. For designers and architects these are challenging new places. 'I am fascinated with the hyper-shopping spaces in airports such as Copenhagen, Heathrow, Singapore and Schiphol. These spaces are in desperate need of some truly inspired retail designs, and we hold out hope to get a chance to try our hand at these part urban, part-mall, part-theatre, and part-duty-free heaven and part-transit hell environments!' says Rashid.

ARE YOU BEING SERVED?

Service is becoming one of the most important elements defining the shopping experience. As the world of commerce is increasingly revolutionized by a trend of dematerialization, there is a move away from the market economy, with its emphasis on physical goods, possessions and ownership, into a new era dominated by service, supply and access. 'In retail, it's the move away from buying and selling mass-produced, manufactured goods into a new understanding that supply is more valuable than that which is being supplied. It's a world of lifestyle and brand identification. A world that treasures customer relations and guards, jealously, the mediation between the consumers and the provider. It's a topsy-turvy world. Sometimes goods are given away for free and profits made from support rather than through mere one-off transactions,' says Neil Churcher, associate professor at the Interaction Design Institute, Ivrea, Italy.

13 Sainsbury's Market at Terence Conran's Bluebird gastrodome, London.

14 The reconstruction of Berlin has resulted in the generation of many innovative store concepts.

15 Epicenter Prada, Tokyo, by Herzog & de Meuron.

13

14

15

Often called the 'service economy', or the 'access economy', its commercial value is often framed within time rather than by physicality. 'A service can only be supplied and judged as it is experienced and that happens in real time. In retail it's the decision to enter a store, or when taking in the atmosphere, identifying with what is on offer or being provided for at the counter. Those intangible moments cannot be possessed like a product, but have weight and impact on retail sales,' says Churcher.

But what are the implications for designers? 'In the way that services are experiences, the creation of services themselves can only be realized by designing the experience itself. It is not enough to specialize in 2D and 3D, products or graphics, or in physical concepts like point of sale or brand image. The designer of services needs to think in time and be able to craft the experience of the consumer, as they themselves would experience it. Service creation is, in many ways, the ultimate design process for the consumer society, because the act of consumption itself is (like service) an experience cycle,' adds Churcher.

Apple is the ultimate example of this shift in retail. Previously only known for the Apple Macintosh computer, a product that was sold and revised into new versions every year, Apple is now a lifestyle choice that is encapsulated by a singular design style that touches everything Apple. Apple is a cool outlet (pages 126–129) of all things Apple. It is a revolutionary way of listening to your music collection and it is a radical change. 'Even Apple's most "product"-like thing, the iPod, is an elusive wrap of style, immersive lifestyle and service,' says Churcher. 'Apple is more lifestyle choice than product sale and that streams right through its outlets. Apple Store is a way for the company to regain the ground

lost by its traditional franchise method of product supply (which always had a reputation for sluggishness). More importantly, Apple wanted to control its identity on the high street. Whether it's hardware, mediated services, software or accessories, the message is the same; the lifestyle is singular. It's a club.'

TECHNOLOGY HAS MADE THE CUSTOMER KING

New technology, 'the digital information revolution', has impacted hugely on the way the world shops. Online access has meant that demand has become increasingly more sophisticated. Defined by some as simply the era of the consumer, the shift in power has swayed towards the customer. 'Yet the technologies that have made this happen are altering aspects of all relationships in the retail chain, from the behavior of the consumer, the means of retail supply, promotions of goods, even the concept of the goods themselves. These alterations are by-products of a much larger technological impact on the market economy,' says Churcher.

Mediation is one altering factor, *i.e.* ways to form closer communications and relationships 'in between' the retail supplier and the customer. 'Any supplier not exploiting this "mediated" space may find the gap filled by techno-opportunists who exploit the space to build their own relationships with consumers as a way of controlling customer desire. Online access to knowledge is a way of controlling the market,' says Churcher. As journalist Paul Markillie points out in the *Economist*'s survey of consumer power (8 April, 2005), '80 percent of Ford's customers in the USA have already researched their purchase on the web before they arrive at a showroom, and most come with a

16 Sainsbury's high-tech pilot store at Hazel Grove, Stockport, UK.

17 Starbucks, South Molton Street, London.

18 H&M store, Germany.

16

17

18

19

20

specification sheet of the precise car from the dealer's stock'. At the other end of the spending power spectrum, many teenagers now find the idea of actually purchasing a DVD or CD somewhat alien. They have grown up in an era of easy access and network download. For them, the cost of the packaging and the medium, as well as the additional retail costs, seem unwarranted, especially as buying a CD or DVD represents the slowest way to get hold of the goods.

For retailers and designers this calls for a new conceptualization of retail space. In the near future retailers are not looking to create places just to sell, but to suggest, evoke and promise the essence of the brand. Volkswagen's impressive Autostadt opened in June 2000 as a 25-hectare (62-acre) 'theme park for cars' at its Wolfsburg, Germany headquarters. The 48-metre (158-foot) -high tower can hold up to 800 new cars, ready for delivery. Autostadt is the architectural embodiment of a move away from conventional showrooms towards an inviting and interactive retail space.

GLOBAL VERSUS LOCAL

In an increasingly globalized world, we like to think of retail as an enterprise that can be easily and successfully exported. But how can retailers translate offers and concepts to other countries and cultures? Brand awareness, advertising and the media have made European shoppers, for example, very similar to each other. The brands on sale in the high street are often the same and, one would assume, so are the shopping patterns. Yet within this process of creeping standardization there are other differences, such as regional variety, different demographics and economic cycles. In consequence, retailers need to cater for an increasingly 'international', yet 'local' customer.

The incredible expansion of Tesco, the UK-based supermarket chain, into Eastern Europe and most recently its entry into the massive Chinese market, makes it one of the largest world retailers, together with the French company Carrefour and US-based Wal-Mart. In retail terms, Tesco could be seen as a successful example of an 'adaptor': a retailer that owns stores in its own country but has also managed to adapt the concept to the regional needs of other countries. By tailoring the offer to local eating habits, the shop has managed to strike a balance between indigenous ranges and universal brands. Food retailer Carrefour is also seen as a positive example of the 'adaptor' model, especially in China, where it is competing in the country's booming retail market. While its sale of snakes and turtles might seem bizarre to a Western customer, it is merely a response to the dietary and cultural requirements of that region.

The success of stores such as B&Q in China, there called 'Bai An Ju', also proves the winning adaptor formula. The UK-based DIY store has entered the country in a time of property development, growth in home ownership and government liberalization of the housing market. These factors, coupled with a rising interest among the Chinese population in home decoration, have ensured the expansion and commercial success of the chain. In addition, retail adaptors see foreign markets as a chance to expand their horizons, perhaps with new store formats. 'In China, shoppers are suddenly given a choice they had never had or seen before,' says Gustafson in 'Crossing Continents', his article in the 2003 summer publication of *Lens* from UK strategy and design consultancy 20/20. 'When Carrefour and B&Q entered China, they went for the latest technology, the

19 Zara store, Oxford Street, London.

20 Tesco supermarket, Lodz, Poland.

21

22

newest store concepts, the most advanced retail offer. So even if they entered a market which is not as developed, consumers quickly got used to a much higher choice and retail offer.'

An alternative retail model, often quoted for international expansion, is the 'repeater', comprising of a simple format and a back-of-house system. This model has been taken up by brands such as the Gap, Starbucks, McDonald's and the Body Shop. Of course there is no such thing as a true 'repeater', and even brands like McDonald's cater to the country's culinary tastes with minor variations. The success of repeaters is that they are cheap to replicate and can expand quickly, although they can also become saturated and seem 'old-hat'. On the other hand, although adaptors might take more market research to set up, once the offer is defined it is perfectly integrated with the consumer's demands and needs. An understanding of the language and cultural patterns of behaviour, price, product qualities and positioning are all crucial elements to consider in global expansion.

This book intends to address some of the current themes in retail design. In 'Glorious Old Brands' it looks at how the revitalization of existing brands happens via retail design. Within the process of reinvention and promotion a flagship store often maintains a stronger impact than a well-orchestrated advertising campaign. 'Technology and Shopping' addresses issues of how technology is being used within retail design – for efficiency, for example, point of sales systems, customer databases, inventory databases, RFID (Radio Frequency Identification) technology, and also as a way of communicating how innovative, forward-thinking and up-to-date a particular brand is. 'Fashionable

Stopovers' questions the issue of whether visiting a shop is similar to visiting a museum or a church and whether the status of the destination can eclipse the merchandise in it. In 'Play and Shopping' the book looks at how irony, play and a slight sense of subversion can be brought in to revitalize the shopping experience – ideas, rather than costly shop fittings, is the theme underlying the collection of case studies.

'New Ways and Places to Shop' looks at how brands, such as telecoms and computers, are favouring the 'service' and the 'lifestyle' model over the sale of goods. It also looks at how brand architecture is being employed to capture the essence of a brand. The lifestyle experience charts the rise of the lifestyle model in retail through food, interiors, jewellery end even eyewear. It shows how retail works at creating an aspirational mode of living as a tool for selling. Finally, 'Fashion and Art' examines how shops have taken to incorporating art and commissioning artists to create a more 'elevated' and entertaining environment. As art curator Germano Celant remarked on the occasion of Prada's presentation of its new Epicenters, 'In the end, it all fits together: art, fashion, architecture, design – even shopping. It's all theatre, really: a modern spectacle for a modern world.'

21 McDonald's restaurant, Germany.

22 Volkswagen Autostadt, Wolfsburg, Germany.

Pringle, in London's New Bond Street, projects an image of modern British glamour while at the same time referencing the company's traditional Scottish roots.

INTRODUCTION

In recent years there has been a spate of established and conventional brands being given a new lease of life through strategic reinvention. This has been achieved through methods such as re-branding and repositioning of the brand values through advertising campaigns and revamping product lines. In particular, the quintessentially British labels Burberry, Aquascutum, Mulberry, Aspreys, Dunhill and Pringle have all been busy reinventing their image by drawing on the qualitative values of their heritage and by replacing outdated values with a sleeker, more contemporary format. Crucial to this ethos has been the flagship store, a synthesis of a glorious old brand's values.

So common has this brand re-evaluation process been, that today it is often referred to by the design press as 'doing a Burberry'. When CEO Rosemary Bravo took over the reins of the company in 1990, Burberry revamped its image through the hiring of new designers and the launch of successful spin-offs, such as the Burberry bikini. New ads, depicting 'Cool Britannia' faces Kate Moss and Stella Tennant, helped the raincoat brand become hip again. In 2004 alone, Burberry opened stores in Houston (Texas, USA), Tokyo (Japan), Americana Manhasset (outside New York, USA), Charlotte (North Carolina, USA), King of Prussia (Pennsylvania, USA), Scottsdale (Arizona, USA), Boca Raton (Florida, USA), Burjuman Centre (Dubai), Rome (Italy), São Paulo (Brazil) and enlarged and refurbished its stores in San Francisco (USA) and Paris (France). Its retail architecture roll-out fittingly reflected the healthy financial status of the company.

Similarly, the British brand Mulberry benefited financially in 2001 from the sale of 41 percent of the business to Club 21, the Singaporean fashion and hotel group owned by husband and wife team Ben Seng and Christina Ong, who also run Armani in the UK. £2.6m was invested in a makeover that was geared to repositioning Mulberry and aimed at expanding its customer base with a complete kit of creative strategic ideas as well as creating several new retail sites.

In March 2002 Pringle of Scotland approached Wells Mackereth to come up with a retail design concept to suit a major repositioning for the luxury fashion brand. London-based Wells Mackereth, comprising Sally Mackereth and James Wells, have a history of working extensively in both retail and leisure. Their other projects include the restaurant Smiths of Smithfield, the restaurant and hotel West Street Bar, Korres Natural Products store, Yoga Studios and Stone Island/CP Company.

INTERVIEW WITH SALLY MACKERETH OF WELLS MACKERETH, LONDON, UK

Wells Mackereth was commissioned to create Pringle's first flagship store in London. What was the brief?

'We were commissioned by Pringle to help them turn shopping into an intriguing and tactile experience. The programme of building involved a store for Heathrow Airport in London, one in Tokyo, a flagship store in New Bond Street, London, a store in Sloane Street, London (with showrooms and company HQ). Other stores were planned for New York and Milan and the production of a design manual for concessions for use by licensees around the world.'

What elements of its heritage and new positioning did you employ as inspiration for the design.

'Pringle has a very strong brand history. It was founded in 1815 as a knitwear company in Scotland and has a royal warrant. You could summarize it as "cabbies and kings" (*i.e.* for taxi drivers and royalty alike). But over the years it lost its identity and developed an extremely different range of clothing. It had no dedicated store, so it was decided to reinvigorate the company by moving it on from the dull, golf sweater image to a cooler, covetable brand. The brief to Wells Mackereth was to turn the flagship into the brand. A site was found on New Bond Street in London, where Armani had a store previously. The challenge was how to seduce people in such a highly charged shopping environment as New Bond Street. There is an element of theatre about the contemporary shopping experience. You have to create a certain thrill.'

How did your retail design help to regenerate the brand?

'With a brand like Pringle it was essential to establish a kind of narrative that translated through the details. The shop was pivotal in Pringle's "new" message, yet the brand had to be cautious in order not to alienate the customers. Just before opening the New Bond Street store, Wells Mackereth was informed of the need to anticipate Pringle's new retail concept with a space at Heathrow Airport's Terminal 3 and in Tokyo, Japan. We found ourselves, therefore, in the odd position of developing a concept manual before the flagship had actually opened.'

Wells Mackereth has worked both in retail and leisure environments. Are the two fields becoming increasingly connected?

'You need to activate the seduction process through a little piece of theatre; the creation of a certain thrill can really only be achieved in three dimensions. You may check "netaporter.com" for fashion's latest arrivals, but you still want to enjoy the physicality of a shop's space. Going shopping is the new "going to church". Pawson's Calvin Klein store is immaculately detailed – it's a cathedral to retail. The fact that some Trappist monks, who had seen images of the store, decided to hire Pawson to design their monastery and robes merely reinforces the idea of a certain type of ascetic architecture that can be applied to both mundane and spiritual places.'

What is the main difference between architects and retail designers?

'Architects know how to create a place instead of a space. They are generally in a better position than retail designers to understand the scale, the pace and the longevity of a space. As architects we can create narratives, which help explain ideas to clients and get people excited. Architecture as a discipline brings into play all the different elements, like the gallery element, the hotel and the entertainment.'

If the building becomes the message, and the flagship becomes the brand, is architecture more potent in its communication than, say, an advertising campaign?

'Flagships need to be seen as a reinforcement of the brand. There needs to be a suitability of the shopping experience to what the brand is trying to do. They are really two different ways. With retail design, you have to work within budgets and consider issues like the rent. With advertising it's difficult to quantify; you can't really say if a double-page spread in *Vogue* has paid for itself. It's really about the power of two dimensions versus the power of three dimensions.'

1

Legendary fashion label Gucci was given a sleek and sexy turnaround by fashion designer Tom Ford when he joined the company in 1990. Before Ford, Gucci had slipped from a 1960s iconic fashion brand into a company ruined by family feuds and with a somewhat relaxed attitude towards licensing. Ford set about successfully reinventing Gucci as the ultimate modern luxury house, every star's favourite and first choice for galas and catwalk struts.

Gucci's two-decade-old Fifth Avenue store reopened its doors in 2000 after a lavish 15-month renovation by architect William Sofield (this after the dramatic 72-month renovation of the whole company under Tom Ford). Studio Sofield's portfolio ranges from landscape design to residential, retail, hospitality and corporate office design.

With 3,252 square metres (35,000 square feet) of space and several floors of corporate offices, Gucci is counting on the beginning of a comeback for the Fifth Avenue shopping district. Banking on its heritage, the New York store aims to be 'a Modernist reinterpretation of Gucci's long-standing, signature marble-and-wood environments, introduced in the 1960s'. Standing at the corner of 54th Street, the new concrete-and-

1 Interlocking display units, within the open floor plan, define the space sculpturally.

2 Banking on its heritage, the New York Gucci store aims to be a Modernist reinterpretation of Gucci's long-standing signature marble-and-wood environments that were introduced in the 1960s.

2

3

4

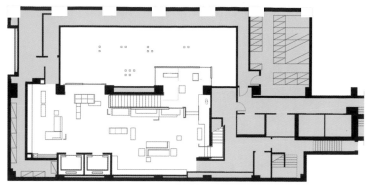

Second floor

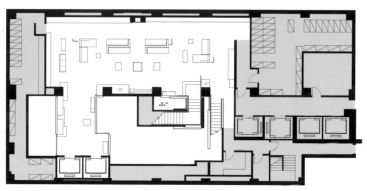

Third floor

limestone embodiment of Gucci Inc., marks the midpoint between the Avenue's two major players: Bergdorf Goodman and Saks Fifth Avenue.

Decked out in rosewood, travertine and stainless steel, the new design is modern throughout and luxurious. The open floor plan is punctuated by interlocking display units that define spaces sculpturally while allowing for dynamic seasonal change. Reflective surfaces, pale lacquers, rich but quiet finishes and generous six-metre (18.5-foot) ceilings on the ground floor complement the horizontal lines of the cantilevered salons, while carefully hand-crafted Modernist fixtures add to a cinematic but subtle interior. Light is treated as a material. A complex combination of HID (High Intensity Discharge), metal halide, incandescent, halogen and fluorescent illumination washes the interiors with a veil of light that complements the sensual, tactile qualities of the store and the sumptuous clothing within it.

With its five floors (increased from three), two elevators, maze of stairways, and umpteen balconies that look out onto other floors, the store is a celebration of luxury consumption and status symbols. The cabinets and finishes are in a seven-layer, hand-rubbed lacquer and the single, central fitting salons are fully upholstered in hand-tufted New Zealand mohair, off of which are the private fitting chambers complete with customer-controlled 'day-to-night' adjustable lighting. An additional private salon and fitting room is located on the fourth floor. Custom-designed and crafted vitrines and cabinets appear to float in space on transparent Lucite bases, providing plateaus of display and luminosity.

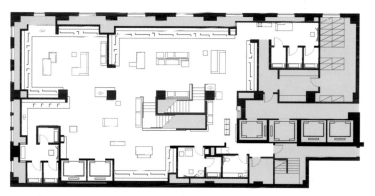

Fourth floor

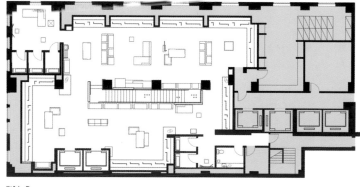

Fifth floor
5

3 Reflective surfaces, pale lacquers and generous six-metre (18.5-foot) ceilings on the ground floor complement the horizontal lines of the cantilevered salons above.

4 Decked out in rosewood, travertine and stainless steel, the design is at the same time both modern and luxurious.

5 Second-, third-, fourth- and fifth-floor plans show the open-plan style of the store with the main circulation staircase at the centre.

For years, the Liberty mock-Tudor building has been a favourite among those in search of the quintessential British shopping experience. The building dates back to 1924 and, although full of heritage, its quaint layout was struggling to keep up with the more theatrical experience offered by nearby London department stores such as Selfridges. In a bid to inject some much-needed contemporary glamour, the London-based design group 20/20 was approached to revitalize the 3,716-square-metre (40,000-square-foot) store overlooking Regent Street.

'The starting point involved a precise definition of what the brand represented, and using this insight to remain faithful to the Liberty brand in all areas of the store design. This resulted in an experience description of an "aesthetic emporium", reflecting the design-centred ethos of the store's founder, Arthur Lasenby Liberty,' says Simon Stacey, then team leader at 20/20 and now a partner at Lippincott Mercer.

A pulsing 'Liberty purple' light installation draws customers to the new entrance. Inside, all three floors have been opened up with windows revealing the store to Regent Street and a new escalator providing greater visibility across the floors and movement between them, again using purple light to create movement and intrigue.

Each floor features a defining 'signature statement' – a distinctive element of product presentation, merchandising or service that creates Liberty's point of difference. On the ground floor, the dramatic-looking cosmetics hall is centred on large, dark-wood 'play tables', where women can indulge in testing their favourite beauty products. The idea of allowing the customers to try out the products creates a warm and relaxed atmosphere. Above them, hang commissioned sculptures – abstracted from Liberty flower prints and using crystal glass, once again in the Liberty purple. Coloured Plexiglas towers, with the signage information inspired by Charles Eames''House of Cards', direct customers up to the first floor and the women's shoes and lingerie department.

1

2

3

LIBERTY Regent House

1
Regent House
♿ WC

Women's Shoes & Lingerie
Link with Tudor House

G
Regent House

Cosmetics & Fragrance
Skincare
Exit to Regent Street

LG
Regent House
🚹🚺 WC

Menswear & Accessories
Men's Shoes
Arthur's bar/restaurant
Link with Tudor House

1 Specially commissioned sculptures using crystal glass are abstracted from Liberty flower prints and hang from the ceiling in the cosmetics hall.

2 Each floor of Liberty is defined by a distinctive element of product presentation that creates the unique Liberty point of difference.

3 On the ground floor, the dramatic-looking cosmetic hall enables women to test and touch their favourite products.

Here, the signature statements are sculptural plinths, which function as display systems for the shoes, allowing them to take centre stage. The contemporary feel of the plinths is contrasted with antique Venetian glass mirrors and Liberty fabric sculptures, commissioned from textile design graduates.

On the lower ground floor, in the menswear, shirts and accessories department, the atmosphere turns to that of a men's club. A 35-metre (115-foot), red Chinese-lacquered shirt and tie 'bar' allows customers to browse for product by colour and fabric. The oriental theme draws on one of Arthur Lasenby Liberty's early inspirations, and is updated for the forms and proportions of the shoe and luggage department, again in red Chinese-lacquer. The café, appropriately named 'Arthur's', is a more obvious testament to the founder. Here, customers can relax surrounded by ever-changing exhibitions of art, photography and sculpture.

'Liberty Regent House translates the richness and colour of the brand's heritage, with a contemporary aesthetic that now gives customers a new, exciting and unique experience of the Liberty brand,' says Stacey.

5

6

4 The shirt and tie counter in the menswear department allows customers to browse by colour and fabric.

5 The newly installed escalator provides greater visibility across the three floors, all of which are bathed in the trademark Liberty purple light.

6 The Chinese red lacquer that is used for the menswear department intends to convey a clubby, decadent feel.

Mulberry was set up in Somerset, England, in the 1970s by Roger Saul, using a family gift of £500 and with his mother, Joan, as a partner. Originally a belt designer, Saul developed a collection of leather accessories from which grew a brand that has since become synonymous with high-quality luxury products ranging from men's and women's clothing and accessories to stationery and home furnishings. By 1992, the annual turnover was £50 million, and on its 25th anniversary, in 1996, Mulberry floated on the AIM market. However, the late 1990s version of luxury failed to be satisfied by a brand like Mulberry, which started to falter. In 2000, 41 percent of the business was sold to Club 21, the Singaporean fashion and hotel group run by husband and wife team Ben Seng and Christina Ong, who also run Armani in the UK.

Design group FOUR IV was appointed by Mulberry to reposition the British brand as a major player in the luxury market. FOUR IV implemented a research strategy geared to find out where Mulberry sat in the landscape of luxury brands. The findings expressed the brand as 'English', 'inspirational' and 'aspirational'. This became the essential communicating elements of the brand, through product, stores, concessions, graphics and other communications. The new Mulberry brand identity, created by FOUR IV, retained the distinctive Mulberry tree logo, redrawn to bring it in line with the new modern luxury values of the company. The tree was also used as a stand-alone logo, particularly on signature leather products, and a new contemporary typeface began to be used in corporate applications.

The New Bond Street store intends to represent Mulberry's heritage as an English, witty brand that specializes in exquisite leathers and detailing. The new store exudes this character – from the leather-panelled staircase to the oak furniture. The re-evaluated brand's newly focused and coherent ranges of leather accessories, contemporary

1

1 The new Mulberry flagship store on New Bond Street embodies the brand's position in the luxury market.

2 A leather-panelled staircase leads to the menswear department on the lower ground floor. The leather-clad back wall contains semi-hidden doors that lead into the changing rooms.

2

3

3 Suede walled changing rooms and low lighting create a
sense of boudoir-style lavishness.

4

4 Leather mannequins and bespoke lighting attempt
to challenge the division that has traditionally existed
between shop fittings and art.

5

clothing and homeware are given individualized areas. Menswear is situated on the lower ground floor and has a leather-clad back wall, containing secret panels leading into changing rooms reminiscent of a stately home. The patterns of the landscaped formal gardens at the Mulberry factory in Shepton Mallet are picked out on the rug. A long table – a piece for the new Mulberry – is oak inset with leather, and amber glass doorknobs, made in Cornwall, complete the look and feel.

British crafted structures focus on the essence and techniques employed by Mulberry. In various departments, bespoke leather mannequins, chandeliers and other ephemera aim to challenge the traditional division between shop fitting and art. Bronze and timber rails hang on leather straps; these clothes-horse-type frames carry gentlemen's trousers. On the ground floor, in leather accessories, luggage and homeware each occupy their own environment, with elements such as chocolate limestone flooring helping to set the various scenes. A leather-panelled staircase leads to womenswear, past a conservatory and bespoke, porcelain chandeliers. Moving into the great hall a huge bevelled mirror reflects the length of two of the signature long tables, and suede-walled changing rooms create boudoir lavishness.

6

5 Bronze and timber are employed throughout the shop for display units.

6 On the ground floor, luggage and home wear is artfully arranged to enact various scenes.

Pringle of Scotland was founded in 1815 by Robert Pringle, a young entrepreneur who recognized the business potential of providing fine-quality, knitted underwear to the well-to-do people of Scotland. Pringle was also one of the first companies to produce machine-knitted garments that could be worn as outerwear, and to coin the term 'knitwear'. In the 1950s, Pringle became famous among Hollywood starlets such as Audrey Hepburn for its figure-hugging twinsets. At the beginning of the Noughties, the fashion label went through a revamp campaign that emphasized the brand's heritage while also injecting a slight edge. From Madonna to Robbie Williams, the quintessential diamond pattern was, as a result, once again present in the wardrobes of the famous.

Pringle's heritage involves fine materials (wool, cashmere and silk) and excellent craftsmanship. With the advertising strapline, 'Be materialistic', the new store in New Bond Street aimed to celebrate the love of materials and to play out the drama between textures – soft against hard, matt against shiny. The design of the space reinforces a subliminal message of the brand's historical Scottish roots through scale, colour, material and reference, while at the same time projecting a bold, new international image of 'British glamour'. The contrasts are embodied by materials such as concrete set against leather detailing by Bill Amberg.

1

2

1 Large tables, covered in felt, are reminiscent of billiard
tables and function as useful display units.

2 Hard materials like concrete and stone play against the
'softer' elements, such as the luxurious leather detailing
by Bill Amberg.

3

The architects, Wells Mackereth, introduced a narrative by juxtaposing images within the two-floor environment. They wanted to create a sense of a story, and to do so they used images, objects that act as references or beacons of an atmosphere. Details and materials such as the silk damask wall, the stone fireplace and the sweeping staircase make subliminal reference to the scale and decadence of a Scottish castle. Slabs of stone, containing fossils, and rich, dark hide transport visitors from the fumes of London to the wild, open Scottish Highlands. To emphasize this, there is a reference to outdoor artist Andy Goldsworthy's work taming nature, as well as to artist Anish Kapoor's sense of scale. A visit to Robert Pringle's library in his home in Scotland inspired the more 'domestic' approach to the various departments. The menswear department, upstairs, has a long plinth with a decanter, bar stools and two large tables covered in felt and leather, reminiscent of billiard tables. A small circular room, designed like the turret of a castle, contains the childrenswear collection. Mackereth chose a rich, deep purple colour as a backdrop for the pastel-hued clothing. Like the collection itself, it was important that aspects of the store were quite playful, such as the clear resin antlers that are mounted in the turret-style winding stairwell.

A second store in Sloane Street was designed to suit a more relaxed, Chelsea spirit. Mixing materials and textures, Wells Mackereth created a distinctly Pringle atmosphere by bringing elements of the great outdoors (Pringle Golf) and London living together within the façade of a grand Victorian townhouse. While the New Bond Street store was conceived as the 'Big House', the Sloane street outlet is viewed as more of a weekend place – a bit younger and more relaxed.

3 The sweeping staircase leads into the menswear department, which is designed to evoke the intimacy of a domestic environment.

4 From left: ground- and first-floor plans, with the curved staircase at the bottom right.

5 The stone fireplace is a direct reference to a Scottish castle, while the clear resin antlers mounted above it inject a dose of humour. The deep purple seating and a rich, dark cowhide on the floor represent the luxurious element.

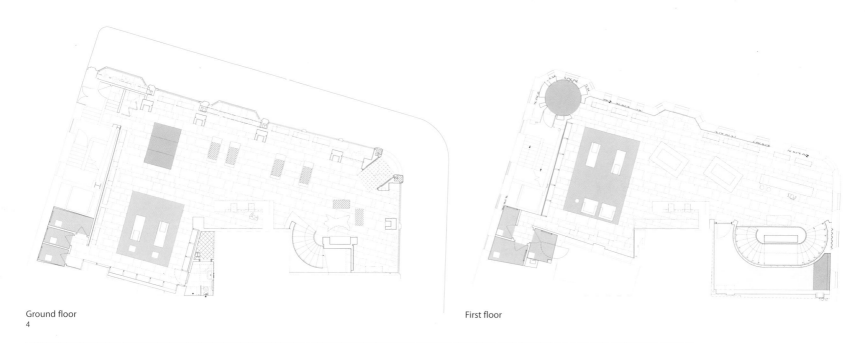

Ground floor
4

First floor

5

TECHNOLOGY AND SHOPPING

INTRODUCTION

Technology has increasingly become a defining element of the shopping experience. With pioneering vision, the Prada Epicenters, commissioned in 2002 in the USA, kick-started an endless discussion about the role that technology has in retail – whether it is about entertainment and/or aiding the act of consumption. While heading the research and concept team at the Office for Metropolitan Architecture (OMA), Markus Schaefer worked closely with architect Rem Koolhaas, Reed Kram from Reed Kram Media Design in Stockholm, Sweden, IDEO and the Prada team on the brand's environment, image and communication.

In 2003, Schaefer joined with Hiromi Hosoya to set up Hosoya Schaefer Architects, a Zurich-based practice that divides its time between creating concepts for clients in field as diverse as politics, university management, integrated regional planning, retail and corporate identity. According to Hosoya Schaefer Architects, digital technologies that provide an alternative to spatial continuity, along with branding and media that affect representation, have fundamentally changed the way we understand and use space. Markus Schaefer talks of the experience of conceiving technology for a retail environment.

INTERVIEW WITH MARKUS SCHAEFER OF HOSOYA SCHAEFER ARCHITECTS, ZURICH, SWITZERLAND

Why is technology used in shopping?

'First, it is used for the efficiency it allows. Point of sale systems, customer databases and inventory databases are tools that were generated strictly for the logistical side of the business. Now, many of these systems are created in order to be seen, and sometimes even used, by clients. In this sense, technology simply is part of how shops are currently organized and run. Second, shopping, especially when it is shopping for fashion and trends, is still associated with newness, and technology is a very important signifier of the new. Shops use technology to show that they are up-to-date. Often the communication that is achieved with displays or projections could also be achieved with print or other media, but that would be seen as old-fashioned. The medium is very much the message in a shopping environment.

When Rem Koolhaas began the collaboration with Miuccia Prada and Patrizio Bertelli several years ago, they were interested in something different, a totally new approach to retailing. With a team of fellow students studying with Koolhaas at Harvard University, we had just completed work on the *Harvard Guide to Shopping*, where we analyzed how shopping had invaded all other activities in the city. The citizen had become a consumer in the museum shop as much as in the university merchandising shop, and in areas as diverse as the airport and the church. We also looked at the relentless drive for newness and its modernizing and innovative, yet often frivolous, force. We were interested in using these insights to respond to the classical questions of architecture – use, the role of the collective, representation and space. Technology integrated into space allowed for interactions that were architectural rather than menu-driven. The system was to allow us, next to increasing efficiency and providing a better service, to represent the company and its cultural context in new ways. We were interested in juxtaposing to the hermetic logic of branded space, information and images that were raw, rough, strange, taken from the public domain or taken from the company and presented without the need to turn them into a seamless story. I believe that companies exist in a spectrum between identity and innovation. Identity, a branded image, is dependent on stability and control; innovation is based on accepting the unexpected. We hoped to use technology to do the latter rather than only the former.'

How do architecture and interaction design relate? How can interaction design bring the whole technological vision together within a retail environment?

'Architecture is the oldest interaction design discipline. Unfortunately, it does not yet have a lot of experience with technology, media and their specific requirements. I strongly believe that digital interaction will increasingly be either constrained to very small devices or become part of environments. I am very interested in using space and movement in space, *i.e.* traditional behaviour understood by architects, as ways of interaction. I think the most successful applications in the stores, the magic mirror and the Privalite wall in Prada's Beverly Hills Epicenter Store, are based on interactions that only involve body movements and result in a playful, spontaneous interaction. Whenever customers need to interact with a screen, or even worse with a menu, their interest is lost rapidly.'

The Prada stores, for many, symbolize the marriage between retail and technology. What has been your participation in it and what were the key concepts that you developed? Also, what was the relationship with IDEO?

'Our interaction and collaboration with Prada was very stimulating because of Miuccia Prada's strong desire to develop the brand's store concept and revolutionize the current perception of retailing. I was heading the research and concept team at OMA at the time. After the stores had been conceptualized, our focus turned to the technology and communications aspect of the project. We invited Reed Kram, who I knew from our studies in Boston, to join us. Together with the creative and technical input from the Prada Group, we defined most of the elements of the store scenario.

We found RFID technology very exciting, as it seemed to promise that physical objects and digital information could seamlessly interact. In our scenarios, information would not be carried around. It would, rather, follow customers and staff to wherever they needed it – displays then became part of the environment rather than part of a device. We conceptualized hanging displays, like garments on hangers that would slide in between clothes hanging on a hangbar. They were still connected to the store system and therefore part of an overall scenario. We were interested in going beyond the simple corporate video playing on a screen. Our displays can be activated by a staff device to show movies, fashion shows or information about a specific product. Later on, Clemens Weisshaar gave these displays a beautiful form. Information was to be managed by the staff through a personal device. Only in specific cases would the customer interact directly with it. The dressing rooms, for example, would provide information and have some sort of digital mirror.

IDEO helped in creating the magic mirror with the idea of elastic time even though the first full-scale demo software was written by Reed Kram. They developed the staff device that, in the New York concept, was the mediator between all the different elements of the scenario. And they were instrumental in implementing the RFID technology as that was, at the time, fairly experimental. When we worked on the second store, technology was already so much further advanced that we could work with much more reliable RFID technology. In addition, the application could be reduced to one flexible and versatile piece of .net software, while the New York store was still based on a server system that mediated between different applications. Thanks to the expertise and valuable contribution of Prada Group IT, we no longer needed the support of IDEO.'

A textbook example of how big a media buzz could be generated from the marriage between high-profile architect and fashion brand, the collaboration between Miuccia Prada and Rem Koolhaas' Office for Metropolitan Architecture (OMA) set international press tongues wagging way before any visualization was even rendered 3D. In spring 1999 Prada asked OMA to develop a unified concept for major outlets in New York, Los Angeles, San Francisco and Tokyo. Prada wanted to create a new retail experience for its customers, something that would reflect the company's credo in shopping 'as a singular experience in which culture and consumerism flow together'. Prada also commissioned Swiss architects Herzog & de Meuron and the Japanese Kazuyo Sejima + Ryue Nishizawa to build stores around the globe.

Following the high-profile opening of the New York Prada Epicenter by OMA in 2002 and the Tokyo Aoyama Epicenter by Herzog & de Meuron in 2003, the Los Angeles store by OMA opened in July 2004. All the stores are defined by the integration of retail and performance space, with an innovative employment of technology. Set in Beverly Hills' Rodeo Drive, the favourite hangout for shopping celebrities, the LA store is a total of 2,230 square metres (24,000 square feet) with 1,370 square metres (14,750 square feet) of retail space on three floors. Inside, are housed the ready-to-wear mens and womens collections, the sports line, handbags, shoes, accessories and beauty.

The absence of a façade and of a logo is arguably the LA store's most defining characteristic. The entire 15-metre (50-foot) width opens up onto the street without a traditional, glass-enclosed storefront, which invites the public to enter the building and creates a continuum between the outside and inside. At night, an aluminum wall is raised to hermetically seal the interior. Inside, the store's architecture remains 'uncovered'. Thanks to the meticulous engineering of Arup, the space is

2

1

1 The Prada façade on Rodeo Drive opens up to the street and merges public with commercial space. Invisible security antennas guarantee the safety of the goods inside.

2 Inside the store, a large wooden stair forms a hill-like structure that supports an aluminium box that floats above the entrance. The stair is framed with laminated glass that fades from translucent to transparent.

an interesting mix of column-free space and certain areas where the structure is exposed. Built using a steel brace frame that features special steel trusses, the building has sheer concrete and the floors are steel, framed with composite metal deck and concrete. One of the most notable structural aspects was the design for the roof, which has a steel frame that supports an all-glass, pitched roof. This also doubles as the seismic-resisting diaphragm.

An oval section arch, faced with polished stainless steel, is hollowed out from the double-sided wood staircase at the centre and contains a replica of the first Prada store opened in Milan in 1913, a poignant reference to the company's growth and development. Surfaces are tactile and ingenious – the staircase is framed with laminated glass that fades from translucent to transparent, shoppers sit on gel-like cushions and the aluminium box that floats above the entrance is lined with a spongy, porous material specifically developed for Prada.

Like the New York Epicenter, interactive technology is key to the shopping experience. Each dressing room is a simple 0.74-square-metre (eight-square-foot) booth with Privalite glass walls that switch from transparent to translucent when a room is occupied. Once inside,

the customer can switch the doors back to transparent at the touch of a button, thus exposing themselves to the onlookers waiting outside the room. Different lighting conditions allow customers to view their selections in a warm evening glow or cool blue daylight. IDEO led the design and development of the interactive dressing rooms, working in close collaboration with OMA and AMO, the research branch of OMA.

The elevator features a series of small, LCD screens, integrated into the cabin that scan virtual imagery while the elevator travels through the shaft. Ubiquitous displays, plasma screens built into the furniture or hung between the merchandise, show news feeds and stock market data. The technology here is designed to work in an non-obtrusive and functional way, as well as helping Prada portray itself as a brand with a deep engagement in current cultural context.

4

5

3 Half matter, half air, the spongy material, specifically developed for Prada, provides a porous, artificial background for the merchandise.

4 The wooden staircase is a novel and open-plan means of display. Here, dismembered legs perch on the display boxes modelling a selection of shoes.

5 The roof structure, spanning the entire floor space, admits daylight to the 'scenario-space', where merchandise is arranged within an open, flexible floor plan.

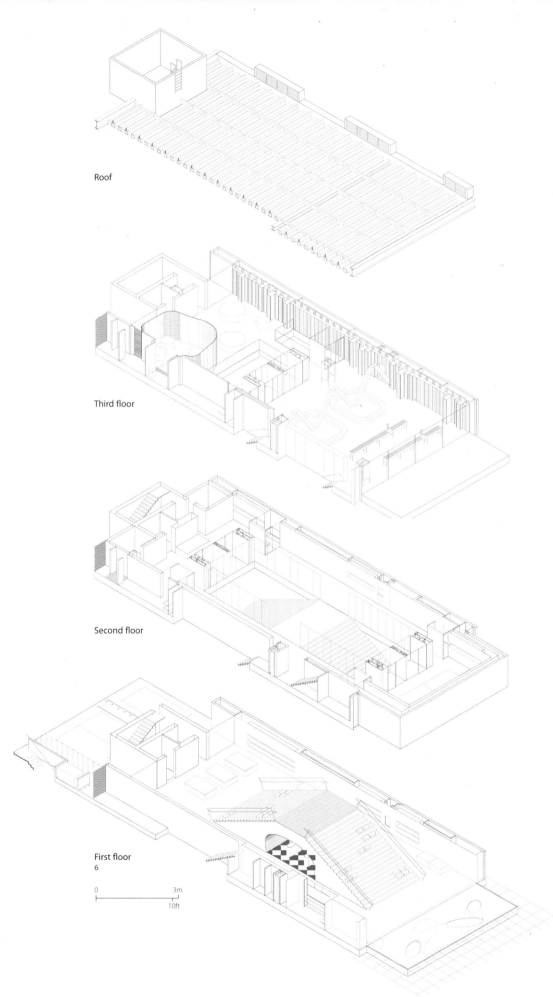

Roof

Third floor

Second floor

First floor
6

0 _____ 3m
10ft

7

6 An axonometric diagram of the building, showing the placement of the alcove beneath the stair-hill.

7 In the mirrored alcove beneath the stair-hill, the black and white marble floor and the vitrines make reference to the first Prada store that was founded in Milan in 1913.

8 Section through the alcove, with stairs above.

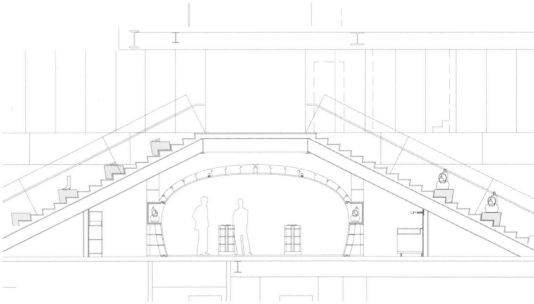

7

Multi-awarded retail concept oki-ni brought new meaning to the introduction of technology into retail. With no display rails, no till or obvious signage, oki-ni (meaning 'thank you' in Osaka dialect) presents itself as a singular installation concept based on the tactile and social opportunities that shopping can provide. The store was set up by Paddy Meehan, the fashion entrepreneur behind the fashion label Beauty:Beast, where limited-edition clothes are sold alongside niche brands such as Fake London, Evisu and UACT.

6a Architects were briefed to create a simple, stylish environment with organic natural lines that were more 'Badly Drawn Boy' and less 'LTJ Bukem' (low-fi, breezy music as opposed to a harder-edged techno sound). Emphasis was put on evoking a communal, user-friendly space that would have a transient, light and portable feel. Inspiration was drawn from the artist Joseph Beuys, whose love for felt is widely reproduced in the interior scheme, and from the metal sculptures by Richard Serra. The idea was that the space should not feel like a shop, but more like a comfortable social setting in which to appreciate clothes.

oki-ni was designed as a huge tray, made of Russian oak, which sits neatly in the triangular-shaped shop and works both as display and as furniture. Low piles of felt replace the traditional arrangement of shelving, rails and furniture and help to define oki-ni's physical landscape. The sparsely arranged clothes hang on deliberately cheap, bare metal coat hangers. Details are minimized or avoided, the focus is instead on good lighting and a few low displays.

oki-ni proposes itself as just a physical space for the looking, choosing and trying out of clothes. All the other transaction (payment and ordering) can be done online, either on the spot by a shop assistant or from your own computer from a website designed by the 'trendy'

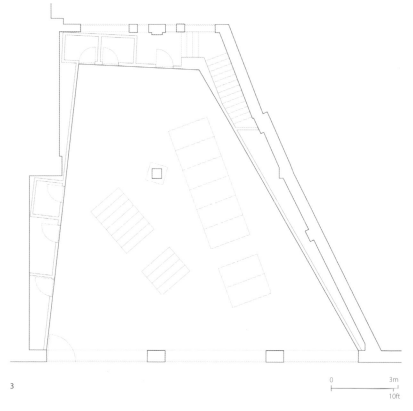

3

0   3m
10ft

2

1 Artist Joseph Beuys and his love of felt were used as inspiration for the sparse interior scheme at oki-ni.

2 oki-ni proposes itself as just the physical space for looking, choosing and trying out clothes. All the economic transactions take place online.

3 The distinctive, triangular floor-plan.

group Fuel. The architects avoided the creation of any point of sale, and proposed the ubiquitous laptop, gently assimilated among the products and visitors, as the sales interface.

The emphasis is not just on online buying, but also on the exclusiveness associated with limited-edition jeans. Against the culture of the quick-fix, power-shopping moment, oki-ni offers individual choice and style, non-conformity and the anticipation that derives from simple waiting (delivery of the final article takes up to three days, no matter what the destination, and can be delivered worldwide). A combination of technology and customization ('rarity is a proof of innocence' reads the epigraph on the oki-ni website) is reinforced by a visual statement similar to the aesthetic of galleries. At oki-ni, the clothes are interspersed with a range of art books and magazines, just like in a museum shop, and display-wise, the hanging items look like they are a part of an art installation or even a project under construction.

6a Architects have an obvious interest in the role of shopping in today's culture. According to them, 'oki-ni is a good example of how the physical environment and a new shopping concept can reinforce each other. oki-ni is a new brand in a world where on line shopping, traditional shopping, leisure and culture have increasingly overlapped.'

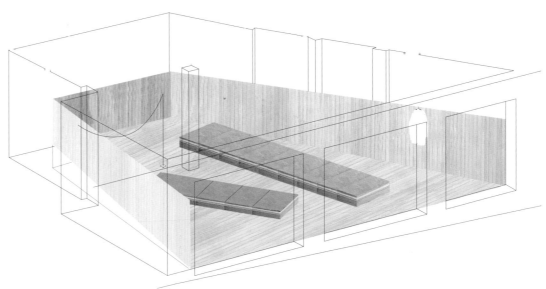

5

4 Designed as a huge oak tray, the layout of oki-ni is both decorative and functional.

5 This computer rendering shows how the oak 'tray' sits in the shop space.

SHOEBALOO

1

A designer-footwear chain, specializing in labels such as Prada, Gucci and Fendi, Shoebaloo prizes itself for its constantly cutting-edge interiors. The original retail concept for the site, located in P.C. Hooftstraat, was created 12 years ago by Czech designer Borek Sipek. Looking for something new, the client commissioned Amsterdam-based Meyer & Van Schooten Architecten to recreate the interior.

Contrary to the many boutiques now present on chic P.C. Hooftstraat, Shoebaloo has no clear display window in a deliberate, reverse attempt to intrigue and attract passers-by. Behind the dark mirror-glass of the display windows only glimpses of a few pairs of shoes, illuminated by spotlights, are visible. The reflective front door mirrors the street and the passers-by, with the intention of stopping them on their steps and luring them inside. The dark façade contrasts with the wildly illuminated inside.

As the mirror doors slide open, the shop interior reveals itself as a futuristic, styled environment, set within a nineteenth-century building. Inside, vacuum-moulded, translucent polyacrylic is used for the ceiling and for wall-mounted shelving that contains niches for the display of

1 The architects chose to design an understated street façade, which employs one-way glass that is only transparent when light is shone behind it.

2 This plan shows the entrance to the right and the egg-shaped display units in the centre.

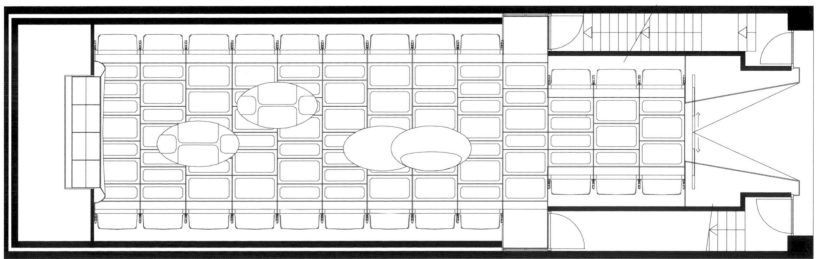

2

shoes. The floor is glass, underneath which sits more polyacrylic panels. Because of the lighting and the reflections of the mirrors at the front of the shop, the depth of the actual space is difficult to grasp.

The egg-shaped display units for accessories are complemented by egg-shaped furniture (two benches and a counter) painted in glossy white paint. Situated behind the shells of all the plastic panels are 540 fluorescent light tubes that create an artificial atmosphere. The colour pattern of the lighting scheme can be changed by the retailer via a computer system. Slow-changing patterns or static configurations can bathe areas of the shop in pink, blue, red or green.

Tones can also be varied at the same time with, for example, a blue light glowing at the front of the store and a red one at the back. The colour change can take about five minutes or even less. Following the success of this Amsterdam shop, the architects are about to design another Shoebaloo, this time in Rotterdam.

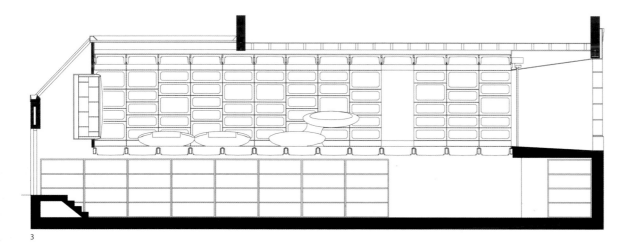
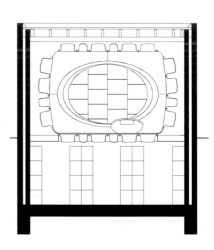

3

4

5

6

7

3 From left: long and short section plans of the shop.

4 The computer-controlled lighting can be set to a series of slowly changing patterns or configured to remain static.

5 The futuristic looking pieces of furniture are seats, a cash desk and display cases for accessories.

6 The floor is made of glass, underneath which sit more acrylic panels.

7 Inside the shop, vacuum-moulded translucent, polyacrylic is used for the ceiling and wall-mounted shelving, with niches for the display of shoes.

Ron Arad's product-design background and penchant for audacious technological innovations that act both as solutions as well as cheerful provocations is well-represented in Y's. In 2002, London-based Ron Arad Associates (RAA) was approached by fashion designer Yohji Yamamoto to design the new Tokyo's flagship store for the company's 'Y's' label. When presenting the preliminary sketches and ideas, RAA was given carte blanche to design the store, while keeping within the constraints of the budget and the physical characteristics of the site. The building of the Y's store coincided with the label's total brand revamp, one that included the way in which the clothes were sold in retail environments.

The store occupies a 570-square-metre (6,135-square-foot) area, divided by three large structural columns. RAA masked the columns in a way that would create an illusion of lightness and movement within the space. Strong reference was drawn from the mechanical automobile parking turntables that are common in Tokyo. The three existing columns,

1

2

plus a 'fake' one, were transformed into sculptures resembling the turntables, and embedded into the floor. Each of these rotating, industrial-looking sculptures is made of 34 tubular, aluminium loops, stacked to occupy the entire distance between the floor and the ceiling around steel column casings – they act almost as structural supports. In fact, the store ceiling and floor appear to be almost held apart by these four, ever-changing elements.

Each of these loops can be rotated 360 degrees, accommodating an infinite number of spatial arrangements. The gentle pirouettes of the sculptures create a flexible environment, one in which the store reconfigures itself several times during a visit. As the customers peruse within this fluid structure, they hardly notice the slow movement of the sculptures, but when the shop closes, the speed of the rotation accelerates, via a lever, with the turntables spinning like the inside of a washing machine. The loops are used as shop-fitting elements. Within the stacks of lozenge-shaped rings, each element can rotate individually to create a rail for Y's clothes. They can also be transformed into wide shelves using special customized 'plug-in' units, and acquire a decorative function as objects are hung on them.

Additional product display units are made from a series of angular glass-fibre, reinforced plastic shelves that can dock into each other to form free-standing shelf stacks. The till is formed by a series of displaced, identical, angular plates that mimic both the shelves and the rotating loops. The changing rooms are located behind gill-like curved walls, and coloured LED lights tell customers whether the room is occupied or not. Outside, the façade is made of a series of curved glass panels forming a refractory glass surface that, when looked through, distorts and stretches the contents of the store. The revolving store entrance door is decorated with the freehand letters 'Y' and 'S'; they had first appeared in Arad's preliminary sketches and ended up becoming the store's logo. When the door is spun open, they shimmer and change colour.

1 The street-facing façade is composed of an array of curved glass panels forming a refractory glass structure that distorts and stretches the contents of the store from the outside.

2 The revolving store entrance is adorned with four layers of coloured glass pieces, forming a freehand Y's logo that, when the door is spun, shimmers and changes colour.

3

4

3 The large structural columns have been masked with tubular aluminium loops to become both decorative and functional elements of the store.

4 These sculptural elements are made of 34 aluminium, tubular loops, stacked to occupy the entire distance between the floor and the ceiling.

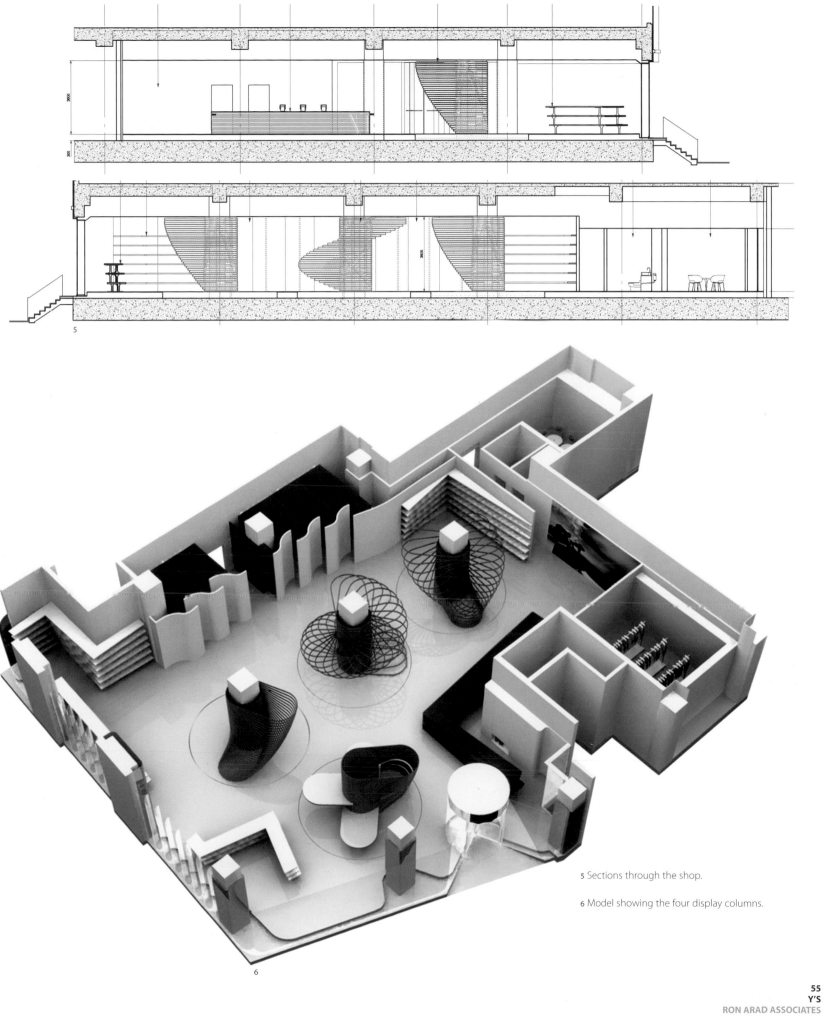

5 Sections through the shop.

6 Model showing the four display columns.

The Tokyo HQ for the Italian shoe and bag brand Tod's is situated on the tree-lined Omotesando Avenue. Architect Toyo Ito drew on the surrounding trees for inspiration when he was designing the distinctive concrete façade, seen here from inside the store.

INTRODUCTION

The love affair between fashion designers and high-profile architects is a commercial fairy tale made in creative heaven. Fashion stores need cultural kudos in a bid to justify their existence, and architects are only too happy to indulge in the ephemeral world of fashion. Retail projects allow for an open brief and superior budgets and they are often perceived as great ways to experiment, the results of which generate worldwide curiosity and concentrated media attention. From John Pawson's minimalist retail temple for Calvin Klein, designed in New York in 1996, to Armani's commissions of Claudio Silvestrin and Massimiliano and Doriana Fuksas, there are very few names that have not been involved in this particular pastime. Even the younger generation of achingly hip fashion designers like Stella McCartney and Alexander McQueen are keen to sign up their own personal architect who can embody their stylish, image-conscious brands.

Designer Rei Kawakubo, who founded Comme des Garçons in 1973, was one the first to initiate the cross-pollination between the two camps. In 1998 she commissioned Future Systems to design her store in New York. Since then, Future Systems has worked with several fashion retailers, such as the Italian retailer Marni, the British fashion chain New Look and the British department store Selfridges. Amanda Levete, of Future Systems, talks about the practice's projects and how shops have become 'fashionable stopovers'.

INTERVIEW WITH AMANDA LEVETE OF FUTURE SYSTEMS, LONDON, UK

How did the relationship with Rei Kawakubo work?

'She is an amazing character, both an artist and the head of a fashion empire. However well she is doing, every ten years she reinvents herself. We did three shops for Comme des Garçons. The New York store (1998) was a rare piece of industrial heritage located in the West Chelsea area, then associated more with art galleries than shops. Rather than refurbish the whole structure, we decided to keep the 1950s' feel of it and designed a transition from the outside to the inside, which was an aluminium tunnel that swept you in. With the Tokyo one (1998), which was a smaller space set within a 1970s' office building, we reduced the size of the entrance and replaced it with inclined curved patterned glass, so as to give it a tunnel effect. The façade was a series of large panels of glass covered with spotted film. In 1999, for the Parfum Shop in Place des Vosges in Paris, we had to work within the restrictions of a nineteenth-century listed apartment building. The question here was how do you transform the perception of a building? We decided to do it through large, flat sheets of coloured glass attached with bolts: both a soft and powerful graphic device. The colour decreases in intensity as it rises up the façade, allowing the original stone front to show through.'

You were at that time approached by Marni, an Italian fashion label only known by the style conscious few.

'For Marni, we created the first flagship store in London and then in Milan, Paris and New York. We needed to reflect the romantic nature of the brand, hence the space could not be another minimalist shop. With London, we came up with this idea of the shop as a landscape. We wanted to get away from the traditional concept of having clothes on rails, so we designed a system in which the clothes were suspended from the ceiling. By creating abstract forms, the clothes worked as artwork, invisibly framed by a romantic landscape.'

Then Vittorio Radice, then chief executive of Selfridges, asked you to build a new department store in Birmingham.

'We had always dreamt of doing something big. Radice had seen the NatWest Media Centre at Lord's Cricket Ground in London. Completed in 1999, the small, streamlined aluminium pod had won architecture's RIBA Stirling Prize. He told us he wanted us to do something for the city of Birmingham. The site was an example of terrible postwar planning and needed some real regeneration. In order for Selfridges to work in Birmingham, it had to do something in a scale that would change the perception of the city. The issue was how to clad a largely opaque building in an affordable way that could turn a doubly curved corner. We looked at fashion influences like Paco Rabanne, we looked at animals and fish scales, and we even looked at baroque churches and how, historically, they have managed to break down mass via plastered forms. Finally we came up with the notion of polished, anodized, aluminium discs. They are a successful device because they really catch the light.'

Your mark was largely on the exterior with the curvaceous shape and the 15,000 anodized aluminum disks, but there is also a striking interior and other designers have been involved in different floors and their concessions.

'Once you have set up such an expectation from the outside, you have to match it on the inside. Each designer was allocated a floor; we chose the food hall downstairs. We strived to do enough for the interior that would hold it all together. For the atrium, we wanted to get away from the department store cliché of the escalator and glass façade. We clad the escalators in matt white plaster to make them more muscular and sensuous. It was important to emphasize the theatricality and the drama of the atrium. We also thought that the rooflight was very important. Often in department stores you have a roof that is illuminated with artificial light; for us it was important to give a sense of the outside, the weather and the clouds. Another important element was the store's relationship with the sixteenth-century church, Saint Martin's, next door. The store is conceived as a backdrop to the church and the juxtaposition works very well. You understand better the scale of the store by seeing it next to another building.'

And of course there is the now the common association of shops being the new churches.

'The church used to be the meeting place, and now the department store is the great meeting place. But the relationship between the two spaces in Birmingham is real, the local priest even organizes a shoppers' service on Sunday.'

Much has been said about shops being a fashionable stopover – not just because of the merchandise, but also because they are spaces that people want to visit with an architectural value and fascination of their own. Some critics have even compared the way museums like the Guggenheim use architecture to attract visitors to commercial brands such as Coca-Cola.

'I'm very wary of these comparisons. Buildings take about four years to complete while a shop is complete within months. They are much more experimental, temporary, and you are constantly going out of fashion. Also, the Bilbao Guggenheim had millions spent on it. Selfridges was built with a developer's budget for the same cost per square metre as the Debenhams store next door, which does not have cultural ambitions. Yet it has become an iconic building, so much so that even Selfridges' store card has the Birmingham building on it as a logo. Selfridges was about selling, but figures says that over 100 million people a year pass by the London store, which is way more than Tate Modern art gallery. It really makes you ask: What is the nature of a public building? Is it visual? Is it creative? Is it an experience?'

4

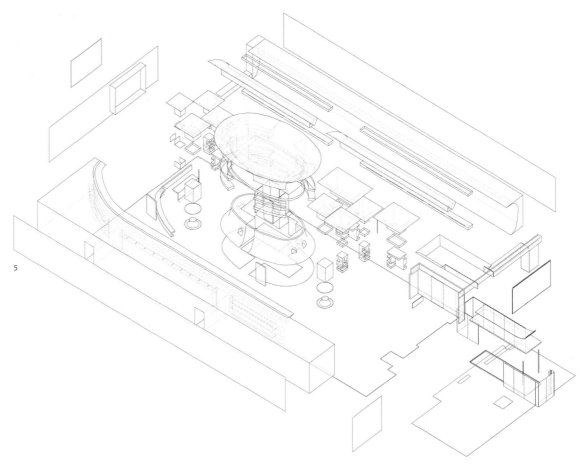

5

6

4 A large ovoid structure, dubbed the 'Mother Ship', functions as the main decorative element in the shop.

5 An exploded axonometric diagram shows the structure of the central ovoid 'Mother Ship'.

6 Wide strips of lighting, embedded in the walls, give the display units and the clothes either a white reflection or a greenish-blue hue.

Taking its cue from the Armani, Milan megastore, an 8,000-square-metre (86,110-square-foot) retail centre, that opened in 2000 and sells all the Armani clothes and accessories lines under one roof) the fashion label repeated the formula in 2002 by opening a 2,000-square-metre (21,530-square-foot) Armani in Hong Kong. Retail-wise, Hong Kong is the perfect springboard from which to conquer China and it appeals to the conspicuous consumption habits of Hong Kong dwellers.

In contrast with the pared-down architectural style of the Italian Claudio Silvestrin, who designed the main body of the five-storey building, Chater House, the Giorgio Armani boutique on the ground floor and the accessories area on the first floor, Rome-based Massimiliano and Doriana Fuksas were commissioned to design a fresher, funkier look for the Emporio Armani store.

According to Massimiliano and Doriana Fuksas, the Emporio Armani project in Hong Kong was born with the insight that 'global culture is an experimental territory of many identities. It is the encounter of diverse modes of sensing the world…' The whole project developed around the idea of fluidity, inspired by the casual movements of visitors and customers. The space was thus conceived as a stage, where the visitor is both the actor and the protagonist of a very special experience.

The result is a store in which the space is filled with lightness, owing mainly to the floor of blue-coloured epoxy resin that shimmers like water and is reflected by the glass-reinforced gypsum ceiling. The bespoke

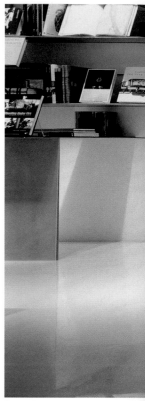

2

1

1 The blue-tinged, epoxy resin floor, reflected by the glass-reinforced gypsum ceiling, gives the store a sense of lightness and fluidity.

2 All the satin stainless-steel display tables and units are designed by Massimiliano and Doriana Fuksas and manufactured by Zeus.

furniture, made of sheets of stainless steel and clad in soft, translucent Plexiglas, reinforces the sense of weightlessness. The merchandise is displayed in sleek, suspended glass boxes or on pared-down clothes rails.

The main feature of the space is the undulating, red fibreglass ribbon that runs through the store, creating a route among the shop, the café, the bookshop, the florist and the cosmetic department. In the restaurant, the ribbon transforms itself into a bar table, rising and dropping to create a dining space, it then transforms into a DJ booth, then into a bar space and finally spirals into a tunnel to form the main entrance to the store. In the bar area, the ribbon is matched by a luminescent curving strip on the ceiling that almost creates the effect of a motorcar ramp. Inspired by the spiralling coloured ribbons used by Chinese gymnasts, the red colour is also a precise cultural reference to China, where it means happiness. Outside, the façade is also decorated

by an illuminated red dragon like motif, which changes intensity to reflect the pulsing life of Hong Kong. These details are a radical departure from the neutral-toned world of Giorgio Armani, but one that works wonders in creating a spectacular retail environment.

3

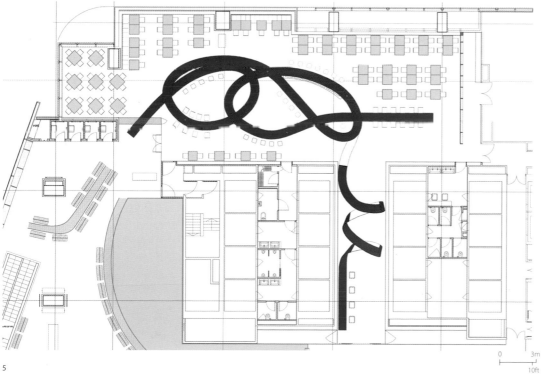

3 The red fibreglass ribbon twirls around the store to define the space and accentuate different areas.

4 The red ribbon is inspired by the spiralling, coloured ribbons of Chinese gymnasts and is also a direct reference to China, where red means happiness.

5 Plan: shoppers follow the red fibreglass ribbon through the entrance corridor (bottom right) into the main store.

4

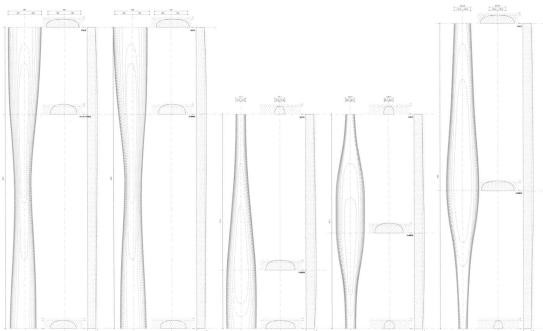

5

4 The architectural practice SANAA was commissioned to focus on the façade of the building, leaving the interiors and shop fitting to Dior's in-house teams.

6

7

The site was constrained by being located within a restricted building area, which had very tall maximum height regulations. The regulated maximum building height is at a ratio of five to one with the maximum floor area. SANAA chose to emphasize both characteristics by creating many floors with different heights and uses – some for shopping, others for events. High ceilings have the effect of making the rooms seem more spacious. In a city like Tokyo where space is so restricted and public areas are not constituted, like in European cities, by a piazza, retail flagships have to work extra hard to make themselves noticed, often on busy, narrow streets. The skin of the building and the outside exterior become defining elements of the growing metropolis.

The imposing silhouette of the simple glass sheath with white horizontals is given even more emphasis by the proximity of a traditional Japanese building next door. At night, the Dior Building is lit and becomes an ethereal, white, glowing city landmark.

5 A drawing of the undulating acrylic interior façade.

6 The high ceilings in the store have the effect of making the room appear more spacious.

7 The building's unusual footprint was dictated by the site and by strict height regulations.

Founded by Eduardo Fendi, the Fendi sisters have been crafting fashion, accessories and furs since 1925, but it was third-generation family member Silvia Venturini, Fendi's creative director, who put the brand on the global map by creating a status symbol for the fashion world, such as the 'Baguette Bag'. Venturini has also been the mind behind the company's new worldwide retail strategy, executed by Rome-based architects Lazzarini Pickering in cities such as Rome, Paris, London and New York.

Located near the elegant shopping heaven of Avenue Montaigne, the Paris store strives hard to stand out amid its luxurious neighbours. While aiming to be immediately recognizable, it was designed to create a unique spatial and shopping experience as well as a space that is reflective of local architectural traditions and materials.

1

2

The entire boutique revolves around the spatial device of a staircase, which is a vortex of sculptural display elements that encourages the shopper to use all of the floors. Three floors are connected by the open staircase in a geometric game of square shapes that spiral towards the top. The shelves, tables and horizontal and vertical hanging fascias are of an architectural scale and proportionate to the space. The shelves are up to 10 meters (33 feet) long; the tables are 7 metres (23 feet) and the hanging fascias up to 20 meters (66 feet) long. Luxurious bags are displayed as if they are in a void, their preciousness heightened by a system of indirect lighting. Clothes are hung or laid out in an informal way – the carefully conceived 'disorder' of the display encourages clients to touch the precious materials and try on the various pieces.

The use of traditional and humble, low-tech materials has provided the opportunity to try out new finishes. Rough, rendered surfaces are finished with a ferromicaceous paint that is normally employed to protect metal surfaces. The crude iron is first treated with a nitrate solvent, to make it virtually stainless, and then it is wax-finished. This in some way reflects Fendi's unconventional attitude towards furs and leathers, both in the treatment and manufacture as well as the combination with other materials.

Following the current retail trend that sees a departure from chilly minimalism as a style that does not encourage shopping or experience, the architects have created an interior palette that is warm with natural grey timber tones, shades of grey, brown and black. The Fendi image is projected as dark, architectural and luxurious.

1 The dark-toned décor offsets the bright garments and accessories on display.

2 The raw steel shelves and wenge tables were designed by the architects.

3

3 Accessories are displayed in a sculptural way, in keeping
with the shop's 3D configuration of shelves, hanging
systems and tables.

4

5

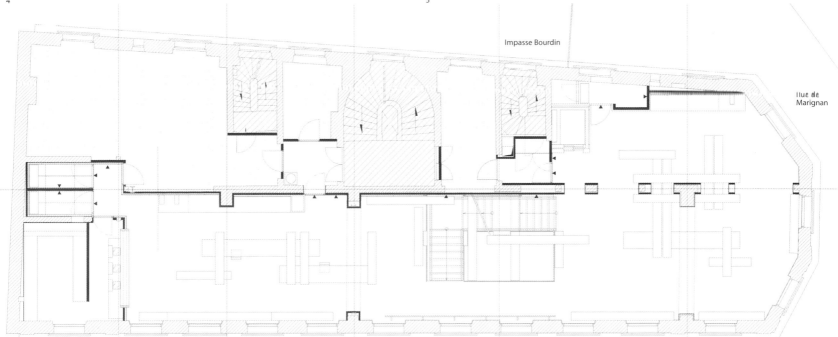

Impasse Bourdin

Rue de Marignan

6

4 The entire store's space revolves around the staircase, which acts as a vortex of sculptural display elements.

5 For the Paris store, the crude iron was treated with a nitrate solvent and then wax-finished.

6 Second-floor plan.

According to Selfridges marketing director, James Bidwell, the store in Birmingham was conceived as a place for cutting-edge individuals to gather and socialize, as well as to shop. The $66.4 million department store was built as the centrepiece of a $750 million redevelopment of the Bull Ring – an area that comprises 16 hectares (40 acres) in the centre of Birmingham. The astounding, armadillo-like building was especially commissioned to rejuvinate people's opinion of the city.

The brainchild of Vittorio Radice, then MD of Selfridges, who notoriously defined the department store as a 'house of brands' and the shopping experience as 'theatre', the Birmingham site was conceived by London-based architects Future Systems. Radice's brief was to create a building that would change the perception of the city.

The actual store is 23,230 square metres (250,000 square feet). The building is curvilinear with no windows, but with a stunning, royal blue outer shell. The exterior surface is covered with 15,000 anodized aluminium discs that create an almost snake-like appearance. This cladding solved the issue of how to turn a doubly curved corner while also being economically sustainable. The discs create a fine, lustrous grain, like the sequins on a Paco Rabanne dress. Above, a sky bridge takes

2

1

1 The striking silhouette of the Birmingham Selfridges stands out against the city's skyline and provides an excellent contrast to St. Martin's Church next door.

2 The store consists of various floors offering fashion, food, homeware, technology and beauty products.

3 Fifteen thousand anodized aluminium discs applied to the stone façade create and armadillo-like appearance.

4

5

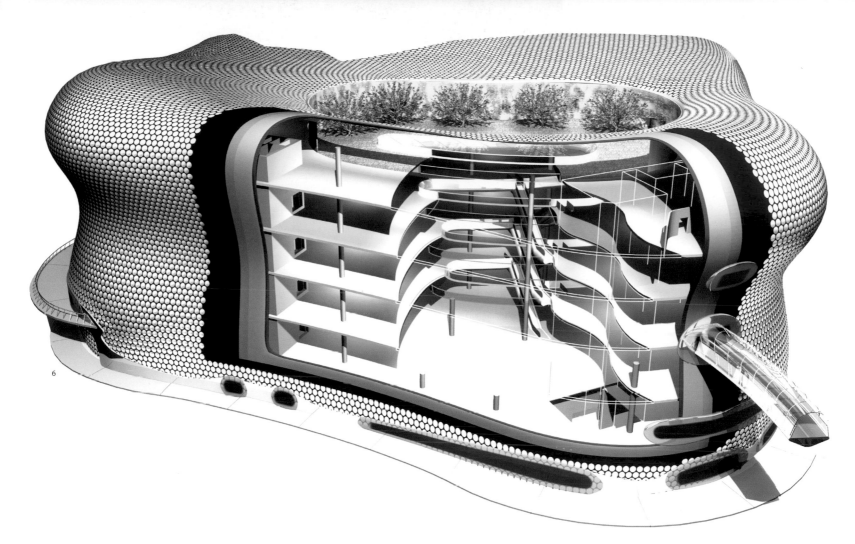

shoppers from the store into an adjacent multi-storey car park. Future Systems chose to illustrate its curvaceous and organic style by making the bridge curved rather than straight; support for it comes from cables attached to a single point on the store's exterior.

Inside, according to Future Systems' partner Amanda Levete, 'circulation was the key' as well as the need to maximize accessibility on every level so that no floor would dominate another. The most spectacular element of the asymmetric interior is the atrium, with its high-gloss white balconies and dizzying array of escalators, recalling a vast skeletal structure. The escalators are clad in robust white plaster, making them sculptural rather than just functional. A glass rooftop allows natural daylight to pour down into the great, canted atrium and gives a clear view of the sky, giving a real sense of the weather conditions outside.

The store has seven floors, four of which are devoted to retail. A different designer was involved in each floor: Milan-based Aldo Cibic and Partners for the fourth and top retail floor; Staunton Williams for the third level; the second was by London-based Eldridge Smerin and the lower level, comprising the food hall, was by Future Systems themselves. Here one can find over ten 'eatover' counters, serving Indian, Japanese and Italian cuisine, among others, and a wine department.

The technology department on the second floor features green rubber floors and walls that are made of expanded foam. Also on the second floor, several brands live in differently designed concessions. The overall look and feel is provided by exposed metalwork, a seamless poured-resin floor and silver photographers' reflectors overhead. The third floor features the menswear department and includes a dark-gray resin floor and an exposed ceiling with overhead cable trays. The top floor, set within an ambience of luxury, fitted with carpets, curved walls and a series of split-level zones, houses the Gallery restaurant and a range of international designers names.

4 The focal point of the store is the atrium, with a dizzying array of escalators and high-gloss balconies.

5 The escalators are clad in robust white plaster, turning the functional into the sculptural.

6 A cutaway computer rendering of the building shows how light enters through the roof and floods the central atrium below.

Stella McCartney's propulsion into the 'A-list' world of fashion designers was no doubt helped by the three stores that were designed for her by budding London architectural practice Universal Design Studio, the retail and interiors arm of furniture designers Barber Osgerby. After a stint at Chloé, Stella McCartney went on to create her own fashion brand, a sassy girl-about-town label endorsed by her celebrity friends and characterized by crisp tailoring and a feminine edge.

Her first store was the New York flagship, located in the trendy meat-packing district. The brief to Universal Design Studio was for a relaxed environment with an air of nature, where customers could feel free to explore and discover the ready-to-wear collection. Set in a gritty urban landscape, the environment wanted to evoke an idealized British landscape, a retreat from the humdrum of the city. As with many retailers today, McCartney was also keen to create a distinctive shopping experience that would attract customers: a space that is defined by clean and modern lines while maintaining a 'soft', rather than a tougher technology driven, interior.

Universal Design Studio simplified the brief into four main themes: relaxation, nature, discovery and differentiation. Nature and relaxation were represented by an 'abstract landscape' built in different scales throughout the 372-square-metre (4,000-square-foot) warehouse |space. The window display is set in a pool of water with lily-like display structures – the water reflects the natural light, thus minimizing the reliance on artificial light. Hanging screens, evocative of blades of grass, create partitions and sway in the air as customers come in. The long eastern wall is crafted out of white ceramic 3D hexagonal tiles, designed by Barber Osgerby, cleverly turning the hard material into a delicate pattern. More decoration comes in the guise of the western wall, covered in a peach fabric and prettily outlined by motifs of hummingbirds,

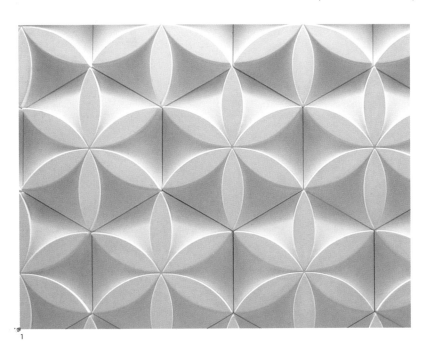

1

2

1 The long eastern wall is crafted out of white ceramic 3D hexagonal tiles.

2 Hanging screens, evocative of blades of grass, introduce the 'nature' theme to the store.

3

4

5

3 The window display is set in a pool of water that reflects the natural light into the shop.

4 Vintage items are cleverly encased in delicate display drawers lined with floral silk inlays.

5 All the furniture in the store is custom-made by Barber Osgerby.

flowers, trees, horseshoes and a female centaur, all designed by McCartney herself.

Other features interpret the differentiation theme. Most of the furniture, display units and hanging rails are flexible and can be rearranged. The rear section is an intimate lounge, featuring bespoke seating by Barber Osgerby that has the period look of mid-century (1950s) pieces. In a bid to remove the financial transaction as much as possible from the shopping experience, the till has been withdrawn from the front of house to a room at the rear where a sales-person conducts all transactions.

Having eliminated the financial aspect, the store's design focuses on emphasizing the social and discovering experience. Customers are encouraged to rummage through several drawers, lined with different floral silk inlays, to discover Stella McCartney's collection of bespoke pieces and vintage finds, such as costume jewellery, accessories and chinaware. Floor-to-ceiling mirrors rotate on their vertical axes, enhancing the spacious atmosphere in a sophisticated game of hide-and-seek.

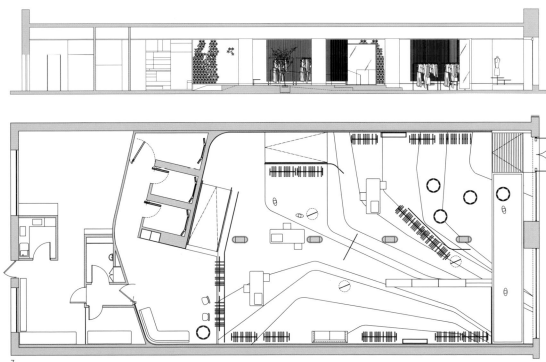

7

6 The themes of 'nature' and 'relaxation' are represented by an abstract landscape built in different scales.

7 From the top: a section and plan showing the varied floor contours in the Stella McCartney store.

Italian shoe and bag brand Tod's decided to go for a piece of the Japanese retail cake with its new Tokyo HQ building located on the shopping strip Omotesando Avenue. Here, wedged between the steel spider web of the Prada Epicenter and the crystal waves of Christian Dior (pages 68–71), stands the seven-storey structure. Keen to give Tod's an identity that would make it stand out from the crowd of places devoted to conspicuous consumption, Chairman Diego Della Valle commissioned the Tokyo architect Toyo Ito with the specific brief to employ high quality materials and colours that would reflect Tod's notion of 'naturalness'. The leather-goods brand is well-known for its impeccably handcrafted shoes and bags as well as its great attention to the natural quality of leathers.

The nature metaphor that has been applied to the store was drawn from Omotesando's long row of zelkova trees. According to Toyo Ito, 'The tree is an autonomous, natural object and therefore its shape has an inherent structural rationality. In a sense, producing a reasonable flow of structural loads with a pattern of superimposed tree silhouettes is a result of a perfectly rational thought process'.

The distinctive concrete façade of the building is thus a tree shaped silhouette made of nine overlapping ramifications. Twenty-seven metres (89 feet) high, the enveloping body opens at the side in a corner that leads west. The 2,550 square metres (27,450 square feet) contains retail spaces on the first three levels, offices in part of the third floor and the fourth and fifth levels, a multifunctional space for events on the sixth floor, and a panoramic meeting room on the roof garden.

1

2

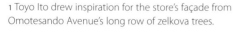

3

1 Toyo Ito drew inspiration for the store's façade from Omotesando Avenue's long row of zelkova trees.

2 At night, the lights from within the store illuminate the 'branches', emphasizing the architectural form of the outer skin.

3 The staircase connecting the store's seven floors allows for views of the distinctive structure of the building as well as the outside.

6

6 The interiors blend Toyo Ito's adventurous forms with Tod's classical Italian style.

7 Ground-floor plan: 1. shop, 2. machine room, 3. stock room.

8 Seating by Zaha Hadid and a blend of natural light and warm artificial light create a relaxed setting.

7

8

Luxury fashion came to the Middle East in 2002 the form of Villa Moda, a fashion emporium that holds the world's leading designer brands, including Gucci, Bottega Veneta, Prada and Fendi. It is the brainchild of Sheik Majed al-Sabah, nephew to the emir of Kuwait and an entrepreneur who first started importing American fashion brands in the 1990s. Realizing the huge potential of supplying solvent, fashion-conscious Arab women customers, Sheik Majed first bought an abandoned warehouse in central Kuwait to stock and sell international brands; when the space became too small, he expanded to a larger space. In order not to pay the premium costs of renting an existing shopping mall space, he decided to commission his own building.

Villa Moda is designed by Italian architect Pierfrancesco Cravel, with interiors by the British design firm Eldridge Smerin, and a brand identity created by Zurich- and London-based Wink Media. The building is a 9,300-square-metre (100,100-square-foot) glass cube emporium that overlooks the Persian Gulf. Inside the structure – a huge, four-way glass cube that resembles a giant, glass aquarium – each fashion label is given its own space and identity. Unusually, Villa Moda is the only civic building in Kuwait City that is not oriented towards Mecca. Instead, it is rotated a couple of degrees in order to afford the customers in the lounge the best view of the Gulf.

The building is set in a sculptural landscape that combines the simplicity of surface with the richness of layering and shadow, produced

2

1

1 Villa Moda resembles a transparent cube, surrounded by a slight frame of pillars.

2 With an identity by Wink Media, architecture by Pierfrancesco Cravel and interiors by Eldridge Smerin, Villa Moda is a hybrid between a commercial centre and a boutique.

3 The building itself is set in a sculptural landscape among 12-metre (39-foot) -high silver steel masts, designed to move with the wind and to light up at night, which surround the building.

Mandarina Duck's London 'destination' store, designed in 2002 by Dutch product designer Marcel Wanders, is intended to represent the specific values of the city. It features 40 breathing mannequins and a giant, seven-metre (23-foot) mannequin, inspired by *Gulliver's Travels*.

INTRODUCTION

In a bid to create an even more stimulating environment for design-savvy, but jaded, shoppers, retailers are increasingly collaborating with product and industrial designers to create concepts that stretch beyond the conventional, sleek, white-box format. Elements of subversion, irony or just an injection of a different perspective from that of architects, seem to have amazing results for some brands. Since 1998, Spanish interior and product designer Marti Guixé has 'overseen' the design of 13 shops around Europe for Camper, the Mallorcan brand that specializes in mid-priced Euro-funky shoes. For each shop, Guixé has developed a distinctive design, while maintaining the same visual language of humorous illustrations – part comic sketch, part user instructions, and part anti-materialistic slogan. The packaging reads, 'If you don't need it, don't buy it'. In 2004 Guixé helped Camper expand its brand with a FoodBALL shop in Barcelona, Spain. This health-food store/restaurant/take-away, also acts as a meeting point for the local community.

Similarly, Italian luggage and clothing brand Mandarina Duck approached Dutch design collective Droog Design to create its Paris store in 2000. Droog literally translates as 'dry wit', which sums up Droog's penchant for the amusing and humorous treatment of everyday objects, crafted with minimal simplicity as well as a careful choice of materials. Droog has made its name on the design scene for the way it has 'humanized' modern design, striking an emotional bond with enthusiasts. For the Paris store, architects Gijs Bakker and Renny Ramakers created a space filled with cocoon-like displays: brightly coloured bending structures that orbit around the rotating spiral staircase. Smaller items were hung on an inventive mutlicoloured rubber-band display system.

In 2002, Mandarina Duck repeated its strategy by commissioning Marcel Wanders to design its London Flagship store. Wanders, a product and furniture designer who has worked with top manufacturers like Cappellini and Flos, is also part of the Droog movement and with them shares the same quirky sense of humour.

INTERVIEW WITH MARCEL WANDERS OF MARCEL WANDERS STUDIO, AMSTERDAM, HOLLAND

You used a lot of irony in the Mandarina Shop in London, was that an attempt to provoke, stimulate, entertain or just a stylistic device?

'Part of the importance of designing Mandarina Duck for me was making sure that the customer loved it. It wasn't just about being featured in the press, but about creating a real experience. I based the design on myself, my needs – not only in terms of fun, but also looking exactly at how you would buy something. We created this idea of mannequins; they are usually boring to see, yet they are the best way to display the clothing, so I decided to create the most exciting mannequins ever. The result were breathing, bizarre yellow mannequins wearing clothes or just naked, but wearing a watch.'

Your background is largely product design – how do you think that informs the way you conceive a shopping experience?

'I think that what creative people are best at is to be generalist. Every time, we push to do things that we did not do before, and we make a new statement – every time. For me to design a shop was a completely different experience and I haven't done another since. On the product-development side, product designers have a tendency to work more on details – to be innovative on the small parts and make to sure they function. We look at an overall 3D plan that works in a functional and scale situation.'

What do you think of the 'patronage' between brands and designers or architects – Prada and Koolhaas, Marni and Future Systems, Pawson and Calvin Klein? Does it aim for a high profile, represent a modern-day version of a patron/artist relationship, or is it just a branding exercise?

'From a marketing point of view, designers are also now, more and more, a brand, so it's a two way brand connection. The marketing side surely exists, but that's not the whole reason. I think collaboration between people who are honest can help both. We can also have fun doing it and it can be very simple. If we can create dreams, why change the winning team?'

How do you think retail design is changing?

'People in the world should be more fun and less boring. The good thing about design now is that stuff is getting less and less functional. And that's not only in retail. Functionality was so important for so many years after the Bauhaus movement, but functionality only counts for stuff we don't have to think about. I think there is a new movement in design that is changing perceptions and that considers the poetic side of things to be more important. The retail world is the perfect example. I was in Rockefeller Square, New York the other day and I just thought, "Even if I had no money in the world I would love to be here – you see so much more beauty, it's such a spectacle". Everybody in this world works to make a buck, but there is also the fun and the visual element to consider.'

More of a concept than a conventional shop, BLESS owes much to a type of retailing spearheaded by Colette, the *über* cool Paris shop that combines cutting-edge fashion, lifestyle and art installations. Indeed, the owners, Desiree Heiss and Ines Kaag, are fashion designers whose early careers were endorsed by Colette. Named after a bakery in a Berlin suburb, the BLESS duo excels at making unexpected juxtapositions and undermining expectations. For example, a DIY trainer kit, made of two New Balance soles, some fabric and instructions for combining the elements, as well as fur wigs made for the designer Martin Margiela, are just some of the duo's creations.

Initiated and created by long-term BLESS supporter and collector, Yasmine Gauster, one of the reasons to open a BLESS shop was the necessity to display, as completely as possible, the whole BLESS product and project range, which would have been difficult in a multibrand shop. It is of no coincidence that the BLESS 'flagship' store is in Berlin, a city that currently seems awash with unconventional retail formats, from the guerrilla shops of Comme des Garçons to low-budget, design-savvy sites.

Another reason to build the shop was to give the itinerant project 'BLESS N°11 BLESS shops' a temporary home. As a reaction to numerous invitations to art and design shows, often curated with a lot of enthusiasm

1

2

1, 2, 3 Innovative 'perpetual home motion machines' incorporate storage furniture and moving display.

4 The interior of the shop is constantly changing, sometimes decorated with plants and at other times with the merchandise.

5 In the summer, the shop expands temporarily into the outdoor space on the street or into a garden café.

6

6 BLESS shops are conceived to display merchandise
as well as art pieces that change constantly.

7

8

but small budgets, in 2000 BLESS came up with the idea of a temporary BLESS shop concept, adapting each time to local room situations and circumstances. The shop sales income manages to cover most of the shipping costs, enabling them to show a whole retrospective of the existing BLESS items. Temporary BLESS shops have opened in Basel, Stockholm, Zurich, Glasgow and Paris, among many others.

According to Desiree Heiss, 'So far, each BLESS shop has come out differently. One of the most interesting BLESS shops was during the Art Biennial in Werkleitz, which is in a region with very high unemployment. We didn't think there was any point in doing a shop, because there wasn't enough demand. So instead of opening a shop space, we looked for local stores that would host different products. The furniture shop had the chairware, the fashion shop had the scarves, and the hairbrush was in the hair salon. Of course, we didn't sell anything. The most abstract piece, The Set, was in the gas station.'

The Berlin location was conceived by Gauster, who has turned it into a main destination stop for BLESS fans. The shop's interior is constantly changing: sometimes its decorated with overgrown plants, other times it's emptied and populated only by BLESS N°22 perpetual home motion machines or used as a tearoom for restless Berlin fashion guests, etc. The dimensions are variable, as one of the main qualities of this concept is the space's flexibility. In the summer the shop can expand temporarily if desired, into the open space next to it, arranging itself as a garden café. It also sometimes crosses to the other side of the street, mixing with other designer's clothes in a multibrand store, or to temporarily occupy other empty locations in the same street.

7 Designed as a space to peruse, purchase or simply to have tea, BLESS shops are based on the idea of flexibility.

8 The BLESS shop was created to display the entire product and project range, something that would have been impossible in a multibrand shop.

MISS SIXTY
ENERGIE EMPORIUM

BARCELONA/SPAIN
STUDIO 63 ARCHITECTURE AND DESIGN/2004

1

1 The Barcelona store is designed as an organic space with curved walls, sculptured counters and bright-yellow colours.

2 The shiny buttercup-yellow epoxy floors contrast well with the cement columns.

3 From top: upper- and lower-level plans.

2

The Miss Sixty brand is the brainchild of Wicky Hassan, the energetic Italian entrepreneur and designer who is also behind the casual menswear label, Energie. Established 20 years ago in Italy, Miss Sixty is fast becoming something of a cult label among young fashionistas and models around the world. This is, no doubt, due to its eclectic selection of natty, vintage-like accessories and perfectly slim-fit jeans and trousers.

Like the collection, the look of the Miss Sixty shops is a careful mix of old and new, with glossy bespoke interiors creating a backdrop for modern period furniture pieces. The historical reference to the 1970s is carried out in the design with shiny surfaces, heavy velvet drapes in rich, saturated colours, and accent lighting, devised to create a warm and feminine atmosphere. The overall look is almost one of a thrift shop, an ironic, hyper-modernist pastiche aimed at the younger, style-conscious generations. Even if the clientele is too young to understand the cultural reference directly, the reference is widely accepted into their culture and is recognizable in the ambience it generates – it communicates an identity of place.

Florence-based Studio 63 Architecture and Design has been commissioned to design all 60 of the new Miss Sixty shops worldwide, of which three opened in the USA in 2003 – Los Angeles, San Francisco and Chicago. The Barcelona site was part of the new roll-out concept. An organic space, designed with curved walls, sculptured counters and

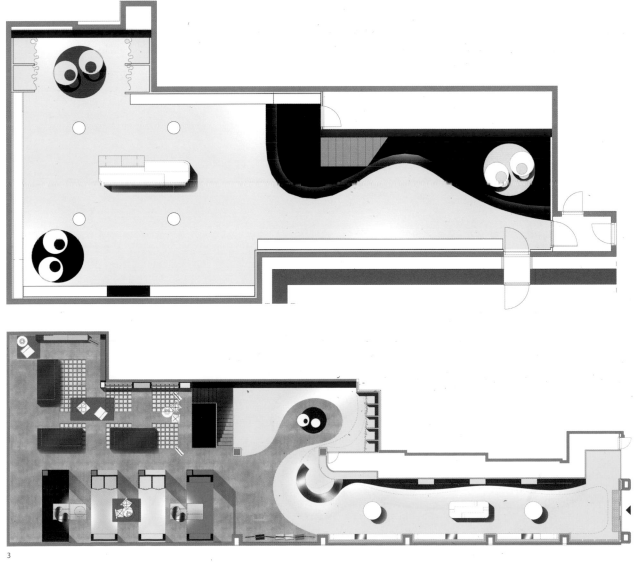

3

soft, cosy surfaces with bright colours is the leitmotif of all the stores worldwide. Each site is also individually conceived to retain the specific characteristics relating to its structure and location.

The Barcelona store features both the Miss Sixty and the Energie lines. Marco Zanuso's Lady chairs sit alongside more obscure 1970s pieces, while the sunny nature of Barcelona is reflected through the choice of bright colours and tones. Graphic design from the 1970s, the performance of David Bowie and the works of Verner Panton are all quoted as references.

4

5

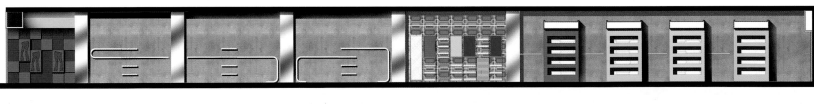

6

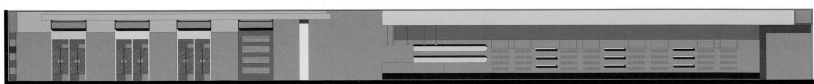

4 Lady chairs by Marco Zanuso add a retro feel to the store.

5 Inspiration from the 1970s can be found in the velvet drapes that hang in the changing rooms, accent lighting and vintage furniture.

6 Internal elevations illustrate varying types of wall display.

7 The in-built display shelves are lined with 1970s patterned wallpaper to enhance the retro feel.

109
MISS SIXTY ENERGIE EMPORIUM
STUDIO 63 ARCHITECTURE AND DESIGN

A strong element of play is arguably one of the defining traits of Mandarina Duck's London 'destination' store, designed in 2002 by Dutch product designer Marcel Wanders. An upmarket, Italian luggage brand, Mandarina Duck has, over the years, created a niche for itself thanks to vividly coloured ranges, wear- and tear-resistant materials and youthful designs of bags and clothing. The collaboration between the company and Marcel Wanders started with the Murano bag collection and then developed with the commission of the London site.

Mandarina Duck calls its shops 'embassies'; each one is conceived to promote the culture of the city in which it is located. With its focus on bags, Mandarina Duck is a company for travellers and therefore the London site was conceived as a shop for international travellers. As part of this 'cultural relativist' approach to retail, the London site was intended to represent the specific values of the city, making it an exciting and desirable destination for discerning shoppers. 'In each city, the brand has some normal Mandarina shops and some very special sites,' explains Wanders. 'They need to be totally special and different from each other; they need to be interesting for a traveller since this is a brand devoted to them.'

The London store was conceived as a place to be experienced – where the atmosphere is changing constantly. In Wanders' words, the shop should be 'not only a place where you buy clothes and bags, but also a store that will sell and hand you over the secrets of the city'.

Design-wise, the concept was initially devised for the Rome site and then moved to London. The underlying idea was that it would be a fun and living place to make purchases. Bathed in the brand's yellow trademark colour, the shop is defined by the presence of 40 bizarre, breathing mannequins that display the brand's clothing and accessories.

2

1

1 The central area of the shop is defined by a giant, yellow mannequin that was inspired by *Gulliver's Travels* and contains an audio system.

2 The store has a double-height ceiling space, no internal walls and a large, swirling silver staircase.

Inside, the construction was overseen by architects Harper MacKay, although it was Wanders' idea to knock down all the internal walls and create a double-height space. The central area is defined by a large, open space filled with a giant seven-metre (23-foot) mannequin, inspired by the giants in *Gulliver's Travels* and with a torso containing an audio system. This archetypical British traveller, Gulliver, lives in the store that is appropriately renamed WanderDuck.

In the middle of the shop is also a swirling silver staircase, around which a large, chromed, two-floor-high wall breathes and changes its surface from convex to concave in a constant fluid rhythm. Outside the building, a fairy-tale-like stream of bubbles float onto the pavement to further amplify the metaphor of a breathing, living building.

The building of the store generated a huge amount of press coverage, reinforcing the notion that often the effect of an imaginative retail design is stronger than any high-profile advertising campaign. For Wanders, the celebration of local culture not only guarantees that customers get more than what they bargained for, but that they will also return. Creating a space that provokes an emotional response, a spectacle rather than a functional environment, was the final effect the Dutch designer was after.

3

4

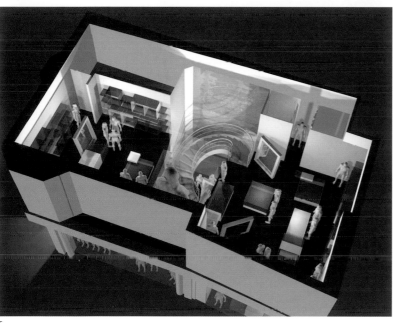

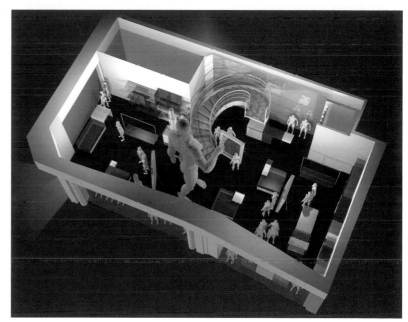

5

3 The large, chromed, double-floor-high wall breathes by changing its surface from convex to concave in a constant fluid rhythm.

4 Luggage, accessories and the clothing line are displayed in glass cabinets or on the yellow mannequins.

5 Computer renderings of the upper and lower levels of the London Mandarina Duck store.

Apple's retail location in the Ginza district of Tokyo allows visitors access to the latest Apple products and aims to promote a stylish, technology-filled lifestyle. The simple and minimal furniture gives emphasis to the elegant computer hardware that is on display.

3

need resolving, there is a 'we're all ears' service desk, specifically for problem solving. All the service desks are highlighted by over-scaled graphic walls, using 3D icons such as hearts, clocks and ears that communicate the service quickly and with a humour that conveys the human dimension of Orange.

The third element, 'play', is key to bringing an exciting experiential dimension to the store, as well as encouraging customers to return to Orange. The 'play' areas allow customers to interact with and learn more about Orange, while browsing the store. All of the phones on the 'merchandising cubes' are live and allow customers to play with and test the product, on their own or with Orange 'phone trainers'. In the centre of the store is the 'play table' – an interactive console where up to four players can engage in digital games that also reveal information on mobile phone content. Above the play table is a large projection cube where moving images and sound provide animation across the store.

At the back of the store are the 'terraces' – a series of rising platforms containing interactive 'pods' where customers can compose and download their own ringtones, as well as create and download screen designs for their mobile phones. The terraces also provide seating to watch the animation, have consultations with phone trainers, or to meet friends. The final social element is where customers can try out the phones, take photos with them and then stick their photos and messages onto a giant Orange logo on the back wall.

3 On the large back wall, at the top of the terraces, customers can try out the phones, take photos and stick them onto the Orange logo.

4 All the service desks are characterized by over-scaled graphic walls using 3D icons such as ears that communicate the service quickly and with humour.

4

For this flagship store, German design group Dan Pearlman translated the brand values of telecoms company O_2 into a 3D interactive space. Conceived to represent a brand experience, rather than just a selling point, the main architectural focus is given by the central 'interactive media band'. This starts on the outer façade with a 3D O_2 logo, then runs across the ceiling and floor inside the shop. The content of the band can be changed according to the seasons and store's needs – for the opening it was set up to evoke a winter mood. When a visitor steps onto the surface of the band, cracks and splits appear on the projected ice surface.

The band runs through the shop and leads into a table area where products, information and prices hover through the ice. When the visitor touches an object, the text or product information fades at the point of touch. On the rear wall, the media band shows excerpts of current O_2 television commercials with testimonials in real-life size or 360-degree product demonstration films. The colour scheme of the store also reiterates the winter, crisp mood with white displays and blue lighting.

1

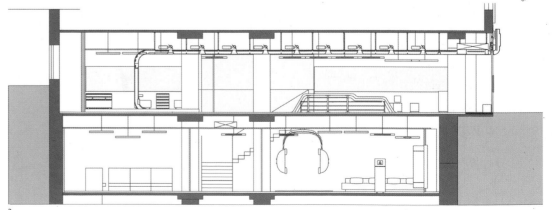

2

3

1 The side of the façade features the O_2 logo and stations for topping up phone cards.

2 A band that starts on the outer façade and unfolds into the store represents O_2's brand.

4

5

6

3 Long section through the ground and basement levels. The entrance is top right.

4 In-store graphics illustrate the changing seasons, while custom-made display units make the products easily accessible to customers.

5 Giant earphones act as a playful, decorative device.

6 The products are displayed in a way that allows customers to touch them and try them out.

APPLE STORE

TOKYO/JAPAN
BOHLIN CYWINSKI JACKSON/2004

1

Since Apple Computers Inc. opened its first retail store in America in May 2001, 70 more, visited by over 24 million visitors, have followed in the USA alone. The 'hands-on Apple Store experience' allows visitors access to the latest Mac computer systems and digital lifestyle applications, including the iconic iPod. All Apple Stores come equipped with an eight-metre (27-foot) long Genius Bar, one of the most popular sections of the Apple retail stores, where visitors can ask a 'Mac Genius' questions or receive product service. In the Internet café, anyone can check e-mail or use Apple's iChat AV and iSight, and customer events every month include a Studio Series of hands-on training classes.

Apple Computer's retail location opened in the Ginza district of Tokyo in 2004. The retail environment aims to replicate the company's success in promoting a stylish, technology-filled lifestyle, with simplicity and efficiency. Like so many buildings in Tokyo, the Ginza store has a vertical orientation. An eight-storey building, it has been renovated by Bohlin Cywinski Jackson into a simple rectilinear form. The façade uses bead-blasted stainless-steel panels at the first three levels, which is where the Apple logo is minimally displayed. The remaining five floors use an

2

3

1 An eight-storey building, the Ginza store's façade is composed of steel and laminated glass panels.

2 The first three floors of the façade, where the Apple logo is displayed, uses bead-blasted, stainless-steel panels.

3 Apple products sit on minimally designed maple tables while the elevators at the end ensure the visitors' flow is extended to the upper floors.

4

5

6

4 Grey limestone and bead-blasted stainless steel on the walls and floors, as well as simple maple tables, are used.

5 Internet stations are kept minimally furnished to give emphasis to the computers and software.

6 The 84-seat, state-of-the-art theatre is used for lectures and presentations.

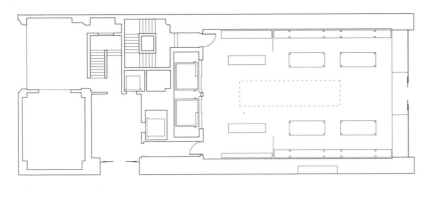

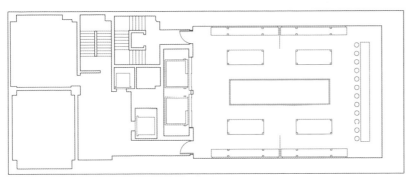

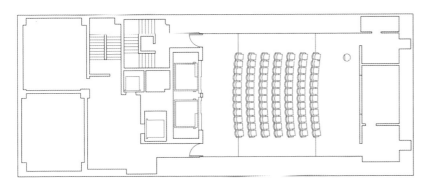

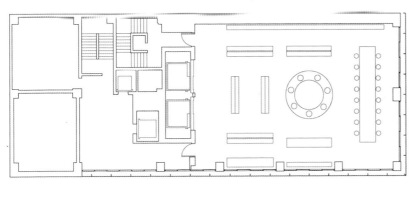

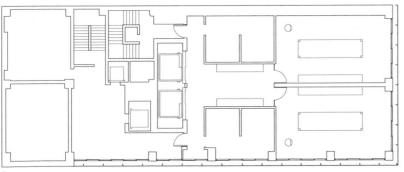

open-joint glass rain-screen system in front of floor-to-ceiling stainless-steel sliding glass doors. The double skin employs ceramic-fitted, laminated glass panels with a special interlayer, creating a minimal, elegant external curtain that provides thermal protection to the internal second skin.

To overcome the vertical structure and to make sure the visitor's flow is uninterrupted, Apple conceived custom-designed, all-glass elevators to create a seamless shopping experience. The elevators were built as transparent as possible, using Otis all-glass doors that require no frames and with the shaft of the elevator exposed to full view behind a large expanse of clear glass. The two cabs operate as shuffle cars rather than traditional elevator cars, which means that the rider does not call the lift, but rather enters the car when it rolls past and is taken automatically to the next floor. The cabs are synchronized to move in opposite directions, passing each other in the middle of the shaft. This stratagem allows for the elevators to feel like a continuation of the shop's space or a sort of vertical moving walkway connecting all five floors.

The five floors offer various ways to experience the Apple product line, from casual browsing on the shop floors to active learning in the studio classrooms or the 84-seat, state-of-the-art theatre. Throughout different levels, grey limestone and bead-blasted stainless steel are used on the floors and the walls. The furniture in the store comprises simply detailed maple tables and benches, minimally arranged to give emphasis to the elegant computers and software on display. Customers can look and touch the products on display, then order and purchase them at the till counter. On the store's third and fifth levels, grey acoustical fabric walls and carpets, coupled with luxurious seating, set the tone for the learning environment of the theatre and demonstration classrooms.

7 From top: plans of the ground through fourth floors. The entrance is to the right of the ground-floor plan.

7

Italian furniture manufacturer B&B Italia, commissioned architects John Pawson and Antonio Citterio for their first flagship store in London. Formerly a car showroom, the airy interiors, designed by Citterio, are bathed in natural light from oversized windows and skylights.

SELLING A LIFESTYLE

INTRODUCTION

In using 'lifestyle', retailers don't just want to sell goods, they want consumers to aspire to a brand as a promise of a way of living. Those retailers that have not so far used lifestyle are gradually realizing it as a means of expanding their range of goods. Fashion brands such as Donna Karan, Armani and Fendi have all jumped on the lifestyle bandwagon, producing their own range of furniture, while the lifestyle champ, Ikea, with its cheap prices and clean design, seems to have conquered almost every corner of Europe, if not the Western world. Vittorio Radice, then executive director of the new Marks & Spencer 'Home' business, made the groundbreaking decision of commissioning minimalist architect John Pawson to create a 'house structure' for Marks and Spencer's innovative 2004 Lifestore building in Gateshead, UK. While the architectural pedigree was excellent, the concept failed to gel with Marks & Spencer's rather disappointing homeware collection.

Perhaps the most interesting novelty is this area was the rise of the concept store in the 1990s. Shops like Colette in Paris, Corso Como in Milan and TAD Conceptstore in Rome are a reflection of the personality of the owners and their editing capacities, not just the brands they sell. Here, what is being proposed is an idealized, holistic lifestyle concept, comprised of clothes and also magazines, flowers, perfumes, homeware and even their own compilation CDs, edited in the same way as the merchandise.

The notion that retail could offer a lifestyle experience arguably started in 1964 with Habitat's first outlet in London. Here, for the first time, customers could pick and choose furniture to create an environment that was reflective of the 1960s' joyous mode of living and that was counterbalanced by informed, modern design. The shop was a huge success in London; John Lennon, George Harrison and film stars like Julie Christie all bought furniture there.

Habitat was, of course, the brainchild of Sir Terence Conran, who went on to build an empire based on retail, restaurants and redevelopment. Habitat was the first shop to identify its products and its image as part of a wider ethos. Its groundbreaking idea was to offer a stylish, affordable way of living to the masses, while introducing products like the chicken brick or the duvet – a reflection of Conran's admiration for Continental ways of living. During the 1970s' Conran went on to open international chains of Habitat stores and The Conran Shop. Today he is still the owner of the The Conran Shop, with stores around the world.

INTERVIEW WITH SIR TERENCE CONRAN OF CONRAN & PARTNERS, LONDON, UK

How has the shopping experience changed from when you started in the UK in the 1960s?

'In the 1960s, stores looked like dreary warehouses. There were rows of stock, all pushed far too close, and bad lighting. There was nothing in it that made it a pleasurable experience. We must remember that we had just come out from an era of rationing, and things had been in short supply. There was no reason why a retailer should make a particular effort, since the shopping experience was driven by needs rather than wants. The real revolution was when retailers discovered that they could create a brand out of the product. As a consequence, the brand became something special and shopping stopped being this endless discounting experience. When we started Habitat, we were also running Mothercare and Next. We soon realized that if we designed the product ourselves, and branded it, we would create a reason to go to our shops. By creating your own brand, which sold at a lower price, you build a house brand and build the loyalty of customers.'

How do you feel Habitat influenced UK shopping and living patterns?

'Habitat was the first lifestyle store. The stores at that time, certainly in the furnishing area, were unfocused, and that was the reason I started Habitat, since I was making furniture and used to get depressed about the totally untargeted selection of merchandise that you found in the stores. I wanted to sell furniture in an environment that was surrounded by a collection that had a point of view. With Habitat I soon realized that if you create a busy store, it becomes a successful store. For example, we were the first to put cafés in shops so the customers could sit down and talk and think. If you want an atmosphere, create an energetic place where visitors feel part of a club. The Habitat philosophy was that you took the thing off the shelf yourself, like a supermarket, and unlike other shops you didn't really have to have an interaction with a salesperson.'

You own and have designed both shops and restaurants. For both of them you emphasize the need to create a 'busy', theatrical experience. What's the difference between retail and leisure?

'The restaurant is really a form of the shop of the future. There is an open kitchen, where you can see everything being made and an incredible busy energy. But also in retail, for example, you can have a manufacturer of glass in the shop showing off his skills or a clothes-alteration service. It creates a spectacle, and it gets rid of the static quality that you see in many shops. Supermarkets are increasingly doing it: for example, by cooking bread on the premises. In Milan, for example, there is a fantastic shop where a guy is cracking Parmesan on a table and there is always a queue of people behind it. That sticks in my memory and I know I will get the best possible cheese and not something old wrapped in clingfilm. It's a ritual and a spectacle, and the only way for smaller shops to survive is to offer something different, a particular service, and to elevate the experience.'

How has the customer changed in the past years? Are they completely jaded or can you still offer possible visions of living?

'Yes, I think you can. Big chains are producing things that are very pleasant. Certainly there is now a huge offer in the high street. When we started Habitat, many were skeptical about it working outside the capital. But we prepared the ground by sending out catalogues in the other parts of the country and then, when we eventually opened a shop there, we had already created demand. I believe that people can't buy what is not offered, so what really informs people's tastes is what the shops offer. And the merchandise is your best message.'

5

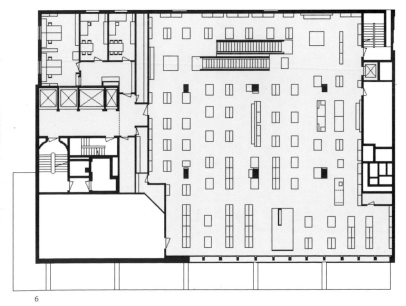

The Italian counter offers piles of fresh pasta in pretty pastel shades; marinated aubergines (eggplant), artichokes, and black, green and purplish olives piled on white dishes. The Japanese counter allows customers to watch a sushi chef slicing and rolling the pink fish and placing it carefully into the neat *bento* boxes. On the shelves are stacked fish sauce, sambal olek, glass noodles, egg noodles, basmati rice, pickled limes and tahini paste. Each shelf has a label to indicate where the food came from – India, Japan, China, even the UK. The aim is to replicate a neighborhood shop, with the familiarity and the customer service that comes with it. The basement atmosphere provides a cellar-like atmosphere, with an emphasis on the fresh and earthy qualities.

The take-away area is at the heart of the ground floor. It is a room with a high, transparent glass wall, which is used as a divider for the different sections that are designed as four big modules – panini/tapas, bar, wok and sushi. Cross-selling shelves across the membrane display the goods range of the delicatessen floor. High-counter tables with chairs allow customers to sit for informal self-service snacks. Sleekly and elegantly designed, the narrow dining tables come equipped with silverware, napkins, condiments and glasses, all ready and waiting for the customers. There's a wine and coffee bar if you want a special drink, and the food counters also dispense mineral water and other simple drinks. Next door are the flower shop, giftware and a very design-oriented home furnishing section, which continues onto the first upper floor and faces directly out onto the street outside.

5 In the basement, wooden floors and dark panelling convey a cellar-like atmosphere for the impressive selection of wines.

6 From top: plans of the lower basement (used for storage and refrigeration), upper basement (delicatessen) and first floor (household items).

6

B&B ITALIA

LONDON/UK
JOHN PAWSON AND ANTONIO CITTERIO/2002

1

1 The B&B Italia showroom is the result of a collaboration between John Pawson and Antonio Citterio.

2 Street elevation: the glass façade (centre right) sits in between existing older buildings.

3 Formerly a car showroom, the site is characterized by a striking façade of sheet glass, natural stone and bronze.

Italian furniture manufacturer B&B Italia decided to commission British architect John Pawson and Italian architect Antonio Citterio for its first flagship store in London. Founded in 1966 by the Busnelli family, B&B has always focused on contemporary furniture born out of an enlightened commissioning relationship with well-known designers. The decision to open a store in London was part of a larger trend that saw many Italian furniture companies such as Artemide and Driade open new concessions or flagship stores in international markets. In the bid for the discerning customer, London had emerged as a ripe market.

Both Pawson and Citterio had previously designed collections for the Italian company, so the project was built on an established working relationship, which benefited from shared values and an understanding of the company's vision. Citterio, in particular, had worked as a product designer and consultant for B&B for 30 years.

2

3

1

1 Old and modern mix seamlessly as custom-made crystal display cabinets show off the Baccarat collection.

2 In this luxurious, decadent atmosphere, mirrors, crystal chandeliers and red tones are employed by Starck to give the space a theatrical air.

The allure of Baccarat's new headquarters in Paris relies on two major assets: the mercurial talents of prolific designer Philippe Starck and the history of its location. This aristocratic townhouse in the sixteenth *arrondissement* was, during the first half of the twentieth century, the home of the Viscountess Marie-Laure de Noailles – art patron, muse and financer of Surrealist 'oeuvres' such as Luis Buñuel's *L'Age d'Or* and Jean Cocteau's *Le Sang d'un Poete*. The viscountess also held memorable parties here, a careful mix of aristocrats and artists set against the backdrop of a cream shagreen and parchment-lined sitting room, designed by Jean Michel Frank.

Starck was given carte blanche to develop the Maison Baccarat headquarters, its boutique and gallery museum, a restaurant and showroom. Inspired by a place so laden with memories and by 'the world of illusion' that the luxury brand evokes, he designed a space filled with contrasts, opulence and modernity. Dadaist and Surrealist touches are a clever nod to the Maison's previous owners.

A crystal chandelier is plunged into a large glass aquarium at the entrance, a 2.4-metre (eight-foot) -tall mirror throne stands on the ground floor, while the hallway is lined with giant mirrors leading to a main staircase illuminated by fibre optics.

3

3 In the private dining room, furnished with pink fabric, a jet-black chandelier hangs in pride of place.

2

4

4 The 12.8-metre (42-foot) custom-made crystal table in the 'transparent' room is used to display glassware.

5

6

Baccarat was founded in 1764, thanks to a grant from the king of France, Louis XV. In just a few years Baccarat had established itself as the leading French crystal manufacturer and soon became the most prestigious in the world. The company, now owned by the Société du Louvre and backed by the Taittinger group, is well-known for its emphasis on techniques and creativity as well as the high standard of its glassblowers, cutters and engravers. More recently, the brand has diversified into luxury accessories and wristwatches.

Some of the most prestigious pieces from the Baccarat collection are housed in the gallery-museum. Crystal thrones created for Indian maharajas; the custom-ordered, monumental Tsar Nicholas II's candelabra; limited-edition collections by Georges Chevalier and Ettore

Sottsass, and dessert plates made for Coco Chanel, decorated with etchings of seamstress scissors. The Crystal Room Restaurant combines exposed brickwork with decadent baroque gilt frames, rooms of pink fabric and satin banquettes as well as bespoke furniture by Starck. In the private dining room a black crystal chandelier hangs in pride of place.

In this glamorous ambience, the shopping experience is elevated to a refined demonstration of discerning taste – a 12.8-metre (42-foot)-long crystal table, which can be custom-ordered at a smaller size, crystal chopsticks and candelabras are just some of the items on sale. The retail space here is conceived as a fluid concept, the focus being the historic narrative of the house and its extraordinary décor.

5 In the ground floor, the specially lit glass case contrasts with the beige concrete walls.

6 The stylized figures that support the glass display cabinets are Starck's subtle nod towards the surrealist past of the building.

8

7 The palatial staircase is illuminated by fibre optic lights.

8 Surrealist humour is displayed by Starck with the 2.4-metre (eight-foot)-high mirror throne that stands on the glass floor.

As much of a showroom as a store, the l.a.Eyeworks shop occupies an existing two-storey building on the corner of Martel and Beverly Boulevards in Los Angeles. Known for its angular frames, l.a.Eyeworks is a brand that has always promoted spectacles as fashion objects to complement a stylish lifestyle. Its advertising campaigns feature famous bespectacled faces along with the slogan: 'A face is like a work of art. It deserves a frame'. The company has always been keen to celebrate an alliance with creative fields through its window displays, website and advertising campaigns.

For the Beverly Boulevard store, l.a.Eyeworks asked Neil Denari to create a space that retained both the temporary qualities of a retail environment and the stability more conventionally associated with institutional or public buildings. Although not tied to a specific budget or brief, the client asked Denari to create a design that would hold up for a long time, not just a few years. While fashion is intentionally based on quick stylistic shifts, the client asked that the design of the store resist not the ephemeral nature of fashion, but rather the fashion of architecture without recurring to minimalism or lack of expression.

Denari tried to make the most of the corner site of the building. He left the upper part of the stucco façade intact, partly to comply with local building regulations. The two main functional requirements – a transparent front and that the products are visible and accessible to the customers – are solved with the use of a glazed front. This engages window-shoppers through the displays for which l.a.Eyeworks is renowned.

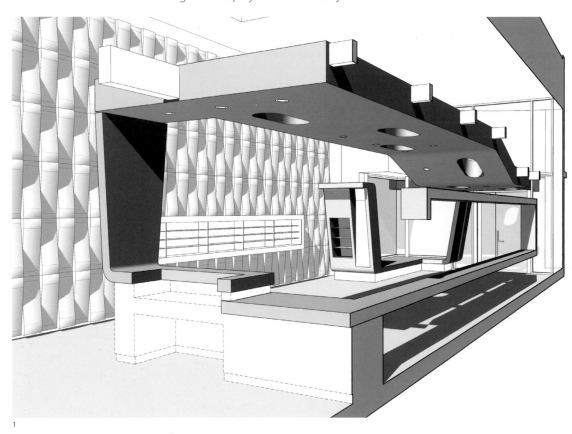

1

1 A computer rendering of the main internal display structure of the store.

2 Denari made the most out of the corner site of the building, leaving the stucco façade intact and creating a transparent frontage.

3 The glazed front engages window-shoppers with a selection of glasses displays.

4 Cutaway computer rendering shows how the display structure occupies the two-storey space.

2

3

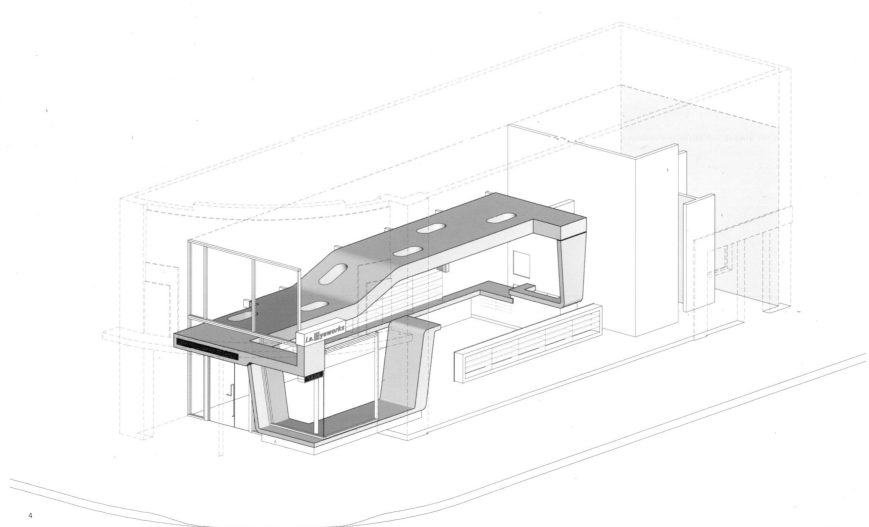

4

9

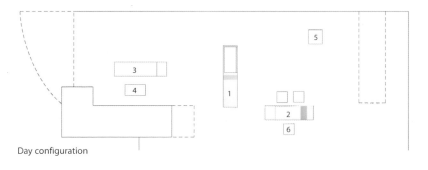

Day configuration

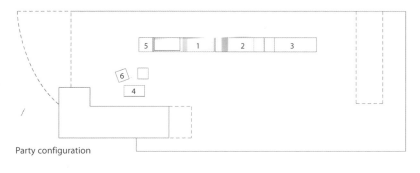

Party configuration

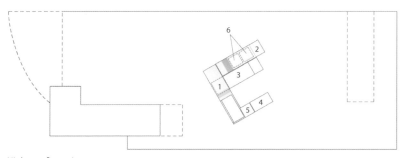

Night configuration

10

8 As much a showroom as a store, l.a.Eyeworks has always been keen to celebrate an alliance with creative fields.

9 The interior of the shop was designed to withstand changes in fashion and architectural style.

10 Moveable benches and shelving units allow various configurations for different uses.

SMART-TRAVELLING STORE

1

The smart-travelling store is arguably what Berlin does best – an independent retail space that combines a quirky taste with a funky, individualistic sense of style. A new retail concept, the smart-travelling store was developed by Nicola Bramigk and her partner and designer, Werner Aisslenger. Inspired by her lust for travel, the store calls itself the first smart-travelling concept store, offering ultimate products for city travellers. Perhaps less of a shop than a travel-related experience, the establishment is housed in a long, 90-square-metre (969-square-foot), double-height space in one of Berlin's historic courtyards in the fashionable Mitte district.

An eclectic treasure trove, the shop sells, among other things, products from or relating to 19 European countries. Many of the items have been sourced by Bramigk on her trips or have been exclusively developed and produced by the smart-travelling brand. The items include travel guides and travel literature and gourmet food from around Europe, such as Austria's Marillenmarmelade and wines and oils from Italy.

2

1 The pink changing cube is to the left and the lamps-cum-clothes racks to the right. Electrical cables are buried under a layer of bark mulch underneath the clothes rails.

2 Simple timber shelving is used to display gifts and gourmet items from different European countries. Aquariums have been illuminated from behind to serve as display boxes.

In the front section of the store, the seven-metre (23-foot)-long fashion area features clothes racks that double up as lamps and a distinctive four-metre (13-foot)-high, freestanding unit made from the same fabric as the lampshades that also serves as a changing room and light box. The racks display clothing designed by Bramigk, with an emphasis on casual travelwear. At the other end of the space, two read/work lounges provide sofas and chairs where visitors can peruse the many books that are for sale. There is also a music station displaying CDs of music from around the world. The store also acts as the office headquarters for the travel services website. A screen set into the wall presents and explains the website and the store's concept.

Apart from the pink that is used in the lampshades and for the light box, the palette comprises neutral colours, with a polished concrete floor, oak shelves and white or black walls. Quirky touches, such as the pink light box, illuminated aquaria (sourced from a zoo), and a large map of Europe enliven the space. The central counter is also strikingly unique – a display cabinet from the 1950s that was bought on an auction website.

To keep it simple, spaces under the clothes racks are filled with bark mulch to cover the exposed electrical cables, done like this to avoid routing grooves in the walls for the cables. The overall design effect is one of sampling, where vintage pieces stand next to ingenious yet simple architectural interventions.

3

4

3 Vintage furniture sits among assorted items that are kept in the timber and glass display units.

4 The store's palette is neutral with a polished concrete floor and white or black walls. The sofas and chairs are provided as comfortable seating for browsing the books that are for sale.

5

6

5 Cheese, bread and a wall-mounted stag's head are just some of the items on display in one section.

6 At the end of the fashion area small, randomly placed shelves display a range of items from European cities.

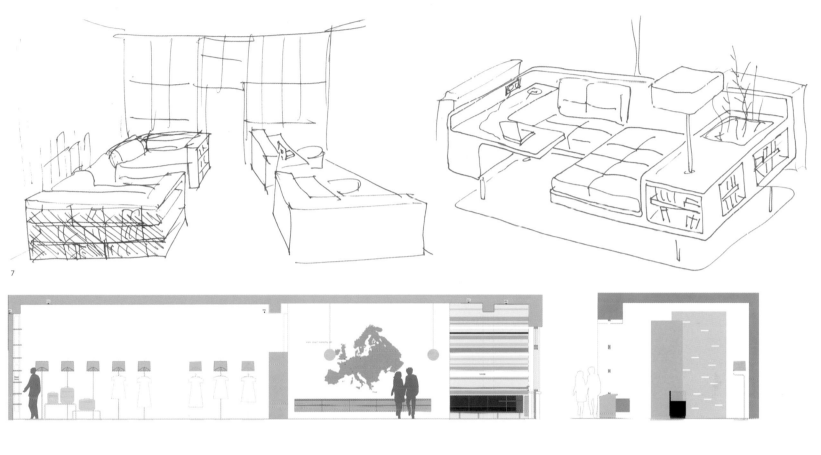

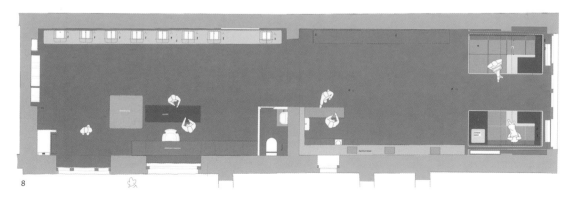

7 Sketches of the seating arrangements in the read/work lounge area.

8 Top and centre: internal elevations. Bottom: plan, with the lounge to the right and the fashion area to the left.

7

8

1

In 2004, in a conscious effort to fuse architectural cool and top-quality produce, Rocco Princi commissioned architect Claudio Silvestrin to create a 'boutique bakery' in the heart of Milan. Entrepeneur Rocco Princi is known locally for being the 'Armani' of bread, hence it was somehow fitting and ironic that he would work with the architect responsible for many of Armani's shops worldwide. Princi also owns four other bakery shops in Milan (the first opened in 1985) all specializing in local and international produce, with a strong focus on smart packaging and customer service via catering, bars and quick-snack food joints.

With Claudio Silvestrin's architecture, Princi wanted to emphasize the traditional, hand-made approach to baking and the quality of the produce. He came up with the idea of making the production visible to customers by moving the street-level kitchen to between the storefront windows and an internal glass wall. The fast-paced action of the 'laboratorio' is intended as a contrast to the calm of the store. Here the bakers knead over 200 types of bread, all visible to the customers and onlookers like a theatrical performance. Clad in chic Armani uniforms, the bakers are elegant and dramatic-looking.

Princi was also keen to employ constant reminders of the Italian artisan tradition. Thus the materials become a way of recalling ancient ways and places. Porphyry slabs of marble are the ones characteristically employed in the old town's *piazze* and historical centres, the laminated elements recall the workshops, while the wood tops are where one traditionally kneads the dough. The essential elements of fire, water, earth and air, each crucial to the art of breadmaking, are strongly present in the architecture as a fusion of an abstract sign and physicality of matter. Silvestrin chose an unusual mixture of colours: brass panels in a scorched-earth tone for the main desks and walls, slabs of smooth porphyry in a grey/violet tone for the floor and rough porphyry for the dwarf wall.

A parapet at the back of the store is a direct reference to Rome, set in a deep niche it houses a wood–burning fireplace. The parapet then turns into a long snack counter and then pierces the glass storefront where water trickles like a fountain from the wall. On the coffee counter, a Venini clear glass designed by Silvestrin is the lone decorative flourish. The seating is several Le Spighe bar stools, produced by Poltrona Frau and designed by Silvestrin, while the lighting is either discreetly set in the white ceiling or hidden in the ankle-level slits in the stairwell walls.

Silvestrin's signature purity and minimalism is, as forever, present – the 209-square-metre (2,250-square-foot), two-level space created for the Princi *panetteria* is stripped down to the bare essentials, so that the simple sensual pleasures of making bread can be fully indulged. The space is more gallery than retail, an oasis of calm and collected style, filled with delectable foodstuffs.

2

3

1 At the back of the store, set in a niche in a parapet, is a wood-burning fireplace.

2 Scorched-earth tones for the walls and desks recall one of the four essential elements.

3 The two-level space is stripped down to its bare essentials in Claudio Silvestrin's trademark, minimalist style.

4

4 Red stools by Poltrona Frau and designed by Claudio Silvestrin are used as seating at the long bar counter.

5 A staircase leads to the lower level, while lighting is hidden in slits in the walls.

5

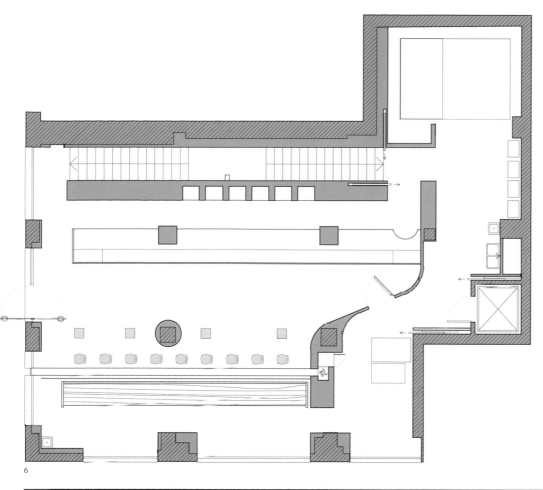

6

7

6 Plan: the entrance is to the left, staircase to the lower level at the top, and the laboratorio at the bottom.

7 In the laboratorio, well-visible to the customers, bakers knead and prepare over 200 types of bread.

1

1 A large metal theatrical mask and an optical pavement create a surreal space.

2 *Waiting for Godot*, by Samuel Beckett, is the text that has been used as decoration in the lower ground area and on the staircase.

3 Two large eyes made of tiles, one brown and one blue, dominate the showroom window.

Italian designer Fabio Novembre, known for his lavish and ornamental installations and love for tiles, was fittingly appointed art director at the German glass mosaic manufacturer, Bisazza, in 2000. Since then, he has designed Bisazza's showrooms in Milan, New York and Berlin. 'Tiles are always architectural elements for me. They are the skin of my spaces,' says Novembre, who likens his architecture to the 'body of a woman, sensual and full of curves'.

For the new showroom at Kantstrasse, Novembre devised a cornucopia of colours and shapes resembling a theatrical design – a theme already employed in the other Bisazza showrooms that also often hold performances and exhibitions. The inspiration for this showroom was Samuel Beckett's play *Waiting for Godot*. The reference to Godot is Novembre's interpretation of the city of Berlin, a metropolis that he believes has been constantly on the verge of 'becoming', and is the historic capital of 'suspense'.

Two large eyes, one brown and one blue, dominate the showrooms windows and attract the attention of passers-by. Made of glass tiles and displayed via a computer system, they are supposed to recall David Bowie's eyes – a man, according to Novembre, who does not wait for any Godot and represents the perfect example of creativity. The exotic, luscious interiors are tiled like canvases and carry many themes throughout the rooms: one has an optical style, another is more decadent in blues and gold, while yet another is decorated with Beckett's text. Downstairs, an all-white lounge with comfortable, white seats for reclining becomes a symbol for the eternal waiting.

2

3

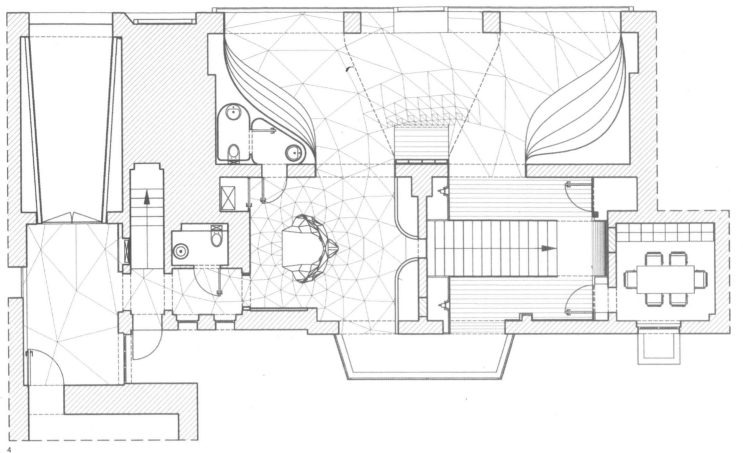

4 Plan: the upper level is dominated by the giant metallic mask (bottom centre)

5

6

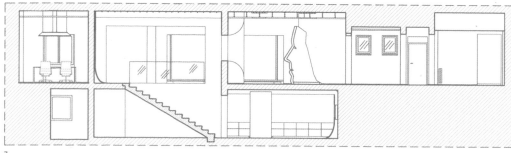
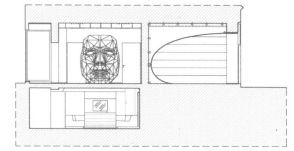

7

5 The staircase, decorated with Godot's text, leads to the downstairs area.

6 The exotic, luscious interiors are tiled like canvases and each room carries a different theme.

7 Long and short sections through the two-storey space.

After the success of her series of 'guerrilla stores' in 2004, Comme des Garçons founder Rei Kawakubo has created Dover Street Market in London's Mayfair. The total antithesis to most designer stores, it has been conceived as more of an artistic collective. The large shed houses the cash desk.

FASHION AND ART

HELMUT LANG

With its love of minimal, clean cut lines, Helmut Lang was always going to need an adequate retail space. The New York flagship opened in 1997 and spearheaded the whole trend of merging art with retail. In an attempt to challenge both traditional retail planning and the consumer experience, architect Richard Gluckman and clothing designer Helmut Lang renovated a 325-square-metre (3,500-square-foot) loft in SoHo, turning it into a space that mimics an art gallery. This retail strategy was expanded with Helmut Lang shops in Paris and Milan. The New York shop has obelisk-like light installations by Jenny Holzer and, in particular, the Paris one also contains works by Louise Bourgeois, with whom Helmut Lang has collaborated many times, and furniture pieces by Jean Prouvé.

The New York space consists of three distinct yet integrated parts. In contrast to traditional retail planning, the merchandising area is at the rear of the store, freeing the front for a reception area that is also visible from the street. A full-height, translucent glass wall draws the customer past the installation by artist by Jenny Holzer and into the main area. In the second of the three spaces, monolithic boxes, in rigorous succession, reveal themselves as freestanding cabinets containing the designer's collections. A long and low cash/wrap table runs parallel to the customer's path. The perimeter walls are not used for any display and act as a blank backdrop to the shop.

1

2

1 In this minimalist setting, the walls are not employed for display, but merely act as a blank back-drop to the shop.

2 One of the three monolithic black boxes that are actually freestanding cabinets containing the designer's collections.

3 Helmut Lang's store in SoHo clearly mimics the space of an art gallery.

3

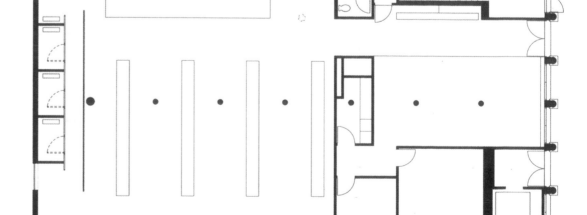

4 Plan: the street façade is to the right and the retail and dressing area to the left.

4

5

Concealed behind the translucent glass wall is the tall, narrow rear space that encloses the dressing room area and creates a private and elegant atmosphere. A continuous skylight above emphasizes the verticality of the space and a large window of blue glass provides views of the exterior space between the buildings behind the store.

Each of the three spaces is further defined by distinct lighting. The reception area is downlit by encapsulated PAR (Parabolic Aluminized Reflector) lamps, mounted in porcelain sockets; the merchandising area is uplit from the top of the cabinets by colour-corrected T8 fluorescent lamps; and the dressing rooms are exposed to natural daylight. The store stocks complete Helmut Lang collections, both for men and women, and a special service is provided, upon request, for VIPs.

6

7

5 The front area of the store is kept empty and used as a reception space.

6 Concealed behind the translucent glass wall is the tall, narrow rear space that encloses the dressing room area.

7 A few items of merchandise are displayed in minimal style on sculptural units.

In an attempt to reverse the now common association between fashion and high architecture, the Japanese Comme des Garçons founder and designer, Rei Kawakubo, opened a series of 'guerrilla stores' in 2004. These temporary flagships were built with very little money and in run-down spaces in unfashionable parts of towns such as Berlin, Singapore and Ljubljana. Understandably, the press was intrigued. This was, after all, the fashion visionary that had kick-started the whole retailer/architect love affair, most notably with the New York Comme des Garçons flagships store designed by Future Systems in the meat-packing district long before it become a location for retail flagships. Almost as a testament to the transient passing of fashion fads, the guerilla stores' life is one year only, after which it closes down.

The Dover Street Market is Kawakubo's latest retail venture, post the guerilla store concept. It is inspired by the energetic, collective anarchy of London's Kensington Market, which compressed the whole eclectic range of the London post-punk, independent designer scene under its one large roof. Dover Street Market is located in a Georgian-fronted property in Mayfair, not far from the chic retail heaven Old Bond Street. Yet Dover Street Market proposes itself as the very antithesis to the elegant, sleek, box format adopted by so many brands. Rather, it is conceived as an artistic collective where fashion, furniture, jewellery and theatre designers come together to realize a unique and eclectic vision.

Bare walls and naked steel beams define the store as anti-flagship par excellence, a concept that is entirely Kawakubo's. A backdrop of

1

1 The large shack-style shed, made of wood and laminated iron, houses the cash desk on the ground floor.

2 Dover Street Market's low-key façade purposely eschews the glitzy style of the more glamorous boutiques on nearby Old Bond Street.

3 Custom-made, low-cost timber display units, bare walls and naked steel beams define Dover Street Market's anti-flagship philosophy.

2

3

4

4 Murals and art pieces sit comfortably alongside vintage furniture and fashion pieces.

5 Limited-edition collections are displayed on simple rail racks while opulent chandeliers clash with the neon lights in the office-style ceiling.

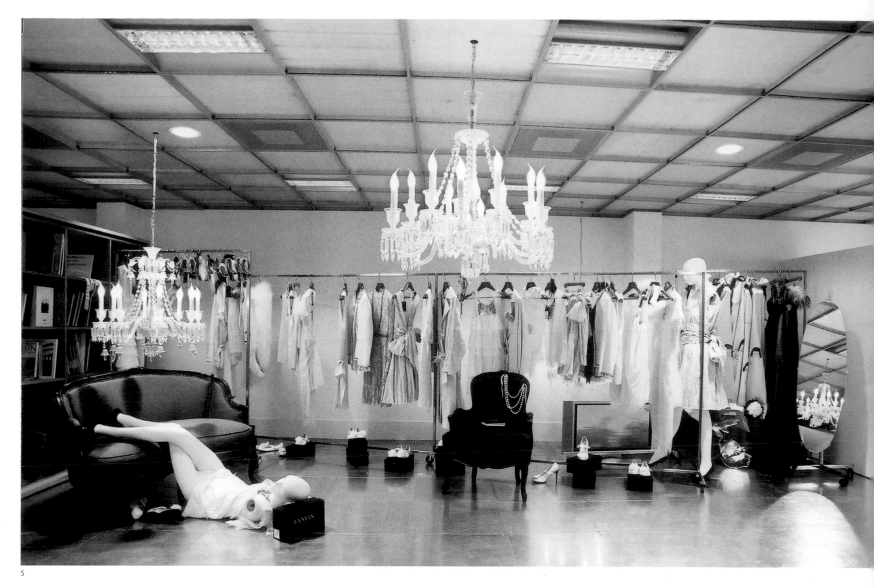

5

houses by the scenographer Elise Capdenat; Minotaurs by theatre designer Michael Howells were inspired by Kawakubo's brief 'Shakespeare meets Picasso'; murals on the walls; draped silk curtains; recycled taxidermy glass cases; a large 'shack shed' made of laminated iron housing the till… all reflect the industrial chic spirit as well as the low budget behind it. The fitting rooms are Portakabins, while collections are displayed behind metallic-bead curtains

The 1,208-square-metre (13,000-square-foot), six-floor shop is packed with freestanding art and fashion pieces, both vintage and bespoke. Jean Prouve chairs sit alongside a limited-edition furniture collection designed by Dior menswear designer Hedi Slimane. Rather than the representation of a single brand or value, it displays a community of designers, gathered together by the selective and discerning eye of Kawakubo. Beside the various Comme des Garçons ranges, Dover Street Market also displays Belgian menswear designer Raf Simmons and his past collections; a boudoir boutique line by East London label Boudicca; hand-signed and hand-decorated Judy Blame jewellery pieces; Lanvin's designer, Alber Elbaz, garments; Fred Perry shirts; and box sets from photographer Nick Knight's archives. On the financial side, the company acts as a mall operator, taking a percentage of sales from each 'stall' to cover the costs of the 15-year lease.

In its bid to create an 'ongoing atmosphere of beautiful chaos' the Dover Street Market blurs the boundary between retail and installation art. Nothing is mass-consumed, nothing is readily available elsewhere, the focus is on the individuality of the purchasing experience.

ISSEY MIYAKE APOC STORE

PARIS/FRANCE

ERWAN AND RONAN BOUROULLEC/2000

French sibling designers Erwan and Ronan Bouroullec were approached in 2000 by Issey Miyake's team to design a space in Paris dedicated to his new clothes collection, APOC. For the Bouroullec brothers this was a first, since their background had been so far been in product and furniture design. Because the commissioner, Issey Miyake, was also a designer, the Bouroullec brothers found that they had to interpret their own brief-specific requirements from Miyake. These were limited to a bespoke cutting table and an ironing table that would evoke the idea of a tailor's workshop, where clothes are made to fit.

'APOC' is an innovative design concept by Miyake. It is made using an industrial knitting or weaving machine, which is programmed by a computer. This process creates continuous tubes of fabric, within which lie both shape and pattern. A thread goes into the machine and re-emerges as a piece of clothing or another shape – accessories or even a chair. The customer cuts sleeves and skirts exactly to the desired length, creating a totally customized final effect. The opposite of the current standard in clothes manufacturing, APOC proposes an interactive method in which customers have a say in the final shape of the product, while benefiting from a new technology. APOC merges the qualities of old-fashioned tailoring with mass production.

The Bouroullec brothers decided to conceive the shop as a playground for Issey Miyake and the APOC collection. 'We tried to design a shop that would be free from our own signature. Our idea was to consider that the experience of the customer would be defined by the clothes presented inside and the way they were arranged. The shop had to be incredibly minimal, but also totally disorganized and eclectic… We also specifically decided to use as little colour as possible, because we thought that the clothes would create a set of their own,' says Erwan Bouroullec.

The shop was designed as a changeable 'presentation tool': it can be full of clothes or alternatively show just one or two garments. Mirrors and tables can be changed around or removed. 'In a way we didn't impose any

1

2

1 The designers' original idea was to create a shop that would be a playground for Miyake and the APOC collection.

2 Most of the furniture is made of Corian, moulded to form continuously flowing, soft shapes.

3 Clothes are either fixed to the walls with magnets or displayed on hangers or rails.

3

4

4 A clothes line rail, made of Corian, allows the garments to be moved around.

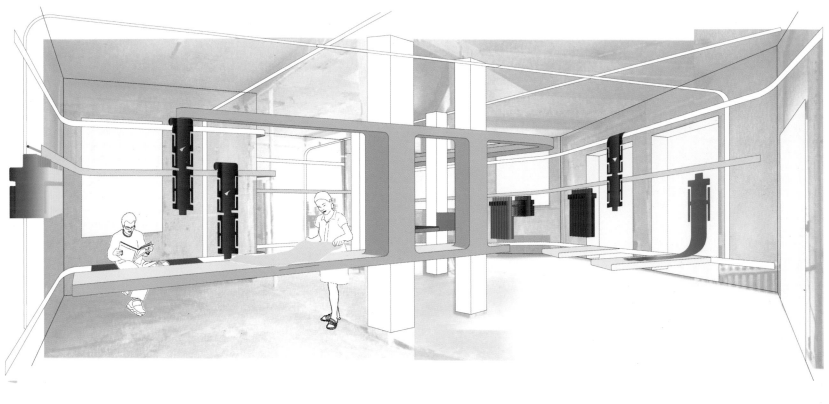

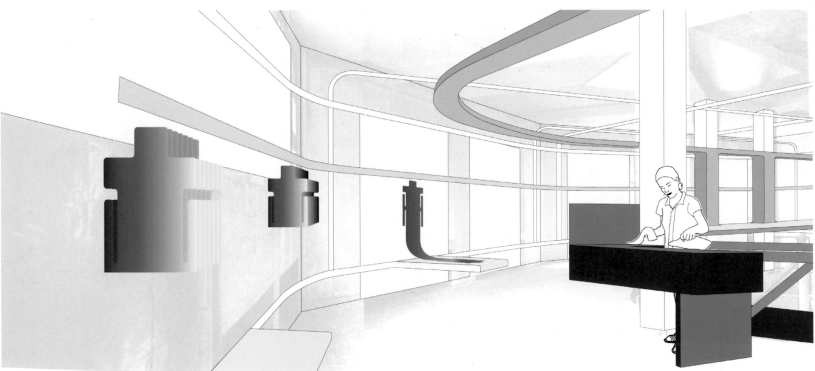

5

5 Renderings of the interior, illustrating the curving display structures and hanging rails that surround the space.

6 The environment is kept minimal and with as little colour as possible to emphasize the clothes.

7 A green partition adds an unusual dash of colour to the store's environment.

6

7

8

presentation set, but opened some different, possible paths that the staff and Miyake could then follow on their own,' says Bouroullec. The interactive, changing environment reflects the nature of the APOC product, where customers participate in the creation of their own garments.

The design of the shop started with details such as the coat hanger, a support for the hanger and so on. There are dresses fixed to the wall with magnets, elastic fabric on rolls, stools for shoes and coloured markings for decoration and orientation. Most of the furniture is made of Corian: tabletops, display surfaces, hangers and 'assembly-line' rails that surround the space and allow 'pieces' to slide along. 'We used a lot of Corian, in a really "carved" way, which at that time was one of the most innovative uses for this material, especially in a large scale like a retail environment,' says Bouroullec. The Corian has been moulded to form continuously flowing, soft shapes. The cutting tables and ironing boards slip into tabletops and merge together without a visible seam. No hooks, no pegs, no strings can be seen because of the use of magnets. The 100-square-metre (1,076-square-foot) boutique is a totally white environment that works as a gallery, an atelier, a factory and a shop.

8 The modular style of the shop fittings reflects the nature of Miyake's APOC product, which can be customized according to the wearer's needs or likes.

Architecture takes on a sculptural function with Carlos Miele's New York flagship designed by Asymptote. The 325-square-meter (3,500-square-foot), single-level space is conceived as a sinuous and curvaceous environment, resplendent in high-gloss liquid finishes and textures. This is a prime example of the flirtation between fashion and art, which sees shops becomes increasingly more like galleries and often even competing for space in same areas of town. The Miele shop presents itself with a luminous façade that leads into a space bathed in a neutral palette of white and shades of pale green, green/blue and grey. The winding central space creates both a welcoming place for gathering as well as providing an ideal catwalk runaway for fashion events.

The design intends to celebrate Miele's perspective and aesthetic attitude towards design in his native country, Brazil. The design and architecture of the store embraces a culture that champions modern aesthetics while being steeped in traditional cultural rituals. The architectural environment becomes a spatial narrative, centred primarily on an abstracted reading of what constitutes Brazilian culture, landscape and architecture, while also being a contemporary experience of downtown, vibrant Manhattan life. The curvilinear forms are arguably an homage to the architecture of the legendary Oscar Niemeyer, and the contrast between technology and tradition reflects the different spirits of São Paulo (Miele's home town) and New York.

1

1 The designer's original concept was for a bright open space using a palette of white, pale green and grey. This was intended to serve as a backdrop for the brightly patterned cloths.

2 The high-gloss, epoxy flooring has embedded glass rings that are illuminated from underneath with neon and halogen lighting. Dresses are strategically suspended so that they appear to float over the rings.

3

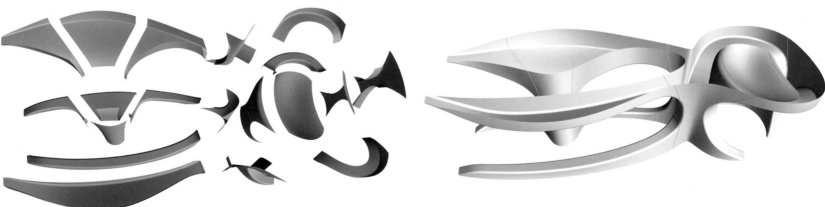

4

3 The central display structure was made from lacquered and bent plywood over a rib-and-gusset substructure.

4 From left: computer models of the display structure, in pieces and assembled.

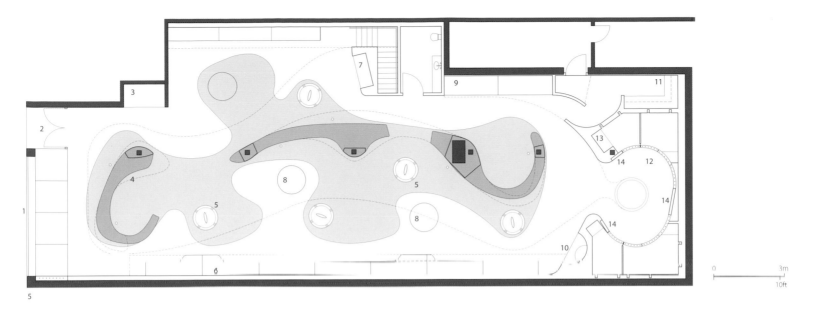

5

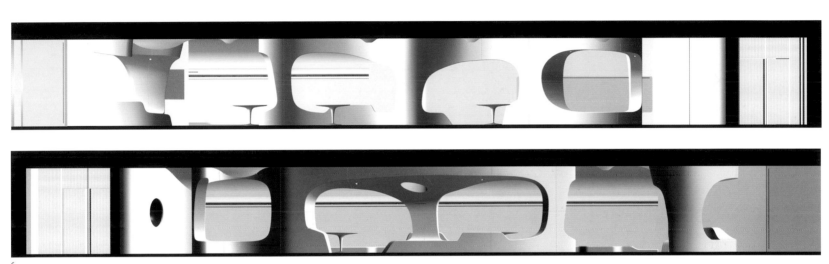

6

This contemporary setting of seemingly disparate, but not irreconcilable, opposite influences sets the stage for the presentation of Miele's brightly patterned clothes. The two-tone, shiny epoxy floor is divided by three sculptural partitions, whose form echoes the fluidity of the exposed clothes. The shape is the result of computer studies of fabric cuttings from the floor of Miele's design studio. A gleaming ceiling, made out of a high-gloss, stretched PVC-based material produced by Barrisol, further adds to the resplendent atmosphere of glossy whiteness. Mannequins float, suspended mid-air by wires. Their shining halos are the result of circular neon fixtures embedded in the floor to visually anchor the floating forms. Interspersed around each ring of light are MR16 lamps. A halo of light emanates overhead from a Par 30 individual fixture, to accent free-hanging mannequins.

The sophisticated environment also features digital art that has been integrated into the architecture in the form of two videos by Asymptote.

While one installation is encased in black, mirrored glass that reflects both viewer and merchandise, a second installation projects images of fire and water against a rear wall. Each piece celebrates an aspect of body and spatiality. These works are extensions of Asymptote's art projects, recently included in Documenta XI and the Venice Biennale.

'One should elevate an experience to the level of the art world,' says Hani Rashid. 'Designing galleries and museums has become somewhat an exhausted project, because the gallery can't seem to rise from the white-box syndrome…. For interesting architectural, spatial and artistic expression, the work has to be rooted in the everyday experience of the city.' With its high-tech organic shapes and cool and collected atmosphere, the Miele space perfectly frames fashion.

5 Plan: 1. West 14th Street, 2. entrance, 3. artwork niche, 4. 'altar', 5. light ring, 6. clothing, 7. display niche, 8. tables, 9. backlit clothing, 10. mirror sphere, 11. cashier, 12. changing area, 13. bench, 14. mirror.

6 Long section through two points in the store, with the entrance to the left.

PROJECT CREDITS

Issey Miyake APOC Store, Paris, France
Design Concept Erwan and Ronan Bouroullec
23 rue du Buisson Saint-Louis
75010 Paris, France
Website www.bouroullec.com
Client Issey Miyake

Alexander McQueen, New York, USA
Designer William Russell Architecture and Design Ltd, now
of Pentagram
Project Team William Russell, Michelle Hotchkin
11 Needham Road
London W11 2RP, UK
Website www.pentagram.co.uk
Client Alexander McQueen
Main Contractor Interior Construction Corporation
Architect of Record STUDIOS Architecture
Mechanical/Electrical/Plumbing MGJ & Associates
Hanging Metal Fixtures/Custom Millwork Mison
Concepts, Inc.
Terrazzo Floors D. Magnan & Co, Inc.

Apple Store, Tokyo, Japan
Architect Bohlin Cywinski Jackson
733 Allston Way
Berkeley, CA 94710, USA
Website www.bcj.com
Project Team Peter Q. Bohlin (design principal), Jon C.
Jackson (principal-in-charge), Karl Backus (principal, project
director), Anastasia Congdon (project manager), Joe
Holsen, David Murray, Mary Beth Coyne, Maria Danielides,
Rachel Lehn, Ben McDonald, Jennifer Rhoades, Lydia So,
Mike Waltner
Design Associate Gensler
Architect of Record/Engineer KAJIMA Design
Client Apple Computer, Inc.
Main Contractor KAJIMA Corporation
Structural Engineer Dewhurst MacFarlane & Partners, Inc.
MEP Engineer Flack & Kurtz, Inc.
Lighting Designer ISP Design

Maison Baccarat, Paris, France
Design Concept Philippe Starck
18/20 rue du Faubourg du Temple
75011 Paris, France
Website www.starck.com
Project Team Dorothée Boissier, Grégoire Maisondieu,
Astrid Courtois, Maud Bury
Project Architect José-Louis Albertini in collaboration with
Hervé Jaillet
Client Baccarat
Project Team Renaud Bereski, Emmanuel Cencig,
Alphonse Goberville, Christophe Schott, Claude Vizelle,
Jean-Claude Weinacker
Graphics Concept Thibaut Mathieu for Cake Design

Glass Blowers Michel Barge, Daniel Denain
Glass Manufacturer/moulder Serge Vanesson
Furniture Suppliers Atelier Thierry Goux, Droog Design,
Drucker, Emeco, ENP, Gaétan Lanzani, Ketta, Laval, Orssi
Engelo, Style et Confort, Techniques Transparents
Woodwork Siam Agencement
Mirrors Mirosyle SARL
Wallpaper Kvadrat, Lelièvrem Pierre Frey
Tapestries Plybe, Mallet
Floors SMD
Carpets Tisca, France
Luminous Carpets Fenaux Createx
Tablecloth in the Crystal Room Rorthault
Stucco L'Atelier Blanch'art
Decorative Paintings Gilles Plagnet
Bronzes Lambert
Sculptures Ion Condiescu
Video and Audio SES Giraudon
Lighting Concept Voyons Voir
Lighting Manufacturer L'Atelier Fechoz
Aquarium Coutant
Fireplaces Bloch

B&B Italia, London, UK
Architect John Pawson
Unit B, 70–78 York Way
London N1 9AG, UK
Website www.johnpawson.com
Collaborating Interior Designer Antonio Citterio with
Patricia Viel
Via Cerva 4
20122 Milan, Italy
Website www.antonio-citterio.it
Project Architect DCM – Denton Corker Marshall
Client B&B Italia
Client Manager David Zimber
Builder John Richards Shopfitters
Lighting Via Bizzuno, Flos

Bisazza, Berlin, Germany
Architect Fabio Novembre
Via Mecenate 76/3
Milan 20138, Italy
Website www.novembre.it
Project Team Giuseppina Flor, Ramon Karges, Carlo
Formisano, Lorenzo De Nicola
Client Bisazza s.p.a
Main Contractor Löhn Hochbau GmbH
Local Architect Arch. Carlo Lorenzo Ferrante – ION
Industrial Design, Berlin
Floorcovering Metron and Logos slabs by Bisazza
Wallcovering Vetricolor by Bisazza
Ceilings Barrisol Stretch lumiere ceiling
Windows, Glass Balustrades and Floor Glass Passage
ABC Gottschalk

Furniture 'Less' table by Molteni s.p.a., 'Aluminum Chair' by
ICF Company, custom-made furniture by F1
Lighting Modular Lighting Instruments, Erco, custom-
made lamps by Se'lux
Plasma Monitor LG Electronics

Bless, Berlin, Germany
Design concept Ines Kaag and Desiree Heiss
Mulackstrasse 38
10119 Berlin, Germany
Website www.bless-service.de
Client Bless Shop

Camper Store, Munich (and Barcelona)
Shop Concept Design Marti Guixé
Calabria 252
08029 Barcelona, Spain
Website www.guixe.com
Client Camper
Project Realization Camper Architecture Department
Lamps – Munich Ingo Maurer
Lamps – Barcelona Marti Guixé

Carlos Miele, New York, USA
Architect Asymptote
561 Broadway, Suite 5A
New York, NY 10012, USA
Website www.asymptote.net
Project Team Hani Rashid, Lise Anne Couture (principals),
Jill Leckner (project architect), Noburu Ota, John Cleater,
Peter Horner, Cathy Jones with Michael Levy Bajar,
Janghwan Cheon, Teresa Cheung, Mary Ellen Cooper,
Shinichiro Himematsu, Michael Huang, Lamia Jallad, AnaSa,
Marjus Schnierle, Yasmin Shahamiri
Client Carlos Miele
Main Contractor Vanguard Construction & Development
Engineers Kam Chiu, Andre Tomas Chaszar
Lighting Design Focus Lighting, Inc.
A/V Consultant Ben Greenfield
Fabricator 555 International

Christian Dior, Tokyo, Japan
Architect Kazuyo Sejima + Ryue Nishizawa/SANAA
7-A, 2-2-35
Higashi-Shinagawa
Shinagawa-ku, Tokyo 140-0002, Japan
Website www.sanaa.co.jp
Project Team Kazuyo Sejima, Ryue Nishizawa, Junya
Ishigami, Koichiro Tokimori, Yumiko Yamada, Yoshitaka
Tanase, Erika Hidaka
Interior Design Christian Dior Couture Architectural
Department
Client Christian Dior
Structural Engineers Sasaki Structural Consultants
Mechanical Engineers P.T. Morimura & Associates

Lighting Designer Kilt Planning
Builder Shimizu Corporation

Dover Street Market, London, UK
Overall Design and Concept Rei Kawakubo
Client Comme des Garçons
Drawings/Realization Ishimaru KK
Construction/Japan Ishimaru KK
Construction/England Mark, Richard, Steve at E.I.T.
Organization Adrian Joffe, Dickon Bowden
4th Floor and Basement Elise Capdenat, Theatre and
Dance Scenographer
1st Floor Michael Howells, film set designer, working on
the brief 'Shakespeare meets Picasso' given to him by Rei
Kawakubo
2nd Floor Jan de Cock, Artist
Ground Floor Reception Vedovamazzei Artists

Emporio Armani, Hong Kong
Architect Massimiliano and Doriana Fuksas/mFuksas Arch
Piazza del Monte di Pietà 30
00186 Rome, Italy
Website www.fuksas.it
Project Team Massimiliano and Doriana Fuksas, Davide
Stolfi (project leader), Iain Wadham, Defne Dilber, Motohiro
Takada (design team), Gianluca Brancaleone, Nicola Cabiati,
Andrea Marazzi (model makers)
Client Giorgio Armani
Floor Sikafloor
Furniture Massimiliano and Doriana Fuksas, manufactured
by Zeus Noto
Glass Showcase Sunglas
Lights iGuzzini
Vases in Armani Fiori Monte di Rovello
Façade Signage Nettuno Neon

Fendi, Paris, France
Architect Lazzarini Pickering Architects
Via Cola di Rienzo 28
Rome 00192, Italy
Project Team Claudio Lazzarini, Carl Pickering, Elisabetta
Biffi, Giuseppe Postet
Executive Architects Sopha Architects
Client Fendi, France
Project Management LVMH Fashion Group Real Estate
Department
Store Fitout Schmit Tradition
Quantity Surveyor Socotec
Services Engineer Espace Temps
Site Coordinator Methodes et Construction
Structural Calculation Staircase Bureau d'Etudes Lefevre

Gallery, Andorra
Architect Francesc Pons
Bonavista 6

Bajos 32
08012 Barcelona, Spain
Website www.estudifrancescpons.com
Client Robert Cassany and Sonia Yebra
Builder Pringeret
Metalworker Talleres fertin
Air Conditioning Trefelca
Carpenter Construmad
Pavement Gra Paviments

Globus Food Hall, Zurich, Switzerland
Architect Brunner Eisenhut Gisi Architects
Letzigraben 114
8047 Zurich, Switzerland
Website www.be-architekten.ch
Project Team ARGE, Eugen Eisenhut, Roger Brunner, Stefan
Gisi
Client Globus Zentralverwaltung
General Management Perolini Baumanagement AG

Gucci, New York, USA
Architect Studio Sofield, Inc. – Designers
380 Lafayette Street
New York, NY 10003, USA
Project Team William Sofield (principal), Emma O'Neill
(vice president), Douglas Gellenbeck (project manager),
Alberto Velez (senior designer)
Collaborators Brennan Beer Gorman (architectural
consultant), Gensler (architect)
Client Gucci Group
Lighting Consultant William Armstrong

Helmut Lang, New York, USA
Architect Gluckman Mayner Architects
250 Hudson Street
New York, NY 10013, USA
Website www.gluckmanmayner.net
Project Team Richard Gluckman (principal-in-charge),
Melissa Cicetti (project manager), Eric Change, Bobby Han,
Perry Whidden
Client Onward Kashiyama (Holding Company), Helmut
Lang
Consultants Ove Arup & Partners, Mechanical and
Structural Engineers
Main Contractors Eurostruct, Inc.
Glass Floral Glass
Cabinets American Woods and Veneers Work, Inc.
GFRC Essex Works

l.a. Eyeworks, Los Angeles, USA
Architect Neil M. Denari Architects, Inc.
12615 Washington Boulevard
Los Angeles, CA 90066, USA
Website www.nmda-inc.com
Project Team Neil M. Denari, Duks Koschitz with Carmen

Hammerer (publication graphics)
Client Gai Gherardi and Barbara McReynolds
Main Contractor Duran and Associates
Design Consultants Gordon Polon (structural engineer),
Julie Reeves of Lighting Design Alliance (lighting
consultants)
Specialized Surface Finishing Boxcar Studio
Mobile Furniture Fabrication K. B. Manufacturing
Fixed Furniture Fabrication John Ballesteros
Vacuum Formed Panel Art Installation Design Jim
Isermann
Custom LED Mandex Motion Displays

Liberty, London, UK
Architect 20/20
20–23 Mandela Street
London, NW1 0DU, UK
Project Team Rune Gustafson, formerly Managing Director
of 20/20 now Lippincott Mercer, Simon Stacey, formerly
Creative Director of 20/20 now of Lippincott Mercer, Sarah
Page (project leader – interiors), Sara Hilden (project leader
– graphics)
Client Liberty
Main Contractors AE Hadleys (shopfitting – cosmetics and
womenswear), JRS (shopfitting – menswear)
Consultants Davis Langdon (project management), INTO
Lighting (lighting designers)

Mandarina Duck, London, UK
Architect Marcel Wanders Studio
Jacob Catskade 25
1052 BT Amsterdam, The Netherlands
Website www.marcelwanders.com
Project Architect Harper Mackay
Client Mandarina Duck
Main Contractor Kingly
Lighting Consultant Modular Lighting
Mannequins, Gulliver free-standing mirrors The Set
Company
Glass Displays Studio LB
Floor Finishes Escopalatino, Desso
Wall Finishes Tyvek, DuPont
Multiple(x) Lighting Modular Lighting NL

Miss Sixty/Energie Emporium, Barcelona, Spain
Architects Studio 63 Architecture and Design
Piazza Santa Maria Sopr'arno 1
50124 Florence, Italy
Website www.studio63.it
Project Team Massimo Dei, Piero Angelo Orecchioni
Interior and Lighting Design Studio 63
Client Miss Sixty of Sixty Group
Furniture Manufactured by Buzzoni SRL
Lighting Manufactured by Nord Light

Mulberry, London, UK
Design Consultants Four IV Design Consultants Ltd
Exmouth House
3 Pine Street
London, EC1R OJH, UK
Website www.fouriv.com
Project Team Chris Dewar-Dixon, Richard Ryan, Louise
Barnard, Ruth Treacher (interiors), Kim Hartley, Paul Skerm,
Julie Austin (graphics)
Client Roger Saul, Godfrey David
Project Managers Mark Alford Associates
Main Contractor Bridport
Consultants EEP (mechanical and electrical), Campbell
(lighting), Michael Hadi Associates (structural engineers),
Kate Henderson (visual merchandising)

O$_2$, Munich, Germany
Architect, Interior Designer, Lead Agency, Multimedia
and Music concept Dan Pearlman Markenarchitektur
Kiefholzstrasse 1
12435 Berlin, Germany
Website www.danpearlman.com
Client O$_2$
Media Band ART+COM AG
Shopfitting/furniture Vizona GmbH
Lighting Ansorg GmbH

oki-ni, London, UK
Architect 6a Architects
6a Orde Hall Street
London WC1N 3JW, UK
Website www.6a.co.uk
Project Team Tom Emerson, Stephanie Macdonald
Client oki-ni (Paddy Meehan)
Main Contractor John Perkins Projects
Brand Consultant JJ Marshall Associates
Structural Engineer Jane Wernick Associates
Project Managers Dobson White Buolcott
Graphics Fuel

Orange, Birmingham, UK
Design Consultants Lippincott Mercer and 20/20
Address of Lippincott Mercer
1 Grosvenor Place, London SW1X 7HJ, UK
Website www.lippincottmercer.com
Address of 20/20
20-23 Mandela Street
London NW1 0DU, UK
Project Team Rune Gustafson, formerly Managing Director
of 20/20 now of Lippincott Mercer, Simon Stacey, formerly
Creative Director of 20/20 now of Lippincott Mercer), John
Regan (project leader – interiors), George Fountain –
project leader – graphics), Sarah Baboo – senior designer
(interiors)

Client Orange Retail UK
Main Contractor Bedford and Havehands (main
shopfitting contractors)
Lighting Designers INTO Lighting

Prada, Los Angeles, USA
Architects Office for Metropolitan Architecture (OMA-
AMO)
Heer Bokelweg 149
3032 AD Rotterdam, The Netherlands
Website www.oma.nl
Project Team Rem Koolhaas (partner-in-charge), Ole
Scheeren (partner-in-charge), Eric Change (project
architect), Jessica Rothschild (project architect), Amale
Andraos (project architect), Christian Bandi, Catarina Canas,
David Moore, Mark Watanabe, Torsten Schroeder, Joecelyn
Low, Keren Engelman, Ali Kops, Jeffrey Johnson
AMO Project Team Markus Schaefer, Clemens Weisshaar,
Reed Kram, Nicolas Firket, Michael Rock, Joakim Dahlqvist,
Stephen Wang, Richard Wang, Sung Kim, Dan Michaelson,
Leigh Devine
Executive Architect Brand+Allen Architects
Client Prada
Main Contractor Plant Construction
Structure Services Arup, Los Angeles
Lighting Kugler Tillotson Associates
Façade Skylight Dewhurst McFarlane
Curtain Inside Outside
Wallpaper and Graphics 2x4
Material Development Chris van Duijn (OMA), Werkplaats
De Rijk, Panelite, Plant Construction

Princi Bakery, Milan, Italy
Architect Claudio Silvestrin Architects
Unit 412 Kingswharf
302 Kingsland Road, London N8 4DS, UK
Website www.claudiosilvestrin.com
Project Team Claudio Silvestrin, Giuliana Salmaso
Client Rocco Rinci, Milan
Main Contractor BOMA
Structural Engineers Giulio Farina
Lighting Claudio Silvestrin in collaboration with
Viabizzuno
Air-conditioning Intesa Impianti
Interior Design Engineering Frontini & Battagin
Brass Covering in terra bruciata Silvestrin Astec
Stone Supplier Polimarmo

Pringle, London, UK
Architects Wells Mackereth Architects
Unit 14, Archer Street Studios
10–11 Archer Street
London W1D 7AZ, UK
Website www.wellsmackereth.com
Project Team Amy Lam, Sally Mackereth, Patricia

Miyamoto, Angelika Richter, Pascale Schulte, Yoko
Watanabe, James Wells
Client Pringle of Scotland
Main Contractor Pat Carter Contracts Ltd
Structural Engineer Whitby Bird
Mechanical Services Sidney Dubbage (H&V) Ltd
Electrical Services MCE Ltd

Selfridges, Birmingham, UK
Architect Future Systems
The Warehouse
20 Victoria Gardens
London W11 3PE, UK
Website www.future-systems.com
Project Team Soren Aagaard, Nerida Bergin, Sarah Jayne
Bowen, Lida Caharsouli, Julian Flannery, Harvinder Gabhari,
Dominic Harris, Nicola Hawkins, Matthew Heywood,
Candas Jennings, Jan Kaplicky, Amanda Levete, Iain
MacKay, Glenn Moorley, Andrea Morgante, Thorsten
Overberg, Angus Pond, Jessica Salt, Severin Soder
Main Contractor Laing O'Rourke
Structure, Services + façade Engineering Arup
Quantity Surveyor Boyden + Co.
Project Manager Faithful + Gould
Main Frame Contractor Sir Robert McAlpine
Glazing Subcontractor Haran Glass
Envelope Subcontractor 5M
Disc Manufacture James +Taylor
Stainless Steel Panelling Subcontractor Baris/Jordan
Sprayed Concrete Subcontractor Shotcrete
GRP.GRG Subcontractor Diespeker
M&E Contractor Haden Young

Shoebaloo, Amsterdam, The Netherlands
Architect Meyer en Van Schooten Architecten BV
Pilotenstraat 35
1059 CH Amsterdam, The Netherlands
Website www.meyer-vanschooten.nl
Project Team Koert Göschel, Oliver Oechsle
Client Shoebaloo BV
Main Contractor GF Deko
Furniture Normania
Installation Lighting Philips Nederland BV
Glazed Entrance Glaverned
Polyester Furniture Meyer en Van Schooten (design),
Normania (manufacturer)
Glass wall covering Altuglas by Atoglas
Glass Floor manufactured by Saint Roch
Curved glass skirting board Tetterode Glas
Lighting Manufacturer Philips Nederland BV

smart-travelling store, Berlin, Germany
Design Concept Werner Aisslinger with Nicola Bramigk
Studio Aisslinger
Oranienplatz 4

10999 Berlin, Germany
Website www.aisslinger.de
Project Team Werner Aisslinger, Thom Spycher, Tina Bunyaprasit, Fred Fréty, Manuel Vital, Till Grosch, Bao-Nghi Droste
Client Nicola Bramigk
Furniture Design Werner Aisslinger

Stella McCartney Store, New York, USA

Architect Universal Design Studio
35 Charlotte Road
London EC2A 3PG, UK
Website www.universaldesignstudio.com
Client Stella McCartney
Main Contractor Interior Construction Corporation
Lighting Design Campbell Lighting Design
Millwork/Specialist Joinery Cappellini Contracts
Tile Designed by Barber & Osgerby, manufactured by Teamwork Italia

TOD's, Tokyo, Japan

Architect Toyo Ito & Associates, Architects
1-19-4 Shibuya
Shibuya-ku
150-0002 Tokyo, Japan
Website www.toyo-ito.co.jp
Project Team Toyo Ito, Takeo Hisashi, Akihisa Hirata, Kaori Shikichi, Leo Yokota, Takuji Aoshima, Yasuaki Mizunuma
Client Holpaf B.V.
Main Contractor Takenaka Corporation
Structural Engineers Structural Design Office OAK, Inc.
Mechanical Engineers ES Associates
Furniture Design Toyo Ito & Associates, Architects
Fixtures and Fittings Design Modar srl, Garde U.S.P Co., Ltd.

Villamoda, Kuwait City, Kuwait

Architects, Concept, Lighting Design, Co-ordination of Interior Design pfcarchitects
Via Giangiacome Mora 7
20123 Milan, Italy
Website www.pfcarchitects.com
Project Team Pierfrancesco Cravel
Collaborators
Eldrige & Smerin Architects (interior design of multibrand areas, external landscaping, restaurant/café, lounge and public areas)
Client Green Cedars spa
Main Contractor Al Ahlia Contracting Group
Engineering Favero & Milan Ingegneria
Building Management Gulf Consult Kuwait
Brand/identity Designers Wink Media (now Winkreative)
Furniture Suppliers Coexistence, SCP, Cappellini

Y's, Tokyo, Japan

Principal Designer Ron Arad, Ron Arad Associates
62 Chalk Farm Road
London NW1 8AN, UK
Website www.ronarad.com
Project Team Ron Arad, Asa Bruno (project architect), James Foster (architectural assistant), Paul Gibbons (3D visualizations)
Executive/collaborating Architect (Japan) Shiro Nakata, Studio Mebius
Client Yohji Yamamoto
Client Representative Mr Fujio Hasumi
Main Contractor Mr Minoru Kawamura, Build Co. Japan
Specialist Subcontractor (loops) Mr Roberto Travaglia, Marzorati-Ronchetti
Lighting Consultant iGuzzini

INDEX

PHOTO CREDITS

The publisher would like to thank the following sources for permission to reproduce images in this book:
Soren Aagaard (78 bottom, 79, 80 bottom), Peter Aaron/ESTO (18–20), Sue Barr/VIEW (10 right), Courtesy Bless (102–103), Luc Boegly/artedia (2, 142–147), Nicola Bramigk (155, 156 left), Richard Bryant/ARCAID (6 left, 7 left, 7 right), Benny Chan/Fotoworks (148–153), Courtesy Comme des Garçons (166–167, 174–177), Courtesy Colette (9 right), Courtesy Conran & Partners (10 left, 11 left), Richard Davies (7 second from left), diephotodesigner.de (122–125), Alberto Ferrero (162–165), Floto + Warner (34–35, 41 left, 42–43), Klaus Frahm/artur (8 right), Dennis Gilbert/VIEW (9 middle), Richard Glover/VIEW (130–131, 138–141), Lydia Gould (38–40, 41 right), David Grandorge (44–47), Courtesy Gucci (6 middle), Roland Halbe/artur (10 middle, 11 right), Ken Hayden (6 right), Heinrich Helfenstein (134–136), Stefan Jaenicke (154, 156 right), Nick Kane/Arcaid (78 top, 80 top), Christoph Kicherer (7 second from right), Inga Knölke (100–101), Morgane Le Gall (174–175, 177), Eric Laignel (60–63), Dieter Leistner/artur (13 right), André Lichtenberg (96–97, 110–112), Aka Son Lindman (92–95), Peter Lippsmeier/artur (13 left), Fredrika Lökholm (11 middle, 12 left), Jeroen Musch (48–51), Nacasa & Partners (52–54, 86 right–91), Tomio Ohashi (86 left), Koji Okumura (114–115, 126–128), Frank Oudeman (82–85), Keith Parry (14–15, 30–33), Andrew Peppard (26–29), Matteo Piazza (72–75, 158–161), Yael Pincus (106–109), Eugeni Pons (76–77), Prat Ramon (64–67), Jörg Schöner/artur (9 left), Shinkenchika-sha (68–71), Edmund Sumner (56–57), Kenichi Suzuki (8 left), Paul Warchol (170–173, 178–180), Adrian Wilson (22–25, 118–121), Łucja Zielińska (12 right)

Author's acknowledgements

A special thanks to all the designers and architects who submitted material for this book. In particular, I would like to thank Rune Gustafson at Lippincott Mercer for his invaluable insight on retail, Neil Churcher for his knowledge of technology and interaction design, Terence Conran, Amanda Levete at Future Systems, Sally Mackereth at Wells Mackereth, everybody at Dan Pearlman, Hani Rashid, Marcel Wanders and Markus Schaefer for taking time to address the different issues explored in this book. Finally, I would like to thank everybody at Laurence King Publishing for making the project possible, especially Jennifer Hudson for all the research.

ALIEN RACE - PETER CHAN

ALIEN RACE · THOM TENERY · PETER CHAN

ALIEN RACE

visual development of an intergalactic adventure

designstudio|PRESS

DEDICATION

"To our friends, families, and Design Studio Press fans, thank you for the support and your patience."

ALIEN RACE
visual development of an intergalactic adventure

Graphic Design: Scott Robertson
Editor: Scott Robertson

Published by
Design Studio Press
8577 Higuera Street
Culver City, CA 90232

Website: www.designstudiopress.com
E-mail: info@designstudiopress.com
Printed in China: First edition, August 2009

10 9 8 7 6 5 4 3 2 1

soft cover ISBN: 978-1-933492-23-0
hard cover ISBN: 978-1-933492-30-8
Library of Congress Control Number: 2006937849

CONTENTS

art both pages: SCOTT ROBERTSON

FOREWORD

A sugar rush for the eyes; a caffeine high for the mind.

I have seen this collection of design in the works for quite some time, so when Scott sent over the final layout for my review, it should have been no surprise as to what my reaction would be. However, I was thoroughly impressed on so many levels.

My first impression was simply the success of finishing this undertaking. When we flip through a book like this, it's easy to take for granted how much work goes into it. Each character is first well thought out...in the mind. This is where each artist indulges in the concept cerebrally. Then there is the multitude of concept sketches. And the immersive illustrations...the level of detail! All of this applied to a huge range of characters, beasties and environments, and with a cohesive narrative and aesthetic throughout. Additionally, Scott has made not just a picture book, but a reference you can use (and will want to use). Images will inspire and techniques will provoke.

It would seem that I have said enough in an exclamatory way, but there was a profound reaction that I had that is almost more important than the sheer enjoyment and appreciation of the content. I was (and am) inspired, educated and motivated. I can't wait to put pencil to paper after having looked at this wonderful collection of ideas. I am chomping at the bit to do more "mirrored madness."

I am moved to speak about what a treat it is, what an honor, and what a validation it is to be a teacher. Except for Scott, the artists in this book were all students of mine while at Art Center (although I think Scott would agree that we have both taught one another a thing or two). To see them take the very little I presented as a teacher and bring it to a whole new level.... What a treat. To have shared in their journey and call them associates and friends.... What an honor. But, what a validation it is to be a teacher. By this I mean to say that their success in this book validates the importance of sharing skills and ideas. Scott and I have always believed in sharing all ideas, and possessing no ownership of them. It does no one any good to harbor selfishly concepts, methods nor techniques. It is with this sharing that the community grows. When the instructor becomes the student, when the teacher is learning—that is successful sharing, that is validation.

I thank you Scott, Justin, Thom, Peter, John and Ben for sharing, inspiring, and teaching me!

Neville Page
Concept Designer: *Avatar, Star Trek, Cloverfield, Watchmen, Tron 2, Piranha 3-D.*
Los Angeles, March 2009

INTRODUCTION

It was in the spring of 2006 that I hired three very talented Art Center College of Design interns, Peter Chan, Justin Pichetrungsi, and Thom Tenery, for the upcoming summer. The question was, what would they work on during those four months? We could do a variety of freelance jobs, as I had done with my interns in summers past, or we could devote the time to the visual development of an original Design Studio Press intellectual property. We chose the latter, and so was born the I.P., *Alien Race.*

As I'm not a creative writer by training, and I wanted to execute not only the pitch art for *Alien Race* but also a great visual development book for DSP, we decided to work toward creating a world of appealing characters for which a compelling story could then be written at a later time. The basic story, written with the help of Julz Chavez, is printed on the next two pages. But this book is about how the concept, before the story, began.

Knowing I had limited time of only a summer, I designed this project so that almost everything that the team produced could be used for the book. Also at the beginning, I wondered whether characters or vehicles should be the main design subject, and what would the genre of the story be? I'm personally averse to violence as entertainment, so I thought about what genres of stories/video games do I like that might be able to compete in the marketplace. I am a big fan of racing games and the drama that dangerous, hard, competitive racing can create. Of course with my history of designing vehicles, this would have been the natural type of story to develop for our I.P. I was thinking, though, that it would be fun in a racing concept to swap the vehicles for creatures, which I know is a very technologically difficult thing to do with today's game engines, but it would make for a great book of concept art and a potentially strong line of toys and an animated film. On a personal skills level, this is a topic I have not spent much time designing and so I thought by pursuing the development of creatures and characters it would provide me with the right project to broaden my own design skills.

So that sets the stage for how the project was conceived. The design of almost any alien rider, human character, racing creature or alien world would work in the book. This meant that very little of the team's efforts would be wasted on doing art that would not be appropriate for the book. As the art came together, a story could then be created with the help of a good writer, such as Julz, and then some of the pieces could be tweaked and refined into pitch art for an animated film or video game. As we did not start the project with a strong plot beyond the idea of humans being invited to take part in an intergalactic alien race with bioengineered racing creatures, this made the early work very design-driven, which

works well for a strong visual development book, for which Design Studio Press is known. We decided on some basic racing creature skeletal forms to use as our starting point, not only for making the execution of "morphable" video-game models more achievable but also so the creatures from various planets would aesthetically work well next to each other. The same idea held true for the alien riders, as we decided early on to stick to anthropomorphic forms. It's always good to retain some elements of the familiar.

That summer of 2006 progressed quickly. The guys did some great work and I did very little art to help out. With my very busy schedule of teaching at Art Center, chairing the Entertainment Design department there, taking on outside freelance work and running Design Studio Press, I knew it was going to be tough to make time for the completion of this project to the level I had envisioned. So it sat idle for about a year and a half as other books and opportunities bumped it further down the to-do list.

Finally last summer there was a ray of hope that I would have enough time to commit to its completion. I hired John Park, another fabulous Art Center entertainment design student, as my summer intern to help finish the book. Thankfully another terrific Art Center student, Ben Mauro, had a little time to help out before his other internships started, so he became the final contributor to the book. During the month of May 2008 we had a great time cranking out some really fun aliens, utilizing a process Neville Page and I had stumbled upon. It is a design process that uses the Photo Booth application on a Mac laptop. You can see the documentation and examples of this process starting on page 50.

The summer moved along and we got sucked into more freelance work and the development of other books. The final push for this book happened during the winter holidays of 2008 and was being tweaked by the entire team on and off through the end of April 2009 when this book went to press...at last.

We hope you enjoy the characters and creatures we have created for *Alien Race.* Hopefully, with a little luck, we all might get to see the content of these pages on the big screen someday. For now though, please enjoy it for hours in this form!

Scott Robertson
Founder of Design Studio Press
Chair of Entertainment Design, Art Center College of Design
Los Angeles, April 2009

STORY OVERVIEW

In the middle of the jungle, a radio telescope locks on-target and sounds the alarm. A head emerges from the SETI Lab, revealing young summer intern, Zeno Cruz, the first to receive "alien contact."

On the southern tip of the constellation Capricornus, a strange alien ship surreptitiously slithers through the cosmos. An unidentifiable flag encrypted on its side displays the Galactic Alien Race Federation.

At the SETI Lab, Zeno frantically announces to well-known planet hunter and mentor, Doc Quan, that first contact has been made and to expect the G.A.R.F. "Bio Lab" to appear on planet Earth! Its target: the East River in New York City.

Days later, an enormous, multi-story high, metallic orb floats near the river's edge alongside the United Nations. Hovering news choppers and military vehicles stand by; ready to take aim and fire! The entire city is paralyzed as the news cameras roll.

Then suddenly, in plain sight, the mysterious orb broadcasts in HD-Alien TV via satellite announcing, "The Galactic Alien Race Federation has overwhelmingly elected to invite planet Earth to race for the future and join the Alien Race across the galactic universe!" The one qualifying rule is this: the official earthling race team must have one representative from each continent. No more, no less.

Foreign lands begin to comb their regions for the best talent their continent has to offer.

Back in New York, the city is seized with unrequited excitement. Camera crews surround the floating orb. Meanwhile the White House fears the United States is under alien attack! The Doc and Zeno argue that this must be the Alien Bio Lab and possibly a transport device to the galactic raceway. But the government can't believe that we finally make contact with intelligent life from another universe, and all they're interested in is...RACING? It is simply absurd! The "Bio Lab" must be destroyed!

The United Nations immediately intervenes in search of a peaceful solution, as the world tunes in to HD-Alien TV to find out who will represent planet Earth.

Before the White House can mutter even a word of objection, in walks Chloe DuBois, the French paratrooper from Europe; Shorty Doongara, the ostrich racer from Australia; Alexia St. Clair, the dog trainer from Antarctica; Baktu, the camel jockey from Africa; Jaya Kumar, the elephant whisperer from Asia; and Dogo Berto, the aviator from South America, all ready to take Earth's greatest journey for all humankind. Time is running out to qualify. There are only six candidates, yet seven are required to represent all the continents of planet Earth.

We then see a familiar cowboy hat rise high in the air. It's Zeno announcing he will be the seventh to join the team. "Make us all proud, space cowboy!" cries the Doc as he gathers the team. There's no time to waste.

With just seconds to spare, Doc directs Zeno and the team down the plank, chased by the security officials. Just in time, the Bio Lab shuts its hatch and locks its doors. Inside, a cool blue light reveals the DNA Lab. Now it is time to design their racing creatures.

Dogo eagerly steps forward, the first to do so. From the DNA panel, he selects various traits from the South American gene pool of animal characteristics and behavioral patterns. Once completed, he steps into the blue light to automatically sync with his "creation" to reveal a sight never-before-seen by earthling eyes!

Candidates step into the DNA Lab to design their very own unique creatures. Now, the true test awaits the newbie riders. How will they fare against the very best the universe has to offer?

Mighty Madden announces, "the world is witnessing the latest and greatest ordinary heroes in such extraordinary times." As shocking as it may seem, all seven "oddball" riders successfully qualify, and must now prepare to join the race for the galactic universe. Sponsors eagerly shower each rider with endorsements. Zeno is voted as team captain since he discovered the initial alien contact. For the first time in human history, the world acts as one nation.

HD-Alien TV broadcasts live: the time has come for planet Earth to enter the great Alien Race across the galactic universe. The US Government insists the team is in danger and breaks into the Bio Lab, only to discover that no one is to

be found, not even the Doc. The large overhead screen projects a message for the entire world to see, "Team Earth has been teleported to the Galaxy of Capricornus to represent planet Earth in the Alien Race hosted by the glorious planet Zyonia...please stay tuned."

The entire population of planet Earth is glued to HD-Alien TV.

Soaring through the cosmos, light years away, we see two dimming suns rise over a strange land of towering peaks and vast valleys. We are now in a place in space that is unrecognizable to the mere human eye. Soaring downward, we rest on the wings of a strange flying alien creature guided by the beautiful princess QBQ of the Zyonian species.

Sire Kannak Nakkan, Zyonian Supreme Elder and founder of the Galactic Alien Race Federation, stands with pride as he witnesses his one and only daughter soar through the brisk Zyonian skies. Just then, Secretary Kinnik of the Syntillian species teleports into the royal sky deck announcing Team Earth's arrival.

QBQ and her winged creature personally welcome Zeno and his team to her planet. She sizes up her competition, giving the once-over to the "newbie riders" and their earthling creatures. Team Earth is surrounded by a wide variety of aliens from all corners of the cosmos ready to compete in the race for the galactic universe. Zeno wonders what on Earth they've gotten themselves into? Doc assures Zeno, "We're not on planet Earth anymore."

The roving HD-Alien TV "digi-bots" surround Sire Kannak Nakkan as Mighty Madden interviews him through the cosmic airwaves. The Sire personally shares the history of the Alien Race and how this may be the last time his glorious planet will host the race due to the vast dimming of the Twin Zyonian Suns. The Sire then announces the winner of the great Alien Race will host the "next generation" of the Galactic Alien Race Federation.

Meanwhile, all galactic teams gather in the stadium while Secretary Kinnik announces from the sacred G.A.R.F scrolls that the race will cover a 300-mile course through the toughest terrain in the most remote locations on planet Zyonia. Teams of three Quadrupeds, two Bipeds and two Flyers must race together, non-

stop, using their skills for three death-defying days. The mandatory rule is simple; each team must complete the race together or otherwise the team and its planet will be disqualified. The qualifying team that clocks in at "top speed" during the Alien Race expedition will be crowned the ultimate winner and "supreme beings" of the galactic universe. The Zyonian crowd applauds with a thunderous roar as each team is handed an official contract to sign prior to entering.

It becomes apparent to the Doc that the race would include strategic navigation from the flyers on the team, and fancy footwork from the riders to conquer the alien terrain. Zeno poses one simple question to the Doc before signing the contract. "What if we don't win?" The Doc eagerly signs the alien contract without hesitation and encourages his team to, "Enjoy the ride."

The race begins with dreams of grandeur and excitement in the brisk Zyonian air. The stadium roars with anticipation as one chosen flyer of each of the racing teams is called forth. They are given a GPS to map the Zyonian Swamplands and three RS-Trackers to help guide their team through its alien terrain.

The crowd rises with a thunderous cheer as Chloe, QBQ and all other alien flyers prepare to "take flight." The starting gun fires! The remaining members of each team charge out of the stadium along the racetrack.

Billions of earthling fans join together on pins and needles while glued to HD-Alien TV. In fact, the world is at peace for the very first time since the beginning of time. Meanwhile, Mighty Madden reports back via HD-Alien TV that the Alien Race is simply, "Out of this world!" One small problem, Zeno and his team are now missing in action.

We pull back to Secretary Kinnik holding Earth's contract in his slimy Syntillian hands. He looks up to the Doc, who is being held captive in a locked cell. "You should always read the fine print before you sign your planet away, Doc." Kinnik gives an evil grin and laughs. The Alien Race to take over the galactic universe has begun.

By Scott Robertson & Julz Chavez

ZENO "Space Cowboy" CRUZ

SCOTT: These are some of the first character sketches done for the project, investigating how Zeno might look. Throughout the book you will see that our work was mostly about experimenting and exploring what the characters, creatures and worlds of *Alien Race* could look like.

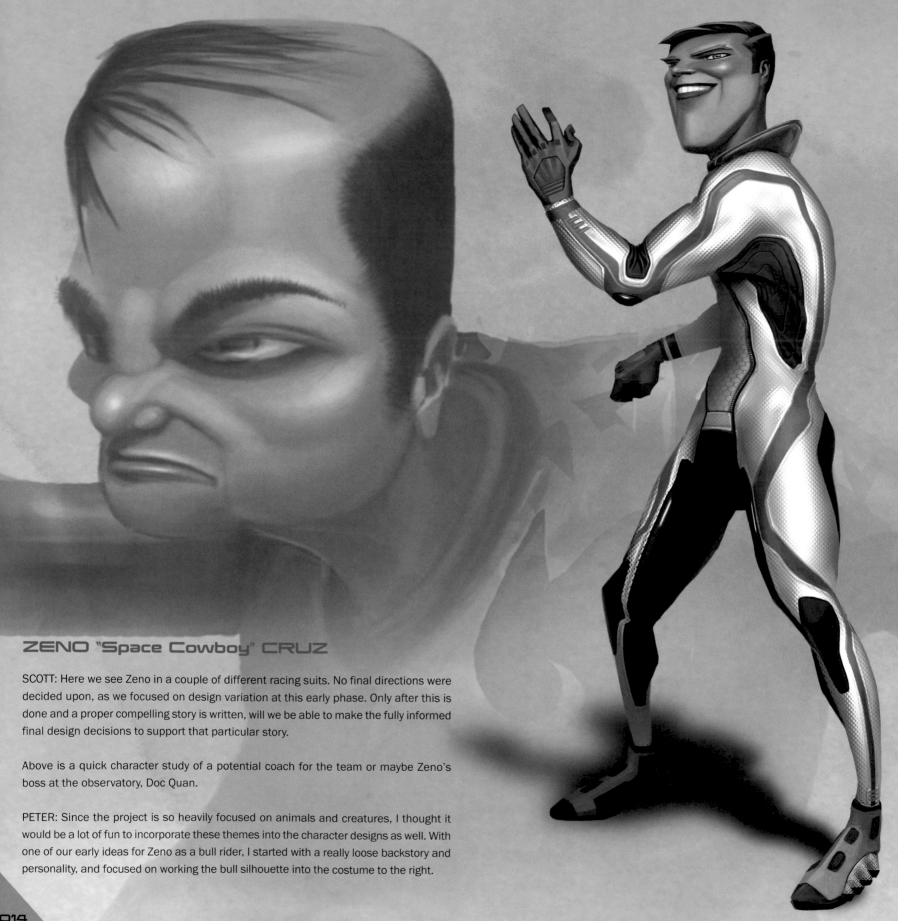

ZENO "Space Cowboy" CRUZ

SCOTT: Here we see Zeno in a couple of different racing suits. No final directions were decided upon, as we focused on design variation at this early phase. Only after this is done and a proper compelling story is written, will we be able to make the fully informed final design decisions to support that particular story.

Above is a quick character study of a potential coach for the team or maybe Zeno's boss at the observatory, Doc Quan.

PETER: Since the project is so heavily focused on animals and creatures, I thought it would be a lot of fun to incorporate these themes into the character designs as well. With one of our early ideas for Zeno as a bull rider, I started with a really loose backstory and personality, and focused on working the bull silhouette into the costume to the right.

CHLOE "Sky Diva" DUBOIS

JULZ: Demure, sultry, austere and French. Sole inheritor of her parents' estate. An extreme paratrooper and best known as the "Sky Diva" of the European skies.

SCOTT: Our early designs of Chloe were sketched using Prismacolor pencils, with Justin leading the way. Since we currently do not have large flying animals on Earth, there would be no one with any prior skills in riding this type of creature; as opposed to rodeo cowboys who already have experience in riding large beasts. So the idea of a character who enjoys being high in the air became our logical choice.

ALIEN RACE · JUSTIN PICHETRUNGSI

CHLOE "Sky Diva" DUBOIS

SCOTT: More early work by Justin shows the idea of Chloe's hair being very full and long, which might provide a fun and very distinctive look for her in the air. And the parachute harness is becoming a large part of the design theme for her costume. The straps and suit elements combine to give Justin plenty to design, and express a variety of graphic looks to her outfit. Throughout the book you will find that we as a team moved between what is a full caricature look found more in animated shows, and a live-action look found in realistic movies. This was fine, as the book is meant to be an exploration of the possibilities of our story concept, not to be heavily art directed other than to encourage variation and originality of the designs and illustrative styles.

ALEXIA ST. CLAIR

JULZ: She's an über-cool snowboarder and "techno geek." A dogsled trainer ready for any extreme challenge, with a unique ability to communicate with the K9s.

SCOTT: The rendering of Alexia on this page is a paintover of one of Peter's sketches, seen below. We had the idea that our human team should be represented equally by all of the continents on Earth. Antarctica presented the biggest challenge and the character you see here is equipped with her snow gear, holding her ski helmet and boots. We thought she might be of Norwegian descent and lead a dogsled team as part of a research group based on Antarctica.

CHLOE "Sky Diva" DUBOIS

SCOTT: On the opposite page are a few more sketches and a rendering of Chloe. The intent was to play up her long, red hair and her attitude. As all of the other human characters have some relation to animals—Zeno is a cowboy, Alexia races dogsleds, and later you will meet the other team members who also know and love animals—Chloe, on the other hand, is great at skydiving and perfectly at home free-falling through the atmosphere, but does not like animals! This could be a fun source of humor throughout the story.

PETER: I wanted the character of Chloe to be very confident, fearless, and a little bit cocky. The large, silky red hair would add a cool visual element while she races, and augment her strategy to mesmerize her competitors.

ALIEN RACE · PETER CHAN ▐ ▌ ▌ ▌ ▌ ▌

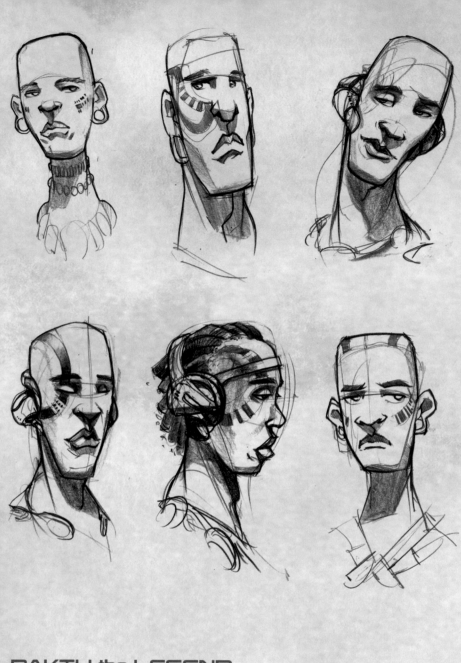

BAKTU the LEGEND

JULZ: He's a famous nomadic camel jockey from the Taureg Tribe of Timbuktu. Wise beyond words, Baktu knows how to survive for days on end in the desert heat.

SCOTT: John joined this project in the second summer of development and did a great job of rounding out Team Earth. On these pages we took a very stylized approach to the suit and character designs, as we imagined *Alien Race* having appeal as an animated show.

DOGO BERTO

JULZ: Legend has it that Dogo was once rescued by a flock of Condors while he was lost up high in the Peruvian Andes.

SCOTT: Our story calls for two flyers, and Dogo is our second. While Chloe's long, red hair provides a nice element to animate while flying, Dogo has a red scarf to achieve a similar goal...helping the viewer to feel the wind through the movement of this costume element.

JAYA KUMAR

PETER: I wanted this character to be cheerful, adventurous and always able to get out of troubled situations during the race because of her positive personality. As with Zeno, I incorporated animal shape influences in the design of her costume, this time with elephants in mind.

JULZ: Daughter of the famous Mahout, best known as the "elephant whisperer." She inherited her father's gift, but the old tradition won't allow her to live her true purpose.

SUKI SAN / SHORTY DOONGARA

JULZ: Suki is Dogo's best friend and trainer. Shorty is an Australian ostrich jockey, a gladiator among men at four feet and three inches tall.

SCOTT: We tried hard to keep our earthling team silhouettes strong and distinctly different from rider to rider. With Shorty, his silhouette is very clearly defined in his name. He might be small in stature, but he is not short of courage!

ALTERNATES

SCOTT: On these and the next pages are a few riders who didn't make the cut. I still like them and they have a place in this book because it is important to explore designs that don't quite fit. That is how you confirm that the design decisions and directions of the final team are correct. I could also image the characters to the right as alternates to the final team and that they might not be too happy about that, hence their expressions.

VOODOO

PETER: With all the other Earth riders being heroic, I thought it would be great to create someone totally evil and devious. The Voodoo's abilities to put a death curse on other riders, or to use magic to slow them, would add some fun game play as a video-game character.

ALIEN RACE · JUSTIN PICHETRUNGSI

HEXLINGS of "Sector Six"

JULZ: Data-driven alien species from the six-sided collective holo-gram of planet Hex. Also known as the "bad boys" of the Galactic Universe and most feared species in the galaxy of Capricornus.

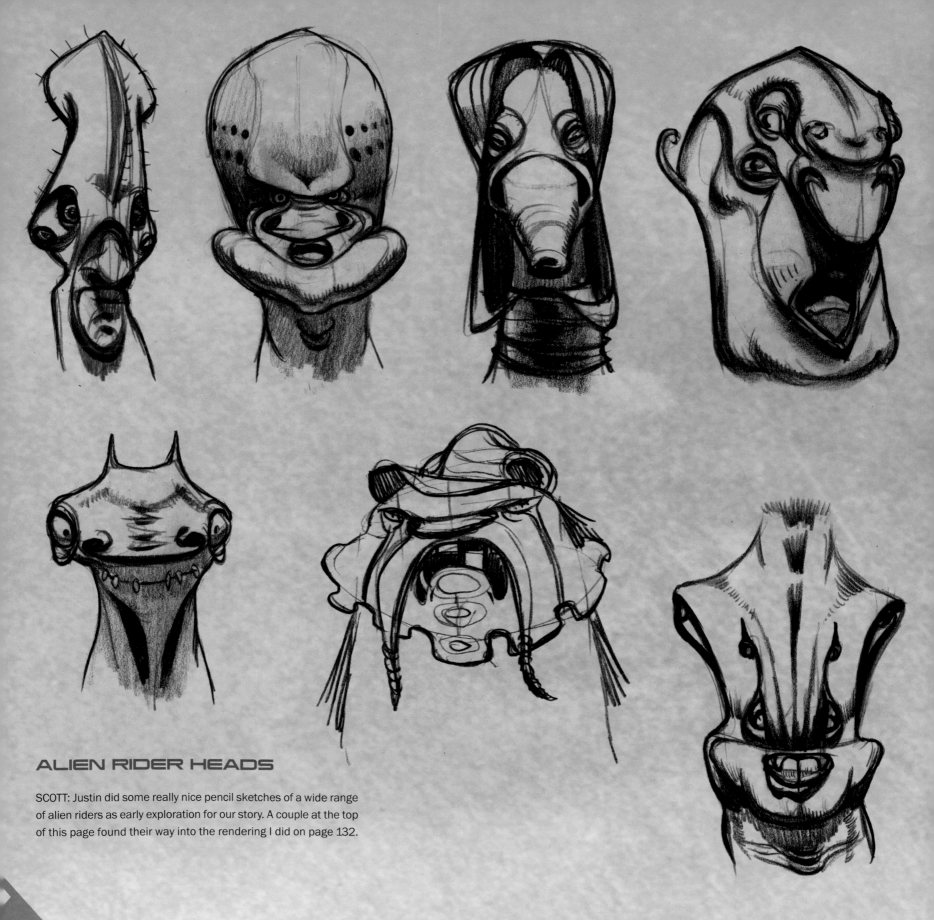

ALIEN RIDER HEADS

SCOTT: Justin did some really nice pencil sketches of a wide range of alien riders as early exploration for our story. A couple at the top of this page found their way into the rendering I did on page 132.

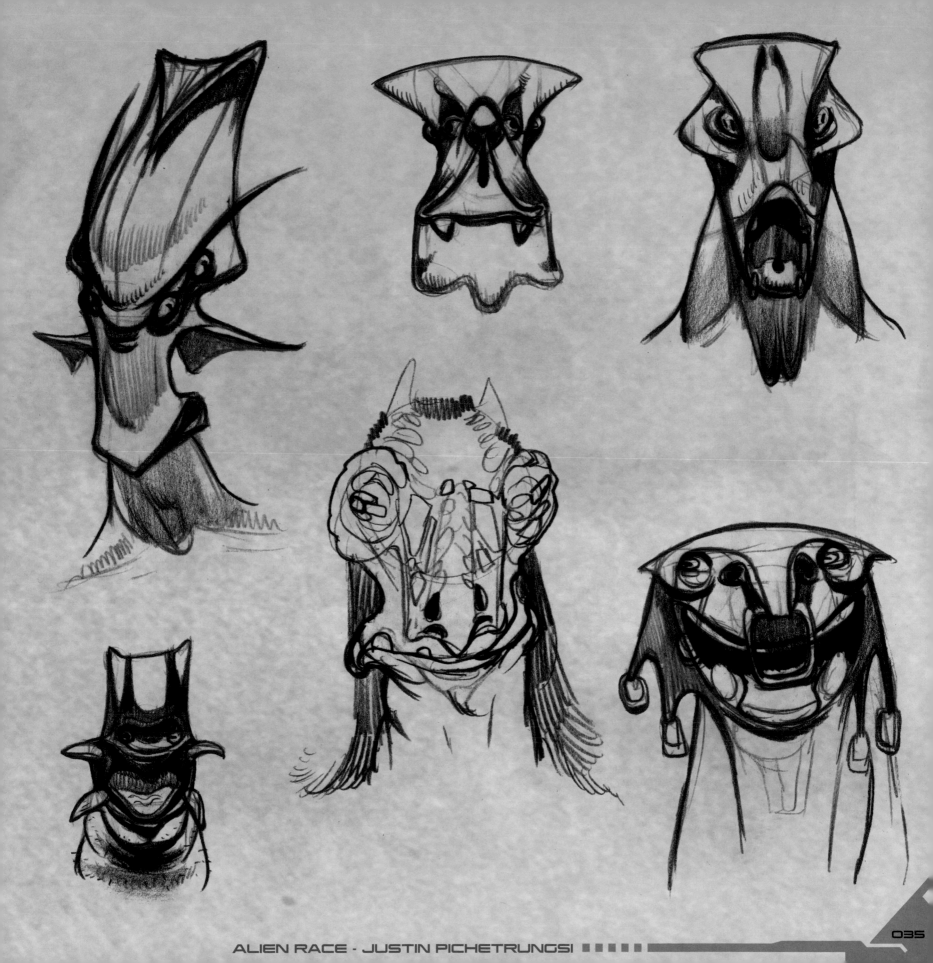

ALIEN RIDER HEADS

SCOTT: Peter also contributed some great alien rider studies with these pencil sketches. As with two of Justin's aliens from the previous spread ending up on page 132, the guy to the far right midway up the page also made it into that rendering. We decided early on to keep our aliens very anthropomorphic so as to make it easier for our audience to relate to them.

ALIEN RIDERS

SCOTT: Here are more of the nice design studies Peter contributed. On page 63 these sketches were used as the basis for a few color renderings. I also used the sketch of the lanky alien second from the left, directly below, as the start for the "Syntillian Diva" on page 146. It's a lot fun to work as a team and share sketches and renderings back and forth, to do collaborative pieces that quite often combine to be more successful than any one of us could have achieved on our own. Fresh eyes and energy can sometimes elevate a design to the next level, just as the original designer is running out of steam to pursue the initial design any further.

ALIEN RACE - PETER CHAN

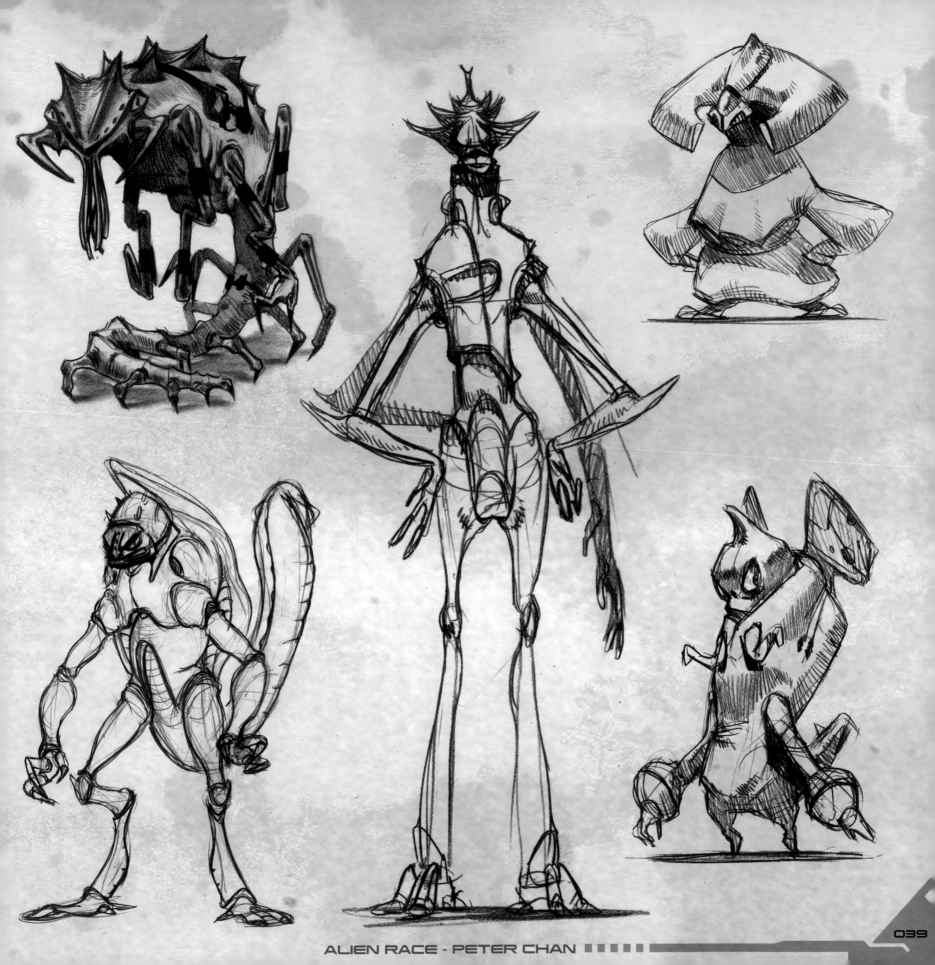

PROGRAMS! PROGRAMS!

BEN: I imagined this character as one of the merchants in the stands who would sell programs to keep the crowds informed of the status of the races. I tried to keep his outfit intentionally low-tech and clunky to contrast with the streamlined, flashy look of the well-funded racers.

SCOTT: I'm not sure of the backstory of John's character on the facing page, but I imagine him as an old past champion.

PETER: I wanted an old veteran alien rider in the story. Maybe he's a retired medal winner from races decades ago. The General feels like he still has the chops and decides to participate again with the younger generation of riders.

opposite: Commentator of the intense alien racing action!

SYNTILLIAN FANBOYS

SCOTT: These are some of the first sketches done to try to define the design of the Syntillians, who host the Alien Race. I really liked the body that Justin came up with to the right, but I was not that excited about the head. The head study on the opposite page was done by Peter and if you turn the page upside down you will see where we found our design direction for the look of the heads of the Syntillian race. When trying to invent original designs, be sure to look at them in different orientations. Occasionally you will discover the unexpected.

SECRETARY KINNIK / PINNIP

JULZ: Secretary Kinnik is wicked, slimy, conniving and of the auspicious genetically-engineered Syntillian Species from the planet of Zyonia. He's a megalomaniac by nature and determined to become the Master of the Galactic Universe and Supreme Ruler over planet Earth.

Pinnip is the sweet, painfully shy and adoringly "plump" scribe and indentured servant to Secretary Kinnik and the Syntillian Tribunal.

SCOTT: Kinnik is our main evil character and a part of the royal Syntillian family. I chose purple as the color for the royal Syntillians as it is frequently associated with past royal families of our own here on Earth.

ALIEN RACE · SCOTT ROBERTSON

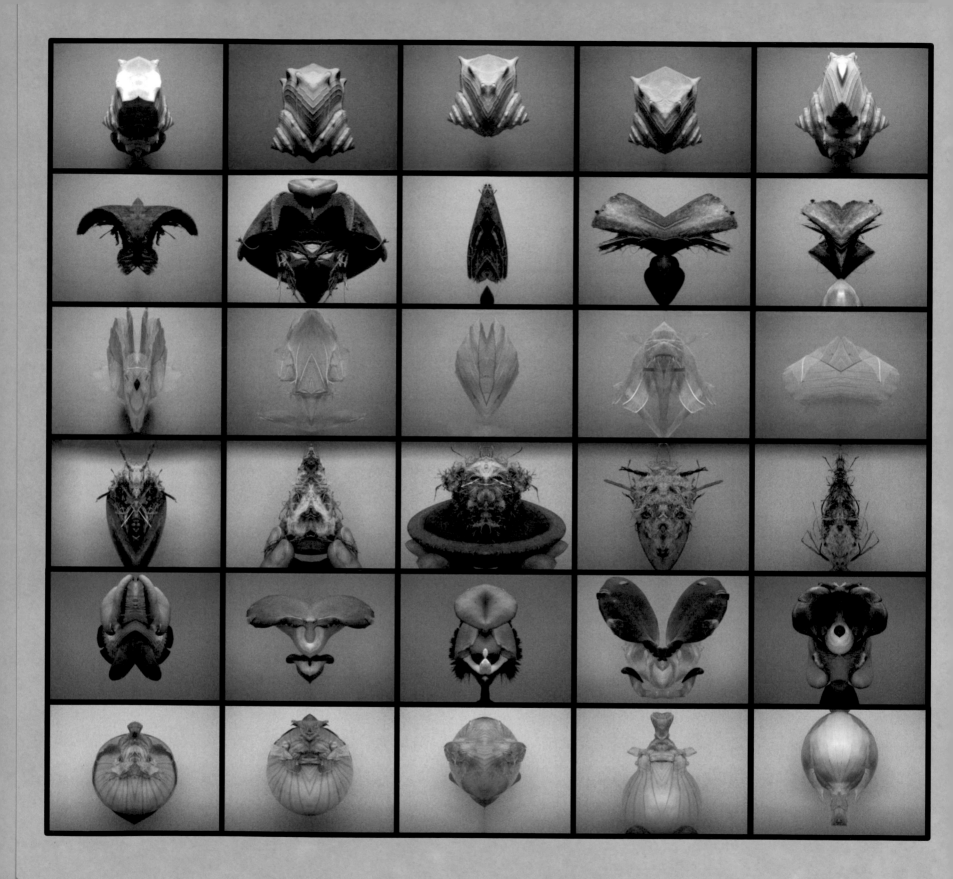

ALIEN RACE - SCOTT ROBERTSON

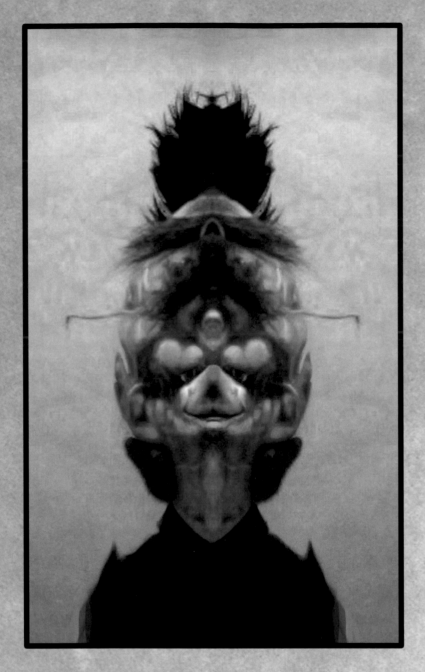

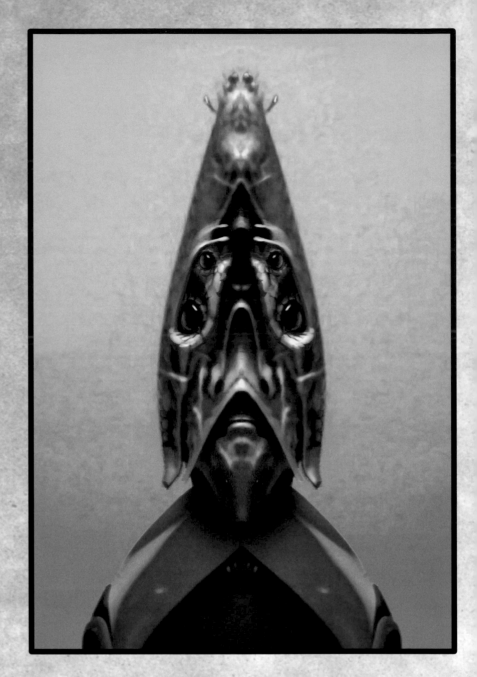

ROOT / MUSHROOM / MEAT

SCOTT: Some of the source images that we captured needed very little in the way of a paintover to fully realize a design direction. The alien in the upper right-hand corner of the opposite page is an example of one of these images. This alien came from a frog sculpture that Neville had done...thanks to Nev for letting me include it here. It required very little painting on my part to find the direction. Generally I would recommend using very abstract sources for design directions, and I usually make it a point to stay away from objects created by others. Found objects from nature often provide the best, most unique and original directions.

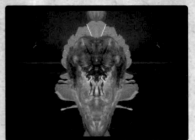

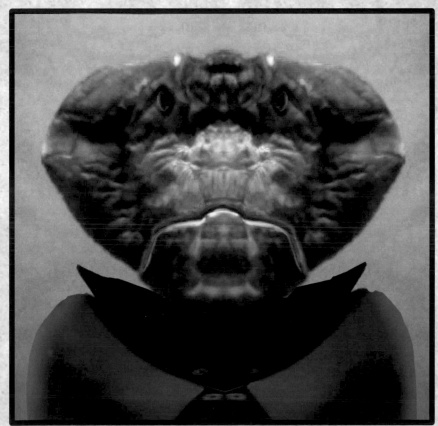

HUSBAND / WIFE

SCOTT: To the right are photos of my wife and me. Not the type of headshots you would send to Grandma! My beauty shot is of my head tilted almost 90 degrees with my hand in front of my face holding a rubber wine stopper with a small rock in the end for the eyes. Melissa's alien double was a combination of my hand holding an iPod and her head tilted 90 degrees behind that. I did a quick paintover and color tweak and there you have it...instant husband and wife aliens! My head was also the source for the alien directly above; the hair should be the clue.

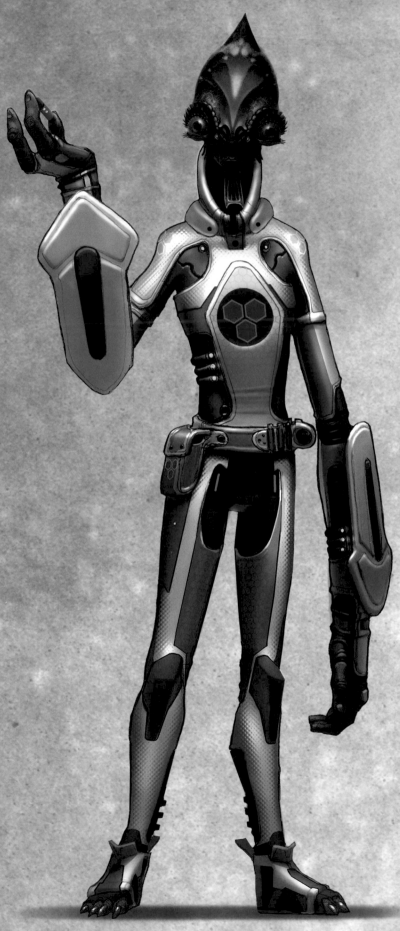

MEAT / POTATO / SHELL

SCOTT: Ben and John painted the aliens above from a variety of sources; I recognize my foot in the two above left. The head on the full-length alien came from a paintover of a red potato I did, and Ben finished off the suit and body. Ben did a wonderful design study and illustration of the alien on the opposite page starting from a seashell source image. As these pages show, we not only used the Photo Booth technique to find the heads of our characters but also for the start of their costumes.

ALIEN BODY STUDIES

SCOTT: John and I went for the full team effort on these aliens. I had done the heads already and later asked John to figure out what their bodies would look like. Several of these body designs started life as earlier sketches by Peter. I have to admit that my favorite is the green guy above, as it reminds me of myself as an alien posing as an Elvis impersonator! Well done, John.

ALIEN RACE · JOHN PARK · SCOTT ROBERTSON ▮▮▮▮▮

REX from HEX

SCOTT: This character started life as the Photo Booth image to the left. It is a seashell I found buried in a basket of shells at my mother's home in Colorado. After a bit of rendering and the addition of a neck, shoulders and a mouth (via more mirroring, this time of a shark ray jawbone), Rex was born. He is the most feared and ruthless rider in the universe, despite his baby blue eyes.

FANDOOT

SCOTT: I always laugh at this one due to the fact that the source photo was of my wife's hand and foot. Adding a pair of goggles and a helmet that appears to be a bit too small, we now have a blockheaded alien not to be taken lightly, as she appears to have attitude to spare!

ALIEN RACE · SCOTT ROBERTSON

ALIEN RACE · SCOTT ROBERTSON

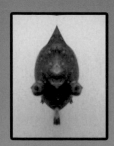

SCOTT: An old red potato provided all the inspiration I needed to find this stylish rider. By adding a suit that came from a bike helmet I had designed, this old potato was transformed into another alien rider. After finding the design direction by painting one side and then duplicating and mirroring it to the other side, it is nice to take a bit of time to go one step further by tilting the head and giving the character a bit more life.

SCOTT: Every good story needs a wise elder. This is one possible direction for that type of character. The source photo in this case was a bird's nest in a wooden bowl. Again, thanks to my mom's shelf of oddities. I left the character study in a symmetrical pose to contrast against the other studies that are tilted and warped a bit. This provides a comparison to illustrate the benefits of manipulating the design direction to add more character.

DR. CAFFEINE

SCOTT: If you know what I look like then you might be able to see my head tilted sideways and my hand holding a seashell for the eyes. I played up the long crazy hair to create Dr. Caffeine!

SHELLAZAR

SCOTT: This study remains one of my personal favorites. On the top of page 52 are the other shell source images I had to chose from. Once I had a direction for this race of aliens, I could more easily go to the other shell images and paint over them to round out a team of alien riders for the great race. The armor is from another Photo Booth series of source images seen at the top of page 51. The original source object was a snowboard helmet. I imagine this character to be a noble past champion, strong and fair in his racing techniques.

HAPOD

SCOTT: My hand holding an iPod in its case makes the basis of this character. After turning the iPod area into a pair of goggles I really warped the shape of the rider to give the study more energy and life. This is one of the hippest riders in the galaxy, but don't underestimate her superior riding skills! She is still a fierce, albeit calm and always collected, rider of one of the most powerful flyers ever to compete in the Alien Race.

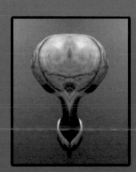

LIL' SPRITEX

SCOTT: One of the cutest riders around, Spritex can finish with the best of them. The source photo above looks a bit spooky though; it was a human anatomical maquette of Neville's. I did quite a bit of painting over this one, but you can still easily see the inspiration of the basic form: big head, small neck. By going "pink" I was trying to get away from the creepy look of the source image.

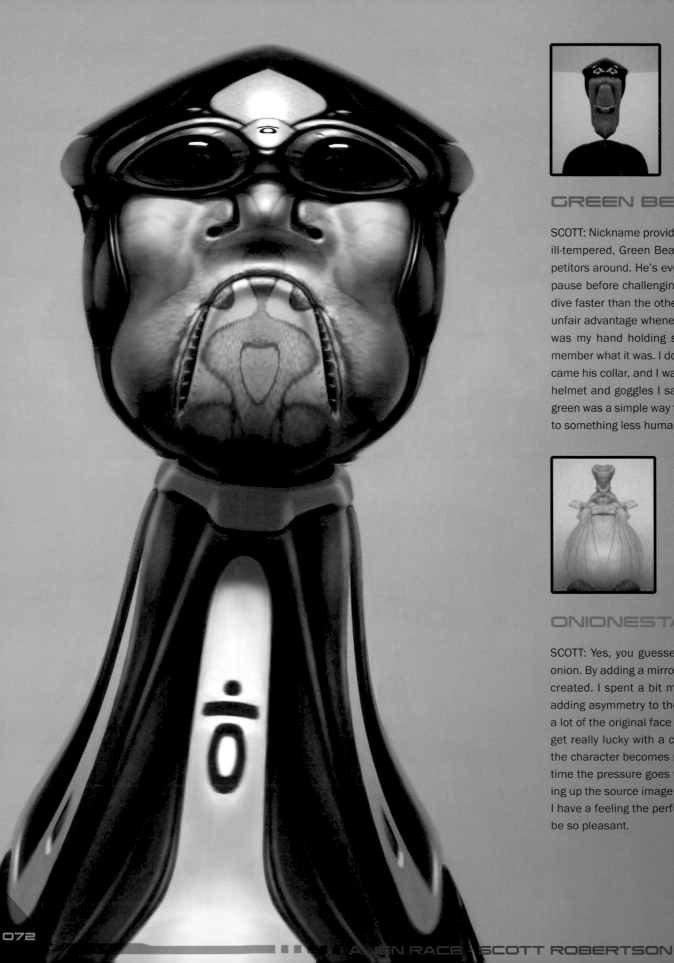

GREEN BEAN

SCOTT: Nickname provided by Zeno. Ace flyer and very ill-tempered, Green Bean is one of the nastiest competitors around. He's even known to give the Hexlings pause before challenging him. In his aero-suit he can dive faster than the others and uses this ability for an unfair advantage whenever he can. The source above was my hand holding something; I do not even remember what it was. I do know that my ring is what became his collar, and I was drawn to this guy by the fun helmet and goggles I saw in the source. Making him green was a simple way to shift the source image color to something less human-looking.

ONIONESTA

SCOTT: Yes, you guessed it, this rider started as an onion. By adding a mirrored piece of bark the suit was created. I spent a bit more time rendering this one, adding asymmetry to the face and pose. You can see a lot of the original face in the onion photo. When you get really lucky with a cool photo, the job of refining the character becomes much easier; but at the same time the pressure goes way up with the fear of messing up the source image and losing its original appeal. I have a feeling the perfume from this alien might not be so pleasant.

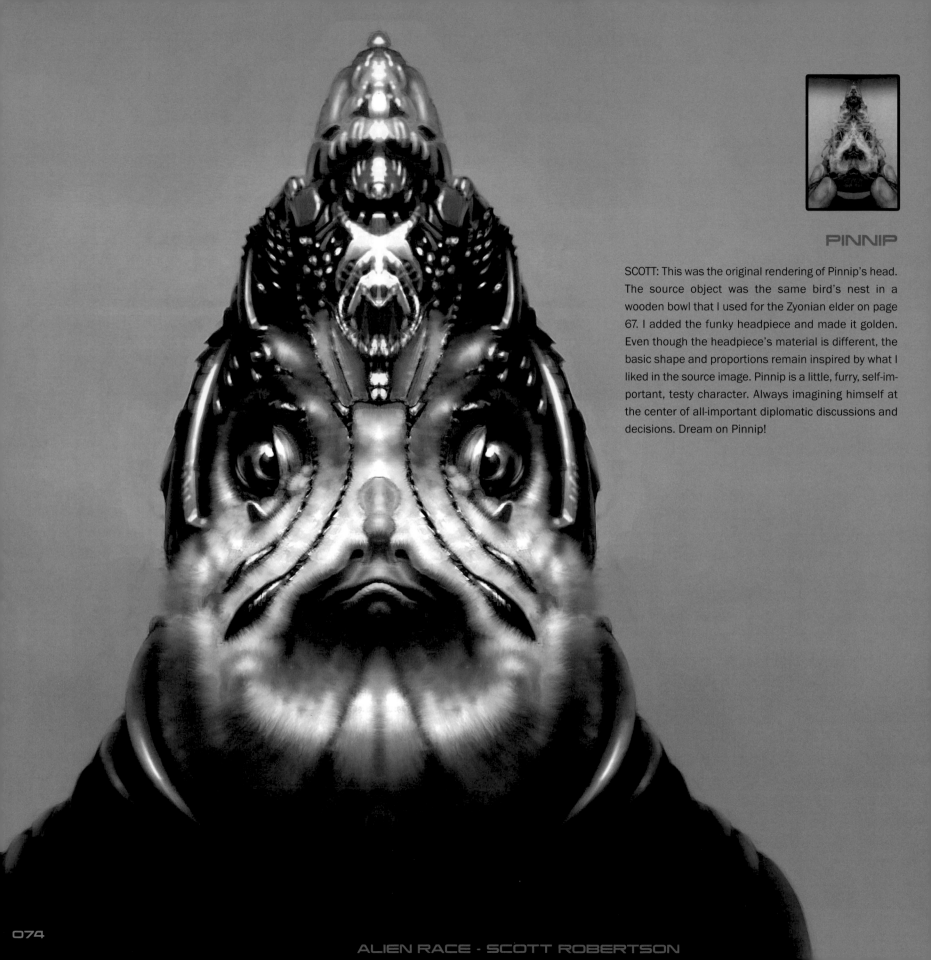

PINNIP

SCOTT: This was the original rendering of Pinnip's head. The source object was the same bird's nest in a wooden bowl that I used for the Zyonian elder on page 67. I added the funky headpiece and made it golden. Even though the headpiece's material is different, the basic shape and proportions remain inspired by what I liked in the source image. Pinnip is a little, furry, self-important, testy character. Always imagining himself at the center of all-important diplomatic discussions and decisions. Dream on Pinnip!

SHELLA

SCOTT: Another source image from a seashell. The eyes, nose and mouth were very clearly defined, to my eye, in the source photo. The little flippers protruding forward from the sides of the head could still use some refinement, but they also might contribute a humorous element to express his emotions if he were ever to be animated. Of course his overly large, bulging eyes would go a long way to communicate his temperament.

INSECTOIDS

SCOTT: These were probably some of the easiest racing creatures for me to design as they were the most like vehicles, with hard shells, pivots, etc.... This was a good place to begin as I ventured into the realm of creatures. For our story we set up three skeletal types for the racing creatures: bipeds, quadrupeds and flyers. In the hope that *Alien Race* will eventually become a video game, this should make it easier to morph the same basic skeleton into a wide range of shapes without having to reinvent the animation rig over and over.

STYLE TESTS

SCOTT: One of the most enjoyable parts of creating any imaginary world is in exploring the infinite illustrative styles that the artwork can take. The art here started with the brush-pen ink sketches from the previous pages. I then spent an afternoon messing about in Photoshop to achieve the range of styles shown here. I happened upon the artistic cutout filter and after some experimentation, I found that it worked best with my simple black and white sketches. The more graphic they were to start with, the better the abstracted results. After a pass with this filter, I had a stylized sketch with various levels of grey within it where none had existed before. The next step was to apply different colors to the range of values using the color-balance sliders. I tried adding a multiply gradient over a few like the one at the top-right of this page and that was it, from black and white brush-pen ink sketch to stylized, colorful, Photoshop happy accident! The final touch was to composite them onto the background. I selected them off of the backgrounds in their original files and layered them onto this spread. Notice how they have varying levels of opacity and some areas drop out all together to let the background color and texture of the page show through.

ALIEN RACE - SCOTT ROBERTSON

ALIEN RACE · JUSTIN PICHETRUNGSI

KNUCKLE WALKERS
MEGA CHICKEN

SCOTT: One of the most fun things that came to mind when we were developing the creatures was to, of course, go BIG! *Alien Race* is a fantasy world; it is place to let our concept design minds run free and explore as we liked, from the behemoth "knuckle walker" on the facing page to the "mega chicken" above. A nIce addition to the sketch on this page was the little flying camera bot. You will see these roaming cam-bots throughout the *Alien Race* world. It would not be a sci-fi racing story without flying cameras!

ALIEN RACE - THOM TENERY

DINO

SCOTT: Here are a few more entrants into the great race, a Manga-inspired character and his racer (above) and a wonderfully colored and stylized biped (opposite). Justin's version of the biped racer explores one of the areas I thought about a lot, which was how can such a small rider control such a large creature? In a few pages you will see one of my design solutions. I did not want the team to lose the relationship of the rider to the creature, which is most challenging in the designs that do not incorporate reins.

PETER: This female biped runner is a specialist in an icy cold climate. Well-developed feet help her to keep steady, and provide more grip with the ground. Her long antennae give her supreme balance as well as detect nearby competitors. When racing during the heavy snow season, Vanilla Ice is almost invisible.

ALIEN RACE · PETER CHAN

DINO STYLE / HARD SHELL

SCOTT: The design below achieves the relationship of the rider to his creature through the use of some very hi-tech reins. The reins slim down to cables that control the appliqués on the sides of creature's head. These sci-fi devices control the movements of the large creature by stimulating certain regions of its brain, which gives this small rider the ability to control the big biped.

I really like the relationship of cowboys to their horse's movement via the reins, but didn't want these reins to appear too familiar. There are many types of reins throughout the book but I think this particular direction is a nice way to go for several of the very large creatures. The image on the facing page was an afternoon paintover of the stylized orange sketch from page 82.

ALIEN RACE · THOM TENERY

095

IIIIII ALIEN RACE - BEN MAURO

SCOTT: Here are a couple of flyers for the race. Lots of attitude on the facing page; not a flyer I would like to race against! The design below features some of the very strong colors bioengineered into many of the racers to play up the festive nature of some alien entrants.

ALIEN RACE - JOHN PARK

JOHN: These flyer concepts were generated through the use of a theme: extreme sports. I tried to keep in mind how the rider would control these bird-like creatures.

ALIEN RACE - JUSTIN PICHETRUNG

BIG NUMBER NINE

SCOTT: This was one of the first flyers done for the project. We found over and over again that the easiest way to start exploring the relationship of rider to creature was to reference creatures that exist on own planet, then bump up their size, add a saddle, reins, a rider, do a nice rendering and we were off to the races!

GREEN SCREAMER

JOHN: The concept behind this particular flyer was inspired by one of my close friends, Justin Pichetrungsi. The snapshot of the screaming creature was a depiction of energy, excitement and determination. The rider controls the bird's wings through the use of direct steering, which is through the bird's scapula. Although the bird is in pain, it screams and swoops for the finish line.

ALIEN RACE - JOHN PARK

ROCK BAND FLYER

JOHN: As music plays into the ears of the alien rider, he drums the rhythm to the bird, to communicate direction and control. Like a concertgoer, each drumbeat stimulates and manipulates the bird's physical patterns. In this way, the bird and the rider fly together in sync.

ALIEN RACE · THOM TENERY

MANTA CANINE / MEAN GREEN

SCOTT: On this page Justin was loosely playing around with combining canine DNA with that of a manta ray. Since our story has a lot of fantasy, it allows for this type of fun creation to be not only believable but encouraged. On the opposite page is a concept Justin had for the nemesis rider Zeno would battle continually throughout the story. The creature is mostly a running quadruped, but also has the ability to jump and glide for short distances.

ALIEN RACE - JUSTIN PICHETRUNGSI

ALIEN RACE · JUSTIN PICHETRUNGSI ▮▮▮▮▮

PHOTOSHOP - ARTISTIC CUTOUT FILTER

SCOTT: These sketches are further investigations of the artistic cutout filter of Photoshop applied to some very simple art, as explained on page 82. The drawings on the facing page started as scanned marker sketches, the drawing below-right was a black ink brush-pen sketch, and the one directly below, the alien on a kind of "speed cow," was originally a pencil and watercolor sketch. I was looking through my early sketches where I was teaching myself how to draw animals, and I thought that by abstracting these a bit they might make for a nice addition to the book as a way to demonstrate how even very simple work can be abstracted and stylized to help find new design directions. A refined and rendered version of the sketch below-right can be seen on page 139. I'm a big fan of manipulating my own work to allow for the "happy accident" to lead me down a different design path than the one I first took while doing the original sketch.

ALIEN RACE · SCOTT ROBERTSON ▮▮▮▮▮

QUADRUPED WARM UP

SCOTT: As a "newbie" to drawing animals, I designed this project partly to force me to figure this out and broaden my own skill sets. I would suggest to any of you who have a similar goal to improve your own animal-drawing skills, that you do what I did, which is to pick up a few good educational drawing books on the subject. Some of my favorites are by Joe Weatherly, a fantastic draftsman, fine artist and teacher. You can find his contact info on the last page of this book. *Thanks for the help Joe, I hope you like the book."*

STARTING SIMPLE

SCOTT: The sketches on the previous two pages, as well as these, were part of my first weekend of drawing animals for this project. They were stylized again in Photoshop and aren't that inventive yet as original designs for *Alien Race,* but they represent an important educational step in learning to draw and design a new subject.

ALIEN RACE - SCOTT ROBERTSON

BIG DOGS

SCOTT: More early brush-pen sketches. This time working with the idea of big bioengineered dogs as the basis for these designs. They served as a good first exploration of the scale of the riders in relation to the size of the animals. As our project began to veer more toward animation than live-action, it allowed us to abstract the animals' anatomy a little more. This was really convenient for me, as I faked the anatomy throughout with all my creatures. I did not even scratch the surface of how much time one should really devote to learning the anatomy of the animals of our own planet before hoping to invent convincing abstractions of those for something taking place on another planet.

THE RENDEZVOUS AT THE START

JULZ: The Alien Race covers a 300-mile course through the toughest terrain in the most remote locations on planet Zyonia. Teams of 3 Quadrupeds, 2 Bipeds and 2 Flyers must race together, non-stop, using their skills for three death-defying Zyonian days. One mandatory rule is simple: each team must complete the race as a team; otherwise the team and its planet will be disqualified. The qualifying team that clocks in at "top speed" during the Alien Race expedition will be crowned the ultimate winner and "supreme beings" of the Master Universe.

ALIEN RACE - BEN MAURO

TEAM EUROPTRA

BEN: I find it helpful to create backstories while working, which adds purpose to the overall aesthetics of each design. Creating a set of parameters allows me get to a finished solution more quickly. The story behind this set of creatures was that an advanced civilization would harvest the most aggressive animals from local planets and retrofit their cutting-edge technology onto them. The saddles are meant to enhance and control the more aggressive qualities of the beasts, to help give the team an edge in the races.

DARSHIAN

BEN: My thoughts on the concept of *Alien Race* were that of a bizarre, futuristic MotoGP. After looking at real-world motorcycles and horse-racing saddles, I took some of the basic mechanics and functionality of the rider/vehicle relationship

and extrapolated it into something (hopefully) new, yet believable. Looking at many of the aggressive, streamlined forms found in modern racing bikes, I attempted to translate a similar form language into the saddles on my creatures.

THE CHALLENGE

SCOTT: While painting this piece I imagined the alien rider on this page to be a grumpy, arrogant, older past champion, engaged in some pre-race taunting of an earthling rider. This does not sit well with the earthling and he responds with his own universal hand gesture.

ALIEN RACE · SCOTT ROBERTSON

SCOTT: Below, a horse-inspired design with a fully armored rider atop. Strong colors and graphics set apart both the rider and the creature from the field of other competitors. This quadruped, named Antigus, has a very long, hinged tail that unfolds to help with balance as it runs around sharp corners. The odd hooves, more like big toes, provide excellent grip. That ability, coupled with the articulating tail, make this one formidable racer!

ALIEN RACE - SCOTT ROBERTSON

PORK GONE WRONG

SCOTT: Both of these color renderings started as simple pig-inspired pencil sketches, like those in the upper right. After scanning them, I looked through my Photo Booth "happy accident" alien-creation database, and collaged together multiple images that became the basis for both of these creatures' heads. The beast to the left started as a kind of large wild boar, and then I thought the human rider from page 28 had the right attitude to pair with it. The perspective worked out so I perched him atop and that one was done. The wacky critter above was thought to be a sort of bucking bronco training ride for the earthling riders. The saddle is fairly slick with no stirrups, and each of our quadruped-riding heroes would train on this guy before heading off to race on alien planets. I worked a lot to establish a dynamic relationship between rider and animal that I wanted all of the action poses to have throughout the book.

THE LOSER

SCOTT: This is one of the first character combinations I painted for the book. Long before we decided to go more hi-tech for the saddles, I had done some research at the local horse-racing track and the photography from that day informed this quick color sketch. One of the easiest ways to communicate that this is a character for a race is to add a number and sponsorship logo. Unfortunately, in this case DSP backed a loser. Hopefully we'll have better luck next time!

SYNTILLIAN DIVA

SCOTT: This is an early concept for QBQ, the Syntillian princess, seen here on her poodle-horse-pelicanesque racing quad. She is all attitude and quite the alien "Diva."

ALIEN RACE · PETER CHAN · SCOTT ROBERTSON

ALIEN RACE - SCOTT ROBERTSON

ALIEN RACE - PETER CHAN

PETER: The royal family of Kaomsh has participated in every intergalactic race for the past 5 centuries, but has failed to achieve results that live up to the expectations of the king. This year, the newly crowned prince is determined to win with his specially bio-engineered stallion, Gold Rush. Gold Rush has swift and accurate reflexes that give him an advantage in overcoming most obstacles and traps. The breathing apparatus on the lower part of his jaw benefits him in the changing climates and protects him from pollutants in the air.

GREEN BERETTA

PETER: Decades after the war, this tribe of mercenaries reached a peace treaty with their enemies. Now having no violent use for their war equipment and trained warriors, they decided to enter the race with the advantage of already being equipped and trained for any kind of combat or strategic situation. The characteristics of Green Beretta are that they are very aggressive, violent, and calculated. They do not believe in mistakes under any circumstances. Many expect this duo to take the race with ease...so put your hard-earned money on Green Beretta!

ALIEN RACE - PETER CHAN

ELECTRO SHOCK

PETER: Electro Shock is an oversized bioengineered bull. He is engineered through Earth's most advanced race-car technology, making him more speed machine than actual animal. His veins run with high voltage electrical cables that generate a maximum amount of nitro, allowing his speed to be paramount. One of the most anticipated performances is Electro's ability to generate magnetic shields, which protect him from harm, as well as temporarily paralyzing aggressive racers. Electro Shock is Earth's last secret weapon that could claim the galactic racing trophy once and for all.

ALIEN RACE · SCOTT ROBERTSON

STRONG TO THE FINISH

SCOTT: This sketch best represents the type of piece I wish I'd had time to do more of—a couple of alien racers hard at it in an interesting alien environment. As I found during our visual development for this story, it is one thing to learn to draw and design a decent racing quad in a static pose—it is altogether another steep learning curve to skillfully compose multiple racers next to each other in the proper perspective in a convincing mid-stride action shot! Alas, not this time around. Hopefully I will find the time to finish more of the pieces I have like this, all in various stages of completion, to be included in a second printing, or at the very least on my blog.

CHECKPOINT BRAVO

SCOTT: This was a fun one to paint. With the wide range of local color I tried to differentiate each racer and their creatures. The scene idea was of a Syntillian race-support crew being directed by their foreman to get the objects at the end of the poles to the riders before they head off for the next leg of the race.

ALIEN RACE · SCOTT ROBERTSON

ALIEN RACE - THOM TENERY

BIO LAB ARRIVAL

THOM: A slow swirling vortex of unnatural weather over the East River was the first indication that this would be no ordinary day in New York City. Hundreds of taxi drivers felt their hair stand on end and heard their car radios crackle and buzz just before the event. Tendrils of green light emerged from the clouds, searching out the perfect location to root a structure. A chaos of light and smoke and inconceivable alien energies preceded the arrival of the bio lab. Everything humankind knew about the universe was about to change....

From the vantage point of a soldier aboard one of the first military vessels ordered to investigate, we can see the alien bio lab towering over the United Nations Building like some colossal, mechanical vegetation growing from the East River. The world's military forces keep their distance, awaiting the U.N.'s decision. The ship's cat hasn't the faintest idea what his animal brethren are in for.

BIO LAB INTERIOR

THOM: The bio lab gave the scientists of Earth the ability to genetically combine the most unrelated species, creating bizarre new creatures with previously unimaginable physical characteristics. The possibilities for creating faster, stronger, more specialized species for racing were almost endless. And with the accelerated growth-rate technology of the lab, it was possible to engineer and produce these animals in real time! Getting accustomed to advanced alien technology was no small feat. The lab came with instructions, of course, but there were bound to be a few unfortunate incidents....

ZYONIAN COLISEUM

SCOTT: This is definitely one of the most awe-inspiring locales in our story, the Zyonian Coliseum, with hundreds of alien racers gathered from throughout the Master Universe, preparing for battle in front of the adoring Syntillian race fans.

ALIEN RACE · JUSTIN PICHETRUNGSI

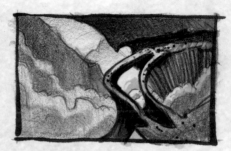

SUB-ZERO TERRAIN

PETER: These sketches focus a bit more on the different terrains of a single racecourse. I was interested in what kinds of movements or actions could occur through various obstacles: from flat ground, sharp turns and precarious ledges, to a grand finish.

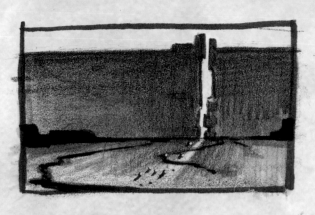
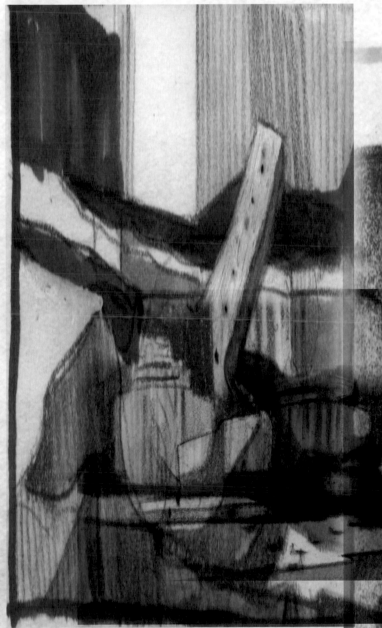

ALIEN RACE - PETER CHAN ▌▐ ▌▐ ▌▐

SEARCH FOR DNA / SKY SPORES

THOM: We had a lot of fun exploring the potential that Photoshop custom brushes bring to the design process. It is a great advantage to have a library of custom brush shapes on hand for the purpose of encouraging "happy accidents." This scene depicts an underwater expedition to capture an animal with a particularly aggressive temperament, for breeding a fiercer racer. The sketch for this scenario came together in about five minutes. One of the first marks I made resembled a large fish head full of sharp teeth. That fish head eventually became the tower of rock in the background, but the initial shapes inspired the narrative that was then fleshed out as a more finished illustration. With just a few brushstrokes an entire world suggested itself. Opposite, the sky atolls provide a particularly dangerous environment for the flyers. At this time every year at high altitudes, the Cococabbages release millions of spores into the tropical winds. Flyers must dodge the spiked spores as they tumble through the sky toward the turquoise waters below.

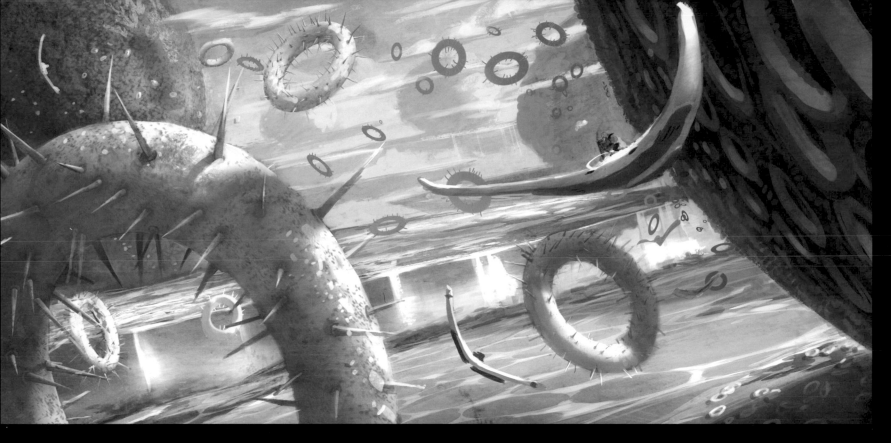

ALIEN RACE - THOM TENERY

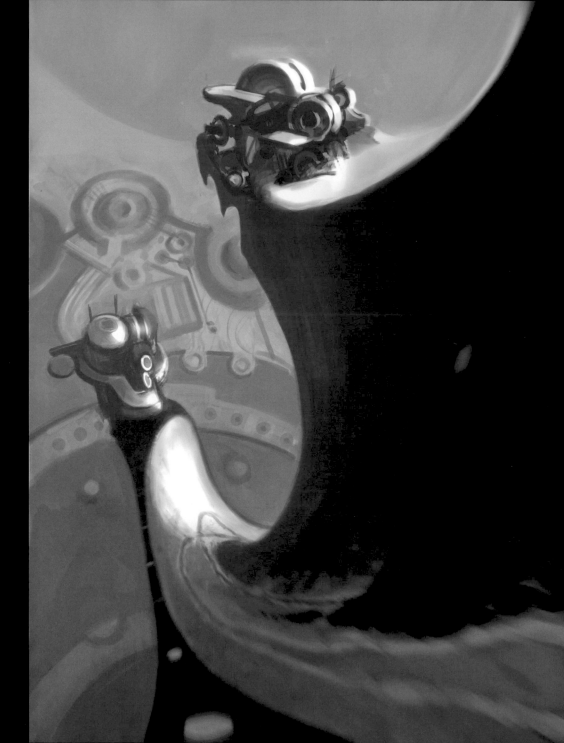

SLOPE OF DEATH

PETER: Wanting to design a cool video-gaming experience, I thought an extreme downhill sliding race would add a lot of excitement. This shot went through an interesting process, starting with pushing the shapes toward more of an animation style, then finishing them off with a little more refinement. Both shots worked well in showing the steep downhill course leading to the coliseum way at the bottom.

ALIEN RACE - PETER CHAN

THE TIPPING POINT

PETER: I wanted to add even more challenges to the race. During the final stretch, the course narrows to a series of small floating platforms that constantly tilt left and right. One misstep and you're out of the game!

GAZIDORE GLACIER

JULZ: The racers are feeling much better now at the top of the Gazidore Glacier, but the celebration stops abruptly when it's realized the only hope they have to "get back on track" is all downhill from here.

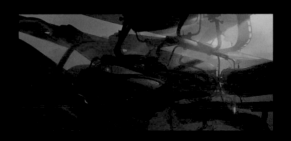

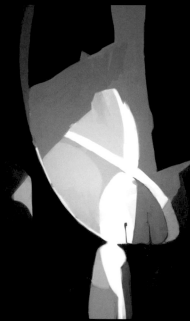

DOWN THE FALLS and ALONG THE CLIFFS

JULZ: The Alien Race is considered to be the most extreme race in the Master Universe. A death-defying race that covers a 300-mile course through the toughest terrain in the most remote locations on planet Zyonia.

ALIEN RACE · JUSTIN PICHETRUNGSI

ALIEN RACE - JUSTIN PICHETRUNGSI

FLYING THROUGH THE GROTTO

SCOTT: Above are a few speed paintings for various environments our racers might encounter. They all started out as images I captured from some layered marker sketches, employing the techniques I share on my educational DVD "Creating Unique Environments." The odd orb shapes to the left were created with a custom brush in Photoshop, and I imagined them to be old gourd-like plants that might serve as dwellings for the aliens living in this large system of old waterworks on Zyonia. John detailed out the flying racers in the piece. Again it was very fun to work as a team on a rendering, with John bringing a fresh set of eyes, energy and of course strong skills to the final painting.

ALIEN RACE · JOHN PARK · SCOTT ROBERTSON

SPOTLIGHT THE LEADERS!

THOM: Natural lanterns lining the forest floor provide ideal lighting for this racecourse. Light levels here are still too low, however, for camera bots and observation vehicles. One of the viewing barges spotlights the race leader rounding a red marker.

ALIEN RACE - THOM TENERY

IRON ORB FOREST

THOM: A medical vessel rushes away from the iron orb forest. To a distant viewer the plants of this forest look like weightless balloons bobbing harmlessly above the landscape. But to a flyer navigating between these 10-ton, methane-filled gasbags, it's a different matter altogether. Thick stalks keep the orbs anchored to the planet's surface, but they are in constant, unpredictable motion. A mistimed pass could easily result in a squashed racer.

THROUGH THE CLAMSHELLS

PETER: With this flying course I really wanted to showcase an environment that racers might not see on the ground. The idea behind it was that an ocean has dried up over the centuries, leaving behind gigantic clamshells as mountain ridges. An indigenous tribe has settled in this remote location, taking advantage of the rich minerals left behind and using the shells as protection from the constant snowstorms that plague this high altitude.

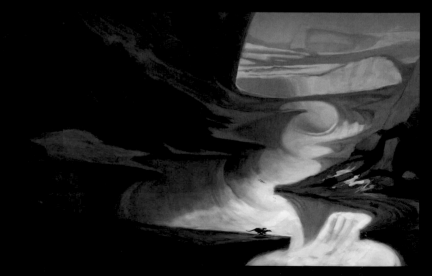

CHECKPOINT ALPHA

SCOTT: Set in a remote industrial region of Zyonia, a racer flies through "checkpoint alpha" as large airships surround it, holding hundreds of the Syntillian upper class who watch on and eagerly await the outcome of today's race.

ALIEN RACE :: JUSTIN PICHETRUNGSI

BIOLUMINESCENCE

THOM: Stilt walkers have a fantastic view of the racers as they wade through the bioluminescent rivers of this remote canyon, its glowing falls just visible in the distance. Flood-sculpted walls of rock make for an unpredictable winding path along narrow ledges and across natural bridges.

ENTERING THE SWAMP

THOM: The jungle course takes racers into a dense tangle of mega-root and twist-wood. All of the high-speed ducking and jumping antics are recorded from camera outposts like this one in the upper right, nestled in tree holes throughout the jungle.

To the left, this quick sketch was the impetus for the illustration on the next page.

THROUGH THE SWAMP

THOM: Where forest gives way to swamp, a slimy swamp-drilling operation sits harvesting noxious gases from the decomposing swamp floor. Racers make a hard left at the rig, careful not to lose their footing in the phosphorescent algal goo that continuously drips from the leaking main tank. A privileged audience gets an up-close-and-personal view of the action from the comfort of a luxury viewing boat.

ALIEN RACE · THOM TENERY

THE CABBAGE PATCH

PETER: While preparing dinner, I got inspired by the cabbage I was cutting. I thought it would be really fun to design a world based on huge cabbage plants that grow to huge sizes, layering giant plates of leaves high into the air. Constant rain and high humidity keep the leaves green but also add a little more challenge for the racers sprinting along the slippery edges of the leaves.

ALIEN RACE · PETER CHAN

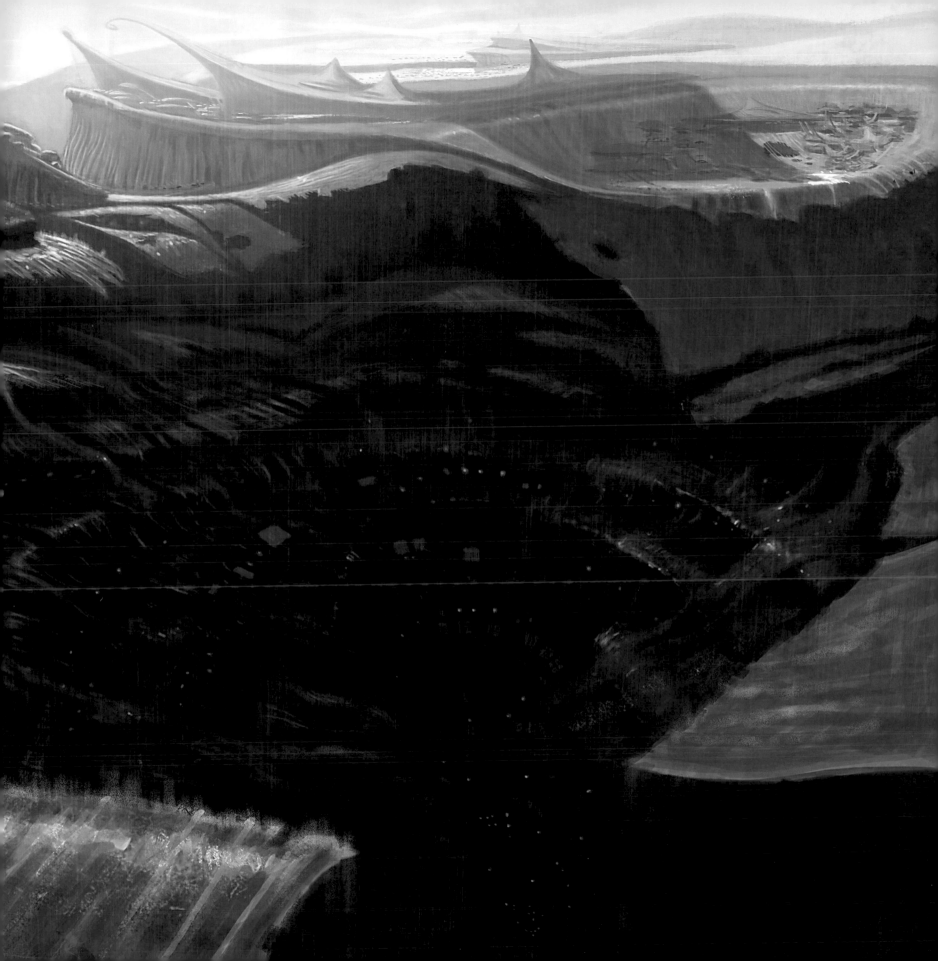

action in the
STRANGLER SWAMP

THOM: The strangler vines of the swamp have relieved more than a few animals of their riders. The experienced rider keeps an eye out for vines and, on occasion, nudges a competitor into a strangler's range. All the action is recorded via light, agile camera bots.

ALIEN RACE - THOM TENERY

DANGERS of CACTICON

THOM: The megalopolis of Cacticon is powered entirely by geo-thermal energy. The city rises above a vast field of geothermal vents, geysers and cascading hot springs. It is surrounded on all sides by this superheated landscape, perpetually shrouded in an at-mosphere of steam. The scalding surface of the Sulfuria Plains has taken its toll on some of the racers. An overheated hornicorn brings up the rear, limping but still keeping pace with the ratamapogs and doodiboars huffing their way toward the next race milestone.

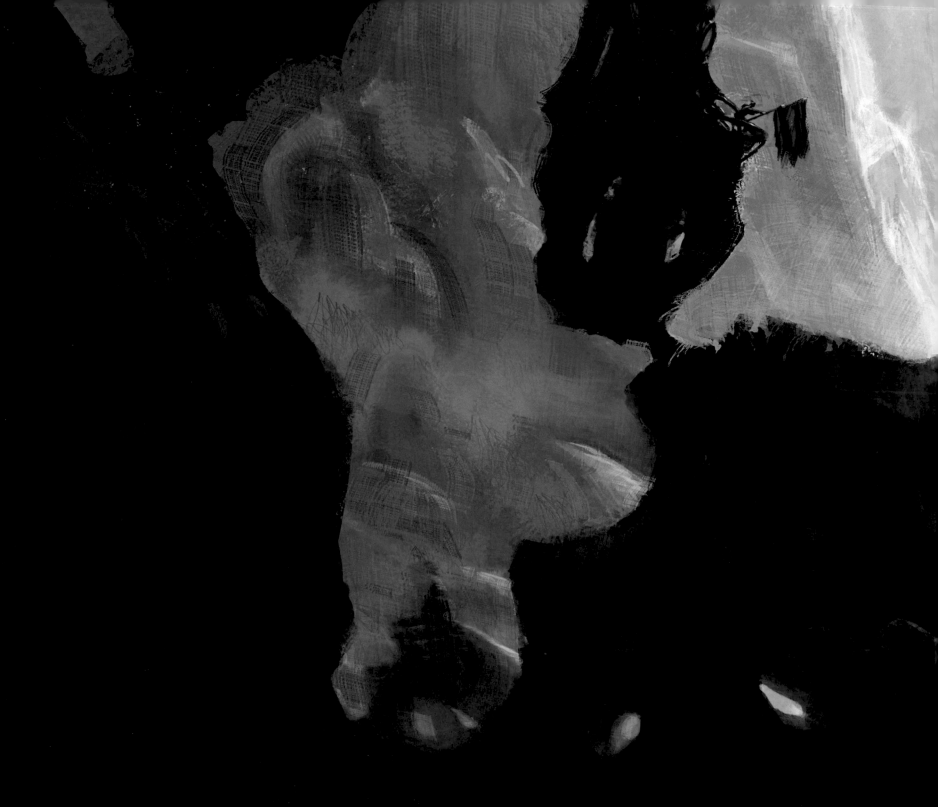

ZYONIAN CORE

JULZ: Racers head straight for the "core of Zyonia" and toward the treacherous and dense cavernous terrain against their aggressive competitors.

FLYING FISH

PETER: Having designed so many scenes of the racecourses with extreme conditions, I decided to chill out a little and work on something a bit more playful. The large structure spanning the water is a piece of commissioned sculpture dedicated to the first winner of the galactic race. The artist referenced the indigenous fish that live in the ocean below for the artwork, now owned by the evil alien, Emperor Kinnik. This amazing piece of art also serves as a museum exhibiting historical facts about the race. There is also a deck and a restaurant where aliens can hang out and enjoy the view.

SCOTT: Peter's painting on the next 2 pages concludes this first edition of the visual development of the *Alien Race* adventure. We hope you have enjoyed the sharing of our design processes, illustrative techniques and visions of this unique story with you. If you are an art and design student or a working professional we hope it will encourage you to gather together your friends and colleagues to create and illustrate your own imaginary stories. With a bit of luck, I hope that someday we can further enjoy *Alien Race* in other mediums beyond that of the printed page.

ALIEN RACE - PETER CHAN

ALIEN RACE · PETER CHAN

peter chan

Peter Chan was born in Taiwan in 1980 and moved to Hong Kong at the age of 10. Interested in drawing and painting, Peter attended Interlochen Arts Academy in Michigan, U.S.A. where he began to focus his skills in fine arts. Afterwards, he received his B.F.A. in Furniture Design from the Rhode Island School of Design. It is not until Peter went to Art Center that he found his passion in the entertainment industry. Peter now works as a concept artist in Los Angeles, and feels very lucky to be drawing and painting everyday with great people!

john park

At a young age, John's creative process began by doodling images from his imagination. He started attending Saturday High at Art Center for high school students, then transitioned into product design at Art Center College of Design. During his early educational terms at Art Center one of his greatest mentors, Scott Robertson, inspired John to commit to entertainment design. Now John is an entertainment design student at Art Center with a few terms left, ready to take on the next challenge ahead.

jparked.blogspot.com
E-mail: Jpforjohnpark@aim.com

justin pichetrungsi

Justin was born in Los Angeles in 1986. At an early age, Justin started recording his experiences and surroundings through drawing, including his doctor visits, family vacations, trains, etc. Inspired by his grandfather, a painter in Thailand, he was determined to pursue the visual arts. Justin took classes in painting, figure drawing and comic book design in his teen years. Later, he attended Saturday High classes at Art Center College of Design, where he was subsequently accepted. For two summers, he interned at Design Studio Press, where he worked on various video games. Justin recently graduated from the Entertainment Design department at Art Center.